Gangs and Adolescent Subcultures

NEWLY REVISED FIRST EDITION

Edited by La Tanya Skiffer

cognella
academic publishing

Bassim Hamadeh, CEO and Publisher
Kassie Graves, Director of Acquisitions
Jamie Giganti, Senior Managing Editor
Natalie Lakosil, Senior Licensing Manager
Miguel Macias, Senior Graphic Designer
Kaela Martin and Rachel Singer, Associate Editors

Cover image credit: Copyright © 2007 iStockphoto LP/Hogogo.

Printed in the United States of America

ISBN:978-1-5165-0697-2 (pbk) / 978-1-5165-0698-9 (br) / 978-1-5165-0717-7 (sb)

www.cognella.com   800-200-3908

CONTENTS

CHAPTER 5: CLASS, GENDER AND GANGS

CHAPTER 6: DRUGS AND GANGS

CHAPTER 7: GANG JOINING AND RISK FACTORS

CHAPTER 8: PUBLIC POLICY, CIVIL GANG INJUNCTIONS, AND GANGS

CHAPTER 9: PRISON GANGS AND DESISTANCE

INTRODUCTION

By Dr. Ginger Silvera,
Dr. Adam G. Sanford,
and Dr. La Tanya Skiffer

At the turn of the 21st century, gangs remain an area of serious concern for researchers, policy makers, and the public alike. From public officials focusing on increases in crime, to teachers fighting gang influence in the classroom, to police dealing with unstable situations on the streets, to parents and social workers at a loss to explain the negative and self-destructive behavior of their children and their clients, the effects of gangs on our society and our citizens cannot be overstated. Currently, the Department of Justice estimates the number of gang members at 1 million members nationwide. This number includes approximately 900,000 gang members within communities and approximately 147,000 in jails or prisons (National Gang Intelligence Center, 2011). According to law enforcement sources, over 90 percent of gang members are nonwhite. However, self-report surveys find that white youth account for 40 percent of adolescent gang members. Although the majority of gang members are still young men, an increasing number of young women are also joining and forming their own gangs.

For individual gang members, substance abuse, physical and sexual abuse, involvement in petty and violent crime, and disconnection from the larger society are serious and common issues that affect not just the gang member's immediate consequences, but his or her long-term prospects as well. Incarceration and early death are unfortunate, but not unusual, outcomes for many gang members. At the societal level, we see the disintegration of family connections, the ongoing school-to-prison pipeline, increases in crime and danger that extend from the inner city to the suburbs, rampant unemployment and lack of education, and grinding poverty—all common causes and effects of gang membership.

News, movies, music, and other media contribute to the problem. Gang lifestyles, fashions, and values are marketed and sold just like any other commodity; to the point where gang and adolescent cultures become all but indistinguishable from one another. Sagging pants, tattoos, hoodies, "colors," and hairstyles are all instantly recognizable as "banger" fashions—and they are worn not just in urban communities but also on the streets of suburbia. Gang music promotes gang values, increasing the chance that adolescents who are not gang members yet will move toward gang membership because it is perceived as the in thing to do.

It is important to understand, too, that gangs are not a new phenomenon. Research dates the first appearances of street gangs in the United States to the 1780s (Anderson, 2000). But understanding the causes and correlates of gang membership is a necessary goal of gang studies; without this understanding, all explanations fail. In the known history of gangs in the United States, institutionalized racism, racial segregation, and an unequal opportunity structure have always informed the formation of gangs and the behavior of gang members. The faces of the gangs may change, but the societal pressures remain the same.

The effects of urban-ecology studies of crime must be mentioned as well. In a poverty-ridden environment with an evaporated social safety net, gang membership and its usual economic activities of drug sales and prostitution, are probably motivated more by economic necessity than by a simple desire for thrills or fun. Adolescents who grow up in these environments are at much higher risk for gang membership, both due to the economic burden of poverty and their ongoing association with deviant peers. Areas with high levels of poverty have higher incidence and prevalence of single-parent households; these communities often face the additional burden of dual-incarceration households, making it virtually impossible for parents to be present in the lives of children. Since school tax support is most often based on property taxes, schools serving predominantly disadvantaged students see higher rates of poor grades and dropping out—and students who drop out often drop right into a gang, if not already a member. The effects of racism on legitimate economic opportunities for these adolescents are profound.

By now, it should be clear that understanding gangs and the reasons why individuals join them must become a central focus for researchers across academic disciplines. Each discipline takes a different perspective on the topic: sociology on the history, causes, and correlates; criminology on methods of prevention and intervention; criminal justice on methods of control; law on punishment; and social work on mitigating and dealing with the effects of gangs and gang membership. However, a diversity of perspectives is necessary to give us a complete picture of the causes and effects of this ongoing social issue.

This textbook provides those various perspectives, mainly in the form of scientific studies and practical applications of policies to the gang problem today. Understanding the various factors that have contributed—and continue to contribute—to the gang problem will make it possible for students to begin considering possible solutions to both this problem and its effects. Whether the student is bound for a career as a community organizer, law enforcement officer, social worker, or researcher, this textbook will provide him or her with a wide variety of perspectives, studies, and findings to use in the investigation of the problem while working toward solutions.

Chapter 1 lays the foundation for an international perspective on gang culture and how it has spread worldwide. Klein (2001) details the findings of the Eurogang program and provides readers with a cross-cultural comparative analysis of gangs in the United States to those in western Europe. Duffy (2004) provides readers with a broader cross-cultural analysis of the differences in gang participation and organization around the world, along with the similarities and differences in response to these problems in several countries. Armed with this broader perspective, students will begin a course in gang studies knowing that gang is not a one-size-fits-all term.

Chapter 2 delves into the issue of delinquency and gang membership, with three studies from three different perspectives. Klein and Maxson (1985) detail the issue of rock (now crack) cocaine sales in Los Angeles during the height of the cocaine crisis in the 1980s, giving readers a look at the specific issues of law enforcement as they relate to dealing with a specific kind of gang crime. Thornberry, Lizotte, Krohn, Farnsworth, and Jang (1994) provide readers with a test of Thornberry's interactional theory of delinquency, using data from the Rochester Youth Development Study, to find that engaging in delinquency increases interactions with delinquent peers. This then increases other negative behaviors and characteristics, including the "hardening" of delinquent beliefs as a lagged effect. Finally, Smith and Thornberry (1995) detail studies from the same data set and demonstrate that child maltreatment significantly increases the risk of later delinquency in teenagers. These three studies offer students a perspective on delinquency that gives the lie to the idea that it is all a matter of free choice. Social conditions matter, in ways that we cannot always see at the time they happen.

Chapter 3 provides readers with two studies on ethnicity—specific outcomes that increase the chance of gang membership. Moore's (1985) discussion of the Chicano movement in Los Angeles and the multigenerational effects of social disapproval and pressure from both within and outside the community shows the effect of ethnic-community belief systems and how they interact with those of the larger society to make gang membership look even more attractive to disaffected and isolated youth. Meanwhile, Farley's (1987) exploration of the underemployment of black and Hispanic men in American metropolitan areas demonstrates that the effects of ethnicity may not be the same as those of race, with black men disproportionately disadvantaged in many areas compared to Hispanic men of the same educational level. This chapter provides students with an understanding that a broad-based condemnation of racism may not get at the problems that each individual ethnic community faces. A more nuanced discourse is needed, and this chapter begins that discussion for its readers.

Chapter 4 deals with race and gangs through five separate studies. Miller (1968) discusses the roots of white Irish gangs in Boston from the 1800s through the 1960s, giving a historical perspective on white ethnic gangs before they were fully assimilated into American society and culture. Lyon, Henggeler, and Hall (1992) provide a study of criminal activity as it relates to race and peer relations by comparing white and Hispanic gang members and non–gang members on their connections to family. The results are not surprising to any who perform ethnic-studies research; nonwhite delinquents felt more connection to their families, whether they were in a gang or not. Adamson (2000) provides a compelling historical overview of four major periods in the development of racially segregated American gangs from the 1780s to the present day, focusing on large metropolitan areas such as New York, Boston, Chicago, and Philadelphia. Berlet and Vysotsky (2006) delve into the issue of white supremacist groups in the United States and their similarities, differences, and connections to skinhead or white-only gangs. Finally, Benson and Decker (2010) detail the internal organization of international (and thus mainly nonwhite) drug smuggling and how it does not function in the same way as organizational studies would normally predict. This chapter provides students with historical context, as well as a better understanding of the true roots of racial segregation in gang life.

Chapter 5 features three studies on class and gender as they relate to gang delinquency. Miller's (1958) study of lower-class culture and how it creates gang delinquency through lower-class values provides students with an overview of the position of gang studies in the 1950s. Miller's (2002) study details the changes in female gang membership observed over a two-decade period, including changes in risk factors and motivations for girls to join gangs. This study also details the consequences girls face for gang membership. Finally, Dorais, Corriveau, and Feldstein (2009) give a brief discussion of the social status of girls in gangs, detailing disturbing findings of sex slavery, group rape as a "jumping-in" ceremony, and the general sexualization of girl gang members' roles in gang operations and behaviors. In this chapter, students learn that even in gangs, there is a gendered and class-based hierarchy, with girls and those of lower class often at the bottom rung.

Chapter 6 deals with the drug problem in gangs, both in terms of drug sales and drug use. Esbensen, Peterson, Freng, and Taylor's (2001) study of eighth-graders in the Gang Resistance Education And Training, or G.R.E.A.T., program, discusses the causes and correlates of initiation patterns for gang membership, drug sales, and drug use, to find out if there is a causal pattern (gang membership leading to drug use, or vice versa). Their study tests the proposed theoretical patterns of gang membership (enhancement, facilitation, or selection) and finds that enhancement (a combination of the other two models) best fits the data. This result makes it clear to the reader that there is no one simple answer to the question of what causes gang membership. Some gang members are already delinquent when they join (selection), but being in a gang causes them to be more so (facilitation). Since the drug-gang connection is so hotly contested in public policy today, this chapter makes it clear to the reader that this connection is not as solid as one might be led to believe by policy positions.

Chapter 7 draws on three studies of the precursors and risk factors that seem to increase gang membership. Dukes, Martinez, and Stein (1997) demonstrate that adolescents who have lower levels of social integration are much more likely than socially connected adolescents to become gang members, while also finding that the facilitation and selection models each partially explain gang membership. Howell and Egley (2005) demonstrate that Thornberry's developmental model shows that different risk factors obtain at different developmental periods in a child and adolescent's life, from preschool through early adolescence, and that these factors can have a cumulative effect on gang joining. Finally, De Coster, Heimer, and Wittrock (2006) discuss three perspectives on the relationship between communities and crime: status characteristics of families, community disadvantage, and violent behavior, finding that status characteristics and their effect on finding residence outside of disadvantaged communities have an indirect but substantial effect on the likelihood of adolescent gang joining and violence. This chapter serves to inform student readers about the controllable and uncontrollable factors that increase the level of gang joining among adolescents.

Chapter 8 moves to a discussion of public policy and law enforcement practice and its response to the gang problem. Huff discusses the effects of prevention, intervention, and suppression tactics, finding that suppression is the most-used and least-effective method of reducing gang activity in a municipality. Braga, Kennedy, and Tita (2001) discuss the "pulling-levers" strategy of eliminating gang activity, and its successes and failures across various municipalities that have tried it. Smith (2000) discusses the implementation and constitutional problems with the use of civil banishment as a gang-control strategy. Maxson, Hennigan, and Sloane (2005) detail the effect of civil gang injunctions on one set of communities in a comparative-analysis study. This chapter gives students insight into the various law enforcement responses to gang behavior and their success and failure rates.

Finally, Chapter 9 examines the special issue of prison gang membership, which is unlike street gang membership in several ways. Rosen and Venkatesh (2007) review literature on the effectiveness of and problems with various intervention methods of controlling crime, with special emphasis on the issue of neighborhood-focused interventions. Fleisher and Decker (2001) discuss the issues of prison returnees and their actual prospects for reintegration into the communities they return to after release, with an emphasis on ways in which the communities can provide a better "landing spot" for them. In the final article of this chapter and volume, Bendixen, Endresen, and Olweus (2006) detail the issues that adolescents face in both joining and leaving gangs, again with an emphasis on determining whether the facilitation or selection model better explains these problems.

This volume provides its readers with historical and current contexts for the various problems to which gangs are a response. It details the ongoing and changing theoretical, policy, and empirical knowledge and positions that inform the study of gangs and gang activity. A student who completes a course with this volume as its text should emerge with a more nuanced understanding of the ways in which historical issues, class issues, race and ethnicity, gender, and many other social concerns both create and perpetuate the gang problem, as well as an informed understanding of what has and has not worked to reduce and eliminate it. While it does not provide the silver bullet or the magic potion that will instantly eliminate all gang problems, it does provide the reader with a framework in which to understand them.

INTRODUCTION

STREET GANGS

A CROSS-NATIONAL PERSPECTIVE

By Malcolm W. Klein

In the fall of the year 2000, an international group of European scholars submitted a proposal for funding to the European Union (Weitekamp, 2000). The purpose was to establish, over a 3-year period, an interactive network of researchers interested in studying street gangs and developing principles for the prevention and control of gang activities. Because it was generally thought up to that time that street gangs were principally an American problem, this chapter will review the history of this new development—known as the Eurogang Program—and place it in the context of this volume of *Gangs in America*. Why should one include a chapter on street gangs outside the United States in such a volume? At least four reasons offer themselves.

1. We have "exported" our American street gang culture abroad. For example, there are Crips in the Netherlands (van Gemert, 2001). As we come to understand foreign variations of our own gang structures, we will learn more about what the sine qua non of street gangs is, and what is peripheral to their necessary nature.

2. The particular forms of European gangs seem similar to those to be found in the United States, although with differences in prevalence and in ethnic makeup. These structural similarities and variations inform us about both European and American youth cultures.

3. The Eurogang Program was initiated by a few Americans on the basis of American gang experiences. We are naturally curious to study our own impact (or lack thereof) in this new setting.

4. The very considerable generic knowledge we have accumulated over the past 70 years in the United States may be quite culture bound. Comparative research

elsewhere can illuminate our own knowledge limitations with respect to such well-studied issues as gang location, diffusion, structure, ethnicity, age, gender, cohesiveness, and behavior patterns (including crime).

GANGS ELSEWHERE

Although this chapter deals principally with the cities of Western Europe, it is clear from a scattered literature that street gangs have been noted in many other locations. Most of this literature, unfortunately, notes but does not describe these gangs: Our empirical knowledge of street gangs in foreign lands is skimpy at best. Here are a number of examples:

- Japan, South Africa, Zambia, Kimshasa, Dakar, the Cameroons, Ceylon (now Sri Lanka), Thailand, Malaysia, Chile, Argentina, India, and Egypt (Clinard & Abbott, 1973)
- Kenya, Tanzania, South Africa, Australia, Mexico, Brazil, Peru, Taiwan, South Korea, Hong Kong, China, and Japan (Spergel, 1995)
- Ghana, Montreal, Australia, Puerto Rico, Jamaica, India, Indonesia, and Thailand (Covey, Menard, & Franzese, 1997). The Ghanaian case is described in sufficient detail to show resemblance to some American street gangs.
- Canada, Mexico, Japan, South Africa, the Philippines, Hong Kong, China, New Zealand, Australia, and Papua-New Guinea (Klein, 1995). The descriptions cited for the Philippines and Papua-New Guinea (Port Moresby in particular) provide some structural and criminal details that both contrast with and exemplify American counterparts.
- A number of Canadian scholars are now reporting on street gangs in Vancouver, Toronto, Winnipeg, and Montreal. They include Caucasian, Aborigine, Vietnamese, Chinese, and Haitian gangs. What structural information exists to date suggests general similarities to U.S. street gangs, although descriptions range from "youth movements" to "criminal business organizations."
- In New Zealand, a more detailed report by Eggleston (1996) depicts primarily Maori gangs that are clearly crime oriented, male dominated, and involved in intergang rivalries. We are told little about their structures, however.
- In El Salvador, both news reports and visits by American gang experts yield a clear picture of gang culture exported to San Salvador, the capital city, by Salvadoran immigrants to the United States who return or are deported back to that country. *Placas* (graffiti) on the walls advertise "homies unidos" (homeboys united).
- In Argentina, DeFleur (1967) many years ago sought counterparts to some highly structured, large, big-city U.S. gangs depicted in American gang treatises of the time.

Instead, she found small, leaderless but internally cohesive gangs, quite different in form from what she had anticipated.

In sum, street gangs, or groups subsumed under similar terminology, have been reported in Asia, Africa, Southeast Asia, Latin America, and Canada. Few of the reports, however, have been based on first-hand research. The "gangs" are mostly of unknown size, structure, and behavior patterns. The exceptions, such as those in Canada, Argentina, Papua-New Guinea, and the Philippines, whet the appetite for further study but provide few clues for new directions. Comparative research is badly needed, and the Eurogang Program at last holds promise for an organized approach to the issues at hand.

THE EUROGANG PROGRAMS DEFINITIONS AND ISSUES

Although a few American researchers initiated the Eurogang Program, it soon became, by design, a decidedly European venture with Americans as principal consultants. The first step was an informal survey I made of European cities, establishing locations in which street gang activity had emerged during 1980s and 1990s. There followed several meetings of a small steering committee (members from the United States, Canada, Belgium, Holland, Germany, and Sweden) and a series of four workshops between 1997 and 2000 in Germany, Norway, Belgium, and Holland. Other countries represented in one or more of these were Finland, Denmark, England, France, Spain, Italy, Slovenia, Croatia, Greece, and Russia. Street gangs, or "gang-like youth groups" as a few preferred to call them, were found to exist, in some cases in small numbers, in almost all of the European nations. A commonality of interests soon developed among more than 100 participants, most of whom were researchers but some of whom were policymakers in public agencies such as ministries of justice and the police.

Throughout the developmental process, four key issues emerged and drew the most attention, issues whose resolution was required before the agreed-upon goals of cross-national and multimethod research could comfortably be undertaken. The first of these was to achieve a common definition of "street gangs" capable of applying to a variety of such groups as well as distinguishing them from other groups. The latter include motorcycle gangs, prison gangs, terrorist groups, and the very large number of other, less troublesome youth groups that exist in all countries (often school and youth culture based) that are not much of a danger to others.

The second issue, shared less among active gang researchers but more among others becoming interested in the Program's research goals, was the possible creation of a "moral panic" (Cohen, 1972). The concern here was that undertaking research on groups specifically labeled "gangs" could reify the concept, create greater public concern about it, and indeed help to create the phenomenon to a degree greater than originally existed. Some felt it might indeed be a wiser policy to deny or ignore gangs, or at least to develop alternative terminology than the gang terms so common in the United States.

Third, and inextricably tied to the first two, was the issue of setting street gangs into the broader context of youth groups generally. If street gangs are in any sense a unique form of group, we can only know and appreciate their unique qualities through contrast with other youth groups not labeled as gangs. Although this issue has not been a central issue in most American gang research, it has greater meaning in many European countries where there has been a tradition of studying youth groups and youth movements over many decades.

The fourth issue was the most engaging, at least to the American gang scholars. It came to be known as the "Eurogang Paradox."[2] Simply stated, the paradox consists of two elements, the first being the denial by numerous European researchers and policy-makers that their jurisdictions have street gangs, because they don't have gangs that are large, highly structured, with strong cultural codes of loyalty and territoriality, and a commitment to violence as seen in American gangs. That is, they don't have "American style" street gangs. The second element of the paradox, of course, is that most American gangs also don't fit this publicly held stereo type of street gangs. Thus the paradox: The denial of gangs in Europe is based on a "typical" American gang that is not at all typical in America.

Very briefly, before moving on to characterizing European gangs as they have been described recently, I will comment on those four issues as they have been addressed in the Eurogang Program. Again, the issues are gang definitions, the concern about moral panic, the context of other youth groups, and the Eurogang Paradox.

Definitions. In a major set of annual surveys of U.S. police agencies designed to assess the prevalence of street gangs, the National Youth Gang Center (NYGC) offered the following approach to defining gangs for its police respondents: "A group of youths or young adults in your jurisdiction that you or other responsible persons in your agency or community are willing to identify or classify as a 'gang.'" The Eurogang participants determined that such a broad definition would be *too* inclusive—almost a "non-definition" as rioted by some. But choosing an accept-able alternative proved—as it has for decades in the United States—to be a thorny problem.

The first solution was to accept, for working purposes, a minimal nominal definition that includes the elements of stability over time, street orientation, and a self-identity based on criminal involvement. The definition drafted for these purposes was this: "A street gang (or a problematic youth group corresponding to a street gang elsewhere) is any stable, street-oriented youth group whose own identity includes involvement in antisocial activity" (Weitekamp, 2000).

Note the phrase in parentheses above. For those wishing to avoid gang terminology, the definition can be applied to "problematic youth groups" without explicitly saying, "this is a gang." The second solution was also adopted to meet the concerns of those wishing or needing to avoid gang terminology This approach, itself having two alternative forms, was to define the issue of whether a group under study is a "gang" or not *operationally,* rather than nominally as above.

The first operational procedure, common to many interview and questionnaire surveys of youth, is to use a set of "funneling" questions. These start with broad questions about one's friends and groups of friends, then narrow slowly to descriptions of groups such as size, activities, reasons for joining, and tendencies to get into trouble. Only at the end is the respondent asked if he or she considers this particular group of friends to be a gang. If the answer is yes, this is generally taken at face value. If the answer is no, the researcher can determine if this is also to be taken at face value or as a denial of "true" gang membership based on the previous answers to the funneling questions. Some of those questions reveal typical gang characteristics.

The second operational procedure is based on the Maxson-Klein typology of gang structures described later in this chapter. The typology describes five gang structures that encompass most gangs found in the United States.[3] It asks youth respondents in two ways to describe their "special group of friends" in line with the five gang types. The first, indirect way is to ask them to describe the group with respect to its size, age range, duration, presence of subgroups, territoriality, and antisocial behavior patterns. These are the dimensions that determine placement of the group in one of the five gang types, or into none of them. The second, more direct way is to present the respondent with very brief scenarios of the five gang types, asking the respondent which of these best describes his special group of friends, or if none of them do.

In sum, the operational definition of a youth's description of his or her group as a street gang can be determined by the funneling questions, or by the indirect or direct approach to the use of the five types of gang structures. The designation of a youth group as nongang or gang is thus achieved by the operations described—that is, by the youth's responses to questions shown in research to distinguish street gangs from other youth groups. These survey approaches can also be applied, with minor modifications, for use in gang observations and ethnographies and for use in surveys of adult experts such as police, school personnel, and community youth agencies. All those procedures are being planned for the developing Eurogang research projects.

Moral Panic. Interestingly, the European colleagues most concerned with creating a moral panic about street gangs tended to be those not yet directly engaged in gang research. Those already so engaged had not found the concern to be very tangible. Nonetheless, the operational definition approach outlined above was designed to make gang research more palatable to those genuinely concerned with the issue. For example, the funneling technique allows one to go all the way through the determination of gang membership by a youth respondent without that youth ever having to admit to gang membership. The phrase adopted—"your special group of friends"—allows avoidance of gang terminology yet permits determination by the researcher of the youth's gang or nongang status.

By the same token, the gang structures approach, both in the questions about size, duration, antisocial activities, and so on, and in the presentation of the five scenarios, uses the word *group,* not gang, in their language. Again, this allows the researcher to determine gang status without directly asking about it. Further, it allows for those youths responding in gang-like fashion to be fitted into one of the five types so that comparisons across sites and with U.S. data can readily be made. Any moral panic resulting from these procedures will not result from the research process, but only from the manner in which the results are presented to the public (if indeed they are made public).

The Youth Group Context. Here, too, the operational approach outlined above serves a secondary purpose, namely the application of gang-relevant survey instruments to a broader array of youth groups. By comparing youth responses from gang and nongang respondents, the distinction between the two types of groups can readily be illuminated. Youth-group researchers will undoubtedly wish to ask a far more extensive set of questions in addition, depending on their particular interests. Having the gang comparisons available to them will simply amplify one issue of concern. A fine example can be found in the comparative study in Bremen, Germany, and Denver, Colorado (Huizinga & Schumann, 2001), using common survey instruments applied to large samples of school students in the two cities. A funneling technique for gang determination was employed amid a far broader set of questions about individuals, families, schools, and communities. Excellent contrasts were thus drawn between gang and nongang youth and between both of these cross-nationally.

The Eurogang Paradox. This fourth issue raised during the development of the Eurogang Program has not yet been fully resolved for two reasons. First, the stereotype of American gangs is fairly fixed in many minds and constantly reinforced by naive, poorly informed representatives of the media and some law enforcement agencies. Second, as the program has expanded its membership, new colleagues continually appear who have not yet been alerted to the nature of the paradox. In my view, following the initiation of the program discussions there have been two principal contributions by the American participants. One is the collaborative process of gang definition statement and measurement. The second, designed to reduce the paradox, is to bring to the European colleagues (admittedly with some repetition and insistence) the most recent data from the 1980s and 1990s on the true nature of U.S. gangs (see, e.g., chaps. 1–7 in

Klein, Kerner, Maxson & Weitekamp, 2001). By showing, with both case studies and national surveys, that the stereotypical gang is the exception rather than the rule, and by illustrating the five structural types of the gang typology, the Americans have attempted to demonstrate the variety of gangs in the United States. By doing this, they have allowed European observers to understand that some of their groups, while not fitting the old stereotype, do indeed resemble some of the other, more common U.S. gangs. The resemblance between U.S. and European gangs has been documented (Klein, 1997) and now allows far more useful comparisons of both similarities and differences. It has been a "hard sell," but progress along these lines has been steady.

CHARACTERISTICS OF AMERICAN GANGS

Though we have established that street gangs probably exist or have existed on every continent, it seems clear that they are most evident in the United States. In attempting to understand street gangs elsewhere, it makes sense to establish their basic elements first in the United States, where seven decades of gang research has taken place. In particular, because American gangs have changed over time and have proliferated in just the past 20 years in particular, it seems sensible to establish the base of knowledge principally on more recent research. The most significant changes have probably taken place with respect to prevalence (there are now thousands of gang-involved jurisdictions), crime patterns (more lethal violence now, due to the availability of modern firearms), and structures (the emergence of several types of nonstereotypical gang forms). In addition to these three characteristics, it seems useful to review several others briefly: location; ethnicity; gender; cultural diffusion; cohesiveness; and two additional crime patterns, versatility and amplification.

Location. In the days of the most "classic" American gang research, from the 1920s to the mid-1970s, gangs known to exist were located principally in large urban centers or their immediate surroundings. These included most notably New York, Philadelphia, Boston, Chicago, Los Angeles, San Francisco, San Antonio, and El Paso. Prior to 1960, there were about 50 communities in these areas with gang problems; street gangs were an urban problem. The number of gang jurisdictions grew slowly but steadily through the mid-1980s, and then exploded to the point that the National Youth Gang Center has reported several *thousand* gang-involved communities, encompassing more than 26,000 gangs and almost 850,000 gang members (NYGC, 2000a).

Almost every urban center is now involved, but there are not 3,000 urban centers in the United States; this means that gangs now exist in many large and even many small towns. Recent data from the NYGC (2000a) show the following (according to police reports and NYGC's very broad definition):

Large cities:	12,538 gangs	482,380 members
Small cities:	8,413 gangs	94,875 members
Suburban counties:	6,040 gangs	176,610 members
Rural counties:	1,716 gangs	26,368 members

The data are a bit misleading, because NYGC defines as large cities those above 25,000 in population. Nonetheless, it is clear from the above figures that gangs *cannot* be considered just a "big city" problem. For those who think of gangs as an East Coast phenomenon, the NYGC data are equally surprising. Seventy-two percent of reporting jurisdictions in the West indicate active gangs, as opposed to 48% in the Midwest and South and only 29% in the Northeast. The *West Side Story* now has a new meaning.

Clearly, as we look at the street gang situation in Europe or elsewhere, we will need to assess their location in urban *and* nonurban areas. The character of gangs is affected by their location on the landscape.

Ethnicity. In the earlier, classic period, American gangs of many backgrounds were reported: German, Scandinavian, Italian, Polish, Irish, Jewish, and other European immigrant populations fueled the inner-city gangs along with black and Hispanic groups. But with the absorption of most immigrant populations into the multiethnic fabric of our nation, it came to be more and more the still-marginalized minorities—blacks, Hispanics, and to a lesser extent various Asian groups—that have composed most of our modern street gangs. This history makes it clear that it is not a particular nationality, ethnicity, or race that makes up the street gang problem, but rather the disadvantaged, marginalized, and alienated status of youth segments that gravitate to the gang world. Even in the case of Caucasian groups such as the Skinheads, a review of their membership reveals that they are drawn from those who perceive themselves to be socially marginalized.

When we look at the composition of street gangs reported in connection with the Eurogang Program, obviously we should not expect to find a preponderance of blacks or Hispanics, but we should be on the lookout for other marginalized populations there.

Gender. Until recently, the prevalence and behavior of girls in street gangs had received moderate attention at best. A very few autonomous female gangs had been described. More commonly, girls were described either as occasional participants in male gangs or as members of auxiliary groups, as small adjuncts to larger male gangs. It was generally acknowledged that female gang members were fewer in number (ratios of from 1 to 10 to 3 to 10 female to male were noted), younger on average by several years, and less criminally involved than males (although manifesting similarly versatile crime patterns). Female gang members were largely ignored by the police and courts, and stereotypes abounded that the females were sex objects for the males ("toys for boys"), carried concealed weapons for the males, spread rumors to incite rivalries between male gangs, and were generally subservient in a male-dominated-street world.

More recently, especially with the advent of feminist criminology, a number of more careful and considered works on female gang members have appeared (see, e.g., Chesney-Lind, Shelden, & Joe, 1996; Fleisher, 1998; Hagedorn, 1999; J. Miller, 2001a; Moore, 1991). Less importance is now given to female subservience and more to female gang participation in serving specific needs, much as male participation serves such needs. Also, it now appears that the prevalence of female gang members is higher than was estimated earlier (percentages in the 20% to 40% range are more common) and fewer auxiliary groups are reported, with more of the girls to some extent integrated with the boys' groups. Male domination, nonetheless, continues to be the typical pattern. Finally, it is still the case that female gang participation is largely unknown to or downplayed by the police and courts.

The Eurogang Program, unlike the earlier days of American gang research, has been alerted to the issues of female gang members (see J. Miller, 2001b). Perhaps attention to females early in the development of European gangs will yield more accurate data, although some European scholars, more than Americans, place heavy weight on the issue of "masculinities" (see, e.g., Kersten, 2001).

Cultural Diffusion. In earlier decades, street gangs seemed to appear in major cities as independent phenomena, arising in each case as responses to local patterns of immigration, central city structure, culture clash, and economic disadvantage. None of the earlier gang literature suggested effective ties between gangs in New York and Chicago and Los Angeles and the other known gang locations. Indeed, one noted scholar almost scoffed at the notion of inter-city gang recognition (Campbell, Munce, & Galea, 1982).[4]

Since the mid-1980s, it has become rather commonplace to assign the responsibility for the proliferation of street gangs across the country to one of three processes. The first is a shadow of the earlier thinking: Gangs have emerged in many localities because of similar conditions that are gang-spawning in their nature. These include racism, relative poverty or deprivation, poor local resources, inadequate employment opportunities for youth (and minority youth in particular), and the general marginalization of black, Hispanic, and other minority groups. Many scholars, my self among them, are inclined to this view, noting that the social and political conservatism of the country over the past 20 years has exacerbated these processes.

A second commonly offered explanation is the advent of crack cocaine and its franchising across the country promulgated principally by law enforcement agencies who saw crack cocaine as a new epidemic being fueled by drug kingpins and distributed through the auspices of organized street gang networks, this explanation did receive support from incidents in widely scattered parts of the country. More careful research, however, has downplayed the importance of gang member migration and street gang capacities to market drugs extensively (Decker & Van Winkle, 1996; Hagedorn, 1988; Howell & Gleason, 1999; Klein, 1995; Maxson, 1998).

The third explanation, propounded by myself (Klein, 1995) and a number of police gang experts in the late 1980s, has gained general acceptance over the past decade. It notes the general diffusion of street gang culture—the dress and ornamentation styles, the postures, the argot of gang members—to the general youth population of the country. The press, gang-oriented movies, television news and documentaries, entertainment venues such as MTV, and "gangsta rap" music forms have ail served to inculcate original street gang culture into a far broader youth culture. Most young people in America recognize the look, the walk, and the talk of gang members. Many mimic it in part or in whole. Many try it out as a personal style, some to discard it and some to retain it. Play groups, break-dancing groups, taggers, and school peer groups experiment with gang life. For some, it becomes all too real (Hagedorn, 1988; Klein, 1995).

In Europe, a number of new street gangs seem to have taken on the trappings of this gang culture. Needed now is a more careful assessment of the degree to which the exportation of the American style is a cause, or merely the external trappings, of European gang forms.

Cohesiveness. Two characteristics of street gangs, important in themselves, lead to a third. The first of these is group cohesiveness, although we must be careful not to overstate the extent to which gang members are tied to each other. Surprisingly few American scholars have paid much attention

The Neotraditional Gang. The Neotraditional gang resembles the Traditional form, but has not been in existence as long—probably no more than 10 years, and often less. It may be medium size—say 50 to 100 members—or also into the hundreds. It probably has developed subgroups or cliques based on age or area, but sometimes may not. The age range is usually smaller than in the classical Traditional gangs. The Neotraditional gang is also very territorial, claiming turf and defending it.

In sum, the Neotraditional gang is a newer territorial gang that looks on its way to becoming Traditional in time. Thus at this point it is sub grouping, but may or may not have achieved territoriality, and size suggests that it is evolving into the Traditional form.

The Compressed Gang. The Compressed gang is small—usually in the size range of up to 50 members—and has not formed subgroups. The age range, is probably narrow—10 or fewer years between the younger and older members. The small size, absence of subgroups, and narrow age range may reflect the newness of the group, in existence less than 10 years and maybe for only a few years. Some of these Compressed gangs have become territorial, but many have not.

In sum, Compressed gangs have a relatively short history, short enough that by size, duration, sub grouping, and territoriality it is unclear whether they will grow and solidify into the more traditional forms, or simply remain as less complex groups.

The Collective Gang. The Collective gang looks like the Compressed form, but bigger and with a wider age range—maybe 10 or more years between younger and older members. Size can be under one hundred, but is probably larger. Surprisingly, given these numbers, it has not developed sub groups, and may or may not be a territorial gang. It probably has a 10-to 15-year existence.

In sum, the Collective gang resembles a kind of shapeless mass of adolescent and young adult members that has not developed the distinguishing characteristics of other gangs.

The Specialty Gang. Unlike these other gangs that engage in a wide variety of criminal offenses, crime in this type of group is narrowly focused on a few offenses; the group comes to be characterized by the specialty. The Specialty gang tends to be small—usually 50 or fewer members—without any subgroups in most cases (there are exceptions). It probably has a history of less than 10 years, but has developed a well-defined territory. Its territory may be either residential or based on the opportunities for the particular form of crime in which it specializes. The age range of most Specialty gangs is narrow, but in others is broad.

Table 15.1 Characteristics of Five Gang Types

Type	Subgroups	Size	Age Range	Duration	Territorial	Crime Versatility
Traditional	Yes	Large (> 100)	Wide (20–30 years)	Long (> 20 years)	Yes	Yes
Neotraditional	Yes	Medium-Large (>50)	(no pattern)	Short (< 10 years)	Yes	Yes
Compressed	No	Small (<50)	Narrow (< 10 years)	Short (< 10 years)	(no pattern)	Yes
Collective	No	Medium-Large (>50)	Medium-Wide (> 10 years)	Medium (10–15 years)	(no pattern)	Yes
Specialty	No	Small (<50)	Narrow (< 10 years)	Short(< 10 years)	Yes	No

In sum, the Specialty gang is crime-focused in a narrow way. Its principal purpose is more criminal than social, and its smaller size and form of territoriality may be a reflection of this focused crime pattern. Typical examples are drug sales gangs and skinhead groups.

Reference to Table 15.1 suggests that modifications may benefit the application of the typology to the European situation. For instance, these relatively new gangs in Europe *at the present time* will seldom reach the size or age-range or duration of the Traditional gangs in the United States. Yet Traditional gangs have been noted in at least three cities—Glasgow, Berlin, and Kazan. The availability of the typology allows a preliminary assessment of the degree to which one can find gangs that are structurally similar in the United States and Europe, thus overcoming the Eurogang Paradox.

Weitekamp's (2001) review of European gang descriptions collected in the book *The Eurogang Paradox* (Klein et al, 2001) reports Traditional gangs in Kazan, Neotraditional and Compressed gangs in Manchester, Specialty Gangs in The Hague and Rotterdam, as well as Compressed gangs in Copenhagen, Frankfurt, and Oslo. Klein (1997) found similar typology counterparts in Paris, Stockholm, Stuttgart, and Brussels. In sum, European nations have street gangs very similar in structure to the street gangs in America. Only future research can reveal variations or prevalence of the types, existence of other types, and the salience of other descriptors.

And what of the seven other gang characteristics listed above; how do they compare in Europe? Here we are severely limited by the few clear depictions currently available in the European gang literature, much of which was written without explicit attention to U.S./European comparisons. I will rely for this analysis on the eight chapters in *The Eurogang Paradox* that describe street gangs in Europe.

Location. The cities involved in these chapters are Rotterdam, den Haag, Manchester, Oslo, Copenhagen, Frankfurt, Kazan, Paris, and Bremen. Within these cities gang locations are described as inner city in Manchester, Oslo, and Kazan. Suburban locations are suggested in Manchester, Oslo, and Paris. In a number of these European cities, the location in suburban areas is explained by the placement there of housing projects designed for or occupied by immigrant and refugee populations.

Ethnicity. Many European countries, especially following the second World War, have welcomed substantial numbers of immigrants—often as "guest workers" to fill low-paying jobs not acceptable to sufficient numbers of the indigenous population. The second-generation offspring of the guest workers have in some locations gravitated toward street gang structures. In addition, some of these same countries have been receptive to large numbers of refugees from countries experiencing various kinds of nationalism and persecution of minority populations. Younger refugees and second-generation offspring have also fueled some of the gang problems. A review of *The Eurogang Paradox* reports reveals the following national and ethnic gang compositions:

Holland:	Moroccan, Antillian, and Surinamese
Manchester:	Afro-Caribbean, indigenous white
Oslo:	Vietnamese, Filipino, Pakistani, Somali, Iranian, Moroccan, Turkish, and indigenous white
Copenhagen:	Muslim, indigenous white
Frankfurt:	Turkish, Croatian, Italian, and Russian
Kazan:	Indigenous white, Tatars
Paris:	Algerian
Bremen:	Turkish, indigenous white

Other reports from Stockholm, London, Berlin, Stuttgart, Spain, and Switzerland confirm this highly varied pattern of both indigenous and, especially, nonindigenous gang composition. The contrast to the United States is obviously fairly striking. It should be added that much of the indigenous white gang activity in these European locations, more so than in the United States, is comprised of skinheads and similar racist groups, most of which fit fairly well into the Specialty gang structure.

Gender. With the exception of a mention in the report from Paris, none of the reports in this collection speaks of female gang participation. Whether this reflects a one-sex gang situation or the absence of researchers' attention to the issue cannot be determined. If the former, this is an important departure from the American experience. If the latter, it may be a reflection of a mostly male research enterprise not unlike that found in earlier American studies. The enrollment of female researchers in the Eurogang Program can certainly be encouraged to help open the window on the gender issue there.

Diffusion. There are no American gangs in Europe, nor have I heard of any American gang members migrating to Europe and influencing gang genesis there. But the reports from Holland, Manchester, and Oslo do suggest that the diffusion of American *gang culture* has had an effect. American gang movies and books (including translations from the English) are specifically cited. And of course much European television fare is imported from the United States, as is gang-oriented popular or rap music. How much we have spread our gang influence is not clear, but it is certain that some level of gang culture diffusion has taken place.

Cohesiveness. The picture on concern for and-measurement of gang cohesiveness in Europe is mixed. The reports from Holland, Paris, and Frankfurt make no explicit reference to the topic. The Manchester report suggests low levels, and the Copenhagen and Bremen reports are of medium levels. Some of the Oslo material suggests high gang cohesiveness, and the Kazan report describes a transformation over time from medium to high cohesiveness as those gangs have become more organized and explicitly criminal in focus. None of these reports uses empirical measures of group cohesiveness, to say nothing of common measures. This, then, is a most promising area for future gang research in European settings.

Crime Patterns. The Dutch gangs observed in The Hague and Rotterdam were small Specialty gangs. In Oslo and Paris, both specialized and versatile crime patterns were reported. In all the other sites, versatility was the reported pattern. The parallel to the American experience is quite striking. The patterns of most concern to American officials—drug sales and violence—are in most cases lower in the European cities, and firearm violence there is practically nonexistent. One can only hope this is a difference that will persist.

Crime Amplification. The major effect on levels of criminal activity occasioned by joining street gangs in the United States is mentioned in only three of the European reports, those from Oslo, Kazan, and Bremen. One suspects that this pattern has simply not been a paramount concern for European gang observers, but only future, focused research can clarify this.

SUMMARY

Although European gang research is quite new, and the gangs themselves have had little opportunity to evolve in form, some comparisons to the U.S. situation are already becoming clear. U.S. gangs are far, far more prevalent, and far more involved in serious and lethal violence. Our ethnic gang composition has over time become narrow, whereas that in Europe is highly varied. Still, on both continents street gangs are composed primarily of youth from marginalized segments of their societies. Gender and cohesiveness patterns may be different, but may also only seem so due to a lack of research attention.

But in contrast to these differences, one is struck by the similarities to be found between American and European gang situations (in the absence of, it should be noted, almost any deliberately comparative research). Two sets of attributes, when compared across the two continents, suggest we are viewing one older and one newer variation on a similar theme attributable to common group processes and similar combinations of societal variables that produce marginalization of some youth populations.

First, there are those attributes of gang structure that produce a typology of five gang types roughly applicable in both the United States and Europe. Group placements on subgrouping, size, age range, duration, territoriality, and crime versatility serve to reduce the "Eurogang Paradox" and reveal that current European street gangs can largely be subsumed under the Maxson/Klein typology developed in the United States. To deny street gang existence in Europe, in these circumstances, would be more foolish than useful.

Second, analyses of European gang reports in eight general locations show that, to the extent they are covered, seven gang-relevant descriptions from U.S. research are applicable to European research. One can obtain clarification of European gangs by reference to such variables as location, ethnicity, gender, cultural diffusion, cohesiveness, crime patterns, and crime amplification. These are variables additional to the structural attributes of the typology (except for crime pattern).

There is much room in all this for future research to elucidate the unique natures of European gangs, and the developing Eurogang Program will likely provide such clarification. But the uniqueness will be bounded by the discovered similarities to American street gangs. This means that the American gang knowledge accumulated over the past 70 years provides a major resource for research in Europe, the kind of research not available to the Americans until only very recently. As suggested above, I would urge special attention to group processes and youth marginalization as pivotal concerns for understanding and controlling street gang developments in Europe.

NOTES

1. The Port Moresby "Rascals" have been described in Biles (1976), and by Sundeen (1981).
2. A book by that name includes many of the papers produced for the first Eurogang workshop: see Klein et al (2001).
3. Klein (1997) and Klein et al. (2001) have expanded on the five gang types revealed in the original research by Maxson and Klein (1995). These types have been confirmed in a statewide study in Illinois by Scott (2000) and by the National Youth Gang Center (2000b) in a comprehensive national survey of law enforcement agencies.
4. Campbell and her coauthors noted, "youth in one part of the country are relatively ignorant of others' activities until it reaches the point of mass movement or violence. The net effect is that New York teenagers, already factioned within the city into their own areas, have virtually no knowledge of the situation of gang members in Chicago, Los Angeles, or Philadelphia."
5. This has also been labeled "cafeteria-style" offending ("Smorgasbord offending" has been suggested by a Swedish scholar). The major exception to this versatile pattern is to be found in Specialty gangs described later in this chapter.

A GLOBAL OVERVIEW OF THE ISSUES OF AND RESPONSES TO TEEN GANGS

By Maureen Duffy

ll of us have a stake in the issues affecting juveniles. In the United States alone, almost 5,000 communities report having juvenile gangs (Moore and Terrett, 1998). These communities document the presence of a total of about 31,000 juvenile gangs with a membership of around 850,000 young people. These numbers reflect the significant impact of juvenile gangs on local communities throughout the United States.

The general public is impacted by youth gangs either through fear of them or by victimization from their crimes. Communities also bear the financial costs of social, legal, and criminal justice services made necessary by young people in gangs. To a greater or lesser extent, young people in gangs in other countries throughout the world are having a similar impact on their societies. Youth gangs raise important questions about the relationship between gang membership and crime. Youth gangs also call attention to the situation of youth who perceive themselves to be excluded from access to societal opportunities and benefits such as jobs and status.

In *Teen Gangs: A Global View*, we have brought together a set of profiles of the youth gang issue in countries throughout the world. The profiles are largely descriptions of the youth gang situation and its relationship to juvenile crime and the larger issues of poverty and politics in the selected countries. Additionally, we have focused special attention on the attempted solutions that government, on the one hand, and private groups such as churches and community-based organizations, on the other hand, have brought to bear on the youth gang problem. Descriptions of the youth gang situation are different from an analysis of the issues raised by the existence of youth gangs. *Teen Gangs: A Global View* provides descriptions of the youth gang situation in countries from the United States to the Caribbean to Central America, from Europe to the Middle East, from Asia to Melanesia and Australia. These descriptions provide a beginning point for both the analysis of the issues raised by the existence of teen gangs and cross-cultural comparisons of the nature of the teen gang problem and attempted solutions.

ISSUES IN DISCUSSION OF TEEN GANGS

Definitions

At this point in time, there is no clear, widely shared definition of what constitutes a youth gang. Neither are there clear criteria for establishing who is a gang member and who is not. In social science research the absence of a consensually shared definition of a youth gang is problematic in developing even basic descriptions of gangs. Social science researchers, theorists, youth workers, government policy-makers, and the public are likely to be operating from different understandings of what constitutes a youth gang. While they all may be using the same word, the meaning of that word for each is likely to vary considerably.

Rob White, in his contribution on youth gangs in Australia (Chapter 1), points out that the media and political leaders may equate youth hanging out on the streets with gang activity. He reminds us that street activity is commonplace among young people and may not necessarily be an indicator of gang activity, although it is often construed as such. Hazlehurst and Hazlehurst (1998) identify "adolescent male membership" (p. 5) as the most basic defining element of a juvenile gang. White (Chapter 1) echoes Howell (1998) and Short (1968) in emphasizing the need to distinguish youth gangs from varieties of other group formations and subcultures, for example, adolescent friendship groups that normally spend a lot of time on the street and other teen subgroups. To further confuse matters, adolescent subgroups, especially in urban areas, may parody gang members in their dress and mannerisms, yet not identify themselves as a gang in the same way as the gang they are parodying.

Illegal activity is the single most important identifier of gang activity (Ball and Curry, 1995), although classic gang theorists such as Thrasher have focused on the sense of solidarity and territoriality of gang members more than on the activities, such as criminal behavior, that gang members may engage in (Thrasher, 1963). Klein (1971) also emphasizes territoriality, along with symbols and, most importantly, the self-identification of the young people as belonging to a gang. Whether a youth gang is defined by where the gang members hang out, how they self-identify, what they look like to others, or whether they act criminally or not, there is still no consensus about what is the most important element in the definition of a youth gang.

The homeless children of the streets of Brazil who engage in crime in order to survive are different from the street gangs of Chicago and Los Angeles. Those American street gangs are not the same as the mixed-age-group gangs linked to organized crime and political patronage that Lorna Black describes in her contribution on the Jamaican posses (Chapter 8). In *Teen Gangs: A Global View,* how gangs are defined and what aspect of gang membership is emphasized will differ somewhat from country to country.

Age and Gender of Youth Gang Members

Indeed, age would seem to be a simple element of a definition of a youth gang, but it is not. There is a trend toward inclusion of both younger and older members in youth gangs, but the most notable increase in membership is among older members (Howell, 1998; Moore, 1990; Spergel, 1995). The age range of the typical youth gang is from 12 to 24 (Howell, 1998); this age range obviously includes young adults.

Mixed-age gangs are not uncommon (Hazlehurst and Hazlehurst, 1998), and some gang theorists, such as Knox (1995), suggest that the very idea of a youth gang makes less and less sense given the increased connections between what are traditionally referred to as youth gangs and organized crime gangs, which include members from a wider range of ages. Bettina Lozzi-Toscano in her contribution on Italian youth gangs (Chapter 7) makes this point very clearly and emphasizes the connections between organized youth gangs and organized crime. However, a modal age for an average youth gang member in the United States is around 17 or 18 (Curry and Decker, 1998). Scott Gillig's article on gang trends in the United States (Chapter 14), notes that females can be gang members, yet it is quite clear that youth gang members across the globe are overwhelmingly male.

Individual Crime, Gang Crime, and Organized Crime

Accepting illegal activity as a central characteristic of gang activity raises significant questions about the relationship between individual crime, gang crime, and organized crime. If an individual who is a gang member commits a crime, when is that crime best understood as an individual crime and when is it best understood as a gang crime? Additionally, if the youth gang has developed a more organized structure and becomes entrepreneurial in nature and linked to organized crime in the community, when is youth gang crime best understood as organized crime? These are very difficult questions to answer, and the distinctions involved are very important ones.

There is a reciprocal relationship between the individual and the gang, with the gang exerting a powerful influence on the individual. At the same time, the individual gang member's needs must be accommodated to a certain extent by the gang. Adolescent gang members commit violent and serious crimes at significantly higher rates than adolescent nongang members (Howell, 1998). Youth gangs demonstrate more serious and more group-based criminal activity, the more formally organized they are (Fagan, 1989). Knox (1995), as noted earlier, raises the question of whether in today's crime environment the idea of a youth gang is even meaningful, given the organized criminal activities, such as drug dealing and money laundering, that gangs as criminal enterprises participate in.

The ability of a youth gang to carry out organized criminal activities is to some extent dependent upon its structure and level of organization. A youth gang composed of young people who hang out together and share similar experiences of demoralization and rejection by society is one view of what a juvenile gang looks like. An alternative view is that of a youth gang as a more formal organization with clear leadership and roles performed by gang members within a framework of rules, expectations, and sanctions for non-compliance. Both forms of youth gangs exist, and the distinction between the two is not necessarily easy to determine from the outside looking in.

More research is needed to understand the relationship between youth gangs and organized crime, in activities such as drug trafficking. Howell (1998) states that "gang involvement appears to increase individual involvement in drug vise, drug trafficking, gun carrying, and violence and, perhaps, to prolong involvement in drug sales" (p. 11), while also noting that the relationship between youth gangs and drug trafficking is still unclear. What is clear though is that the more formally structured and organized a youth gang becomes, the more likely it is that it will eventually start participating in organized criminal enterprises, in particular, drug dealing and trafficking.

MARGINALIZATION, EXCLUSION, AND INCLUSION

A theme running through this collection of profiles of youth gangs from around the globe is the concept of marginalization. Marginalization refers to the state of being on the edges or the fringes of society, being left out and not fully included. Alienated or marginalized youth are more likely to join gangs than are young people who fully participate in school and work. Inclusion in society involves some degree of personal ownership of the dominant values of one's culture and community. At the personal level, included members of society feel that they belong, that they are a part of what is going on, and that what they think about things is important and will make a difference. Included members of society feel respected and that they have a voice. Being socially included means having ties to one's community that connect one to other people in meaningful ways. Inclusion means access and opportunity. Included people are insiders; excluded people are outsiders.

Within particular societies, certain groups are often more marginalized than other groups. Young people and minorities are examples of groups that are frequently marginalized. There are a number of social indicators that point to a state of marginalization within a community. These indicators include poverty, unemployment, increased crime, increased school dropout rates, and increased rates of substance abuse and homelessness. People in marginalized communities generally have lower levels of education than those in more socially integrated communities and often lack the job skills necessary to move into a state of fuller social participation. Young people living in poorer communities who have dropped out of school and whose lives are disorganized through substance abuse and lack of job skills are most likely to experience themselves as socially excluded and as outsiders. This combination of social and psychological circumstances makes a young person more at risk for gang membership, and gang leaders recruit in these depressed environments. The term "underclass" is also used to describe people living in these marginalized situations.

A number of theorists about gangs identify the presence of this underclass of excluded members of society as fertile ground for the development and survival of youth gangs (Bursik and Grasniick, 1993; Huff, 1992; Moore, 1991). Individual psychological and family factors can serve as either protective factors or as additional predisposing factors for those in marginalized communities. Adult role models in the family, order and routine within the family, and absence of family violence and addiction are protective. Family disorganization, substance abuse, and parental attitudes negative toward authority and community increase the risk that an already marginalized young person will become a gang member (Esbensen, Huizinga, and Weiher, 1993).

In *Teen Gangs: A Global View*, a number of contributors address the issue of marginalization and emphasize its importance in understanding the cultural context giving rise to youth gang formation. In Chapter 10, Sinclair Dinnen discusses the growth of raskolism in Papua New Guinea against the backdrop of rapid urban growth following independence from colonial rule. The indigenous people of Papua New Guinea, as a result of the country's change in political status and subsequent rapid growth, experienced the disruption of their traditional kinship networks, leaving many alienated and without support. Edil Torres Rivera and Loan Phan clearly implicate a history of colonialism, injury to cultural pride, and associated economic exploitation in the emergence and tenacity of the youth gang problem in Puerto Rico (Chapter 11). Perhaps the most shocking discussion of the relationship between social exclusion and the youth gang problem can be found in Anthony Borrow and Jennifer Walker's contribution on Honduras (Chapter 4). They trace the origins of Honduran youth gangs to deported Salvadoran gang members from the street gangs of Los Angeles, who upon returning to El Salvador laid the groundwork for the spread of youth gangs to neighboring

Central American countries. Borrow and Walker document the claims of groups inside Honduras who believe that government sanctioned extrajudicial murder of youth gang members has been used as a form of social cleansing of a both troubled and troubling segment of society.

Schneider (2002) addressed the issue of marginalization and exclusion of adolescent gang members in post-World War II United States in this way:

> Adolescents responded to a labor market that exploited them by quitting or getting fired from jobs, to a school system that did not educate by dropping out, and to families that failed to nurture them by hanging out on street corners. Although the institutions of adolescent socialization encouraged only individual rebellion, adolescents in acts of creativity and imagination established street gangs and forged a gang culture so evocative that its forms were repeatedly commercialized. Gangs were a collective response to the difficulties of adolescent life in poor neighborhoods. (p. 660)

Schneider's position suggests that the very formation of youth gangs was a solution attempt—an attempt on the part of excluded young people to construct a culture of acceptance and participation that the larger institutions of society had failed to provide.

DRUGS AND YOUTH GANGS

The relationship between drugs and youth gangs is graphically portrayed in the chapter on Ireland's youth gang problem (Chapter 5). In this chapter the infamous "needle muggings," in which blood-filled syringes were used as weapons to intimidate victims and extort money and goods from them, are discussed. As with so many issues relating to youth gangs, the relationships among drug use, drug trafficking, and gangs are not clear. About one thing there is not much doubt, however: gang members do use drugs more frequently and at higher levels than do nongang members (Esbensen, Huizinga, and Weiher, 1993; Fagan, 1989).

By its very nature, drug dependency opens the door to increased crime and violence. Addiction requires a steady stream of drugs, and many addicted young gang members increase their criminal activities in order to obtain the drugs needed to support their habits. This is the vicious cycle of drug abuse leading to drug dependency leading to increased crime leading to increased drug use, and on and on.

The sale, distribution, and trafficking of drugs is another matter, and the distinction between organized criminal drug enterprises and youth gangs is less clear. In Ireland (Chapter 5), for example, the emergence of gang violence coincided with the widespread introduction of drugs, especially heroin, into the country in the late 1970s and early 1980s. Jill Duba and Marty Jencius, in their discussion of youth gangs in the Bahamas (Chapter 2), also point to the fact that job opportunities are available in the underworld of drug trafficking for youth gang members and that legitimate jobs are much harder to get. Richard Van Dorn, in his contribution about street gangs in Britain (Chapter 3), makes the point that the drug trade is attractive to adolescent youth gangs whose members are relatively economically disadvantaged and who also suffer from a loss of a sense of identity and place.

Howell and Decker (1999), in their comprehensive review of the primarily U.S.-focused literature related to youth gangs, drugs, and violent crime, document the relationship between the crack cocaine epidemic in the inner cities and increased youth gang violence. They also point out that it can be difficult to distinguish youth gangs from organized crime gangs and that more research and analysis of the relationship between the two is needed. In her discussion of how schools can respond to youth gangs and juvenile crime in Taiwan (Chapter 12), Julia Yang indicates that Taiwanese youth gangs are connected to organized crime, as does Lorna Black in her discussion of gangs in Jamaica (Chapter 8). Black describes Jamaican gangs as having juvenile members, but points out that these members are controlled by the older gang members higher up in the crime gang organization, suggesting a more formal and organized structure.

In many cases, drug use and the sale and distribution of drugs are simply assumed to be a part of youth gang life. As discussed, the research confirms that gang members do more drugs more often, Howell and Decker (1999) emphasize the need for caution in making a direct connection between youth gangs and organized drug crime and counsel against equating the two. The contributors to *Teen Gangs: A Global View*, while not methodologically examining the distinction between youth gangs and organized criminal drug gangs, point suggestively in the direction of youth gang involvement in organized drug crime.

RESPONSES AND FUTURE DIRECTIONS

Responses by government and nongovernmental organizations to the juvenile gang situation can range from minimization and denial of a problem to gross overreaction. Fear of a gang problem's hurting the image of a community or country can lead to understatement and denial. A few particularly vicious or sensational crimes, or frustration with groups of youths hanging out on the streets, can lead to a public perception of a greater problem than actually exists. Both minimizing and exaggerating the nature of a youth gang problem can give rise to inappropriate and counterproductive responses by governmental bodies and nongovernmental organizations. In Chapter 6, Sloane Veshinski discusses youth gangs and juvenile crime in Israel and concludes that the existence of youth gangs in Israel is not widely acknowledged within the country and suggests this could be a function of Israel's larger struggles for its security and survival in a highly turbulent part of the world. Sylvia Fernandez, in her contribution about teen gangs in Malaysia (Chapter 9), notes that behavior that in the past would have been brushed off as the usual school fights or bullying is now described as "teen gangsterism," indicating the significant shift in public perception and tolerance that has occurred.

Responding to a gang problem requires a focus on relationships, both cooperative and adversarial. Gang members have significant relationships with one another, and for a gang to function, there must be some degree of cooperation and coordination among its members. They also have relationships with other gangs, relationships that may be cooperative or adversarial and that alternate between cooperation and conflict, depending upon the time and situation. As discussed, gangs and gang members also have relationships with the larger communities within which they are located. These relationships are often failed ones, marked by a sense of mutual suspicion, anger, and distrust. Gang members' relationships with their communities are characterized by the experiences of rejection, exclusion, futility, and, not uncommonly, overt anger and a demand to be recognized. In turn, communities frequently respond by relating to the gangs with fear, avoidance, and a desire to separate or remove the gangs and gang members from their midst so that they do not have to deal with them.

It makes sense, therefore, that interventions aimed at reducing gang involvement and gang activities, particularly those of a criminal nature, must take into account the complexity of the relationships between the gang and the community and ideally involve collaboration among all stakeholders. The key stakeholders are the gang members, law enforcement, the business and economic community, churches and community organizations, and citizens most impacted by gang related crime.

Responses to gang activity in a community can be to prevent or to intervene or both. Preventive responses are designed to reduce the proliferation of gangs in a community and divert young people from joining them. Interventions are designed to reduce gang activity that already exists, particularly criminal activity, and to provide opportunities for gang members to leave gangs for productive legitimate employment.

Preventive responses are often educational in nature, focusing on antigang and antidrug education. Antidrug education appears to be especially important since research does show an increase in gang involvement among drug using and drug-selling youth (Esbensen, Huizinga, and Weiher, 1993; Fagan, 1989). Hill, Howell, Hawkins, and Battin (1999) are quite clear in identifying early drug use as a risk factor for gang involvement later. In addition, antigang education programs similar in philosophy to the antidrug education programs such as Drug Abuse Resistance Education (DARE) may also be effective. School-based antigang programs such as GREAT (Gang Resistance Education and Training), based on the DARE model, focus on helping young people develop gang refusal skills and are being more formally examined (Esbensen and Osgood, 1999). Julia

Yang, in her comprehensive research about the youth gang problem and at-risk youth in Taiwan (Chapter 12), describes in detail a host of school-based programs that have been put in place to address these problems. Community policing, a gang intervention that can be both preventive and suppressive, is a gang response strategy that Joanna Headley describes in her contribution on teen gangs in Trinidad and Tobago (Chapter 13).

Interventive responses to youth gangs include: (1) gang suppression through law enforcement activities; (2) community-based programs designed to offer meaningful alternatives to gang membership, primarily by giving gang members access to legitimate jobs; (3) innovative restorative justice programs such as gang and weapons surrenders and victim-offender mediation; and (4) setting of national policy agendas to include resources for addressing youth issues. Gang suppression is usually understood as prosecution and incarceration of gang members and supervision by law enforcement and probation departments.

Community-based gang alternative programs are varied. They focus on providing opportunities to gang members to learn basic job skills. The more effective programs in this category also provide access to legitimate employment through mentoring. Other rehabilitation programs, such as addiction treatment, can be structured to support the goals of community based gang alternative programs.

In many ways, restorative justice programs seem to offer the most promise for addressing the problems of marginalized youth and teen gangs. Such programs attempt to address the needs of the victim, the offender, and the community by connecting them in a circle of responsibility, amends, and restitution. Ireland's extremely successful Garda Juvenile Diversion Programme (Chapter 5), is an example, as is the gang surrender described in Sinclair Dinnen's contribution on Papua New Guinea (Chapter 10). In promoting a restorative justice focus, Bazemore (1998) states that "a relational approach to rehabilitation cannot be clinical in its focus, but must instead emphasize community socialization networks and naturally occurring processes in its analysis of how most delinquents grow up to be normal, productive adults" (p. 790). As Dinnen notes, however, in his discussion of the gang surrender in Papua New Guinea, the public's enthusiasm for programs like the gang surrender seems to wane in the face of increased crime and threat.

Finally, the policies set by governments at the national level about at-risk youth and juvenile crime are convincing indicators of the direction a country is heading in addressing youth issues. Zero-tolerance and get-tough policies are accompanied by resource allocation to prosecution and incarceration. Resources tend to be allocated toward prevention when risk reduction is the government's policy priority. There is still much unexplored ground in the development of gang alternative and restorative justice programs. The development and refinement of these kinds of programs would be helped considerably by national policies promoting and supporting them.

CONCLUSIONS

Teen Gangs: A Global View provides a window to the world of teen gangs. In each of the cultural descriptions in this volume, the teen gang situation is discussed within the larger framework of associated social and economic conditions. The unique character of the teen gang situation in each country is presented, and important questions are raised by the contributors. These questions address issues related to the nature of teen gangs, the degree of threat posed by teen gangs, their connection to organized crime, and the issues of social exclusion and marginalization of youth. The contributors also invite us to reflect upon the strategies and solutions utilized by various countries across the globe to deal with at-risk youth and teen gangs. Perhaps most important of all, the global view of teen gangs presented in this volume invites us, as thoughtful citizens, to think broadly about at-risk youth and teen gangs and to participate more fully in conversations about how best to respond to them.

REFERENCES

Ball, R. A., and G. D. Curry. "The logic of definition in criminology: Purposes and methods for defining gangs." *Criminology,* 33 (1995): 225–245.

Bazemore, G. "Restorative justice and earned redemption: Communities, victims, and offender reintegration." *American Behavioral Scientist,* 41 (1998): 768–813.

Bursik, R. J., and H. G. Grasmick. *Neighborhoods and crime: The dimensions of effective community control* (New York: Lexington Books, 1993).

Curry, G. D., and S. H. Decker. *Confronting gangs: Crime and community* (Los Angeles: Roxbury Publishing Co., 1998).

Esbensen, F. A., D. Huizinga, and A. W. Weiher. "Gang and non-gang youth: Differences in explanatory variables." *Journal of Contemporary Criminal Justice,* 9 (1993): 94–116.

Esbensen, F., and D. W. Osgood. "Gang resistance education and training (GREAT): Results from the national evaluation." *Journal of Research in Crime and Delinquency,* 36 (1999): 194–225.

Fagan, J. "The social organization of drug use and drug dealing among urban gangs." *Criminology,* 27 (1989): 633–669.

Hazlehurst, C., and K. M. Hazlehurst. "Gangs in cross-cultural perspective." In *Gangs and youth subcultures: International Explorations,* edited by C. Hazlehurst and K. M. Hazlehurst (New Brunswick, NJ: Transaction Publishers, 1998), pp. 1–34.

Hill, K. G., J. C. Howell, J. D. Hawkins, and S. R. Battin. "Childhood risk factors for adolescent gang membership: Results from the Seattle Social Development Project." *Journal of Research in Crime and Delinquency,* 36 (1999): 300–322.

Howell, J. C. "Youth gangs: An overview." *Juvenile Justice Bulletin* (Washington, DC: U.S. Department of Justice, Office of Justice Programs, Office of Juvenile Justice and Delinquency Prevention, 1998).

Howell, J. C., and S. H. Decker. "The youth gangs, drugs, and violence connection." *Juvenile Justice Bulletin* (Washington, DC: U.S. Department of Justice, Office of Justice Programs, Office of Juvenile Justice and Delinquency Prevention, 1999).

Huff, R. C. "The new youth gangs: Social policy and malignant neglect." In *Juvenile justice and public policy: Towards a national agenda*, edited by I. M. Schwartz (New York: Lexington Books, 1992), pp. 22–44.

Klein, M. W. *Street gangs and street workers.* (Englewood Cliffs, NJ: Prentice Hall, 1971).

Knox, G. W. *An introduction to gangs*, rev. ed. (Bristol, IN: Wyndham Hall Press, 1995).

Moore, J. P. "Gangs, drugs, and violence." In *Drugs and violence: Causes, correlates, and consequences*, edited by M. de La Rosa, E. Y. Lambert, and B. Cropper. Research Monograph No. 103 (Rockville, MD: National Institute on Drug Abuse, 1990), pp. 160–176.

—*Going down to the barrio: Homeboys and homegirls in change.* (Philadelphia: Temple University Press, 1991).

Moore, J. P., and C. P. Terrett. *Highlights of the 1996 National youth gang survey.* Fact Sheet (Washington, DC: U.S. Department of Justice, Office of Justice Programs, Office of Juvenile Justice and Delinquency Prevention, 1998).

Schneider, E. "Eric Schneider's response to Andrew Diamond." *Journal of Urban History,* 28 (2002): 659–660.

Short, J. F., ed. *Gang delinquency and delinquent subcultures.* (New York: Harper and Row, 1968).

Spergel, I. A. *The youth gang problem.* (New York: Oxford University Press, 1995).

Thrasher, F. M. *The gang: A study of one thousand three hundred thirteen gangs in Chicago.* (Chicago: University of Chicago Press, 1963).

DELINQUENCY AND GANGS

"ROCK" SALES IN SOUTH LOS ANGELES

By Malcolm W. Klein
and Cheryl L. Maxson

Throughout the Black residential areas of Los Angeles County, there has been a recent, dramatic increase in cocaine dealing. This has resulted in large part from the proliferation of cocaine "rocks" and fortified "rock houses" which, with certain refinements, constitute a new technology and organization for cocaine distribution.

An increasing trend in the distribution system is the use of street gang members in various dealing roles.

What follows is a brief description of this phenomenon, gleaned from a preliminary research foray into the local "rock" world in order to develop a retrospective study of changes in gang involvement in the rock cocaine trade. Included are the increased potentials for expanding the demand for cocaine and for serious violence in the sales system, as well as the implications of this new technology for the Investigation of cocaine distribution and control.

Data for this report derive from media reports, on site observations, and numerous conversations with police officers, personnel from community organizations, our colleagues in both gang and drug research, and various individuals with insight into the local drug scene.

A cocaine "rock" is a pebble-sized crystaline form of cocaine base, obtainable currently for $25.00-, an amount making it available to virtually any interested potential

Malcolm W. Klein and Cheryl L. Maxson, ""Rock" Sales in South Los Angeles," *Sociology and Social Research*, vol. 69, pp. 561-565. Copyright © 1985 by Malcolm W. Klein and Cheryl L. Maxson. Reprinted with permission.

user. Double rocks at $50.00 are also available. A rock is produced by cutting cocaine powder with a common substance such as baking soda or a baby laxative and then cooking the substance in a test tube or—preferably, to avoid open fire—agitating it in hot water. The rocking process is simple, quick, and clearly more advantageous than free-basing. Purity of rocks is estimated to range from five percent to thirty per cent (corresponding to non-rock estimates in the East: Schnoll, 1979; Johnson, personal communication, 1985) to as high as 95 percent. Narcotics analyses have placed rocks from .05 to .50 grams of cocaine, but most typically at about .25 grams. At this latter estimate, the $25 price is not much below the average pre-rock price for cocaine of $125 to $250 per gram. (Information received from LAPD narcotics officers, LASD Narcotic Information Network, LASD narcotics officers, LAPD Narcotics Analysis Laboratory, Torrance Regional Crime Laboratory; Dr. Sidney Cohen of the Neuro-Psychiatric Institute, UCLA). The rock form is not new (Anon, 1972), but knowledge of it evidently is.

Rocks are generally smoked through a pipe (water pipes are preferred), often with other substances such as marijuana or rum. They yield a brief but intense high. Rocks are easily manufactured, hidden, passed, and disposed. They are a boon to dealer and user alike. As a police informant noted, "the real value is not that you get so much for the dollar, but that it's easy to carry, easy to get rid of in a bust. You drop it and it's hard to find on the ground; step on it and it's history."

A "rock house" is a small home or an apartment from which rocks are distributed to customers. Manufacture of rocks may take place in a rock-house, but often the house is merely the last station in the distribution system of rocks manufactured elsewhere.

Some rock houses are little more than low level sales points where, as one of our informants noted, you get a "drive-up-and-honk-your-horn buy." But more critical, if less common, are the fortified rock houses. Fortifications take many forms, but can be so formidable that if they are not broken into in a raid within 20 seconds (one officer claimed-entry in 10 seconds with the right equipment), it may take several hours to break in.

Typical fortifications include barred windows, windows with thick wood that "is stronger than the walls, windows with steel mesh inside, doors with three inch solid iron bars, barred doors leading to interior doors of four inches of solid wood, wooden doors secured by bars drilled into floor and ceiling and 4 x 4s across top and bottom. Some houses have a TV surveillance camera with monitor. Rock houses of this sort have been entered by enforcement groups employing special door springing devices, tow trucks with one-inch ropes or cables attached to the bars which may eventually yank door and porch across the neighbor's yard, and by explosive devices (including "flash bang" grenades which temporarily blind and confuse residents as a diversion to discourage the destruction of evidence and to facilitate a safe entry. Swat teams are often used, but their careful approach often yields no contraband. The problem is that, prior to entry, drugs, equipment, and paraphernalia have been destroyed or flushed. In some cases, plumbing modifications create direct and immediate access to sewer lines. Narcotics team entries are faster, aimed at immediate entry and recovery of evidence, but far more dangerous because of their more single-minded goal; guns are commonly found in rock houses, but are sought after the drug search. The newest wrinkle, mobile rock houses, give witness to the acceleration of move and countermove between distributors and enforcement agencies, as does the LAPD's battering ram attached to the front of an armored personnel carrier.

Rock houses are generally manned by several individuals working in concert. Roles may include lookout, dealer (unseen by the customer who obtains his rock by slipping his hand and and money through a slot in the inner door), guard (armed, often with a shotgun through another slot to prevent rip-off), a manufacturer, and someone to manage the funds. Estimates on the number of such establishments in South Los Angeles, a Black area where the phenomenon is concentrated, range from one to two hundred at a time to as many as a thousand. "That phenomenon is incredible," reports a police official actually involved in assessing the scope of the problem, "I've never seen the likes of it in 22 years in enforcement." Estimates are minimal because (a) locations are switched very often and (b) so many residences in the area have barred windows and doors that rock houses are usually distinguishable only by the heavy traffic in and out of houses. As one police officer noted, "a frightened grandmother and a rock house can be next to each other and, if we don't make a buy first, we may mistake the one for the other."

While the fortified distribution center is not a new phenomenon, it has been reported in such widely divergent sites as Harlem and Bridgeport, Connecticut (Bruce Johnson and Dana Hunt, personal communications)—rocks and rock houses constitute the new "technology" of cocaine sales in the Black community. What makes them of particular interest to the writers is the acknowledged but as yet poorly measured infusion of street gang members into this distribution system. Gang involvement is a connected part of a very rapid process by which this system has become institutionalized. For example, in addition to the reported formal recruitment of gang members, the system has involved other formal accoutrements:

1. There is now evidence of a coordinated construction apparatus for fortifying rock houses. Equipment found on busted houses and secretly marked by the police has shown up shortly thereafter on new rock houses.
2. There is evidence of coordinated transport systems. For instance, one Mercedes dealership is said to be used for car leases in certain distribution networks.
3. Some suppliers, transporters, and dealers are using commercial radio beeper systems with coded messages. While the police plug into these systems they can

do little because the systems are legitimate (i.e., have legitimate customers such as physicians) and are protected by federal legislation.

4. There are now numerous examples in police files of multi-house ownerships. In one case, a rock house "franchise" was reportedly sold recently for $30,000—the amount was for the franchise, not for the house. What we have described then is a rapidly spreading increasingly institutionalized cocaine distribution technology which yields ready access to inexpensive cocaine to a high demand in a very large Black community in Los Angeles. How serious is the problem posed by this situation? The following points, at least, seem relevant to an assessment of seriousness.

5. The phenomenon, at least currently, seems to be ethnically specific. Cocaine is found widely in the Black community in Los Angeles, but is almost totally absent from the Hispanic areas. The distribution seems custom-made for other Black gang centers (Philadelphia, New York, Washington, Chicago, etc.). Early confirmation of this suggestion may be seen in the recent press description of rock houses appearing in Black areas of Pasadena, a development confirmed by the gang unit of the Los Angeles Sheriff's Department, and in Inglewood, another racially transitional middle class community. As Blum noted, "Like the legitimate trade, the illicit one is likely comprised of ERROR deaths, put the recent related killings at 25 people. Another estimate places the number at 65. Blum's comments seem apropos, that dealing provides a role and identity, individual power, adventure, and flouting of the law, and opportunity for aggression "and sometimes to kill. Is this not a violent pie to set before the delinquent king" (1972:111).

6. The level of rook sales leaves no doubt that a ready, cheap supply can result in a dramatic increase in demand. The daily "take" from a rock house operation has been placed at a few thousand dollars in some in-stances, and up to $25,000 a house on the 1st and 15th of each month when welfare checks arrive. As a result, treatment centers are reporting rock-related clientele increases of 40, 70, even 100%. Just as treatment requests increase, so do arrests. The LAPD's South Bureau narcotics unit reported more than a fourfold increase from 1983 to 1984 in coke-related arrests of juveniles alone. Supply and demand, enforcement and treatment are all tied together in this increased activity. The importance is underscored by David Nurco's comments to a Senate Subcommittee: "Thus we may conclude that individuals who currently use cocaine are at risk to become heavily dependent upon it, should the price of cocaine go down and the availability go up. Should this circumstance occur, and it appears it is imminent, we can expect to have a major problem in this country with severely dependent cocaine users" (Nurco, 1984:4).

7. Finally, and perhaps most serious of all, there is both to respond to existing demand and, when supply exceeds demand, to enhance it" (1972:6).

8. The phenomenon "explodes" so rapidly that only two months after public awareness was achieved in Los Angeles through press reports, there has been a report from a special task force appointed by Mayor Bradley, the appointment of another task force in the office of Chief Gates (LAPD) to coordinate gang and narcotics units in South Los Angeles, the formation of a special narcotics task force of 40 officers pulled off patrol in LAPD's South Bureau, and a mandated coordination of heretofore totally separated gang and narcotics units in the Los Angeles Sheriff's Department. The field director of the County's very large neighborhood gang program has added his summary view of this "whole new challenge for us." And, the first rock house "sting, has been mounted by the LAPD. That is, there has been a definite organizational Acknowledgment of the gang/cocaine distribution connection.

9. Associated with the rock technology development, but at levels in considerable dispute among enforcement and other agency informants, is serious violence associated with rock sales, or gang involvement, or both. Certainly the potential for violence is there; most rock houses (38% by one estimate), when busted, yield firearms upon search. A recent raid yielded dozens of automatic weapons, with ammunition, purchased from a nearby munitions store—legally. A gang unit officer, commenting on a recent gang shooting related to a drug deal that resulted in five absolutely nothing inherent in this distribution technology, nor in the Los Angeles context of its development, that would prevent its exportation to many other urban centers. Indeed, exportability seems very high. There is the easily distributable and low cost rock form; there is the rock house which is easily fortified against enforcement, protects distributors and consumers alike, and provides high accessibility for consumers; and there; is a well organized distribution network, especially with gang involvement, yielding minimal risk to dealers through various levels of the distribution system. All this makes for an intelligent well-organized system that is maximally effective—in short, it works efficiently, is very impressive, and could easily explode across the nation.

That the trade itself has grown is not in dispute. We found clear documentation of increases from a brief review of law enforcement records. LAPD Narcotic Bureau arrests for cocaine sales or possession with the intent to sell were 605 in 1982, 919 in 1983, and 1490 in 1984, an overall increase of 146 per cent.

During the same period, arrests for possession increased 114 per cent: supply and demand climb together. In the three LAPD divisions where rock houses are most common, the sales figures grew three-fold from 210 in 1983 to 628 in 1984. The first monthly figures for 1985 show a continuation of the trend. In these same stations, possession arrests rose 125 per cent from 1983 to 1984. The Narcotics Bureau director for

South Bureau (which includes these stations) reports that almost all cocaine arrests now are for rock; cocaine in powder form is now seldom seen in the area.

We also reviewed LAPD South Bureau Narcotic Division activity reports from January of 1982 to the present. From January to April of 1982 there are notes of cocaine increase with free base as the most popular method. In May there is a random comment about "rock hard" pre-free based cocaine. With continuing increases in arrests, the first real mention of rocks came in September, 1982, in the Southeast Division. It showed up in 77th Division after another five months. Thereafter, monthly reports continued to report the presence of rock cocaine throughout the Bureau in increasing amounts.

For the Sheriff's Department, we have department-wide cocaine figures which include arrests by both patrol and narcotics officers. They show sales and possession-for-sale arrests mounting from 699 in 1982 to 850 in 1983 to 1,311 in 1984, an increase of 88 per cent. LASD gang offense statistics for 1983 and 1984 indicate that while major categories remained relatively stable or actually decreased, murder and attempted murder rose, as did narcotic violations. The changes are instructive:

- assaults:-2 per cent
- shooting into inhabited dwellings:-6 per cent
- robbery:-5 per cent
- murder and attempted murder: +19 per cent
- burglary: +2 per cent
- narcotics offenses: +12 per cent
- auto theft:-6 per cent.

Finally, we can add a recent update from Black areas of Inglewood and Pasadena. Narcotic sales arrests there, cited by the police as being principally cocaine, and mostly in rock form, have jumped 76 per cent and 183 per cent, respectively.

What the statistics in each jurisdiction suggest is what most professionals report; cocaine sale is increasing dramatically, in rather direct proportion to the development of the rock and rock house technology. We are no longer surprised to learn of operators who run a string of rock houses, of 250 buys a day in a two-house set-up, or of a $25,000 take at one house. Corroborating reports of the sales impact are provided by various treatment agencies with rapid and dramatic increases in cocaine users seeking help.

In contrast to the consensus on the cocaine problem, the agreement on the level (but not the existence) of gang involvement is not high. In part, this is due to the isolation of gang from narcotics intelligence within enforcement agencies.

It is also due in part to the narrow mandates of both gang and narcotics units, and the low level of information-sharing between both groups and community programs for both gang and drug-prevention.

The Sheriff's Department personnel seem least convinced of a major street gang intrusion into the rock phenomenon, although this varies by administrative level. LAPD personnel are somewhat more concerned, and cite various estimates such as: fewer than 50 per cent of South Central dealers are gang members 24 out of 155 recent narcotics arrestees are known gang members approximately 25 gang-related murders last year were associated with dealing drugs.

As with the Sheriff's Department, it seems true in LAPD that officers closer to the street action find more evidence of gang involvement. It Is not surprising, then, that community gang workers report the greatest level of gang intrusion. From them come reports, for example, that two third of gang violence is now drug-related; that gangs are now "heavily involved in cocaine sales"; that workers have been threatened and are justifiably afraid on the streets in certain areas because of the new violence levels; that truces and amnesties are being declared to permit cross-turf expansion of sales networks, and while the enforcement agencies tend to down-play the violence as gang-initiated, community workers suggest just the opposite. They report gang members as "drug assassins" of dealers in the wrong territory, cheaters on drug quality, and rip-off offenders.

In this climate, it is not possible to draw definitive conclusions about gang involvement in the new cocaine arena in South Los Angeles. It is clear, however, that the potential is very considerable and requires independent assessment. At this point, a reasonable conclusion might be similar to the conservative comments drawn from a "White Paper" circulated in the Sheriff's Department:

1. "We can firmly establish that many members of certain Black street gangs are involved in narcotics dealing, and they are involved to some degree in the operations of the so-called "rock houses."
2. The gang member involved in trafficking "still maintains a loose relationship with the street gang of his youth and quite naturally has a ready-made consumer market—his former "Shomeboys' (who are prime candidates to become the low level street dealers for the organization."
3. Black gang members "are more apt to use random violence to obtain their goals. It would be logical to assume that drug dealers, knowing the gangs' propensity for malevolent behavior, would use them as street enforcers.

In considering the exportability of this Los Angeles situation it is useful to consider the reaction of an experienced researcher in the area of gangs and drugs in Chicago. He states that while rocks and rock houses are unknown there, there has been a dramatic increase in cocaine availability. Gangs, gang violence, and street sales commonly go together, with the modal age being 18 to 24 as in Los Angeles. A major gang advantage is protection, as in a recent ease of a gang member paid $4,000 for a "contract" on a dealer who cheated (Irving Spergel, personal communication).

Finally, and very briefly, we comment on investigative matters within our collaborating enforcement agencies. It has become apparent that the rock house phenomenon has forced a marriage—really a flirtation—between gang and narcotics units. Both in the LAPD and the LASD, management has required a greater level of coordination to be forged than has been known before, and in both agencies the liaison is being handled cautiously. There are police "turfs" to be defended, differing procedures for dealing with informants and disclosing confidential information, and concerns for "credit" for successful efforts.

Traditionally, arrests for use and especially sales are handled by narcotics units. Patrol narcotics arrests are seldom very substantial (but see Brown, 1981). Since narcotics officers are not sophisticated about gang matters, both about gang organizations and about member recognition, the intrusion of gangs into the drug arena is a matter of considerable concern. How the investigative implications are handled will affect the effectiveness of the police response to the rock situation and, by inference, the levels of supply and demand which are an ultimate concern. Perhaps solutions attempted in Los Angeles may find the prevailing winds and move eastward in anticipation of the new rock technology.

REFERENCES

Anonymous. 1972. *The Gourmet Cokebook: A Complete Guide to Cocaine*, (cited by M. Schatzman,

A Sabbadini, and L. Forti, "Coka and cocaine," *Journal of Psychedelic Drugs*, 1976, 8 (April-June) pp. 95–125.

Blum, R.H. 1972. *The Dream Sellers*. San Francisco: Jossey-Bass.

Brown, M.K. 1981. *Working the Street: Police Discretion and the Dilemmas of Reform*. New York: Russell Sage Foundation.

Scholl, S.H. 1979. "Pharmacological aspects of youth drug abuse," in G.M. Beschner and H.S. Friedman (ed.), *Youth Drug Abuse: Problems, Issues and Treatment*. Toronto: D.C. Heath.

Nurco D. 1984. "Letter to Senator Paula Hawkins," 6/21/84, cited by permission.

Rock Sales in Los Angeles

Ryan Long
Donna Belvin
LaShell Long

"Rock" Cocaine

According to the National institute on drug abuse, Cocaine is a powerfully addictive stimulant drug. The powdered hydrochloride salt form of cocaine can be snorted or dissolved in water and then injected. Crack is the street name given to the form of cocaine that has been processed to make a rock crystal, which, when heated, produces vapors that are smoked. The term "crack" refers to the crackling sound produced by the rock as it is heated.

History of "rock" sales in los Angeles

► Cocaine was a status drug for the wealthy in the late 1970's and early 1980's. It was not widely used in South Central Los Angeles in 1980, because it was not affordable to many drug users. Phencyclidine (PCP) was still common in that era. PCP was manufactured and distributed mainly by Los Angeles street gangs, according to the Los Angeles Police Department.

► Press accounts also set South Central Los Angeles' crack crisis as beginning in or about 1984. The press did not begin reporting on the issue of crack cocaine until 1984, but those articles suggested that the growing crack problem had existed prior to that time.

► The first coverage of crack cocaine by a major newspaper was a November 25, 1984, Los Angeles Times article entitled, "South Central Cocaine Sales Explode Into $25 'Rocks.'" The article recounted concerns about the "sale of hardened cocaine called 'rocks'" that reportedly swept through South Central Los Angeles' black community during the prior 18 months.

How is rock cocaine distributed?

► For the better part of a decade, a Bay Area drug ring sold tons of cocaine to the Crips and Bloods Street Gangs of Los Angeles and funneled millions in drug profits to a Latin American guerilla army ran by the U.S. Central Intelligence Agency, a Mercury News investigation has found.

► This drug network opened the first pipeline between Colombia's cocaine cartels and the black neighborhoods of Los Angeles, a city now known as the "crack" capital of the world. The cocaine that flooded in helped spark a crack explosion in urban America and provided the cash and connections needed for L.A.'s gangs to buy automatic weapons.

Where is rock distributed?

- Crack house is a term mainly used in the United States used to describe an old, often abandoned or burnt-out building often in inner an inner-city neighborhood where drug dealers and drug users buy, sell, produce, and use illegal drugs, including, but not limited to, crack cocaine.
- October 21, 1990 | From Times Staff and Wire Reports Police in Colton seized $400,000 worth of methamphetamine and $13,000 in cash in a raid prompted by a business card that advertised "good, high quality, uncut cocaine." The card, confiscated in neighboring Banning during a warrant search, announced "Colton's newest crack house" and gave an address, police said. "If you offer good, high quality, uncut cocaine, at a reasonable price, Southern California will beat a path to your door," the card said.

How is rock cocaine ingested?

- According to Malcolm Klein and Cheryl Maxson rocks are generally smoked through a pipe and often taken with other drugs such as marijuana or taken with rum.
- In this photo Addicts help each other shoot up in a crack house in Loiza Aldea. The owners of this crack house pay the police to stay away so addicts can use drugs without worrying about being arrested.

Cocaine Issues in Los Angeles Communities

▶ Crime Rate—We have all heard numerous times on the news of murders, robberies, and other types of violence have being connected with drug use.

▶ School Dropout—Dropouts are five times more likely to use cocaine and are arrested more often for violent crime than teenagers who remain in school, according to a study released on Monday. Superintendent of Public Instruction Delaine Eastin said nearly 71,000 California students failed to complete high school last year. Of the 71,000, 1,243 California high school drop-outs revealed that they have experimented with cocaine.

▶ Effects on Babies—Drug abuse by pregnant women is rising rapidly. In the first six months of 1985 alone, more than 300 babies were born in Los Angeles County showing symptoms of drug withdrawal, according to the Department of Health Services. Jean McIntosh of the Department of Children's Services said that, since 1981, her department had recorded a 453% increase in infant and child drug problems.

Source Citing

▶ Cleaver, Jim. 1995. "Dropouts Use More Drugs Than Students." Los Angeles Sentinel, August, 23. Retrieved November 30, 2010.

▶ Roark, Clark. 1985. "Effects of PCP, Cocaine on Unborn: A Tragic Picture" Los Angeles Times, December, 5. Retrieved December 1, 2010.

THE RELATIONSHIP BETWEEN CHILDHOOD MALTREATMENT AND ADOLESCENT INVOLVEMENT IN DELINQUENCY

By Carolyn Smith
and Terence P. Thornberry

Recent research suggests a link between childhood maltreatment and later involvement in delinquency. This study examines this issue using official and self-report data from the Rochester Youth Development. Study. The analysis addresses three central issues: the magnitude of the relationship between early child maltreatment and later delinquency, official and self-reported; the possibility of spuriousness in this relationship; and the impact of more extensive measurement of maltreatment on later delinquency. A significant relationship between child maltreatment and self-reported and official delinquency is found and this relationship, especially for more serious forms of delinquency, remains when controlling for other factors. The results also suggest that more

Carolyn Smith and Terence P. Thornberry, "The Relationship Between Childhood Maltreatment and Adolescent Involvement in Delinquency," *Criminology*, vol. 33, no. 4, pp. 451-479. Copyright © 1995 by American Society of Criminology. Reprinted with permission.

extensive maltreatment is related to higher rates of delinquency. Implications and suggestions for further research are discussed.

I n recent years researchers have become increasingly concerned with the long-term consequences of childhood abuse and maltreatment (Cicchetti and Toth, 1993; Widom, 1994; Wolfe, 1987; Zingraff et al., 1993, 1994). An accurate understanding of the extent to which maltreatment is a significant risk factor for negative outcomes is particularly crucial because recent estimates of the prevalence of child maltreatment suggest that it is a much more substantial problem than ever suspected (Garbarino, 1989; National Center on Child Abuse and Neglect, 1981, 1988). In addition, evidence is increasingly found of an extensive range of potentially harmful sequelae for children and adolescents who are victims of maltreatment, including involvement in various forms of delinquent and criminal behavior (Lewis et al., 1989; Widom, 1989a, 1989c). The precise effect of experiences of child maltreatment on later involvement in delinquency, especially violent delinquency, however, is somewhat controversial and not clearly resolved based on the current literature. This article examines the impact of childhood maltreatment on various indicators of delinquency in an effort to further understanding of this relationship. We begin with a brief review of prior studies of this issue and then, based on that review, pose the specific research questions addressed in this analysis.

LITERATURE REVIEW

Initial estimates of the link between early childhood maltreatment and later delinquency were based on clinical, cross-sectional, or retrospective studies (see, e.g., Kratcoski and Kratcoski, 1982; Lewis et al., 1979; Mouzakitis, 1981; Silver et al., 1969; Steele, 1976; Wick, 1981). While these studies sensitized the field to this issue, they produced widely varying estimates—ranging from 10% to 85%—of the proportion of delinquents who have a maltreatment background. Moreover, since these studies suffered from a number of methodological problems, such as retrospective designs, unrepresentative samples, and uncontrolled confounding variables, it is hazardous to base a firm understanding of the relationship between maltreatment and delinquency upon them. The results and methodological limitations of these earlier studies have been reviewed by Garbarino and Plantz (1986), Howing et al. (1990), and Widom (1989a), and, because of that, our review is limited to more recent studies that use prospective designs, include control groups, and trace childhood maltreatment victims forward in time to see if maltreatment increases the risk of later delinquency.

Bolton et al. (1977) were among the first researchers to use a prospective design. They studied a sample of 5,392 children reported for child maltreatment in Arizona and a comparison group of about 900 nonmaltreated siblings. Sixteen percent of the maltreated group had juvenile court records for delinquency compared with 8% of the nonmaltreated siblings. By using siblings as comparison subjects, many important confounding variables—such as class and race—were held constant, although the effect on siblings of living in a maltreating family was not explored.

Alfaro (1981) studied 4,465 children referred to New York State protection agencies for maltreatment during 1952 and 1953. He investigated their juvenile court histories through 1967 and found that about 10% of the maltreated children were later reported as being delinquent or ungovernable. This compared with 2% of juveniles in the state overall.

McCord (1983) used early case records on 233 males, collected between 1939 and 1945, to identify subjects who were "neglected," "abused," "rejected," or "loved." Subjects in these categories did not differ in terms of the proportion living in poverty or from broken homes. In a followup of official records 40 years later, McCord found significant differences among the groups with respect to delinquency. During the juvenile years the rejected youngsters had substantially higher rates of delinquency than the loved youngsters, with the neglected and abused groups falling in between. McCord also reported that "close to half (45%) of the abused or neglected boys had been convicted for serious crimes, became alcoholics or mentally ill, or had died while unusually young" (1983:270).

In a series of recent articles Widom (1989a, 1989b, 1989c, 1991b) examined involvement in criminal and delinquent behavior for maltreated subjects and matched nonmaltreated subjects. The matching design controls for the impact of major demographic variables, including age, sex, race, and social class. Her prospective research finds that earlier maltreatment increased the rates of official delinquency. The prevalence of official delinquency among those who were maltreated is 26% compared with 17% in the matched control group; in other words, maltreatment increases the risk of offending by about 50%. On average, maltreated children began offending earlier and had a greater number of offenses than the matched comparison children. In addition, Widom (1989a) suggests that physical abuse is less strongly related to delinquent outcomes than is a history of neglect.

Social learning theory and more generic theoretical assumptions about the intergenerational transmission of violence suggest that the association between maltreatment and violent delinquency should be stronger than the association between maltreatment and other forms of delinquent behaviors (Lewis et al., 1989; Simons et al., 1993; Widom, 1989c). Widom (1989a), however, does, not find clear-cut evidence of increased violent delinquency among maltreated adolescents. She concludes that maltreated children appear to have higher rates of general delinquency, especially status and property offenses, but not necessarily higher rates of violent delinquency.

Another recent study also indicates that maltreatment may be a risk factor for general delinquency but not violent delinquency. Zingraff and his associates (1993,1994) randomly sampled one in three cases reported to the Registry of Child Abuse and Neglect in a North Carolina county during 1983–1989. They compared these maltreated children with two smaller random samples of 281 children from the general school population and 177 children from a caseload of welfare recipients (to represent impoverished children). Maltreated children were excluded from each of the two comparison groups. Zingraff et al. (1993) found that the maltreated children had higher rates of juvenile court referrals than either of the comparison groups. These effects, however, were only observed for general delinquency and status offenses; they were not observed for violent and property offenses. When age, sex, race, and family structure were held constant, a history of maltreatment significantly increased the odds of general delinquency when the comparison group was the school sample. In the comparison with the poverty sample, however, Zingraff and associates found that the maltreatment effect was no longer significant except when status offenses were used to measure delinquency. Finally, Zingraff et al. (1993) report little distinction in the effect of different types of maltreatment on the risk for later delinquency.

The studies reviewed so far rely entirely on official records to measure delinquency and there is little information in the literature about whether maltreatment is also a risk factor for self-reported delinquency. This is an important gap in knowledge since it is possible that the link between maltreatment (especially when it is measured through official records) and *official* delinquency simply reflects the tendency of some families to be dealt with by official agencies. It may or may not indicate that maltreatment is a risk factor for behavioral involvement in delinquency.

We have found only two studies that used self-report measures of delinquency and both are based on retrospective designs. Doerner (1987) studied a convenience sample of college students, a marginally appropriate group for the study of this topic. He measured maltreatment and delinquency retrospectively and found that maltreatment is correlated with certain types of self-reported delinquency, including serious offenses. Kruttschnitt and Dornfeld (1993) compared a clinical sample of the children of abused women and a community sample of children matched for sex, race, and poverty. Measures of family violence were gathered retrospectively from maternal respondents and self-reported delinquency data were gathered from the children. Results indicate earlier initiation and more frequent delinquency among those exposed to family violence. However, these results are not strictly comparable with those of other studies cited here, since the independent variable, family violence, is operationalized to include spousal violence as well as maltreatment, and the maltreatment measures are based on retrospective reports by the mother.

In sum, a number of studies have examined the role of early childhood maltreatment as a risk factor for later involvement in delinquency. Although these studies generally indicate that maltreatment is a risk factor, there are a number of unresolved issues about the relationship between these variables. First, estimates of the strength of the effect of maltreatment on delinquency vary substantially (compare, e.g., Widom, 1989a, and Zingraff et al., 1993), and there are no prospective estimates of the effect of maltreatment on self-reported delinquency. Second, researchers have yet to examine the role of maltreatment as a risk factor for delinquency in representative samples of the population not preselected on the basis of maltreatment. Third, findings of past research are inconclusive about the effect of maltreatment on different categories of offending, especially serious and violent offending. Finally, research in this area has inconsistently considered the impact of different dimensions of maltreatment, such as exposure to multiple types of maltreatment or the seriousness and extensiveness of the maltreatment, on later involvement in delinquency. This issue is particularly important because reliance on a global measure of maltreatment may underestimate the impact of maltreatment on delinquency by combining less severe and more severe cases in a single measure.

In order to help resolve these issues, we pose the following questions in this analysis:

1. Is childhood maltreatment a significant risk factor for official and self-reported measures of delinquency?
2. Is childhood maltreatment a risk factor for various types of delinquent behavior, including violent offending?
3. Is the relationship between maltreatment and delinquency spurious, or is it maintained when relevant variables are held constant?
4. Are more refined measures of maltreatment—for example, measures that incorporate such dimensions as the extensiveness and severity of abuse—more strongly related to delinquency than simple, global measures of abuse?

This study offers a number of methodological features that facilitate a more detailed look at these issues. The study is based on a representative sample that is not preselected on the basis of abuse or delinquency. The data allow for the measurement of a number of possible confounding variables to examine the issue of spuriousness. There is also great breadth in the measurement of maltreatment and delinquency; the measurement of maltreatment is based on a comprehensive and validated classification system (Cicchetti and Barnett, 1991), and delinquency is measured by both self-report and official data.

METHODS

The data are drawn from the Rochester Youth Development Study (RYDS), a multiwave panel study in which youth and their primary caretakers were interviewed every six months over four and a half years. In addition, data were collected from the Rochester public schools, Police Department, Department of Social Services, and other agencies that have contact with RYDS subjects. This analysis makes use of interview data collected in waves 2 through 8, data on maltreatment from the Monroe County Child Protective Service records, and arrest data from the Rochester Police Department. At wave 2 the subjects were in the fall semester of the eighth or ninth grade, and at wave 8 they were in the fall semester of the eleventh or twelfth grade.

SAMPLE

The target population for the RYDS were students attending the seventh or eighth grade of the Rochester, New York, public schools in the spring of 1988. A stratified sample was selected from this population so that students at high risk for delinquency and drug use were proportionally overrepresented and the findings could be weighted to represent the target population.

To accomplish these objectives, the sample was stratified on two dimensions. Males were oversampled (75% vs. 25%) because they are more likely than females to engage in serious delinquency (Blumstein et al, 1986) and students from high-crime areas were oversampled since living in a high-crime area increases the risk of offending. Areas with high crime rates were identified by assigning each census tract a resident arrest rate reflecting the proportion of the tract's total population that was arrested by Rochester police in 1986.

Of the 4,103 students in the seventh and eighth grades in the spring of 1988, 3,372 (84%) were eligible for the sample.[10] To generate a final panel of 1,000 students, 1,334 were initially selected based on an estimated nonparticipation rate of 25% (Elliott et al., 1983). All students in the census tracts with the highest resident arrest rates (approximately the top one third) were asked to participate, whereas students in the remaining census tracts were selected at a rate proportionate to the tract's contribution to the overall resident arrest rate. Once the number of students to be selected from each tract was determined, the student population was stratified by sex and grade, and students were selected from those strata at random. Based on these stratification procedures, a

---

10 Students were considered ineligible if they moved out of the Rochester school district before the wave 1 cases were fielded, if neither English nor Spanish was spoken in the home, if a sibling was already in the sample, or if they were older than the expected age for the cohort.

final panel of 1,000 students and their primary caretakers was selected for the study. Because the probability of a youth living in a particular census tract is known, this sampling strategy provides a means for weighting the cases to represent the initial panel of all seventh and eighth graders in the Rochester public schools. The sample is weighted in the analyses presented here.

The number of cases used in the following analyses varies somewhat depending on the particular variables that are included. The smallest number of cases—823—represents 82% of the original sample and there is no evidence of differential attrition. In the total panel males are over-represented by approximately 3 to 1 (74% to 26%), African-Americans make up the majority of the sample (68%), 15% are white, and 17% Hispanic. More complete discussions of the sampling plan and retention rates are presented in Thornberry et al. (1993) and Farnworth et al. (1990).

Adolescent interviews were typically conducted in a private room provided by the schools. Students who had dropped out of school, moved to a different school district, or were institutionalized were tracked and interviewed in an appropriate setting. Caretakers were interviewed in their homes. Adolescents and caretakers were not present at each others' interviews, and each interview lasted approximately one hour.

MEASUREMENT

Maltreatment

Our measure of maltreatment is based on data obtained from the Child Protective Service records of the Monroe County Department of Social Services, the county of residence for all subjects at the start of the RYDS project. For each of our subjects, we recorded any instance of substantiated abuse or maltreatment, from birth through 1992.

These records provide detailed information on a number of important dimensions of maltreatment, including the type and the severity of maltreatment. To capture this information we used the classification system developed by Cicchetti and Barnett (1991), for which there is ample evidence of validity and reliability (Barnett et al., 1993). For each incident of maltreatment, the Cicchetti-Barnett schema encodes such information as the dates the case was opened and closed, the age of the victim, victim-offender relationships, the type or types of abuse, and for each type, its level of severity.

Seven types of maltreatment are included in the classification system. They are physical abuse, sexual abuse, emotional maltreatment, moral/legal maltreatment, educational maltreatment, physical neglect, and lack of supervision. In addition, the classification system assesses the severity of each of these types of maltreatment on a 5-point scale. Physical abuse, for example, can vary from overly severe spankings to life-threatening assaults that result in permanent injuries. Exemplars of each level of severity for each maltreatment type have been developed (see Appendix 1 for exemplars for physical abuse) and coders use these exemplars to score each incident of maltreatment (Barnett et al., 1993).[11]

Five indicators of maltreatment are used in this analysis:

1. Prevalence of maltreatment. This variable denotes whether or not the subject was a victim of any type of maltreatment prior to the age of 12.
2. Frequency of maltreatment. This measure is the number of different substantiated incidents of maltreatment up to the age of 12.
3. Duration. This variable indicates the duration of the official investigation and monitoring of the family subsequent to the initial report of maltreatment. It can be viewed as a proxy for the severity and complexity of the case. If the subject experienced more than one incident of maltreatment, the duration scores are summed across all incidents for this analysis.
4. Number of types of maltreatment. As indicated above, the classification scheme includes seven types of maltreatment. This variable indicates the number of distinct types of maltreatment that the subject experienced. As such, it ranges from 1 to 7 and is akin to the "ever variety" scores that are often used in self-reported delinquency studies.[12]
5. Total severity score. Each incident of maltreatment receives a severity score based on the scoring system described above. Instances of maltreatment can involve more than one subtype, and severity scores are summed across subtypes for each incident. The total severity score used in this analysis is the sum of severity scores across all incidents of maltreatment for each subject.

Outcome Measures

Unlike prior research in this area, which has relied almost exclusively on official measures of delinquency, the RYDS data set contains official and self-report measures. Each is briefly described here.

---

11 Interrater reliability was assessed throughout the coding process and the coders agreed on 88% of the assessments. Disagreements were resolved by consensus scoring and by discussion with a trained social worker with extensive clinical experience.

12 There are a total of only 219 different incidents of maltreatment in this data set and we find, as have others (Cicchetti and Barnett, 1991), that many incidents involve multiple types of maltreatment. Because of that, there are too few cases to reliably analyze the impact of different types and combinations of types of maltreatment on delinquency. Moreover, Zingraff et al. (1993) do not find significant differences by type of maltreatment. For these reasons we examine only the impact of the simple variety of maltreatment experiences in this article.

Official Data

The official measure of delinquency is based on the number of times each subject had an official contact with the police as a juvenile or an arrest as an adult. Official contacts include cases in which the juvenile was "warned and released" by the police and an official record of the event was maintained, as well as cases in which the juvenile was referred to Family Court. These data were collected from the files of the Rochester Police Department but cover all police agencies in Monroe County, as the Rochester Police Department maintains a countywide registry. The official data cover the time period from the subject's first official contact through 1992, when the subjects averaged 17 years of age.

Self-Report Measures

A self-report inventory containing 32 delinquency items is administered at each interview. The items range from petty theft and public rowdiness to armed robbery and serious assault. Respondents are asked if they committed each offense during the past six months and, if so, how often. Prior to analysis, coders screen all responses to ensure that they fit the category of delinquency being measured and that they are not such trivial actions that they would be ignored by law enforcement officials.

In this analysis we use cumulative prevalence and frequency measures of self-reported delinquency covering waves 2 through 8, the period from eighth and ninth grades to eleventh and twelfth grades. The cumulative prevalence measures indicate any involvement in a particular type of delinquency during these seven waves, and the cumulative frequency measures sum all instances of each of the delinquent acts included in a particular self-report index. Since the frequency measures are positively skewed, a log transformation is used in this study. Five self-report indexes are used:

1. General delinquency: a 26-item omnibus delinquency index consisting of minor and serious offense types.
2. Serious delinquency: an eight-item index of serious delinquent behaviors focused on violent and property offenses, including such items as armed robbery and burglary.
3. Moderate delinquency: a nine-item index of moderately serious offenses, including joyriding and simple assault.
4. Minor delinquency: a two-item index consisting of minor theft and being loud and rowdy in a public place.
5. Violent delinquency: a six-item index of involvement in violent offenses.[13]

---

13 The items composing each index are presented in Appendix 2. There are no duplicate items on the serious, moderate, and minor indexes, but the six items on the violent delinquency index are also

Control Variables

A number of variables are held constant in the following analysis. Our measure of maltreatment is based on Monroe County Department of Social Services case records. Since not all subjects were residents of Monroe County for their entire lives, some subjects could be erroneously classified as nonmaltreated if they lived outside Monroe County at the time of the maltreatment. To control for this effect we include a dummy variable, mobility, indicating whether the subjects began their first grade in the Rochester public schools. Of the total panel, 791 subjects (79%) began their schooling in the Rochester schools and only 21% entered the Rochester schools at a later grade. While this measure obviously does not cover mobility prior to the first grade, it is the best measure available in this data set.[14] In addition to including this variable as a control in the multivariate analysis, we reestimated all the results reported below for only the 791 subjects who began first grade in the Rochester schools and none of the substantive results reported here changes.

We also hold constant race/ethnicity, sex, underclass status, and family structure since these factors have been shown to be related to maltreatment and to delinquency. "Sex" is a dichotomous dummy variable with females as the comparison group; "African-American" and "Hispanic" are dummy variables with non-Hispanic whites as the comparison group. "Underclass status" is a measure of social class representing those who are most socioeconomically disadvantaged. If the principal household wage earner is unemployed, if the family received welfare benefits, or if the household income is below the federally defined poverty guidelines for a family of that size, the family is classified as underclass (Farnworth et al., 1994). "Family structure" is a dichotomous variable denoting households in which both biological parents are in the home, in comparison with other types of family structures. Both underclass status and family structure were measured temporally prior to the estimate of delinquency.

The temporal order of the key variables in the analysis, maltreatment and delinquency, is an important issue since the main question for analysis is whether childhood maltreatment is a risk factor for adolescent delinquency. For the purposes of this study, we define child maltreatment as that which occurs before the subject's 12th birthday. The cumulative delinquency measures begin at wave 2, when the mean age of the subjects was 13.9 years. Since the self-report questions cover the six-month period prior to the interview, all of the subjects were at least age 12 during this recall period. Thus,

---

included on either the serious or moderate indexes.

14   The problem of misclassification brought about by mobility works against the study hypothesis. That is, we run the risk of including maltreated subjects in the nonmaltreated group, which would make it harder to show that maltreatment is a risk factor for delinquency. In other words, this introduces a conservative bias to this test of the hypothesis.

the occurrence of maltreatment in fact precedes the delinquency that is measured in this analysis.

We considered the possibility that early onset of delinquency not captured by our dependent variable may actually precede maltreatment since a number of researchers have drawn attention to the possibility that delinquency is a stable individual phenomenon, which may cause disturbances in parenting (Mowing et al., 1990; Lytton, 1990; Sampson and Laub, 1993).[15] Ideally, therefore, one would want to see if maltreatment leads to *changes* in delinquency, taking into account preexisting levels of delinquent behavior. We have no direct data to measure the impact of early delinquency, however, since delinquency that occurred prior to wave 1 is not measured in detail in our data. Subjects do, however, report the age of onset for each delinquent act in the wave 1 interview, and very small numbers of subjects report age of onset prior to age 8 (for no item more than 7%). In order to reduce the possibility of confounded temporal order between maltreatment and delinquency, we repeated all the analyses reported below restricting the cases to those who were under age 8 at the time of the maltreatment. The substantive findings are the same as those reported here: There is no change in the significance of maltreatment in any of the analyses. In order to maximize the number of subjects in the maltreated group, however, we use the age 12 cutoff for maltreatment in the analysis to follow.

RESULTS

We begin by examining the prevalence of childhood maltreatment for the members of the Rochester Youth Development Study. Restricting the analysis to cases of maltreatment under age 12 results in a prevalence rate of 13.6, as reported in Table 1. These subjects were maltreated in a total of 219 separate incidents, for an average of 1.5 incidents per subject. This prevalence rate is somewhat higher than rates reported in national data (National Center on Child Abuse and Neglect, 1981, 1988), and it is probably related to the urban population and the high proportion of minority youth in the sample, factors that have been related to higher rates of official maltreatment (Garbarino and Ebata, 1987; Hampton, 1987; Hampton and Newberger, 1985).

Table 1 also presents the prevalence of maltreatment for major demographic subgroups. There are no significant differences in the prevalence of maltreatment by sex or race. There are, however, substantial differences by social class and family structure.

---

15   It is more likely that delinquency would affect maltreatment during adolescence, when the power balance between parents and adolescents shifts, and maltreatment may well represent reactions to very challenging youth behavior (Garbarino, 1989). For this reason, youth with maltreatment reports only at adolescence are not counted as maltreated in this study.

Almost one fifth (19.5%) of the youngsters reared in underclass families were victims of maltreatment, while 8.2% of the nonunderclass respondents were maltreated. The largest difference is observed for family structure. Only 3.2% of the boys and girls who resided with both biological parents at wave 1 had a history of maltreatment, but 18.6% of those in other family situations had been maltreated. With this demographic information as a backdrop, we turn now to the central issue of this analysis—the relationship between earlier maltreatment and later involvement in delinquency.

Table 1. Prevalence of Reported Maltreatment Prior to Age 12, by Demographic Characteristics

	Abused		
	Yes	No	N
Total Sample	13.6%	86.4%	1,000
Sex			
Male	13.0	87.0	500
Female	14.1	85.9	500
Race			
White	16.4	83.6	179
African-American	14.0	86.0	659
Hispanic	8.7	91.3	162
Underclass Status			
Yes	19.5	80.5	450
No	8.2	91.8*	452
Family Structure			
Both Biological Parents	3.2	96.8	299
Other Structures	18.6	81.4*	647

$* p < .05.$

MALTREATMENT AND DELINQUENCY

The relationship between childhood maltreatment and involvement in adolescent delinquency is presented in Table 2. Panel A of the table examines this relationship for the prevalence of delinquency, and Panel B does so for the frequency of delinquency.

Bivariate relationships and multivariate relationships, controlling for sex, race/ethnicity, underclass status, family structure, and mobility, are presented.[16]

Table 2. Relationship Between Childhood Maltreatment and Adolescent Involvement in Delinquency

	A. Prevalence of Delinquency					
	Official	General	Serious	Moderate	Minor	Violent
Maltreated						
Yes	45.1	78.8	42.4	71.3	45.3	69.6
No	31.7*	69.8*	32.7*	55.6*	37.2*	56.0*
(N)	(1,000)	(889)	(889)	(889)	(889)	(889)
Logistic Regression Coefficient[2]	.54*	.23	.29	.55*	.32	.45*
Change in Probability [b]	.13	.05	.07	.13	.08	.11
(N)	(892)	(823)	(823)	(823)	(823)	(823)
	B. Frequency of Delinquency					
Maltreated						
Yes	1.4	79.4	5.4	13.0	2.4	11.0
No	.8*	49.4*	2.8*	8.1*	2.6	5.9*
(TV)	(1,000)	(889)	(889)	(889)	(889)	(889)
OLS Unstandardized Coefficient[a]	.21*	.33	.23*	.33*	.06	.30*
(N)	(892)	(823) .	(823)	(823)	(823)	(823)

[a] Holding constant sex, race/ethnicity, underclass status, family structure, and mobility.
[b] The change in the probability of delinquency is assessed at the mean of the dependent variable.
* $p < .05$, one-tailed test.

There is a significant bivariate relationship between maltreatment and the likelihood of official delinquency. Forty-five percent of the maltreated subjects had an arrest record compared with 31.7% of the nonmaltreated subjects. In addition, the logistic regression coefficient is significant, indicating that maltreatment affects the prevalence of official delinquency even when the control variables are held constant. At the mean of the dependent variable, which is .32, a history of maltreatment increases the probability of having an official record by .13. In other words, the probability of official delinquency,

---

16   Coefficients for the control variables are not presented since the focus of attention is the impact of maltreatment on delinquency after these variables are controlled; the results are available upon request.

given a history of maltreatment, would move from .32 to .45, which is almost identical to the observed prevalence rate of .451. This indicates that the control variables have a minimal impact on the relationship between maltreatment and delinquency. This finding replicates those reported by Widom (1989b) and Zingraff et al. (1993) concerning official measures of delinquency.

The remaining data in Table 2A examine the relationship between maltreatment and self-reported delinquency, an issue that has not been examined in prior prospective studies. All of the bivariate relationships are significant, suggesting that maltreatment is not only related to later official delinquency but also to self-reported delinquency. Only two of these relationships remain significant once the control variables are held constant, however. They are the effects for moderate delinquency and for violent delinquency. For moderate delinquency a history of maltreatment increases the probability of delinquency by .13 and for violent delinquency it increases the probability by .11; both changes are assessed at the means of the dependent variables (.57 in both cases). As was the case for official delinquency, these results suggest that the control variables have a rather minor impact on the relationship between maltreatment and delinquency. For moderate delinquency, a history of maltreatment increases the probability of delinquency from .57 to .70, only slightly less than the observed prevalence rate of .713; for violent delinquency it moves the probability of delinquency from .57 to .68, again only slightly below the observed prevalence rate of .696.

Table 2B examines the impact of childhood maltreatment on the logged frequency of involvement in delinquency during adolescence. Beginning first with the official measure, the nonmaltreated subjects were arrested an average of .8 times compared with 1.4 times for the maltreated subjects. This relationship is maintained when the control variables are held constant $(b = .21, p < .05)$.[17]

Turning to the self-report measures, with the exception of minor delinquency, all the bivariate relationships are significant. Moreover, the bivariate relationships appear particularly strong for serious delinquency and violent delinquency; maltreated subjects report almost twice as many serious delinquencies and violent offenses as nonmaltreated subjects. The ordinarily least squares (OLS) results examine this relationship when sex, race/ethnicity, underclass status, family structure, and mobility are held constant. They indicate that maltreatment continues to exert a significant impact on serious, moderate, and violent delinquency, but not on general or minor delinquency.

The results presented in Table 2 allow us to answer the first three research questions posed earlier—Is maltreatment related to official and self-reported delinquency? Is

---

17   The unstandardized coefficients refer to a one-unit change in the independent variable (un-logged) on the log of the dependent variable and are therefore not easily interpretable. An assessment of the antilogged values indicates that, when significant, the impact of maltreatment on delinquency is sizeable even when other variables are held constant.

it related to involvement in violent delinquency? And, are these relationships spurious? The results suggest that childhood maltreatment is a significant and nonspurious risk factor for official delinquency, violent self-reported delinquency, and moderate self-reported delinquency. It is inconsistently related to serious delinquency, being a significant predictor for the frequency but not the prevalence of serious delinquency. Finally, childhood maltreatment is not a significant risk factor for minor delinquency or general delinquency, the omnibus scale containing a mixture of serious and trivial delinquencies. Overall, maltreatment appears to be a risk factor for the more serious forms of delinquency and not to be a risk factor for the less serious forms of delinquency.

THE MEASUREMENT OF MALTREATMENT

The final question that guides this analysis concerns the impact of the way in which maltreatment is measured. To this point we have measured maltreatment as a simple dichotomy, comparing adolescents who did and did not have an official record of maltreatment as children. This measure ignores the fact that maltreatment can vary along such dimensions as frequency, severity, duration, and type. Indeed, we hypothesize that children exposed to more extreme levels of maltreatment will have higher rates of delinquency than children exposed to less extreme levels of maltreatment. Whatever causal mechanisms link early maltreatment to later delinquency ought to operate most strongly as the frequency, severity, duration, and variety of maltreatment increase.

To examine this hypothesis, for each of these four dimensions of maltreatment, we have divided the maltreated children into two groups: those falling into the lowest two thirds of the distribution and those falling into the highest one third of the distribution. This cutting point was chosen to identify better youth who experienced the most serious forms of maltreatment. Because the distributions for these variables are skewed, the actual cutting points are slightly above or below the target of the 67th percentile.[18] Table 3 presents the frequency of delinquency for the nonmaltreated youth, those in the bottom two thirds, and those in the top one third on each of these four dimensions of maltreatment, along with one-way analyses of variance (ANOVAs) and Scheffe tests. The Scheffe test for multiple comparisons "is known to be conservative in terms of both α and power" (Toothaker, 1993:51). Only the measures of delinquency consistently found to be significantly related to maltreatment in the previous analysis are included.

The results for self-reported moderate delinquency differ substantially from those for the other three indicators of delinquency. For moderate delinquency none of the

---

18 For the number of incidents it is the 72nd percentile; for the total severity of maltreatment it is the 58th percentile; for the duration of all incidents it is the 62nd percentile; and for the number of types of maltreatment it is the 77th percentile.

ANOVAs or Scheffe tests is significant. Moreover, higher delinquency rates are associated with those below the 67th percentile. This finding is consistent with the thrust of findings reported above; maltreatment does not appear to be strongly related to the less serious forms of delinquent involvement. Given this finding, the following discussion refers only to the other three indicators of delinquency—official delinquency, self-reported serious delinquency, and self-reported violent delinquency.

When only the three measures are examined, there is mixed support for the hypothesis that children exposed to the most serious forms of maltreatment will be at the greatest risk for later involvement in delinquency. On the one hand, all 12 ANOVAs (three types of delinquency by four dimensions of maltreatment) are significant and in all 12 cases the highest rates of delinquency are observed for those in the top one-third of the maltreatment distributions. Moreover, the elevation in risk of delinquency for these youngsters, as compared with the nonmaltreated group, is quite substantial. Consider, for example, the data in panel A concerning the number of different incidents of maltreatment. Those in the top third of the distribution were arrested 2.8 times as often as the nonmaltreated subjects, and they reported 2.3 times as many serious offenses and 1.9 times as many violent offenses. All of these results suggest that exposure to more serious forms of maltreatment is a substantial risk factor for serious forms of delinquency.

On the other hand, a comparison of those exposed to less extreme and more extreme forms of maltreatment offers less support for this hypothesis. While it is true that the highest rates of delinquency are found for those above the 67th percentile, the distinction between these subjects and those below the 67th percentile is generally rather modest. Only 4 of the 12 Scheffe tests comparing these groups are significant, and all four are for official arrests. The data in Panel A can again illustrate the general pattern of results. While there is a substantial difference in number of arrests (1.11 versus 2.34) for those below and above the 67th percentile, there are rather modest differences in self-reported serious delinquency (5.11 versus 6.22) and violent delinquency (10.95 versus 11.29). Similar patterns can be seen in the other three panels of Table 3.

Overall, the data in Table 3 confirm the general finding that there is a relationship between childhood maltreatment and later delinquency and offer some support for the notion that the strength of this relationship increases as the seriousness of the maltreatment increases. The highest rates of delinquency are observed for those maltreated youngsters in the top third of the distributions on each of these dimensions of maltreatment, but the differences between them and those in the bottom two thirds are not very large.[19]

---

19   One reason the differences between the maltreatment subgroups may not be very large is that the sample of maltreated children may be too small to detect these differences. In analysis not presented here, we repeated the analysis reported in Table 3 for a larger sample of maltreatment incidents by

Table 3. Relationship Between the Frequency of Delinquency and Indicators of the Frequency, Severity, Duration, and Type of Child Maltreatment, for Maltreatment Occurring Prior to Age 12

Delinquency	A. Non-Maltreated	Number of Incidents of Maltreatment		Scheffe Testsa
		Less Than 67th Percentile	Greater Than 67th Percentile	
Official	.82	1.11	2.34*	1,3 2,3
Serious	2.75	5.11	6.22*	—
Violent	5.89	10.95	11.29*	1,2
Moderate	8.09	13.35	12.09	—
Nb	763	87	37	
		B. Total Severity of All Incidents		
Official	.82	1.04	2.02*	1,3 2,3
Serious	2.75	4.31	6.83*	1,3
Violent	5.89	11.05	11.07*	1,2 1,3
Moderate	8,09	14.05	11.66	—
Nb	763	68	56	
		C. Duration of All Incidents		
Official	.83	1.01	2.12*	1,3 2,3
Serious	2.75	4.74	6.69*	—
Violent	5.89	10.94	11.44*	1,2 1,3
Moderate	8.18	12.69	12.14	—
Nb	763	74	49	
	D. Number	of Types of Maltreatment Across		All Incidents
Official	.82	1.21	2.29*	1,3 2,3
Serious	2.75	4.73	7.80*	—
Violent	5.89	10.99	11.26*	1,2
Moderate	8.09	13.30	11.87	—
Nb	763	96	29	

a Significant Scheffe tests ($p < .05$) are noted by numbers referring to the different groups: 1 = none, 2 = less than 67th percentile, and 3 = greater than 67th percentile.

b The N's presented are for the self-report measures. The N's for official delinquency are somewhat larger, totaling at least 995 cases in these analyses.

* Significant one-way ANOVA ($p < .05$).

relaxing the temporal order and including also those incidents that occurred after the subjects were 12 years of age. For this larger sample, there appeared to be more support for the hypothesis that more serious forms of maltreatment are more strongly related to delinquency.

DISCUSSION

In the past few decades increasing attention has been paid to the phenomenon of child maltreatment and its long-term impact on youth development. A growing body of research (e.g., Cicchetti and Carlson, 1989; Widom, 1994; Wodarski et al., 1990) suggests that being maltreated as a youngster increases the risk of a variety of negative consequences during childhood, adolescence, and adulthood. This study has examined the impact of childhood maltreatment on one particular outcome, adolescent involvement in delinquency. Using data from the Rochester Youth Development Study, the study replicates and extends the results of previous studies examining this issue.

First, like previous studies (e.g., Widom, 1989b; Zingraff et al., 1993), we found that a history of childhood maltreatment significantly increases the chances of involvement in delinquency. While maltreatment is certainly no guarantee of later delinquency, a history of maltreatment significantly increases the risk of being arrested and the frequency of arrests. Moreover, the results clearly indicate that the impact of maltreatment is not limited to increasing the risk of official delinquency. A history of maltreatment was found to be related to more serious forms of self-reported delinquency, including violent, serious, and moderate forms of delinquency. Maltreatment is not, however, significantly related to minor delinquency or an omnibus index that includes a mixture of offense types.

In addition, we found that maltreatment is a significant predictor of the prevalence of official, moderate, and violent delinquency when race/ethnicity, sex, social class, family structure, and mobility are held constant. It is also a significant predictor of the frequency of official, serious, moderate, and violent forms of delinquency when these same variables are controlled. These data provide some confidence that the effects of maltreatment are not spurious and are independent of such variables as underclass status and family structure.

Previous studies have not explored the substantial heterogeneity that exists within the category of maltreatment with respect to the extensiveness and variety of maltreatment and, as a result, may underestimate the impact of maltreatment on delinquency. We hypothesized that if exposure to maltreatment increases risk for later delinquency, exposure to more extensive maltreatment should have an even stronger impact on later delinquency. To test this hypothesis we measured the frequency, severity, duration, and variety of maltreatment in the child's history and compared subjects falling above the 67th percentile on each of these dimensions with those falling below the 67th percentile and with the nonmaltreated subjects.

The results are somewhat mixed. The differences between subjects in the top third of the distributions and those in the lower two thirds were not large and most of the Scheffe tests comparing those above the 67th percentile with those below were insignificant.

The more extensively maltreated subjects, however, consistently exhibited the highest rates of delinquency.

Overall, these results indicate that having a history of childhood maltreatment serious enough to warrant official intervention by child protective services is a significant risk factor for later involvement in serious delinquency. Within this highly select group there appears to be at least preliminary evidence that experiencing more extreme forms of maltreatment is associated with higher rates of subsequent delinquency. That distinction, however, appears to be overwhelmed by the threshold effect of simply experiencing maltreatment serious enough to elicit official recognition.

Some qualifications to our findings are in order based on design and measurement limitations. First, while the stratified random sample used here results in a representative sample, it yields fewer cases of maltreatment than would be available for analysis were the sample preselected on the basis of maltreatment. Because of that, it was not possible to look at sex-by-race comparisons even though some studies suggest that the effects of maltreatment may be conditioned by race and sex (Kruttschnitt et al., 1986; Widom, 1989a, 1989b). Also, as indicated above, we were unable to evaluate clearly the differential impact of our measures of maltreatment, although our data suggest the importance of finer grained measures of maltreatment that capture dimensions of extensiveness and severity.

Second, there are limitations to the validity of our maltreatment measure. Our measure is based entirely on official records of maltreatment, and researchers have noted the biases inherent in such data. For example, race and class biases may enter into an official determination of maltreatment, and this may simply reflect the tendency of disadvantaged families in urban places to be labeled by official agencies, with an iatrogenic effect on the behavior of family members, including adolescents (Pagelow, 1984). This would inflate the apparent link between maltreatment and delinquency. However, a recent study compared founded and unfounded cases of maltreatment and discovered little difference between the groups in the association between maltreatment and delinquency (Leiter et al., 1994). It is also possible that our findings understate the magnitude of the relationship since we do not know of all instances of maltreatment in the sample.

Finally, we acknowledge that we have incompletely addressed the issue of temporal order between maltreatment and delinquency. Although we conducted the analysis using only instances of maltreatment that occurred prior to age 12 (and replicated it using only instances of maltreatment prior to age 8), it is indeed possible that the behaviors that are reported as maltreatment may be reinforced by antisocial behavior patterns in some children. Indeed, interactional theory (Thornberry, 1987) suggests the importance of reciprocal effects, such that the impact of exogenous variables may be amplified or moderated by their consequences.

Nevertheless, if as the results reported here suggest, childhood maltreatment is a significant risk factor for adolescent delinquency, investigating the processes by which maltreatment translates itself into delinquency is warranted. While our research strengthens and clarifies the empirical link between maltreatment and later delinquency, a direct causal link is not implied by these data. An important theoretical and practical issue is to identify the intervening variables that translate early maltreatment into delinquency on the one hand, or into resilient outcomes on the other. Understanding these mechanisms may more directly lead to suggestions for how to reduce that risk.

A number of intervening mechanisms that translate risk into negative outcomes have been suggested in the literature (e.g., Cicchetti, 1989; Widom, 1994; Wodarski et al., 1990; Wolfe, 1987). These include immediate developmental malfunction, changes in physiological responses, maladaptive styles of coping, and disordered behavior. Early childhood maltreatment may also affect children's attitudes toward themselves or others, through the development of faulty attributions. This range of social, behavioral, and attitudinal outcomes may, in turn, contribute to patterns of behavior that are then related to delinquency, such as aggressiveness, lack of school achievement, and inability to form prosocial peer and family attachments. Maltreated children tend to behave more aggressively and may be rejected by or isolate themselves from conventional peers. This may lead them to seek associations with other antisocial children, leading to peer group associations that are further conducive to delinquency (Mueller and Silverman, 1989; Patterson et al., 1989; Thornberry et al., 1994).

Moreover, some research suggests that the effect of maltreatment may be potentiated by the presence of other forms of violence, such as spousal abuse and media and community violence (Kruttschnitt et al., 1986; Thornberry, 1994). It is also likely that since poverty and family disruption are linked to the occurrence of maltreatment, they will continue to interact with (and may exacerbate) the effects of maltreatment (Garbarino and Plantz, 1986; Paget et al., 1993). In order to reduce negative behavioral consequences, research should address the range of possible intervening mechanisms that link maltreatment to delinquency.

Although these results demonstrate an association between maltreatment and delinquency, they also demonstrate that the majority of maltreated youngsters are not arrested and do not report involvement in serious delinquency (see Table 2). Many maltreated youth are, therefore, resilient—at least with respect to delinquent behavior. Factors related to resilience to maltreatment appear to parallel the factors that operate more generally to protect children at high risk (Rutter, 1987; Werner and Smith, 1992), for example, compensating parental support (Herrenkohl et al., 1994; Kendziora and O'Leary, 1993; Kruttschnitt et al., 1987) and intellectual capacity and school achievement (Smith et al., 1995; Wodarski et al., 1990; Zingraff et al., 1994). Additional research is needed to extend this line of inquiry. For example, research is needed to determine whether there are protective factors that operate uniquely for different aspects of maltreatment and whether such factors change over the course of adolescent development. Identifying the buffering factors that help youth avoid the consequences of maltreatment is important because it would help elucidate the mechanisms that disrupt the link between early maltreatment and later delinquency (Herrenkohl et al., 1994; Mrazek and Mrazek, 1987; Widom, 1991a). Interventions with maltreated children that focus on the development of such protective factors may make the difference in youth making a transition past the maltreatment experience into productive adulthood.

Evidence also indicates that researchers should consider the maltreated child in a range of developmental subsystems and environments (Aber and Cicchetti, 1984; Wodarski et al., 1990). This study has examined only the consequences of childhood maltreatment in one area—delinquency. A history of maltreatment may have a range of possible negative consequences, for example, drug use, involvement in juvenile gangs, precocious sexual behavior, suicidal behavior, teenage parenthood, violence toward partners, and subsequent maltreatment of the next generation of children (Thornberry and Smith, 1994; Widom, 1991b, 1994). Past research (Huizinga et al., 1991; Jessor et al., 1991) indicates that the most serious offenders have high rates of co-occurring problem behaviors, but it does not explain the role that maltreatment plays as a risk factor for this. Based on the results of this study, it would be reasonable to hypothesize that maltreatment—and probably more extreme forms of maltreatment—may lead to disruption in several developmental domains and to multiple, co-occurring problem behaviors. Further research is needed to address this issue. If the hypothesis is correct, that would again imply that intervention programs designed to counteract the consequences of maltreatment would have to deal with multiple and interacting problem behaviors (see Thornberry et al., forthcoming) and conversely, that programs for multiproblem youth would have to detect and address prior experiences of maltreatment. As researchers solidify findings about the range of long-term consequences that may flow from experiences of maltreatment, they will be in a better position to design and evaluate interventions that remove barriers to optimal functioning and promote long-term resilience.

REFERENCES

Aber, J. Lawrence and Dante Cicchetti. 1984. "Socioemotional development in maltreated children: An empirical and theoretical analysis." In Hiram Fitzgerald, Barry Lester, and Michael Yogman (eds.), *Theory and Research in Behavioral Pediatrics*. Vol. 11. New York: Plenum.

Alfaro, Jose D. 1981. "Report on the relationship between child abuse and neglect and latersocially deviant behavior." In Robert J. Hunner and Yvonne Elder Walker (eds.), *Exploring the Relationship Between Child Abuse and Delinquency*. Montclair, N.J.: Allanheld, Osmun.

Barnett, Douglas, Jody Todd Manly, and Dante Cicchetti. 1993. "Defining child maltreatment: The interface between policy and research." In Dante Cicchetti and Sheree L. Toth (eds.), *Child Abuse, Child Development, and Social Policy.* Norwood, N.J.: Ablex.

Blumstein, Albert, Jacqueline Cohen, Jeffrey A. Roth, and Christy A. Visher. 1986. *Criminal Careers and Career Criminals.* 2 vols. Washington, D.C.: National Academy Press.

Bolton, Frank G., John W. Reich, and Sarah E. Gutierres. 1977. "Delinquency patterns in maltreated children and siblings." *Victimology*, 2:349–357.

Cicchetti, Dante. 1989. "How research on child development has informed the study of child development: Perspectives from developmental psychopathology." In Dante Cicchetti and Vicki Carlson (eds.), *Child Maltreatment: Theory and Research on the Causes and Consequences of Child Abuse and Neglect.* Cambridge, Mass.: Harvard University Press.

Cicchetti, Dante and Douglas Barnett. 1991. "Toward the development of a scientific nosology of child maltreatment." In William Grover and Dante Cicchetti (eds.), *Thinking Clearly About Psychology: Essays in Honor of Paul E. Meehl. Vol. 2: Personality and Psychopathology.* Minneapolis: University of Minnesota Press.

Cicchetti, Dante and Vicki Carlson (eds.). 1989. *Child Maltreatment: Theory and Research on the Causes and Consequences of Child Abuse and Neglect.* New York: Cambridge University Press.

Cicchetti, Dante and Sheree L. Toth (eds.). 1993. *Child Abuse, Child Development, and Social Policy.* Norwood, N.J.: Ablex.

Doerner, William G. 1987. "Child maltreatment seriousness and juvenile delinquency." *Youth and Society*, 19:197–244.

Elliott, Delbert S., Suzanne S. Ageton, David Huizinga, Brian A. Knowles, and Rachelle J. Canter. 1983. *The prevalence and incidence of delinquent behavior 1976–1980.* National Youth Survey Report No. 26. Boulder, Colo.: Behavioral Research Institute.

Farnworth, Margaret, Terence P. Thornberry, Alan J. Lizotte, and Marvin D. Krohn. 1990. *Sampling and Design Implementation. Technical Report No. 1.* Hindelang Criminal Justice Research Center, The University at Albany.

Farnworth, Margaret, Terence P. Thornberry, Marvin D. Krohn, and Alan J. Lizotte. 1994. "Measurement in the study of class and delinquency: Integrating theory and research." *Journal of Research in Crime and Delinquency*, 31:32–61.

Garbarino, James. 1989. "Troubled youth, troubled families: The dynamics of adolescent maltreatment." In Dante Cicchetti and Vicki Carlson (eds.), *Child Maltreatment: Theory and Research on the Causes and Consequences of Child Abuse and Neglect.* Cambridge, Mass.: Harvard University Press.

Garbarino, James and Aaron Ebata. 1987. "The significance of ethnic and cultural differences in child maltreatment." In Robert L. Hampton (ed.), *Violence in the Black Family.* Lexington, Mass.: D.C. Heath.

Garbarino, James and Margaret C. Plantz. 1986. "Child abuse and juvenile delinquency: What are the links?" In James Garbarino (ed.), *Troubled Youth, Troubled Families*. New York: Aldine de Gruyter.

Hampton, Robert L. (ed.). 1987. *Violence in the Black Family*. Lexington, Mass: D.C. Heath.

Hampton, Robert L, and Eli H. Newberger. 1985. "Child abuse incidence and reporting by hospitals: Significance of severity, class, and race." *American Journal of Public Health*, 75:56–60.

Herrenkohl, Ellen C, Roy C. Herrenkohl, and Brenda Egolf. 1994. "Resilient early school-age children from maltreating homes: Outcomes in late adolescence." *American Journal of Orthopsychiatry*, 64:301–309.

Howing, Phyllis T., John S. Wodarski, P. David Kurtz, James M. Gaudin, Jr., and Emily N. Herbst. 1990. "Child abuse and delinquency: The empirical and theoretical links." *Social Work*, 35:244–249.

Huizinga, David, Rolf Loeber, and Terence P. Thornberry (eds.). 1991. *Urban Delinquency and Substance Use: Technical Report*. Prepared for the Office of Juvenile Justice and Delinquency Prevention, U.S. Department of Justice, Washington D.C.

Jessor, Richard, John E. Donovan, and Frances M. Costa. 1991. *Beyond Adolescence: Problem Behavior and Young Adult Development*. New York: Cambridge University Press.

Kendziora, Kimberly T. and Susan G. O'Leary. 1993. "Dysfunctional parenting as a focus for prevention and treatment of child behavior problems." In Thomas H. Ollendick and Ronald J. Prinz (eds.), *Advances in Clinical Child Psychology*. Vol. 15. New York: Plenum.

Kratcoski, Peter C. and Lucille Dunn Kratcoski. 1982. "The relationships of victimization through child abuse to aggressive delinquent behavior." *Victimology*, 7:199–203.

Kruttschnitt, Candace and Maude Dornfeld. 1993. "Exposure to family violence: A partial explanation for initial and subsequent levels of delinquency?" *Criminal Behavior and Mental Health*, 3:61–75.

Kruttschnitt, Candace, Linda Heath, and David A. Ward. 1986. "Family violence, television viewing and other adolescent experiences related to violent criminal behavior." *Criminology*, 24:235–267.

Kruttschnitt, Candace, David A. Ward, and Mary Ann Sheble. 1987. "Abuse-resistant youth: Some factors that may inhibit violent criminal behavior." *Social Forces*, 66:501–519.

Leiter, Jeffrey L., Kristen A. Myers, and Matthew T. Zingraff. 1994. "Substantiated and unsubstantiated cases of child maltreatment: Do their consequences differ?" *Social Work Research*, 18:67–82.

Lewis, Dorothy Otnow, Shelley S. Shanok, Jonathan H. Pincus, and Gilbert H. Glaser. 1979, "Violent juvenile delinquents: Psychiatric, neurological, psychological and abuse factors." *Journal of the American Academy of Child Psychiatry*, 18:307–319.

Lewis, Dorothy Otnow, Catherine Mallouh, and Victoria Webb. 1989. "Child abuse, delinquency and violent criminality." In Dante Cicchetti and Vicki Carlson (eds.), *Child Maltreatment: Theory and Research on the Causes and Consequences of Child Abuse and Neglect*. New York: Cambridge University Press.

Lytton, Hugh. 1990. "Child and parent effects in boy's conduct disorder: A reinterpretation." *Developmental Psychology*, 26:683–697.

McCord, Joan. 1983. "A forty year perspective on child abuse and neglect." *Child Abuse and Neglect*, 7:265–270.

Mouzaldtis, Chris M. 1981. "An inquiry into the problem of child abuse and juvenile delinquency." In Robert J. Hunner and Yvonne Elder Walker (eds.), *Exploring the Relationship Between Child Abuse and Delinquency*. Montclair, N.J.: Allanheld, Osmun.

Mrazek, Patricia J. and David A. Mrazek. 1987. "Resilience in child maltreatment victims: A conceptual exploration." *Child Abuse and Neglect*, 11:357–366.

Mueller, Edward and Nancy Silverman. 1989. "Peer relations in maltreated children." In Dante Cicchetti and Vicld Carlson (eds.), *Child Maltreatment: Theory and Research on the Causes and Consequences of Child Abuse and Neglect*. New York: Cambridge University Press.

National Center on Child Abuse and Neglect. 1981. *National Study of the Incidence and Severity of Child Abuse and Neglect* (Document No. 81–30325). Washington, D.C.: U.S. Department of Health and Human Services.

—1988. "Study Findings: Study of National Incidence and Prevalence of Child Abuse and Neglect." Washington, D.C.: U.S. Department of Health and Human Services.

Pagelow, Mildred Daley. 1984. *Family Violence*. New York: Praeger.

Paget, Kathleen D., Joel D. Philp, and Lois W. Abramczyk. 1993. "Recent developments in child neglect." In Thomas H. Ollendick and Ronald J. Prinz (eds.), *Advances in Clinical Child Psychology*. Vol. 15. New York: Plenum.

Patterson, Gerald R., Barbara D. DeBaryshe, and Elizabeth Ramsey. 1989. "A developmental perspective on antisocial behavior." *American Psychologist*, 44:329–335.

Rutter, Michael. 1987. Psychosocial resilience and protective mechanisms. American Journal of Orthopsychiatry 57:316–331.

Sampson, Robert and John Laub. 1993. *Crime in the Making: Pathways and Turning Points Through Life*. Cambridge, Mass.: Harvard University Press.

Silver, Larry B., Christina C. Dublin, and Reginald S. Lourie. 1969. "Does violence breed violence? Contributions from a study of the child abuse syndrome." *American Journal of Psychiatry*, 126:152–155.

Simons, Ronald L., Chyi-In Wu, Rand D. Conger, and Les B. Whitbeck. 1993. *A test of theoretical perspectives on the intergenerational transmission of domestic violence*. Unpublished paper, Department of Sociology and Center for Research in Rural Mental Health, Iowa State University.

Smith, Carolyn A., Alan J. Lizotte, Terence P. Thornberry, and Marvin D. Krohn. 1995. "Resilient youth: Identifying factors that prevent high-risk youth from engaging in delinquency and drug use." In John Hagan (ed.), *Delinquency in the Life Course*. Greenwich, Conn.: JAI Press.

Steele, Brandt. 1976. "Violence in the family." In Ray E. Heifer and C. Henry Kempe (eds.), *Child Abuse and Neglect: The Family and Community*. Cambridge, Mass.: Ballinger.

Thornberry, Terence P. 1987. "Toward an interactional theory of delinquency." *Criminology*, 25:863–891.

—1994. *Violent families and youth violence. Fact Sheet.* Office of Juvenile Justice and Delinquency Prevention, U.S. Department of Justice, Washington, D.C.

Thornberry, Terence P. and Carolyn Smith. 1994. *The effect of childhood victimization on adolescent deviance and criminal activity.* Paper presented at the 46th Annual Meeting of the American Society of Criminology, Miami.

Thornberry, Terence P., Beth Bjerregaard, and William Miles. 1993. "The consequences of respondent attrition in panel studies: A simulation based on the Rochester Youth Development Study." *Journal of Quantitative Criminology*, 9:127–158.

Thornberry, Terence P., Alan J. Lizotte, Marvin D. Krohn, Margaret Farnworth, and Sung Joon Jang. 1994. "Delinquent peers, beliefs, and delinquent behavior: A longitudinal test of interactional theory." *Criminology*, 32:601–637.

Thornberry, Terence P., David Huizinga, and Rolf Loeber. "The prevention of serious delinquency and violence: Implications from the Program of Research on the Causes and Correlates of Delinquency." In James C. Howell, Barry Krisberg, J. David Hawkins, and John J. Wilson (eds.), *Sourcebook on Serious, Violent and Chronic Juvenile Offenders*. Thousand Oaks, Calif.: Sage.

Toothaker, Larry E. 1993. *Multiple Comparison Procedures.* Newbury Park, Calif.: Sage.

Werner, Emmy E. and Ruth S. Smith. 1992. *Overcoming the Odds: High Risk Children from Birth to Adulthood.* Ithaca, N.Y.: Cornell University Press.

Wick, Steven C. 1981. "Child abuse as a causation of juvenile delinquency in central Texas. "In Robert J. Hunner and Yvonne Elder Walker (eds.), *Exploring the Relationship Between Child Abuse and Delinquency*. Montclair, N.J.: Allanheld, Osrnun.

Widom, Cathy Spatz. 1989. "Child abuse, neglect, and violent criminal behavior." *Criminology*, 27:251–271.

Widom, Cathy Spatz. 1989. "The cycle of violence." *Science*, 244:160–166.

Widom, Cathy Spatz. 1989. "Does violence beget violence? A critical examination of the literature." *Psychological Bulletin*, 106:3–38.

Widom, Cathy Spatz. 1991. "Avoidance of criminality in abused and neglected children." *Psychiatry*, 54:162–174.

Widom, Cathy Spatz. 1991. "Childhood victimization: Risk factor for delinquency." In Mary Ellen Colton and Susan Gore (eds.), *Adolescent Stress: Causes and Consequences*. New York: Aldine de Gruyter.

Widom, Cathy Spatz. 1994. "Childhood victimization and risk for adolescent problem behavior." In Michael E. Lamb and Robert Ketterlinus (eds.), *Adolescent Problem Behaviors*. New York: Lawrence Erlbaum.

Wodarski, John S., P. David Kurtz, James M. Gaudin, Jr., Phyllis T. Howing. 1990. "Maltreatment and the school-age child: Major academic, socioemotional, and adaptive outcomes." *Social Work*, 35:501–513.

Wolfe, David A. 1987. *Child Abuse: Implications for Child Development and Psychopathology.* Beverly Hills, Calif.: Sage.

Zingraff, Matthew T., Jeffrey Leiter, Kristen A. Myers, and Matthew C. Johnson. 1993. "Child maltreatment and youthful problem behavior." *Criminology,* 31:173–202.

Zingraff, Matthew T., Jeffrey Leiter, Matthew C. Johnson, and Kristen A. Myers. 1994. "The mediating effect of good school performance on the maltreatment delinquency relationship." *Journal of Research in Crime and Delinquency,* 31:62–91.

ABOUT THE AUTHORS

Carolyn Smith is an Assistant Professor of Social Welfare at the University at Albany, State University of New York. She holds an MSW as well as a Ph.D. in Criminal Justice, and has spent several years in clinical practice with youth and families in the child welfare and juvenile justice fields. Her interdisciplinary research is in the area of family influences on youth behavior, and she has published in journals in criminology, sociology, and social work.

Terence P. Thornberry is Professor, and former Dean, at the School of Criminal Justice, University at Albany, State University of New York. He is the author of The Criminally Insane *and* From Boy to Man—From Delinquency to Crime, *as well as numerous articles and book chapters. His research interests focus on the longitudinal examination of the development of delinquency and crime, as well as the construction of an interactional theory to explain these behaviors. Professor Thornberry is the director of the Rochester Youth Development Study, the recipient of awards including the American Bar Association's Gavel Award Certificate of Merit, the President's Award for Excellence in Research at the University at Albany, and is a Fellow of the American Society of Criminology.*

APPENDIX 1

Exemplars From The Cicchetti-Barnett Classification System to Indicate Different Levels of Severity for Physical Abuse

1. The caregiver inflicted minor marks on the child's body during a spanking; and there were no marks to the neck or head.

2. Reports indicated that the caregiver had beaten the child; no other information was given.

3. The child received injuries that were documented to have occurred by nonaccidental means. The details of the report were not specific enough to warrant a higher rating.

4. The caregiver was reported to have spanked the child with an open hand or an object likely to inflict only minor marks in most cases (e.g., a switch, a soft belt, a ruler, a paddle), with the child sustaining marks on or below the shoulders.

5. The caregiver inflicted numerous or nonminor marks to the child's body from any incident.

6. The caregiver spanked the child with an object likely to leave a nonminor mark (e.g., a hair brush, a belt buckle, an electrical cord), or kicked or punched the child with a fist, leaving marks on the child's body below the neck.

7. The caregiver inflicted marks on the child's head, face, or neck (e.g., a black eye).

8. The caregiver's rough handling of the child resulted in serious bruises or minor lacerations (e.g., required stitches or minor medical attention).

9. The caregiver inflicted minor burns (e.g., minor cigarette burns) to the child's body.

10. The caregiver hit the child with an object (e.g., a baseball bat, a telephone) likely to result in serious injury (e.g., nonminor lacerations, second-degree burns, fracture, or concussion), or threw the child against the wall, but injuries that were sustained did not require hospitalization, according to available medical information.

11. The caregiver attempted to choke or smother the child, but no emergency medical care was required.

12. The caregiver inflicted serious burns (second degree) to the child's body, but the injury did not require hospitalization. The caregiver inflicted an injury which required some hospital care, such as treatment in the Emergency Room, but did not require hospitalization for more than 24 hours (e.g., stitches, fractures, nonminor sprain).

13. The caregiver inflicted an injury to the child that required hospitalization (e.g., severe/multiple burns, internal injuries), and/or that was permanently physically damaging, or disfiguring (e.g., resulting in brain damage, severe scarring, crippling). The caregiver inflicted a fatal injury.

* Prepared under Grant 86-JN-CX-0007 (S-3) from the Office of Juvenile Justice and Delinquency Prevention, Office of Justice Programs, U.S. Department of Justice; Grant 5 RO1 DA05512–02 from the National Institute on Drug Abuse; and Grant SES-8912274 from the National Science Foundation. Points of view or opinions in this document are those of the authors and do not necessarily represent the official position or policies of the funding agencies. We would like to thank Bonnie Carlson, Richard Felson, Marvin D. Krohn, Alan J. Lizotte, and Cathy Spatz Widom for their helpful comments on earlier drafts of this paper.

The Relationship Between Childhood Maltreatment & Adolescent Involvement in Delinquency by Smith & Thornberry

PowerPoint by:
Derek Reddick
Florence Lowe
Stefanie Watkins

Maltreatment

FIVE INDICATORS OF MALTREATMENT:

- Prevalence
- Frequency
- Duration
- Number of Types
- Total Severity Scores

SELF-REPORT MEASURES-5 SELF-REPORT INDEXES:

- General
- Serious
- Moderate
- Minor
- Violent
- Child maltreatment occurs before 12th birthday

Results

► No significant differences by sex or race
► Significant differences by class and family structure
 — *Class* 19.5% to 8.2% abused
 — *Family* 18.6% to 3.2%

► Table 2 – Significant relationship between maltreatment & likelihood of delinquency

Accurate Understanding

► The extent to which maltreatment is a significant risk factor for negative outcomes is particularly crucial because recent estimates of the prevalence of child maltreatment suggest that it is a much more substantial problem than ever suspected.
► In sum, a number of studies have examined the role of early childhood maltreatment as a risk factor for later involvement in delinquency. Although these studies generally indicate that maltreatment is a risk factor, there are a # of unresolved issues about the relationship between these variables.

Resolutions

►   In order to resolve these issues, we pose the following questions in this analysis:

1. Is childhood maltreatment a significant risk factor for official & self-reported measures of delinquency?

2. Is childhood maltreatment a risk factor for various types of delinquent behavior, including violent offending?

3. Is the relationship between maltreatment & delinquency spurious, or is it maintained when relevant variables are held constant?

4. Are more refined measures of maltreatment—*for example, measures that incorporate such dimensions as the extensiveness & severity of abuse*—more strongly related to delinquency than simple global measures of abuse?

Methods:

► Data is drawn from the Rochester Youth Development Study (RYDS)
  — Youth & Caretakers
  — Every 6 mos. for 4 ½ yrs
► Rochester public school, police dept., & dept. of social services.

Measurements:

► Record of abuse from birth until 1992
► Classification system (Cicchetti & Barnett)
► 7 types or Maltreatment
  — physical abuse
  — sexual abuse
  — emotional
  — moral/legal
  — educational
  — neglect
  — lack of supervision
► 5 Point Scale

Elevation in Risk: Maltreated Vs. Nonmaltreated

▶ Maltreated persons
  — *Arrests = 2.8 times as often*
  — *Serious offenses = 2.3 times as many*
  — *Violent offenses = 1.9 times as many*

▶ Childhood Maltreatment & Later Delinquency
  — *linked to seriousness of Maltreatment*
  — *childhood, adolescence, and adulthood*

Limitations of Measure:

▶ Based entirely on official records
  — biases inherent
  — race & class biases
  — behavior of family members

▶ Direct Causal Links (delinquency vs. resilience)
  — intervening variables = developmental, physiological, coping styles, disordered behavior
  — Effects potentiated by spousal abuse, media, community, poverty (sociological issues)

▶ Range of outcomes: drug use, gangs, sexual behavior, suicidal, teen parenthood, violence toward partners

ETHNICITY AND GANGS

ISOLATION AND STIGMATIZATION IN THE DEVELOPMENT OF AN UNDERCLASS

THE CASE OF CHICANO GANGS IN EAST LOS ANGELES

By Joan W. Moore

A good deal of our concern in the study of social problems has to do with the emergence in American society of a predominantly minority urban underclass. Generally, social scientists rely on one or a combination of two approaches in explaining this phenomenon. The first approach—the culture of poverty—argues for the existence of a tangle of pathology which is "... capable of perpetuating itself without assistance from the white world" (Moynihan, 1967:47). All that is required to sustain this underclass culture is a welfare state. An alternative approach, equally over-simplified here, argues that the minority underclass is a product of institutionalized racism, which operates in education, the job market, the housing market, and the criminal justice system.

But both the culture of poverty and racism explanations focus on categories of people rather than on communities. The culture of poverty approach emphasizes individuals and their families. The discrimination argument looks at individuals in relation to their roles in the institutions of the larger society. Neither recognizes the dynamics working within the communities in which underclass families live. I suggest here that it would be fruitful to focus on differentiation within poor minority communities. Further, since deviance and potential deviance are also part of our image of the underclass, we may borrow from the labeling perspective to understand how deviants, and by extension, underclass families come to be differentiated further in their own minority communities. A case history—the development of Chicano youth gangs—shows some of these processes at work, and also demonstrates that it is possible for these trends to be reversed. Thus we can also identify some of the dynamics involved in the reabsorption of members of the under-class into a less deviant or stigmatized segment of the minority poor.

LABELING, DEVIANCE, AND MINORITIES

I became interested in the relevance of the labeling perspective after looking again at John Kitsuse's 1979 SSSP presidential address. He was surprised and a little delighted when he noticed that stigmatized persons were collectively rejecting the labels that he and other theorists of deviance had analyzed so effectively. "Deviants were coming out all over … to profess and advocate the lives they live and the values that those lives express" (Kitsuse, 1980:8).

One of the controversial issues in his paper and to other labeling theorists was the extension of the labeling analysis to minority persons. They implied that to be a minority person—or a woman, for that matter—is to be stigmatized. Thus Goffman talks about "tribal stigma of race, nation and religion" (1963:4), and Kitsuse adds "genetic stigma" to include gender, left-handedness, and other genetically-determined attributes (1980:2). This is a rather blurry area, particularly in the case of minorities. Labeling and its consequences for generating distinctive lifestyles (or secondary deviance) evoke images of *deviance*—not "otherness." As Kitsuse acknowledged, many people were uneasy about this extension. After all, women and minorities were not really deviants. And, are the subcultures of minorities "secondary deviance?" Some interpretations of the labeling perspective imply that these subcultures would not have emerged without public labeling. Obviously, this is not true.[10]

---

10   In his own work, Kitsuse is concerned with the "social differentiation of deviants as a process by which others make persons different, often independent of whether or not they 'really are different'" (personal communication, April 19, 1985). However, Shur, for one, struggles with "the line between reactions to … perceived deviance [on the one hand] and devaluing responses to racial and ethnic minorities, and to women [on the other hand]" (1984:23). Being placed in an "other" category is

However, there may be some truth in this perspective that is worth untangling. Stigma involves a stereotype, and for minorities the stereotypes include perceptions of deviance. The larger society certainly does label *some* minority persons, a priori, as "probably deviant." Thus to be young, male, and black or Chicano in white America *is* to be a suspect person (cf. Wilkinson, 1977). To be a visible member of a population that many Anglos associate with violent crime is to evoke hostile and fearful responses. I would like to call this "ascribed deviance," and to distinguish it from the "achieved deviance" of the criminal or the drug addict.[11] The ascription of deviance is based, of course, on generalized stereotypes, but it is focused on a particular segment of the minority population. Ascribed deviance, then, is deviance that is ascribed to minority young men on the basis of visible characteristics (or, if you like, ascriptive characteristics). Young black males need only appear in an Anglo neighborhood to evoke fear.

The ascription of deviance to young minority males by Anglos has some direct consequences. We might reasonably expect that these consequences would be trivial for law-abiding minority youth, even if *all* Anglos thought that *all* minority young men were likely to be violent or criminal. Young men in the "wrong" place—e.g., wandering in an Anglo neighborhood—might be harassed. However, real damage is done when suspicious Anglos control the police, schools, and organized services for youth, and structure these institutions in order to avert and control *possible* deviance. The functions of these socializing institutions are thus distorted and the result is socialization destined for social control.

There are also indirect effects, which operate through community social structure. How do the law-abiding members of minority communities react when their children are groundlessly assumed to be deviant? I suspect that they turn on the "real," achieved young deviants in their midst. After all, isn't it those "real" deviants and their deserved reputation that caused all this trouble with the Anglo community in the first place? The targeted ascription of deviance by Anglos—to young minority males—generates processes inside minority communities which are very different from the consequences of

---

taken by some writers as tantamount to being labeled as deviant, and by Schur as the equivalent of devaluation.

11 James Orcutt has called my attention to the fact that Milton Mankoff (1971) used similar terms—"ascriptive rule breaking" and "achieved rule breaking." However, Mankoff uses "ascriptive rule breaking" to summarize the existing work of labeling theorists with regard to the "physically and visibly handicapped" in a more general critique of the validity of labeling theory for understanding the development of deviant careers. I am interested in the impact of the ascriptive labeling of minority males in general and on minority community treatment of gang members and ex-offenders. Clearly, I am not describing physically handicapped persons. My interest is in processes—in communities where all the members are in jeopardy of labeling—rather than in individual career issues.

general discrimination. General discrimination makes minority people mad at Anglos, but ascriptive labeling makes those same minority people mad at other minority people. Achieved deviants and innocent members of their families become the target of enhanced labeling within the communities—labeling which might not have occurred without the Anglo ascription of deviance. This generates more secondary deviance, laying the conditions for the development of a distinctive underclass.

But minority communities are internally differentiated, and some people are highly likely to transmit and amplify the Anglo labeling, while others correctly view it as yet another form of racism. Three cross-cutting bases of differentiation concern me. First, there is the distinction between respectable and disreputable poor found in writings on the American class structure from Warner (Warner and Lunt, 1941) through Matza (1966) and Banfield (1970). The distinction refers not only to law-abiding vs. law-violating *behavior*, but even more importantly to variations in the degree of "concern with 'front' and respectability," as Drake and Cayton make clear about the black middle class (1962:661). I suggest that it is those who are preoccupied with maintaining their own front of respectability that are the most likely to transmit Anglo labeling.[12] Thus the distinction between law-abiding people and law-breakers is reinforced and given much more moral impact by the desire of some to prove to themselves, to each other, and to label-prone Anglo contacts that *they*, at least, are decent people.

The second cross-cutting basis of differentiation is the equally familiar cut between accommodationists and the protest-oriented. Many poor people (both white and minority) define the reward structure of the dominant system in "either deferential or aspirational terms" (Parkin, 1972:81), and adjust to inequality without much interest in collective improvement. But *many* minority persons define the dominant system as unfair, and are preoccupied with changing it for their group.[13] Many law-violating and

---

12   There is a hint in some of the literature that even the respectable in poor communities tolerate deviance. I have not found that criminality is accepted; rather, the law-abiding minority poor learn that they can rarely count on responsive and fair police work. However, neither is it true that all law-abiding families reject the form of young male deviance that is expressed in barrio gang membership. Minorities cannot be expected to share Anglo moral orders that are closely linked to Anglo stereotypes, i.e., that the neighborhood gang is an inherently criminal phenomenon. Thus, the minority community violates what Kitsuse identifies as one of Goffman's postulates for effective stigmatization: that "those who impose stigma ... [share a moral order with] those on whom they are imposed" (Kituse, 1980:4).

13   Parkin (1972) and other English writers on the class structure are extremely useful, but are difficult to apply to American class structures because the concept of race is so important in the United States. Thus Parkin discusses both radical and accommodationist value sets, but white working class radicals are not the same as protest-oriented minorities.

law-abiding persons are accommodationist, while both law-violating and law-abiding persons have protested injustice and racism. Accommodationists are most prone to transmit the labels, while the protest-oriented are more likely to become alienated from the larger system.

There is a third dimension of differentiation within poor minority communities. Many people in these communities are first-generation urbanites. During and after the Second World War large-scale migration of blacks and Hispanics to American cities filled the ghettos and barrios with newcomers. More recently, a heavy influx of non-European immigrants is having a similar impact on the composition of American cities in the 1980s (cf. Maldonado and Moore, 1985). Invariably this means that newcomers—law-abiding and law-violating alike—struggle with both urban ways and American ways. Many also bring highly traditional and individualistic values.

I think that Kitsuse (1980) and others missed these distinctions. But this is understandable. Kitsuse, for example, focused on the processes during a peculiar point in history, the days of "the Movement"—the Great Egalitarian Movement of the 1960s and early 1970s. When he gave his presidential address to the SSSP in 1979, Kitsuse was very much impressed by the effects of the "politics of social and legal entitlement." Stigmatized deviants (gays and young blacks in Hunters Point, for example) were collectively "confront[ing] ... assess[ing] ... and reject[ing] ... the negative identity embedded in secondary deviation and were transform [ing] ... that identity into a possible and viable self-conception" (1980:9). He called this "tertiary deviance"—the flaunting of a stigmatized lifestyle and the transcendence of stigma.

Since much of Kitsuse's argument draws on the Egalitarian Movement, it may be worth looking at that epoch a little more closely and see who was flaunting what stigmatized lifestyle. Thus, among minorities, it is true that conventional demonstrators (conflict and political groups) marched side-by-side with groups of actual, achieved minority deviants.[14] But there is something very peculiar about the "tertiary deviance" that was expressed in these public affirmations of minority identity and solidarity. At least among the Chicanos, it was *not* achieved deviants such as ex-convicts and gang youth who flaunted the street style—*they* wore conventional clothing. It was the college students, symbolically associating with the stigmatized Chicano gang youth, who adopted the street style. Their style was a challenge—to "colonialist" teachers and accommodationist relatives—a courting of ascription of deviance from Anglos that was designed to separate themselves from hints that they aspired to assimilationist lifestyles.[15] By contrast, the style of the achieved deviants was *not* designed for an Anglo

---

14 The gang members of the Young Lords and Blackstone Rangers and the ex-convicts of the Black Panthers

15 Thus the High Potential program at UCLA, designed to recruit minority students, rapidly became known as the "High Pot" program, permitting the implication that all of these promising

audience. Rather, they were coming out more cautiously to the respectable people living inside the minority community. For Kitsuse, tertiary deviance involves an affirmation of a stigmatized lifestyle. This is not too hard for college students, plainly on their way to respectability, but much harder for the achieved deviants—the street people and ex-offenders, black and Hispanic. There are two steps in the transformation of this stigmatized identity. First, respectable minority persons must be convinced that the street lifestyle does not necessarily involve danger to the community, and that these persons should, indeed, be reintegrated. Only then, with respect-able allies, can gang youth and ex-offenders directly confront the labeling of the larger society. There had to be two steps because the initial labeling of these achieved deviants went through two steps over many years. The first step involved continuous labeling by Anglos of all young minority males as probable deviants. The second step was continuous reactive labeling of gang people *inside* the minority community, further isolating and stigmatizing achieved deviants. Therefore, as a first step to redress, the street people of the 1960s made claims for acceptance in a specialized role in the Movement—as militants. The claims were successful: young college militants redefined the gang people as "specialists" in resistance to authority and symbolically adopted the street style. This second step, then, meant that ex-offenders and gang members had found respectable minority allies to confront the larger system about their grievances. In turn, the ex-offenders backed up Chicano professionals and paraprofessionals in *their* confrontations with health care institutions, schools, and community development agencies.

Ultimately, the Movement provided an opportunity for minority communities to reabsorb their achieved deviants. However, this was not to last. Minority responses to both achieved and ascribed deviance are complicated and fluctuate from time to time. We must analyze the cross-cutting social differentiation within the communities in order to understand this. Under some conditions the community labelers prevail; under others, their influence is submerged. Similarly, there are variations in the extent to which minority achieved deviants "come out," as they did in the days of the Movement, or remain mired in secondary deviance that begins to resemble an underclass subculture. To ground this discussion, I will turn to a more detailed history of the gangs in Chicano East Los Angeles.[16]

---

minority students were high on pot all the time.

16 I am indebted to Diego Vigil for his insights into this process, in which he participated. It is probable that there were parallels in the black community.

Youth gangs are particularly susceptible to labeling as deviant, regardless of their behavior. In Chicano communities of the 1980s, a "disreputable" lifestyle is closely associated with the development are well-known, but the mix of Chicano demonstrators is less well known. In the major street protests of Los Angeles on August 29, 1970, the march was led by the striking farmworkers of Cesar Chavez' Huelguistas. Then came a self-help group of ex-offenders (LUCHA). Next came two traditional middle-class Mexican American political organizations (MAPA and LULAC). Then, the Brown Berets, the Chicano versions of the Young Lords with many gang members, were followed by the staff members of militant publications and by a large group of Chicano college student organizations (Acosta, 1973). Over the past two generations of a *cholo* or street lifestyle which derives from the youth gangs (Vigil, 1985a, 1985b). *Cholismo* includes considerable pessimism about adult life chances, anticipates some time in prison, and incorporates deep fatalism about the prospects for conventional careers. The *cholo* lifestyle approaches, but cannot yet be called the culture of an "underclass" or "lumpenproletariat" either on subjective or objective grounds. Youth gang members neither feel ostracized nor do they all in fact graduate to an adulthood of degradation. The following history may sound like a classic illustration of deviance, labeling, and secondary deviance. But the point of it is that the gangs evolved within a community that was extremely sensitive and responsive to Anglo ascription of deviance to its members.

I will trace four turning points in the evolution of these gangs.[17] All four are related both to changes in actual or achieved deviance and to the ascription of deviance from the larger society. The first two developments permitted the labelers within the community to stigmatize the gangs; the third reversed the trend and reintegrated gang members, and the fourth again isolated the gangs. Community differentiation figured into each turning point, as did the behavior of gang members. Newcomers, old-timers, accommodationists, and protesters all played distinct roles.

The "gang" in Mexican and Mexican American life is not necessarily delinquent. Aggressive male youth groups have been a documented feature of town and rural life as far back as the nineteenth century (Redfield, 1941:28). They appeared in rural Texas in the guise of *palomillas* (Rubel, 1965) and continued in American cities, attached to specific neighborhoods or barrios as they had been in Mexican cities. In Los Angeles in the 1920s Bogardus (1926) called them "boy gangs" to distinguish them from "real" gangs. In the 1930s the precursors of the three Los Angeles gangs we have studied were respectable groups of young men. In fact, in one of the neighborhoods, White Fence,

---

17   This history is derived in part from interviews conducted during a series of studies funded largely by grants from the National Institute on Drug Abuse, especially DAO 3114, and the National Institute of Mental Health, MH 33104. Of course, neither agency is responsible for opinions expressed here.

the gang was attached to the barrio church and called by the church name, *La Purissima*, as late as the 1940s. The early barrio gangs of the Mexican agricultural laborers of Los Angeles' San Fernando Valley in the 1930s were much like the rural *palomillas*. We know they formed a baseball league, and outside the league went from one town to another crashing Saturday night dances and fighting with each other (Moore et al., 1979a). Even the local police didn't seem to make much fuss about the gangs.[18]

Then, in the 1940s, the gangs developed a style which soon evoked a sharp reaction from the Anglo community. It is the first clear instance of ascriptive labeling. This was the *pachuco* fad. It swept the second-generation youth culture with its flamboyant zoot-suit clothing and English-Spanish slang. It was the dominant youth style throughout the community, although the gang youth may have been particularly fond of the exaggerated "drapes" and double-soled shoes.[19] But the gangs did not seem to be deviant. To be sure, there were fights, occasional serious wounds, and even deaths. But this was in the tradition of aggressive barrio-based youth groups. The *pachuco* gangs of the 1940s were sharing a version of the larger youth culture (zoot-suiters) that involved innovation in language and lifestyle. Not surprisingly, Mexican-born parents were often baffled (Burma, 1954; Griffith, 1948). The 1940s Chicano gangs were culturally innovative; however, our research suggests that the innovation remained strictly within a Mexican youth tradition. Thus, in the semi-rural San Fernando Valley, the *pachuco* Polviados of San Fernando were seen as "peculiar"—even a little sissified—by other San Fernando Valley gangs because they "dressed fancy and smelled pretty," and spent a lot of money to achieve these affects. They were no longer Mexican gangs but Chicano gangs (Moore et al., 1979a). Still, no one inside or outside these gangs seems to have defined them as dangerous, even when a subclique began to use heroin. Heroin use, in fact, seems to have been an extension of older patterns of marijuana use. Casual use was overlooked.

---

18   Thus, in one of the barrios that we studied—Hoyo Maravilla—a sheriff's deputy was quoted in 1932, "There is not much we can do to break up the gangs. ... We talk to the boys and take them home and talk to the parents. Some of the parents don't seem to care what their kids do and others lick the tar out of them ... The kids themselves know that we are not likely to really do anything to them" (Lanigan, 1932:67).

19   One academic who grew up in Los Angeles at the time comments, "Young people of my generation lived on various levels of pachuquismo (acculturation). Everyone, for example, wore drapes or the equivalent for women. Really straight/square dress was rare, truly rare. Mexicans from Mexico wore square clothes upon arrival, but not for long. It was stylish to wear drapes and sharp calcos (shoes). But again, this was the style set by the movies for all American youth. There was a very large element of 'semis,' i.e. young Chicanos who were stylishly pachuco, but not extreme. Their language and behavior and such was also 'semi.' The 'semis' operated between pachuco culture and gabacho (Anglo) society" (Ralph Guzmán, personal communication, 1985).

Zoot-Suit Riots

This comparatively halcyon state was not to last. The sweep arrests accompanying the Sleepy Lagoon murder case and the later zoot-suit riots of the early 1940s were the first turning point in the Anglo labeling of young Mexicans as deviant (Acuña, 1981; Gonzalez, 1981; Mazón, 1976; McWilliams, 1949). Mexican communities east of downtown Los Angeles were invaded by servicemen. Youths wearing the zoot-suit costume anywhere in the city were chased and beaten, regardless of their behavior. Most of the victims were not members of gangs. Newspapers went well beyond the facts of the race riots and greatly stirred up racial feeling. For instance, the term "ratpack" was coined by a reporter to refer to Mexican youth gangs. The net result was a new and strongly established image of Mexican young men as savage. This ascription of deviance was never reversed. It was said to be genetic—"blood lust" inherited from the Aztecs. While there is no doubt the Chicano gangs were aggressive, this was the first time gangs and youthful Mexican violence became part of the media stereotype (Gonzalez, 1981).

How did this development affect the barrios? These were new labels and many Mexican Americans reacted with great concern. Thus, when the Anglo press labeled Mexican American youth gangs as "vicious," many respectable people accepted the label.[20] They may have felt it was exaggerated, but it was important that they dissociate themselves. Over the next decade the increase in police harassment and sensationalist press coverage reinforced this reaction. As one young activist put it in 1954, "it is becoming more and more difficult to walk through the streets of Los Angeles—and look Mexican!" (Guzmán, quoted in Acuña, 1984:337). Basically the respectables thought that the police harassment made no distinction between good kids and bad kids. Therefore, people who needed a respectable front may have been especially punitive toward the youth gangs.

But, on the other hand, many people in the barrios tolerated the gangs for years. They saw the gangs as little more than nuisances and defined the police reaction as

---

20 In fact, 20 years later, when I began a large-scale study of Mexican Americans, many "respectable" Mexican Americans found it difficult to believe that Anglo liberals could define the zoot-suiters as victims, given the overwhelming effect of the media. Members of our project's community advisory committee urged us not to study marijuana use in the barrios because it would further stigmatize them. "Square" youth, some of whom are now Chicano professionals, had been ridiculed as lambion ("kiss-ass") or had their school lunches or movie money stolen by these same pachucos—or had watched barrio fights from a safe distance. But not all gang members were hostile to achievers. As one source notes, "Many squares then and today are protected by gang members. There is much evidence that pachucos (then) and cholos (today) exhibit raza pride for Chicano achievers" (Ralph Guzmán, personal communication, 1985).

racist.[21] Throughout this period gang members recall that perfectly respectable barrio residents *did* hide them from police and *did* lie in order to protect them (Moore et al., 1979b). Of course, in small communities, even outside the Mexican barrios, perfectly respectable people are likely to know somebody with a kid in the local gang or to have a child or relative in the gang themselves. At that time there were few if any "gang families" or families with a *cholo* tradition of street life over several generations. We must not forget that to be upwardly mobile in those days usually implied movement into the Anglo world, since opportunities within Chicano communities were limited. Thus, there was probably concern with "front" and correspondingly greater sensitivity to Anglo stereotypes. In addition, there was a continuing trickle of new immigrants from Mexico to cluck in disapproval at the youthful violators of tradition.

Heroin Indictments

During the 1950s still other processes were at work inside the gangs. Increasing sigmatization and isolation probably encouraged further deviance. Most importantly, the spread of heroin in the barrios generated intensified law enforcement (see Moore et al., 1979a). This led to a second turning point in ascriptive labeling. Some major changes in police practice led to widely publicized indictments of young gang men for heroin marketing in 1950. Other cases were also widely publicized. Subsequently, California narcotics laws became more punitive and, for the first time, barrio men went to prison in large numbers. Barrio gang subcultures began to incorporate mythologies about coping with prison. This had predictable effects on younger members. The earlier naivete of the gangs was destroyed; tension and secrecy mounted, and there was even greater reliance on "homeboy" networks. Mexican Americans long had been stereotyped as marijuana users and now the image of the evil dope dealer was added to the "ratpack" image of the gangs.

Chicano Movement

The community reaction to these gangs was now negative. But, by the late 1960s the community reversed itself for a third stage. As noted earlier, street gangs and ex-offenders were integrated into the Chicano Movement. This happened for several reasons.

---

21   In a recent study of a Dallas barrio, Achor (1978) notes a similar situation: "Barrio residents sometimes speak of lospelados (poor, wretched people) … but they do not consider them sufficiently numerous to constitute a large and threatening element of the barrio's social world. They usually explain that problem families have suffered severe and prolonged hardship" (1978:131). Again, "many residents … view their neighborhood as relatively safe … [and] the people … do not seem to fear their neighbors—but many do show signs of fearing the police." (1978:104).

First, gangs began to be romanticized as social bandits in the century-old Mexican tradition of resistance and opposition to Anglo authority.[22] This romanticization was partly a revisionist account of accommodationist histories of the barrios—an attempt to demonstrate an unbroken history of Chicano resistance to Anglo repression.

Second, gangs (and their ex-offender adult members, the *pintos*) had a specialized role: they were seen as a sort of fighting branch of the Chicano movement. *Pintos* responded to the image of themselves as "soldiers." The Brown Berets (gang members and younger ex-offenders) marched and solemnly posted guards during rallies. In the bloody riot of August 29, 1970, a line of *pintos* spontaneously came out of the crowd to keep a police charge at bay, giving the women and the children in the crowd a few minutes to escape before being overrun. Only two weeks later an ex-offender organization undertook to organize security for a Mexican Independence Day parade, drawing on a network of Chicano gangs in the Los Angeles metropolitan area. This general eagerness to defend the entire community *(la raza)* was at least in part an extension of the gang's propensity to defend its own tiny neighborhood or turf.

The *pintos* and the young men of the barrios were integrated into the Chicano Movement through other means than a romantic ideology and their specialized role as soldiers. Kinship linkages also contributed to this end. Relatives of members of ex-offender self-help groups were scattered throughout the growing set of community-based organizations established as part of the War on Poverty. In addition, some of the paraprofessionals in these new agencies had themselves been gang members as teenagers and were unusually sensitive to the needs of their clientele.[23] Many older, conventional Mexican Americans—some in professional positions—appeared in support of these groups. An ex-offender organization held a weekly *menudo* breakfast, served by women relatives. For many relatives of the ex-offenders, this was the first chance to come out into the open about the incarceration of a family member. The family shame

---

22   Thus Diego Vigil identified Joaquin Murietta and Tiburcio Vasquez, bandits of the post-Conquest era, as "Early Chicano Guerilla Fighters" (1974) and dedicated his paper to a man killed in an armed robbery in 1971 as a "modern prototype of a Chicano social bandit" (also see Cortes, 1972). Vigil suggests further that the Californios were the accommodationists of their time and reacted to these desperados much as the 1940s accommodationists reacted to their modern counterparts, the gangs.

23   Ramon Salcido (1979) found significant differences in background and attitudes between professional and paraprofessional gang workers. Most of the paraprofessionals had been affiliated with gangs; most of the professionally trained social workers had not. Paraprofessionals with early gang affiliations had far more complex perceptions of the composition and nature of the gangs. The professionals, trained largely in psychological models, seemed to focus more on individualistic theory-derived views. Paraprofessionals tended to emphasize community intervention; professionals emphasized casework intervention tactics.

could be redefined as a community issue. Many community leaders saw the Chicano Movement as an extension of their life-long struggle for the advancement of Mexicans and sympathized with the *pintos* as a segment of the community needing reintegration into barrio life—not rejection or further stigmatization. These networks facilitated the reintegration of achieved deviants into a protest-oriented community movement.[24]

Very clearly, this appears to be what Kitsuse calls "coming out all over" or the development of "tertiary deviance." But was it? Ex-offender groups were actually being consciously political, trying to gain broad community support for prison reform, for change in laws about sentencing narcotics offenders, and for community programs for gang youth, ex-offenders and addicts. It was during this era—the early 1970s—that heroin addiction began to be a recognized and defined as a serious problem within these communities, and local medical people began to deal with it as a medical issue rather than as a purely criminal activity. Thus Kitsuse's tertiary deviants, the militant squares, were working in a different direction from the achieved deviants. The young militant squares adopted the style of younger gang members in their symbolic "tertiary deviance" to mark their identification with the politics of entitlement. But older gang members worked with change-oriented squares to reintegrate *pintos* and addicts into conventional careers.

Prison "Super-Gangs"

However, this was not to last. During the last 10 years or so, the push toward accepting the "achieved deviants" back into the community has waned. A wave of violence in California prisons heralded a fourth turning point in the history of barrio gangs. Community-based convict and addict organizations were swept away, as *all* ex-offenders were suspected of association with the prison-based Mexican Mafia or *La Familia*, two prison "super-gangs" (Adams, 1977). Once again, Anglo authorities and the media ascribed deviance to all Chicano convicts—over generalizing from the real, achieved deviance. Each of the five cultural and structural bases for the movement inspired integration of the gangs into the community dissolved. First, the street people were again defined as criminals rather than as social bandits. Now this criminal definition was even stronger. When some younger researchers recently showed an interest in studying

---

24 There was, of course, no more consensus on reintegration than there had been on stigmatization. The tipping of the balance was shown when traditionalist spokespersons protested the formation of a small heroin detoxification unit in a hospital ward funded by Model Cities. The Mexican-born representative for Model Cities appeared before the City Council to denouce the "shameful" fact that an ex-offender group had been involved in this unit and to demand the elimination of the program and the presence of ex-offenders from the overall city planning. She was soundly defeated.

and working with ex-offenders, older Chicano scholars advised against it. They argued that *pintos* are just "lumpenproletariat"—a liability and not a resource for the Chicano Movement.[25] Second, there were no more street demonstrations and the *pintos* lost their value as soldiers. Third, families of ex-offenders reverted to an earlier adaptation: hiding their shame.[26] Fourth, former gang members who had turned respectable and "come out of the closet" to support the street people were now discredited for their association with individuals later proven to be linked to the Mexican Mafia. Fifth, many of the older paraprofessional activists retired, and community-based organizations became increasingly professionalized. Federal and state funds were cut and paraprofessional street workers, who were generally more empathetic with the gangs, were forced into marginal positions or eliminated.

In sum, there was a major erosion in the presence and legitimacy of structural and cultural resources for integrating street people into conventional roles. The end result was predictable: prison self-help groups dissolved and community-based agencies serving ex-offenders were eliminated, only to emerge, transformed, as part of the criminal justice system. Gang programs began to be replaced by Sheriff's and Police Department anti-gang efforts, which were strengthened in the 1980s. Gang isolation increased, as did gang violence.

Other shifts in community differentiation reinforced these trends. The increased pace of immigration from Mexico in the late 1970s meant that the barrios began again to fill with men and women who were very traditional in their values and generally contemptuous of Americanized Chicanos—and of the *cholo* gang members in particular. No matter how poor they might be, Mexican immigrants often display an attitude of superiority toward Chicanos whom they view as inept with the Spanish language and unfamiliar with Mexican ways. Some community activists feel that this immigrant rejection of *"pocho"* or Chicano culture underlies the refusal of newer community groups to take up the cause of reintegrating street people. Thus, in Los Angeles the church-based UNO (United Neighborhood Organization, affiliated with Saul Alinsky's Industrial Areas Foundation) actively rejected work with gang youth and, in fact, asked for enhanced policing as a solution to the gang problem—even though UNO and its counterpart organizations have played a different role in other cities. These changes all occurred against a constant barrage of media coverage, which continues to sensationalize the barrio gangs and dramatize police responses. Similarly, the media paint lurid pictures of prison gangs and applaud the "get-tough" correctional responses.

---

25   This echoed the advice given to the UCLA Mexican American Study Project in the mid 1960s.

26   Evidence from interviews with the parents and siblings of ex-convict gang members shows that in many cases the family as a whole, rather than just the individual law-breaker, is labeled as criminal and made to feel less comfortable in its neighborhood (Moore and Long, 1981).

In sum, we find four critical turning points in the reputation of gangs in Chicano East Los Angeles: the zoot-suit riots, the large-scale indictments of gang men for heroin dealing, the political "coming out" and reintegration of gang members during the Chicano Movement and, finally, the appearance of the violent prison gangs and corresponding repression in the community. Three of these four turning points involved further isolation and intra-community stigmatization of the gangs. Across these four periods, media coverage of the gangs has always been negative.

This is a rather depressing history. But it does not imply that law-abiding Mexican Americans in East Los Angeles are eternally and unremittingly hostile to gang youth, any more than it shows overwhelming acceptance of gangs during the heyday of the Chicano Movement. There are always mixed feelings. Thus, when PCP recently became a major drug in East Los Angeles, there was a wave of sympathy for the youngsters— and their families—who were caught up with this dangerous drug. The sympathy soon faded. Gangs, gang members, and their families are more and more isolated, and increasingly are left to the attention of law enforcement. Remnants of an integrative approach survive in a few programs that hire or work with young gang people, but these efforts run against the dominant trend. The East Los Angeles version of gang culture has spread into other communities in the metropolitan area, into other cities of the Southwest, and even into the border cities of Mexico. Thus East Los Angeles is a center for the diffusion of the *cholo* subculture. Predictably, it is also a center of information and techniques for reactive institutions—specifically, the media, the police, and the prisons that wish to combat gang violence.

PROCESS AND MINORITY COMMUNITIES

It is often argued that we should not look at the processes within minority communities for the answers to their problems. Many researchers feel the answers obviously lie elsewhere. This argument is particularly persuasive in the late 1980s, when we try to disentangle the twin effects of drastic shifts in the economy and changes in the political support structures. But this view implies that these communities are passive victims of external social conditions, and this is not entirely true. If an underclass is developing in poor minority communities, respectable members of these communities *will* react. Exactly *how* they react depends both on the cues from the larger society and on their own location within the community social structure. In the history just sketched, a major indirect effect of ascriptive labeling of minority youth has been to exacerbate cleavages within minority communities. In the 1940s diffuse racist sentiments became focused, with media and institutional targeting on the youth; what was "just another riot"—a seven-days' wonder—to the press had devastating impacts on the communities involved. In the scramble to establish that there were "good" Mexican kids and that "race" wasn't the issue, respectable Hispanics stigmatized and isolated the "bad" kids—the then comparatively innocuous gang kids and their almost totally innocent families. Then, during the 1960s and the politics of entitlement, the community was reminded that race *is* the stigma, and the achieved deviants and their families were reintegrated both symbolically and structurally. Once again, this alliance has disintegrated, as have the policies and programs that helped to promote it.

The case of East Los Angeles is not an isolated instance, only of esoteric concern. In city after city, the minority youth gang is either clearly defined as a social problem, as in Los Angeles and Chicago, or is currently being created, as in my own city of Milwaukee (Office of Juvenile Justice and Delinquency Prevention, 1983). In these "new" cities, many of the processes in the historical sequence outlined earlier are recurring. These include media sensationalism, an enhanced criminal justice system response,[27] and an effective breakup of solidarity within minority communities. Times have changed. The fact that more minority members have risen into the middle classes is taken, through a perversion of Wilson's (1978) complex sociological argument, as evidence that race no longer holds people down.

There are still voices of protest even as there were in Los Angeles during the 1940s. Some of these voices echo our recent history. Thus the Eisenhower Foundation report defines minority youth crime as "a form of slow rioting" that calls for major developmental efforts within minority communities (Curtis, 1985:8). It urges that crime prevention in the inner city be viewed not as an end in itself by as a "means to secure the neighborhood for development" and to alleviate the causes of crime. This is a sophisticated analysis but it continues to neglect intra-community differentiation.

It seems, therefore, that as welfare state and civil rights initiatives weaken, these intra-community processes become more rather than less important. Furthermore, the history that I have presented suggests that the "tangle of pathology" or the growth of a so-called "underclass" is not a simple process. Nor is it even self-perpetuating.

REFERENCES

Achor, Shirley. 1978. *Mexican Americans in a Dallas Barrio.* Tucson: University of Arizona Press.

Acosta, Oscar Zeta. 1973. *The Revolt of the Cockroach People.* San Francisco: Straight Arrow Press.

Acuña, Rodolfo. 1981. *Occupied America.* New York: Harper and Row.

---

27   The rate of juvenile incarceration increased nationally from 167 per 100,000 in 1979 to 184 per 100,000 in 1982. In California it increased from 378 per 100,000 in 1979 to 456 per 100,000 in 1982. As of 1982, 56 percent of adult state and federal prisoners were members of minority groups (U.S. Department of Justice, Bureau of Justice Statistics, 1984).

——1984. *A Community Under Seige: A Chronicle of Chicanos East of the Los Angeles River, 1945–1975*. Los Angeles: University of California-Los Angeles Chicano Studies Research Center Publications.

Adams, Nathan. 1977. "America's newest crime syndicate—the Mexican mafia." *Reader's Digest,* 111:97–102.

Banfield, Edward. 1970. *The Unheavenly City*. New York: Little, Brown.

Bogardus, Emory S. 1926. *The City Boy and His Problems: A Survey of Boy Life in Los Angeles*. Los Angeles: Rotary Club.

Burma, John. 1954. *Spanish-speaking Groups in the United States*. Durham, NC: Duke University Press.

Cortes, Carlos. 1972. "The Chicano social bandit as romantic hero." Unpublished paper.

Curtis, Lynn (ed.). 1985. *American Violence and Public Policy*. New Haven: Yale University Press. Drake, St.

Clair and Horace Cayton. 1962. *Black Metropolis*. New York: Harper and Row. [1945]

Goffman, Erving. 1963. *Stigma*. Englewood Cliffs, NJ: Prentice-Hall.

Gonzalez, Alfredo. 1981. *Mexican/Chicano Gangs in Los Angeles: A Sociohistorical Case Study*. Unpublished Ph.D. Dissertation, University of California-Berkeley.

Griffith, Beatrice. 1948. *American Me*. Boston: Houghton Mifflin.

Kitsuse, John. 1980. "Coming out all over: deviants and the politics of social problems." *Social Problems,* 28:1–13.

Lanigan, Mary. 1932. *Second Generation Mexicans in Belvedere*. Unpublished M. A. Thesis, University of Southern California.

McWilliams, Carey. 1949. *North from Mexico*. New York: Greenwood Press.

Maldonado, Lionel and Joan Moore (eds.). 1985. *Changing Urban Ethnicity: New Immigrants and Old Minorities*. Beverly Hills: Sage.

Mankoff, Milton. 1971. "Societal reaction and career deviance: a critical analysis." *Sociological Quarterly*. 12:204–18.

Matza, David. 1966. "The disreputable poor." pp. 289–302 in Reinhard Bendix and S. M. Lipset (eds.), *Class, Status and Power*. New York: The Free Press.

Mazon, Mauricio. 1976. *Social Upheaval in World War II: "Zoot-suiters" and Servicemen in Los Angeles, 1943*. Unpublished Ph.D. Dissertation, University of California-Los Angeles.

Moore, Joan, Robert Garcia, Carlos Garcia, Luis Cerda, and Frank Valencia. 1979. *Homeboys*. Philadelphia: Temple University Press.

Moore, Joan, Ramon Salcido, Diego Vigil and Robert Garcia. 1979. *A Model for Chicano Drug Use and for Effective Utilization of Employment and Training Resources by Barrio Addicts and Ex-Offenders*. Los Angeles: Chicano Pinto Research Project.

Moore, Joan W. and John Long. 1981. *Barrio Impact of High Incarceration Rates*. Los Angeles: Chicano Pinto Research Project.

Moynihan, Daniel Patrick. 1967. "The Negro Family: The Case for National Action." In L. Rainwater and W. L. Yancey (eds.), *The Moynihan Report and the Politics of Controversy.* Cambridge, M.I.T. Press.

Office of Juvenile Justice and Delinquency Prevention. 1983. *Police Handling of Gangs.* Washington, DC: National Juvenile Justice Assessment Center.

Parkin, Frank. 1972. *Class Inequality and the Political Order.* New York: Praeger.

Redfield, Robert. 1941. *Folk Culture of Yucatan.* Chicago: University of Chicago Press.

Rubel, Arthur. 1965. "The Mexican American palomilla." *Anthropological Linguistics,* 4:29–97.

Salcido, Ramon, 1979. "Gang workers." pp. 126–137 in Joan Moore, Ramon Salcido, Diego Vigil and Robert Garcia, *A Model for Chicano Drug Use and for Effective Utilization of Employment and Training Resources by Barrio Addicts and Ex-Offenders.* Los Angeles: Chicano Pinto Research Project.

Schur, Edwin. 1984. *Labeling Women Deviant: Gender, Stigma and Social Control.* New York: Random House. U.S. Department of Justice, Bureau of Justice Statistics

—1984. *Prisoners in State and Federal Institutions on December 31, 1982.* Washington, DC: U.S. Department of Justice.

Vigil, Diego. 1974. *Early Chicano Guerilla Fighters.* Upland, CA: JDV Publications.

—1985. *Street Youth in Mexican American Barrios.* Unpublished manuscript.

—1985. "Chicano gangs: one response to Mexican urban adaptation in the Los Angeles area." *Urban Anthropology,* 12:45–75.

Warner, W. Lloyd and Paul Lunt. 1941. *The Social Life of a Modern Community.* New Haven, CT: Yale Univerity Press.

Wilkinson, Doris. 1977. "The stigmatization process." pp. 145–58 in Doris Wilkinson and Ronald Taylor (eds.), *The Black Male in America.* Chicago: Nelson-Hall.

Wilson, William J. 1978. *The Declining Significance of Race.* Chicago: University of Chicago Press.

Isolation and Stigmatization in the Development of an Underclass: The Case of Chicano Gangs in East Los Angeles

By Joan W. Moore

PowerPoint by:
Erik Negron, Evelin Perez, Raquel Avina

Introduction

- The study of social troubles has a great "deal to do with emergence in American society of a predominantly minority urban underclass" (Moore).
- First approach - Culture of poverty
- Second approach - Minority underclass is a product of institutionalized racism
- "...Culture of poverty and racism explanations focus on categories of people rather than on communities (Moore).
- "A case history - the development of Chicano youth gangs— shows some of these processes at work, and also demonstrates that it is possible for these trends to be reversed" (Moore).

Labeling, Deviance, and Minorities

- ▶ "Deviants were coming out all over...to profess and advocate the lives they live and the values that those lives express" (Kitsuse, 1980:8).
- ▶ "They implied that to be a minority person - or a woman, for that matter - is to be stigmatized"
- ▶ Stigma involves a stereotype, so for minorities stereotypes meant deviance. A "probably deviant" as labeled by society, would be if you were young, a male and black or Chicano in white America.
- ▶ Ascribed Deviance - is deviance that is ascribed to minority young men on the basis of visible characteristics as opposed to those youth that already achieved their deviant behavior.
- ▶ To understand this points more we need to go more into the history of Chicano gangs. To were the Movement started back in the 1960's and helped minority communities reabsorb their achieved deviants by working together for a cause.

Case History: Gangs in East Los Angeles

- ▶ "In Chicano communities of the 1980s, a "disreputable" lifestyle is closely associated with the development over the past two generations of a *cholo* or street lifestyle which derives from the youth gangs." (Vigil, 1985a, 1985b).
- ▶ Four turning points in the development of these Chicano gangs are known as credit to deviance from the larger society.
  - — 1 & 2. "Allowed the labelers within the community to classify these gangs."
  - — 3. "Reversed the trend and reintergrated gang members."
  - — 4. "Again, isolated the gangs." (Moore)
- ▶ In the 1940s, the gangs developed a new style called *Pachuco*.

Zoot-Suit Riots

▶ "The sweep arrests accompanying the Sleepy Lagoon murder case and the later zoot-suit riots of the early 1940s were the first turning point in the anglo labeling of young Mexicans as deviant." (Acuna, 1981: Gonzales, 1981: Mazon, 1976: Mc Williams, 1949).
— The Sleepy Lagoon Murder case began on August 2, 1942, when the body of a man named Jose Diaz was found at a reservoir, known as Sleepy Lagoon, located in southeast Los Angeles.

▶ "Communities of east Downtown Los Angeles were raided by servicemen. " (Moore)
▷ Young Men who wore zoot-suits were followed and hit even though they were not involved in any activity.
▷ As a result of this, it was considered to be the first ocassion were a Mexican blowup became part of the news' stereotype.

Heroin Indictments

▶ "In the 1950s, Heroin spread in the Barrios, generating a more intense law enforcement." (Moore)
▶ Leading to a another turning point in pertaining to Labeling.
▶ "California narcotic laws became more punitive and, for the first time, barrio men went to prison in large numbers." (Moore)
▶ "Mexican American long had been stereotyped as marijuana users and now the image of the evil dope dealer was added to the "ratpack" image of the gangs." (Moore)

Chicano Movement

- By the late 1960's when the Chicano community was already looked upon as negative they tried one more time to reverse themselves.
- there were two reasons why in this movement street gangs and ex offenders were integrated to help: first the gangs were romanticized as social bandits on a Mexican tradition to resist and oppose the Anglo authority and second the ex offenders especially adult members were looked as a sort of fighting branch, they were soldiers.
- **Brown Berets:** They would attend rallies and special celebrations and watched out for the neighborhood when cops would try to stop them.
- Many community leaders saw the Chicano movement as an extension of their life long struggle for advancement ....of the community needing reintegration into barrio life- not rejection or further stigmatization. While others saw it as "tertiary deviance".

Prison "Super-Gangs"

- The acceptance of achieved deviants back into the community started decreasing because of a wave of violence over California when all ex offenders were suspected off having associations with two prison super gangs: Mexican Mafia and La Familia.
- Once again the Anglo authorities and the media ascribed deviance to all Chicano youth making their cultural and structural bases for the movement dissolve.
  - ▷ first street people were once again described as criminals.
  - ▷ second, there were no more rallies and the "pintos" lost their value as soldiers.
  - ▷ third, ex offender families would rather hide their shame.
  - ▷ fourth, the former gang members that helped out in the movement were now associated with the prison gangs.
  - ▷ finally, the professionals and organizations that helped were either retired or lost funds from the federal and state government.
- The four turning points of the reputation of gangs in Chicano ELA were the zoot suit riots, the indictments of gang men and heroin, the reintegration of ex offenders into the community and the appearance of violent prison gangs.

Process and Minority Communities

- "If an underclass is developing in poor minority communities, respectable members of these communities *will* react" (Moore).
- Communities began to establish differences between their own youth. "Good" Vs "Bad"
- "Race" is a stigma
- Minority youth gangs are already social problem or are currently being created
- Breaking up solidarity
- Race no longer holds people down, but the, "...growth of a so called "underclass" is not a simple process. Nor is it even selp perpetuating (Moore).

Work Cited

- Del Castillo, R.G. "Sleepy Lagoon Murder Mystery." Sleepy Lagoon. November 23, 2010 (http://www.sleepylagoon.com/H/sltrial.htm)
- Moore, Joan W. "Isolation and Stigmatization in the Development of an Underclass: The Case of Chicano Gangs in East Los Angeles." *Social Problems. Vol. 33, No. 1* (October 1985). Print.

RACE AND GANGS

WHITE GANGS

By Walter B. Miller

I f one thinks about street corner gangs at all these days, it is probably in the roseate glow of *West Side Story,* itself the last flowering of a literary and journalistic concern that goes back at least to the late 40's. Those were the days when it seemed that the streets of every city in the country had become dark battlefields where small armies of young men engaged their honor in terrible trials of combat, clashing fiercely and suddenly, then retiring to the warm succor of their girl cohorts. The forward to a 1958 collection of short stories, *The Young Funks,* captures a bit of the flavor:

> These are the stories behind today's terrifying headlines—about a strange new frightening cult that has grown up in our midst. Every writer whose work is included in this book tells the truth. These kids are tough. Here are knife-carrying killers, and thirteen-year-old street walkers who could give the most hardened call girl lessons. These kids pride themselves on their "ethics": never go chicken, even if it means knifing your own friend in the back. Never rat on a guy who wears your gang colors, unless he rats on you first.

Old men on crutches are fair game. If a chick plays you for a sucker, blacken her eyes and walk away fast.

Today, the one-time devotee of this sort of stuff might be excused for wondering where they went, the Amboy Dukes and all those other adolescent warriors and lovers who so excited his fancy a decade ago. The answer, as we shall see, is quite simple—nowhere. The street gangs are still there, out on the corner where they always were.

The fact is that the urban adolescent street gang is as old as the American city. Henry Adams, in his *Education,* describes in vivid detail the gang fights between the Northsiders and Southsiders on Boston Common in the 1840's. An observer in 1856 Brooklyn writes: "… at any and all hours there are multitudes of boys … congregated on the corners of the streets, idle in their habits, dissolute in their conduct, profane and obscene in their conversation, gross and vulgar in their manners. If a female passes one of the groups she is shocked by what she sees and hears. …" The Red Raiders of Boston have hung out on the same corner at least since the 1930's; similarly, gang fighting between the Tops and Bottoms in West Philadelphia, which started in the 30's, is still continuing in 1969.

Despite this historical continuity, each new generation tends to perceive the street gang as a new phenomenon generated by particular contemporary conditions and destined to vanish as these conditions vanish. Gangs in the 1910's and 20's were attributed to the cultural dislocations and community disorganization accompanying the mass immigration of foreigners; in the 30's to the enforced idleness and economic pressures produced by the Great Depression; in the 50's to the emotional disturbance of parents and children caused by the increased stresses and tensions of modern life. At present, the existence of gangs is widely attributed to a range of social injustices: racial discrimination, unequal educational and work opportunities, resentment over inequalities in the distribution of wealth and privilege in an affluent society, and the ineffective or oppressive policies of service agencies such as the police and the schools.

There is also a fairly substantial school of thought that holds that the street gangs are disappearing or have already disappeared. In New York City, the stage of so many real and fictional gang dramas of the 50's and early 60's, *The Times* sounded their death-knell as long ago as 1966. Very often, the passing of the gang is explained by the notion that young people in the slums have converted their gang-forming propensities into various substitute activities. They have been knocked out by narcotics, or they have been "politicized" in ways that consume their energies in radical or reform movements, or their. Members have become involved in "constructive" commercial activities, or enrolled in publicly financed education and/or work-training programs.

As has often been the case, these explanations are usually based on very shaky factual grounds and derived from rather parochial, not to say self-serving, perspectives. For street gangs are not only still widespread in United States cities, but some of them appear to have again taken up "gang warfare" on a scale that is equal to or greater than the phenomenon that received so much attention from the media in the 1950's.

In Chicago, street gangs operating in the classic formations of that city—War Lords, High Supremes, Cobra Stones—accounted for 33 killings and 252 injuries during the first six months of 1969. Philadelphia has experienced a wave of gang violence that has probably resulted in more murders in a shorter period of time than during any equivalent phase of the "fighting gang" era in New York. Police estimate that about 80 gangs comprising about 5,000 members are "active" in the city, and that about 20 are engaged in combat. Social agencies put the total estimated number of gangs at 200, with about 80 in the "most hostile" category. Between October 1962 and December 1968, gang members were reportedly involved in 257 shootings, 250 stabbings and 205 "rumbles." In the period between January 1968 and June 1969, 54 homicides and over 520 injuries were attributed to armed battles between gangs. Of the murder victims, all but eight were known to be affiliated with street gangs. The assailants ranged in age from 13 to 20, with 70 percent of them between 16 and 18 years old. Most of these gangs are designated by the name of the major corner where they hang out, the 12th and Poplar Streeters, or the 21 W's (for 21st and Westmoreland). Others bear traditional names such as the Centaurs, Morroccos and Pagans.

Gangs also continue to be active in Boston. In a single 90-minute period on May 10, 1969, one of the two channels of the Boston Police radio reported 38 incidents involving gangs, or one every 21½ minutes. This included two gang fights. Simultaneous field observation in several white lower-class neighborhoods turned up evidence that gangs were congregating at numerous street corners throughout the area.

Although most of these gangs are similar to the classic types to be described in what follows, as of this summer the national press had virtually ignored the revival of gang violence. *Time* magazine did include a brief mention of "casual mayhem" in its June 27 issue, but none of the 38 incidents in Boston on May 10 was reported even in the local papers. It seems most likely, however, that if all this had been going on in New York City, where most of the media have their headquarters, a spate of newspaper features, magazine articles and television "specials" would have created the impression that the country was being engulfed by a "new" wave of gang warfare. Instead, most people seem to persist in the belief that the gangs have disappeared or that they have been radically transformed.

This anomalous situation is partly a consequence of the problem of defining what a gang is (and we will offer a definition at the end of our discussion of two specific gangs), but it is also testimony to the fact that this enduring aspect of the lives of urban slum youth remains complex and poorly understood. It is hoped that, the following examination of the Bandits and the Outlaws—both of Midcity—will clarify at least some of the many open questions about street comer gangs in American cities.

Midcity, which was the location of our 10-year gang study project (1954–64), is not really a city at all, but a portion of a large one, here called Port City. Midcity is a predominantly lower-class community with a relatively high rate of crime, in which both criminal behavior and a characteristic set of conditions—low-skill occupations, little education, low-rent dwellings, and many others—appeared as relatively stable and persisting features of a developed way of life. How did street gangs fit into this picture?

In common with most major cities during this period, there were many gangs in Midcity, but they varied widely in size, sex composition, stability and range of activities. There were about 50 Midcity street corners that served as hangouts for local adolescents. Fifteen of these were "major" "corners, in that they were rallying points for the full range of a gang's membership, while the remaining 35 were "minor," meaning that in general fewer groups of smaller size habitually hung out there.

In all, for Midcity in this period, 3,650 out of 5,740, or 64 percent, of Midcity boys habitually hung out at a particular comer and could therefore be considered members of a particular gang. For girls, the figure is 1,125 out of 6,250, or 18 percent. These estimates also suggest that something like 35 percent of Midcity's boys, and 80 percent of its girls, did *not* hang out. What can be said about them? What made them different from the approximately 65 percent of the boys and 20 percent of the girls who did hang out?

Indirect evidence appears to show that the practice of hanging out with a gang was more prevalent among lower-status adolescents, and that many of those who were not known to hang out lived in middle-class or lower-class I (the higher range of the lower-class) areas. At the same time, however, it is evident that a fair proportion of higher-status youngsters also hung out. The question of status, and its relation to gang membership and gang, behavior is very complex, but it should be borne in mind as we now take a closer look at the gangs we studied.

THE BANDIT NEIGHBORHOOD

Between the Civil War and World War II, the Bandit neighborhood was well-known throughout the city as a colorful and close-knit community of Irish laborers. Moving to a flat in one of its ubiquitous three-decker frame tenements represented an important step up for the impoverished potato-famine immigrants who had initially settled in the crowded slums of central Port City. By the 1810's the second generation of Irish settlers had produced a spirited and energetic group of athletes and politicos, some of whom achieved national prominence.

Those residents of the Bandit neighborhood who shared in some degree the drive, vitality and capability of these famous men assumed steady and fairly remunerative positions in the political, legal and civil service world of Port City, and left the neighborhood for residential areas whose green lawns and single houses represented for them what Midcity had represented for their fathers and grandfathers. Those who lacked these qualities remained in the Bandit neighborhood, and at the outset of World War II made up a stable and relatively homogeneous community of low-skilled Irish laborers.

The Bandit neighborhood was directly adjacent to Midcity's major shopping district, and was spotted with bars, poolrooms and dance halls that served as meeting places for an active neighborhood social life. Within two blocks of the Bandits' hanging-out corner were the Old Erin and New Hibernia dance halls, and numerous drinking establishments bearing names such as the Shamrock, Murphy and Donoghue's, and the Emerald Bar and Grill.

A number of developments following World War II disrupted the physical and social shape of the Bandit community. A mammoth federally-financed housing project sliced through and blocked off the existing network of streets and razed the regular rows of wooden tenements. The neighborhood's small manufacturing plants were progressively diminished by the growth of a few large establishments, and by the 1950's the physical face of the neighborhood was dominated by three large and growing plants. As these plants expanded they bought off many of the properties which had not been taken by the housing project, demolished buildings, and converted them into acres of black-topped parking lots for their employees.

During this period, the parents of the Bandit corner gang members stubbornly held on to the decreasing number of low-rent, deteriorating, private dwelling units. Although the Bandits' major hanging corner was almost surrounded by the housing project, virtually none of the gang members lived there. For these families, residence in the housing project would have entailed a degree of financial stability and restrained behavior that they were unable or unwilling to assume, for the corner gang members of the Bandit neighborhood were the scions of men and women who occupied the lowest social level in Midcity. For them low rent was a passion, freedom to drink and to behave drunkenly a sacred privilege, sporadic employment a fact of life, and the social welfare and law-enforcement agencies of the state, partners of one's existence.

The Bandit Corner was subject to field observation for about three years—from June 1954 to May 1957. Hanging out on the corner during this period were six distinct but related gang subdivisions. There were four male groups: The Brigands, aged approximately 18 to 21 at the start of the study period; the Senior Bandits, aged 16 to 18; the Junior Bandits, 14 to 16, and the Midget Bandits, 12 to 14. There were also two distinct female subdivisions: The Bandettes, 14 to 16, and the Little Bandettes, 12 to 14.

The physical and psychic center of the Bandit corner was Sam's Variety Store, the owner and sole employee of which was not Sam but Ben, his son. Ben's father had founded the store in the 1920's, the heyday of the Irish laboring class in the Bandit neighborhood. When his father died, Ben took over the store, but did not change its name. Ben was a stocky, round-faced Jew in his middle 50's, who looked upon the whole of the Bandit neighbor-hood as his personal fief and bounden responsibility—a sacred legacy from his father. He knew everybody and was concerned with everybody; through his store passed a constant stream of customers and noncustomers of all ages and both sexes. In a space not much larger than that of a fair-sized bedroom Ben managed to crowd a phone booth, a juke box, a pinball machine, a space heater, counters, shelves and stock, and an assorted variety of patrons. During one 15-minute period on an average day Ben would supply $1.37 worth of groceries to 11-year-old Carol Donovan and enter the sum on her mother's page in the "tab" book, agree to extend Mrs. Thebodeau's already extended credit until her A.D.C. check arrived, bandage and solace the three-year-old Negro girl who came crying to him with a cut forefinger, and shoo into the street a covey of Junior Bandits whose altercation over a pinball score was impeding customer traffic and augmenting an already substantial level of din.

Ben was a bachelor, and while he had adopted the whole of the Bandit neighbor-hood as his extended family, he had taken on the 200 adolescents who hung out on the Bandit corner as his most immediate sons and daughters. Ben knew the background and present circumstances of every Bandit, and followed their lives with intense interest and concern. Ben's corner-gang progeny were a fast-moving and mercurial lot, and he watched over their adventures and misadventures with a curious mixture of indignation, solicitude, disgust, and sympathy. Ben's outlook on the affairs of the world was never bland; he held and freely voiced strong opinions on a wide variety of issues, prominent among which was the behavior and misbehavior of the younger generation.

This particular concern was given ample scope for attention by the young Bandits who congregated in and around his store. Of all the gangs studied, the Bandits were the most consistently and determinedly criminal, and central to Ben's concerns was how each one stood with regard to "trouble." In this respect, developments were seldom meager. By the time they reached the age of 18, every one of the 32 active members of the Senior Bandits had appeared in court at least once, and some many times; 28 of the 32 boys had been committed to a correctional institution and 16 had spent at least one term in confinement.

Ben's stout arm swept the expanse of pavement which fronted his store. "I'll tell ya, I give up on these kids. In all the years I been here, I never seen a worse bunch. You know what they should do? They should put up a big platform with one of them stocks right out there, and as soon as a kid gets in trouble, into the stocks with 'im. Then they'd straighten out. The way it is now, the kid tells a sob story to some soft-hearted cop or social worker, and pretty soon he's back at the same old thing. See that guy just comin' over here? That's what I mean. He's hopeless. Mark my word, he's gonna end up in the electric chair."

The Senior Bandit who entered the store came directly to Ben. "Hey, Ben, I just quit my job at the shoe factory. They don't pay ya nothin', and they got some wise guy nephew of the owner who thinks he can kick everyone around. I just got fed up. I ain't gonna tell Ma for awhile, she'll be mad." Ben's concern was evident. "Digger, ya just gotta learn you can't keep actin' smart to every boss ya have. And $1.30 an hour ain't bad pay at all for a 17-year-old boy. Look, I'll lend ya 10 bucks so ya can give 5 to ya Ma, and she won't know."

In their dealings with Ben, the Bandits, for their part, were in turn hostile and affectionate, cordial and sullen, open and reserved. They clearly regarded Ben's as "their" store. This meant, among other things, exclusive possession of the right to make trouble within its confines. At least three times during the observation period corner boys from outside neighborhoods entered the store obviously bent on stealing or creating a disturbance. On each occasion these outsiders were efficiently and forcefully removed by nearby Bandits, who then waxed indignant at the temerity of "outside" kids daring to consider Ben's as a target of illegal activity. One consequence, then, of Ben's seigneurial relationship to the Bandits was that his store was unusually well protected against theft, armed and otherwise, which presented a constant hazard to the small-store owner in Midcity.

On the other hand, the Bandits guarded jealously their own right to raise hell in Ben's. On one occasion, several Senior Bandits came into the store with a cache of pistol bullets and proceeded to empty the powder from one of the bullets onto the pinball machine and to ignite the powder. When Ben ordered them out they continued operations on the front sidewalk by wrapping gunpowder in newspaper and igniting it. Finally they set fire to a wad of paper containing two live bullets which exploded and narrowly missed local residents sitting on nearby doorsteps.

Such behavior, while calculated to bedevil Ben and perhaps to retaliate for a recent scolding or ejection, posed no real threat to him or his store; the same boys during this period were actively engaged in serious thefts from similar stores in other neighborhoods. For the most part, the behavior of the Bandits in and around the store involved the characteristic activities of hanging out. In warm weather the Bandits sat outside the store on the sidewalk or door-stoops, playing cards, gambling, drinking, talking to one another and to the Bandettes. In cooler weather they moved into the store as the hour and space permitted, and there played the pinball machine for such cash payoffs as Ben saw fit to render, danced with the Bandettes to juke box records, and engaged in general horseplay.

While Ben's was the Bandits' favorite hangout, they did frequent other hanging locales, mostly within a few blocks of the corner. Among these was a park directly adjacent to the housing project where the boys played football and baseball in season. At night the park provided a favored locale for activities such as beer drinking and lovemaking, neither of which particularly endeared them to the adult residents of the project, who not infrequently summoned the police to clear the park of late-night revellers. Other areas of congregation in the local neighborhood were a nearby delicatessen ("the Delly"), a pool hall, and the apartments of those Bandettes whose parents happened to be away. The Bandits also ran their own dances at the Old Erin and New Hibernia, but they had to conceal their identity as Bandits when renting these dance halls, since the proprietors had learned that the rental fees were scarcely sufficient to compensate for the chaos inevitably attending the conduct of a Bandit dance.

The Bandits were able to find other sources of entertainment in the central business district of Port City. While most of the Bandits and Bandettes were too young to gain admission to the numerous downtown cafes with their rock 'n' roll bands, they were able to find amusement in going to the movies (sneaking in whenever possible), playing the coin machines in the penny arcades and shoplifting from the downtown department stores. Sometimes, as a kind of diversion, small groups of Bandits spent the day in town job-hunting, with little serious intention of finding work.

One especially favored form of downtown entertainment was the court trial. Members of the Junior and Senior Bandits performed as on-stage participants in some 250 court trials during a four-year period. Most trials involving juveniles were conducted in nearby Midcity Court as private proceedings, but the older Bandits had adopted as routine procedure the practice of appealing their local court sentences to the Superior Court located in downtown Port City. When the appeal was successful, it was the occasion for as large a turnout of gang members as could be mustered, and the Bandits were a rapt and vitally interested audience. Afterwards, the gang held long and animated discussions about the severity or leniency of the sentence and other, finer points of legal procedure. The hearings provided not only an absorbing form of free entertainment, but also invaluable knowledge about court functioning, appropriate defendant behavior, and the predilections, of particular judges—knowledge that would serve the spectators well when their own turn to star inevitably arrived.

THE SENIOR BANDITS

The Senior Bandits, the second oldest of the four male gang subdivisions hanging out on the Bandit corner were under intensive observation, for a period of 20 months. At the start of this period the boys ranged in age from 15 to 17 (average age 16.3) and at the end, 17 to 19 (average age 18.1). The core group of the Senior Bandits numbered 32 boys.

Most of the gang members were Catholic, the majority of Irish background; several were Italian or French Canadian, and a few were English or Scotch Protestants. The gang contained two sets of brothers and several cousins, and about one third of the boys had relatives in other subdivisions. These included a brother in the Midgets, six brothers in the Juniors, and three in the Marauders.

The educational and occupational circumstances of the Senior Bandits were remarkably like those of their parents. Some seven years after the end of the intensive study period, when the average age of the Bandits was 25, 23 out of the 27 gang members whose occupations were known held jobs ordinarily classified in the bottom two occupational categories of the United States census. Twenty-one were classified as "laborer," holding jobs such as roofer, stock boy, and trucker's helper. Of 24 fathers whose occupations were known, 18, or 83 percent, held jobs in the same bottom two occupational categories as their sons; 17 were described as "laborer," holding jobs such as furniture mover and roofer. Fathers even held jobs of similar kinds and in similar proportions to those of their sons, e.g., construction laborers: sons 30 percent, fathers 25 percent; factory laborers: sons 15 percent, fathers 21 percent. Clearly the Senior Bandits were not rising above their fathers' status. In fact, there were indications of a slight decline, even taking account of the younger age of the sons. Two of the boys' fathers held jobs in "public safety" services—one policeman and one fireman; another had worked for a time in the "white collar" position of a salesclerk at Sears; a fourth had risen to the rank of Chief Petty Officer in the Merchant Marine. Four of the fathers, in other words, had attained relatively elevated positions, while the sons produced only one policeman.

The education of the Senior Bandits was consistent with their occupational status. Of 29 boys whose educational experience was known, 27 dropped out of school in the eighth, ninth, or tenth grades, having reached the age of 16. Two did complete high school, and one of these was reputed to have taken some post-high-school training in a local technical school. None entered college. It should be remarked that this record occurred not in a backward rural community of the 1800's, nor in a black, community, but in the 1950's in a predominantly white neighborhood of a metropolis that took pride in being one of the major educational centers of the world.

Since only two of the Senior Bandits were still in school during the study, almost all of the boys held full-time jobs at some time during the contact period. But despite financial needs, pressure from parents and parole officers and other incentives to get work, the Senior Bandits found jobs slowly, accepted them reluctantly, and quit them with little provocation.

The Senior Bandits were clearly the most criminal of the seven gangs we studied most closely. For example, by the time he had reached the age of 18 the average Senior Bandit had been charged with offenses in court an average of 7.6 times; this compared with an average rate of 2.7 for all five male gangs, and added up to a total of almost 250 separate charges for the gang as a whole. A year after our intensive contact with the group, 100 percent, of the Senior Bandits had been arrested at least once, compared with an average arrest figure of 45 percent, for all groups. During the 20-month contact period, just about half of the Senior Bandits were on probation or parole for some period of time.

To a greater degree than in any of the other gangs we studied, crime as an occupation and preoccupation played a central role in the lives of the Senior Bandits. Prominent among recurrent topics of discussion were thefts successfully executed, fights recently engaged in, and the current status of gang members who were in the process of passing through the successive states of arrest, appearing in court, being sentenced, appealing, re-appealing and so on. Although none of the crimes of the Senior Bandits merited front-page headlines when we were close to them, a number of their more colorful exploits did receive newspaper attention, and the stories were carefully clipped and left in Ben's store for circulation among the gang members. Newspaper citations functioned for the Senior Bandits somewhat as do press notices for actors; gang members who made the papers were elated and granted prestige; those who did not were often disappointed; participants and non-participants who failed to see the stories felt cheated.

The majority of their crimes were thefts. The Senior Bandits were thieves *par excellence,* and their thievery was imaginative, colorful, and varied. Most thefts were from stores. Included among these was a department store theft of watches, jewelry and clothing for use as family Christmas presents; a daylight raid on a supermarket for food and refreshments needed for a beach outing; a daytime burglary of an antique store, in which eight gang members, in the presence of the owner, stole a Samurai sword and French duelling pistols. The gang also engaged in car theft. One summer several Bandits stole a car to visit girl friends who were working at a summer resort. Sixty miles north of Port City, hailed by police for exceeding speed limits, they raced away at speeds of up to 100 miles an hour, overturned the car, and were hospitalized for injuries. In another instance, Bandits stole a car in an effort to return a drunken companion to his home and avoid the police; when this car stalled they stole a second one parked in front of its owner's house; the owner ran out and fired several shots at the thieves, which, however, failed to forestall the theft.

The frequency of Senior Bandit crimes, along with the relative seriousness of their offenses, resulted in a high rate of arrest and confinement. During the contact period somewhat over 40 percent of the gang members were confined in correctional institutions, with terms averaging 11 months per boy. The average Senior Bandit spent approximately one month out of four in a correctional facility. This circumstance prompted one of the Bandettes to remark, "Ya know, them guys got a new place to hang—the reformatory. That bunch is never together—one halfa them don't even know the other half. ...

This appraisal, while based on fact, failed to recognize an important feature of gang relationships. With institutional confinement a frequent and predictable event, the Senior Bandits employed a set of devices to maintain a high degree of group solidarity. Lines of communication between corner and institution were kept open by frequent visits by those on the outside, during which inmates were brought food, money and cigarettes as well as news of the neighborhood and other correctional facilities. One Midcity social worker claimed that the institutionalized boys knew what was going on in the neighborhood before most neighborhood residents. The Bandits also developed well-established methods for arranging and carrying out institutional escape by those gang members who were so inclined. Details of escapes were arranged in the course of visits and inter-inmate contacts; escapees were provided by fellow gang members with equipment such as ropes to scale prison walls and getaway cars. The homes of one's gang fellows were also made available as hideouts. Given this set of arrangements, the Bandits carried out several highly successful escapes, and one succeeded in executing the first escape in the history of a maximum security installation.

The means by which the Senior Bandits achieved group cohesion in spite of recurrent incarcerations of key members merit further consideration—both because they are of interest in their own right, and because they throw light on important relationships between leadership, group structure, and the motivation of criminal behavior. Despite the assertion that "one halfa them guys don't know the other half," the Senior Bandits were a solidaristic associational unit, with clear group boundaries and definite criteria for differentiating those who were "one of us" from those who were not. It was still said of an accepted group member that "he hangs with us"—even when the boy had been away from the corner in an institution for a year or more. Incarcerated leaders, in particular, were referred to frequently and in terms of admiration and respect.

The system used by the Senior Bandits to maintain solidarity and reliable leadership arrangements incorporated three major devices: the diffusion of authority, anticipation of contingencies, and interchangeability of roles. The recurring absence from the corner of varying numbers of gang members inhibited the formation of a set of relatively stable cliques of the kind found in the other gangs we studied intensively. What was fairly stable, instead, was a set of "classes" of members, each of which could include different individuals at different times. The relative size of these classes was fairly constant, and a member of one class could move to another to take the place of a member who had been removed by institutionalization.

The four major classes of gang members could be called *key* leaders, standby leaders, primary followers, and secondary followers. During the intensive contact period the gang contained five key leaders—boys whose accomplishments had earned them the right to command; six standby leaders—boys prepared to step into leadership positions when key leaders were institutionalized; eight primary followers—boys who hung out regularly and who were the most dependable followers of current leaders; and 13 secondary followers—boys who hung out less regularly and who tended to adapt their allegiances to particular leadership situations.

Predictably, given the dominant role of criminal activity among the Senior Bandits, leadership and followership were significantly related to criminal involvement. Each of the five key leaders had demonstrated unusual ability in criminal, activity; in this respect the Senior Bandits differed from the other gangs, each of which included at least one leader whose position was based in whole or in part on a commitment to a law-abiding course of action. One of the Senior Bandits' key leaders was especially respected for his daring and adeptness in theft; another, who stole infrequently relative to other leaders, for his courage, stamina and resourcefulness as a fighter. The other three leaders had proven themselves in both theft and fighting, with theft the more important basis of eminence.

Confinement statistics show that gang members who were closest to leadership positions were also the most active in crime. They also suggest, however, that maintaining a system of leadership on this basis poses special problems. The more criminally active a gang member, the greater the likelihood that he would be apprehended and removed from the neighborhood, thus substantially diminishing his opportunities to convert earned prestige into operative leadership. How was it possible, then, for the Senior Bandits to maintain effective leadership arrangements? They utilized a remarkably efficient system whose several features were ingenious and deftly contrived.

First, the recognition by the Bandits of five key leaders—a relatively large number for a gang of 32 members—served as a form of insurance against being left without leader ship. It was most unlikely that all five would be incarcerate ed at the same time, particularly since collective crime were generally executed by one or possibly two leaders along with several of their followers. During one relatively brief part of the contact period, four of the key leaders were confined simultaneously, but over the full period the average number confined at any one time was two. One Bandit key leader expressed his conviction that exclusive reliance on a single leader was unwise: "… since we been hangin' out [at Ben's corner] we ain't had no leader. Other kids got a leader of the gang. Like up in Cornerville, they always got one kid who's the big boss … so far we ain't did that, and I don't think we ever will. We talk about 'Smiley and his boys,' or 'Digger and his clique,' and like that. …"

It is clear that for this Bandit the term "leader" carried the connotation of a single and all-powerful gang lord, which was not applicable to the diffuse and decentralized leadership arrangements of the Bandits. It is also significant that the gangs of Cornerville which he used as an example were Italian gangs whose rate of criminal involvement was relatively low. The "one big boss" type of leadership found in these gangs derives from the "Caesar" or "I Duce" pattern so well established in Italian culture, and it was workable for Cornerville gangs because the gangs and their leaders were sufficiently law-abiding and/or sufficiently capable of evading arrest as to make the removal of the leader an improbable event.

A second feature of Bandit leadership, the use of "stand-by" leaders, made possible a relatively stable balance among the several cliques. When the key leader of his clique was present in the area, the standby leader assumed a subordinate role and did not initiate action; if and when the key leader was committed to an institution, the standby was ready to assume leadership. He knew, however, that he was expected to relinquish this position on the return of the key leader. By this device each of the five major cliques was assured some form of leadership even when key leaders were absent, and could maintain its form, identity and influence vis-a-vis other cliques.

A third device that enabled the gang to maintain a relatively stable leadership and clique structure involved the phenomenon of "optimal" criminal involvement. Since excellence in crime was the major basis of gang leadership, it might be expected that some of those who aspired to leadership would assume that there was a simple and direct relationship between crime and leadership: the more crime, the more prestige; the more prestige, the stronger the basis of authority. The flaw in this simple formula was in fact recognized by the actual key leaders: in striving for maximal criminal involvement, one also incurred the maximum risk of incarceration. But leadership involved more than gaining prestige through crime; one had to be personally involved with other gang members for sufficiently extended periods to exploit won prestige through wooing followers, initiating noncriminal as well as criminal activities, and effecting working relationships with other leaders. Newly-returned key leaders as well as the less criminally-active class of standby leaders tended to step up their involvement in criminal activity on assuming or reassuming leadership positions in order to solidify their positions, but they also tended to diminish such involvement once this was achieved.

One fairly evident weakness in so flexible and fluid a system of cliques and leadership was the danger that violent and possibly disruptive internal conflict might erupt among key leaders who were competing for followers, or standby leaders who were reluctant to relinquish their positions. There was, in fact, surprisingly little overt conflict of any kind among Bandit leaders. On their release from confinement, leaders were welcomed with enthusiasm and appropriate observances both by their followers and by other leaders. They took the center of the stage as they recounted to rapt listeners their institutional experiences, the circumstances of those still confined, and new developments in policies, personnel and politics at the correctional school.

When they were together Bandit leaders dealt with one another gingerly, warily and with evident respect. On one occasion a standby leader, who was less criminally active than the returning key leader, offered little resistance to being displaced, but did serve his replacement with the warning that a resumption of his former high rate of crime would soon result in commitment both of himself and his clique. On another occasion one of the toughest of the Senior Bandits (later sentenced to an extended term in an adult institution for ringleading a major prison riot) returned to the corner to find that another leader had taken over not only some of his key followers but his steady girl friend as well. Instead of taking on his rival in an angry and perhaps violent confrontation, he reacted quite mildly, venting his hostility in the form of sarcastic teasing, calculated to needle but not to incite. In the place of a direct challenge, the newly returned key leader set about to regain his followers and his girl by actively throwing himself back into criminal activity. This course of action—competing for followers by successful performance in prestigious activities rather than by brute-force confrontation—was standard practice among the Senior Bandits.

THE JUNIOR BANDITS

The leadership system of the Junior Bandits was, if anything, even farther removed from the "one big boss" pattern than was the "multi-leader power-balance" system of the Seniors. An intricate arrangement of cliques and leadership enabled this subdivision of the gang to contain within it a variety of individuals and cliques with different and often conflicting orientations.

Leadership for particular activities was provided as the occasion arose by boys whose competence in that activity had been established. Leadership was thus flexible, shifting and adaptable to changing group circumstances. Insofar as there was a measure of relatively concentrated authority, it was invested in a collectivity rather than an individual. The several "situational" leaders of the dominant clique constituted what was in effect a kind of ruling council, which arrived at its decisions through a process of extended collective discussion generally involving all concerned. Those who were to execute a plan of action thereby took part in the process by which it was developed.

A final feature of this system concerns the boy who was recognized as "the leader" of the Junior Bandits. When the gang formed a club to expedite involvement in athletic activities, he was chosen its president. Although he was an accepted member of the dominant clique, he did not, on the surface, seem to possess any particular qualifications for this position. He was mild-mannered, unassertive, and consistently refused to take a definite stand on outstanding issues, let alone taking the initiative in implementing policy. He appeared to follow rather than to lead. One night when the leaders of the two subordinate factions became infuriated with one another in the course of a dispute, he trailed both boys around for several hours, begging them to calm down and reconcile their differences. On another occasion the gang was on the verge of splitting into irreconcilable factions over a financial issue. One group accused another of stealing club funds; the accusation was hotly denied; angry recriminations arose that swept in a variety of dissatisfactions with the club and its conduct. In the course of this melee, the leader of one faction, the "bad boys," complained bitterly about the refusal of the president to take sides or assume any initiative in resolving the dispute, and called for a new election. This was agreed to and the election was held—with the result that the "weak" president was re-elected by a decisive majority, and was reinstated in office amidst emotional outbursts of acclaim and reaffirmation of the unity of the gang.

It was thus evident that the majority of gang members, despite temporary periods of anger over particular issues, recognized on some level the true function performed by a "weak" leader. Given the fact that the gang included a set of cliques with differing orientations and conflicting notions, and a set of leaders whose authority was limited to specific areas, the maintenance of gang cohesion required some special mechanisms. One was the device of the "weak" leader. It is most unlikely that a forceful or dominant person could have controlled the sanctions that would enable him to coerce the strong-willed factions into compliance. The very fact that the "weak" leader refused to take sides and was noncommittal on key issues made him acceptable to the conflicting interests represented in the gang. Further, along with the boy's nonassertive demeanor went a real talent for mediation.

THE OUTLAW NEIGHBORHOOD

The Outlaw street corner was less than a mile from that of the Bandits, and like the Bandits, the Outlaws were white, Catholic, and predominantly Irish, with a few Italians and Irish-Italians. But their social status, in the middle range of the lower class was sufficiently higher than that of the Bandits to be reflected in significant differences in both their gang and family life. The neighborhood environment also was quite different.

Still, the Outlaws hung out on a classic corner—complete with drug store, variety store, a neighborhood bar (Callahan's Bar and Grill), a pool hall, and several other small businesses such as a laundromat. The corner was within one block of a large park, a convenient locale for card games, lovemaking, and athletic practice. Most residents of the Outlaw neighborhood were oblivious to the deafening roar of the elevated train that periodically rattled the houses and stores of Midcity Avenue, which formed one street of the Outlaw corner. There was no housing project in the Outlaw neighborhood, and none of the Outlaws were project residents. Most of their families rented one level of one of the three-decker wooden tenements which were common in the area; a few owned their own homes.

In the mid-1950's, however, the Outlaw neighborhood underwent significant changes as Negroes began moving in. Most of the white residents, gradually and with reluctance, left their homes and moved out to the first fringe of Port City's residential suburbs, abandoning the area to the Negroes.

Prior to this time the Outlaw corner had been a hanging locale for many years. The Outlaw name and corner dated from at least the late 1920's, and perhaps earlier. One local Boy who was not an 'Outlaw' observed disgruntledly that anyone who started a fight with an Outlaw would end up fighting son, father, and grandfather, since all were or had been members of the gang. A somewhat drunken and sentimental Outlaw, speaking at a farewell banquet for their field worker, declared impassionedly that any infant born into an Outlaw family was destined from birth to wear the Outlaw jacket.

One consequence of the fact that Outlaws had hung out on the same corner for many years was that the group that congregated there during the 30-month observation period included a full complement of age-graded subdivisions. Another consequence was that the subdivisions were closely connected by kinship. There were six clearly differentiated subdivisions on the corner: the Marauders, boys in their late teens and early twenties; the Senior Outlaws, boys between 16 and 18; the Junior Outlaws, 14 to 16: and the Midget Outlaws, 11 to 13. There were also two girls groups, the Outlawettes and the Little Outlawettes. The number of Outlaws in all subdivisions totalled slightly over 200 persons, ranging in age, approximately, from 10 to 25 years.

The cohesiveness of the Outlaws, during the 1950's, was enhanced in no small measure by an adult who, like Ben for the Bandits, played a central role in the Outlaws' lives. This was Rosa—the owner of the variety store which was their principal hangout—a stout, unmarried woman of about 40 who was, in effect, the street-corner mother of all 200 Outlaws.

THE JUNIOR OUTLAWS

The Junior Outlaws, numbering 24 active members, were the third oldest of the four male subdivisions on the Outlaw Corner, ranging in age from 14 to 16. Consistent with their middle-range lower-class status, the boys' fathers were employed in such jobs as bricklayer, mechanic, chauffeur, milk deliveryman; but a small minority of these men had attained somewhat higher positions, one being the owner of a small electroplating shop and the other rising to the position of plant superintendent. The educational status of the Junior Outlaws was higher than that of the Bandit gangs, but lower than that of their older brother gang, the Senior Outlaws.

With regard to law violations, the Junior Outlaws, as one might expect "from their status and age, were considerably less criminal than the lower-status Bandits, but considerably more so than the Senior Outlaws. They ranked third among the five male gangs in illegal involvement during the observation period (25 involvements per 10 boys per 10 months), which was well below the second-ranking Senior Bandits (54.2) and well above the fourth-ranking Negro Kings (13.9). Nevertheless, the two-and-a-half-year period during which we observed the Juniors was for them, as for other boys of their status and age group, a time of substantial increase in the frequency and seriousness of illegal behavior. An account of the events of this time provides some insight into the process by which age-related influences engender criminality. It also provides another variation on the issue, already discussed in the case of the Bandits, of the relation of leadership to criminality.

It is clear from the case of the Bandits that gang affairs "were ordered not by auto-cratic ganglords, but rather through a subtle and intricate interplay between leadership and a set of elements such as personal competency, intra-gang divisions and law viola-tion. The case of the Junior Outlaws is particularly dramatic in this regard, since the observation period found them at the critical age when boys of this social-status level are faced with a serious decision—the amount of weight to be granted to law-violating behavior as a basis of prestige. Because there were in the Junior Outlaws two cliques, each of which was committed quite clearly to opposing alternatives, the interplay of the various elements over time emerges with some vividness, and echoes the classic morality play wherein forces of good and evil are locked in mortal combat over the souls of the uncommitted.

At the start of the observation period, the Juniors, 13-, 14- and 15-year-olds, looked and acted for the most part like "nice young kids." By the end of the period both their voices and general demeanor had undergone a striking change. Their appearance, as they hung out in front of Rosa's store, was that of rough corner boys, and the series of thefts, fights and drinking bouts which had occurred during the intervening two-and-one-half years was the substance behind that appearance. When we first contacted them, the Juniors comprised three main cliques; seven boys associated primarily with a "good boy" who was quite explicitly oriented to law-abiding behavior; a second clique of seven boys associated with a "bad boy" who was just starting to pursue prestige through drinking and auto theft; and a third, less-frequently congregating group, who took a relatively neutral position with respect to the issue of violative behavior.

The leader of the "good boy" clique played an active part in the law-abiding activities of the gang, and was elected president of the formal club organized by the Juniors. This club at first included members of all three cliques; however, one of the first acts of the club members, dominated by the "good boy" leader and his supporters, was to vote out of membership the leader of the "bad boy" clique. Nevertheless, the "bad boy" leader and his followers continued to hang out on the corner with the other Juniors, and from this vantage point attempted to gain influence over the uncommitted boys as well as members of the "good boy" clique. His efforts proved unsuccessful, however, since during this period athletic prowess served for the majority of the Juniors as a basis of greater prestige than criminal behavior. Disgruntled by this failure, the "bad boy" leader took his followers and moved to a new hanging corner, about two blocks away from the traditional one.

From there, a tangible symbol of the ideological split within the Juniors, the "bad boy" leader continued his campaign to wean away the followers of the "good boy" leader, trying to persuade them to leave the old corner for the new. At the same time, behavior at the "bad boy" corner became increasingly delinquent, with, among other things, much noisy drinking and thefts of nearby cars. These incidents produced complaints by local residents that resulted in several police raids on the corner, and served to increase the antagonism between what now had become hostile factions. Determined to assert their separateness, the "bad boy" faction began to drink and create disturbances in Rosa's store, became hostile to her when she censured them, and finally stayed away from the store altogether.

The antagonism between the two factions finally became sufficiently intense to bring about a most unusual circumstance—plans for an actual gang fight, a "jam" of the type characteristic of rival gangs. The time and place for the battle were agreed on. But no one from either side showed up. A second battle site was selected. Again the combatants failed to appear. From the point of view of intragang relations, both the plan for the gang fight and its failure to materialize were significant. The fact that a physical fight between members of the same subdivision was actually projected showed that factional hostility over the issue of law violation had reached an unusual degree of bitterness: the fact that the planned encounters did not in fact occur indicated a realization that actual physical combat might well lead to an irreversible split.

A reunification of the hostile factions did not take place for almost a year, however. During this time changes occurred in both factions which had the net effect of blunting the sharpness of the ideological issue dividing them. Discouraged by his failure to win over the majority of the Outlaws to the cause of law-violation as a major badge of prestige, the leader of the "bad boy" clique began to hang out less frequently. At the same time, the eight "uncommitted" members of the Junior Outlaws, now moving toward their middle teens, began to gravitate toward the "bad boy" corner—attracted by the excitement and risk of its activities. More of the Juniors than ever before became involved in illegal drinking and petty theft. This trend became sufficiently pronounced to draw in members of the "good boy" clique, and the influence of the "good boy" leader diminished to the point where he could count on the loyalty only of his own brother and two other boys. In desperation, sensing the all-but-irresistible appeal of illegality for his erstwhile followers, he increased the tempo of his own delinquent behavior in a last-ditch effort to win them back. All in vain. Even his own brother deserted the regular Outlaw corner, although he did not go so far as to join the "bad boys" on theirs.

Disillusioned, the "good boy" leader took a night job that sharply curtailed the time he was able to devote to gang activities. Members of the "bad boy" clique now began a series of maneuvers aimed at gaining control of the formal club. Finally, about two months before the close of the 30-month contact period, a core member of the "bad boy" clique was elected to the club presidency. In effect, the proponents of illegality as a major basis of prestige had won the long struggle for dominance of the Junior Outlaws.

But this achievement, while on the surface a clear victory for the "bad boy" faction, was in fact a far more subtle process of mutual accommodation.

The actions of each of the opposing sides accorded quite directly with their expressed convictions; each member of the "bad boy" faction averaged about 17 known illegal acts during the observation period, compared to a figure of about two per boy for the "good boy" faction. However, in the face of these sharp differences in both actions and sentiments respecting illegality, the two factions shared important common orientations. Most importantly, they shared the conviction that the issue of violative behavior as a basis of prestige was a paramount one, and one that required a choice. Moreover, both sides remained uncertain as to whether the choice they made was the correct one.

The behavior of both factions provides evidence of a fundamental ambivalence with respect to the "demanded" nature of delinquent behavior. The gradual withdrawal of support by followers of the "good boy" leader and the movement toward violative behavior of the previously "neutral" clique attest to a compelling conviction that prestige gained through law-abiding endeavor alone could not, at this age, suffice. Even more significant was the criminal experience of the "good boy" leader. As the prime exponent of law-abiding behavior, he might have been expected to serve as an exemplar in this respect. In fact, the opposite was true; his rate of illegal involvement was the highest of all the boys in his clique, and had been so even before his abortive attempt to regain his followers by a final burst of delinquency. This circumstance probably derived from his realization that a leader acceptable to both factions (which he wanted to be) would have to show proficiency in activities recognized by both as conferring prestige.

TO BE A MAN

It is equally clear, by the same token, that members of the "bad boy" faction were less than serenely confident in their commitment to law-violation as an ideal. Once they had won power in the club they did not keep as their leader the boy who had been the dominant figure on the "bad boy" corner, and who was without question the most criminally active of the Junior Outlaws, but instead elected as president another boy who was also criminally active, but considerably less so. Moreover, in the presence of older gang members, Seniors and Marauders, the "bad boy" clique was far more subdued, less obstreperous, and far less ardent in their advocacy of crime as an ideal. There was little question that they were sensitive to and responsive to negative reactions by others to their behavior.

It is noteworthy that members of both factions adhered more firmly to the "law-violation" and "law-abiding" positions on the level of abstract ideology than on the level of actual practice. This would suggest that the existence of the opposing ideologies and their corresponding factions served important functions both for individual gang members and for the group as a whole. Being in the same orbit as the "bad boys" made it possible for the "good boys" to reap some of the rewards of violative behavior without undergoing its risks; the presence of the "good boys" imposed restraints on the "bad" that they themselves desired, and helped protect them from dangerous excesses. The behavior and ideals of the "good boys" satisfied for both factions that component of their basic orientation that said "violation of the law is wrong and should be punished;" the behavior and ideals of the "bad boys" that component that said "one cannot earn manhood without some involvement in criminal activity."

It is instructive to compare the stress and turmoil attending the struggle for dominance of the Junior Outlaws with the leadership circumstances of the Senior Bandits. In this gang, older and of lower social status (lower-class III), competition for leadership had little to do with a choice between law-abiding and law-violating philosophies, but rather with the issue of which of a number of competing leaders was *best* able to demonstrate prowess in illegal activity. This virtual absence of effective pressures against delinquency contrasts sharply with the situation of the Junior Outlaws. During the year-long struggle between its "good" and "bad" factions, the Juniors were exposed to constant pressures, both internal and external to the gang, to refrain from illegality. External sources included Rosa, whom the boys loved and respected; a local youth worker whom they held in high esteem; their older brother gangs, whose frequent admonitions to the "little kids" to "straighten out" and "keep clean" were attended with utmost seriousness. Within the gang itself the "good boy" leader served as a consistent and persuasive advocate of a law-abiding course of action. In addition, most of the boys' parents deplored their misbehavior and urged them to keep out of trouble.

In the face of all these pressures from persons of no small importance in the lives of the Juniors, the final triumph of the proponents of illegality, however tempered, assumes added significance. What was it that impelled the "bad boy" faction? There was a quality of defiance about much of their delinquency, as if they were saying—" We know perfectly well that what we are doing is regarded as wrong, legally and morally; we also know that it violates the wishes and standards of many whose good opinion we value; yet, if we are to sustain our self respect and our honor as males we *must,* at this stage of our lives, engage in criminal behavior." In light of the experience of the Junior Outlaws, one can scarcely argue that their delinquency sprang from any inability to distinguish right from wrong, or out of any simple conformity to a set of parochial standards that just happened to differ from those of the legal code or the adult middle class. Their delinquent behavior was engendered by a highly complex interplay of forces, including, among other elements, the fact that they were males, were in the middle range of the lower class and of critical importance in the present instance were moving through the age period when the attainment of manhood was of the utmost concern.

In the younger gang just discussed, the Junior Outlaws, leadership and clique structure reflected an intense struggle between advocates and opponents of law-violation as a prime basis of prestige.

Leadership in the older Senior Outlaws reflected a resolution of the law-conformity versus law-violation conflict, but with different results. Although the gang was not under direct observation during their earlier adolescence, what we know of the Juniors, along with evidence that the Senior Outlaws themselves had been more criminal when younger, would suggest that the gang had in fact undergone a similar struggle, and that the proponents of conformity to the law had won.

In any case, the events of the observation period made it clear that the Senior Outlaws sought "rep" as a gang primarily through effective execution of legitimate enterprises such as athletics, dances, and other non-violative activities. In line with this objective, they maintained a consistent concern with the "good name" of the gang and with "keeping out of trouble" in the face of constant and ubiquitous temptations. For example, they attempted (without much success) to establish friendly relations with the senior priest of their parish—in contrast with the Junior Outlaws, who were on very bad terms with the local church. At one point during the contact period when belligerent Bandits, claiming that the Outlaws had attacked one of the Midget Bandits, vowed to "wipe out every Outlaw jacket in Midcity," the Senior Outlaws were concerned not only with the threat of attack but also with the threat to their reputation. "That does it," said one boy, "I knew we'd get into something. There goes the good name of the Outlaws."

Leadership and clique arrangements in the Senior Outlaws reflected three conditions, each related in some way to the relatively low stress on criminal activity: the stability of gang membership (members were rarely removed from the area by institutional confinement), the absence of significant conflict over the prestige and criminality issue, and the importance placed on legitimate collective activities. The Senior Bandits were the most unified of the gangs we observed directly; there were no important cleavages or factions; even the distinction between more-active and less-active members was less pronounced than in the other gangs.

But as in the other gangs, leadership among the Senior Outlaws was collective and situational. There were four key leaders, each of whom assumed authority in his own sphere of competence. As in the case of the Bandit gangs there was little overt competition among leaders; when differences arose between the leadership and the rank and file, the several leaders tended to support one another. In one significant respect, however, Outlaw leadership differed from that of the other gangs; authority was exercised more firmly and accepted more readily. Those in charge of collective enterprises generally issued commands after the manner of a tough army sergeant or work-gang boss. Although obedience to such commands was frequently less than flawless, the leadership style of Outlaw leaders approximated the "snap-to-it" approach of organizations that control firmer sanctions than do most corner gangs. Compared to the near-chaotic behavior of their younger brother gang, the organizational practices of the Senior appeared as a model of efficiency. The "authoritarian" mode of leadership was particularly characteristic of one boy, whose prerogatives were somewhat more generalized than those of the other leaders. While he was far from an undisputed "boss," holding instead a kind of *primus inter pares* position, he was as close to a "boss" as anything found among the direct-observation gangs.

His special position derived from the fact that he showed superior capability in an unusually wide range of activities, and this permitted him wider authority than the other leaders. One might have expected, in a gang oriented predominantly to law-abiding activity, that this leader would serve as an exemplar of legitimacy and rank among the most law-abiding. This was not the case. He was, in fact, one of the most criminal of the Senior Outlaws, being among the relatively few who had "done time." He was a hard drinker, an able street-fighter, a skilled football strategist and team leader, an accomplished dancer and smooth ladies' man. His leadership position was based not on his capacity to best exemplify the law-abiding orientation of the gang, but on his capabilities in a variety of activities, violative and non-violative. Thus, even in the gang most concerned with "keeping clean," excellence in crime still constituted one important basis of prestige. Competence as such rather than the legitimacy of one's activities provided the major basis of authority.

We still have to ask, however, why leadership among the Senior Outlaws was more forceful than in the other gangs. One reason emerges by comparison with the "weak leader" situation of the Junior Bandits. Younger and of lower social status, their factional conflict over the law-violation-and-prestige issue was sufficiently intense so that only a leader without an explicit commitment to either side could be acceptable to both. The Seniors, older and of higher status, had developed a good degree of intragang consensus on this issue, and showed little factionalism. They could thus accept a relatively strong leader without jeopardizing gang unity.

A second reason also involves differences in age and social status, but as these relate to the world of work. In contrast to the younger gangs, whose perspectives more directly revolved around the subculture of adolescence and its specific concerns, the Senior Outlaws at age 19 were on the threshold of adult work, and some in fact were actively engaged in it. In contrast to the lower-status gangs whose orientation to gainful employment was not and never would be as "responsible" as that of the Outlaws, the activities of the Seniors as gang members more directly reflected and anticipated the requirements and conditions of the adult occupational roles they would soon assume.

Of considerable importance in the prospective occupational world of the Outlaws was, and is, the capacity to give and take orders in the execution of collective enterprises. Unlike the Bandits, few of whom would ever occupy other than subordinate positions, the Outlaws belonged to that sector of society which provides the men who exercise direct authority over groups of laborers or blue collar workers. The self-executed collective activities of the gang—organized athletics, recreational projects, fund-raising activities—provided a training ground for the practice of organizational skills—planning organized enterprises, working together in their conduct, executing the directives of legitimate superiors. It also provided a training ground wherein those boys with the requisite talents could learn and practice the difficult art of exercising authority effectively over lower-class men. By the time they had reached the age of 20, the leaders of the Outlaws had experienced in the gang many of the problems and responsibilities confronting the army sergeant, the police lieutenant and the factory foreman.

The nature and techniques of leadership in the Senior Outlaws had relevance not only to their own gang but to the Junior Outlaws as well. Relations between the Junior and Senior Outlaws were the closest of all the intensive contact gang subdivisions. The Seniors kept a close watch on their younger fellows, and served them in a variety of ways, as athletic coaches, advisers, mediators and arbiters. The older gang followed the factional conflicts of the Juniors with close attention, and were not above intervening when conflict reached sufficient intensity or threatened their own interests. The dominant leader of the Seniors was particularly concerned with the behavior of the Juniors; at one point, lecturing them about their disorderly conduct in Rosa's store, he remarked, "I don't hang with you guys, but I know what you do. ..." The Seniors did not, however, succeed in either preventing the near-break-up of the Junior Outlaws or slowing their move toward law-breaking activities.

THE PREVALENCE OF GANGS

The subtle and intricately contrived relations among cliques, leadership and crime in the four "subdivisions of the Bandits and Outlaws reveal the gang as an ordered and adaptive form of association, and its members as able and rational human beings. The fascinating pattern of intergang variation within a basic framework illustrates vividly the compelling influences of differences in age and social status on crime, leadership and other forms of behavior—even when these differences are surprisingly small. The experiences of Midcity gang members show that the gang serves the lower class adolescent as a flexible and adaptable training instrument for imparting vital knowledge concerning the value of individual competence, the appropriate limits of law-violating behavior, the uses and abuses of authority, and the skills of interpersonal relations. From this perspective, the street gang appears not as a casual or transient manifestation that emerges intermittently in response to unique and passing social conditions, but rather as a stable associational form coordinate, with and complementary to the family, and as an intrinsic part of the way of life of the urban low-status community. How then can one account for the widespread conception of gangs as somehow popping up and then disappearing again? One critical reason concerns the way one defines what a gang is. Many observers, both scholars and non-scholars, often use a *sine qua non* to sort out "real" gangs from near-gangs, pseudo-gangs, and non-gangs. Among the more common of these single criteria are: autocratic one-man leadership, some "absolute" degree of solidarity or stable membership, a predominant involvement in violent conflict with other gangs, claim to a rigidly defined turf, or participation in activities thought to pose a threat to other sectors of the community. Reaction to groups lacking the *sine qua non* is often expressed with a dismissive "Oh, them. That's not a *gang*. That's just a bunch of kids out on the corner."

On the Corner Again

For many people there are no gangs if there is no gang warfare. It is that simple. For them, as for all those who concentrate on the "threatening" nature of gang, the phenomenon is defined in terms of the degree of "problem" it poses: A group whose "problematic" behavior is hard to ignore is a gang; one less problematic is not. But what some people see as a problem may not appear so to others. In Philadelphia, for example, the police reckoned there were 80 gangs, of which 20 were at war; while social workers estimated there were 200 gangs, of which 80 were "most hostile." Obviously, the social workers' 80 "most hostile" gangs were the same as the 80 "gangs" of the police. The additional 120 groups defined as gangs by the social workers were seen as such because they were thought to be appropriate objects of social work; but to the police they were not sufficiently troublesome to require consistent police attention, and were not therefore defined as gangs.

In view of this sort of confusion, let me state our definition of what a gang is. A gang is a group of urban adolescents who congregate recurrently at one or more nonresidential locales, with continued affiliation based on self-defined criteria of inclusion and exclusion. Recruitment, customary places of assembly and ranging areas are based in a specific territory, over some portion of which limited use and occupancy rights are claimed. Membership both in the gang as a whole and in its subgroups is determined on the basis of age. The group maintains a versatile repertoire of activities, with hanging out, mating, recreational and illegal activity being of central importance; and it is internally differentiated on the basis of authority, prestige, personality and clique-formation.

The main reason that people have consistently mistaken the prevalence of gangs is the widespread tendency to define them as gangs on the basis of the presence or absence of one or two characteristics that are thought to be essential to the "true" gang. Changes in the forms or frequencies or particular characteristics, such as leadership, involvement in fighting, or modes of organization, are seen not as normal variations over time and space, but rather as signs of the emergence or disappearance of the gangs themselves. Our work does not support this view; instead, (our evidence indicates that the core characteristics of the gang vary continuously from place to place and from time to time without negating the existence of the gang. Gangs may be larger or smaller, named or nameless, modestly or extensively differentiated, more or less active in gang fighting, stronger or weaker in leadership, black, white, yellow or brown, without affecting their identity as gangs. So long as groups of adolescents gather periodically outside the home frequent a particular territory, restrict membership by age and other criteria, pursue a variety of activities, and maintain differences in authority and prestige—so long will the gang continue to exist as a basic associational form.

FURTHER READING SUGGESTED BY THE AUTHOR

The Gang: A Study of 1313 Gangs in Chicago by Frederic M. Thrasher (Chicago: University of Chicago Press, 1927) is the classic work on American youth gangs. Although published in the 1920's, it remains the most detailed and comprehensive treatise or gangs and gang life ever written.

Delinquent Boys: The Culture of the Gang by Albert K. Coher (Glencoe, 111.: Free Press, 1955) is the first major attempt to explain the behavior of gang members using modern sociologies theory.

Delinquency and Opportunity: A Theory of Delinquent Gangs by Richard A. Cloward and Lloyd E. Ohlin (Glencoe, 111.: Free Press 1960) explains the existence, both of gangs, and major types gangs. It has had a profound impact on American domestic policy

Group Process and Gang Delinquency by James F. Short Jr. and Fred L. Strodtbeck (Chicago: University of Chicago Press, 1965) An empirical "test" of divergent theories of gangs and delinquency, it includes the first extensive application of statistic techniques and the first systematic application of the social-psychological conceptual framework to the study of gangs.

White Gangs

Carol Ajimavo
Leah Venegas

Sociology 362

History of street gangs (Quantitative Study)

- Street Corner gangs were thought to have originated in the early 1940s
    - West Side Story style
    - Territorial
- Gangs actually originated around the 1840s
    - Boston, Massachusetts

► Every generation of gangs feels that they are innovative, but gangs have continued historically

► Today's gangs are based on social injustices
  ▷ racial discrimination
  ▷ unequal education and work opportunities
  ▷ unequal distribution of wealth

The Bandit Neighborhood

► Between the Civil War and WWII
► Close-knit group of Irish Laborers
► In the midst of shopping centers and pool halls bars and dance-halls which was their meeting places
► Their favorite meeting place was Ben's (A store owned by guy who supported the bandits)
► Post WWII developments disrupted the physical social shape of this community

- ► Four major subdivisions of the gangs included:
  - ▷ The Brigands (18 to 21)
  - ▷ Senior Bandits (16–18)
  - ▷ Junior Bandits (14–16)
  - ▷ Midget Bandits (12–14)

- ► Two Female subdivisions
  - ▷ Bandettes (14–16)
  - ▷ Little Bandettes (12–14)

The Senior Bandits

- ► The core members totaled 32 members
  - ▷ Mostly Irish Catholic some Italian and French Canadian
  - ▷ Most Members were related (brothers and cousins)
  - ▷ Low socioeconomic status
  - ▷ Most were laborers like their fathers (stock boys, roofers, trucker helpers)
  - ▷ Most were high school dropouts
- ► The most criminal of all of the Bandits
  - ▷ Mostly thefts (watches, jewelry clothing, food, weapons, cars)
  - ▷ gang-related fights
  - ▷ arrests, court appearances, sentences, appeals

The Outlaw Neighborhood
(The Outlaw Street Corner)

► Consisted of, white, Catholic, predominantly Irish, with a few Irish and Irish Italians
► Social structure was in the mid-range of the lower class, higher than 'the bandits'
► There were no housing projects in Outlaw neighborhoods, and none were residents of housing projects
 ▷ Few owned homes, most rented one level of a three decker wooden tenement

1950S

► African-Americans started moving in to the neighborhood
 ▷ Most Whites left their houses and moved to the first fringe of Port City's residential suburbs.

The Outlaws

- The Marauders: boys in their late teens, early twenties
- The Senior Outlaws: boys 16–18
- The Junior Outlaws: boys 14–16
- The Midget Outlaws: boys 11–13
- The Outlawettes: girl group
- The Little Outlawettes: girl group
- There were over 200 people on the Outlaw corner, ranging from 10–25 years old
- Rosa, "mother of the Outlaws"

Junior Outlaws

- 24 active members, aged 14–16
- 3rd ranked in illegal involvement
- Three cliques:
  - ▷ 7 boys with a law abiding "good boy" behavior
  - ▷ 7 boys with a "bad boy" behavior
    - — Pursued prestige through drinking and auto theft
  - ▷ 3rd group held a neutral position, with respect to violent behavior

Senior Outlaws

- ▶ Stayed consistent with the "good boys" name in "keeping out of trouble"
- ▶ Leadership and Arrangements:
  - ▷ Most unified of all the gangs
  - ▷ Authority was exercised firmly and accepted readily
  - ▷ Accepted a strong leader without jeopardizing the gang's unity
  - ▷ Provided a training ground for practice for their future by working together, enterprising, and executing directives of legitimate supervisors

Prevalence of Gangs

- ▶ Relationships in both Bandits and Outlaw gangs are an ordered and adaptive form of association
  - ▷ Members are able and rational human beings
- ▶ Gangs serve lower-class adolescent as a flexible and adaptable training instrument for knowledge
  - ▷ Value of individual competence
  - ▷ Limits of law-violating behavior
  - ▷ Uses and abuses of authority
  - ▷ Interpersonal skills

On the Corner Again

▶ Most people believe there are no gangs if there is no warfare (between the gangs)
  ▷ A group of people who are problematic are a gang; a group of people who are less problematic are not a gang
▶ As long as groups of adolescents gather up together, frequent a certain place (territory), restrict membership, maintain authority and prestige gangs will continue to exist.

References

▶ AL BAKER and JOEL STONINGTON. (2009, April 7). The History of Postwar Street Gangs Lives in Musicals, Books and Memories: [Metropolitan Desk], *New York Times* (Late Edition (east coast)), p. A.21. Retrieved December 4, 2010, from ProQuest National Newspapers Core. (Document ID: 1674575171).

▶ Allan Lengel. (2003, September 18). Nation Has Long History Of Gangs: [FINAL Edition], *The Washington Post*, p. A.10. Retrieved December 4, 2010, from ProQuest National Newspapers Core. (Document ID: 406567291).

THE FAMILY RELATIONS, PEER RELATIONS, AND CRIMINAL ACTIVITIES OF CAUCASIAN AND HISPANIC-AMERICAN GANG MEMBERS

By Jean-Marie Lyon,
Scott Henggeler,
and James A. Hall

Juvenile gang members present serious problems to society, yet few empiri-cal studies have examined their criminal activity, family relations, and peer relations in comparison with other highly antisocial youths. In a 2 (Gang Membership) x 2 (Ethnicity: Hispanic-American vs. Caucasian) design, 131 incarcerated male juvenile offenders were administered a battery assessing criminal activity, family relations, and peer relations. Results demonstrated (a) higher rates of criminal behavior (i.e., general delinquency, index offenses, school delinquency) among gang members than among offenders who did not belong to gangs, (b) higher rates of general delinquency and home delin-quency among Caucasian offenders than among Hispanic-American offend-ers, and (c) greater aggression and less social maturity in the peer relations of gang members" than in the peer relations of offenders who did not belong to

Jean-Marie Lyon, Scott Henggeler, James A. Hall, "The Family Relations, Peer Relations, and Criminal Activities of Caucasian and Hispanic-American Gang Members," *Journal of Abnormal Child Psychology,* vol. 20, no. 5, pp. 439-449. Copyright © 1992 by Springer Science+Business Media. Reprinted with permission.

gangs. In addition, gang membership mediated sociocultural differences in hard drug use. Findings are integrated with the extant literature.

J uvenile gang members are thought to have become increasingly violent as participation in drug trafficking has increased (California Council on Criminal Justice, 1989). Likewise, Klein and Maxson (1989) suggested that juvenile offenders who are gang members have higher rates of violent criminal activity than offenders who are not gang members. In light of the increased tendency for gang members to continue their gang affiliation into adulthood (Hagedorn, 1988) and the extremely detrimental emotional, physical, and economic effects that violent crime has on victims, victims' families, and the community as well as on gang members themselves (Gottfredson, 1989; Thompson & Jason, 1988), a better understanding is needed of delinquent youths who comprise juvenile gangs.

Studies of the correlates and causes of delinquency have consistently implicated the significance of family relations and peers relations (Henggeler, 1989; Quay, 1987). Indeed, the numerous correlates of antisocial behavior in adolescents have prompted the development of multidimensional structural models of delinquency (for a review, see Henggeler, 1991), at least two of which examined the predictors of serious criminal activity. In a national probability sample, Elliott, Huizinga, and Ageton (1985) found that involvement with delinquent peers directly predicted self-reported index offenses, and family difficulties predicted involvement with delinquent peers. Similarly, in a survey of violent delinquents, Fagan and Wexler (1987) found that association with deviant peers was the strongest predictor of violent criminal activity. Findings such as these demonstrate the significance of family relations and peer relations in the study of juvenile offenders.

In the general delinquency literature, the pertinence of low family cohesion and ineffective parental monitoring/discipline are well-documented (Henggeler, 1989; Snyder & Patterson, 1987). Regarding family correlates of gang membership, Vigil (1988) suggested that parents of gang members frequently are unable to provide adequate supervision for their children, and gangs provide emotional support that is often lacking in the family. Few studies, however, have used standardized measures to assess the family relations of gang members, and such relations have not been contrasted with the family relations of juvenile offenders who do not belong to gangs.

The peer relations of gang members have been viewed as highly adaptive and cohesive by some investigators and as quite dysfunctional by others. Several theorists and reviewers (e.g., Hagedorn, 1988; Quicker, 1983; Vigil, 1988) have suggested that many gang members experience an intense emotional closeness born of children growing up together on the streets and turn to each other for support in times of need. In contrast, other authors (e.g., Johnstone, 1983; Klein, 1971; Spergel, 1991) have argued that the socioemotional deficits of gang members restrict their capacity for genuine friendships. Moreover, Short and Strodtbeck (1965/1974) viewed aggression and mistrust as the underlying themes of gang members' interactions, especially considering the constant threat of having to prove oneself.

This study has several purposes. First, as suggested by Klein and Maxson (1989), we assessed whether juvenile offenders who are gang members report more frequent and serious criminal activity than offenders who do not belong to gangs. Second, we examined the unique family and peer correlates of gang membership, and whether such correlates are mediated by ethnicity (Hispanic-American vs. Caucasian). Hispanic-American youths are the most rapidly increasing incarcerated population (Martinez, 1987), but little evidence suggests that the correlates of antisocial behavior differ among ethnic groups. On the other hand, Rodriguez and Zayas (1990) proposed that Hispanic cultural norms concerning parental respect and loyalty to family are likely to attenuate rates of criminal behavior among Hispanic-American youth. To the best of our knowledge, this represents the first study to evaluate the social systems of gang members with standardized instruments while controlling for the presence of serious antisocial behavior.

METHOD

Participants

Participants meeting all screening criteria included 131, 13-to 18-year-old incarcerated male juvenile offenders divided into four groups in a 2 (Gang Membership) x 2 (Ethnicity: Hispanic-American vs. Caucasian) design. Thus, groups were comprised of Hispanic-American gang members (HG; $n = 50$), Hispanic-Americans who did not belong to a gang (HN; $n = 26$), Caucasian gang members (WG; $n = 25$), and Caucasians who did not belong to a gang (WN; $n = 30$). Across groups, the mean adolescent age was 16.1 years ($SD = 1.1$), 64% of youths were from two-parent families (both biological parents or one biological parent and a mate), and the mean social status (Hollingshead, 1975) score was 34 ($SD = 14$), reflecting skilled craft workers, clerical and sales workers. Between-groups differences were not observed for age and family structure, but Caucasian youths were of higher social status than Hispanic-American youths, $F(1, 127) = 86.33$, p < .001. Consequently, social status was used as a covariate in subsequent analyses.

Procedure

Adjudicated minors, recently referred to a county Assessment Center that serves several juvenile detention facilities, were screened for ethnicity (Hispanic-American or Caucasian). Next, a researcher, who was a mental health professional, met with eligible youths (either individually or in pairs) to explain the purpose of the study. Procedures to guarantee confidentiality were emphasized, and eventual anonymity was assured. The researcher stressed that participation was completely voluntary and would have no bearing on services provided by the Center. If agreeable, the participants signed the consent form and were administered an assessment battery. Ninety-six percent of the eligible youths agreed to participate. Because reading difficulties are widespread among delinquents, all items were read aloud by the researcher while the participants read along. Four youths lacked sufficient command of the English language and were excluded from the study. Each youth was given a soft drink at the completion of the 45-min assessment session.

Independent Variables

Ethnicity. Ethnicity was determined by self-report responses on a demographic questionnaire. The majority of minors committed to the county's detention facilities are Caucasian (non-Hispanic; 42%) or Hispanic-American (44%). Youths of other ethnic backgrounds were excluded.

Gang Membership. Status as a gang member was based on criteria of the county Gang Violence Suppression Unit. To be considered a gang member, the youth must have admitted gang membership and must have responded affirmatively to at least two other criterion items (e.g., tatoos related to a gang, a particular style of dress or grooming related to a gang). Youths were defined as not belonging to a gang if they denied gang membership and did not meet the other criteria for gang membership. As noted above, these criteria identified 75 gang members and 56 youths not belonging to a gang. Twelve other youths were excluded from the study because they did not fit the criteria either for gang membership or no gang membership (e.g., youth denied gang membership but responded affirmatively to two criterion items).

Dependent Variables

Criminal Activity. Criminal activities during the past year (excluding time incarcerated) were assessed with the Self-Report Delinquency (SRD; Eiliott & Ageton, 1980) scale used in the National Youth Survey. The SRD includes a broad range of criminal acts and is the most well-validated of the self-report delinquency indices (Henggeler, 1989). Four summary scales were examined: general-delinquency, index offenses, school delinquency (e.g., hit teacher, strongarmed students), and home delinquency (e.g., damaged family property, stole from family). In addition the hard drug use offense-specific scale was evaluated.

Arrest histories were not included for two primary reasons. First, to guarantee anonymity after the assessment, increase participation rates, and enhance internal validity, participant names were not written on research forms and a master list matching names with identification numbers was not compiled. Second, we were concerned about possible biases in arrest records (see e.g., Fagan, Slaughter, & Hartstone, 1987).

Family Relations. The 20-item Family Adaptability and Cohesion Evaluation Scales-Ill (FACES-Ill; Olson, Portner, & Lavee, 1985) assesses two central dimensions of family relations: cohesion and adaptability. The validity of FACES has been supported in numerous studies of juvenile offenders (e.g., Biaske, Borduin, Henggeler, & Mann, 1989; Henggeler, Burr-Harris, Borduin, & McCallum, 1991; Tolan, 1988). In light of debate regarding the linearity vs. curvilinearity of the subscales (Henggeler et al., 1991), analyses determined that the subscales were linearly associated with the SRD summary scales. Thus, the scales are treated linearly in subsequent analyses.

The 30-item Children's Report of Parental Behavior Inventory (CR-PBI-30; Schludermann & Schludermann, 1988) is a brief version of the CR-PBI (Schaefer, 1965) and assesses three important dimensions of mother-adolescent and of father-adolescent relations: acceptance, psychological control, and firm control. Such dimensions have been consistently linked with antisocial behavior in adolescents (Henggeler, 1989; Snyder & Patterson, 1987). The CRPBI-30 subscales are highly correlated with their counterparts in the CRPBI-108, have high test-retest reliabilities (all rs > .94), and acceptable internal consistencies (alpha coefficients >.63).

Peer Relations. The 13-item Missouri Peer Relations Inventory (MPRI; Borduin, Blaske, Treloar, Mann, & Hazelrigg, 1989) evaluates three qualitative dimensions of adolescent friendships: emotional bonding, aggression, and social maturity. The inventory was normed on juvenile offenders and normal controls and recent studies have supported its validity with serious delinquents (Blaske et al., 1989) and hearing impaired adolescents (Henggeler, Watson, & Whelan, 1990).

RESULTS

A 2 (Gang Status) X 2 (Ethnicity: Hispanic-American vs. Caucasian) multivariate analysis of variance (MANCOVA), with social status as a covariate, was performed on the subscales of each research instrument. When the multivariate effect was significant, an ANCOVA was conducted on each measure in the set.

Criminal Activity
Significant multivariate effects for gang status, $F(4, 123) = 14.92$, $p<.001$, and ethnicity, $F(4, 123) = 2.89$, $p < .05$, emerged for the SRD summary scales. Univariate analyses revealed significant gang status effects for general delinquency, $F(1, 126) = 13.28$, $p < .001$, index offenses, $F(1, 126) = 41.44$, $p < .001$, and school delinquency, $F(1, 126) = 16.78$,

$p < .001$. In each case, gang members reported much higher rates of criminal activity than did youths who did not belong to gangs (see Table I). Univariate ethnicity effects emerged for general delinquency, $F(1, 126) = 8.36$, $p < .01$, and home delinquency, $F(1, 126) = 4.40$, $p < .05$, with Caucasian youths reporting higher rates of criminal behavior than Hispanic-American youths. In addition, a significant interaction effect, $F(1, 126) = 6.92$, $p < .01$, and a main effect for ethnicity, $F(1, 126) = 8.89$, $p < .01$, emerged for hard-drug use. *Post hoc* comparisons showed that Hispanic-American offenders who did not belong to gangs reported significantly less hard drug use than their counterparts in each of the other groups.

Family Relations

Separate MANCOVAs were conducted on the FACES-III (cohesion and adaptability), the CRPBI-30 for mother (acceptance, psychological control, and firm control), and the CRPBI-30 for father. No significant multivariate effects were observed.

Although the primary purpose of conducting multivariate analyses was to limit Type 1 error, one univariate finding emerged (the only significant univariate effect among the family relations measures) that has important implications for interpreting ethnicity differences in self-reported delinquency. Hispanic-American youths reported significantly more psychological control from their mothers than did Caucasian youths, $F(1, 126) = 5.63$, $p < .02$.

Peer Relations

A significant multivariate effect for gang status, $F(3, 124) = 3.33$, $p < .05$, emerged for the MPRI. Gang status univariate effects were observed for aggression, $F(1, 126) = 5.53$, $p < .05$, and social maturity, $F(1, 126) =$

Table 1. *Group Means, Standard Deviations, and Analyses for Dependent Measuresa*

		HG	HN	WG	WN	Significant Multivariate	Effects Univariate
SRD						E, G	
General							
delinquency	M	359	110	448	366		E, G
	SD	(289)	(211)	(424)	(339)		
Index offenses	M	73	16	73	39		G

	SD	(68)	(45)	(83)	(74)	
School delinquency	M	67	18	83	53	G
	SD	(58)	(27)	(94)	(54)	
Home delinquency	M	4	2	4	9	E
	SD	(9)	(5)	(7)	(14)	
Hard-drug use	M	33	5	24	47	EG, G
	SD	62	25	43	72	
CRPBI-30: Mother						n.s.
Acceptance	M	24.8	25.8	24.3	24.7	
	SD	(4.5)	(6.0)	(5.5)	(4.8)	
Psychological control	M	20,9	20.6	18.0	18.4	
	SD	(4.6)	(4.7)	(4.5)	(5.0)	
Firm control	M	19,2	20.2	18.9	20.4	
	SD	(4.4)	(3.8)	(5.6)	(4.1)	
CRPBI-30: Father						n.s.
Acceptance	M	21,6	23.1	20,7	20.4	
	SD	(5.7)	(6.6)	(7.3)	(5.1)	
Psychological control	M	20.7	18.7	19.0	19.1	
	SD	(4.2)	(4.4)	(4.9)	(6.7)	
Firm control	M	20.4	20.5	23.4	22.0	

		HG	HN	WG	WN			
	SD	(5.7)	(3.9)	(5.6)	(6.0)			
FACES-III								n.s.
Cohesion	M	32.7	34.8	29.6	32,8			
	SD	(9.5)	(8.6)	(9.8)	(9.4)			
Adaptability	M	24.4	23.1	22.6	24.2			
	SD	(5.8)	(5.6)	(6.2)	(5.8)			
MPRI								G
Emotional bonding	M	16.8	17.3	17,9	17.6			
	SD	(3.3)	(2.5)	(2.5)	(2_4)			
Aggression	M	12.8	12.4	14.1	11.7			G
	SD	(3.1)	(3.8)	(3.7)	(2.6)			
Social maturity	M	9.6	10.5	10.6	11.1			
	SO	(1.7)	(1.7)	(2.0)	(2.0)			G

[a] Note: HG = Hispanic-American gang members; HN = Hispanic-American offenders who are not gang members; WG = Caucasian gang members; WN = Caucasian offenders who are not gang members. G = main effect for gang membership; E = main effect for ethnicity; EG = interaction effect. SRD = Self-Report Delinquency scale; CRPBI-30 = 30-item Children's Report of Parental Behavior; FACES-III = 20-item Family Adaptability and Cohesion Evaluation Scales-III; MPRI = Missouri Peer Relations Inventory, 4.80, p < .05. The friendships of gang members were more aggressive and less socially mature than the friendships of offenders who did not belong to gangs.

DISCUSSION

The first purpose of this study was to evaluate the view that gang members present an inordinately high rate of serious antisocial behavior (Klein & Maxson, 1989; Spergel, 1991). Results clearly demonstrated a higher rate of reported criminal behavior among incarcerated gang members than among incarcerated youths who were not gang members. For example, gang members reported a mean of 73 index offenses during the past year, which was more than twice that reported by serious offenders who were not gang members. As another point of comparison, the mean number of index offenses reported by adolescents in the National Youth Survey was less than 1.0 (Elliott, Ageton, Huizinga, Knowles, & Canter, 1983). Moreover, because gang membership may enhance the probability of incarceration due to increased scrutiny by the juvenile justice system (Zatz, 1985), between-groups differences in reported offenses are even more striking.

In addition, results revealed that Caucasians reported more general delinquency and home delinquency than did their Hispanic-American counterparts. The finding for general delinquency may reflect underreporting on self-report indices by minorities (e.g., Dunford & Elliott, 1984), racial discrepancies in decisions to arrest and incarcerate (e.g., Huizinga & Eiliott, 1987), greater psychological control exercised by Hispanic-American mothers (as suggested in the results section), and/or better monitoring via larger extended families and more cohesive ethnic neighborhoods among Hispanic-Americans. Regarding home delinquency, findings may reflect the greater respect for parental authority reported for Hispanic-American families (Rodriguez & Zayas, 1990) as well as the aforementioned use of psychological control by mothers of Hispanic-American youths. The finding that hard drug use was relatively low among Hispanic-Americans who did not belong to gangs is consistent with extant sociocultural differences in substance abuse (Delgado, 1990). Moreover, the high rate of hard drug use reported by Hispanic-American gang members suggests that gang membership mediates this sociocultural difference.

The second purpose of this study was to assess the family relations and peer relations of gang members in comparison to juvenile offenders who do not belong to a gang, and to determine whether such relations were mediated by ethnicity. Between-groups differences were not observed for family relations, mother-adolescent relations, or father-adolescent relations. The lack of between-group differences does not discount the important role of family relations in serious antisocial behavior, but such findings suggest that family problems are no more associated with gang membership than with serious antisocial behavior in general.

Regarding peer relations, gang members were more aggressive and less socially mature than offenders who did not belong to gangs. These findings support Short and Strodtbeck's (1965/1974) view that aggression underlies the friendships of gang members, and that much of the pseudo-aggression (e.g., body-punching) displayed in gang members' relationships may be due to social disabilities that prelude more mature ways of relating. Similarly, Romig, Cleland, and Romig (1989) reported that incarcerated gang members presented poor social and interpersonal skills.

Interestingly, in contrast to previous qualitative research, gang members did not report greater emotional bonding with their friends than did offenders who did not belong to gangs.

The social contexts of gang members were not moderated by ethnicity. All groups reported similar family relations, and Hispanic-American gang members reported similar peer relations as Caucasian gang members. Such findings support the view that the correlates and causes of serious antisocial behavior are similar across ethnic groups (Henggeler, 1989).

Finally, the limitations of this study are noted, and directions for future research are suggested. First, the use of an incarcerated sample limits the external validity of the study, though a very high percentage of eligible youths agreed to participate. Second, the inclusion of a nondelinquent control group might have improved internal validity. However, we were primarily interested in the unique correlates of gang membership, and, consequently, the present comparison group was most pertinent. Third, construct validity was limited by use of only one measurement method (i.e., adolescent self-report). Nevertheless, this represents the first study to use standardized instruments to evaluate the social systems of gang members while controlling for the presence of serious antisocial behavior. Future investigators should consider the inclusion of community samples and the assessment of constructs from multiple perspectives (e.g., parent and peer reports).

REFERENCES

Blaske, D. M., Borduin, C. M., Henggeler, S. W., & Mann, B. J. (1989). "Individual, family, and peer characteristics of adolescent sex offenders and assaultive offenders." *Developmental Psychology*, 25, 846–855.

Borduin, C. M., Blaske, D. M., Trcloar, L., Mann. B. J., & Hazelrigg, M. (1989). *Development and validation of a measure of adolescent peer relations.* Unpublished manuscript, University of Missouri, Department of Psychology, Columbia.

California Council on Criminal Justice. (1989). *State task force on gangs and drugs.* Sacramento: Author.

Delgado, M. (1990). "Hispanic adolescents and substance abuse: Implications for research, treatment, and prevention." In A. R. Stiffman & L. E. Davis (Eds.), *Ethnic issues in adolescent mental health* (pp. 303–320). Newbury Park, CA: Sage.

Dunford, F. W., & Elliott, D. S. (1984). "Identifying career offenders using self-reported data". *Journal of Research in Crime and Delinquency,* 21, 57–86.

Elliott, D. S., & Ageton, S. S. (1980). "Reconciling race and class differences in self-reported and official estimates of delinquency." *American Sociological Review,* 45, 95–110.

Elliott, D. S., Ageton, S. S., Huizinga, D., Knowles, B. A., & Canter, R. J. (1983). *The prevalence and incidence of delinquent behavior: 1976–1980* (Project Report No. 26). Boulder, CO: Behavioral Research Institute.

Elliott, D. S., Huizinga, D., & Ageton, S. S. (1985). *Explaining delinquency and drug use.* Beverly Hills, CA: Sage.

Fagan, J., Slaughter, E., & Hartstone, E. (1987). "Blind justice? The impact of race on the juvenile justice process." *Crime & Delinquency*, 33, 244–258.

Fagan, J., & Wexler, S. (1987). "Family origins of violent delinquents." *Criminology*, 25, 643–669.

Gottfredson, G. D. (1989). "The experience of violent and serious victimization." In N. Ao Weiner & M. E. Wolfgang (Eds.), *Pathways to criminal violence*. Newbury Park, CA: Sage.

Hagedorn, J. M. (1988). *People and folks: Gangs, crime, and the underclass in a rustbelt city*. Chicago: Lake View Press.

Henggeler, S. W. (1989). *Delinquency in adolescence*. Newbury Park, CA: Sage.

Henggeler, S. W. (1991). "Multidimensional causal models of delinquent behavior." In R. Cohen & A. Siegel (Eds.), *Context and development*. Hillsdale, NJ: Erlbaum.

Henggler, S. W., Burr-Harris, A. W., Borduin, C. M., & McCallum, G. (1.991). "Use of the Family Adaptability and Cohesion Evaluation Scales in child clinical research." *Journal of Abnormal Child Psychology*, 19, 53–63.

Henggeler, S. W., Watson, S. M., & Whelan, J. P. (1990). "Peer relations of hearing-impaired adolescents." *Journal of Pediatric Psychology*, 15, 721–731.

Hollingshead, A. B. (1975). *The four-factor index of social status*. Unpublished manuscript, Yale University, New Haven, CT.

Huizinga, D., & Elliott, D. S. (1987). "Juvenile offenders: Prevalence, offender incidence, and arrest rates by race." *Crime and Delinquency*, 33, 206–223.

Johnstone, J. W. C. (1983). "Recruitment to a youth gang." *Youth and Society*, 14, 281–300.

Klein, M. W. (1971). *Street gangs and street workers*. Englewood Cliffs, NJ: Prentice-Hall.

Klein, M. W., & Maxson, C. L. (1989). "Street gang violence." In N. A. Weiner & M. E. Wolfgang (Eds.), *Violent crime, violent criminals* (pp. 198–234).

Newbury Park, CA: Sage. Martinez, O. (1987). "Minority youth and crime." *Crime and Delinquency*, 33, 325–328.

Olson, D. H., Portner, J., & Lavee, Y. (1985). *FACES-III*. St. Paul: University of Minnesota, Department of Family Social Science.

Quay, H. C. (Ed.). (1987). *Handbook of juvenile delinquency*. New York: Wiley.

Quicker, J. C. (1983). *Seven decades of gangs: What has been learned, what has been done, and what should be done*. Sacramento: California Commission on Crime Control and Violence Prevention.

Rodriguez, O., & Zayas, L. H. (1990). "Hispanic adolescents and antisocial behavior: Sociocultural factors and treatment implications." In A. R. Stiffman & L. E. Davis (Eds.), *Ethnic issues in adolescent mental health* (pp. 147–171). Newbury Park, CA:Sage.

Romig, D. A., Cleland, C. C., & Romig, L. J. (1989). *Juvenile delinquency: Visionary approaches*. Columbus, OH: Merrill.

Schaefer, E. S. (1965). "Children's reports of parental behavior: An inventory." *Child Development*, 38, 417–424.

Schludermann, E., & Schludermann, S. (1988). *Notes on the CRPBI-30*. Unpublished manuscript, University of Manitoba, Department of Psychology, Winnipeg, Canada.

Short, J. F., & Strodtbeck, F. L. (1974). *Group process and gang delinquency* (4th impression). Chicago: The University of Chicago Press. (Original work published in 1965).

Snyder, J., & Patterson, G. R. (1987). "Family interaction and delinquent behavior." In H. C. Quay (Ed.), *Handbook of juvenile delinquency* (pp. 216–243). New York: Wiley.

Spergel, I. A. (1991). *Youth gangs: Problem and response.* Unpublished manuscript, University of Chicago, School of Social Service Administration, Chicago.

Thompson, D. W., & Jason, L. A. (1988). "Street gangs and preventative interventions." *Criminal Justice and Behavior*, 15, 323–333.

Tolan, P. (1988). "Socioeconomic, family, and social stress correlates of adolescent antisocial and delinquent behavior." *Journal of Abnormal Child Psychology*, 16, 317–331.

Vigil, J. D. (1988). *Barrio gangs.* Austin: The University of Texas Press.

Zatz, M. S. (1985). "Los Cholos: Legal processing of Chicano gang members." *Social Problems*, 33, 13–30.

The Family Relations, Peer Relations and Criminal Activities of Caucasian and Hispanic-American Gang Members

PowerPoint by:
Aundria Anderson
Karena Campbell
David Mouy

- ► Violence among juveniles have increased
- ► Klein and Maxson
  - ▷ Do gang members have higher rates of violent criminal activity than non gang members?
  - ▷ Is delinquency related to family and peer relations?
  - ▷ Is ethnicity relevant to those relations? (Hispanic-American or Caucasian)
- ► **Family Relation** (Vigil)
  - ▷ Gang member's parents lack the means to provide and supervise them
  - ▷ *Results*: Joining a gang; provides emotional support
- ► **Peer Relation** (Hagedorn, Quicker, Vigil)
  - ▷ Gang members have become close to their childhood friends
  - ▷ Use each other for support on the streets

Procedure

- ▶ Each participant was screened for ethnicity
  - ▷ Either Hispanic-American or Caucasian (131 participants)
- ▶ Researcher explained the purpose of the study
  - ▷ Participants were guaranteed confidentiality
  - ▷ Strictly voluntary
  - ▷ 96% agreed to participate
  - ▷ Signed consent forms
  - ▷ Were given an assessment battery
  - ▷ Quantitative Study
- ▶ The researcher read aloud the terms and conditions of the study
  - ▷ The delinquents had trouble reading

Variables

Independent Variables

- ▶ *Ethnicity:* Only Caucasians and Hispanic-Americans could participate
- ▶ *Gang membership:* Those identified as gang members were accepted
  - ▷ **Identified by:** Tattoos, apparel, admitting to being in a gang
  - ▷ All non-gang members were dismissed

Dependent Variables

- ▶ *Criminal Activity:*
  - ▷ General delinquency
  - ▷ Index offenses
  - ▷ School delinquency
  - ▷ Home delinquency
- ▶ *Family Relations:*
  - ▷ Relationship of the parents w/ the adolescent
- ▶ *Peer Relations:*
  - ▷ According to the MPRI (Missouri Peer Relations Inventory), they evaluated peer relations by:
    - – Emotional bond
    - – Aggression
    - – social maturity

Results

Criminal activity
- Youth gang members rates higher for criminal activity than youths that are not in a gang
- Caucasians youth have highest rate of criminal activity
- Hispanic youth gang members show higher hard drug use

Family Relations
- Mother of Hispanic youth show more control psychologically than Caucasian mothers

Peer Relations
- Relationships of youth gang members more aggressive and low rates in social maturity

---

Home Versus School Environments and their Influences on the Affective and Behavioral States of African American, Hispanic, and Caucasian Juvenile Offenders (Caldwell, Silver, Sturges, 2006)

Purpose to investigate
- Effects of adolescents home vs. school environment on behavior and affective state
- Race/Ethnicity/Gender
- Differences between home and school environment

Results for behavior
- High score related to home environment(uncomfortable and unsupported home life)
- Positive relation to compliance (disregarding) rules
- Positive relationship between home environment and impulsity(acting out)

Purpose and Results

Results for affective states
- Caucasian and Hispanic males has correlation with home environment, depression and anxiety
- Males home environment associated with moods anger and irritable thoughts

Results for affective states
- Females (African American and Caucasian high relationship between home environment, compliance and impulsity
- Males more likely to have school related problems(effects of school environment

Methods

- 626 participants 516 males/110 females
- 23% African American, 45.3% Caucasian and 31.7% Hispanic
- Manova 2 × 3
- Quantitative study
- Moss T/F report scale
- Home environment scale
- School environment scale and depressed-anxious (yes/no questions)

Socio-Demographic Variability in Adolescent Substance Use: Mediation by Parents and Peers (Farhart, Luk, Simons-Morton, Wang, 2009)

Purpose
- ► Investigate socio-demographic variability in adolescent substance use and the dependent roles of maternal and paternal knowledge and peer substance use in a diverse sample

Methods
- ► Used data from HBSC(Health and Behavior in school aged children) 2005/2006
- ► Grades-6-10
- ► Sample 8,795
- ► Measured gender, race(Caucasian, African American, Hispanic and others), Family structure- 2 parent home, single mother or father, mothers-stepfather or the reciprocal and others

Results

10th graders
- ► (highest use in last 30 days)
  1. Alcohol
  2. Cigarettes
  3. Marijuana

Hispanic
- ► Highest use of alcohol cigarettes and marijuana

Father-Stepmother
- ► Highest for alcohol and cigarettes

Single father
- ► Highest for marijuana

Socioeconomic
- ► No significant difference in gender
- ► Hispanic more substance use
- ► Only two parent family show low substance use

References

Caldwell, R.M., Sturges, S.M, & Silver, N.C. (2007).Home Versus School Environment and their Influences on the Affective and Behavioral States of African American, Hispanic, and Caucasian Juvenile offenders. Journal of Child and Family Studies, 10, 119–132

Lyon, J.M., Henggeler, S., & Hall, J. A., (1992). The Family Relations, and Criminal Activities of Caucasian and Hispanic-American Gang Member. Journal of Abnormal Child Psychology, 20, 439–447.

Wang, J., Bruce, G., Morton, S.S., Farhart, T., Luk, J.W. (2009). Socio-Demographic Variability in Adolescent Substance use: Mediation by Parents and Peers, Prevention Science

DEFENSIVE LOCALISM IN WHITE AND BLACK

A COMPARATIVE HISTORY OF EUROPEAN-AMERICAN AND AFRICAN-AMERICAN YOUTH GANGS

By Christopher Adamson

ABSTRACT

The activities of European-American and African-American youth gangs have been closely linked to the operation of changing racial and class structures. In this article, I compare European-American and African-American youth gangs in four historical periods: the seaboard city, 1787–1861; the immigrant city, 1880–1940; the racially changing city, 1940–1970; and the hypersegregated city, 1970–1999. I show that the differences between European-American and African-American gangs can be traced to the race specific effects of labour, housing and consumer markets, government policies (especially crime control policies), local politics and organized crime on European-American and African-American communities. I conclude that European-American youth gangs facilitated cultural assimilation because of their close ties with formal and informal political authorities and organizations which commanded substantial social and economic power, whereas African-American youth gangs reinforced cultural separation because of

Christopher Adamson, "Defensive Localism in White and Black: A Comparative History of European-American and African-American Youth Gangs," *Ethnic and Racial Studies*, vol. 23, no. 2, pp. 272-298.

their embeddedness in racially segregated, economically marginalized and politically powerless communities.

Keywords: Youth gangs; United States; ethnicity; race; assimilation; segregation.

I n a country like the United States in which race and class have been the central structuring principles of urban life, we would expect significant differences in the patterns of historical development of European-American and African-American youth or street gangs. Indeed, the effects of racial and class structures on the behaviour of American youth gangs have been so profound that scholars who have sought to develop race-invariant theories of gangs and delinquency have been stymied.[1] Over the last fifty years, those criminologists and sociologists who have been sensitive to the differential effects of joblessness, residential segregation and the availability of public services on white and black communities have acknowledged the absurdity of attempts to construct a single, race-invariant model of youth-gang behaviour.[2]

This is not to say that there are not similarities between white and black gangs.[3] It is true, for example, that both white and black youth gangs have been affected by economic disadvantage, family disruption and social disorganization. Gangs of both races have been predators upon, and protectors of, the communities in which they are embedded. For black and white teenagers, the gang has been a place in which to forge an identity and achieve social status. And just as white youth gangs have attacked vulnerable blacks, black youth gangs have attacked vulnerable whites. For both races, the gang has performed important community functions which can be subsumed under the rubric of defensive localism. These functions include the defence of territory, the policing of neighbourhoods, the upholding of group honour, and the provision of economic, social, employment, welfare and recreational services.

Despite these similarities, white and black youth gangs are profoundly different historical creations. They originated at different times, and their respective relationships to labour, housing and consumer markets, governmental institutions, formal and informal political authority, organized crime and agencies of crime control have been different. In the historical analysis which ensues, I compare the effects of these structural relationships on white and black youth gangs.

WHITE YOUTH GANGS IN THE SEABOARD CITY, 1787–1861

Black youth gangs did not exist as a recognized social problem until the great migration of the 1910s when large numbers of African-Americans came to the northern cities. Indeed, it was only with the massive second great migration of the mid-twentieth century, when a far more intractable urban ghetto was created, that politicians, prosecutors, police officials and social workers began to view African-American youth gangs as a threat to social order. In the nineteenth century, the assumptions of caste militated against the formation of territorial gangs of free black youth. No doubt groups of three or more young blacks got together on many occasions, and certain newspapers, such as the *North American and United States News Gazette* in 1853, did point to the existence of black youth gangs in Philadelphia (Davis 1982, p. 190). It is significant, however, that these black gangs were neither named nor territorial. At a time when African-American gatherings and parades were regarded with suspicion, the appearance of boisterous gangs of black teenagers on street corners, even in areas inhabited by many blacks, would have been dangerously provocative (Litwack 1961, p. 102).

White youth gangs, in contrast, existed at the very inception of the republic. In the late 1780s, for example, prison reformers commented on the baneful presence of gangs of young people hanging out on Philadelphia's street corners (Meranze 1996, p. 94). The activities of white gangs, which became an increasingly visible presence in the antebellum city, were geared to the defence of local neighbourhoods. Gang youth, who were generally subservient to prominent adults in the community, upheld the local racial order.

By the 1820s white boys in their teens and early twenties were gathering on street corners in New York's Bowery and Five Points districts, Boston's North End and Fort Hill, and the outlying Southwark and Moyamensing sections of Philadelphia. These gangs of boys fought youths from other neighbourhoods for control of street corners and open lots. For example, New York's Smith Vly Boys, a gang which took its name 'from the marsh, or lowlands (Dutch *Vly)* in the lower, eastern part of the city', fought several Broadway gangs for control of the high ground on present-day Grand Street, then called Bunker Hill (Gilje 1987, p. 261). The Roach Guards, named in honour of a Five Points liquor seller, took on the Chichesters, the Plug Uglies and the Dead Rabbits. The Roach Guards' battle uniform was 'a blue stripe on the pantaloons, while the Dead Rabbits adopted a red stripe, and at the head of their sluggers carried a dead rabbit impaled on a pike' (Asbury 1928, p. 23). The impoverished suburbs of Philadelphia were home to a large number of turf defending white gangs whose 'verminous designations', as *New York Tribune* reporter George Foster (1848, p. 35) put it, 'were written in chalk or charcoal on every dead-wall, fence, and stable door'.

It is important to recognize that white gangs were often multi-ethnic, especially in neighbourhoods that were not rigidly segregated by ethnicity. Dutch, English, Welsh, Scots-Irish, Irish Catholics, Germans and persons of mixed ancestry could be found in the same territorially denned youth gang. Territory was often more important than ethnicity in shaping the formation of white youth gangs. New York's Bowery gangs, such as the O'Connell Guards, the Atlantic Guards, the American Guards and the True Blue Americans—some of which were nativist and Protestant, others Irish Catholic—put aside their ethnic differences in order to defend their territory against Five Points gangs[4] (Asbury 1928, p. 28; Sante 1991, p. 200).

It is central to this article's argument to recognize that white youth gangs enjoyed a measure of support from the adult population. To be sure, gang boys annoyed adults by swearing and carrying on loudly in the streets; and their drinking, fighting, disrespect for property and theft disrupted the fabric of social life. But white gangs were sponsored by politically powerful adults, who rewarded them for defending the local neighbour-hood. In some instances, youth gangs served an informal policing function. Gang boys in New York, for example, 'served as informal neighborhood constabularies'. They 'stood about on street corners with a studied watchful glower, making sure, as one New Yorker recalled, that anyone who was 'exotic or unfamiliar' would not cause trouble or linger too long' (Wilentz 1984, p. 262). Gang boys also considered it their duty to protect young women in the neighbourhood. In the Bowery young toughs chased after prowling outsiders and voyeuristic 'aristos' seeking sexual liaison with Bowery girls (Stansell 1987, p. 95).

It was thus a hallmark of white defensive localism that street gangs were subservient to powerful adults in the community. Gangs allied themselves with social and political clubs and often took direction from political bosses, who depended on them to mobilize the vote and protect polling places on election days. Membership in a youth gang could lead to a career in local politics. Thus William McMullen, Philadelphia's influential saloon keeper, alderman, prison inspector and political boss, started his career as a member of the Killers, one of the city's violent Irish-Catholic fighting gangs.

White youth gangs patrolled streets and secured neighbourhood boundaries. The Killers, for example, won the support of the people of Moyamensing by protecting them from nativist invaders and by occasionally distributing food to the poor (Silcox 1989, p. 46). However, white youth gangs like the Killers also participated in collective attacks on free blacks. Given the caste assumption of black ontological inferiority, white gang boys looked upon black Americans as a people to whom the rules of honour-based conflict did not apply, and viciously assaulted inoffensive black women and elderly black men during riots.

In the 1830s young Irish and native-born workingmen expressed their contempt for New York's African Americans by savagely attacking black patrons of white drinking and eating houses, and by destroying the property of successful black tavern keepers (Kaplan 1995, pp. 606–9). In Philadelphia, in 1834, a 'party of half grown boys' pre-cipitated a three night riot by attacking a tavern with an interracial clientele. A mob then invaded the streets and alleys of Moyamensing, assaulting free blacks, looting their homes, destroying their furniture and bedding, and forcing many of them to flee into the city or across the Delaware. Many of the rioters described their activities as 'hunting the nigs' (Runcie 1972, p. 190). In 1849 Philadelphia's Killers burnt down the California House Tavern, an establishment owned by a mulatto who had married a white woman.

As in 1834, a mob then proceeded to hunt down pedestrians on the streets of the African-American section of Moyamensing, killing three blacks and injuring at least two dozen others (Feldberg 1980, p. 59; Laurie 1980, p. 156).

The Irish antipathy towards African Americans was partly fuelled by competition for jobs on the docks, shipyards and building construction sites, and partly rooted in a *herrenvolk* republicanism which sought to deprive free blacks of any of the rights enjoyed by white citizens and members of the producing classes (Roediger 1991, p. 147). This antipathy found its ugliest expression in New York City's draft riot of 1863 and in Philadelphia's voting day riot of 1871 (Lane 1986, p. 10; Bernstein 1990, p. 66). The impulse of Irish-Catholic youth gangs to victimize African Americans became an undeniable element in the century-long cultural transformation of the United States from a haven of Protestant purity to a white republic that included Catholics. Poor Irish immigrants strove to assimilate or, as Noel Ignatiev (1995, pp. 163–76) has put it, to 'become white' by victimizing African Americans. As early as the antebellum period, then, belonging to a white gang facilitated the cultural assimilation of European immigrants.

WHITE YOUTH GANGS IN THE IMMIGRANT CITY, 1880–1940

A significant number of the 13.5 million people who came to the United States from South, Central, and Eastern Europe between 1880 and 1924 settled in the cities of the Northeast and Midwest. The economic hardship and cultural dislocation experienced by many immigrant parents made it difficult for them to adequately discipline their children, let alone supervise their school work or guide them into rewarding employment. Immigrant children, who found themselves caught between the oldworld communal practices of their parents and the norms of an often hostile host society, frequently got together in corner groups and gangs.

White youth gangs in the immigrant city were often multi-ethnic, generally subservient to ward politicians, resolutely territorial, delinquent in varying degrees and virulently racist. In 1927 the country's foremost gang expert, Frederic Thrasher, highlighted the involvement of immigrants in the youth gangs of Chicago. He noted that 70.4 per cent of Chicago's 10-24-year-old males were boys of foreign extraction, while a 'whopping' 87.4 per cent of the city's gangs were gangs of foreign boys. In contrast, 25.7 per cent of Chicago's 10-24-year-old males were American (that is, native white parentage) boys, while a 'miniscule' 5.3 per cent of the city's gangs were gangs of American boys (Thrasher 1936, p. 193, Table 5).

Progressive-era white youth gangs, like their antebellum predecessors, were often multi-ethnic. Thrasher's data include myriad examples of ethnically mixed white gangs. For example, the Tent Gang, which stole tinned goods from railroad cars, was made up of Italian and Polish boys. The Elstons, who fought 'innumerable battles of fists and bricks' against the Polish Belmonts, were Irish and Swedish. The O'Brien Juniors, known for their tradition of initiating new members by 'kicking them around', included Irish, Scottish, and Swedish boys. The Twelfth Street Boundary Gang was composed of Polish, Bohemian and Greek lads. Italian boys were invited to join a Jewish gang in the Maxwell Street area 'because of their compatibility and their residence in the area' (Thrasher 1936, pp. 136, 180, 258, 282, 310).

Thrasher determined the race and ethnicity of 880 out of the 1,313 gangs known to exist in Chicago at the time. If we exclude the sixty-three Negro gangs, the twenty-five mixed Negro-white gangs, and the five miscellaneous gangs, as shown in Table 1, then 787 of these 880 gangs were European-American gangs. Of this number, 351 gangs (or 44.6 per cent) were of mixed European-American ethnicity. Such a large percentage of ethnic mixing within gangs reflected the fact that immigrant Chicago was ethnically heterogeneous. As Thomas Philpott (1978, pp. 139–42) has revealed, the average number of nationalities in Chicago's immigrant neighbourhoods was twenty-two. None of the immigrant groups represented more than 50 per cent of the population in their neighbourhoods, except for the Poles, who constituted 54 per cent of their neighbourhood.

As in the antebellum period, white youth gangs often attached more importance to the defence of territory than to the promotion of the honour of a specific ethnic identity. Feuds between rival white gangs were typically about turf, and so persisted even when the ethnic composition of the feuding gangs changed. Moreover, many white gang boys interviewed by Thrasher expressed an existential disinterest in the question of ethnicity. 'Aw, we never ask what nationality dey are', said a Polish boy. 'If dey are good guys, dey get in our gang. Dat's all we want.' To be sure, ethnicity and territory sometimes converged. For example, Jewish boys in Chicago were at risk when they travelled unprotected through solidly Polish territory (Thrasher 1936, pp. 215, 197). In ethnically polyglot white areas, however, the impetus for gang conflict was usually territorial rather than ethnic.

Table I Race and nationalities (ethnicities) of gangs in Chicago

Race or ethnicity	Number of gangs	Percentage of total gangs
Mixed ethnicities	351	39.89
Polish	148	16.82
Italian	99	11.25
Irish	75	8.52
Negro	63	7.16
American white	45	5.11
Mixed negro-white	25	2.84
Jewish	20	2.27

Slavic	16	1.82
Bohemian	12	1.36
German	8	.91
Swedish	7	.79
Lithuanian	6	.69
Miscellaneous	5	.57
Total	880	100.00

Source: Thrasher (1936, p. 191). The term ethnicity has been substituted for nationality.

Politically powerful adults did not approve of many of the things that white gangs did, such as breaking windows, reporting false fire alarms, cutting cable lines, defacing street signs, disturbing the peace at night, insulting people on the sidewalk, pilfering from stores, breaking into private dwellings, and looting factory yards and construction sites (Philpott 1978, p. 73). Nevertheless, those adults sponsored white street gangs, and rewarded them for playing a key role in neighbourhood defence, especially since urban governments and police forces were weak, ineffective and often corrupt. While adults frowned on activities which undermined the quality of community life, they approved of the youth gang's role in keeping strangers, especially blacks, off their streets and beaches, and out of their parks, baseball diamonds, swimming pools, saloons and dance halls (Spear 1967, p. 206; Kusmer 1976, p. 185).

Ward politicians and street gang leaders often reached a mutually beneficial understanding. The former would pay the rent of an apartment that could serve as a gang clubhouse, while the latter would distribute campaign leaflets, put up posters, hustle up votes, and chase opponents from polling booths on election days. Ward bosses could mitigate the police harassment of gangs, and gangs could turn over a share of the proceeds of their illegal activities.

Local politicians legitimized street gangs by sponsoring neighbourhood athletic clubs. Cook County's Democratic Commissioner, Frank Ragen, set up the Ragen Athletic Club on Chicago's Halsted Street. This club was home to Ragen's Colts, a fighting gang of Irish youth ranging in age from seventeen to thirty. This gang, whose motto was 'Hit me and you hit a thousand', provided a *de facto* policing service for the community. Ragen Colt territory was the Back of the Yards district west of Wentworth Avenue extending south from 43rd to 63rd Street. Any black who made the mistake of crossing Wentworth Avenue risked being seriously injured. In 1918 the poet, Langston Hughes, then a high school student, made this mistake and was badly beaten up. Yet, every working day, thousands of black labourers had to cross Wentworth Avenue and make their way through hostile Irish and Polish streets in order to get to the stockyards (Tuttle 1970, pp. 103, 199).

Youth gangs served as nuclei for the white mob during the race riots in East St. Louis in 1917, Philadelphia in 1918 and Chicago in 1919 (Rudwick 1964, pp. 41–57; Tuttle 1970, pp. 32–66; Franklin 1975, p. 340). The Chicago Commission on Race Relations, which investigated the causes of the city's five-day riot, concluded that 'the riot would not have gone beyond the first clash' were it not for the involvement of local gangs and athletic clubs (1922, pp. 11–17). Members of Ragen's Colts, for example, drove into the Black Belt at night, setting fire to wooden porches and shacks, and firing their guns at the windows and roofs of tenement buildings.

Approximately two-fifths of the violent confrontations between whites and blacks during the Chicago riot occurred in Bridgeport. Young people in this cohesive Irish-Catholic neighbourhood belonged to the Hamburg Social and Athletic Club. The youth gang known as the Hamburgs or Hamburgers were active participants in the street fighting. As the journalist Mike Royko (1971, p. 37) has noted, it is likely that one of the Hamburgs, the seventeen-year-old boy, Richard J. Daley, future mayor of the city, was caught up in the violence.

Another gang active in the riot, the Dirty Dozen, armed themselves with 'revolvers, blackjacks, and knives, and started out to get the "niggers"'. An ex-gang member recounted that about twenty gang members stopped a 'street car filled with colored people' at 35th and State Streets, which was about 'five miles or more from their own territory'. In the ensuing fracas, a 'colored woman' slashed a boy by the name of Shaggy Martin across the heart with a razor. Infuriated by this, the white gang extracted vengeance by killing two blacks and seriously injuring five others (Thrasher 1936, p. 47). This kind of racial violence was an offshoot of the politics of white defensive localism in the cities of the Progressive era.

BLACK YOUTH GANGS IN THE IMMIGRANT CITY, 1880–1940

The immigrant city was the birthplace of the African-American youth gang. Most of our knowledge of the black youth gangs of this period comes from Thrasher's research. Whereas African-American boys accounted for approximately 3.8 per cent of Chicago's total boy population, African-American gangs made up 7.4 per cent of the total number of city gangs (Thrasher 1936, p. 193). The finding that the involvement of African-American boys in gangs was greater than their representation in the overall population of young people makes sense in the light of the fact that they were barred from unionized factory jobs, clerical positions and even unskilled, part-time positions.

Thrasher also found some racial mixing in the gangs of Progressive-era Chicago. As Table 1 reveals, twenty-five of the 880 gangs of known race and ethnicity were mixed 'Negro-white' gangs. Although only 2.8 per cent of the total, this percentage is relatively high when considered in the light of the small number of racially mixed gangs reported in the far more racially segregated cities of the second half of the twentieth century.

To be sure, white ethnic mixing in gangs was far more extensive than racial mixing. As Table 1 shows, 28 per cent (25 of 88) of Chicago's African-American gangs were racially mixed, while 44.6 per cent (351 of 787) of the city's European-American gangs were of mixed white ethnicity. The existence of racially mixed youth gangs was because African Americans often lived interspersed among whites. The arrival of southern blacks in Chicago's Jewish neighborhoods created friction, but 'the Negro boys brought in by this migration', one of Thrasher's informants stated (1936, p. 216), 'are being received in a friendly way by Jewish boys, and Jewish gangs are now fraternizing with the negroes'.

Whereas the white youth gangs of this period derived support from local political authorities and were aggressive in the defence of turf, black youth gangs existed in communities that were not yet large enough or ecologically distinct enough to sanction the vigorous defence of turf.[5] In Washington and Philadelphia, African Americans, many of whom worked as domestic servants, lived in unmapped alleys and streets behind the elegant houses of their white employers (Borchert 1980, p. 135; Lane 1986, p. 21). In New York, prior to the black settlement of Harlem in the 1910s, African Americans lived on many different blocks between 20th and 63rd Streets (Osofsky 1966, p. 12). On Chicago's South Side, less than a dozen blocks were 'entirely Negro' in 1910 (Spear 1967, p. 20). 'We have no LITTLE AFRICA in Cleveland,' an African-American clerk boasted in 1915. 'There is not yet a single street in this city that is inhabited by nothing but Negroes' (Kusmer 1976, p. 42). As late as 1930, following two decades of migration from the South, blacks were widely dispersed throughout Pittsburgh (Gottlieb 1987, pp. 66–67). In the same year, most of Milwaukee's blacks lived in white residential areas (Trotter 1985, p. 67). In none of these cities was the black population large enough for the formation of territorially aggressive black youth gangs. In the 1919 Chicago riot, according to the Commission investigating its causes, African-American gangs played an insignificant and largely defensive role (1922, pp. 11–17).

The exclusion of African Americans from urban political structures, their subordinate role in organized crime and the hostility of predominantly white police forces also inhibited the rise of turf-defending black street gangs. The white business elite, real estate developers, city politicians, police forces and dominant figures in organized crime conspired to locate the vice industry in areas of the city that were inhabited by large numbers of black people.[6] Yet, the illegal economy associated with prostitution, gambling and the provision of bootleg alcohol was largely controlled by whites. In Chicago's 'Levee', Detroit's 'Paradise Valley', or Cleveland's 'Roaring Third', white crime syndicates hired young black males to work as bouncers in speakeasies, as lookouts in brothels, and as numbers runners. Black entrepreneurs who attempted to establish their own rackets were ruthlessly suppressed. In Harlem, for example, Dutch Schultz relied on the police to wrest control of the policy racket away from Stephanie St. Clair (Schatzberg and Kelly 1996, p. 90). The racial order upheld by corrupt politicians, police forces, and white criminal syndicates permitted neither collective forms of illegality by black adults nor the aggressive defence of turf by black youth.

White youth gangs at mid-century continued to defend turf and uphold the racial order, and derive support for doing so from political leaders and organized crime figures. Ethnically heterogeneous areas continued to produce ethnically mixed gangs. Irish, Italian, Polish, Serbian and Mexican boys who lived on the same block or street in South Chicago joined the same gang and fought similarly mixed gangs from other blocks (Kornblum 1974, p. 74). In New York's Spanish Harlem, one particular Italian gang included 'maybe twenty guys who were Puerto Rican' (Wakefield 1957, p. 126). In Boston's Roxbury, the Senior Bandits and the Outlaws were predominantly Irish Catholic, but also included a few Protestants of British ancestry, French Canadians, and Italians (Miller 1969, pp. 16–20).

Elsewhere in Boston, the intermarriage of Irish and Italian families affected gang fighting. For many years, Charlestown's Irish-American gangs had been at feud with Italian-American youth from the North End. The bridge across the river was the site of battles which dragged on for hours and involved hundreds of adolescents armed with bottles, two-by-fours (timber planks), and slingshots. With the intermarriage of Irish and Italian families, however, Italian families began to settle in Charlestown. Thereafter Charlestown's residents began to view 'the Champas, Saccos, and Castranovas as "our Italians" or "white Italians" to distinguish them from "the goddamned Italians" across the bridge' (Lukas 1985, p. 155).

The traditional role which white youth gangs played in neighbourhood defence became more important during the 1950s when the influx of southern blacks created a tidal wave of urban racial transition.[7] Adults seeking to keep their neighbourhoods white formed neighbourhood improvement and homeowners' associations which mobilized youth gangs to do much of their dirty work. In the housing riots which occurred in the Chicago neighbourhoods of Fernwood and Englewood in 1947 and 1949, roving youth gangs terrorized the South Side, hauling blacks off streetcars and attacking University of Chicago students assumed to be sympathetic to racial desegregation (Hirsch 1983, p. 54). White youth gangs targeted black teenagers in neighbourhoods like Oakland, Kenwood, Hyde Park, Woodlawn, Park Manor and Englewood that were undergoing partial or complete racial transition. In the early 1960s, a large white gang attacked participants in the so-called 'wade-ins'—protests against the segregation of Chicago's beaches. This kind of activity was supported by adults. Gang boys who chased black pedestrians out of their neighbourhoods were, James Short and Fred Strodtbeck (1965, pp. 193, 114) noted, 'spurred on to greater efforts by adults of the area who offered advice and encouragement'.

In Detroit, white homeowners' associations relied on youth support in their militant response to racial change. When a black family purchased a home in a white neighbourhood, youth gangs could be counted on to throw stones and bottles at the newcomer's house, pile garbage on his lawn, block his driveway or slash his tires (Sugrue 1996, pp. 247–58). During the late 1950s, in what was then still the Italian section of Manhattan on the Upper East Side, much of the gang fighting was, according to a local settlement house worker, 'a reflection of the insecurity of the adults, who felt very hostile toward the Puerto Ricans and Negroes' who were moving in (Spergel 1964, p. 64). In mid-1960s Brooklyn, white adults moving out of Crown Heights, East Flatbush, Brownsville, Bushwick and Red Hook sanctioned youth gang violence directed at minority newcomers. Italian youth gangs in East New York vandalized a black realty office and grocery store, and armed themselves with lug wrenches to keep blacks off their streets and out of their parks (Connolly 1977, p. 134).

White street gangs were active at Chrysler Corporation's Dodge Main Plant in Detroit's Hamtramck municipality during the 1950s. The local chapter of the United Automobile Workers, in its efforts to uphold male white supremacy, 'drew support from neighborhood street gang members who had taken work in the plant' (Boyle 1997, p. 507). However, the usual way for white street gangs to uphold white supremacy was by terrorizing black newcomers in neighbourhoods threatened with racial change. In this regard, multi-ethnic white gangs signified that social solidarity among whites at mid-century was increasingly founded on a common identification with territory rather than on a particularistic identification with a specific European ethnic or cultural heritage (Kornblum and Beshers 1988, p. 219).

AFRICAN-AMERICAN YOUTH GANGS IN THE RACIALLY CHANGING CITY, 1940–1970

The rapidly growing urban black population led to an increase in the number of African-American youth gangs.[8] With the creation of large areas of concentrated black poverty, black youth gangs began to defend themselves and enter adjoining white territory. However, extreme ghettoization ultimately cut black youth off from white areas of the city so that black youth gangs began to prey on each other. While black gang boys received moral support from adults for defending turf, they received little concrete political or economic support because of the relative powerlessness of adults in disadvantaged black communities. The exclusion of black youth from legal jobs as well as from opportunities in white controlled criminal syndicates resulted in an increase in violent gang feuding among black youth.

Initially, the geographic expansion of the black ghettos led to an increase in fighting between black and white youth gangs. As early as the 1940s, teenagers in Detroit's densely populated ghetto, Paradise Valley, hung out on street corners and got into fights with white gangs in parks and playgrounds (Thomas 1992, p. 119). During the 1943 riot, black youth gangs adopted the same tactics that white gangs had traditionally used against black people. They assaulted white students and factory workers returning home on streetcars, and they hurled bricks at unsuspecting white motorists (Lee and Humphrey 1943, p. 28). In Chicago, black youth were no longer the passive victims of white violence. In 1957, when a white gang killed a black youth at 59th Street and Kedzie, black gangs retaliated and seriously assaulted twelve whites (Hirsch 1983, p. 291). Black gangs increasingly challenged whites over the use of streets, bridges, beaches, parks, school playgrounds, restaurants, ballrooms and roller rinks. Black teenagers on Chicago's South Side took on the Diablos, a white gang which tried to keep them out of the Capitol Theater. Reminiscing about the night his gang fought their way into the theatre, a former gang member, interviewed for the film *The Promised Land* (1995), remarked ironically, 'that was my first experience of integration'.

However, one effect of the doubling of black spatial isolation in northern cities between 1930 and 1970 was that turf-oriented black youth gangs became increasingly likely to prey on each other (Massey and Denton 1993, p. 46) .[9] Turf rivalries on Chicago's West Side enmeshed the Imperial Chaplins and the Clovers, forerunners of the Vice Lords and the Egyptian Cobras (Perkins 1987, p. 28). Black-on-black gang warfare was endemic to the massive public housing estates constructed in the middle of slum neighbourhoods. One of wartime Chicago's largest youth gangs, the Deacons, was born in the Ida B. Wells housing project just a few years after its completion in 1941. The Deacons took on the Destroyers, who lived to the north of the projects, and the 13 Cats, who occupied the area south of Oakwood Boulevard (idem). From the Governor Henry Horner Homes, a project which opened on the Near West Side in 1957, the Vice Lords and Black Souls, a faction of the Devil's Disciples, fought with white gangs located in the neighbourhood to the north. When the whites moved away, the Vice Lords and Black Souls fought each other (Kotlowitz 1991, p. 18). In the early 1960s, Devil's Disciples, Blackstone Rangers, and Vice Lords began to carve up sections of the twomile-long, quarter-of-a-mile-wide strip of twenty-eight identical sixteen-storey buildings along State Street that comprised the Robert Taylor Homes (Lemann 1991, p. 226).

As the population of vast areas of Philadelphia's north side became exclusively black in the 1960s, gang fighting became increasingly intraracial. In 1973, for example, two North Philadelphia gangs, the Valley gang and the Norris Street gang, fought over an abandoned area known as the 'graveyard' which consisted of '3 or 4 acres of smashed brick and twisted tailpipe' (Lieber 1975, p. 42). In Los Angeles, conflict-oriented black gangs began to form in the housing projects in Watts during the 1950s. A little farther north in the Florence/Firestone district, which was undergoing racial transition, the Slausons emerged partly in response to attacks by whites on defenseless blacks. However, white flight led to turf-and honour-based rivalries between the Slausons and various Watts gangs. A few years after the formation of the first Crip gang in 1969, marauding Crips, belonging to different sets, such as the West Side Crips, Main Street

Crips and Grape Street Watts Crips, began to victimize youth living on Piru Street in Compton, who then banded together for protection. The Pirus, Brims, Bishops, Blood Fives, Swans, and other gangs formed the nucleus of the Blood Nation. By the early 1980s not only were Crips fighting Bloods, but different Crip sets were also locked in deadly turf and honour-based feuds (Valentine 1995, pp. 45–50; Quicker and Batani-Khalfani 1998, pp. 18–20).

Extreme racial segregation in Chicago, Milwaukee, St. Louis and Cleveland has virtually eliminated confrontations between black and white youth gangs (Dawley 1973; Hagedorn 1988; Decker and Van Winkle 1996; Huff 1996). In New York, however, black-white gang violence has persisted in places where black housing projects were built near white working-class neighbourhoods. In South Brooklyn, for example, the proximity of the predominantly black Red Hook Houses to Carroll Gardens, an Italian neighbourhood of brownstones, has been the source of more than thirty years of inter-racial youth violence (Barron 1997; Martin 1997).

The increased violence associated with gang fighting in impoverished African-American neighbourhoods can be traced to growing joblessness among youth, especially in cities like Philadelphia, Cleveland, Detroit and St. Louis. Another reason why a destructive conflict subculture began to emerge among African-American youth was that opportunities for illegal work as bouncers or numbers runners declined. By 1940 Italian gangsters had seized control of numbers gambling in Boston, New York, Philadelphia, Cleveland and Detroit, and, in 1952, Sam 'Mooney' Giancana took over Chicago's lucrative black-operated policy racket (Pinderhughes 1987, p. 147; Schatzberg and Kelly 1996, pp. 78,102). The failure of black street gangs during the 1950s and 1960s to develop into criminal organizations, or even to provide major services to white criminal organizations, reflected their inability to influence the operation of crime or to launder money because of the political and economic marginality of urban black communities (Ianni 1974).

Richard Cloward and Lloyd Ohlin were among the first sociologists to recognize, in their influential book, *Delinquency and Opportunity* (1960), that social disorganization and community breakdown brought about by political and economic marginality tend to decrease the involvement of youth in income-producing illegality and increase their participation in gang-fighting. A weakened community fabric, they argued, increases the degree to which gang youth resort to violence to win social status. Their argument was empirically extended by Irving Spergel (1963, p. 250), who discovered that sophisticated, income-producing forms of youth crime, such as burglary, larceny and narcotics selling, were more frequent on Chicago's South Side, whereas crimes of violence, such as murder, manslaughter, assault and robbery, occurred more frequently among youthful offenders on the West Side. Gangs on the South Side, a much older, established ghetto community, engaged in criminally oriented behaviour, whereas the trend on the newly settled and rapidly growing West Side pointed towards a future in which growing numbers of black youth, unable to find legal work and excluded from illegitimate economic opportunities, would participate in turfand honour-based gang violence.

The social scientists who undertook detailed studies of gang delinquency during the 1950s and early 1960s recognized that the greater social disorganization of black neighbourhoods made it more difficult for adults to control the violence of young people. Spergel (1964, pp. 40–43) compared patterns of delinquency in Slumtown, a structurally isolated, mixed Puerto Rican and African-American ghetto in Manhattan north of 100th Street and east of Fifth Avenue, with those in Racketville, an Italian section of Manhattan north of 86th Street between Second Avenue and the East River. He found that 'bopping' or gang fighting was four times more frequent in Slumtown. Not only were parents in Slumtown unable to help their children find either legal or illegal jobs, they were also unable to supervise their children's activities at school and in the street.

Whereas the youth of Slumtown resorted to fighting as a means of achieving 'rep', the Italian youth of closely knit Racketville rarely fought among themselves. As a local street-club worker reported, these kids may decide every few months to go out and get a "spick," but there isn't a constant tension or pressure to participate in a gang fight as in other neighborhoods. Fighting isn't the usual subject of conversation among the Italian kids (Spergel 1964, p. 41).

Racketville's white youth gangs were discouraged from fighting each other by politically powerful adults. Moreover, those adults, some of whom were affiliated with locally tolerated organized crime families, rewarded youth gangs and street-corner groups for upholding the racial order by chasing Puerto Ricans and blacks out of Racketville. A similar situation existed in Chicago's white neighbourhoods (Short and Strodtbeck 1965, pp. 107–14).

The behaviour of white and African-American youth gangs during the 1960s reflected the profound differences in the social organization of white and black neighbourhoods. The journalist Walter Bernstein (1968), in a 1957 article in *The New Yorker,* described how local community resources, such as the availability of the American Legion Hall for dances, were effectively used to discourage Italian-American gangs from fighting in the Park Slope neighbourhood of Brooklyn. Adults in socially organized, resource-rich white communities were able to control the violent excesses of their young people, whereas the growing joblessness, political powerlessness and social disorganization of inner-city black neighbourhoods made it far more difficult for adults in those neighbourhoods to prevent young people from fighting over turf and honour.

Continued suburbanization during the 1970s and 1980s decreased the number of white youth gang members relative to minority youth gang members.[10] Nevertheless, just as in previous eras, white youth gangs and corner groups were positively sanctioned by politically powerful adults for their role in upholding the racial order. During the late 1970s in South Philadelphia, members of a white youth gang called the Counts, according to a local informant, 'had the blessing and support of their parents' when they attacked blacks who ventured into their turf (Skogan 1990, p. 25). The people of Canarsie, an Italian-Jewish enclave in South Brooklyn, who, in 1972, objected to the busing of African-American children from Brownsville, approved of youth groups who armed themselves with iron pipes and heavy sticks and attacked 'blacks they took to be suspiciously out of place' (Reider 1985, p. 179).

Similar incidents occurred in Boston during that city's busing crisis of the mid-1970s. Charlestown's notorious Green Store Gang won approval from adults in the community for intimidating black families living in the Bunker Hill projects and adjacent Charles Newton development (Lukas 1985, pp. 157–8). In Dorchester, four street-corner gangs—the Roseland Street gang, the Shawmut Station gang, the Mather Street gang and the Wainright Park gang—tried to force a black family, the Debnams, out of the neighbourhood. The boys in these gangs did what the adults in the neighbourhood wished they could do but felt self-conscious about doing. They drove by the Debnam's house at all hours honking and shouting racial slurs, threw rocks and bottles through their windows, exploded firebombs in their driveway, and removed planks of wood from their fence. The boys recalled that the community had failed to defend itself 'when their parents lived west of Washington Street', and vowed that this time they would not 'let the colored push us out' (Lukas 1985, p. 525).

In the Bensonhurst section of Brooklyn, an 80 per cent white neighbourhood which experienced significant job loss and a decline in its Italian population during the 1980s, white youth gangs upheld the racial order (Alba 1995, p. 12). In the 1990s, Bensonhurst's Avenue T Boys specialized in the practice of going on 'missions'.[11] 'That's when,' as one boy described it, 'you go look for people who don't belong in the neighborhood and you beat 'em up. Sometimes we go out lookin' for blacks to jump. Sometimes we look for anybody who ain't supposed to be there'. Another boy revealed that by 'taking care of people who don't belong in the neighborhood, you get respect. Especially if it is some of the blacks from the Marlboro projects' (Pinderhughes 1997, pp. 132, 134).

The adult population within communities like Bensonhurst and Charlestown, besides sanctioning youth gangs for upholding the racial order, strove to curb gang behaviour, such as petty theft, vandalism, disorderly conduct and drug dealing, which detracted from the quality of life in the neighbourhood. Their ability to do so was facilitated by their political influence, their close ties with local police forces, and, most important, their economic power. White parents used their contacts with neighbours and local employers to get their children jobs and keep them out of trouble. The father of one of the Avenue T Boys, for example, owned a construction business and hired his son and other gang members (Pinderhughes 1997, p. 57). Even in economically declining blue-collar neighbourhoods, then, white adults were rarely so cut off from the labour market that they were unable to find entry-level jobs for their children. Boys with jobs were more likely to leave the gang in their early twenties, and the youth gang itself was less likely to be a troublesome presence.

BLACK YOUTH GANGS IN THE HYPERSEGREGATED CITY, 1970–1999

Since 1970 one effect of declining manufacturing and service employment on black ghettos is that black youth gangs have become far more troublesome. Between 1970 and 1982, the number of black men aged between 18 and 29 in the country's central cities who were either unemployed or marginally attached to the labour force increased from 24 per cent to 54 per cent (Lichter 1988, p. 782). The growing concentration of joblessness in increasingly segregated African-American ghettos has meant that black parents have been less effective than white parents in finding jobs for their children (Sullivan 1989, p. 74; Kasinitz and Rosenberg 1996, p. 187). Moreover, the kinds of job available to young inner-city black males are typically poorly paid, part-time positions in the secondary labour market which fail to insulate them from the influence of gangs (Crutchfield 1995, p. 205).

Black male joblessness, which more than doubled levels of ghetto poverty during the 1970s, has also disrupted family and community life (Lynn and McGeary 1990). The withdrawal or breakdown of government services in jobless ghettos has aggravated the difficulties which impoverished African-American parents face in caring for, supervising and educating their children (Sampson 1987; Anderson 1990).[12] The fact that policing policies in places like North Philadelphia have been lax, on the one hand, or irrationally severe, on the other, has created an atmosphere of danger on the streets, giving rise to a code of violence and legitimizing the tendency of young men to join a corner group of running buddies or a street gang for physical protection and psychological peace of mind (Anderson 1998, p. 81).[13]

The vast majority (84 per cent) of the gang members in St. Louis interviewed by Decker and Van Winkle (1996, p. 65) said they joined a gang because they found it impossible to live without some form of protection against the violence of rival gangs in nearby neighbourhoods. Young males growing up in underpoliced housing estates are most likely to live in fear of assault. A boy who joined Chicago's Black Disciples at the age of fifteen explained:

Around here, if you're not in a gang, they still think you're in a gang. You can't walk to school. You can't go where you want, when you want, so you might as well be in a gang. Then at least when trouble starts, you ain't by yourself. You got some aid and assistance (Terry 1994, p. A26).

Police have also contributed to the inner-city gang problem by the harshness and irrationality of certain of their responses (Tonry 1995, pp. 105–16; Miller 1996, pp. 80–86). William Chambliss (1994) has described policing and sentencing policies in Washington, DC whereby deproletarianized black males were repeatedly arrested and given long prison sentences for minor drug offences. Blacks have been five times more likely than whites to be arrested for drug-related offences, and thus account for much of the nearly fourfold increase in the proportion of drug offenders in US prisons—from 5.7 per cent in 1979 to 21.5 per cent in 1991 (Sampson and Lauritsen 1997, pp. 327, 354). The incarceration of adults has hurt black teenagers by depriving them of parental guidance at home, and the incarceration of teenagers has led directly to their future job-lessness by isolating them from job networks and exposing them to the gangs operating behind bars. The mutually reinforcing effects of joblessness, incarceration and gang involvement have made it increasingly difficult for gang members to 'age out' of black street gangs (Hagedorn 1988; 1994a; 1998).

Adult authority has been particularly powerless in curbing gang violence in African-American housing projects. Certainly the fact that women and children comprise over 90 per cent of the population of many housing estates has made it easy for young male gang members to intimidate tenants. But the real reason why tenants have found it difficult to stand up to gangs is that they cannot rely on the social services of city and county governments. Whereas parents in white communities have relied on social workers, school teachers, truant officers and the police to deal with troublesome youth, African-American parents living in isolated housing projects have discovered that so-cial workers, school teachers and truant officers are often reluctant to visit, and city and housing police are often incompetent. In the early 1990s tenants at Chicago's Robert Taylor Homes felt that gangs did a better job of protecting them than did the housing police.

At least the gangs is giving us something, so lot of us prefers to help them 'cause we can *always* go to them and tell them to stop the shooting. Police don't do anything for us and they can't stop no shooting anyway (quoted in Venkatesh 1997, p. 95).

Parents in many of Chicago's housing projects have been unable to insulate their children from gang sniper fire, or prevent gangs from commandeering apartments as places to store weapons and stash drugs (Venkatesh 1996, p. 250; Belluck 1997, p. A1).

Because of the breakdown of public services, some gangs have taken on a *de facto* community service role. As early as the 1960s, the Blackstone Rangers helped to pay the rents of the destitute elderly and obtained medical service for prostitutes (Sale 1971, p. 76). Since then, gangs have tried to provide a range of welfare, maintenance and recreational services. They have repaired apartments, sponsored picnics, barbecues and basketball tournaments, paid bail bonds for people in trouble with the law, and purchased groceries, clothing and sneakers for needy children (Kotlowitz 1988; Venkatesh 1997, p. 101).

African-American street gangs have progressed further in the direction of organized crime in Chicago than in the larger, less rigidly segregated, and more ethnically diverse cities of New York and Los Angeles. Over the years, the FBI and local agencies of law enforcement have targeted Jimmie Lee's Conservative Vice Lords, Larry Hoover's Black Gangster Disciples, and Jeff Fort's Black P. Stone Nation, a branch of which evolved into the criminal mob known as El Rukns, for their involvement in prostitution, drug-selling, gambling, theft, intimidation and extortion (Spergel 1995, p. 45; Schatzberg and Kelly 1996, pp. 200–4). Although unable to corrupt a white-controlled police force, Chicago street gangs have increasingly left their imprint on local politics. As Kotlowitz (1991, p. 39) noted, politicians aligned with one gang have not been safe on the turf of a rival gang.

One of Chicago's most powerful gang leaders, who derived much of his income from illegal activities occurring at rundown housing projects, made his home in a solidly middle-class black neighbourhood (Pattillo 1998). In this respect, he resembles Italian mafia leaders who have purchased homes in quiet residential districts. Despite this similarity, it would stretch the meaning of the term to suggest that black street gangs in Chicago or other American cities have become a mafia. At best, they are a proto-mafia. While the spread of the illegal drug economy has blurred the boundaries between organized drug gangs and turf-defending street gangs, the consensus among criminologists is that most African-American street gangs lack the organizational structure, leadership and discipline needed to operate highly sophisticated illegal drug manufacturing and selling businesses.[14]

The name of one of Chicago's street gangs, the Vice Lords, conveys the nature of much African-American organized crime. Vice or vicerelated illegality is contingent on a form of lordship—the military capacity to use violence or the threat of violence to control territory. In the 1990s, for example, Larry Hoover required heroin and crack-dealing individuals and crews operating in Gangster Disciple turf to 'devote one day a week to selling drugs strictly for him' (Terry 1997, p. 12). The Italian and Jewish syndicates of the 1920s were unable to completely prevent bloodshed related to factional disputes over the extraction of tributary surplus from illegal operations. Black street gangs have been even less successful in preventing bloodshed, especially since 1985. In Milwaukee, a surge in gang-related violence during the 1990s resulted from battles to control the cocaine market (Hagedorn 1998, p. 95). In Chicago, two 'brother gangs' that were not traditionally in dispute—the Black Gangster Disciples and the Black Disciples—quarrelled over drug markets, resulting in forty-five feud-related homicides between 1987 and 1994 (Block *et al.* 1996, pp. 11–12).[15]

The relative organizational weakness of contemporary African-American street gangs, their orientation towards extracting tribute from small-scale, local illegal operators and the intensity of their fights over turf are indicative of the fact that African-American neighbourhoods remain ghettoized and excluded from both legitimate and illegitimate opportunity structures.

CONCLUSION

Over the last two hundred years, white youth gangs have facilitated the cultural assimilation of non-Hispanic European immigrants into American society. Irish Catholic, German, Swedish, Polish, Bohemian, Slovak, Lithuanian, Jewish, Italian, Serbian and Greek boys internalized from the culture of the ethnically mixed gang a sense of whiteness and Americanness. For white immigrants, the youth gang facilitated cultural assimilation because of its close ties with formal and informal political authorities and organizations which commanded substantial political and economic power. For African Americans, in contrast, the youth gang has reinforced cultural separation because of its embeddedness in racially segregated, economically marginalized and politically powerless communities.

Black youth gangs only appeared with the shift from caste- to class-specific forms of segregation which did not really get underway until the second quarter of the twentieth century. Racially mixed gangs were rare in Thrasher's day, and, with increasing racial segregation since then, have become even more rare. Since 1950 continuous economic restructuring resulting from deindustrialization and commercial disinvestment has progressively weakened institutions of social control in the poorest urban black neighbourhoods. Lacking access to the organizational resources available to white parents, African-American parents and community leaders have found it difficult to curb youth gang violence. This was the case during the crack-related epidemic of violence which spread throughout the inner cities in the late 1980s.

The evidence of this article shows, first, that the causes of this epidemic were structural, not cultural; and, second, that a cultural predisposition towards violence has been far more characteristic of white than black youth gangs. African-American youth gangs have certainly resorted to violence in coping with social and cultural structures of racism and class oppression, but these same structures have been continuously reinforced by white youth gangs which, in performing their role in neighbourhood defence, have engaged in much socially harmful, violent and vicious conduct.

ACKNOWLEDGMENTS

I am grateful to an anonymous *ERS* reviewer for a helpful critique, and thank Arnold Hirsch, Irving Spergel, Walter Miller, John Quicker, Joan Moore, and Frederick Wright for responding to my requests for information. Tom Finlay, librarian at the Centre of Criminology, University of Toronto, kindly obtained research material through Interlibrary loan.

NOTES

1. I use the terms youth gang and street gang interchangeably. A great deal of youth or street gang activity is non-delinquent. Some scholars (for example, Klein 1995, p. 75) insist that a predisposition towards law-violating behaviour be a defining element of the youth or street gang. Others (for example, Short, Jr. 1997, pp. 81–2) do not. Walter B. Miller (1982) introduced the term 'law-violating youth group' to cover the countless cliques, crews, crowds, bands, rings and groups of three or more associates or running buddies which are not recognized as youth or street gangs by urban police forces.

2. See, for example, discussions by Miller (1969), Suttles (1969; 1972), Spergel (1984; 1986), Bursik and Grasmik (1993, p. 134).

3. The word 'white' in this article refers only to persons of non-Hispanic European background. On the links between the country's various Latino ethnicities and cultures and youth gangs, see Moore (1978; 1991); Horowitz (1983); Vigil (1988); Sullivan (1989); Sanchez-Jankowski (1991) and Padilla (1992). On the impacts of residential segregation, economic restructuring and government neglect on Latino communities and their youth gangs, see Moore and Pinderhughes (1993); Moore and Vigil (1993); Chincilla, Hamilton, and Loucky (1993); and Sullivan (1993).

4. In pointing out that some antebellum youth gangs were multi-ethnic, I am not denying the existence of violent conflict between nativist and Irish Catholic gangs. One of Philadelphia's powerful nativist gangs, the Shifflers, named itself after George Shiffler, a nativist political leader who was killed during the Kensington riots of 1844. This disturbance also radicalized the Schuylkill Rangers, one of the city's violent Irish Catholic gangs (Clark 1973, p. 11; Laurie 1980, p. 151).

5. In 1920 African Americans accounted for 7.4 per cent, 4.3 per cent, 4.1 per cent, 4 per cent, and 2.7 per cent of the populations of Philadelphia, Cleveland, Detroit, Chicago and New York respectively (Osofsky 1966, p. 128; Spear 1967, p. 16; Kusmer 1976, p. 10; Lane 1986, p. 7; Thomas 1992, p. 26).

6. On the zoning of vice in black areas of New York, Chicago, Detroit, Cleveland, Pittsburgh, Milwaukee and Philadelphia, see, respectively, Osofsky (1966, p. 14);

Spear (1967, p. 25); Katzman (1973, p. 171); Kusmer (1976, p. 48); Bodnar, Simon and Weber (1982, p. 227); Trotter (1985, p. 24); Lane (1986, p. 122).

7. From 1950 to 1960, the percentage of African Americans in northern cities increased dramatically, from 18 to 29 per cent in Philadelphia, from 16 to 29 per cent in both Cleveland and Detroit, and from 14 to 23 per cent in Chicago (Massey and Denton 1993, p. 45).

8. By 1970 African Americans accounted for 21 per cent of the population of New York City, around 33 per cent of the population of both Philadelphia and Chicago, 38 per cent, 41 per cent, and 44 per cent of Cleveland's, St. Louis' and Detroit's populations, respectively, 54 per cent of Newark's population, and 71 per cent of the population of Washington, DC (US Bureau of Census 1975, p. 23).

9. For an analysis of how the public housing, urban renewal, and highway building initiatives taken by governments and the private sector ghettoized African Americans during the 1950s and 1960s, see Bowly (1978), Hirsch (1983), Goldstein and Yancey (1986), Bauman (1987), Massey and Kanaiaupuni (1993), Mohl (1993), Kusmer (1995), Sugrue (1996). For an analysis of how suburbanization and suburban shopping mall construction siphoned off tax revenue and eroded the fabric of the central cities, leading to housing deterioration and abandonment, see Taub, Taylor and Dunham (1984, pp. 6–7); Jackson (1985, p. 284); Darden et al (1987, p. 24); Miller and Wheeler (1990, p. 159); Lazare (1991, p. 270); Wilson (1996, pp. 34–50).

10. Curry (1995, n.p. Table 10) reviewed surveys of recent law enforcement data on the race and ethnicity of gang members in the United States, and concluded that between 1975 and 1992 white gang membership declined from 8.8 to 4.4 per cent of total gang membership, while African-American gang membership remained constant at about 48 per cent. Interpretation of these data is problematic, since the surveys defined gangs differently and were not based on random samples.

11. This name is fictitious. The gang's real name did, however, derive from the turf it defended. Although loosely organized and lacking a leadership hierarchy, specialized roles, and initiation rites, this gang was well-known throughout the metropolitan area. It was 'a community institution, having existed for years, with its membership being continually regenerated by the newer, younger members of the community' (Pinderhughes 1997, p. 54).

12. On housing abandonment, unsafe buildings, inadequate trash collection, the withdrawal of fire and ambulance services, underfunded schools and the closing of libraries, parks and recreational facilities, see Wallace (1990a; 1990b); Skogan (1990, p. 36); Weir (1994, p. 337); Kelley (1997, pp. 49–53).

13. At Chicago's Robert Taylor Homes during the late 1970s, city police officers rarely got out of their cars after dark (Lemann 1991, pp. 295–7). At Chicago's Henry Horner Homes during the 1980s, the city police frequently ignored reports of gang shootings (Kotlowitz 1991, p. 18). In North St. Louis during the early 1990s, officers in the 5th

Police District freely admitted that they did not always respond to calls from residents, and often failed to file reports or follow up on assaults and vandalism (Ward 1997, p. 183).

14. See Fagan (1989); Klein, Maxson and Cunningham (1991); Hagedorn (1994b); Maxson (1995). Decker and Van Winkle (1996, p. 153) reported that gang involvement in drug selling in St. Louis during the early 1990s was 'generally poorly organized, episodic, non-monopolistic, carried out by individuals and cliques on their own' and never the gang's raison d'être. Hagedorn (1998, p. 391) concluded that Milwaukee's black street gangs, despite their increasing involvement in drug dealing between 1988 and 1993, were not likely to mutate into organized criminal syndicates. For a description of Detroit's specialized drug gangs, see Mieczkowski (1986); Taylor (1990); Adler (1995).

15. African-American gangs have also feuded with Hispanic-American gangs in areas where the two groups live in relatively close proximity. In Los Angeles, for example, fighting between the African-American Venice Shoreline Crips and the Hispanic-American Culver City Boys resulted in eleven deaths during the summer of 1997 (New York Times, 20 June 1999, "Courts in Los Angeles Help Fight Gang Crime").

REFERENCES

ADLER, WILLIAM M., 1985. *Land of Opportunity*, New York: Atlantic Monthly Press ALBA, RICHARD D., 1995. "Assimilation's quiet tide", *The Public Interest*, no. 119, pp. 3–18

ANDERSON, ELIJAH, 1990. *Streetwise: Race, Class, and Change in an Urban Community*, Chicago, IL: University of Chicago Press 1998. "The social ecology of youth violence", in Michael Tonry and Mark H. Moore (eds), *Youth Violence. Crime and Justice: A Review of Research*, Chicago, IL: University of Chicago Press, vol. 24, pp. 65–104.

ASBURY, HERBERT, 1928. *The Gangs of New York*, New York: Knopf

BARRON, JAMES, 1997. "Beating shatters a fragile Brooklyn truce", *The New York Times*, 23 September, p. C27

BAUMAN, JOHN F., 1987. *Public Housing, Race, and Renewal: Urban Planning in Philadelphia, 1920–1974*, Philadelphia, PA: Temple University Press

BELLUCK, PAM, 1997. "Chicago school in gang crossfire tries to duck but not run", *The New York Times*, 17 November, p. A1.

BERNSTEIN, IVER, 1990. *The New York City Draft Riots*, New York: Oxford University Press.

BERNSTEIN, WALTER, 1968. "The cherubs are rumbling", (first published in *The New Yorker*, 1957), in James F. Short, Jr. (ed), *Gang Delinquency and Delinquent Subcultures*, New York: Harper & Row, pp. 22–55.

BLOCK, CAROLYN, CHRISTAKOS, ANTIGONE, JACOB, AYAD and PRZYBYL-SKI, ROG-ER, 1996. "Street gangs and crime: patterns and trends in Chicago", Chicago, IL: Illinois Criminal Justice Information Authority

BODNAR, JOHN, SIMON, ROGER and WEBER, MICHAEL P., 1982. *Lives of Their Own: Blacks, Italians, and Poles in Pittsburgh, 1900–1960*, Urbana, IL: University of Illinois Press.

BORCHERT, JAMES, 1980. *Alley Life in Washington: Family, Community, Religion, and Folk life in the City, 1850–1970*, Urbana, IL: University of Illinois Press

BOWLY, JR., DEVEREUX, 1978. *The Poorhouse: Subsidized Housing in Chicago, 1895–1976*, Carbondale, IL: Southern Illinois University Press

BOYLE, KEVIN, 1997. "The kiss: racial and gender conflict in a 1950s automobile factory", *Journal of American History*, vol. 84, no. 2, pp. 496–523

BURSIK, JR., ROBERT J. and GRASMIK, HAROLD G., 1993. *Neighborhoods and Crime*, New York: Lexington

CHAMBLISS, WILLIAM J., 1994. "Policing the ghetto underclass: the politics of law and law enforcement", *Social Problems*, vol. 41, no. 2, pp. 177–94

CHICAGO COMMISSION ON RACE RELATIONS, 1922. *The Negro in Chicago*, Chicago, IL: University of Chicago Press

CHINCHILLA, NORMA, HAMILTON, NORA and LOUCKY, JAMES, 1993. "Central Americans in Los Angeles: an immigrant community in transition," in Joan W. Moore and Raquel Pinderhughes, (eds), *In the Barrios: Latinos and the Underclass Debate*, New York: Russell Sage, pp. 51–78

CLARK, DENNIS J., 1973. *The Irish in Philadelphia*, Philadelphia, PA: Temple University Press.

CLOWARD, RICHARD A. and OHLIN, LLOYD E., 1960. *Delinquency and Opportunity*, New York: Free Press

CONNOLLY, HAROLD X., 1977. *A Ghetto Grows in Brooklyn*, New York: New York University Press

CRUTCHFIELD, ROBERT D., 1995. "Ethnicity, labor markets and crime", in Darnell F. Hawkins, (ed.), *Ethnicity, Race, and Crime*, Albany, NY: SUNY Press, pp. 194–211

CURRY, G. D., 1995. "National youth gang surveys: a review of methods and findings", *Report Prepared for the National Youth Gang Center*, December, Tallahassee, Florida

DARDEN, JOE T., HILL, RICHARD C, THOMAS, JUNE and THOMAS, RICHARD, 1987. *Detroit: Race and Uneven Development*, Philadelphia, PA: Temple University Press

DAVIS, SUSAN G., 1982. "Making night hideous": Christmas revelry and public order in nineteenth-century Philadelphia", *American Quarterly*, vol. 34, no. 2, pp. 185–99

DAWLEY, DAVID, 1973. *A Nation of Lords: The Autobiography of the Vice Lords*, Garden City, NY: Anchor

DECKER, SCOTT H. and VAN WINKLE, BARRIK, 1996. *Life in the Gang*, New York: Cambridge University Press

FAGAN, JEFFREY, 1989. "The social organization of drug use and drug dealing among urban gangs", *Criminology*, vol. 27, no. 4, pp. 633–69

FELDBERG, MICHAEL, 1980. *The Turbulent Era: Riots and Disorder in Jacksonian America*, New York: Oxford University Press

FOSTER, GEORGE G. ,1969. "Philadelphia in slices", (1st edn 1848), *The Pennsylvania Magazine of History and Biography*, vol. 93, no. 1, pp. 23–72

FRANKLIN, VINCENT P., 1975. "The Philadelphia race riot of 1918", *The Pennsylvania Magazine of History and Biography*, vol. 99, no. 3, pp. 336–50

GILJE, PAUL A., 1987. *The Road to Mobocracy: Popular Disorder in New York City, 1763–1834*, Chapel Hill, NC: University of North Carolina Press

GOLDSTEIN, IRA and YANCEY, WILLIAM L., 1986. "Public housing projects, blacks, and public policy: the historical ecology of public housing in Philadelphia", in John M. Goering, (ed.), *Housing Desegregation and Federal Policy*, Chapel Hill, NC: University of North Carolina Press, pp. 262–89

GOTTLIEB, PETER, 1987. *Making Their Own Way: Southern Blacks' Migration to Pittsburgh, 1916–1930*, Urbana, IL: University of Illinois Press

HAGEDORN, JOHN M., 1988. *People and Folks: Gangs, Crime and the Underclass in a Rustbelt City*, Chicago, IL: Lake View Press

———1994a. "Homeboys, dope fiends, legits, and new jacks", *Criminology*, vol. 32, no. 2, pp. 197–219

———1994b. "Neighborhoods, markets, and gang drug organization", *Journal of Research in Crime and Delinquency*, vol. 31, no. 3, pp. 264–94

———1998. "Gang violence in the postindustrial era", in Michael Tonry and Mark H. Moore (eds), *Youth Violence, Crime and Justice: A Review of Research*, Chicago, IL: University of Chicago Press, vol. 24, pp. 365–19

HIRSCH, ARNOLD, R. 1983. *Making the Second Ghetto: Race and Housing in Chicago, 1940–1960*, New York: Cambridge University Press

HOROWITZ, RUTH, 1983. *Honor and the American Dream*, New Brunswick, NJ: Rutgers University Press

HUFF, C. RONALD, 1996. "The criminal behavior of gang members and nongang at-risk youth", in C. Ronald Huff (ed.), *Gangs in America*, 2nd edn, Newbury Park, CA: Sage, pp. 75–102

IANNI, FRANCIS A. J., 1974. "New mafia, black, Hispanic and Italian styles", *Society*, vol. 11, no. 3, pp. 26–39

IGNATIEV, NOEL, 1995. *How the Irish Became White*, New York: Routledge

JACKSON, KENNETH T., 1985. *Crabgrass Frontier: The Suburbanization of the United States*, New York: Oxford University Press

KAPLAN, MICHAEL, 1995. "New York city tavern violence and the creation of a working-class male identity", *Journal of the Early Republic*, vol. 15, no. 4, pp. 590–617

KASINITZ, PHILIP and ROSENBERG, JAN, 1996. "Missing the connection: social isolation and employment on the Brooklyn waterfront", *Social Problems*, vol. 43, no. 2, pp. 180–96

KATZMAN, DAVID M., 1973. *Before the Ghetto: Black Detroit in the Nineteenth Century*, Urbana, IL: University of Illinois Press

KELLEY, ROBIN D. G., 1997. *Yo' Mama's DisFUNKtional: Fighting the Culture Wars in Urban America*, Boston, MA: Beacon Press

KLEIN, MALCOLM W., MAXSON, CHERYL L. and CUNNINGHAM, LEA C., 1991. " "Crack," Street Gangs, and Violence", *Criminology*, vol. 29, no. 4, pp. 623–50

KLEIN, MALCOLM W., 1995. *The American Street Gang: Its Nature, Prevalence and Control*, New York: Oxford University Press

KORNBLUM, WILLIAM, 1974. *Blue Collar Community*, Chicago, IL: University of Chicago Press

KORNBLUM, WILLIAM and BESHERS, JAMES, 1988. "White ethnicity: ecological dimensions", in John H. Mollenkopf (ed.), *Power, Culture and Place: Essays on New York City*, New York: Sage, pp. 201–221

KOTLOWITZ, ALEX, 1988. "Chicago street gangs treat public housing as private fortresses", *The Wall Street Journal*, 30 September

———1991. *There Are No Children Here*, New York: Anchor

KUSMER, KENNETH, 1976. *A Ghetto Takes Shape: Black Cleveland, 1870–1930*, Urbana, IL: University of Illinois Press

———1995. "African Americans in the city since World War II: from the industrial to the postindustrial era", *Journal of Urban History*, vol. 21, no. 4, pp. 458–504

LANE, ROGER, 1986. *Roots of Violence in Black Philadelphia 1860–1900*, Cambridge, MA: Harvard University Press

LAURIE, BRUCE, 1980. *Working People of Philadelphia, 1800–1850*, Philadelphia, PA: Temple University Press

LAZARE, DANIEL, 1991. "Collapse of a city: growth and decay of Camden, New Jersey", *Dissent*, vol. 38, Spring, pp. 267–75

LEE, ALFRED M. and HUMPHREY, NORMAN D., 1943. *Race Riot*, New York: Dryden Press

LEMANN, NICHOLAS, 1991. *The Promised Land*, New York: Vintage

LICHTER, DANIEL T., 1988. "Racial differences in underemployment in American cities", *American Journal of Sociology*, vol. 93, no. 4, pp. 771–92

LIEBER, J. B., 1975. "Philadelphia's brotherly death", *The Nation*, no. 220, pp. 42–7

LITWACK, LEON, 1961. *North of Slavery: The Negro in the Free States, 1750–1860*, Chicago, IL: University of Chicago Press

LUKAS, J. ANTHONY, 1985. *Common Ground*, New York: Knopf

LYNN, JR. LAURENCE E. and McGEARY, MICHAEL G. H. (eds), 1990. *Inner-City Poverty in the United States*, Washington, DC: National Academy Press

MARTIN, DOUGLAS, 1997. "At the scene of a beating, a line divides 2 worlds", *The New York Times*, 28 September, pp. A19

MASSEY, DOUGLAS S. and DENTON, NANCY A., 1993. *American Apartheid: Segregation and the Making of the Underclass*, Cambridge, MA: Harvard University Press

MASSEY, DOUGLAS S. and KANAIAUPUNI, SHAWN M., 1993. "Public housing and the concentration of poverty", *Social Science Quarterly*, vol. 74, no. 1, pp. 109–22

MAXSON, CHERYL L., 1995. "Street gangs and drug sales in two suburban cities", *Research in Brief*, September, Washington, DC: National Institute of Justice

MERANZE, MICHAEL, 1996. *Laboratories of Virtue: Punishment, Revolution, and Authority in Philadelphia, 1760–1835*, Chapel Hill, NC: University of North Carolina Press

MIECZKOWSKI, THOMAS, 1986. "Geeking up and throwing down: heroin street life in Detroit", *Criminology*, vol. 24, no. 4, pp. 645–66

MILLER, CAROL POH and WHEELER, ROBERT, 1990. *Cleveland: A Concise History, 1796–1990*, Bloomington, IN: Indiana University Press

MILLER, JEROME G., 1996. *Search and Destroy: African-American Males in the Criminal Justice System*, New York: Cambridge University Press

MILLER, WALTER B., 1969. "White gangs", *Transaction*, vol. 6, no. 10, pp. 11–26

———1982. "Gangs, groups, and serious youth crime", in Rose Giallombardo (ed), *Juvenile Delinquency*, 4th edn, New York: Wiley and Sons, pp. 311–28

MOHL, RAYMOND A., 1993. "Race and space in the modern city: interstate-95 and the black community in Miami", in Arnold R. Hirsch and Raymond A. Mohl (eds), *Urban Policy in Twentieth-Century America*, New Brunswick, NJ: Rutgers University Press, pp. 100–58

MOORE, JOAN W., 1978. *Homeboys: Gangs, Drugs and Prisons in the Barrios of Los Angeles*, Philadelphia, PA: Temple University Press

———1991. *Going Down to the Barrio: Homeboys and Homegirls in Change*, Philadelphia, PA: Temple University Press

MOORE, JOAN W. and PINDERHUGHES, RAQUEL, 1993. "Introduction", in Joan W. Moore and Raquel Pinderhughes (eds), *In the Barrios: Latinos and the Underclass Debate*, New York: Russell Sage, pp. xi–xxxix

MOORE, JOAN W. and VIGIL, JAMES DIEGO, 1993. "Barrios in Transition", in Joan W. Moore and Raquel Pinderhughes (eds), *In the Barrios: Latinos and the Underclass Debate*, New York: Russell Sage, pp. 27–9

OSOFSKY, GILBERT, 1966. Harlem, *The Making of a Ghetto: Negro New York, 1890–1930*, New York: Harper and Row

PADILLA, FELIX M., 1992. *The Gang as an American Enterprise*, New Brunswick, NJ: Rutgers University Press

PATTILLO, MARY E., 1998. "Sweet mothers and gangbangers: managing crime in a black middle-class neighborhood", *Social Forces*, vol. 76, no. 3, pp. 747–74

PERKINS, USENI EUGENE, 1987. *Explosion of Chicago's Black Street Gangs: 1900 to Present*, Chicago, IL: Third World Press

PHILPOTT, THOMAS L., 1978. *The Slum and the Ghetto: Neighborhood Deterioration and Middle-Class Reform, Chicago, 1880–1930*, New York: Oxford University Press

PINDERHUGHES, DIANNE M., 1987. *Race and Ethnicity in Chicago Politics: A Reexamination of Pluralist Theory*, Urbana, IL: University of Illinois Press

PINDERHUGHES, HOWARD, 1997. *Race in the Hood: Conflict and Violence among Urban Youth*, Minneapolis, MN: University of Minnesota Press [THE] PROMISED LAND, 1995 Film Narrated by Morgan Freeman, The BBC

QUICKER, JOHN C. and BATANI-KHALFANI, AKIL, 1998. "From boozies to bloods: early gangs in Los Angeles", *Journal of Gang Research*, vol. 5, no. 4, pp. 15–21

REIDER, JONATHAN, 1985. *Canarsie: The Jews and Italians of Brooklyn Against Liberalism*, Cambridge, MA: Harvard University Press

ROEDIGER, DAVID R., 1991. *The Wages of Whiteness*, New York: Verso

ROYKO, MIKE, 1971. *Boss: Richard J. Daley of Chicago*, New York: Signet

RUDWICK, ELLIOTT M., 1964. *Race Riot at East St. Louis, July 2, 1917*, Carbondale, IL: Southern Illinois University Press

RUNCIE, JOHN, 1972. " "Hunting the nigs" in Philadelphia: the race riot of August 1834", *Pennsylvania History*, vol. 39, no. 2, pp. 187–218

SALE, R. T., 1971. *The Blackstone Rangers*, New York: Random House

SAMPSON, ROBERT J., 1987. "Urban black violence: the effect of male joblessness and family disruption", *American Journal of Sociology*, vol. 93, no. 2, pp. 348–82

SAMPSON, ROBERT J. and LAURITSEN, JANET L., 1997. "Racial and ethnic disparities in crime and criminal justice in the United States", in Michael Tonry (ed.), *Crime and Justice*, vol. 21, Chicago, IL: University of Chicago Press, pp. 311–74

SANCHEZ-JANKOWSKI, MARTIN, 1991. *Islands in the Street: Gangs and American Urban Society*, Berkeley, CA: University of California Press

SANTE, LUC, 1991. *Low Life*, New York: Farrar, Strauss, Giroux

SCHATZBERG, RUFUS and KELLY, ROBERT J., 1996. *African-American Organized Crime, A Social History*, New York: Garland

SHORT, JR. JAMES F., 1997. *Poverty, Ethnicity and Violent Crime*, Boulder, CO: Westview Press

SHORT, JR. JAMES F. and STRODTBECK, FRED L., 1965. *Group Process and Gang Delinquency*, Chicago, IL: University of Chicago Press

SILCOX, HARRY C., 1989. *Philadelphia Politics from the Bottom Up: The Life of Irishman William McMullen, 1824–1901*, Philadelphia, PA: The Balch Institute Press

SKOGAN, WESLEY G., 1990. *Disorder and Decline: Crime and the Spiral of Decay in American Neighborhoods*, New York: Free Press

SPEAR, ALLAN H., 1967. *Black Chicago: The Making of a Negro Ghetto, 1890–1920*, Chicago, IL: University of Chicago Press

SPERGEL, IRVING A., 1963. 'Male young adult criminality, deviant values, and differential opportunity in two lower-class neighborhoods', *Social Problems*, vol. 10, no. 3, pp. 237–50

———1964. Racketville, Slumtown, Haulburg, Chicago, IL: University of Chicago Press

———1984. "Violent gangs in Chicago: in search of social policy", *Social Service Review*, vol. 58, no. 2, pp. 199–226

———1986. "The local gang in Chicago: a local community approach", *Social Service Review*, vol. 60, no. 1, pp. 94–131

———1995. *The Youth Gang Problem: A Community Approach*, New York: Oxford University Press

STANSELL, CHRISTINE, 1987. *City of Women: Sex and Class in New York, 1789–1860*, Urbana, IL: University of Illinois Press

SUGRUE, THOMAS J., 1996. *The Origins of the Urban Crisis: Race and Inequality in Postwar Detroit*, Princeton, NJ: Princeton University Press

SULLIVAN, MERCER, 1989. "Getting Paid": Youth, *Crime and Work in the Inner City*, Ithaca, NY: Cornell University Press

———1993. "Puerto Ricans in Sunset Park, Brooklyn: poverty amidst ethnic and economic diversity", in Joan W. Moore and Raquel Pinderhughes (eds), *In the Barrios: Latinos and the Underclass Debate*, New York: Russell Sage, pp. 1–25

SUTTLES, GERALD, 1969. Anatomyof a Chicago slum", *Transaction*, vol. 6, no. 4, pp. 16–25

———1972 The Social Construction of Communities, Chicago, IL: University of Chicago Press

TAUB, RICHARD P., TAYLOR, D. GARTH and DUNHAM, JAN D., 1984. *Paths of Neighborhood Change: Race and Crime in Urban America*, Chicago, IL: University of Chicago Press

TAYLOR, CARL S., 1990. *Dangerous Society*, East Lansing, MI: Michigan State University Press

TERRY, DON, 1994. "Gangs: Machiavelli's descendants", *The New York Times*, 18 September, p. A26

———1997. "Chicago trial could end long reach of man said to run gang from jail", T*he New York Times*, 23 March, p. A2

THOMAS, RICHARD W., 1992. *Life for Us Is What We Make It: Building a Black Community in Detroit, 1915–1945*, Bloomington, IN: Indiana University Press

THRASHER, FREDERIC, 1936. *The Gang: A Study of 1,313 Gangs in Chicago*, (1st edn 1927), 2nd edn, Chicago, IL: University of Chicago Press

TONRY, MICHAEL H., 1995. *Malign Neglect: Race, Crime and Punishment in America*, New York: Oxford University Press

TROTTER, JR., JOE W., 1985. *Black Milwaukee: The Making of an Industrial Proletariat*, 1915–1945, Urbana, IL: University of Illinois Press

TUTTLE, JR. WILLIAM M., 1970. *Race Riot: Chicago in the Red Summer of 1919*, New York: Atheneum

VALENTINE, BILL, 1995. *Gang Intelligence Manual: Identifying and Understanding Modern-Day Gangs in the United States*, Boulder, CO: Paladin Press

VENKATESH, SUDHIR A., 1996. "The gang in the community", in C. Ronald Huff (ed.), *Gangs in America*, 2nd edn, Newbury Park, CA: Sage, pp. 241–55 1997 "The social organization of street gang violence in an urban ghetto", *American Journal of Sociology*, vol. 103, no. 1, pp. 82–111

VIGIL, JAMES DIEGO, 1988. *Barrio Gangs: Street Life and Identity in Southern California*, Austin, TX: University of Texas Press

WAKEFIELD, DAN, 1957. *Island in the City: The World of Spanish Harlem*, Boston, MA: Houghton Mifflin

WALLACE, RODRICK, 1990a. "Urban desertification, public health and public order: "planned shrinkage," violent death, substance abuse and AIDS in the Bronx", *Social Science and Medicine*, vol. 31, no. 7, pp. 801–13

WALLACE, DEBORAH, 1990b. "Roots of increased health care inequality in New York", *Social Science and Medicine*, vol. 31, no. 11, pp. 1219–27

WARD, CAROLYN M., 1996-97. "Policing in the Hyde Park neighborhood of St. Louis: racial bias, political pressure, and community policing", *Crime, Law and Social Change*, vol. 26, no. 2, pp. 161–86

WEIR, MARGARET, 1994. "Urban diversity and defensive localism", *Dissent*, vol. 41, Summer, pp. 337–2

WILENTZ, SEAN, 1984. *Chants Democratic: New York City and the Rise of the American Working Class, 1788-1850*, New York: Oxford University Press

WILSON, WILLIAM J., 1996. *When Work Disappears: The World of the New Urban Poor*, New York: Knopf

Defensive Localism in White and Black: A Comparative History of European-American and African-American Youth Gangs (Adamson, 2000)

Changing Racial and Class Structures:
- ► Four Historical Periods
1. Seaboard City 1787–1861
2. Immigrant City 1880–1940
3. Racially Changing City 1940–1970
4. Hypersegregated City 1970–1999

Differences Between European-American and African-American Gangs

Race Specific Effects:
1. Labor
2. Housing and Consumer Markets
3. Government Policies (especially crime control)
4. Local Politics
5. Organized Crime

Defensive Localism

- Defensive localism—a political and ideological strategy that supports local actions and makes localities responsible only for the problems that occur within their communities or jurisdictions.
- Localism can be based on a category of "otherness" that reduces the scope of whom we care about.
  - NIMBY

European-American Gangs

- Facilitated Cultural Assimilation
  - Close ties with formal and informal political authorities and organizations.
  - Commanded social and economic power

African-American Gangs

►   Reinforced Cultural Separation
►   Embeddedness in communities that are:
1.   Racially segregated
2.   Economically marginalized
3.   Politically powerless

"Black youth gangs did not exist as a recognized social problem until the great migration 1910s" 273

Seaboard City, 1787–1861 Ante-bellum Era

White Youth Gangs:
► Multi-ethnic Dutch, English, Welsh, Scots-Irish, Irish Catholic, Germans, mixed.
► Territory, rather than ethnicity:
  ▷ NY's Bowery and Five Points districts;
  ▷ Boston's North End and Fort Hill;
  ▷ Philadelphia's Southwark and Moyamensing sections.
► Activities
  ▷ Defense of local neighborhoods, street corners, open lots.
  ▷ Uphold racial order (attacking blacks)
  ▷ Supported by/subservient to prominent social and political clubs
  ▷ Careers in local politics

African American Youth Gangs:
► Not named or territorial
► Few in number
► Blacks targeted for attacks by white ethnic gangs.
► Competition for jobs e.g. docks, shipyards, building construction sites with Irish.
► Herrenvolk republicansim-sought to deprive blacks of rights enjoyed by white citizens and producing classes.
► NY draft riot 1863; Philly voting day riot 1871.

Gangs In Immigrant City, 1880–1940 Progressive Era

White Youth Gangs(Multi-Ethnic) and White Defensive Localism
Immigrant Parents
► Economic hardship, cultural dislocation—inability to discipline, supervise, direct immigrant children.
Immigrant Children
► Old—world communal practices vs. new world norms-formed corner groups and gangs.
Politicians and Powerful Adults—sponsored white gangs in mutually beneficial way e.g. white business elite, real estate developers, city politicians, police forces, dominant figures in organized crime.
    ▷ role in neighborhood defense of beaches, parks, diamonds, pools, saloons, halls.
        — strangers, blacks.
        — Riots East St. Louis 1917
        — Neighborhood Athletic Clubs
           — Mayor Richard Daley member of Hamburgs Irish-Catholic gang

Gangs In Immigrant City, 1880–1940 Progressive Era

African American Youth Gangs and Black Defensive Localism
► Overrepresented - 3.8% of boy population, 7.4% of city gangs.
    ▷ Excluded from unionized factory jobs, clerical positions, unskilled/part-time positions.
    ▷ 28% (25/88) racially mixed.
        — Lived in communities not large enough or ecologically distinct enough, unmapped alleys and streets behind elegant houses of white employers.
► Not territorially aggressive
    ▷ smaller black population, exclusion urban political structures, subordinate role in organized crime, hostile police.
► 1919 Chicago riot insignificant, primarily defensive role.
► "The racial order upheld by corrupt politicians, police forces, and white criminal syndicates permitted neither collective forms of illegality by black adults nor the aggressive defense of turf by black youth." 280

White Youth Gangs Racially Changing City, 1940–1970 Mid-Century

"Multi-ethnic white gangs signified that social solidarity among whites at mid-century was increasingly founded on a common identification with territory rather than on a particularistic identification with a specific European ethnic or cultural heritage ." (Kornblum and Beshers 1988, p. 219)

► Continued turf and uphold to defend racial order with support of political leaders and organized crime figures.
► Ethnically mixed in ethnically heterogeneous areas e.g. South Chicago- Irish, Italian, Polish, Serbian, Mexican; NY Spanish Harlem—Italian, Puerto Rican; Boston Roxbury—Irish Catholic, Protestant Brits, French Canadian (Miller 1969).
► 1950s Urban Racial Transition–Upholding White Supremacy
  ▷ Neighborhood improvement and homeowners' associations mobilized youth gangs
  ▷ Chrysler Corporation's Dodge Main Plant, Detroit's Hamtramck municipality.
  ▷ United Automobile Workers, Detroit
1950s Urban Racial Transition–Upholding White Supremacy

African American Youth Gangs Racially Change City, 1940–1970

► Increase in number of black gangs
  ▷ Rapid pop. Growth/doubling of black spatial isolation
  ▷ Concentrated black poverty
  ▷ Defense
► Begin to defend themselves and enter adjoining white territory.
► Rec'd moral support from adults, but little political/economic support due to adult powerlessness in disadvantaged communities.
► Ghettoization—cut black youth off from white areas of city.
  ▷ Black youth started to prey on each other.

African American Youth Gangs Racially Change City, 1940–1970

- ▶ Exclusion from legal jobs and white-controlled syndicates increased violent gang feuding of black youth.
  - ▷ Initially expansion of black ghetto increased black and white gang fights e.g. Paradise Valley, Detroit.
  - ▷ 1943 riot assaulted white students/factory workers, motorists (historic white gang tactics).
    - — Chicago 1957 12 whites assaulted after white gang killed a black youth.
- ▶ Neighborhoods & cities became exclusively black, gang fighting became increasing intraracial e.g. jobless youth, illegal work decline (bouncers/runners).
- ▶ Philadelphia's N. side, N. & S. Chicago, Watts, Florence/Firestone district
- ▶ Public housing estates constructed.

- ▶ Delinquency and Opportunity (Cloward & Ohlin, 1960)
- ▶ Social disorganization and community breakdown due to political/economic marginality, decreases youth involvement in income-producing illegality and increases involvement in gang-fighting.
- ▶ Spergel (1963) found burglary, larceny, drug sales, Chicago S. Side, murder, assault, robbery West Side.
  - ▷ Weakened community fabric, increases degree gang youth resort to violence to win social status. 284
  - ▷ Example-Slumtown (Puerto Rican/Black) vs. Racketville (Italian section, differences in gang fighting in Manhattan.

Hypersegregated City, 1970–1999

White youth gangs-
Cont. suburbanization 70s-80s
► Sanctioned by politically powerful adults to uphold racial order by arming themselves and attacking blacks.
  ▷ Tried to curb theft, vandalism, drug dealing…
  ▷ Facilitated by political influence, ties to local police, economic power e.g. social capital, got their children jobs via neighbors/local employers.
► S. Philly Counts (white youth) 1970s, S. Brooklyn Canarsie gang 1972 (Italian-Jewish enclave), Boston 1975, Bensonhurst (Brooklyn) 80s.

Hypersegregated City, 1970–1999

Black youth gangs:
► Black youth gangs became more troublesome:
  ▷ 1970s decline manufacturing/service work.
► Black males 18–29 unemployment rate (central cities)
► 1970 24%; 1982 54%

"The growing concentration of joblessness in increasingly segregated African-American ghettos has meant that black parents have been less effective than white parents in findings jobs for their children" (Sullivan 1989)

Hypersegregated City, 1970–1999

Black Youth Gangs:
- ▶ Black male joblessness disrupted family/community life.
- ▶ Adult authority powerless in housing projects…
  - ▷ Breakdown in caring for, supervising, educating children.
    84% St. Louis gang members joined for protection (Decker & Van Winkle (1996).

Harsh/irrational police response to gangs.
- ▶ Chambliss (1994) D.C. black arrests for minor drug offenses high.
  - ▷ incarcerated parents, cannot supervise teens.
  - ▷ incarcerated teens face joblessness, isolation from job networks, and prison gangs.
  - ▷ Cannot simply 'age out'

Lack of Equal Access City/County Social Services

- ▶ Social workers-fail to visit
- ▶ School teachers
- ▶ Truant officers
- ▶ Police
- ▶ Generally not helpful in black communities.

Blackstone Rangers (Chicago)-paid rents, got medical services for prostitutes.
- ▷ provided welfare services, maintenance, recreational services (1960s).
- ▶ African-American neighborhoods remain ghettoized and excluded from legitimate & illegitimate opportunity structures.

DEFENSIVE LOCALISM IN WHITE AND BLACK: HOMEWORK ASSIGNMENT

Please define the following terms/concepts using this week's article. Additionally, provide one example for each term from your reading. Please bring your homework to the next class.

1. **Ethnicity** –

2. **Race** –

3. **Assimilation** –

4. **Segregation** -

OVERVIEW OF U.S. WHITE SUPREMACIST GROUPS

By Chip Berlet,
Political Research Associates
Stanislav Vysotsky
Northeastern University

White Supremacist groups in the United States share certain common elements and characteristics. In addition to a view of racial hierarchy, there is usually some form of antisemitism, dualism, apocalypticism, a reliance on conspiracy theories, a masculinist perspective, and antipathy towards gays and lesbians. They also share some common elements with all social movements. At the same time, there are distinctive differences among White Supremacist groups. There are several ways to illustrate these differences. In order to better explain how these groups operate in the public sphere, we separate them into the categories of: political, religious, and youth cultural (racist skinhead, racist gangs, etc.) This typology, proposed by Vysotskv (2004), focuses on how these groups recruit and mobilize supporters around specific ideologies or cultural frames. We also look at several complexities and controversies in the study of White Supremacist organizations.

Organized White Supremacist groups in the United States evolved from their historic base of various predecessor Ku Klux Klan and neo-Naziorganizations (Schmaltz 1999; Trelease 1995; Chalmers 1965). Overtime, they spread into a wide range of competing forms and ideologies.

Chip Berlet, Stanislav Vysotsky, "Overview of U.S. White Supremacist Groups," *Journal of Political & Military Sociology,* vol. 34, no. 1, pp. 11-48. Copyright © 2006 by Transaction Publishers. Reprinted with permission.

These groups and organizations constitute what some have broadly termed the "radical right." While there are some areas where the extreme right White Supremacist movement and right-wing dissident groups (usually listed as being part of the Patriot or armed militia movements) overlap, we do not include the latter in this study because there are important boundaries separating them from White Supremacist race hate groups (Durham 2000).

Despite their many differences, there are some common elements across the boundaries of organized white supremacy, or at least a collection from which certain aspects are selected. Gardell describes a "smorgasbord" in the "white-racist counterculture" consisting of the lore of the Ku Klux Klan, national socialism, the culture of White Power music and racist skinheads, the ideal of the heroic warrior, conspiracism, anti-semitism, right-wing populism, and White Separatism. He also includes the idea of race as integrated intoreligion, and two mutually exclusive religious worldviews; Christian Identityand pagan Odinism (2003:78–79). It is in this similarity of worldview that we find the first in a number of common elements to most White Supremacist groups. While individual members of White Supremacist movements may appear to be deviant or engage in criminal activity, they are also rational individuals who are acting in accordance with complex belief systems and responding to their material reality, cultural forces, and the requirements of movement organizations and ideologies.

A social movements analysis of White Supremacist groups provides a clear understanding of the complexity of such a varied movement. "The use of this approach presents an alternative view to the deviance perspective," suggest Jipson and Becker, and assumes that White Supremacists"are social movement actors, like mainstream social movement actors and institutions, and are socially, politically, and ideologically constructed" (2000:111). As McVeigh explains, "forms of structural differentiation ... make the worldview [that is] constructed within racist organizations seem plausible to a critical mass of individuals ... racial and ethnic heterogeneity, industrial heterogeneity, income inequality, and changes in the economic structure within local communities provide 'evidence' that may appear to be consistent with white supremacists' claims if individuals lack an alternative interpretation" (2004).

All social movements develop a common ideology and establish a set of frames through which they view a struggle over power (Zald 1996; Snow, Rochford, Worden, and Benford [1986] 1997; Goffman 1974). Social movements also pick (or create) narratives or stories that teach members and potential members about what is to be admired and what is to be opposed (Davis 2002; Polletta 1998; Ewick and Silbey 1995). White Supremacist groups are no different (Berlet 2001; Dobratz and Shanks-Meile 2000, 1995). The complexity of framing processes, intellectualization, psychological undercurrents, and mobilization among White Supremacists is gaining increased attention, and replacing older, more simplistic, models of understanding these groups and their members (See, for example: Ferber 2004, 1999; Gardell 2003; Flint 2003; Blee

2002; Goodrick-Clark 2002, 1985; Dobratz and Shanks-Meile 1996; Kaplan 2000, 1997a; Arena and Arrigo 2000; Berbrier 1998a, 1998b, 1999; Kaplan and Bjorgo 1998; Kaplan and Wcinberg 1998; Barkun [1994] 1997; Daniels 1997). The White Supremacist movement relies on several overarching metaframes (or stylistic master frames), especially conspiracism, dualism and a pocalypticism.

Conspiracism is the idea that most major historic events have been shaped by vast, long-term, secret conspiracies that benefit elite groups and individuals. Stories explaining the alleged conspiracy are narratives about good and evil that select specific targeted groups, and justify aggression against them by combining dualism and a pocalypticism with populist rhetoric calling for an uprising against the evil plotters (Barkun 2003; Goldberg 2001; Berlet and Lyons 2000; Mintz 1985). Populism, in this setting, is primarily used as a style of rhetoric used to generate specific emotions of displacement (Durham 2000;Berlet and Lyons 2000, Kintz 1997. Kazin 1995, Canovan 1981). The conspiracism in the White Power subculture centers on imagined Jewish intrigues. This is mingled with the faulty view that Jews belong to a single race, and thus White Supremacists promote antisemitism in a way that involves religious bigotry as well as racism. This racist and antisemitic mindset employs two other elements common across organized white supremacy: dualism and apocalypticism.

Dualism is the idea that the world is divided into the forces of good and evil with no middle ground. Anthony and Robbins (1997) coined the term "exemplary dualism" to describe how some social and political struggles are turned into cosmic battles that are believed to involve the fate of the entire world, Wessinger (2000b) describes certain types of worldviews that can create a form of "radical dualism" that demonizes perceived enemies. The White Supremacist movement presents the world as a place where heroic warriors white, heterosexual, (mostly) Christian men and women are in constant battle with a number of "others": non-white races, Jews, homosexuals, etc. (Bushart, Craig, and Barnes 2000). The warrior element of dualism helps significantly to buttress the apocalyptic visions of many movement leaders and texts.

Apocalyptic and millenarian visions of an ideal future after a cataclysmic battle help shape the ideologies of contemporary right-wing political and social movements in the United States (Wessinger 2000a, 2000b; Berlet and Lyons 2000; Robbins and Palmer 1997;). These include the Christian Right (Brasher and Berlet 2004, Brasher 2001, 2000); through the Patriot and militia movement (Lamy 1996); to the White Supremacist subculture (Gardell 2003; Blee 1999; Kaplan 1997a; Barkun [1994] 1997; Goodrick-Clarke [1985]2004). Apocalypticism is the idea that there is an approaching confrontation that will change the nature of the world, during which important hidden truths will be revealed (O'Leary 1994; Boyer 1992). Apocalyptic frames and narratives trace back thousands of years, and were shaped by specific interpretations of the Bible's book of Revelation and the millennial battle of Armageddon (Weber 1999, Cohn 1993. [1957] 1970). Apocalypticism seeped into secular political ideologies including Hitler's "thousand year Reich" and other forms of sacralized political ideology (Redles 2005; Gentile 2004. 1996; Griffin 2004, 1991; Berlet 2004b; Ellwood 2000; Vondung 2000; Wistrich 1985; Rhodes; 1980). White Supremacist apocalyptic belief predicts a fast approaching and inevitable confrontation between good and evil, pitting the white race against people of color, Jews, and race traitors.

Women are increasingly encouraged to be active participants in the movement, however they are generally kept in relatively subordinate positions (Blee 2002), and overall. White Supremacist groups tend to exhibit some form of male supremacy (Ferber 1998, 2000). Most groups also stigmatize and denounce gay men, lesbians, and other non-heterosexuals, and generally blame "the Jews" for promoting tolerance of such difference (Perry 2004; Blee 2002,1991; Dobratz and Shanks-Meile 2000).[10]

White supremacy is based on pseudo-scientific theories of the genetic superiority of the white "race." Many of these claims track back to four books arguing that perceived racial differences are both hierarchical and vitally important to the proper social order: Count Arthur de Gobineau's 1853 *The Inequality of Human Races* (Tucker 1994:88–91; Poliakov 1974:215–238; Biddiss 1970); Frances Galton's 1870 *Hereditary Genius: An Inquiry into Its Laws and Consequences* (Tucker 1994:49–53); Madison Grant's 1916/1924 *The Passing of the Great Race* (Tucker 1994:88–96, 124–125; Mintz 1985:32–35), and T. Lothrop Stoddard's 1920 *The Rising Tide of Color Against White World Supremacy* (Kuhl 1994:61–63; Tucker 1994:92–93). In the 1920s. American eugenicists traded ideas with their counterparts in the German Nazi movement (Lombardo 2002; Tucker 2002, Kühl 1994). There are many other sources of information that defend white supremacy, both historic and contemporary, and members of White Power groups use them as a justification for their beliefs.

In the racially-diverse contemporary U.S. military, the problem of White Supremacists entering with a variety of ulterior motives has created investigative and disciplinary issues since the 1990s. According to Scott Barfield, a gang detective with the Department of Defense, the presence of neo-Nazis stretches "across all branches of service, they are linking up across the branches once they're inside, and they are hard-core." There is even a problem with "Aryan Nations graffiti in Baghdad," Barfield told the SPLC (Holthouse 2006).

Since their views are widely rejected by mainstream media. White Supremacist groups often turn to alterative forms of media, especially the Internet, to get their

---

10 There has long been a tiny subculture of gay neo-Nazis. However, this subculture may be more intimately linked to a sado-masochist or "fetish" sexual under ground than an organized White supremacist movement. In July of 2006, a group calling itself the Aryan Anarchist Skins staged a demonstration in Illinois, with a spokesperson stating: "We accept homosexuals, bisexuals lesbians." Rival groups immediately denounced it as a hoax, an issue that remained unresolved when this article was submitted.

message out (Simi and Futrell 2006; Kim 2005; Gerstenfeld, Grant, and Chiang 2003; Schroer 2001; Burris, Smith, and Strahm 2000). They also engage in what Oberschall calls public "identification moves" in which social movement leaders collect their members together for rallies, literature distribution, and other group activities that show movement members, the media, a target group, or the government that they are a force to be reckoned with (1973: 308–309). Ezekiel (1995) has noted that in the White Supremacist subculture, such rallies serve to bring greater attention to marginal groups and build the prestige of leaders within their own organization and the movement as a whole. While this is true for all social movements, the controversial content of the White Supremacist messages often is seen as more provocative and confrontational, especially by the mainstream media.

In organized white supremacy, ideology and activity need to be assessed separately. Some groups with a virulent ideology can choose not to engage in violence, while individual members of any group can engage in acts of violence, no matter what the stated or normative methodology of the group (Kittrie 1995, 2000). With the growth of White Supremacist activity on the Internet and a rise in the belief in a methodology called "leaderless resistance" (Beam 1983), organizations have been able to actively distance their ideological and "theoretical" positions from the activities of individuals who may share their beliefs. Since movement participation often involves symbolic displays (wearing of insignias, tattoos, etc.) that are readily available to the public, direct links between leadership and individuals is hard to establish.

DATA COLLECTION ISSUES

The study of extreme right groups by scholars presents a number of unusual problems (Blee 2002; Dobratz and Shanks-Meile 2000; Himmelstein 1998). Members of these groups are usually highly suspicious of academics, membership numbers are difficult to verify, and scholars can find it difficult to retain a neutral approach with groups that often promote race hate, religious bigotry, and even genocide. At the same time, the mainstream media and non-profit watch groups face persistent questions regarding accuracy of reporting and the exaggeration of the threat posed to civil society. Kaplan devoted a whole chapter to his criticisms of "Anti-Cult" and "Watchdog" groups (1997a: 127-163. 170–171). This prompted a dialogue over these issues. (Robbins. 1997; J.Kaplan. 1997b; Wright. 1999). Chermak (2002) reopened the debate with criticisms over how watch groups and the media portray dissident right-wing groups, with a lengthy look at the militia movement. Nonetheless, a number of scholars cautiously rely on data from groups such as the Southern Poverty Law Center (SPLC) and the

Anti-Defamation League (ADL) in studies looking at the Patriot and armed militia movements and the extreme right White Supremacist movements.[11]

Freilich (2003) and Van Dyke and Soule (2002) have used group location data to study the militia movement. Other scholars have used similar data and other materials from SPLC and ADL to study a range of right-wing groups including the Ku Klux Klan and other White Supremacist groups (Ferber and Kimmel 2004; Beck 2000). According to Freilich, "the prudent course of action is to utilize the data, while recognizing the potential problems associated with it." (2003:93) Researchers at both SPLC and ADL say they are aware of these criticisms, and have responded to them by both urging caution, and refining their data collection and reporting (Berlet 2004c). The SPLC divides their reporting of the "Radical Right" into two categories: Race hate and Supremacists, and other antigovernment activists in the Patriot movement, including the militia movement. In the race hate category, SPLC lists Black Separatist, Christian Identity, Ku Klux Klan, Neo-Confederate, Neo-Nazi, Racist Skinhead, and Other.[3] We do not cover the Black Separatist and Neo-Confederate movements in this study, nor the Patriot movement and anti government militias. SPLC has also begun tracking the anti-immigrant movement, due to its overlap with white supremacy (SPLC 2005).

TYPOLOGIES AND DESCRIPTIONS

In studying the diversity of the modern. American White Supremacist movement, researchers have often tried to develop typologies that seek to group the significant tendencies within the broader movement. These typologies have often limited the movement to the Ku Klux Klan. Neo-Nazis, racist skinheads, and Christian Identity (Blee 2002; Ferber 1999; Marks 1996). While these four types do present certain organizational trends, they also miss a number of significant developments in the movement, such as the expansion to youth cultures other than the skinheads and the influence of religious belief systems that reject Christianity. As an alternative to previous typologies, we suggest a typology based on ideology and activity of organizations within the movement. The modern White Supremacist movement can be seen as being composed of political, religious, and youth cultural organizations. This typology is based on analysis of social movement activity taking the form of instrumental, subcultural, and counter cultural groups (Kriesi et al. 1995).

---

11 Leaderless resistance encourages actions by small cells or lone individuals with ideological ties to the White Supremacist movement without direct organizational affiliation. This philosophy is espoused by many leaders and rank-and-file members of the movement as a means for promoting acts of violence and intimidation without directly implicating other movement members; and therefore, shielding them from criminal liability.

By relying on the inconsistent criteria of ideology (Neo-Nazi), specific organizational affiliation (Ku Klux Klan), and a distinct youth subculture (racist skin head), the dominant typologies of White Supremacist groups engage in over-generalization, while simultaneously focusing on distinct organizations and subcultures. In the dominant typologies Neo-Nazi groups can include those with a secular political orientation, or those allied with religious forms such as Christian Identity or Odinism. In fact, it could be argued that virtually any White Supremacist organization may be categorized as Neo-Nazi as a result of the historical influence of the Nazi party on the movement of today (see Figure 1).

We believe that the Neo-Nazi category common in previous typologies more closely approximates the political category of our typology because it is designed to reflect the ideological influence of fascist and Nazi political philosophy. Also, while it is important to acknowledge the historic role of the Ku Klux Klan in the history of the American White Supremacist movement, typological references to the Klan obscure the decline of its influence on the broader movement, rifts between various Klan groups, and important ideological changes such as the increasing influence of Christian Identity. Finally, there are also major divides within youth culture groups, as well as conflicts between them and established groups that primarily consist of older political or religious movement members. Inevitably, attempts at placing groups into the categories listed above often result in a number of organizations, ideological trends, and counter cultural shifts being labeled as "other" for lack of a better term. In addition, many of the groups studied are fractious and fractioning with splits, collapses, and new groups occurring at frequent intervals. This has led some scholars to refer to them as the "Groupuscular Right" (Griffin 2003, *Patterns of Prejudice* 2002). Because of this constant ebb and flow within and between organizations, typologies of the White Supremacist movement that focus solely on dominant organizations are likely to be problematic.[12]

We think it is easier to understand White Supremacist groups by placing them into broadly defined political, religious, and youth culture categories. Groups within each individual category can consist of a handful of young people hanging out on a corner, a religious belief shared by tens of thousands, or a specific organization with hundreds of members. By creating a typology that organizes groups using ideological similarity and group activity (particularly through the construction of counterculture), we believe that this model allows one to adequately categorize the various elements of the modern White Supremacist movement. The typology suggested presents broad categories to distinguish between individual groups and allows for the development of further distinction within categories such as those explored by Dobratz's (2001) research into religious White Supremacists. These categories allow multiple organizations to be

---

12   See the Southern Poverty Law Center's Hate Groups in the United States map at: http://www.splcenter.org/intel/map/hate.jsp.

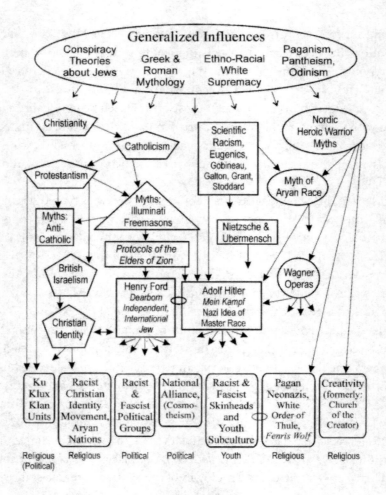

FIGURE 1 Genealogy Of White Surpemacy & Antisemitism

placed into a broad category without creating exclusive group/sub cultural types such as Ku Klux Klan or racist skinhead. Groups that demonstrate similarities in philosophy may be placed into a single category that roughly encompasses similar organizations. By generally defining the categories in this typology, the need for a "catchall" category such as other is reduced significantly. Using similarity of ideology and activity as base criteria organizations within the political and youth cultural categories may be distinguished further.

This typology creates broad, yet specific categories that allow the classification of White Supremacist groups by focusing on their activities and the source of their ideology. It allows social scientists, as well as criminal justice professionals to develop an understanding of the belief systems, recruitment tactics, and organizational activities of typologically similar groups, as well as the possibility for mapping alliance structures and organizational changes due to the aforementioned splits and conflicts within and between groups. This is not to depreciate the value of other models of taxonomy, but to argue that this typology is a useful addition, especially for law enforcement professionals who will encounter these groups on the street or inside the military. Using this typology, they may be able to identify more accurately the organizational affiliation of individuals involved in white supremacy, and respond appropriately to their

Ideas about valor, heroic warriors, nationalism, and race were widely circulated throughout Europe in the late 1800s and early 1900s, with one vehicles parking discussion being performances of Wagnerian operas, which Adolf Hitler as a youth greatly admired. These concepts were reinforced by the development of scientific racism and theories of white supremacy advanced by writers including Gobineau, Galton, Grant, and Stoddard.

Mythical claims about sinister anti-Christian conspiracies by Freemasons and the Illuminati society circulated in the 1790's: then were transformed into claims by Protestants about plots by the Roman Catholic Church in the 1820s. The Freemason myths were melded into the hoax document, the *Protocols of the Elders of Zion* in the early 1900s, blaming Jews for global subversive machinations. Industrialist Henry Ford widely circulated these antisemitic claims in a series of articles in his *Dearborn Independent* newspaper, later collected in book form as *The International Jew.* Allies of Ford also promoted Christian Identity.

Hitler, who read a German translation of *The International Jew,* synthesized an ideology of antisemitic conspiracy theories and white supremacy in his autobiography, *Mein Kampf* which also assumed the existence of an Aryan race. (Aryan actually refers to a linguistic subgroup, not a bloodline). Hitler also developed an idiosyncratic understanding of Nietzsche's concept of the *Ubermensch* or "superior" men, which Hitler elaborated into the Nazi idea of a master race.

Various amalgams of these ideas are found across the spectrum of organized White Supremacist groups in the United States activities or ideological motivations in ways that are sensitive to Constitutional issues.

The typology that we suggest is based on a New Social Movement analysis of social movement activity that divides movements into instrumental, sub cultural, and counter cultural (Kriesi et al. 1995). To the casual observer of the White Supremacist movement, every organization within the movement would qualify under the counter cultural category because they are very strongly identity oriented, engage in exclusive mobilizations, follow a radical, confrontational action repertoire, and have very few alliances with mainstream political groups and parties. However, an analysis of the action orientation of individual organizations within the movement allows one to categorize the groups using the model developed by Kriesi, et al. The groups characterized as political in our typology are in many ways similar to instrumental social movements that are goal-oriented and engage in traditional as well as non-traditional forms of political participation. White Supremacist youth cultures in many ways exemplify counter cultural movements which seek to create alternative lifestyles and social structures as precursors to radical social change through confrontational actions. Religious movements may be classified as sub cultural movements because of their focus on instrumental goals coupled with a reliance on prefigurative spiritual practice.

By relying on the typology that we suggest, the organizations, ideological tendencies, and sub cultural trends that make up the modern White Supremacist movement are situated in the context of their ideology and activity. A broad overview of the movement then can be organized by placing groups into the political, religious, and youth cultural sectors of our suggested typology.

THE POLITICAL SECTOR

Most White Supremacist organizations we characterize as Political find their ideological inspiration rooted in neo-fascist or neo-Nazi ideology. Many organizations in this category view themselves as direct political descendents of Hitler's Nazi party while others would prefer to cast themselves as unique organizations with ideologies that are more suited for modern, post-industrial societies. There are a number of key ideological elements that all organizations within the political category share.

Fascist movements are authoritarian. Within such organizations, hierarchies of leadership are seen as natural, and the model for a future society. Elite leadership is acknowledged as both natural and necessary for societies to operate with the sense of order that is a crucial promise of fascist states. Politically, fascists exalt the authority and status of political elites embodied in the fascist party and leaders, ensuring their control over both the state and the populace. Fascist leaders assert and enforce proper social roles and structures; and they use moral rhetoric that extols social stability and values the nation as superior to individual rights (Paxton 2004. Payne 1995; Lyons 1995; Griffin 1991). According to Lyons:

> Fascism rejects the liberal doctrines of individual autonomy and rights, political pluralism, and representative government, yet it advocates broad popular participation in politics and may use parliamentary channels in its drive to power. Its vision of a "new order" clashes with the conservative attachment to tradition-based institutions and hierarchies, yet fascism often romanticizes the past as inspiration for national re birth. (1995: 245)

Fascist movements frequently use authoritarianism and appeals to traditional values to develop narrow and exclusionary definitions of nation, race, and proper citizenship in order to increase unity among their idealized and homogenous constituents. National identity is lauded as the ultimate social identity in fascist states. This nationalism is racialized and equated with the racial identity of the social group seen as naturally superior. This sense of national and racial identity serves to delineate in-group and out-group members and allows for scape goating of minorities and other "enemies" in fascist societies. The pattern of scape goating seen in fascist movements is a matter of policy as victims provide a practical target for fascist beliefs in superiority through conflict, violence, and war and the pursuit of power for its own sake. Fascist movements are ideologically committed to the achieving power through violence and often take a stance of revolutionary opposition to dominant political systems. When they gain power, fascists are likely to expand their ideological imperative towards violence into war and colonial conquest of other states (Payne 1995; Lyons 1995; Griffin 1991).

Political White Supremacist organizations are likely to engage in activities similar to other marginal political parties. Their primary purpose is to build an organization for what they believe to be a coming racial conflict or the political overthrow of the state. This is achieved mostly through legal activities. A primary focus for political organizations is the spreading of ideas via active development of literature on any number of socially or politically relevant topics that often takes the form of fliers, pamphlets, and magazines. Members are encouraged to distribute literature in locations where potential new members may be recruited. It should be noted that literature distribution is also sometimes used as a means to threaten communities of color, Jewish communities, as well as institutions and communities that are open to homosexuals. The Internet serves as a primary location for such organizations to provide literature for distribution, news that has been adapted or properly framed as racist, and communication for group members (Vysotsky 2004; Gerstenfeld, Grant, and Chiang 2003).

Political organizations, however, are not limited to the relatively passive activity of literature distribution. Many organize and hold public rallies, protests, and meetings as a means of spreading their message and recruitment of potential new members. These events are often carefully planned and occur in what Green, Strolovich, and Wong (1998) term "defended neighborhoods," areas where racial or ethnic tensions are heightened due to a perception of threat from newly arriving or integrating groups. The goal of such events is to heighten existing tensions and build the organization's membership by attracting sympathetic individuals from the community.

Most political White Supremacist organizations operate openly as non-violent political parties or similar organizations. However, behind the public image of a reactionary voice in America's pluralist system lies a criminal underground of militants who receive ideological guidance and tacit support from such a movement. In response to prosecutions of key leaders of the movement following the terrorist activities of the Order in the 1980s, the White Supremacist movement has taken to advocating "leaderless resistance," which urges a series of individual or small-cell acts of violence against the state and racially, religiously, ethnically, and sexually subordinate groups that will trigger a larger race war and place White Supremacist organizations in power (Shanks-Meile 2001; Ezekiel 1995). This strategy allows political White Supremacist organizations to keep a "legitimate" public presence while encouraging the violent overthrow of the United States.

We have singled out the following historic and contemporary groups to profile briefly here: National Alliance, White Aryan Resistance. National Socialist Movement, White Revolution, Volksfront, and National Vanguard.

NATIONAL ALLIANCE

The National Alliance promotes the revolutionary overthrow of the American political system. For a time in the 1990s, the National Alliance was the leading neo-Nazi organization in the United States. The group was founded by William Pierce, author (under the pseudonym Andrew Macdonald) of *The Turner Diaries* and *Hunter* (Durham 2004, 2002; Ware and Back 2002; ADL 2002; Burghart 1999). The National Alliance is based on a metaphysical belief called Cosmotheism, a form of apocalyptic millenarianism (Whitsel 1998). In practical terms, however, the National Alliance is a revolutionary right-wing political organization with few members paying attention to the religious basis in a meaningful way. According to Durham (2004), Pierce hoped that followers of the National Alliance would embrace Cosmotheism, but it was not a requirement, although rejection of Judaism and Christianity was a necessity.

While the organization is based out of a national headquarters in West Virginia, local contacts and active chapters may be found throughout the United States. Its website contains essays by members, a number of publications, Internet radio, and links to organizations affiliated with the NA. It sponsors a competing version (pitted against National Vanguard) of the weekly radio program American Dissident Voices, distributed on the Internet and broadcast on short wave radio. Members of the National Alliance also engage in public propaganda campaigns through active leafleting of their local communities.

In 1999, Pierce paid some $250,000 for Resistance Records, a White Power music company producing and marketing CD's and paraphernalia to a primarily youthful audience. The music business became a moneymaker for the National Alliance. According to SPLC (2002c), by the year 2002, "the Alliance was bringing in more than $1 million a year, had a paid national staff of 17 full-time officials, and was better known than at any time in its history. In just five days in June, Alliance members in 20 states distributed 70,000 leaflets." That same year Pierce died, and since then the primary activity for the NA has been to spread propaganda and maintain the organization, a task made much more difficult by bitter battles over control of the organization and its resources (SPLC 2002a).

Shaun Walker eventually emerged as the chairman of the National Alliance, however in June 2006 Walker and two associates were indicted by a federal grand jury in Salt Lake City for civil rights violations stemming from an alleged campaign of intimidation and assaults against members of minority groups in that city during 2002 and 2003 (ADL 2006). This further accelerated the declining influence of the National Alliance.

WHITE ARYAN RESISTANCE (WAR)

White Aryan Resistance was a very active group that was essentially put out of business after its founder, former California Klan leader Tom Metzger, lost a civil lawsuit stemming from a murderous racial attack by several of his followers. We mention WAR here because it pioneered the spread of a particular revolutionary "national socialist" ideology, which Metzger summarized at the 1987 Aryan Nations Congress:

> WAR is dedicated to the White working people, the farmers, the White poor. … This is a working class movement. … Our problem is with monopoly capitalism. The Jews first went with Capitalism and then created their Marxist game. You go for the throat of the Capitalist. You must go for the throat of the corporates. You take the game away from the left. It's our game! We're not going to fight your whore wars no more! We've got one war, that is right here, the same war the SA fought in Germany, right here; in the streets of America. … (Center for Democratic Renewal 1988)

This type of rhetoric is associated with a national socialist form of neo-Nazi ideology called the "Third Position," a political tendency that challenges globalization as part of a call for organic, localized, cooperative economic systems—rejecting both capitalism and communism (Gardell 2003; Berlet and Lyons 2000; Coogan 1999). This form of neo-Nazism has been carried forward by groups such as White Revolution, the National Socialist Movement, and Volksfront.

NATIONAL SOCIALIST MOVEMENT

The National Socialist Movement describes itself as "fighting for Race and Nation," and an "organization dedicated to the preservation of our Proud Aryan Heritage, and the creation of a National Socialist Society in America and around the world." NSM calls itself a Nazi Party that cooperates and works with "many like minded white nationalist groups such as the KKK (Ku Klux Klan), Aryan Skinheads, the Racial Nationalist Party of America and many others which are either Nazi or at least racially aware of our Aryan

Heritage." Currently based in Minneapolis, Minnesota, NSM was founded in 1974 as the National Socialist American Workers Freedom Movement. It was later renamed and taken over in 1994 by current leader 31-year-old Jeffrey Schoep (ADLn.d.(b)).

Schoep outlined an aggressive agenda of expanding activities and membership, launching an estimated 45 units in 29 states by 2004, with "new chapters in Indiana, Kansas, California. Massachusetts, and Canada" (ADLn.d.(b); Jackson and Potok 2004). It favors literature distribution as a recruitment and publicity technique.

As some other White Supremacist groups declined. NSM "rapidly achieved a higher profile," than its closest new competitors. While Revolution and National Vanguard, according to SPLC. By early 2006, the NSM count rose to "59 units in 32 states as the NSM continued to salvage and reassemble" the neo-Nazi movement in the United States. High profile and aggressive public demonstrations and publicity-conscious activities helped attract media attention and recruits (SPLC 2006).

WHITE REVOLUTION

White Revolution was founded by Billy Roper, deputy membership coordinator of the National Alliance, who was ousted in a power struggle after the death of NA founder William Pierce in 2002 (Potok 2002). The group lays out its worldview on its website:

> Any culture can be destroyed and rebuilt over and over again, so long as the founding race of that culture survives. Once the founding race has lost its genetic identity, though, culture, which is a product of race, also becomes moot. Race, therefore, is more important than culture. Better to have the whole world burn except for one White boy and one White girl raised by wolves, than a world of ten billion mulattos who can quote Shakespeare and play classical violin. (White Revolution n.d.)

One of White Revolution's greatest successes has been in building coalitions and ties to other White Supremacist groups. White Revolution is best known for staging rallies "that attract a wide array of racist participants, ranging from young skinheads to Identity Christians to neo-Nazis and Klansmen" (ADLn.d.(c)). As such, "White Revolution ('The Only Solution')" declares its intent to "'serve as an umbrella coalition of racial activists from every pro-White organization.' and unaffiliated 'Patriots,'" reported SPLC (2002b). The organization encourages members of other groups to attend its events and reciprocates by participating in events organized by other movement organizations. White Revolution urges members to belong to other White Supremacist groups, which allows it to build stronger networks within the movement. The organization has worked to promote itself through active use of the media. Its members are active on a variety of White Supremacist Internet message boards, run their own website, and produce a television program known as "White Revolution Television" (ADL n.d.(c)).

White Revolution, however, has not been able to dominate the White Supremacist movement, and its "unity efforts" have not been as successful as they had hoped, according to ADL (2005).

VOLKSFRONT

Volks front is another national socialist group and calls itself the "independent voice of the white working class" (Volksfront 2005). The organization was founded in the mid-1990s by then neo-Nazi skinhead, Randall Lee Krager, as a means of organizing other White Supremacist skinheads in and around Portland, OR. The organization has since transformed itself into a group that we would argue is more political in its orientation.

Volksfront's political ideology can best be described as belonging to the "third position" discussed earlier. The organization describes its enemies as "agents of the Stalinist police state, capitalists, communists, Zionists and other enemies of White Self-Determination" (Volksfront 2005) with opposition to capitalism being a critical element of the group's ideology. The organization's program and mission statement reserve several points for discussion of the need to "support and protect the rights of workers from capitalist and communist manipulation and exploitation" (Volksfront 2005) and urge its members to engage in political activity to defend its political base. The program calls for the creation of white owned businesses, land ownership projects and other small-scale economic activities designed to create economic autonomy for the white race.

The modem incarnation of Volksfront encourages its members to engage in political propaganda campaigns in order to promote its agenda. The group's website takes pains to disavow the organization from violent activity and encourages its members to use "media, music, and literature" to promote their cause. However, the group also reserves the right to use violence in "self-defense" and has been associated with a number of violent White Supremacist activists through its prisoner support program (Beirich and Potok 2004; Vysostky 2004).

Members and affiliates of the group have tended to get involved in violent incidents. For example, in 2004 a judge sentenced a 20-year-old linked to Volksfront to life in prison for the murder of a homeless man (Beirich and Potok 2004).

By blending political ideology that rejects dominant left and right-wing discourse in favor of racial populism and public activity that promotes itself as a mainstream political organization, Volksfront has been successful in establishing chapters across the United States and Europe. While the organization is still small, it has been growing in recent years and building ties to other White Supremacist groups.

National Vanguard, run by Kevin Alfred Strom, and based in Charlottesville, Virginia, disclaims that it is a White Supremacist group, calling itself "an intelligent and responsible organization that stands up for the interests of White people. If other races and interest groups can organize, so can we. Finally, White men and women have joined together—under the banner of National Vanguard. It's about time" (National Vanguard n.d.).

NV sponsors a competing version (pitted against National Alliance) of the weekly audio program American Dissident Voices, distributed on the Internet and broadcast on short wave radio. NV has gained attention for creating visually stunning flyers and posting them online in high resolution where local activists download them and print them out for distribution. These flyers, on the surface, tend to avoid naked race hate rhetoric.[13] National Vanguard, along with Stormfront (Kim 2005), are examples of White Supremacist groups that design a "micro-frame" as a recruitment tool for consumption by the public; and which does not, in fact, represent the frame presented by leaders to followers (Johnston 1995).

THE RELIGIOUS SECTOR

The category of religious White Supremacist groups includes any organization that derives its core ideology from a spiritual belief system and has members who are expected to practice that religion. Religion plays a powerful yet complicated role in shaping the ideologies and activities of social movements, including those on the Political Right (Eatwell 2003; Steigmann-Gall 2003; Kintz 1997; Williams 1994; Jeansonne 1988; Ribuffo 1983). Members of religious White Supremacist groups often look to religious text as the inspiration for their ideas regarding race, and the appropriate behavior and role for members in the larger world (Dobratz 2001). Religious White Supremacist groups frequently construct the idea of a dualistic apocalyptic "holywar" between their faithful allies and their unholy enemies who are seen as plotting vast conspiracies (Berlet 2004a, 2004b; Barkun [1994] 1997). This type of a pocalypticism is complementary to a masculinist and authoritarian model of behavior (Quin by 1994).

In addition to constructing a spiritual foundation for racial ideology, religious groups engage in prefigurative activities based around adherence to religious beliefs. Even though members of religious movements often engage in White Supremacist activities

---

13 See for example, the images at http://www.nationalvanguard.org/docs/love-your-race.pdf; http://www.nationalvanguard.org/docs/missing.pdf

that are similar to political movements, they are also likely to be highly involved in a complex subculture based around their spiritual beliefs. Members of groups that fit into the religious category structure their lives to include religious services, meetings dedicated to the study of sacred texts, and special rituals and ceremonies limited to loyal adherents (Futrell and Simi, 2004). Finally, the organizational structure of religious groups derives itself from the individual's status in the religious group. Movement leaders are likely to be spiritual leaders within the faith and often are recognized as such through official titles such as the use of the title "reverend" in both Christian Identity and Creativity. While religious groups share common structural and ideological elements, there are a number of competing spiritual tendencies. The three primary spiritual forms of white supremacy today are Christian Identity, Creativity, and Odinism; each with its own interpretation of sacred texts or mythology that serves as a basis for racialist beliefs (Dobratz 2001).

CHRISTIAN IDENTITY

Christian Identity is a racialized version of Protestantism that evolved from a mid 1800s theology called British Israelism, which claimed the Biblical lost tribes of Israel were the ancestors of people who settled in the British Isles. The more overtly racist version of Christian Identity, developed in the United States, believes that White Aryan Christians are therefore God's chosen people, and that America is the Biblical Promised Land. Identity has no central church structure, and exists in the United States as a series of autonomous small churches and religious communities (Blee 2002; Dobratz 2001; Ferber 1999;Kaplan 1997a:l–10, Marks 1996; Ridgeway 1995; Barkun [1994] 1997).

The current version of racist Christian Identity began to emerge in the mid-1940s but did not generate substantial published articulations until the 1960s. Key early ministers were Conrad Gaard, Bertrand Comparet, and Wesley Swift (Good rick-Clark 2002). The theology passed through Swift to William Potter Gale in the mid 1950s, to Richard G. Butler. In the mid 1970s, Butler moved to Idaho and established the Aryan Nations compound from which would be built a racially-pure separatist nation carved out of the United States and composed solely of people from the various historic and genetic "Aryan Nations," (Levitas 2002; Kaplan 1997a; Barkun [1994] 1997). Aryan Nations became one of the most visible institutional outposts of Christian Identity.

The theology of Christian Identity sees "all of history as a Manichaean struggle between white, divine, Anglo-Saxon Christians, and Satanic Jews." (Levitas 2002; 81). The main view within Identity sees Jews as evil, in part because they are believed to be the literal biological descendants of a race conceived by Satan and Eve in the Garden of Eden. Identity followers believe that crafty and clever Jews install racially inferior (and subhuman) Black people and other non-Aryan people of color in positions of power.

Identity sees the prophetic apocalyptic battle described in the Bible's book of Revelation as an approaching race war that requires immediate preparation. Identity believers are premillennialist like many evangelicals in the United States, but they reject the notion of the Rapture, and thus expect to wage the race war during the prophesied Tribulations (Berlet 2004b; Kaplan 1997a; Minges 1995; Barkun [1994] 1997).

The property on which the Aryan Nations compound was located was lost in 2000 following a civil lawsuit filed by the SPLC on behalf of local residents who had been assaulted by compound security personnel. Butler died in 2004, and there have been disputes over who will retain the mantle of leadership for the Aryan Nations group, with competing headquarters and websites. Currently, the two factions are Ayran Nations (Kindred Awake), led by August B. Kreis, III in Lexington, SC; and Ayran Nations: Church of Jesus Christ Christian led by Jonathan Williams in Lincoln, Alabama. The influence of Aryan Nations continued to diminish from 2004 to 2006. Christian Identity, however, continues to exist as a religion and a movement outside of Aryan Nations (Berlet 2004b).

CREATIVITY MOVEMENT

Ben Klassen invented the Creativity religion in 1973 under the name World Church of the Creator, but a New Age group with a similar name forced a name change in 2003 through a civil court ease (Hightower 2002). The battle cry of Creativity is "RAHOWA!" which stands for Racial Holy War. Creativity believes that people of color and Jews are "mud races" that are inferior to the "Aryan race." When Creativity takes power, the "mud races" and white "racetraitors" will be expelled from the United States or eliminated (CNC, MHRN, and NCHD 2003; Beirich and Potok 2003; Hightower 2002). Matt Hale eventually became the national leader *(Pontifex Maximus)* of the Creativity movement, although he was later jailed after his conviction on charges of soliciting the assassination of the federal judge who issued the ruling in the civil litigation over the name. (SPLC 2004; CNC, MHRN. and NCHD 2003). Although claiming to operate within the law. Hale has explained:

> It cannot be denied that Ben Klassen envisioned that one day, there would probably be an all-out war with the mud races. After all, he did not speak the words, "RAHOWA! This Planet is Ours!" for nothing. In [Klassen's book *Nature's Eternal Religion*], he describes how once we get the White Race's thinking straight, the White Race will cease to subsidize the mud races, and they shall wither on the vine. Then, the White Race under the banner of Creativity shall expand its territory until all of the good lands of this planet

earth are ours. The mud races may very well offer some resistance and that resistance will have to be destroyed. (Hale n.d.)

Creativity considers Christianity to be polluted by Judaism, and teaches the importance of maintaining racial purity to keep the white race superior (Dobratz 2001). The religion believes that spirituality is expressed through nature as the collective will of the white race (Klassen [1973] 1992). In addition to *Nature's Eternal Religion*, Klassen's other two core founding texts include *The White Man's Bible* (1981), and *Salubrious Living* (1982). In the past. Creativity was very successful at organizing neo-Nazi skinheads through an affiliation with a racist record label and its rejection of traditional Christianity (Burghart 1999).

In many ways, Creativity functions more like a revolutionary rightwing political organization similar to the National Alliance. Yet Creativity has a more developed founding religious text from which to draw, and its members tend to see their struggle as a "holy war," regardless of their familiarity with the intricacies of Creativity's spiritual basis.

For example, a March 1998 issue of the group's newsletter *The Struggle* carried a full-page advertisement urging members to "Order the Holy Books of Creativity," and suggested the books be read so that members could "fully understand the power and greatness of our religious Movement." At the same time the cover story by Matt Hale urging a "fruitarian diet as set forth in our Holy Books," conceded there "is no requirement that Creators practice salubrious living (as outlined in Creative Credo 5 through 9 *of The White Man's Bible),* but you will be extremely glad that you did" (Hale 1998).

RACIST NORSE PAGANISM: ODINISM, ÁSATRÚ, ANDWOT AN ISM

Odinism, Ásatrú, and Wotanism are related forms of paganism based on the spiritual themes of Norse mythology. Gardell uses the term Ásatrú toencompass Odinism (2003:153), Others use Ásatrú/Odinist (Kaplan and Bjorgo1998:109–110), but we find it less awkward to simply refer to Odinism, as did Dobratz (2001). Most Odinists are not racists, but the racist form of Odinism claims it is the true religion of the white northern Europeans, especially Scandinavians. Norse gods are therefore the true gods of the Aryan race. Odinism has appealed to young people looking for an alternative to Christianity or atheism (Gibbons 2004; Gardell 2003; Goodrick-Clarke 2002; Dobratz 2001; Kaplan 1997a).

Small circulation print newsletters and magazines such as *Fenris Wolf* also help network the movement, as do Internet sites and online stores. A major publisher of racist Odinists books and tracts was 14 Word Press. The "14 words" are from the statement by jailed White Supremacist David Lane: "We must secure the existence of our people and a future for White children" (ADLn.d.(a); Lane 1999, pp. xix, 6, 27, 83–99, 102–105, 126). In 2001, Micetrap Distribution took over the catalog from 14 Word Press, adding it to an online distributorship of racist music and print materials.

The White Order of Thule is a racist Odinist movement built around Norse war-rior myths. ("Thule" is pronounced "Two-Lee"). According to Burghart and Massa (2001) the group "teaches its few members everything from Practical Occultism," 'Jungian psychology.' and 'Archetypal Path working,' to 'Folkish Hygiene' and 'Hermetic Philosophy.'" Recommended books include Hitler's *Mein Kampf,* Yockey's *Imperium,* Spengler's *The Decline of the West,* Redbeard's *Might is Right,* Evola's *Revolt Against the Modern World,* and Nietzsche's *Twilight of the Idols* (Burghart and Massa 2001).

THE YOUTH CULTURAL SECTOR

Despite an almost total lack of ideological cohesion, youth subcultures play a major role in the White Supremacist movement. The late Aryan Nations leader Richard G. Butler conducted specific outreach to young White Power advocates, inviting them to national gatherings and even holding neo-Nazi rock concerts at the Aryan Nations compound in Hayden Lake, ID. These events drew hundreds of skinheads from across the country, and significantly influenced the construction of ties among various neo-Nazi skinheads who were then better able to build a skinhead movement in the United States (Burghart 1999; Ferber 1999; Hamm 1993).

The youth culture sector of the White Supremacist movement displays relatively unique features in terms of primary activities. Youth cultural elements in the White Supremacist movement tend to cluster around activities particular to their sub cultural affiliations. At the same time, certain other activities are common elements of most White Supremacist youth subcultures. Members of youth subcultures are often able to identify themselves as holding White Supremacist beliefs through active displays of neo-Nazi and other White Supremacist symbols as part of a deliberate aesthetic. Watch organizations such as the Anti-Defamation League (www.adl.org) and Center for New Community (www.tumitdown.com) have collected information on dozens of symbols used to identify oneself as a White Supremacist. Members of White Supremacist youth cultures are likely to communicate with one another through small-scale publications or "zines" which often combine elements of specific youth subcultures and the politics of white supremacy. The skillful construction of a White Supremacist zine inextricably links white supremacy to the subculture in a way that forces youth involved to adopt the ideology as a condition of membership. Most importantly, youth subcultures help to sustain and develop the movement through the development of prefigurative spaces. Rock concerts, parties, and subcultural "crash pads" and "hangouts" are locations where new recruits are exposed to the politics of white supremacy and the subculture of themovement. Older members (who are respected by all the members of the sub-culture, new and old alike) reinforce the ideals and norms in these settings. Finally, prefigurative spaces give recruits a sense of belonging and community that often leads them to seek out such movements as a solution to feelings of strain (Futrell and Simi 2004; Blazak 2001; Ezekiel 1995).

SKINHEADS

The skinhead subculture has its roots in England in the late 1960s. A wave of immigration from Britain's former Caribbean colonies, especially Jamaica, brought the youth culture of the region to the UK. The earliest skin heads were interracial groups of working class youth who maintained short, clean cut hair and a "mod" appearance and organized around Jamaican "ska" and American soul music. As reggae and Rastafarianism began to dominate Jamaican youth subculture in the 1970s, the skinhead subculture lost much of its interracial character and became a white phenomenon. Economic hardship and a reputation for violence led many skinheads to adopt nationalist politics and engage in sporadic attacks against immigrants from Asia and South Asia. The change in the subculture, combined with the influence of early Punk rock nihilism and the development of a musical style known as "Oi!" (a mid-tempo form of Punk rock which contained lyrics that often reflected the working class lifestyles of the audience), opened the door for the British neo-Nazi National Front to look to the skinhead subculture as a source of potential recruits. Skrewdriver, the first neo-Nazi Oi! Band (which was fronted by a member of the National Front) would make the term, skinhead, virtually synonymous with racism and violence in 1980s England. Nazi skinheads began to appear in the United States around 1984 with the formation of the neo-Nazi organization (read: youth gang) known as Romantic Violence by skinhead Clark Martell. The group began its activities by publishing leaflets and distributing records by European White Supremacist bands such as Skrewdriver, No Remorse, and Brutal Attack in Chicago area record stores and through the mail. Martell also formed the first American neo-Nazi skinhead band. Final Solution, in 1985 (Burghart 1999: Hamm 1993).

The "traditional" skinheads in Europe and the United States resisted the influx of racist polities into the subculture, and a culture war for the hearts and minds of new members exists within much of the subculture between racists and anti-racists. Violence often attributed to "rival skinhead gangs" or within the Punk rock and skinhead subculture may be the result of conflicts between rival political tendencies. Such conflict is part of a repressive effort against the influence of White Supremacist politics on the subculture by anti-racist activists. What may appear to many law enforcement and/or social science professionals as a conflict between groups of "deviant" youth may in fact be a conflict between rival political organizations for influence within a cultural space, and a battle for potential recruits to their respective social movements.

The culture war within the Punk rock and skinhead subculture, combined with the limited appeal of the genre, has forced the White Supremacist movement to diversify its musical propaganda efforts. It found a more fruitful breeding ground within certain genres of the heavy metal scene. In recent years, many acts within the heavy metal music scene have grown to national prominence. Despite metal's mainstream acceptance, a growing group of bands and artists has focused on maintaining the underground status of some elements of the subculture. Beginning in the late 1980s, underground heavy metal has developed a style of music that "features fast and heavy guitars, double drumbeats, and growling vocals" (Burghart 1999:52) with lyrics that focus on horror movie style topics related to violence. While this music was designed to shock, it had little political message and songs that may have been deemed "political" often focused on populist anti-elitist themes. Deriving from the "Death" metal of the underground scene. Black metal sought to upstage this earlier form by focusing on clearly establishing their group identity as evil rebels through the bold rejection of mainstream society, religion, and polities (Burghart 1999).

The Black metal underground consists of individuals who view themselves as intellectuals and philosophers. Much of the appeal of the music style and subculture is based on the outsider status of its adherents who view themselves as inherently superior to most people. The pursuit of "evil" status, and belief in the intrinsic superiority of the Black metal audience, led many of its initial artists to seek out philosophies that matched the music's message. Many of these people quickly gravitated to neo-Nazi ideologies and Adolf Hitler as a symbol of ultimate evil. Black metal's rejection of religion allows the subculture to mask antisemitic polities under the guise of atheism (Burghart 1999).

While music subcultures are not particularly dangerous in and of themselves, Black metal has produced a coherent social movement that values turning philosophy into action. As with many other subcultures, the Black metal scene communicates with its members via fanzines, music, and the Internet. Yet, unlike in many other subcultures, there are several organized networks of neo-Nazis, whose overall effect has been to associate permanently the Black metal genre with the politics of National Socialism. The largest of these groups is the Pagan Front, "an international conglomeration of record labels, individuals, organizations, and bands that seek to promote 'black music for white people'"(Burghart 1999, 60). This quasi organization lists among its ideological principles that it is "pro-Aryan," consists of "proud national socialists," and consists of "serious activists" with "zero tolerance for enemies of [their] race" (www.thepaganfront. com), The Black metal subculture has earned a reputation for turning words into deeds. Some of the founding members of bands in the genre have been arrested and convicted of crimes ranging from arson attacks on churches to murder (Burghart 1999). With its focus on seeking out and valorizing "pure" evil, philosophical attachment to neo-Nazi ideology, and propensity for violence, the Black metal subculture has proven a fruitful recruiting ground for White Supremacists. While National Socialist Black metal represents one subset of a larger culture, there appears to be little internal critique of its polities within the subculture under the guise of remaining "apolitical."

INDUSTRIAL/NOISE/APOCALYPTIC FOLK/GOTHIC

The musical styles that fall under the industrial, noise, apocalyptic folk, and gothic labels vary greatly. However, the fan base for all of these genres contains a great amount of crossover with many individuals following some or all of them. Some of the artists who choose these musical styles also often "crossover" within the broad subculture. Much like Black metal, this subculture prides itself on examining the more sinister aspects of modern society and many of its members also view themselves as intellectuals pursuing taboo subjects. Many of the early performers in these genres used Fascist and Nazi imagery as a means of criticizing what they saw as growing social control and authoritarianism in their societies. These bands and individuals would generally be identified with political movements of the left in their criticism of industrialization, war, environmental destruction, and animal experimentation. However, there are clearly performers within the genre that have chosen to address similar issues using neo-fascist and neo-Nazi ideologies. For these individuals the fascist imagery of the subculture allows them to actively advocate for white supremacy, Odinism, and race war (Burghart 1999).

Much like the Punk rock/skinhead and Black metal subcultures, the industrial/noise/apocalyptic folk/gothic subculture appeals to youth who are experiencing some form of strain and provides an outlet for their anger as well as a means to reject mainstream society. The White Supremacist movement is aided in its recruitment within this subculture by the fact that certain pioneers of these musical genres are also some of the most ardent advocates of neo-fascism and/or neo-Nazism. This lends legitimacy to supremacist attempts to "infiltrate" the subculture and use it as a recruiting base (Burghart 1999).

White Supremacist elements within the industrial/noise/apocalyptic folk/gothic subculture appear to have a limited influence on the scene as a whole. Although many members of the culture view themselves as "apolitical" and the pattern of White Supremacist recruitment within this subculture follows that of Black metal, it would appear that there is somewhat more internal criticism of neo-fascist/Nazi ideology and recruitment.

CONCLUSIONS

While researching the movement, scholars have often attempted to categorize the major ideologies, organizations, and cultural tendencies that makeup modern, organized white supremacy. These varying typologies have generally shared four categories Ku Klux Klan, Neo-Nazi, racist skinhead, and Christian Identity (Blee 2002; Ferber 1999; Marks 1996). These typologies do reveal certain organizational trends, but do not take into account a number of significant changes such as the influence of White Supremacist ideology on youth cultures other than skinheads, and the development of religious belief systems that reject Christianity in favor of pagan or other spiritualities.

Using the typology of New Social Movements developed by Kriesi, et al. (1995), we suggest an alternative typology based on ideology and activity of organizations within the movement. This typology organizes the movement into "instrumental" political organizations that engage in the political process however marginal they may be; "countercultural" youth cultural groups that rely on alternative forms of communication, social activity, and symbols as well as direct confrontation with the state and "mainstream" society; and "subcultural" religious movements that focus on attaining concrete goals while engaging in alternative spiritual practices.

By categorizing organizations using this typology, one can begin to make important distinctions in the types of individuals involved with a specific group, the type of propaganda an organization produces, the recruitment tactics and style of the members within it, and its propensity for violence. This not only assists scholarly research, but has an applied societal value in helping develop practical plans for minimizing violent confrontations when members of these groups become involved in disputes, criminal investigations, or issues of military discipline.

Despite the ideal typical construction of this typology, there is nonetheless significant crossover between groups within these categories. Political and religious groups often seek new recruits by allying themselves with youth cultural trends. The history of one of the largest White Supremacist music labels. Resistance Records, serves as a perfect case example of the importance of ties between political and/or religious groups and youth culture. Resistance was founded in the early 1990s by Creativity movement member, George Burdi, as a means for releasing music by his band Ra Ho Wa. Burdi actively promoted White Supremacist counterculture through CD releases and a glossy magazine and actively built a skinhead base for the Creativity movement. After Burdi experienced legal and financial trouble, the label was sold to a fellow movement member, and then Resistance was sold again to William Pierce of the National Alliance. Resistance's ties to the National Alliance gave greater legitimacy to the organization in the late 1990s and increased skinhead participation. The label also began to expand into other musical styles to promote white supremacy in Burdi's final years of ownership and much more actively after it became the property of the National Alliance (Burghart

1999). Further study of the relationship between political and/or religious organizations and youth culture should be conducted; however, there is anecdotal evidence that a similar relationship exists between NSBM and Odinism.

The overlap that exists between organizations may have more than a strategic basis. While alliances between organizations are common, individuals may find themselves associating with multiple types of organizations through a combination of ideological and personal motivations. Instrumental movements that are perceived as successful may gain members, yet spiritual beliefs or the emotional benefits of counter cultural participation that such movements provide (Polletta and Jasper 2001; Jasper 1997) may not be affected by the success or failure of a particular organization.

In addition, there are a number of prefigurative spaces where White Supremacists may meet across the various typologies. Large scale gatherings are often purposely organized to draw together the various organizations and elements within the broader White Supremacist social movement in order to facilitate movement growth and expansion, as well as to solidify participation by members (Futrell and Simi 2004). Furthermore, the Internet serves as a space where members of various organizations can interact, particularly on "non-sectarian" websites such as stormfront.org where participation by members of abroad White Nationalist movement is tolerated and intercommunication is actively encouraged.

While the phenomenon of trans movement fluidity may undermine the typology provided, we believe that it serves to underscore the important differences and identities of individual movement members and provides a clear organizational tool for identifying specific movement organizations within the broad White Supremacist movement.

In the past, many of the groups mentioned here have been described in public discourse as crazy "extremists." Traditional scholarly conceptions of the White Supremacist movement have often focused on the ideological and criminal "deviance" of movement participants. Detailed sociological study of movement members, however, has found that they are no different from other social movement participants who develop complex ideologies and respond to material forces, cultural changes, and the influence of organizations and ideologies (Jipson and Becker 2000). By locating White Supremacist groups within the context of how all social and political movements operate, one can begin to see how specific frames guide White Supremacist ideology, analysis, and action; especially the meta frames of conspiracism, dualism, and apocalypticism (Berlet 2004a), Understanding how these groups assemble their ideologies, pick their goals, and justify their actions, makes them easier to understand.

REFERENCES

Anthony, Dick and Thomas Robbins. 1997. "Religious Totalism, Exemplary Dualism, and the Waco Tragedy." Pp. 261–84 in *Millennium, Messiahs, and Mayhem,* edited by Thomas Robbins and Susan Palmer. New York: Routledge.

Anti-Defamation League of B'nai B'rith (ADL). 2006, "Neo-Nazis Indicted for Civil Rights Violations in Utah," Anti-Defamation League of B'nai B'rith, June 9. Retrieved July 18, 2006 (http://www.adl.org/leam/ extremism in the news/White Supremacy/ walker arrested national_allianee.htm?LEARN_Cat=Extremism&LEARN SubCat=F. xtremism_in_the_News).

———. 2005. "White Revolution: Billy Roper's Unity Efforts Not Particularly Successful," Anti-Defamation League of B'nai B'rith, Retrieved January15, 2006 (http://www.adl.org/ learn/extremism_in_ America_updates/groups/white_revolution/white+revolution_update 0501.htrn).

———. 2002, "National Alliance: Extremism in America." Anti-Defamation League of B'nai B'rith. Retrieved January 15, 2006 (http://www.adl.org/leam/ext%5Fus/n%5Falliance. asp).

n.d.(a). "David Lane," Online resource: Extremism in America, Law Enforcement Agency Resource Center. Anti-Defamation League of B'naiB'rith. Retrieved January 15, 2006 (http://www.adl.org/leam/Ext_US/lane.asp?xpicked=2anditem=lane).

n.d.(b). "The National Socialist Movement," Anti-Defamation League of B'nai B'rith. Retrieved January 15, 2006 (http://www.adl.org/leam/ext_us/.The_National_Socialist_Movement.asp?)

n.d.(c), "White Revolution / Billy Roper." Anti-Defamation League of B'nai B'rith. Retrieved January 15, 2006 (http://www.adl.org/leam/ext_us/w_revolution.asp).

Arena, Michael P. and Bruce A. Arrigo. 2000. "White Supremacist Behavior: Toward an Integrated Social Psychological Model." *Deviant Behavior* 21:213–44.

Barkun, Michael. [1994] 1997. Religion and the Racist Right: The Origins of the Christian Identity Movement. Chapel Hill, NC: University of North Carolina Press

———. 2003. *A Culture of Conspiracy: Apocalyptic Visions in Contemporary America.* Berkeley: University of California Press.

Beam, Louis. 1983. "Leaderless Resistance" *Inter-Klan Newsletter & Survival Alert.* Undated, circa May, pages not numbered, on file at PRA.

Beck, E. M. 2000. "Guess Who's Coming to Town." *Sociological Focus* 33:153–74.

Beirich, Heidi and Mark Potok. 2003. "Creator Crack Up." *Intelligence Report,* Spring 2003. Retrieved January 15, 2006 (http://www.splcenter.org/intel/intelreport/article.jsp?aid=23)

———. 2004. "Two Faces of Volks front." *Intelligence Report,* Summer 2004. Retrieved January 15, 2006 (http://www.splcenter.org/intel/intelreport/article.jsp?aid=475;)

Berbrier, Miteh. 1998a, "Half the Battle": Cultural Resonance, Framing Process, and Ethnic Affectations in Contemporary White Separatist Rhetoric." *Social Problems* 45: 43 1-47.

———1998b. "White Supremacists and the (Pan-)Ethnic Imperative: on 'European Americans' and 'White Student Unions.'" *Sociological Inquiry* 68:498–516.

———1999. "Impression Management for the Thinking Racist: A Case Study of Intellectualization as Stigma Transformation in Contemporary White Supremacist Discourse." *Sociological Quarterly* 40:411–33.

Berlet, Chip. 2001. "Hate Groups, Racial Tension and Ethnoviolence in an Integrating Chicago Neighborhood 1976–1988." Pp. 117–63 in Dobratz, Waldner, and Buzzell, eds., 2001.

———2004a. "Mapping the Political Right: Gender and Race Oppression in Right-Wing Movements," Pp, 19–48 In *Home-Grown Hate: Gender and Organized Racism.*, edited by Abby L. Ferber. New York, NY: Routledge.

———2004b.' "Christian Identity: The Apocalyptic Style, Political Religion, Palingencsis and Neo-Fascism." *Totalitarian Movements and Political Religions* 5.469–506.

———2004c. "Militias in the Frame." *Contemporary Sociology* 33:514–21.

Berlet, Chip and Matthew N. Lyons, 2000. *Right-Wing Populism in America: Too Close for Comfort.* New York, NY: Guilford Press.

Biddiss, Michael D. 1970. *Father of Racist Ideology: The Social and Political Thought of Count Gobineau* New York: Weybright and Talley.

Blazak, Randy. 2001. "White Boys to Terrorist Men: Target Recruitment of Nazi Skinheads." *American Behavioral Scientist* 44:982–1000.

Blee, Kathleen M. 1991. *Women of the Klan: Racism and Gender in the 1920s.* Berkeley, CA: University of California Press.

———. 1999. "Racist Activism and Apocalyptic/Millennial Thinking." *Journal of Millennial Studies* 2(1). Retrieved July 4. 2004 (http://www.mille.org/publications/summer99/blee. PDF).

———. 2002. *Inside Organized Racism: Women in the Hate Movement.* Berkeley, CA: University of California Press.

Boyer, Paul S. 1992. *When Time Shall Be No More: Prophecy Belief in Modern American Culture.* Cambridge, Mass.: Belknap/Harvard University Press.

Brasher, Brenda E. 2000. "From Revelation to The X-Files: An Autopsy of Millennialism in American Popular Culture." *Semeia* 82:281–95.

———2001. "When Your Friend is Your Enemy: American Christian Fundamentalists and Israel at the New Millennium." Pp. 135–45 in *Millennial Visions: Essays on Twentieth-Century Millenarianism,* edited by M.F. Lee. Westport, CT: Greenwood Publishing Group.

Brasher, Brenda E. and Chip Berlet. 2004. "Imagining Satan: Modem Christian Right Print Culture as an Apocalyptic Master Frame." Presented at the Conference on Religion and the Culture of Print in America, Center for the History of Print Culture in Modern America, September 10–11, University of Wisconsin-Madison.

Burghart, Devin and Justin Massa. 2001. "Damned, Defiant and Dangerous: Continuing White Supremacist Violence in the U.S." *Searchlight* July, online archive.

Burghart, Devin, ed. 1999. *Soundtracks to the White Revolution: White Supremacist Assaults on Youth Music Subcultures.* Chicago, IL: Center for New Community [in cooperation with Northwest Coalition for Human Dignity].

Burris, Val, Emery Smith, and Ann Strahm. 2000. "White Supremacist Networks on the Internet." *Sociological Focus* 33:215–35.

Bushart, Howard L., John R. Craig and Myra Barnes. 2000. *Soldiers of God: White Supremacists and their Holy War for America.* New York, NY: Kensington Books.

Canovan, Margaret. 1981. *Populism.* New York: Harcourt Brace Jovanovich. Center for Democratic Renewal, "Metzger Begins Move to the Top," *The Monitor,* January 1988, p. 5; cited in Berlet and Lyons 2000, p. 269, footnote 11 (p. 394).

Center for New Community, the Montana Human Rights Network, and the Northwest Coalition for Human Dignity (CNC, MHRN, and NCHD). 2003. *Creating a Commotion: Matt Hale and the "World Church of the Creator."* Chicago, IL.

Chalmers, David M. 1965. *Hooded Americanism: The First Century of the Ku Klux Klan. 1865–1965.* Garden City, N.Y.: Doubleday and Company.

Chermak, Steven M. 2002. *Searching for a Demon: The Media Construction of the Militia Movement.* Boston: Northeastern University Press.

Cohn, Norman. [1957] 1970. *The Pursuit of the Millennium: Revolutionary Millenarians and Mystical Anarchists of the Middle Ages.* New York, NY: Oxford University Press.
———1993. *Cosmos, Chaos and the World to Come: The Ancient Roots of Apocalyptic Faith.* New Haven: Yale University Press.

Coogan, Kevin. 1999. *Dreamer of the Day: Francis Parker Yockey and the Postwar Fascist Intetrnational.* Brooklyn. N.Y.: Autonomedia.

Daniels, Jessie. 1997. *White Lies: Race Class. Gender, and Sexuality in White Supremacist Discourse.* New York, NY: Routledge.

Davis, Joseph, ed. 2002. *Stories of Change: Narrative and Social Movements.* Albany, NY: State University of New York Press.

Dobratz, Betty A. 2001. "The Role of Religion in the Collective Identity of the White Racialist Movement." *Journal for the Scientific Study of Religion* 40:287–302.

Dobratz, Betty A. and Stephanie Shanks-Meile. 1995. "Conflict in the White Supremacist/Racialist Movement in the United States." *International Journal of Group Tensions* 25:57–75.
———1996. "Ideology and the Framing Process in the White Separatist/Supremacist Movement in the United States." *Quarterly Journal of Ideology* 19:3–29.
———2000. *The White Separatist Movement in the United States "White Power. White Pride!"* Baltimore, MD: Johns Hopkins University Press.

Dobratz, Betty A., Lisa K. Waldner, and Timothy Buzzell, eds. 2001. "ThePolitics of Social Inequality," *Research in Political Sociology. Vol, 9.* Amsterdam: JAI/Elsevier.

Durham, Martin. 2000. *The Christian Right, the Far Right and the Boundaries of American Conservatism.* Manchester, England: Manchester University Press.

————2002. "From Imperium to Internet: the National Alliance and the American Extreme Right" *Patterns of Prejudice* 36:50–61.

————2004. "The Upward Path: Palingenesis, Political Religion and the National Alliance." *Totalitarian Movements and Political Religions* 5:454–68.

Eatwell, Roger. 2003. "Reflections on Fascism and Religion." *Totalitarian Movements and Political Religions* 4: 145–66.

Ellwood, Robert. 2000. "Nazism as a Millennialist Movement." Pp. 241–60 in *Millennialism, Persecution, and Violence: Historical Cases,* edited by Catherine Wessinger. Syracuse, NY: Syracuse University Press.

Ewick, Patricia and Susan S. Silbey. 1995. "Subversive Stories and Hegemonic Tales: Towards a Sociology of Narrative." *Law and Society Review* 29:197–226.

Ezekiel, Raphael S. 1995. *The Racist Mind: Portraits of American Neo-Nazis And Klansmen.* New York, NY: Viking.

Ferber, Abby L. 1998. *White Man Falling: Race. Gender, and White Supremacy.* Lanham, MD: Rowman and Littlefield.

————1999. "The White Supremacist Movement in the United States Today." Pp. 346–54 in *Race and Ethnic Conflict: Contending Views on Prejudice, Discrimination, and Ethno violence,* edited by Fred L. Pincus and Howard J. Ehrlich. Boulder, CO: Westview Press.

————2000. "Racial Warriors and Weekend Warriors: The Construction of Masculinity in Mythopoetic and White Supremacist Discourse." *Men and Masculinities* 3: 30–56., ed. 2004. *Home-Grown Hate: Gender and Organized Racism.* New York, NY: Routledge.

Ferber, Abby L. and Michael S. Kimmel. 2004. "'White Men are this Nation:' Right-Wing Militias and the Restoration of Rural American Masculinity." Pp. 143–60 in *Home-Grown Hate: Gender and Organized Racism,* edited by Abby L. Ferber. New York: Routledge.

Flint, Colin, ed. 2003. *Spaces of Hate Geographies of Discrimination and Intolerance in the U.S.A.* New York, NY: Routledge.

Freilich, Joshua D. 2003. *American Militias: State Level Variations in Militia Activities.* New York: LFB Scholarly Publishing.

Futrell, Robert and Pete Simi. 2004. "Free Spaces, Collective Identity, and the Persistence of U.S. White Power Activism." *Social Problems* 51:16–42.

Gardell, Mattia. 2003. *Gods of the Blood: The Pagan Revival and White Separatism.* Durham, N.C.: Duke University Press.

Gentile, Emilio. 1996. *The Sacralization of Politics in Fascist Italy,* translated by Keith Botsford. Cambridge, MA.: Harvard University Press.

————2004. "Fascism, Totalitarianism and Political Religion," *Totalitarian Movements and Political Religions* 5:326–75.

Gerstenfeld, Phyllis, Diana R. Grant and Chau-Pu Chiang. 2003. "Hate Online: A Content Analysis of Extremist Internet Sites." *Analyses of Social Issues and Public Policy* 3:29–44.

Gibbons, Tom. 2004. "Shadows from a Black Sun." Review of *Gods of the Blood: The Pagan Revival and White Separatism,* by M. Gardell. *Quadrant* 48(4). Retrieved September 3, 2006 (http://www.quadrant.org.au/php/ archive_details_list.plip?article_id=754).

Goffman, Erving. 1974. *Frame Analysis: An Essay on the Organization of Experience.* Cambridge, Mass: Harvard University Press.

Goldberg, Robert Alan. 2001. *Enemies Within: The Culture of Conspiracy in Modern America.* New Haven: Yale University Press.

Goodrick-Clark, Nicholas. [1985] 2004. *The Occult Roots of Nazism.* London: I. B. Tauris
———. 2002. *Black Sun: Aryan Cults. Esoteric Nazism, and the Politics of Identity.* New York: NYU Press.

Green, D. P., D.Z. Strolovich, and J.S. Wong. 1998. "Defended Neighborhoods, Integration, and Racially Motivated Crimes." *American Journal of Sociology* 104: 372–403.

Griffin, Roger. 1991. *The Nature of Fascism.* New York, NY: St. Martin's Press.
———2003. "From Slime Mould to Rhizome: an Introduction to the Groupuscular Right." *Patterns of Prejudice* 37:27–50.
———2004. "Introduction: God's Counterfeiters? Investigating the Triad of Fascism, Totalitarianism and Political Religion." *Totalitarian Movements and Political Religions* 5:291-325.

Hale, Matt. 1998. "The Suffering Which Can Be Avoided." *The Struggle.* Issue 33 (XXXIII), p. I. Dated "March XXV AC" in a system that sets dates from the founding of Creativity by Klassen in 1973. n.d. (circa 2002). "Creativity's Strategy for White Victory," originally on Creativity website which is now offline, periodically posted on web, various wordings and punctuation, this version on tile at Political Research Associates.

Hamm, Mark S. 1993. *American Skinheads: The Criminology and Control of Hate Crime.* West Port, CT: Praeger Publishers.

Hightower, Nia. 2002. "What's in a Name?" *Intelligence Report,* Winter 2002. Retrieved January 15, 2006 (http://www.splcenter.org/intel/intelreport/ article.jsp?sid=64).

Himmelstein, Jerome L. 1998. "All But Sleeping with the Enemy: Studying the Radical Right Up Close." Presented at the annual meeting of the American Sociological Association, August 21–24, San Francisco, CA.

Holthouse, David. 2006. "A Few Bad Men," Southern Poverty Law Center website news story, July 7. Retrieved July 18. 2006 (http://www.splcenter. org/ intel/news/item.jsp?aid=66).

Jackson, Camille and Mark Potok. 2004. "National Socialist Movement," Southern Poverty Law Center. Summer 2004. Retrieved January 15, 2006 (http://www.splcenter.org/intel/intelreport/article.jsp?aid=473)

Jasper, James. 1997. *The Art of Moral Protest.* Chicago, IL: Chicago University Press.

Jeansonne. Glen. 1988. *Gerald L. K. Smith: Minister of Hate.* New Haven, CT: Yale University Press.

Jipson, Arthur and Paul Becker. 2000. "The Social Significance of White Supremacy." *Sociological Focus* 33:111–112.

Johnston, Hank. 1995. "A Methodology for Frame Analysis: From Discourse to Cognitive Schemata." Pp. 217 246 in *Social Movements and Culture. Social Movements. Protest, and Contention 4,* edited by Hank Johnston and Bert Klandermans, Minneapolis, MN: University of Minnesota Press.

Kaplan, Jeffrey and Tore BJorgo, eds. 1998. *Nation and Race: The Developing Euro-American Racist Subculture.* Boston: Northeastern University Press.

Kaplan, Jeffrey and Leonard Weinberg. 1998. *The Emergence of a Euro-American Radical Right.* New Brunswick, N.J.: Rutgers University Press.

Kaplan, Jeffrey. 1997a. *Radical Religion in America: Millenarian Movements from the Far Right to the Children of Noah.* Syracuse, N.Y.: Syracuse University Press.

———1997b. "Interpreting the Interpretive Approach: A Friendly Reply to Thomas Robbins." *Nova Religio* 1:30–49.

———2000. "Ku Klux Klan." Pp. 163–66 in *Encyclopedia of White Power: A Sourcebook on the Radical Racist Right,* edited by Jeffrey Kaplan. Walnut Creek, CA: Altamira Press (Rowman and Littelfield).

Kazin, Michael. 1995. *The Populist Persuasion: An American History.* New York, NY: Basic Books.

Kim, T.K. 2005. "Electronic Storm: Stormfront Grows a Thriving Neo-Nazi Community," *Intelligence Report.* Summer 2005. Retrieved January 15, 2006 (http://www.splcenter.org/intel/intelreport/article.jsp?aid=551).

Kintz, Linda. 1997. *Between Jesus and the Market: The Emotions that Matter in Right-Wing America.* Durham, NC: Duke University Press.

Kittrie, Nicholas N. 1995. *The War Against Authority: From the Crisis of Legitimacy to a New Social Contract.* Baltimore. MD: Johns Hopkins University Press.

———2000. *Rebels With a Cause: The Minds and Morality of Political Offenders.* Boulder, CO: Westview Press.

Klassen, Ben. [1973] 1992. *Nature's Eternal Religion.* Milwaukee, WI: Milwaukee Church of the Creator.

———[1981] *The White Man's Bible.* Lighthouse Point, FL: The Church of the Creator.

Klassen, Ben and Arnold De Vries. 1982. *Salubrious Living.* Lighthouse Point, FL: The Church of the Creator.

Kriesi, Hanspeter, Ruud Koopmans, Jan Willem Duyvendak, and Marco G. Guigni. 1995. *New Social Movements in Western Europe: A Comparative Analysis.* Minneapolis, MN: University of Minnesota Press.

Kühl, Stefan. 1994. *The Nazi Connection: Eugenics. American Racism and German National Socialism.* New York, NY: Oxford University Press.

Lamy, Philip. 1996. *Millennium Rage: Survivalists. White Supremacists and the Doomsday Prophecy.* New York, NY: Plenum.

Lane, David. 1999. *Deceived, Damned and Defiant: The Revolutionary Writings of David Lane.* St. Maries, ID: 14 Word Press.

Levitas, Daniel. 2002. *The Terrorist Next Door: The Militia Movement and the Radical Right.* New York, NY: Thomas Dunne/St. Martin's.

Lombardo, Paul A. 2002. "'The American Breed': Nazi Eugenics and the Origins of the Pioneer Fund." *Albany Law Review* 65:743–830.

Lyons, Matthew. 1995. "What is Fascism?" Pp. 244–45 in *Eyes Right! Challenging the Right Wing Backlash,* edited by Chip Berlet. Boston, MA: South End Press.

Marks, Kathy. 1996. *Faces of Right Wing Extremism.* Boston. MA: Branden Publishing.

McVeigh, Rory. 2004. "Structured Ignorance and Organized Racism in the United States." *Social Forces* 82:895–936.

Minges, Patrick. 1995. "Apocalypse Now! The Realized Eschatology of the "Christian Identity' Movement." *Union Seminary Quarterly Review* 49:83–107.

Mintz, Frank P. 1985. *The Liberty Lobby and the American Right: Race. Conspiracy, and Culture.* Westport, CT: Greenwood.

National Vanguard. No date. "What is National Vanguard?" Charlottesville, VA: National Vanguard. Retrieved January 15, 2006 (http://nationalvanguard.org/intro.pdf).

Oberschall, Anthony. 1973. *Social Conflict and Social Movements.* Englewood Cliffs, NJ: Prentice-Hall.

O'Leary, Stephen D. 1994. *Arguing the Apocalypse: A Theory of Millennial Rhetoric.* New York, NY: Oxford University Press.

Patterns of Prejudice. 2002. Special issue on the "Groupuscular Right," 36(3).

Paxton, Robert O. 2004. *The Anatomy of Fascism.* New York, NY: Alfred A. Knopf.

Payne, Stanley G. 1995. *A History of Fascism. 1914–45.* Madison, WI: University of Wisconsin Press.

Perry, Barbara. 2004. "White Genocide: White Supremacists and the Politics of Reproduction." Pp. 75–95 in *Home-Grown Hate: Gender and Organized Racism,* edited by Abby L. Ferber. New York, NY: Routledge.

Poliakov, Leon. 1974. *Aryan Myth: A History' of Racist and Nationalist Ideas in Europe.* New York, NY: Basic Books.

Poiletta, Francesca. 1998. "Contending Stories: Narrative in Social Movements." *Qualitative Sociology* 21:219–46.

Poiletta, Francesea and James Jasper. 2001. "Collective Identity and Social Movements." *Annual Review of Sociology* 27:283–305.

Potok, Mark. 2002. "Divided Alliance" *Intelligence Report,* Winter 2002. Retrieved January 15, 2006 (http://www.splcenter.org/intel/intelreport/ article.jsp?pid=148).

Quinby Lee. 1994. *Anti-Apocalypse: Exercises in Genealogical Criticism.* Minneapolis, MN: University of Minnesota Press.

Redles, David. 2005. *Hitler's Millennial Reich: Apocalyptic Belief and the Search for Salvation,* New York, NY: New York University Press.

Rhodes, James M. 1980. *The Hitler Movement: A Modern Millenarian Revolution.* Stanford, CA: Hoover Institution Press. Stanford University.

Ribuffo, Leo P. 1983. *The Old Christian Right: The Protestant Far Right from the Great Depression to the Cold War*. Philadelphia, PA: Temple University Press.

Ridgeway, James. 1995. *Blood in the Face: The Ku Klux Klan, Aryan Nations, Nazi Skinheads: and the Rise of a New White Culture*. New York, NY: Thunder's Mouth Press.

Robbins, Thomas and Susan J. Palmer, eds. 1997. *Millennium, Messiahs, and Mayhem: Contemporary Apocalyptic Movements*. New York: Routledge.

Robbins, Thomas. 1997. "Religious Movements and Violence: A Friendly Critique of the Interpretive Approach." *Nova Religio* 1:13–29.

Schmaltz, William H. (1999). *Hate: George Lincoln Rockwell and the American Nazi Party*. Washington, DC: Brassey's.

Schroer, Todd J. 2001. "Issue and Identity Framing within the White Racialist Movement: Internet Dynamics." Pp. 207–231 in "The Politics of Social Inequality," *Research in Political Sociology, Vol.* 9, edited by B. Dobratz, L. Waldner, and T. Buzzell. Amsterdam: JAI/Elsevier.

Shanks-Meile, Stephanie. 2001. "The Changing Faces of the White Power Movement and the Anti-Racist Resistance." Pp. 191–195 in "The Politics of Social Inequality." *Research in Political Sociology. Vol. 9,* edited by B. Dobratz, L. Waldner, and T. Buzzell. Amsterdam: JAI/ Elsevier.

Simi, Pete and Robert Futrell. 2006. "White Power Cyberculture: Building a Movement," *Public Eye Magazine*. Summer. Retrieved July 18, 2006 (http://www.publiceye.org/magazine/ v20n2/simifutrellwhite powcr.html). Adapted from a paper presented at the annual meeting of the American Sociological Association. August 13–16, 2005, Philadelphia, PA.

Snow, David A., E. B. Rochford, Jr., S. K. Worden. and Robert D. Benford. [1986] 1997. "Frame Alignment Process. Micromobilization, and Movement Participation." Pp. 211 228 in *Social Movements: Perspectives and Issues,* edited by Steven M. Buechler and F. Kurt Cylke, Jr. Mountain View. Calif.: Mayfield Publishing. Southern Poverty Law Center (SPLC).

———2002a. "Facing the Future," *Intelligence Report*. Winter 2002. Retrieved January 15, 2006 (http://www.splcenter. org/intel/intelreport/article.jsp?pid=92).

———2002b. "A Group Is Born," *Intelligence Report*. Winter 2002. Retrieved January 15. 2006 (http://www.splcenter.org/intel/intelreport/article.jsp?sid= 53).

———2002c. "William Pierce: A Political History." *Intelligence Report,* Fall 2002. Retrieved January 15, 2006 (http://www.splcenter.org/intel/ intelreport/ article.jsp?sid=35)

———2004. "Pontifex Ex," *Intelligence Report*. Summer 2004. Retrieved January 15, 2006 (http://www.splcenter.org/intel/intelreport/article.jsp?aid=476).

———2005. "Center Newsletter Tracks Anti-Immigration Movement. Montgomery. AL: Southern Poverty Law Center. Retrieved January 15, 2006 (http://www.splcentcr.org/news/ item.jsp?aid=129).

——— 2006. "Nazis Rising," *Intelligence Report,* Spring 2006. Retrieved July 18. 2006 (http:// www.splcenter.org/intel/intelrepon/article.isp?aid=61 7)

Steigmann-Gall, Richard. 2003. *The Holy Reich: Nazi Conceptions of Christianity, 1919–1945.* Cambridge: Cambridge University Press.

Trelease, Allen W. 1995. *White Terror: The Ku Klux Klan Conspiracy and Southern Recon-struction.* Baton Rouge: Louisiana State University Press.

Tucker, William. 1994. *The Science and Politics of Racial Research.* Urbana, IL: University of Illinois Press.

———2002. *The Funding of Scientific Racism: Wickliffe Draper and the Pioneer Fund.* Urbana. IL: University of Illinois Press.

Van Dyke, Nella and Sarah A. Soule. 2002. "Structural Social Change and the Mobilizing Effect of Threat: Explaining Levels of Patriot and Militia Mobilizing in the United States." *Social Problems* 49:497–520.

Volksfront. 2005. "Introduction to Volksfront." Portland, OR: Volksfront international. Retrieved January 15, 2006 (http://www.volksfront international.com).

Vondung, Klaus. 2000. *The Apocalypse in Germany.* Columbia, MO: University of Missouri Press.

Vysotsky, Stanislav. 2004. "Understanding the Racist Right in the Twenty First Century: A Typology of Modern White Supremacist Organizations." Presented at the annual meeting of the American Sociological Association, August 14–17, San Francisco, CA.

Ware, Von and Les Back. 2002. "Wagner and Power Chords: Skinheadism, White Power Music, and the Internet." Pp. 94–132 in *Out of Whiteness: Color, Politics, and Culture.* Chicago, IL: University of Chicago Press.

Weber, 1999. *Apocalypses: Prophecies, Cults and Millennial Beliefs through the Ages.* Cambridge, MA: Harvard University Press.

Wessinger, Catherine, ed. 2000a. *Millennialism, Persecution, and Violence: Historical Cases.* Syracuse: Syracuse University Press.

———2000b. "Introduction." Pp 3–39 in *Millennialism, Persecution, and Violence: Historical Cases,* edited by C. Wessinger. Syracuse. NY: Syracuse University Press.

Whitsel, Brad. 1998. "The Turner Diaries and Cosmotheism: William Pierce's Theology of Revolution." *Nova Religio* 1:183–97.

White Revolution. No date. "Introduction." Russellville, AR: White Revolution. Retrieved January 15, 2006 (http://www.whitcrevolution.com).

Williams, Rhys H. 1994. "Movement Dynamics and Social Change: Transforming Fundamentalist Ideology and Organization." Pp. 785–833 in *Accounting for Fundamentalisms,* edited by Martin E. Marty and R. Scott Appleby. Chicago, IL: The University of Chicago Press.

Wistrieh, Robert. 1985. *Hitler's Apocalypse: Jews and the Nazi Legacy.* New York: St. Martin's Press.

Wright, Stuart A. 1999, "Radical Religion in America: Millenarian Movements from the Far Right to the Children of Noah," Review of *Radical Religion in America: Millenarian Movements from the Far Right to the Children of Noah,* by J. Kaplan. *Sociology of Religion,* Summer. Retrieved September 1, 2006 (http://www.ftndatticles.com/p/anicles/mi_mOSOR/is_2_60/ai55208526).

Zald, Mayer N. 1996. "Culture, Ideology, and Strategic Framing." Pp. 261–74 in *Comparative Perspectives on Social Movements: Political Opportunities, Mobilizing Structures, and Cultural Framings* edited by Doug McAdam, John D. McCarthy, and Mayer N. Zald. Cambridge, UK: Cambridge University Press.

LIST OF GROUPS BY CATEGORY

All of the websites below were online at some point in 2005–2006, Websites that were offline as of July 20, 2006 arc crossed out and listed as (offline). This list (along with URLs from the works cited) is online at http://www.publiceye.org/racism/jpms34.html.

POLITICAL

American Defense League, http://americandefenseleague.com/
American Renaissance, http://www.amren,com
Aryan Militia, http://www.aryan-militia,com/
Aryan Nations-New Hampshire
Aryan Network, (offline)
Blood and Honour/Combat 18, http://www.bloodandhonour-usa.com/
Index1.html
German Defense League, http://www.compuserb,com/gemiandefenseleagueHeritage
Front (Canada), http://www,heritagefront,com
Ku Klux Klan units not primarily based on religion Free Knights of the Ku Klux Klan
Libertarian National Socialist Green Party, http://www.nazi.orgNational Alliance, http://www.natall.com, www.natvan.com
National Association for the Advancement of White People (NAAWP), (offline)
National Socialist Movement, http://www,nsm88.com
National Vanguard, http://www.nationalvanguard.org.
Nationalist Movement (Crosstar), http://www.nationalist.org
New Order, NSDAP/AO (Gerhard Lauck), http://www.nazi-lauck-nsdapao.com
Order of White Knights, http://www.orderofwhiteknights.org
Political Soldier (3rd Positionists)
Rebel Army
Stormfront (White Nationalist Community), http://www.stormfront.org
Volksfront, http://www.volksfrontintemational,com/
White Aryan Resistance
White Nationalist Party
White Nationalist Party (UK), http://www.white.org.uk

White Revolution, http://www.whiterevolution.com
Women for Aryan Unity (Canada), http://www.crusader.net/texts/wau/

RELIGIOUS

Christian Identity
Aryan Nations (factional split)
Ayran Nations, (Kreis), http://www.aryan-nations.org
Ayran Nations: Church of Jesus Christ
Christian. (Williams),
http://www.twelvearyannations.eomChildren of Yahweh, http://www.childrenofyah-weh.com
Christian Separatist Church Society, http://www.christianseparatist.org
Church of True Israel, http://www.churchoftrueisrael.com
Imperial Klans of America (Imperial Knights), http://www.k-k-k.com
Kingdom Identity Ministries, http://www.kingidentity.com
Kinsman Redeemer Ministries, http://www.kinsmanredeemer,com
Ku Klux Klan units primarily based on Christian Identity Knights Party (Ku Klux Klan—Thomas Robb), http://www.kkk.com
Mission to Israel, http://www.missiontoisrael.org
Posse Comitatus (many autonomous units)
Scriptures for America, http://www.scripturesforameriea.org
Sheriffs Posse Comitatus (James Wickstrom (offline)
Creativity Movement
Creativity Movement International, (offline)
Creativity Movement Ohio, (offline)
Creativity Movement U.S., (offline)
Klassen was Right, (offline)
Matt Hale, (offline)
Rahowa, (offline)
Rahowa (Klassen's Teachings), http://www.rahowa.eom
Skinheads of the Racial Holy Way, http://www.creatorforum.com
SS Rahowa, (offline)
White Faith, (offline)
White Struggle, http://www.whitestruggle.net
Odinist
14 Word Press, (offline)
Heathen Front, (Allgerinanische Heidnische Front), http://www.heathenfront.org
White Order of Thule

Skinhead

Golden State Skinheads, (offline)

Gutz Skinhead Crew, (offline)

Hammerskin Nation, http://www.hammerskins,net

Keystone State Skinheads, http://www.kss88.com

Maryland Skinheads, http://www.marylandskinheads.com

West Virginia Skinheads, (offline)

Black Metal

National Socialist Black Metal, http://www.nsbm.org

Pagan Front, http://www.thepaganfront.cot

Music Labels, etc.

Diehard Records, http://www.diehardrecords.net

Free Your Mind Productions (formerly Panzerfaust Records),

http://www,freeyourmindproductions.com

Micetrap Distribution (Micetrap Records), http://www.micetrap.net

NS88 Videos (skinhead videos), http://www,ns88.com/shop

Resistance Records, http://www.resistanee.eom

Overview of White Supremacist Groups (Berlet & Vysotsky, 2004)

Typology:

1. Political
2. Religious
3. Youth Cultural—racist skinheads, racist gangs

Explains how the groups recruit and mobilize supporters around ideologies or cultural frames.

Characteristics of White Supremacist Groups

1. Racial hierarchy
2. Antisemitism
3. Dualism
4. Apocalypticism
5. Conspiracy theories
6. Masculinist perspective
7. Antipathy towards gays/lesbians

Similar to other social movements.
Explains how white supremacist groups operate in the public sphere.

Radical Right

► Organized White Supremacist groups evolved from Ku Klux Klan and Neo-Nazi organizations.
  — Spread into a wide range of competing forms and ideologies.
Not focused on right-wing dissident groups (Patriot, armed militia movements)

White-Racist Counter Culture

► White-racist counter culture (Gardell)—Ku Klux Klan, national socialism, culture of White Power music and racist skinheads, the idea of the heroic warrior, conspiracism, antisemitism, right-wing popularism, White separatism.
► "While individual members of White Supremacist movements may appear to be deviant or engage in criminal activity, they are also rational individuals who are acting in accordance with complex belief systems and responding to their material reality, cultural forces, and the requirements of movement organizations and ideologies."

Social Movements

- ▶ Alternative to deviance perspective.
- ▶ Assumes they "are social movement actors, like mainstream social movement actors and institutions, and are socially, politically, and ideologically constructed." (Jipson and Becker 2000).
- ▶ All social movements develop a common ideology and establish a set of frames through which they view a struggle over power (Zaid 1996; Snow, Rochford, Worden, and Benford [1986] 1997; Goffman 1974).

Social Movements (Cont.)

- ▶ Social movements also pick (or create) narratives or stories that teach members and potential members about what is to be admired and what is to be opposed (Davis. 2002; Poiletta 1998; Ewick and Silbey 1995).
- ▶ Overarching metaframes (or stylistic master frames), especially conspiracism. dualism and apocalypticism.

Conspiracism

- Conspiracism—idea that most major historic events have been shaped by vast, long-term, secret conspiracies that benefit elite groups and individuals.
- "Stories explaining the alleged conspiracy are narratives about good and evil that select specific targeted groups, and justify aggression against them e.g. imagined Jewish Intrigues, also the faulty view that Jews belong to a single race or antisemitism that involves religious bigotry and racism."

Dualism

- Dualism-the idea that the world is divided into the forces of good and evil with no middle ground.
- Exemplary dualism-where social and political struggles are cosmic battles, fate of world. (Anthony & Robbins, 1997)
- Radical dualism-worldviews that demonizes perceived enemies (Wessinger, 2000b).

Dualism (Cont.)

▶ "The White Supremacist movement presents the world as a place where heroic warriors—white, heterosexual, (mostly) Christian men and women- are in constant battle with a number of "others": non-white races, Jews, homosexuals, etc." (Bushart, Craig, and Barnes 2000).

White Supremacist Beliefs- Ideology and Activity

▶ Apocalypticism-the idea that there is an approaching confrontation (between white race and people of color, Jews, and race traitors.
   ▷ It will change the nature of the world, during which important hidden truths will be revealed (O'Leary 1994; Boyer 1992).
▶ Hitler
▶ Bible's book of Revelation and the millennial battle of Armageddon (Weber 1999, Cohn 1993. [1957] 1970).
▶ Women subordinate—male supremacist.

Four Books

- Pseudo-scientific theories of the genetic superiority of the white "race."
1. Count Arthur de Gobineau's 1853 *The Inequality of Human Races (Tucker 1994:88–91; Poliakov 1974:215–238;* Biddiss 1970);
2. Frances Galton's 1870 *Hereditary Genius: An Inquiry into Its Laws and Consequences (Tucker 1994:49–53);*
3. *Madison Grant's 1916/1924 The Passing of the Great Race (Tucker 1994:88–96, 124–125; Mintz 1985:32–35)*
4. T. Lothrop Stoddard's 1920 *The Rising Tide of Color Against hite World Supremacy (Kuhl 1994:61–63; Tucker 1994:92–93).*

- In the 1920s. American Eugenicists traded ideas with their counterparts in the Gennan Nazi movement (Lombardo 2002; Tucker 2002, Kuhl 1994).

US Military 1990s

- White Supremacists
- "Aryan Nations graffiti in Baghdad,"
- Identification moves-collect their members together for rallies, literature distribution to show movement members, the media, a target group, government that they are a force (Oberschall1973).
- Leaderless resistance—organizations actively distance ideological and "theoretical" positions from the activities of individuals (Beam 1983).
- Southern Poverty Law Center (SPLC)
- Anti-Defamation League (ADL)

Modern White Supremacist Movement

▶   Ideology and Activity Typology
1. Political-ideological influence of fascist and Nazi political philoso-
    phy e.g. Neo-Nazi. Goal oriented
2. Religious
3. Youth cultural organizations
▶   Social movement activity-instrumental, subcultural, and coun-
    tercultural groups (Kriesi et al. 1995).

Political

▶   Political-goal oriented
▶   Authoritarian–elite leadership hierarchy natural and exalted,
    ensuring control over state and populace.
    — Appeal to-traditional values, racialized national identity (in-group/
    out-group), scapegoating.
        ▷ Fascist movements are ideologically committed to achiev-
        ing power through violence.
        ▷ Expand to war/colonial conquest.

Political White Supremacist Organizations

► Openly operate as non-violent, underneath is criminal underground of militants receiving ideological guidance and tacit support for smallcell/individual acts of violence (race war).

— Preparing for coming racial conflict or political overthrow of the state.

► Literature, rallies, protests, internet to spread ideas and recruit.

► Defended Neighborhoods-areas where racial/ethnic tensions heightened due to threat of integrating groups.

---

1. National Alliance-neo-Nazi, revolutionary overthrow of US political system. Cosmotheism (W. Pearce)-apocalyptic millenarianism, Resistance Records (White Power music company)

2. White Aryan Resistance-CA Klan leader Tom Metzger, founder.
   — Third position–national socialist form of neo-Nazism against globalization

3. National Socialist Movement-fighting for race and nation. Nazi party 52 units, 32 states (2006)

4. White Revolution-Billy Roper, founded umbrella coalition Skinheads, Identity Christians, KKK, etc.

5. Volksfront-Randall Lee Kragar (neo-Nazi skinhead) Third Position against capitalism, creation of white businessess. OR

Religious White Supremacist Groups

► Complex subculture based on spiritual belief systems and practice of the religion.
  — Ideas about race, behavior, roles based in religious text.
  — Services, study sacred text, rituals, ceremonies, spiritual leaders (reverend).

Holy war—dualistic apocalyptic

1. Christian Identity
2. Creativity
3. Odinism

3 Spiritual Forms of White Supremacy

1. Christian Identity-racialized Protestantism made of small churches/religious communities (1800s British Israelism).
   — White Aryan Christians God's chosen and America is Promised Land. US 1940s/60s.
   — Aryan Nations compound Idaho
   — Manichacan—white Christian/Jewish struggle (install people of color in powerful positions).

2. Creativity Movement-Ben Klassen founded under World Church of Creator (1973).
   — RAHOWA-Racial Holy War against mud races (blacks/jews) to expel/eliminate them and race traitors.
   — Christianity polluted by Judaism
   — Organized new-Nazi skinheads—record label
3. Odinism-paganism (Asatru, Wotanism) based on Norse mythology (true gods Aryan race).
   — Newsletters, Internet, magazines, 14 Word Press
   "We must secure the existence of our people and a future for White children." David Lane

Youth Cultural Sector

1. Lack ideological cohesion.
2. Aryan Nation leader Richard Butler recruited young White Power advocates e.g. neo-Nazi skinheads.
3. Symbols (Aesthetic)-Neo-Nazi, White Supremacist
4. Prefigurative Spaces-sustain and develop the movement.
   1. rock concerts, parties, crash pads, hangouts used to expose youth to politics of white supremacy and the subculture .
5. Zines—publications used by White Supremacist youth subcultures to communicate their politics.
   — Must adopt ideology to be member.
   — Community, belonging

Youth Cultural Sector

Strain Theory-gap between culturally approved goals and legitimate means for achieving said goals, strain causes frustration and leads to crime.

▶ Skinheads-England 1960s, influx Jamaican immigrants.
  — Interracial early on, mod, ska, soul.
  — 1970s white
  — nationalist politics, economic hardship, violence
  — Asia, S. Asia
  — Punk rock , Oi!, Skrewdriver
  — British neo-Nazi National Front

▶ US 1984 Romantic Violence (youth gang) neo-Nazi organization
  — No Remorse, Brutal Attack, Final Solution (US neo-Nazi band 1985)
  — Punk rock and skinhead political conflict/violence

Youth Cultural Sector

▶ Black Metal—alternative White supremacist musical propaganda born from Death metal.
  — Themes and deeds of horror and violence via fanzines, music, internet.
  — Outsiders-evil rebels, reject of mainstream society, religion, politics.
    ▷ Intellectuals and philosophers, superior
    ▷ Neo-Nazi, Hitler, antisemitic politics, disguised as atheism
    ▷ Pagan Front–National socialist, international record labels, organizations, and bands promoting black music for whites.

Youth Cultural Sector

- Industrial/Noise/Apocalyptical Folk/Gothicdiverse fan base.
  — Fascist, neo-fascist, Nazi, neo-Nazi imagery
  — Focus on the most sinister aspects modern society.
- Intellectuals, taboo topics
  — Industrialization, war, environmental destruction, animal experimentation.
  — Some internal critique

Southern Poverty Law Center (SPLC)

- <u>932 known hate groups</u> (2009) operating across the country, including <u>neo-Nazis, Klansmen</u>, <u>white nationalists</u>, <u>neo-Confederates</u>, <u>racist skinheads</u>, <u>black separatists</u>, border vigilantes and others.
  ▷ Up 54% since 2000
- 512 "Patriot" groups active in 2009.

OVERVIEW OF WHITE SUPREMACIST GROUPS:
HOMEWORK ASSIGNMENT

Please define the following terms/concepts using the article. Additionally, provide one example for each term from your reading. Please bring your homework to the next class.

1. **Ideology** –

2. **Leaderless resistance** –

3. **White Supremacy** –

4. **Racial hierarchy** -

THE ORGANIZATIONAL STRUCTURE OF INTERNATIONAL DRUG SMUGGLING

By Jana S. Benson
and Scott H. Decker

ABSTRACT

While most group offending is not well organized, it is generally assumed that high levels of organization can be found in group offending that generates revenue, such as white-collar crime, drug sales, and smuggling drugs or humans. The organizational structure of international drug smuggling has typically been viewed as highly rational and formally structured. Employing interviews with thirty-four federal prisoners convicted of smuggling large volumes of cocaine into the United States, this study explored the organizational structure of high level international drug smuggling. The subjects described a general lack of formal structure and depicted the drug smuggling operations as composed of isolated work groups without formal connections among each other. These findings bring into question the idea that these groups are rationally organized around pursuing efficiency and support

Jana S. Benson, Scott H. Decker, "The Organizational Structure of International Drug Smuggling," *Journal of Criminal Justice*, vol. 38, no. 2, pp. 130-138. Copyright © 2010 by Elsevier Press. Reprinted with permission.

recent research that suggests network security or minimizing risk are key organizing principles of drug trading organizations.

INTRODUCTION

How well are offenders organized? What are the characteristics of the group in offenses where multiple offenders are involved in committing a crime? The criminological literature is replete with discussions of group offending (McCord & Conway, 2002; Reiss, 1988; Warr, 2002). While rates of co-offending are higher among juveniles (Klein, 1995; McCord & Conway, 2002; Warr, 2002), co-offending among adults is also substantial (Reiss, 1988; Warr, 2002). What is missing in the existing understanding of the group context of offending is how well organized groups of offenders are, the characteristics of those groups, and the influence of organization on offending patterns.

Several characteristics of the offending process must be accounted for if criminologists are to promote a broader understanding of crime. The motivation to offend typically receives the most attention, while other important aspects of offending receive scant attention, particularly the degree to which groups of offenders are organized, the characteristics of those organizations, and the impact of organizational structure on behavior. A better understanding of how criminal groups are organized would have implications for theory development as well as policy responses to crime. It is not enough to know that a group of individuals were present at a crime scene or participated in concert with each other. The structure of their interactions is a central feature to this process that must be understood. Specifically, organizational features of group offending such as the adaptability of the group, specialization, hierarchy, roles, and communication are key aspects that must be accounted for.

This article examines the question of how well organized groups of offenders are and builds on the previous literature on the organization of drug smugglers by focusing exclusively on high level offenders who have personal experience smuggling drugs into the United States. The analysis begins by examining the literature on organizational structure of offending to establish a context for the current study of the organizational structure of high level international drug smugglers. Following a discussion of the sample included in this study, six key characteristics of organizational structure are reviewed for their presence in both complex and less formally organized groups. Using thirty-four offender interviews, the organization of international drug smuggling groups is illustrated. Finally, conclusions are drawn and directions for future research are discussed.

One of the long-standing "major facts" in criminology (Klein, 1967) is the group context of most offending. Group offending is especially pronounced among youthful offenders, with most estimates that 80 percent (or more) of delinquency occurs in a group context (Shaw & McKay, 1931; Warr, 1996). Group offending is particularly pronounced in offenses that generate revenue, such as burglary, larceny, drug sales, and auto theft, but less common in violent offenses, particularly serious assault. Co-offending may have a larger impact, net of the number of individuals involved, than solo offending. Felson (2003) noted that such offending is more likely to generate additional offenses and generate more harm to victims and offenders. Accordingly, criminologists must pay careful attention to the characteristics of co-offending.

Offending groups tend to be relatively small, between two and four individuals (Warr, 2002), but these groups of offenders are typically nested in larger groups of associates, many of whom are also involved in crime or delinquency. Warr (2002, p. 36) identified the former as offending groups and the latter as accomplice networks. He noted that there was little clarity with regard to roles in offending and that most offenders moved between group and individual offending with relative ease, thus addressing the issue of specialization of roles. Offending groups, particularly delinquent offending groups, have a short life span and display little evidence of the kind of rational planning or calculation often thought to characterize group behavior. Reiss (1988) noted that little is known about co-offending patterns among adults. He described adult offending groups as transitory in nature with individuals drifting in—and out—of the groups on a frequent basis.

There is considerable variation in offending groups and to treat them as all the same would be to mischaracterize the nature of such groups. Reiss (1988) suggested that distinctions among gangs, groups, and networks would be a useful starting point in attempting to understand the nature of offender organizations and their impact on offending. Cressey (1972) used the core concept of rationality to characterize the extent and nature of organization within offending groups. Role specialization, hierarchy, and coordination are all key concepts by which he described variation among offending groups from organized crime to street criminals. For this reason, these characteristics were also employed in the present study to distinguish between varying degrees of organization of drug smuggling groups. Waring (2002) argued that the organization of co-offenders rarely follows a market-driven approach or corresponds to the structure of formal organizations, even among organized crime groups. Her key focus was on behavior within offending networks, not elements of the structure, as a means to avoid a strict focus on hierarchy or structure. This approach was consistent with that championed by Burt (1992), who argued that all social structures are built on relationships between individuals.

There have been several attempts to describe more fully the characteristics of co-offending groups, networks, and criminal organizations. Best and Luckenbill (1994, p. 5) created a descriptive typology of co-offending groups using the nature of the association among individuals involved in offenses together. While they concentrated on explaining deviance rather than serious offending, they contended that deviance is generally not well organized. In addition, relationships among offenders were not formal, had short temporal spans, and were specific to individual offenses. Central to their description of these relationships was the idea that the most prominent features of organizations of co-offenders are not part of group structure, but rather in the interactions and transactions. To examine the nature of the interactions between group members in drug smuggling organizations, the present article examines communication within and between these groups.

Many researchers have concluded that offenders do not organize themselves effectively. These studies included ethnographic work done with burglars (Cromwell, Olson, & Avary, 1994; Shover, 1996; Wright & Decker, 1990); robbers (Einstadter, 1969; Wright & Decker, 1997); carjackers (Jacobs, Topali, & Wright, 2003); and gang members (Decker, Bynum, & Weisel, 1998; Decker, Katz, & Webb, 2007). In this context, Donald and Wilson (2000) differentiated between teams and co-acting. Teams, they argued, display a considerable level of interdependence among actors and produce outputs greater than the simple sum of individuals. Co-acting was characterized by low levels of interdependence among offenders who create little additional output beyond what the sum of the individuals would produce. Ram raiders, individuals who engaged in a pattern of smash, grab, and flee at jewelry stores, rarely exhibited permanence in their relationships, specialization, or high levels of long-term interdependence. They observed that offenders were connected in ways that allowed them to assemble teams, identify targets, commit crimes together, and dispose of the proceeds. These relationships were the consequence of generalized offending roles, weak ties and fluid relationships, not a formal, rational structure. The current study examined interdependence as a characteristic of highly organized groups by investigating the coordination of activities within and among the smuggling organizations.

Gangs merit additional discussion in this context because they are a common example of organization among offenders. Many portrayals of gangs by law enforcement and the media depict youth gangs as instrumental-rational organizations. From this perspective, gangs are described as formal organizations that advance their self-interest in rational ways. Researchers have suggested that drug sales in gangs reflect a high degree of organization that is also visible in their use of violence, neighborhood intimidation, and property offenses (Mieczkowski, 1986; Padilla, 1992; Sanchez-Jankowski, 1991; Skolnick, Correl, Navarro, & Robb, 1988). They asserted that gangs embrace common goals, engage in common enterprise, regulate the revenue generating activities of their members, and thus have a formal structure. This view emphasized the formal, rational, and instrumental aspects of the organization. This research also highlighted the vertical nature of the gang and the role of internal controls on gang member behavior in pursuing common goals. It thus recognized the vertical hierarchy of authority as a central feature of highly organized groups.

A competing view described gangs as somewhat disorganized groups, recognizing that although gangs are united by several common features, they are best characterized as having a diffuse organizational structure. Much research has provided support for this contention (Decker & Van Winkle, 1996; Fagan, 1989; Hagedorn, 1988; Klein, Maxson, & Cunningham, 1991). Findings from this research emphasized the lack of a corporate use for the money generated by drug sales, robbery, and property crime among gang members, noting that most profits from such activities are used for individual purposes. This is evidence of a somewhat disorganized, unstructured gang organization.

The focus of this study was on the organizational structure of international drug smuggling. Burt (1992) and Williams (1998) noted that formal organizations can be composed of a number of smaller cells and co-offending groups that engage in drug smuggling, money laundering, human trafficking, or terrorism may have access to information and technology that allows them to operate independently of a larger organizational structure. Indeed, Williams (1998) argued that the key to understanding such groups is to view them as networks; a series of loosely connected nodes (individuals, organizations, firms, and information sharing tools) that are linked across and within organizations. In fact, descriptions of human trafficking and smuggling (Zhang, 2007, 2008); terrorist groups (Kean & Hamilton, 2004; Sageman, 2008); international trafficking in stolen vehicles (Clarke & Brown, 2003); and international drug smuggling (Decker & Chapman, 2008; Morselli, 2001; Williams, 1998) have depicted such groups as small networks of individuals who lack much in the way of a formal structure.

Zaitch (2002) studied drug importation from Colombia to the Netherlands and found little evidence of vertical hierarchies in drug smuggling. The structure of drug distribution was flexible, horizontal, and relied on ethnic and kinship ties to facilitate relationships among smugglers. These characteristics can hardly be described as inductive of a formal organization. Accordingly, the current study examined the recruitment and promotion procedures used in the organization to gain a better understanding of the nature of the bonds that draw people into drug smuggling organizations.

Zaitch (2002) also depicted drug smuggling operations as flexible networks comprised of dynamic, insulated groups that could quickly change tactics and were relatively separate from those earlier or later in the smuggling transaction chain. Organizational adaptability was addressed in the current article through the subjects' descriptions of the how flexibly their group dealt with a variety of changes. Similarly, Schiray (2001) described the organizational structure of drug distribution markets in Sao Paulo as ad hoc, unstable, and not longterm operations. Where specialization is found in international drug trade, it can be quite episodic, and smugglers are often absorbed into other forms of crime. The ad hoc or unplanned quality of drug smuggling organizations was inspected here through the subjects' descriptions of the statement of rules and objectives prior to a trip being made. These findings were consistent with exploratory research on high-level drug smugglers (Reuter, 1983; Reuter & Haaga, 1989) as well as research on street-level dealers (Adler, 1985).

While research on group offending and drug smuggling in particular has contrasted criminal organizations to formally organized hierarchies, recent research has moved away from the hierarchy—decentralization dispute and examined organized crime within the social network framework (McIllwain, 1999; Morselli, 2005, 2008; Raab & Milward, 2003). Instead of viewing group offenders as either hierarchical or decentralized, this perspective emphasized the dynamic interactions between individuals in these groups and the utility of pooling their resources. Using the social network framework and the case-study approach, Morselli (2008), a salient author in this field of research, examined the organizational structure of various criminal networks, including street gangs, drug distribution networks, and other forms of organized crime. He concluded that these criminal networks were less centralized and structured than previously believed and created a flexible order thesis, which suggested that despite some degree of hierarchy and levels of authority among these groups, they maintain some adaptability that benefited the group in terms of managing resources and detecting law enforcement. The current study examined similar aspects of organizational structure, specifically in high-level drug smuggling groups.

A REVIEW OF THE ORGANIZATIONAL LITERATURE

To better understand the organizational structure of international drug smuggling groups, the authors reviewed commonly recognized characteristics of complex organizations. By establishing the qualities that typify complex organizations, it was possible to examine the organizational context of international drug smugglers. The following six characteristics were addressed: (1) hierarchy, (2) statement of rules, (3) communication, (4) adaptability, (5) specialization/coordination, and (6) recruitment/promotion procedures.

In his discussion of the structure of offending organizations, Cressey (1972) noted that the degree of organization is directly related to the rationality of that group. Following the description of formal or complex organizations, as those most rationally arranged in pursuit of its goals it is logical that many of the structural characteristics discussed below are attempts at maximizing rationality and efficiency. Other researchers have suggested, however, that networks are sometimes forced to sacrifice efficiency for other concerns such as security, depending on such traits as the time-to-task and degree of centrality of the organization (Morselli, 2008; Morselli, Giguère, & Petit, 2007). When considering the following characteristics of formally organized networks, it is important to keep in mind that they are not composed of distinct categories. Rather, as previous researchers have observed (e.g., Cressey, 1972; Morselli, 2008), their differences in organization are a matter of degree.

Hierarchy of Authority

One of the most prominent and readily identifiable characteristics of a complex organization is the existence of a formal hierarchy. Formal hierarchies have ranked levels of authority that clearly delineate super-and subordinates, where those in superordinate positions are responsible for overseeing those in lower offices (Weber, 1946). This organization is based on the rationale that having the most qualified person in each position will place an organization in a position to be most effective. The organizational structures of these groups tend to be pyramidal in nature and have a definite vertical quality due to the ranked nature of positions.

Complex or formally organized groups can also have a structure that is horizontally organized. These organizations do not have such graded positions as in a vertical hierarchy and resemble a line connecting various functions rather than a centralized source of control. It is important to note that these rationally organized groups still have a formal designation of responsibilities, but the span of control no longer functions vertically. Decision-making powers flow across various units rather than coming down from a chain of command that originated from a single, ultimate authority.

In contrast to vertical hierarchies or horizontal structures, some groups are organized in a less formal or rational manner. Williams (1998) suggested that some drug smuggling organizations are more accurately described as networks of connected nodes. There is no definite vertical or horizontal chain of command, as individual units are more independent from the larger organization. Decision-making authority, therefore, does not move freely or continuously between nodes, leaving stages of the drug smuggling process isolated from the others to some degree. Such groups exhibit less coordination among their components.

Statement of Rules

In addition to hierarchical structures, another common feature of complex organizations is the formal or written statement of rules, responsibilities, and operating procedures. The structure of organizations is rooted in the rational pursuit of efficiency; therefore, it is necessary to state the group's objectives clearly and the means to reach those goals. Positions are created based on what is found to be the "best" technique or approach, and individuals in those positions are expected to follow rules accordingly.

Less complex organizations or networks typically do not provide members with such explicit expectations. Instead of written rules, objectives and responsibilities are communicated orally or sometimes simply implied. Since individuals are not placed in such organizations because of rational considerations of the fit between their skills and the needs of the organization, there may not be a formal set of rules to communicate to members of the organization.

Communication

Stemming from the hierarchy of authority and formal expression of rules and objectives, complex organizations are typically characterized by indirect communication between members. Communication in these groups is indirect in two senses. First, because of the vertical ranking of positions and formal directives for member's actions, communication with anyone except one's immediate supervisor is rare. Messages and information must flow through the appropriate channels in the chain of command before they reach their target audience. Communication is also indirect in the sense that little personal interaction occurs in these groups. Instead, information tends to be exchanged through more formal channels, where correspondence is more easily documented. Krebs' (2001) examination of terrorist networks demonstrated that groups characterized by distance between members tended to have lower levels of communication, which in turn resulted in increased security for the networks' activities.

Whereas complex organizations are plagued by slow, indirect passing of information from one party or level to another, the opposite is true for groups with a less complex organizational structure. Messages move more directly between members of different units because the units tend not to be separated by various levels of authority. The absence of formal regulations leaves open the possibility to transmit information through personal contacts instead of written communication. In addition, because units tend to be independent within these networks, it is unlikely that a message would successfully reach its target when it is transmitted by any means other than a direct contact with that individual.

Adaptability

The rational model on which most complex organizations are established leaves these groups in a position where they are unable to adapt quickly to changes. Research has noted that organizations characterized by hierarchy and formal rules are typically unsuited to be flexible in their norms and regulations (Heimer, 1992). Rational goal directed behavior is based on contingencies that exist in a given space and time. Organizational components are then selected and positioned for their contribution to that goal and formal rules for actions are established. While these written regulations ensure success under certain conditions, most organizations cannot control the environment and market in which they operate. These groups are therefore unable to change methods of operation or procedures quickly when necessary. This is particularly difficult to accomplish in dynamic environments, where change is more common than stability. Watts (2003) noted that highly centralized, formal networks are "vulnerable to cascade failures," but also have the benefit of structural resources that support recovery.

On the other hand, less complex organizations typically enjoy high levels of adaptability. Due to their lack of established procedures for maximizing efficiency and direct communication between units, less complex organizations are better able to change in response to a dynamic environment. These adaptations can be stimulated by changes in market conditions or specific to offending groups, improvements in law enforcement technologies, or changes in law enforcement tactics (Bouchard, 2007; Degenhardt, Reuter, Collins, & Hall, 2005). Consistent with the social network perspective, Morselli (2008) noted that more flexible networks are not the result of a predefined form. Instead, they emerge from a process of interactions among the individuals in the group. Zaitch (2002) observed that segments of drug smuggling groups were quickly able to change their modus operandi without disturbing the entire operation because the subunits were relatively isolated from other steps in the process due to their non-hierarchical nature.

Specialization and Coordination of Activities

Along with the presence of a formal hierarchy, specialization (or division of labor) is a commonly cited indicator of a complex organization. Division of labor is a product of the rational search for maximum efficiency and contributes to that goal in two ways. First, specialization guarantees that multiple people are not performing the same task. Every member or unit focuses his or her attention on one element of the larger organizational function, in effect becoming an expert at it. Second, by assigning only one task to a position, the organization is able to seek the most qualified person for that role and place them accordingly. This division of labor recognizes that members vary in their skills and abilities and uses individuals' specializations to benefit the larger organization.

Specialization alone, however, is not sufficient for maximum rationality. Complex organizations must also coordinate the activities of each unit to ensure that the ultimate objective is reached. These groups, therefore, are characterized by high levels of interdependence between subunits. For the organization as a whole to be successful, it is imperative that each individual task be performed in the most efficient manner. Coordinating activities in complex organizations is illustrated in the hierarchical distribution of authority discussed previously. With regard to producing and transporting drugs, research has demonstrated the level of specialization required to produce special substances influences not only individual members' activities, but also the complexity of the overall organizational structure (Reuter & Greenfield, 2001).

Networks that are not as complex or rational rely less on specialization and coordination than do their counterparts. While these groups might have some division of labor, they are unlikely to place the most "specialized" individual in any given position because clearly delineated objectives and rules to establish the best means for fulfilling that role do not exist. Placement in the group could be based on other criteria other than specialization, such as convenience, cost, or patrimony. In addition, because these groups are best described structurally as a series of connected nodes, coordinating activities across the entire organization is highly unlikely. Instead, the success of the entire operation depends less on the efficiency of individual tasks, as is the case with complex organizations. Lack of coordinating activities can also be understood to contribute to the high adaptability of these networks.

Recruitment and Promotions

High levels of specialization and rationality are also associated with merit-based recruitment and promotional systems. Selecting and placing members in the group based on their skills and formal qualifications increases the odds that an organization is operating in the most efficient means possible. Promotions in complex organizations are typically merit based, adding an element of competition to motivate members to be efficient. As individuals who have accomplished the most for the organization are promoted up the chain of command, a direct link between member productivity and advancement is established.

In contrast to complex organizations, less rationally organized networks rely less on merit or qualifications. This could be attributed to their lack of clearly enumerated role expectations, which makes developing criteria specific to a position more difficult. The absence of a vertical hierarchy for members to "climb" makes promotions less likely in these groups of connected, but isolated nodes. Recruitment and placement could be based on prior working relationships, kinship, ethnicity, or in more short-term assignments, the nature of the task, as opposed to competency (Donald & Wilson, 2000; Schiray, 2001; Zaitch, 2002). The role of patrimony, kinship, and social capital in recruitment and promotion in organized crime has been documented in the empirical literature (e.g., Block, 2006; Morselli, 2003).

THE DRUG SMUGGLER STUDY

The following analysis was based on interviews conducted with thirty-four individuals held in federal prisons in the United States. The interviews were conducted as part of a larger investigation into the effects of various law enforcement and interdiction techniques on high-level drug smuggling. While the organizational structure of these groups was not a central focus of the original study, information about the way drug smugglers organized themselves was unavoidable in the discussion. A semi-structured, open-ended questionnaire, which was used to elicit information during in-depth interviews, was created from information obtained from interviews with U.S. Customs, U.S. Coast Guard, and prior literature on drug smuggling. The interviews lasted approximately two hours and were conducted in the federal facility where the individual was currently serving time. To acquire the most useful information from the convicted smugglers, a Spanish translator was used when necessary, and all interviews were recorded and transcribed for later analysis.

To focus on high-level drug smuggling, the sample for the current study was selected from individuals serving time for federal drug trafficking convictions from 1992 to 1998. Individuals were selected based on their pre-sentencing investigations and the severity of their score according to the federal sentencing guidelines. Of the 135 "high-level" drug smugglers located in federal prisons, 73 were asked to participate. This produced a sample of 35 individuals that were heavily involved in drug smuggling.

To better understand the characteristics of the interviewed individuals, it is useful to describe them in broad terms. Table 1 presents descriptive characteristics for individuals included in the sample. While the majority of subjects indicated the United States as their country of origin, such nations as Colombia, Cuba, Venezuela, and the Bahamas were also reported. Smuggling activity was described in various locations in the Caribbean and South America, including Colombia, the Bahamas, Panama, Cuba, the Dominican Republic, Mexico, Haiti, Peru, Puerto Rico, and Venezuela.

Of the thirty-four subjects, the modal category for age at time of arrest was forty to forty-nine, and the extreme categories of twenty to twenty-nine years old and seventy to seventy-nine years old each contained one subject. The mean year of arrest was 1993, with reported values ranging from 1988 to 1997. Twenty-two members of the sample were serving a sentence of twenty years or more, with six doing a sentence of thirty years or more, and five doing life. The mean amount of cocaine with which the smugglers in the sample were caught was 1,136 kilograms, just less than 2,500 pounds. None of the smugglers in the sample was caught on their first act of smuggling.

The individuals interviewed for this study were heavily involved in international drug smuggling. Table 1 demonstrates that they played a diversity of roles in the smuggling event for which they were caught, ranging from broker or organizer to transporter or manager. Only one of the individuals could be described as playing a minor role in drug smuggling (off-loader), giving the researchers confidence that this sample of drug smugglers were in positions that afforded them significant knowledge of the organizational structure of their networks. In addition, the smugglers employed a variety of smuggling techniques. Smuggling methods ranged from commercial and private vessels to private and commercial airplanes and included the combination of vessels and airplanes. In short, this diverse and high-level group of drug smugglers was in a position to know and understand the structure of drug smuggling organizations.

Table 1 Summary of subject characteristics

Country of origin	Role	Smuggling region	Age range	Weight of drugs
Bahamas	Recruiter	Colombia/Bahamas	40–49	480 kilos
Colombia	Organizer	Colombia	40–49	1,500 kilos
Colombia	Manager	Colombia	40–49	630 kilos
Colombia	Supervisor	Colombia	40–49	165 kilos
Colombia	Organizer	Colombia	40–49	1,500 kilos
Colombia	Organizer	Bahamas	40–49	3,345.5 kilos
Colombia	Leader	Colombia	60–69	500 kilos
Cuba	Recruiter	Colombia	50–59	40 kilos
Cuba	Broker	Panama	30–39	59 kilos
Cuba	Leader	Cuba/Dom. Republic	30–39	515 kilos
Cuba	Leader	Cuba	40–49	2,350.5 kilos
Cuba	Organizer	Colombia	30–39	728 kilos
Cuba	Transporter	Mexico	40–49	5,000 kilos
Cuba	Captain	Colombia/Haiti	30–39	150+kilos
Cuba	Off-loader	Colombia	40–49	500 kilos
Venezuela	Organizer	Peru	50–59	500 kilos
Venezuela	Leader	Bahamas/Cuba	40–49	50 kilos
U.S.	Manager	Venezuela	30–39	605.5 kilos
U.S.	Leader	Bahamas	50–59	414 kilos
U.S.	Recruiter	Colombia	50–59	15–50 kilos
U.S.	Leader	Caribbean	50–59	1,450 kilos
U.S.	Manager	Haiti	40–49	2,200 kilos
U.S.	Captain/ investor	Bahamas	70–79	776.3 kilos
U.S.	Organizer	Panama	30–39	800–1,000 kilos
U.S.	Organizer	Bahamas	50–59	488 kilos
U.S.	Broker	Colombia	30–39	4,500 kilos and 14,000 lbs
U.S.	Organizer	Puerto Rico/ Dom. Republic	40–49	480 kilos
U.S.	Leader	Colombia	20–29	500–600 kilos
U.S.	Leader	Hong Kong/	60–69	86 kilos and

U.S.	Leader	Puerto Rico Colombia/Puerto Rico	60–69	39 lbs 1,000 kilos and 1,000 lbs
U.S.	Manager	Bahamas	60–69	600 kilos
U.S.	Leader	Caribbean	30–39	15–50 kilos
U.S.	Manager	Caribbean	50–59	5,543.8 kilos
U.S.	Owner/financier	Bahamas	30–39	757 kilos

It should be noted that the sampling procedure employed in the current study had its limitations. While the purpose of this study was to gain a better understanding of all aspects of drug smuggling organizations, the sample only included interviews with individuals who were arrested and convicted for that offense. It was possible that some characteristic of these convicted individuals differentiated them from others who had not been caught; for example, the degree of organization of their smuggling group. This concern brought into question the representativeness of the sample and the generalizability of the findings.

The information obtained from this sample was adequately representative of drug smuggling organizations working in the Caribbean during the period of time these offenders were active. First, most of the subjects interviewed were smuggling drugs internationally for many years prior to their arrest and had been involved in multiple trips to various locations. Due to the high-involvement in and experience with international drug smuggling, the experiences the subjects reported were believed to be similar to those of other active high-level offenders. In addition, the results of the study were consistent with most of the findings from earlier work on drug smuggling specifically and that of other types of offenders more generally.

ANALYZING THE ORGANIZATIONAL STRUCTURE OF INTERNATIONAL DRUG SMUGGLING

Hierarchy of Authority

When considering all distribution groups as part of a larger organization of drug smugglers, one finds an example of this formal hierarchy in the former Colombian trafficking groups of the Medellin and Cali cartels. During this era, drug smuggling operations had clear leadership positions in charge of various functions in addition to a clearly defined area of control over which they ruled (Filippone, 1994). Consistent with traditional conceptions of highly organized cartels, subjects who had longtime involvement in drug smuggling described the drug trade during the 1970s as follows:

RESPON DENT 26: Those were the people that we met during that time, and they had an organization, a big organization. They were organized. They paid on time. Once it comes in, they've got the cars. They've got everything.

RESPONDENT 24: Well, it's kind of like a company where you have a person in charge, which would be your chairman of the board, CEO, whatever. And he delegates his other officer of his vice presidents, which would be lieutenants … Then from there you had different workers for him that did different jobs.

When asked about the organization of drug trafficking more recently, it became clear that a formal, complex structure had given way to a less organized network of connected units, as was described by Williams (1998):

RESPONDENT 8: Well, it's different if its smaller groups now. Like before, it was all cartels. It was a group of gentlemen, it was like a board. We make decisions together and stuff. Not it's all broken up—all of those brokers became chiefs, became bosses— they know all of the connections. They have their own networking, they have clients. [Now they are] … smaller groups, unknown small groups like two, three guys, that have people that say, you know, make a batch of 1,000 keys, and they will distribute it differently.

RESPONDENT 20: There is no such thing as the Cali cartel; there are Cali groups, but not a Cali Cartel. Right now that is destroyed. Right now there are thousands of small groups called small offices—So there is not such a thing as a cartel, but a bunch of people together. This finding is consistent with Morselli's (2001) in-depth examination of high-level marijuana smugglers. Morselli observed that the high status achieved by an individual within the organization was not attributable to his ability to control others and excessive use of force, as is typical in mafia and cartel-linked networks. Rather, the high-ranking position of the individual was a result of his ability to serve as a "network vector"(p.228), mobilizing the drug trade by connecting key actors.

By exploring the relationship between the groups that are responsible for moving drugs from the supplier to transporter to distributor, one can better understand the nature of the connections between individuals in the organization. Interviews with the thirty-four smugglers revealed that these groups were not well connected between different functions and the units tended to operate in-dependently of the larger organization. Many times, individuals were only aware of their portion of the operation and had very limited knowledge about the other stages and workers:

RESPONDENT 4: I only knew one guy—two guys in this enterprise, and there were about thirteen or fourteen people in the deal, involved there.

RESPONDENT 2: Transportation is one thing, okay. That office in Colombia is supposed to get the people in Miami to do the smuggling, right? And I was the head, you know, my own group. Got twenty people working for me doing the smuggling, ten people, whatever, and it was my responsibility. They got nothing to do with that. They just pay me for me to do the job.

Further evidence of the independent nature of the smuggling networks was found in the description of how loads of drugs are assembled and the autonomy of individuals involved in various stages of the smuggling process. First, subjects reported that many times loads of drugs to be transported to the Unites States were not assembled by a single organization, but rather they were financed by contributions from multiple offices and individuals. Second, the lack of a formal authority structure or chain of command was illustrated by a boat captain who demonstrated independence in decision making about his stage of the process:

RESPONDENT 30: A bunch of people will invest in the load. It's like selling shares of stock. This person will put up this amount of money. Another person will put up another amount of money, and they in effect maybe own 2 or 3 keys. Then the collector, or whoever, whatever you want to call him, puts all this together, and this joint venture goes on a plane.

RESPONDENT 14: I'm the transport. I'm the one that tells them this is how we're going to play the game. We're going to do it this way. We're not going to use this. We're going to do this because I'm in charge, and I'm aware of surveillance. I know how the Government is running things, how things are happening. So I keep constant contact with the office. All the broker does is pick up the drugs and give me the money for my services.

With regard to formal rules, this study found that expectations and objectives were rarely codified. Agreements about payments for loads were made informally and some aspects of the smuggling operations lacked established procedures. This resulted in a variety of methods being employed, some of which were more successful than others.

There were aspects of the transaction that were uncertain and highly variable within and between trips:

RESPONDENT 1: I think [payment] would have happened after they took the merchandise, after they sold it. There wasn't any date—we never talked about it—we don't sign no contract. All we do, we shake hands on it because my word is my vow, and I have to keep it.

RESPONDENT 21: The pickups were usually about the middle of the night. Now I have done it during the day. I pull right up to the seawall, and they'd offload right out of the house. One of them was a boat transfer, but others they just offload right off the seawall right into the boat.

RESPONDENT 1: I would get everybody in a room, the guys that was supposed to be involved in it, and in the planning of the project, how we're going to do it. I always figure that if all of them would come to the same conclusion that this is the best way to do it, then the police and the DEA, too, would think this was the best way to do it. So to me, the best way was to go all different [techniques].

The rational organization of these international drug smuggling organizations is also challenged by the indirect and informal nature of their communications. Consistent with prior literature on communication in smuggling networks (Morselli et al., 2007), information obtained during the interviews described communication in international drug smuggling groups as commonly involving face-to-face contact, even between bosses and distant workers. Communication between groups was frequent and quick, relying on such means as phones or radios, and less on written exchanges.

RESPONDENT 20: A group of two or three Colombians owned the load. I started [doing business] with intermediaries, but then went to Barranquilla and went straight to an owner. At that time we were thinking about using ships, commercial cargoes, to transport the cocaine. That was the reason why I went from the island to Barranquilla, to talk about how we were going to do it in the future.

RESPONDENT 8: It's just a matter of a phone call. I say, "I have this package for you. Would you take care of it?" And [the broker] says "Okay, I'll take care of it."

RESPONDENT 29: I would be notified that the drugs had moved from Colombia to the Bahamas. Communicating with the boat crew? I saw them and talked to them almost every day.

RESPONDENT 23: We were in the house, waiting for [the boats] to come and unload. We knew when they were coming because we got a call from the one that I told you it was, the chief, the boss.

Regarding the flexibility of the organizational networks, this sample of offenders suggested that high-level drug smuggling organizations were adaptable to a variety of stimuli. Such stimuli included law enforcement activity, a country's market for the drug, or removing an individual from a position. In addition, the subjects related that changes to the plan of action occurred frequently, often on very short notice. The interviews provided many instances that illustrate rapid change in both the techniques of smuggling and the organizations that smuggle drugs:

RESPONDENT 14: When I met him, we started running things a whole different since that boat got caught and that whole operation, that whole route got caught, we changed everything. I met this Colombian gentleman and we started working in the Bahamas. We started air-dropping marijuana. Then after the plane crash, I stopped moving through the Bahamas and moved from cigarette boats to lobster boats. Cigarette boats were already obsolete. They were, like we say, hot. Too suspicious.

RESPONDENT 1: Right now the United States is a very—the market is lucrative. But the profit, it isn't there like it used to be. Now, if you do your research and you look at all the countries, Australia, a kilo of coke goes for $8,000. Japan, it goes for $100,000 … I had that set up, but like I said … you got to look for different places to go. You got to move on.

RESPONDENT 16: When organizing a group of captains and people who could sell these drugs, they were still able to do it once I was caught. They do it with somebody else. They find somebody, they find somebody. To stop drug smuggling, they [the government] keep on [using] prison, putting people in jail. It stopped me, but 20 more come in.

RESPONDENT 3: That's why people are going from heroin—from marijuana—to coke ... You're bringing 80,000 pounds of marijuana. You need 50, 60, 70 [people]. To bring 500 kilos of cocaine, you need only four people. The money is there.

RESPONDENT 5: We would constantly change the routes through the Caribbean. You go around through the Peninsula to the west or you go to the east around the Caribbean Basin.

The convicted smugglers described the levels of specialization and coordination in their groups to be relatively low. Many of the subjects did not specialize in drug smuggling, as they reported also being involved in a range of other legitimate and illegitimate endeavors. In addition, instead of employing the best person doing a particular task, there were often many people doing the same job, even with some redundancy.

RESPONDENT 34: I am an accountant. I wanted more money, and I saw the money from the drugs ... I also had legal businesses ... I had a paint franchise ... a company for remodeling and interior design ... an import-export company for clothes, bicycles, toys and those types of things.

RESPONDENT 5: [In response to "What was your favorite offense?"]: Money laundering ... drugs-robbing the bank ... frauds ... there's no such thing as a favorite offense. I don't like being caught.

RESPONDENT 14: We don't own certain routes. I mean, there's multiple people working. Doing exactly the same thing I am.

Coordination was also absent or minimal in the drug smuggling process. Interviews suggested that a lack of integration commonly occurred between the transportation and pick-up stages. As expected with less formally organized groups, inconsistencies during important activities did not cause the entire operation to fail.

RESPONDENT 21: The[y] just give me Loran coordinates. I've got the maps. And they give me a time. Sometimes I'd go [from Miami to the Bahamas] and nothing would ever happen. And then I would come back empty.

RESPONDENT 17: I had a freighter, I knew the owner of the land strip in Guajira. Sometimes they had the loads waiting there for two or three weeks and no one would show up to pick it up. So this guy would call me to ask if I pick it up, I said yes, and the other people would call me.

In the experiences of the men interviewed, recruitment and promotions in drug smuggling organizations were not based on merit. In fact, many interviewed recounted that at the time of their initial involvement in drug smuggling they were at a low point in their lives, experiencing marital, financial, or drug-related problems. Actual placement into a position in the group was based on shared ethnicity or previous interactions, often based on family connections. In either case, the subjects made clear that establishing trust was the key aspect of recruiting new members.

RESPONDENT 24: When we got divorced, I just really didn't care about anything … So when I was getting a pair of pants done, some guys comes and talks to me, and he said "Listen, how's it going? I see you're from Miami." He asked me if I wanted to make some money, and I said sure, that's cool.

RESPONDENT 30: I met Jorge in prison … We became friends. We kept in contact after we got out. That's where I met him.

RESPONDENT 6: I arrived [in Colombia]. I used to live there, fishing. I meet a girl. Then she die, and I get so damn crazy. That's when I start using [cocaine]. Then I meet people that I knew … I knew them before. They was lobster fishermen, poor people. I find out they are all rich. Then they give me work smuggling drugs … they were Cubans, all the time Cubans. There is a bond between Cubans … you trust another Cuban more than a Colombian or Haitian.

The interviews also revealed that promotions within drug smuggling organizations were not based on productivity, time in the network, or merit. Instead, individuals moved into more autonomous positions once they had amassed enough money and connections to do so, typically resulting in them having their own operation.

RESPONDENT 1: I was a bodyguard for the off-loader … One day, one of the guys was sick. He could not drive the boat, and I said I can drive the boat … So I got in the boat and I was the driver then. [The first trip] was a forty mile trip, and I spent three days looking for the place because I could not find it. I didn't know how to navigate.

RESPONDENT 29: The fellow whose deal it was ran short on money, and he started offering back seven to one to anyone who wanted to invest. So I had a little bit of money. Because of a shortage of trustworthy people … I ended up being on one of these two boats going out to meet a coastal freighter coming up from Colombia … The fellow whose deal it was, was a cokehead … so, finally we said the hell with it. We'd buy our own boat. We went down and bought an old fishing boat, and we started in the marijuana-smuggling business. We had people with the connections through him.

CONCLUSION

This study examined the commonly held features of formal organizations, and contrasted them with descriptions of drug smuggling organizations provided by a sample of high-level international drug smugglers. The six organizational features examined here included hierarchy, statement of rules, communication, adaptability, specialization/coordination, and recruitment/promotion procedures. These attributes are commonly taken to be attributes of formal organizations.

Little evidence was found to support the view that drug smugglers work in groups that are organized in a manner consistent with such organizations. Rather than being characterized as efficient or rational, drug smugglers work in groups that are horizontal rather than vertical. That is, orders or commands seldom come from a centralized authority communicated down an organizational structure. Instead, drug smugglers work in loosely connected nodes where communication is informal. Such groups of drug smugglers described their groups as having few rules, and seldom relied on a meritocracy for selecting, recruiting, or promoting members in the group. Rather, informal associations ... personal knowledge, kinship ties, or common experiences ... characterized how most decisions were made in this regard. These groups were highly adaptable to their environment. The environment could include threats posed by new law enforcement tactics or technologies, inclement weather, dynamic supply or demand for the drug, or other factors. Rather than working to the detriment of the goal of making profit through drug smuggling, these organizational characteristics seemed to provide a rational means to success. This description of international drug smuggling groups itself must be regarded as dynamic and evolutionary. The horizontal, informal, and loosely connected nodes succeeded the more tightly organized cartels that preceded them. This work has illustrated the adaptability of groups of offenders to their environment.

It should be noted that the generalizability of these findings was limited. The qualitative nature of this study, however, was selected to produce more descriptive findings, specifically about how high-level smugglers move drugs into the United States. A concern that this research failed to incorporate information from active drug smugglers is minimized when one considers the research on organization of groups of other active offenders (see e.g., Decker et al., 2007; Jacobs et al., 2003; Shover, 1996; Wright & Decker, 1997). Qualitative research on active burglars, armed robbers, carjackers, and gang members had concluded that these offenders are not well organized either. This suggested that the finding that drug smuggling groups were not well organized could not be attributed to the fact that only individuals who were arrested and convicted were interviewed. Future research in this area should attempt to tap into information from active drug smugglers—difficult as this may be—to evaluate whether their organization is, indeed, as disorganized as those offenders included in the present sample.

As previously suggested, to gain a more complete understanding of how groups operate, it is essential to examine not only their structure, but the interactions and transactions that occur between individuals (see e.g., Best & Luckenbill, 1994; Burt, 1992; Waring, 2002). While this article certainly addresses the structure of drug smuggling groups, it only briefly touches on the way members behave and interact with each other. Future research should focus on this aspect of the organization to better understand how these interactions influence the group's offending patterns.

Cressey (1972) noted that the foundation of formal organization is based in a rational search for efficiency and maximized profits. Similarly, Warr (2002) suggested that a low degree of specialization and an absence of clearly stated rules indicated a group is not rationally organized. The findings in this study revealed that was not the case with international drug smuggling groups. Although they failed to demonstrate many of the characteristics of a formally organized group, the interviews suggested that minimizing risk is an essential rationale within these operations and might account for the high adaptabiity of these groups. For example, research has suggested that drug supply chains without a centralized power source are more vulnerable to interdiction because they lack the organized network support and resources associated with a more formal, centralized chain (Reuter, 1983; Tremblay, Cusson, & Morselli,1998). Research on social systems and networks supports the idea that networks can be organized around a variety of rationalities beyond profit-maximization, depending on their particular organizational norms (Machado & Burns, 1998).

While some might suggest loosely connected individuals would make these smuggling operations less successful than more formally organized drug cartels, this is not necessarily the case. Although it appears that these groups are not highly structured organizations, they still exhibit elements of rationality in their attempts to reduce risk of detection. It is possible, therefore, that instead of being organized around efficiency, which results in the formal structure discussed above, these groups ensure their success by arranging their activities around minimizing risk. For example, Morselli et al. (2007) suggested that the quick, informal communication between central actors in drug trafficking networks actually serves to increase security of the network by creating a periphery that insulates participants at the core. In addition, Reuter (1985) suggested that centrally organized illegal networks are more vulnerable to detection because of their increased visibility. If this true, then it might be the case that drug smuggling groups are not disorganized, but instead merely organized around an alternative rationale.

Future research should therefore consider how the pursuit of minimized detection risk affects smuggling operations and consequently its organizational structure. For example, while it was shown here that these organizations rely more on trust or association-based recruitment procedures to reduce risk of detection, research has yet to examine the impact of this practice on the offending of the group. In addition, future research should consider the size of the production source when exploring the rationale of minimized risk. Bouchard (2007) found that risk of detection in marijuana distribution networks depended both on the number of cultivators as well as the size of the sites they operate, two variables not examined in the preceding analysis. Undoubtedly, the current research was more descriptive than causal in nature. It described the structure of drug smuggling organizations, with little emphasis on the impact of organizational structure on operational processes. How does a less structured organization drug smuggling group influence that group's offending patterns? What effect, if any, does a rational organization based on minimizing risk versus maximizing profit have on the activities and life span of an organization? Future research should consider these questions and others to move toward better understanding the organization of international drug smuggling groups and offending groups in general.

REFERENCES

Adler, P. A. (1985). *Wheeling and dealing: An ethnography of an upper-level drug dealing and smuggling community.* New York: Colombia University Press.

Best, J., & Luckenbill, D. (1994). *Organizing deviance.* Englewood Cliffs, NJ: Prentice Hall.

Block, A. A. (2006). "The snowman cometh: Coke in the progressive New York." *Criminology,* 17, 75–99.

Bouchard, M. (2007). "A capture-recapture model to estimate the size of criminal populations and the risks of detection in a marijuana cultivation industry." *Journal of Quantitative Criminology,* 23, 221–241.

Burt, R. S. (1992). *Structural holes.* Cambridge, MA: Harvard University Press.

Clarke, R. V., & Brown, R. (2003). "International trafficking in stolen vehicles." In M. Tonry (Ed.), *Crime and justice: A review of research* (Vol. 30, pp. 197–228). Chicago: University of Chicago Press.

Cressey, D. (1972). *Criminal organization: Its elementary forms.* New York: Harper and Row.

Cromwell, P., Olson, J., & Avary, D. W. (1994). *Breaking and entering.* Thousand Oaks, CA: Sage.

Decker, S. H., Bynum, T. S., & Weisel, D. L. (1998). "A tale of two cities: Gang organization". *Justice Quarterly,* 15, 395–425.

Decker, S. H., & Chapman, M. T. (2008). *Drug smugglers on drug smuggling: Lessons from the inside.* Philadelphia: Temple University Press.

Decker, S. H., Katz, C., & Webb, V. (2007). "Understanding the black box of gang organization: Implications for involvement in violent crime, drug sales and violent victimization." *Crime and Delinquency,* 54,153–172.

Decker, S. H., & Van Winkle, B. (1996). *Life in the gang: Family friends and violence.* New York: Cambridge.

Degenhardt, L., Reuter, P. H., Collins, L., & Hall, W. (2005). "Evaluating explanations of the Australian heroin shortage." *Addiction,* 100, 459–469.

Donald, I., & Wilson, A. (2000). "Ram raiding: Criminals working in groups." In D. Canter & L. Allison (Eds.), *The social psychology of crime* (pp. 191–246). Burlington, VT: Ashgate.

Einstadter, W. (1969). "The social organization of robbery." *Social Problems,* 17, 64–83.

Fagan, J. (1989). "The social organization of drug use and drug dealing among urban gangs". *Criminology,* 27, 633–669.

Felson, M. (2003). "The process of co-offending." *Crime Prevention Studies,* 16, 149–167.

Filippone, R. (1994). "The Medellin Cartel: Why we can't win the drug war." *Studies in Conflict and Terrorism*, 17, 323–344.

Hagedorn, J. (1988). *People and folks: Gangs, crime, and the underclass in a rustbelt city.* Chicago: Lakeview Press.

Heimer, C. A. (1992). "Doing your job and helping your friends: Universalistic norms about obligations to help particular others in networks." In N. Nohria & R. G. Eccles (Eds.), *Networks and organizations: Structure, form and action* (pp. 143–164). Boston: Harvard Business School Press.

Jacobs, B., Topali, V., & Wright, R. (2003). "Carjacking, streetlife and offender motivation." *British Journal of Criminology*, 43, 673–688.

Kean, T. H., & Hamilton, L. (2004). *The 9/11 Commission report: Final report of the National Commission on Terrorist Attacks upon the United States.* Washington, DC: U.S. Government Printing Office.

Klein, M. W. (1967). *Criminological theories as seen by criminologists: An evaluative review of approaches to the causation of crime and delinquency.* Albany, NY: Governor's Special Committee on the Criminal Offender.

Klein, M. W. (1995). *The American street gang.* New York: Oxford University Press.

Klein, M. W., Maxson, C. L., & Cunningham, L. C. (1991). "Crack, Street gangs, and violence." *Criminology*, 29, 623–650.

Krebs, V. E. (2001). "The network paradigm applied to criminal organizations." *Connections*, 24, 53–65.

Machado, N., & Burns, T. R. (1998). "Complex social organization: Multiple organizing modes, structural incongruence, and mechanisms of integration." *Public Administration*, 76, 355–386.

McCord, J., & Conway, K. P. (2002). "Patterns of juvenile delinquency and co-offending." In E. Waring & D. Weisburd (Eds.), *Crime and social organization* (pp. 15–30). New York: Transaction.

McIllwain, J. S. (1999). "Organized crime: A social network approach." *Crime, Law, and Social Change*, 32, 301–324.

Mieczkowski, T. (1986). "Geeking up and throwing down: Heroin street life in Detroit." *Criminology*, 24, 645–666.

Morselli, C. (2001). "Structuring Mr. Nice: Entrepreneurial opportunities and brokerage positioning in the cannabis trade." *Crime, Law, and Social Change*, 35, 203–244.

Morselli, C. (2003). "Career opportunities and network-based privileges in the Costa Nostra." *Crime, Law, and Social Change*, 39, 383–418.

Morselli, C. (2005). "Contacts, opportunities and criminal enterprise." Toronto, Ontario, Canada: University of Toronto Press.

Morselli, C. (2008). *Inside criminal networks.* New York: Springer.

Morselli, C., Giguère, C., & Petit, K. (2007). The efficiency/security trade-off in criminal networks. *Social Networks*, 29,143–153.

Padilla, F. M. (1992). *The gang as an American enterprise.* New Brunswick, NJ: Rutgers University Press.

Raab, J., & Milward, H. B. (2003). "Dark networks as problems." *Journal of Administration Research and Theory*, 13, 413–439.

Reiss, A. J., Jr. (1988). "Co-offending and criminal careers." In N. Morris & M. Tonry (Eds.), *Crime and justice* (Vol. 10, pp. 117–170). Chicago: University of Chicago Press.

Reuter, P. H. (1983). *Disorganized crime: The economics of the visible hand.* Cambridge, MA: MIT Press.

Reuter, P. H. (1985). *Organization of illegal markets: An economic analysis.* Washington, DC: National Institute of Justice.

Reuter, P. H., & Greenfield, V. (2001). "Measuring global drug markets." *World Economics*, 2, 159–173.

Reuter, P. H., & Haaga, J. (1989). *The organization of high-level drug markets: An exploratory study.* Santa Monica, CA: Rand.

Sageman, M. (2008). *Leaderless Jihad: Terror networks in the twenty-First century.* Philadelphia: University of Pennsylvania Press.

Sanchez-Jankowski, M. (1991). *Islands in the street: Gangs and American urban society.* Berkeley: University of California Press.

Schiray, M. (2001). "Introduction: Drug trafficking, organised crime, and public policy for drug control." *International Social Science Journal*, 53, 351–358.

Shaw, C., & McKay, H. (1931). "Report on the causes of crime: No. 13." Washington, DC: National Commission on Law Observance and the Administration of Justice. Shover, N. (1996). *Great pretenders: Pursuits and careers of persistent thieves.* Boulder, CO: Westview Press.

Skolnick, J., Correl, T., Navarro, E., & Robb, R. (1988).*The social structure of street drug dealing.* Report to the Office of the Attorney General of the State of California. Berkeley: University of California.

Tremblay, P., Cusson, M., & Morselli, C. (1998). "Market offenses and limits to growth." *Crime, Law, and Social Change*, 29, 311–330.

Waring, E. (2002). "Co-offending as a network form of social organization." In E. Waring & D. Weisburd (Eds.), *Crime and social organization* (pp. 31–48). New Brunswick, NJ: Transaction.

Warr, M. (1996). "Organization and instigation in delinquent groups." *Criminology*, 34, 11–37.

Warr, M. (2002). *Companions in crime: The social aspects of criminal conduct.* New York: Cambridge University Press.

Watts, D. J. (2003). *Six degrees: The science of a connected age.* New York: W.W. Norton.

Weber, M. (1946). Bureaucracy. In H. H. Gerth & C. W. Mills (Eds.), Max Weber: *Essays in sociology* (pp. 196–244). New York: Oxford University Press.

Williams, P. (1998). "The nature of drug-trafficking networks." *Current History*, 97, 154–159.

Wright, R., & Decker, S. H. (1990). *Burglars on the job: Streetlife and residential burglary.* Boston: Northeastern University Press.

Wright, R., & Decker, S. H. (1997). *Armed robbers in action: Stickups and street culture.* Boston: Northeastern University Press.

Zaitch, D. (2002). *Trafficking cocaine: Colombian drug entrepreneurs in the Netherlands.* The Hague, Netherlands: Kluwer.

Zhang, S. X. (2007). *Smuggling and trafficking in human beings: All roads lead to America.* Westport, CT: Praeger.

Zhang, S. X. (2008). *Chinese human smuggling organizations.* Stanford, CA: Stanford University Press.

The Organizational Structure of International Drug Smuggling

Important Questions:
1. Are offenders organized? How well?
2. What are the characteristics of group offending and co-offenders?
3. What is the influence of group organization on offender patterns?

Group Offending

► Characteristics of offending process-structure of their interactions i.e. adaptability, specialization, hierarchy, roles, communication.
► Group Context of offending (Klein, 1967)-80% or more of delinquency occurs in a group context (Shaw & McKay, 1931). More offenses and harm…
— Youthful offenders
 ▷ Burglary, larceny, drug sales, auto theft.
 ▷ Violent offenses, serious assault
► Complex groups versus less formally organized groups…

Nature of Offender Organizations and Impact Offending (Warr 2002, Reiss 1988)

Nature of Offender Organizations:
- ► Gangs
- ► Offending Groups-relatively small 2 to 4 individuals.
- ► Accomplice Networks-groups of offenders nested in larger groups of associates (Warr 2002).

Variation Among Organizations & Offending Groups:
1. Hierarchy
2. Rules
3. Role specialization
4. Communication/Coordination
5. Adaptability
6. Recruitment/Promotion

Organization (Donald & Wilson, 2000)

- ► Teams-interdependence, outputs greater than sum of individuals e.g. highly organized.
- ► Co-acting-low interdependence, little additional output over what individuals produce e.g. lack organization.
  - — Ram raiders, lack permanence, specialization, long-term interdependence.
    - ▷ Assemble teams, identify targets, co-offend, dispose proceeds.
      - — Generalized offending roles, weak ties, fluid relationships vs. formal, rational structure.

Gangs

- Disorganized Groups-diffuse structure, common features, no corporate use for profits (drug sales, robbery, property crimes), profits used for individual purposes (Decker & Van Winkle, 1996).
- Instrumental-Rational Organizations-formal organizations advancing self-interest in rational ways.
  - Embrace common goals, engage in common enterprise, regulate revenue generating activities.
    - ▷ Drug sales-highly organized, like violence, intimidation, property offenses (Mieczkowski, 1986; Sanchez-Jankowski, 1991).
    - ▷ Vertical hierarchy and internal controls (Benson and Decker, 2010)

Organizational Structure of International Drug Smuggling

- Networks-series of loosely connected nodes linked across/ within organizations (Williams, 1998).
  - Nodes-Individuals, organizations, firms, information sharing tools.
  - Human trafficking/smuggling, terrorist groups, international stolen vehicles, international drug smuggling (small networks of informally organized individuals.)
- Formal Organizations-many smaller cells/cooffending groups engaged in smuggling, laundering, trafficking, terrorism.

Social Networks versus Hierarchy-Decentralization

- ▶ Drug importation Columbia to Netherlands (Zaitch, 2002):
  - — No vertical hierarchies
  - — Flexible structure, adaptability, quickly change tactics
  - — Horizontal
  - — Dynamic, insulated groups, unconnected to earlier and later smuggling transaction chain.
  - — Ethnic/kinship ties relationships among smugglers e.g recruitment promotion procedures.
- ▶ Drug distribution Sao Paulo (Schiray, 2001):
  - — Ad hoc/unplanned, unstable, no long term operations
  - — Episodic specialization

Social Networks (Morselli, 2008)

Criminal networks-street gangs, drug distribution networks.
- ▶ Criminal networks less organized than previously thought.
  - — Flexible Order Thesis-criminal networks some hierarchy and levels of authority, but also adaptabile to manage resources and detect law enforcement.
  - — Less centralized and structured

The Drug Smuggler Study

- ► US, Caribbean, South America
  - — Columbia, Bahamas, Panama, Cuba, Dominican Republic, Mexico, Haiti, Peru, Puerto-Rico, Venezuela.
- ► Diversity of roles-recruiter, off-loader, broker, organizer, transporter, distributor, supervisor, manager, captain, leader, investor, owner/financier.

Sample—1,136kilos or 2,500lbs.

- ► 22 – 20 years or more
- ► 6 – 30 years or more
- ► 5 – life
- ► Commercial/private vessels, private/commercial airplanes.

Networks of Connected Units

Groups of 2 to 3 chiefs or bosses, clientele, multiple small offices will invest in loads.

Marijuana smugglers (Morselli, 2001)

Network Vector-a person that mobilizes the drug trade by connecting key actors.

- — Power stems from ability as vector.
- — Not well connected between different functions, units operate independently, limited knowledge others stages or workers.

1) Hierarchy of Authority—various functions/control

- ► Medellin, Cali cartels (1970s)-Columbian—Power stems from formal control , force

2) Rules-expectations and objectives rarely codified i.e. payments lacked established procedures.
3) Flexibility-very adaptable to variety of stimuli
   1. law enforcement
   2. plan changes—air-dropping, cigarette/lobster boats, routes
   3. drug markets-AUS $8,000, JAP $100,000
   4. demotions

50–70 people (80,000lbs marijuana), 4 people (500kilos coke)
4) Communication-indirect and informal in nature. Frequent/quick.
   — Phones, radios

Coordination-absent, minimum. Lack integration transportation and pick-up stages.

5) Specialization—not specialized and some redundancy, accountant, paint franchise, remodeling/interior design, import-export clothes, toys, bikes.
6) Recruitment-shared ethnicity, previous interactions, family connections.
   ▷ Initial involvement due to marital, financial, drug-related problems.
7) Promotion-money, connections

THE ORGANIZATIONAL STRUCTURE OF INTERNATIONAL DRUG SMUGGLING: HOMEWORK ASSIGNMENT

Please define the following terms/concepts using the article/chapter. Additionally, provide one example for each term from your reading. Please bring your homework to our next class session!

1. **Drug smuggling**

2. **White-collar crime**

3. **Group offending**

4. **Co-offending**

5. **Organizational Structure**

CLASS, GENDER AND GANGS

THE GIRLS IN THE GANG

WHAT WE'VE LEARNED FROM TWO DECADES OF RESEARCH

By Jody Miller

I t is no longer accurate to say that female involvement in youth gangs is an under-studied phenomenon. Since Anne Campbell's (1984) groundbreaking book *The Girls in the Gang,* a number of scholars have dedicated themselves to understanding the lives of young women in gangs. In the past 4 years, two monographs and an edited collection have specifically addressed girls' gang activities (Chesney-Lind & Hagedorn, 1999; Fleisher, 1998; J. Miller, 2001a). This is in addition to Joan Moore's (1991) landmark *Going Down to the Barrio,* the important ongoing research on female gang involvement in San Francisco (Hunt, Joe-Laidler, & Mackenzie, 2000; Hunt, Mackenzie, & Joe-Laidler, 2000; Joe-Laidler & Hunt, 1997; Lauderback, Hansen, & Waldorf, 1992), and other informative studies (see Joe & Chesney-Lind, 1995; Nurge, 1998; Portillos, 1999; Portillos, Jurik, & Zatz, 1996). In fact, though some gang researchers continue to ignore girls, a number of scholars have become attentive to the importance of examining gender in the context of gangs (see Bjerregaard & Smith, 1993; Curry, 1998; Curry & Decker, 1998; Deschenes & Esbensen, 1999a, 1999b; Esbensen & Deschenes, 1998; Esbensen, Deschenes, & Winfree, 1999; Esbensen & Winfree, 1998; Pagan, 1990; Hagedorn, 1998b; Klein, Maxson, & Miller, 1995).

It is safe to say that we now have more information about girls in gangs, and from a variety of methodological perspectives, than at any point in the long history of gang research. In fact, as David Curry (1999) points out in a recent essay, the foundations for contemporary research on girls in gangs were actually laid down earlier. As Curry reviews, Walter Miller (1973) first described two female gangs, the Molls and the Queens, active in the middle part of the 20th century. Waln Brown (1978) reported on his observations of African American female gang members in Philadelphia, and John Quicker (1983) studied Chicana gang members in Los Angeles around the same period. We also have historical evidence of the nature of female gang involvement from Laura Fishman's (1995) analysis of data collected on the Vice Queens for James Short and Fred Strodtbeck's (1965) Chicago-based research during the 1960s. Joan Moore's (1991) research was based on interviews with adults active in street gangs in the 1950s and 1970s; and Malcolm Klein's research during the same era documented the widespread involvement of young women in street gangs (see Klein, 2001; see also Bowker, Gross, & Klein, 1980; Bowker & Klein, 1983).

This early research is especially important to highlight, as it tempers popular claims of "new violent female offenders" routinely depicted as young women in gangs (see Chesney-Lind, 1993, and Chesney-Lind, Shelden, & Joe, 1996, for a discussion). From the available information, it appears that there has been both continuity and change in young women's participation in gangs. But overall the proportion of gang members who are girls, and the nature of girls' gang involvement, does not appear to have shifted substantially over the years. Klein documented that approximately a quarter of the gang members in his study were girls. Moore reports that females were nearly a third of the gang members she studied. As important, research from this earlier era shows that although there was variation in young women's gang involvement, girls were actively involved in violence, most often fighting. In addition, their place in gangs was never as mere "tomboys" or "sex objects." Instead, girls' roles and activities in gangs were negotiated, with varying results, in the context of male-dominated settings.

In the contemporary era, scholarly concern with young women's gang involvement has grown substantially. In part this is because of the growth in gangs since the 1980s and the tremendous growth in gang research during this same period. As other chapters in this volume illustrate, recent estimates suggest that there are now more than 1,000 cities and towns across the United States reporting gangs in their communities—more than five times the number that existed as recently as 1980 (Klein, 1995; Maxson, Woods, & Klein, 1995). This alone is not sufficient to account for the growth in research on girls in gangs, however. Instead, the move away from a primarily androcentric approach to the study of gangs is in large part because of the expansion of feminist criminology and its requisite attention to the experiences of women.

So then, what have we learned in the past two decades? For starters, we have come to recognize that young women's involvement in youth gangs is a varied phenomenon.

Girls' experiences in gangs and the consequences of their gang involvement vary by—among other things—their ethnicity, the gender composition of their gangs, and the community contexts in which their gangs emerge. In this chapter, I provide an update of our current state of knowledge about girls in gangs. My focus is on four issues:

1. The level of female gang involvement
2. Risk factors for gang membership and girls' pathways into gangs
3. The level and character of gang girls' delinquency and its context in gang life for girls
4. The consequences of gang involvement for girls, including both victimization risks within gangs and evidence of long-term costs associated with gang involvement for girls

In discussing each of these issues, I draw from my own research (J. Miller, 2001a) and collaborations with others (Miller & Brunson, 2000; Miller & Decker, 2001; Peterson, Miller, & Esbensen, 2001), as well as from the wide range of studies documented at the start of this chapter. I take this approach to emphasize the comparisons that can be drawn across research methodologies, study sites, ethnicity, and gang structures. As Klein (2001) aptly notes, the examination of such differences is "instructive and remind[s] us properly that while we can generalize about gangs, we had best do so while recognizing that they reflect [a range of] different … contexts" (p. x).

LEVELS OF FEMALE GANG INVOLVEMENT

Recent estimates suggest that female participation in gangs is more widespread than has typically been believed. Data from official sources continue to underestimate the extent of girls' gang membership. For instance, Curry, Ball, and Fox (1994) found that some law enforcement policies officially exclude female gang members from their counts. Controlling for data from these cities, they still found that females were only 5.7% of gang members known to law enforcement agencies. Part of law enforcement's underestimation of girls' gang involvement is attributable to male gang members' greater likelihood of being involved in serious crime, as well as average age differences between males and females in gangs (see Bjerregaard & Smith, 1993; Fagan, 1990). Whereas young men are more likely to remain gang involved into young adulthood, gang membership for girls is much more likely to remain a primarily adolescent undertaking (see J. Miller, 2001a; Moore & Hagedorn, 1996).

On the other hand, results from survey research with youths indicate that young women's gang involvement is relatively extensive and at levels only slightly below that of young men, particularly in early adolescence. For instance, findings from the Rochester Youth Development Study, based on a stratified sample of youths in high-risk, high-crime neighborhoods, actually found that a slightly larger percentage of females (22%) than males (18%) claimed gang membership when self-definition was used as a measure (Bjerregaard & Smith, 1993). Later evidence from this longitudinal study suggests that girls' gang involvement tends to be of a shorter duration than boys', with girls' peak gang involvement around eighth and ninth grades (Terence P. Thornberry, personal correspondence, April 2, 1999). Similarly, based on a sample of eighth graders in 11 cities, Esbensen and Deschenes (1998) report a prevalence rate for gang membership of 14% for males and 8% for females.

In addition to prevalence rates, two additional issues are important in considering the level of girls' participation in gangs. One is the proportion of gang members that are female versus male, and the other is the distribution of female gang involvement across various gang types. Estimates of the ratio of female to male members suggest that young women approximate between 20% and 46% of gang members (Esbensen & Huizinga, 1993; Esbensen & Winfree, 1998; Pagan, 1990; Moore, 1991; Winfree, Fuller, Vigil, & Mays, 1992). There is wide variation, however, across gangs. In my comparative study of female gang involvement in Columbus, Ohio, and St. Louis, Missouri, girls in mixed-gender gangs (i.e., gangs with both male and female membership) were as few as 7% or as many as 75% of the members of their gangs (J. Miller, 2001a). Overall, these girls were in predominantly male gangs: of the 42 girls in my sample who were in mixed-gender gangs, 74% were in groups that were majority-male, with just under a third (31%) in gangs in which 80% or more of the members were males. Male gang members in St. Louis provide even more extreme accounts. Although 39% of the boys we spoke to described their gangs as male-only, of the 61% of young men who described having both male and female membership in their gangs, two thirds reported that their membership was at least 80% male (Miller & Branson, 2000).[2]

Though standard approaches for categorizing (presumably or implicitly) male gangs continue to focus on a broad range of issues exclusive of gender (see, e.g., Maxson & Klein, 1995; Spergel & Curry, 1993), studies of female gang types focus specifically on gender organization, most often drawing from Walter Miller's (1975) tripartite classification: (a) mixed gender gangs with both female and male members; (b) female gangs that are affiliated with male gangs, which he refers to as "auxiliary" gangs; and (c) independent female gangs. Several scholars have noted that this tripartite division misses some of the complexity of gang formations, and also that it is androcentric to focus on gender organization when examining female but not male gang involvement (Hagedorn & Devitt, 1999; Nurge, 1998). Nonetheless, as I will discuss throughout this chapter, research on the gendered organization and gender ratio of girls' gangs has yielded important information.

There are several case studies of the various gang types Miller describes (see Fleisher, 1998; Lauderback, Hansen, & Waldorf, 1992; Quicker, 1983; Venkatesh, 1998), but less evidence of their prevalence. Curry's (1997) study of female gang members in three cities found that only 6.4% of girls described being in autonomous female gangs, whereas 57.3% described their gangs as mixed-gender, and another 36.4% said they were in female gangs affiliated with male gangs. It appears that there is some variation across ethnicity in the likelihood of each gang type. For example, Chicana/Latina gang members are those most likely to describe their gangs as female groups affiliated with male gangs, and African American young women are more likely to describe there gangs as mixed-gender. The handful of all-female gangs documented by scholars has largely been African American as well (Curry, 1997; Joe-Laidler & Hunt, 1997; Lauderback et al., 1992; J. Miller, 2001a; Venkatesh, 1998).

Nurge (1998) reports that the majority of girls in her study of girls in Boston gangs were in groups that were mixed-gender rather than auxiliary or female-only, but with varying gender compositions. She further differentiated mixed-gender gangs according to whether the groups were territorial and whether they referred to themselves as gangs or cliques. Likewise, in my comparative study of gangs in St. Louis and in Columbus, Ohio, the vast majority of girls interviewed were African American, and all of their gangs were predominantly African American. In all, 85% of girls described their gangs as mixed gender, with only three girls each describing their gangs as a female group affiliated with a local male gang, or as an independent female gang (J. Miller, 2001a). Because sampling was not representative, it is difficult to ascertain how generalizable such patterns are.

A recent analysis of the Gang Resistance Education and Training (G.R.E.A.T.) program data (Peterson et al., 2001) supports the finding that most youth gangs are composed of both male and female members. Of the 366 gang members reporting, 84% of male gang members described their gangs as having both female and male members and 16% said they were in all-male gangs. In terms of the ratio of males to females in their groups, approximately 45% of male gang members described their gangs as having a majority of male members; 38% said their gangs had fairly equal numbers of males and females; and just under 1% (2 cases) reported being in gangs that were majority female. Young women were more likely than young men to describe belonging to gender-balanced, rather than majority-male, mixed-gender gangs. Fully 64% of girls described their gangs as having equal numbers of males and females, followed by 30% in majority-male gangs, and 13% in majority female (8 cases) or all-female (10 cases) gangs. Thus, just 7% of girls described their gangs as having only female members.

Unfortunately, the measure of gender composition in the G.R.E.A.T. study did not allow an assessment of the prevalence of the gang types described above (i.e., affiliated vs. integrated groups). However, this and several additional studies suggest that the gender composition of gangs has a significant impact on the nature of gang members' activities, including their participation in delinquency (Joe-Laidler & Hunt, 1997; J. Miller, 2001a; Miller & Brunson, 2000; Peterson et al., 2001). I will highlight these findings further below.

GIRLS' RISK FACTORS FOR GANG MEMBERSHIP AND PATHWAYS INTO GANGS

Gang membership doesn't happen overnight. Research shows that youths typically hang out with gang members for some time—often as much as a year—before making a commitment to join (Decker & Van Winkle, 1996). The young women in my study typically began hanging out with gang members when they were quite young—around age 12 on average—and they joined at an average age of 13. In fact, 69% of the girls in the sample described joining their gangs before they turned 14. This is quite similar to reports from other research, and appears to be relatively consistent across ethnic groups. Joe and Chesney-Lind's (1995) study of Samoan and Filipino gang youths in Hawaii reports an average age of entrée of 12 for girls and 14 for boys. Based on his study in Phoenix, Portillos (1999) reports that most of the Chicana girls in his study joined between ages 12 and 13. Recall also that the Rochester Youth Development Study found the highest prevalence rates of female gang participation in the early waves of their study, again suggesting that girls' gang membership starts quite young (see also Maxson & Whitlock, Chapter 2 of this volume).

Research on why girls join gangs has generally included two approaches. First are analyses of etiological risk factors for gang membership from survey research; second, qualitative analyses of girls' accounts of why they join gangs, what they gain from their gang participation, and their life contexts both prior to and at the time of joining. Though differing in approach, most studies focus on several or more of five sets of issues: structural and neighborhood conditions, the family, school factors, the influence of peers, and individual factors.

To account for the proliferation of gangs in recent decades, many scholars have focused on compelling evidence that much, though not all, of this growth has been spurred by the deterioration in living conditions for many Americans caused by structural changes brought about by deindustrialization (see Hagedorn, 1998b; Huff, 1989; Klein, 1995). The resulting lack of alternatives and sense of hopelessness are believed to have contributed to the growth of gangs in many cities, as scholars point to the gang as a means for inner-city youths to adapt to oppressive living conditions imposed by their environments. Though much of the focus of this research has been on gangs in general, or male gang members in particular, a few scholars have linked these conditions to female gang involvement as well. For example, findings from the Rochester Youth Development Study (RYDS) suggest that growing up in disorganized, violent neighborhoods is a risk factor for gang involvement for young women[3] (Thornberry, 1998).

Qualitative research highlights the importance of this link even further. Campbell (1990) notes that in addition to the limited opportunities and powerlessness of underclass membership shared with their male counterparts, young women in these communities also face the burden of child care responsibilities and subordination to men. The youths in Joe and Chesney-Lind's (1995) study were from impoverished communities, in what they note was a "bleak and distressing environment." They conclude from their research that "the gang assists [both] young women and men in coping with their lives in chaotic, violent and economically marginalized communities" (p. 411; see also Moore, 1991). Moreover, because these neighborhoods are often dangerous, gangs may assist young women in protecting themselves both by providing them the opportunity to learn street and fighting skills (Fishman, 1995), and by offering protection and retaliation against victimization in high-crime communities (J. Miller, 2001a).

The characteristics of the neighborhoods from which the young women in my study were drawn were very much in keeping with this image of urban poverty and racial segregation. In both cities, the vast majority of girls lived in neighborhoods that were economically worse off and more racially segregated than the cities as a whole (see J. Miller, 2001a). My project also included a comparative sample of nongang girls from the same communities. Although the neighborhood conditions were similar for both gang and nongang girls, there were important differences in girls' descriptions, particularly in relation to their exposure to gangs. In both Columbus and St. Louis, the vast majority of young women described some exposure to gangs in their neighborhoods. However, the extent and proximity of gang activity in girls' neighborhoods was a feature distinguishing gang and nongang girls' descriptions. More than four fifths of the gang members reported both "a lot" of gang activity in their neighborhoods and other gang members living on their streets, as compared to about half of the nongang girls. It appears that coupled with other risk factors, living in neighborhoods with gangs in *close* proximity increases the likelihood that girls will decide to join gangs.

Although impoverished and dangerous neighborhood conditions help answer the question of why girls come to join gangs, this remains only a partial explanation. Research shows that less than one quarter of youths living in high-risk neighborhoods claim gang membership (Bjerregaard & Smith, 1993; Winfree et al., 1992), and researchers have not found differences in perceived limited opportunities between gang and nongang youths in these communities (Esbensen, Huizinga, & Weiher, 1993). A factor that has received quite a bit of attention is the family, which has long been considered crucial for understanding delinquency and gang behavior among girls.

Findings from survey research have been somewhat inconsistent with regard to the family. Esbensen and Deschenes (1998), in a multisite study of risk factors for delinquency and gang behavior, found that weak supervision and low parental involvement were significant risk factors, though they suggest that lack of maternal attachment was more predictive of gang membership for males than females. Bjerregaard and Smith (1993) measured both parental supervision and parental attachment within the family, and found neither to be significantly related to gang membership for girls. However, Thornberry (1998) in his analysis including later waves of the RYDS project reports low parental involvement as a significant risk factor for girls.

Ethnographic and other qualitative studies are much more likely to suggest that serious family problems contribute significantly to girls' gang involvement. Joe and Chesney-Lind (1995) observe that the girls in their study had parents who worked long hours, or who were un- or underemployed—circumstances they suggest affected both girls' supervision and the quality of family relationships. Fleisher's (1998; see also Campbell, 1984) ethnographic study of gangs in Kansas City, Missouri, documents intergenerational patterns of abuse and neglect, exacerbated by poverty and abject neighborhood conditions, which he suggests are at the heart of the gang problem. Likewise, Moore (1991) documents a myriad of family problems that contribute to the likelihood of gang involvement for young women: childhood abuse and neglect, wife abuse, alcohol and drug addiction in the family, witnessing the arrest of family members, having a family member who is chronically ill, and experiencing a death in the family during childhood. Her conclusion, based on comparisons of male and female gang members, is that young women in particular are likely to come from families that are troubled. Portillos's (1999) study of Chicana gang members suggests that girls are also drawn to gang involvement as a means of escaping oppressive patriarchal conditions in the home.

In my study, gang members were significantly more likely than girls who were not in gangs to come from homes with numerous problems. Gang girls were significantly more likely to have witnessed physical violence between adults in their homes and to have been abused by adult family members. In addition, they were much more likely to report regular drug use in their homes. Most important, gang members were significantly more likely to describe experiencing *multiple* family problems—with 60% (vs. 24% of nongang girls) describing three or more of the following five problems: having been abused, violence among adults, alcohol abuse in the family, drug abuse in the family, and the incarceration of a family member. In fact, 44% reported that four or more of these problems existed in their families, compared to only 20% of the nongang girls (see J. Miller, 2001a).

In the in-depth interview portion of my study, the most common family-related themes described by young women as contributing to their gang involvement were drug addiction among primary caregivers and being physically and/or sexually abused by family members.[4] The ways in which family problems facilitated girls' gang involvement were varied, but they shared a common thread—young women began spending time away from home as a result of difficulties or dangers there, and consequently sought to get away and to meet their social and emotional needs elsewhere. A number of researchers have suggested that "the gang can serve as a surrogate extended family for adolescents who do not see their own families as meeting their needs for belonging, nurturance, and acceptance" (Huff, 1993, p. 6; see also Campbell, 1990; Joe & Chesney-Lind, 1995; but see Decker & Van Winkle, 1996; Hunt, Mackenzie, & Joe-Laidler, 2000). The gang can offer a network of friends for girls whose parents are unable to provide stable family relations; moreover, girls' friendships with other gang members may provide a support system for coping with family problems, abuse, and other life problems (Joe & Chesney-Lind, 1995). Regardless of whether gangs actually fulfill these roles in young women's lives,[5] it is clear that many girls believe they will when they become involved.

Some girls who lack close relationships with their primary caregivers can turn to siblings or extended family members to maintain a sense of belonging and attachment. However, if these family members are gang involved, it is likely that girls will choose to join gangs themselves. Moreover, even when relationships with parents or other adults are strong, having adolescent or young adult gang members in the family often heightens the appeal of gangs (see also Joe & Chesney-Lind, 1995; Moore, 1991). In fact, Hunt, Mackenzie, and Joe-Laidler (2000) have challenged the dichotomous treatment among gang researchers between "gang" and "family," noting that there are many cases in which both "real" and "fictive" kin are members of girls' gangs. Thus, when young women speak of the familial nature of their gang relationships, they sometimes are literally speaking about their family members.

In my own research, this was often the case. As compared with nongang girls, gang girls in my study were much more likely to have siblings in gangs and were more likely to have two or more gang-involved family members. Moreover, in the qualitative portion of the study, many young women described the significant influence that older siblings and relatives had on their decisions to join their gangs. More often than not, young women who joined gangs to be with or like their older siblings did so in the context of the types of family problems noted earlier (J. Miller, 2001a). In fact, in my study the themes just reviewed—neighborhood exposure to gangs, family problems, and gang-involved family members—were overlapping in most gang girls' accounts, further distinguishing them from nongang girls in the sample.[6] These were the primary issues I identified as contributing to girls' gang involvement.

Although qualitative studies are most likely to find family problems and community conditions at the heart of girls' gang involvement, a number of studies based on surveys of juvenile populations note school-based problems (see Thornberry, 1998, for an overview). Bjerregaard and Smith (1993) found that low expectations of completing school were a significant predictor of gang membership for young women. Likewise, Bowker and Klein (1983) report that female gang members are less likely than nonmembers to intend to finish high school or go to college. More recently, Esbensen and Deschenes

(1998) report that school commitment and expectations are associated with gang involvement for girls, and Thornberry (1998) also describes negative attitudes toward school as a risk factor for girls.[7]

Survey research has also examined individual characteristics and behaviors as risk factors for gang membership, as well as relationships with delinquent peers. Based on their analysis of the G.R.E.A.T. project, Esbensen, Deschenes, and Winfree (1999) report that gang girls were more socially isolated and had lower self-esteem than their male gang peers. Comparing male and female nongang members, their findings were similar; however, the difference was more pronounced between gang girls and boys. G.R.E.A.T. findings also suggested that risk seeking was a predictor of female, but not male, gang membership (Esbensen & Deschenes, 1998). On the other hand, Bjerregaard and Smith (1993) did not find self-esteem predictive of gang membership for girls. With regard to values, activities, and exposure to antisocial peers and situations, Esbensen and Deschenes (1998) report that commitment to negative peers was associated with gang membership for girls; Thornberry (1998) reports that delinquency, drug use, and positive values about drugs are risk factors for girls; and Bjerregaard and Smith (1993) also report that both delinquent peers and early onset of sexual activity were associated with gang membership for girls. As Maxson and Whitlock (Chapter 2, this volume) suggest, these survey results suggest a "lack of stable, unique predictors" of gang membership for young women. Combined, however, survey and qualitative research highlight many of the salient issues researchers are continuing to examine.

GANG LIFE, DELINQUENCY, AND VIOLENCE AMONG GIRLS

One reason gangs have received so much attention among criminologists is that we know from quite a bit of research that young people who are in gangs—male and female—are substantially more involved in delinquency than their nongang counterparts. Research comparing gang and nongang youths has consistently found that serious criminal involvement is a feature that distinguishes gangs from other groups of youths (see Battin, Hill, Abbott, Catalano, & Hawkins, 1998; Esbensen & Huizinga, 1993; Fagan, 1990; Klein, 1995; Thornberry, 1998; Thornberry, Krohn, Lizotte, & Chard Wierschem, 1993). This pattern holds for female gang members as well as their male counterparts (Bjerregaard & Smith, 1993; Deschenes & Esbensen, 1999a, 1999b; Esbensen & Winfree, 1998; J. Miller, 2001a). The enhancement effect of gang membership is most noticeable for serious delinquency and marijuana use (Thornberry et al, 1993). Bjerregaard and Smith (1993) summarize:

> Our study suggests that for females [as well as males], gangs are consistently associated with a greater prevalence and with higher rates of delinquency and

substance abuse. Furthermore, the results suggest that for both sexes, gang membership has an approximately equal impact on a variety of measures of delinquent behavior. (p. 346)

Perhaps what's most significant about this research is evidence that female gang members are more delinquent than their female nongang counterparts, but also more so than their *male* nongang counterparts. For instance, Fagan (1990) reports that "prevalence rates for female gang members exceeded the rates for non-gang males" for all the categories of delinquency he measured (see also Esbensen & Winfree, 1998). Fagan summarizes his findings in relation to girls as follows:

> More than 40 percent of the female gang members were classified in the least serious category, a substantial difference from their male counterparts. Among female gang members, there was a bimodal distribution, with nearly as many multiple index offenders as petty delinquents. Evidently, female gang members avoid more serious delinquent involvement than their male counterparts. *Yet their extensive involvement in serious delinquent behaviors well exceeds that of non-gang males or females.* (Fagan, 1990, p. 201, my emphasis).

As Fagan's findings suggest, there is also evidence of gender differences within gangs with regard to criminal involvement. Fagan (1990, pp. 196–197) reports greater gender differences in delinquency between gang members than between nongang youth. Male gang members were significantly more involved in the most serious forms of delinquency, while for alcohol use, drug sales, extortion, and property damage, gender differences were not significant. Specifically, as noted above, Fagan reports a bimodal distribution among young women in gangs: Approximately 40% of the gang girls in his study were involved only in petty delinquency and a third were involved in multiple index offending, compared to 15% and 56%, respectively, for young men. Moreover, evidence from a number of studies suggests that gun use is much more prevalent among male than female gang members (Decker, Pennell, & Caldwell, 1997; Fleisher, 1998; Hagedorn & Devitt, 1999; Miller & Brunson, 2000; Miller & Decker, 2001).

Several explanations have been offered for these differences. In keeping with a large body of literature showing that gender stratification is a key organizational element of delinquent and criminal street networks (see Maher, 1997; Miller, 1998b), there is evidence of the "structural exclusion of young women from male delinquent activities" within mixed-gender gangs (Bowker et al, 1980, p. 516; J. Miller, 2001a; Miller & Brunson, 2000). Bowker et al's (1980) male respondents suggested that not only were girls excluded from the planning of delinquent acts, but when girls inadvertently showed up at the location of a planned incident, it was frequently postponed or terminated. Likewise, the majority of young women in my study did not participate routinely in the most serious forms of gang crime, such as gun use, drive-by shootings, and (to a lesser extent) drug sales. This was in part a result of exclusionary practices by male gang members, but in addition, many young women purposively chose not to be involved in what they considered dangerous and/or morally troubling activities (J. Miller, 2001a). Like Fagan (1990), I found that only about a quarter to a third of gang girls were routinely involved in serious delinquency.

Other researchers suggest that gender differences in norms supportive of violence and delinquency accounts for differences in gang girls' and gang boys' delinquency. Joe and Chesney-Lind (1995; see also Campbell, 1993), for example, suggest that participation in violence is a stronger normative feature of male gang involvement than it is for young women in gangs. They argue that for girls, "violence (gang and otherwise) is not celebrated and normative; it is instead more directly a consequence of and a response to the abuse, both physical and sexual, that characterizes their lives at home" (Joe & Chesney-Lind, 1995, p. 428). As noted, some girls in my study suggested they avoided violence because they found it morally troubling, but I did not find this to be a consistent pattern. Instead, many young women in my study did describe violence as a normative activity for girls, though rarely at extreme levels such as gun use or homicide (J. Miller, 2001a; see also Hagedorn & Devitt, 1999).

There is growing evidence that part of the answer to these competing explanations for gender differences in gang delinquency and violence, as well as variations in young women's participation in gang crime, can be found by examining the gender organization and composition of girls' gangs (Joe-Laidler & Hunt, 1997; Miller & Brunson, 2000; Peterson et al., 2001). It may also be the case—though more comparative research is needed—that ethnic differences may account for variations as well. Moore and Hagedorn (1996) suggest that Latina gang members are more bound by "traditional" community patriarchal norms than are African American gang girls (see also Portillos, 1999). Likewise, as noted, the young women in Joe and Chesney-Lind's (1995) study were from communities (Samoan and Filipino) with strong patriarchal norms for girls, particularly with regard to sexuality.

I did not find strong supportive relationships among most gang girls in my study; instead, many girls identified with masculine status norms in the gang and desired acceptance as "one of the guys." Given the extent to which this finding contradicted other research on girls in gangs (Campbell, 1984; Joe & Chesney-Lind, 1995; Lauderback et al, 1992), I sought explanation in gang structure. Kanter (1977) notes that often conclusions drawn about differences between males and females, and attributed to "gender roles" or cultural differences between women and men, are in fact more appropriately attributable to situational or structural factors such as the gender composition of groups. As I described above, the vast majority of girls in my study were in mixed-gender gangs that were numerically male dominated. Examining the data more closely, it did appear that the handful of girls in female-only gangs, or gangs with a substantial representation of female members, were more likely to emphasize the social and relational aspects of their gangs, particularly their friendships with other girls.

This also suggests that differences in girls' levels of participation in violence, and the normative salience of violence for girls, might also be influenced by the gender organization of their gangs. In an analysis of gang boys' perceptions of girls' activities in their gangs, we found that young men in gender-balanced groups highlighted the social aspects of their interactions with female gang members, but differentiated males' and females' participation in delinquent activities. Young men in gangs with a vast majority of male members embraced the few young women in their gangs as "one of the guys" and described these girls as essentially equal partners in many of their delinquent endeavors (Miller & Branson, 2000).

Peterson et al.'s (2001) analysis of the G.R.E.A.T. project, described above, allowed for further examination of this question. We classified youths' gangs according to four types of gender composition: all male, majority-male but with female membership, gender-balanced, and majority-or all female. We compared youths' descriptions of their gangs' activities, as well as individual delinquency rates for males and females across these groups, and our findings offer support for the importance of gender composition in shaping both the nature of gang activities, and individual gang members' delinquency. Based on member characterizations of their *gangs,* majority-/all-female gangs were the least delinquent groups, followed by all-male gangs. Both gender-balanced and majority-male gangs were similar with regard to the gangs' involvement in delinquent activities. To the extent that these descriptions are a reflection of the goals and norms of respondents' gangs, these differences are noteworthy and suggest that delinquency, particularly of a serious nature, is a less normative feature of primarily female gangs than other gangs.

On the other hand, our findings are not fully supportive of the notion of "gender differences" between girls and boys with regard to the normative acceptance of violence and delinquency.[8] Instead, we found significant within-gender differences for both girls and boys with regard to their level of participation in delinquency across gang types (Peterson et al, 2001). Specifically, comparing youths by gender and across gang types, we founds that girls in all-/majority-female gangs had the lowest rates of delinquency. They were followed by girls in gender-balanced gangs. Next lowest were *boys* in all-male gangs, followed by girls in majority-male gangs, boys in gender-balanced gangs, and finally, boys in majority-male gangs. For both boys and girls, but especially girls, membership in majority-male gangs was correlated with the highest rates of delinquency.[9] Thus, girls' (and boys') gang-related delinquency appears to be strongly associated with the gender organization of their groups.

Other research offers additional support for the importance of examining the types of gangs girls are involved in. For instance, Lauderback et al. (1992) provide one of the few thorough descriptions of an autonomous female gang (see also Venkatesh, 1998), the Potrero Hill Posse (PHP), a group that was heavily involved in drug sales in San Francisco. Lauderback and colleagues (1992) suggest that PHP actually came about because these young women were dissatisfied with a "less than equitable ... distribution of the labor and wealth" (p. 62) that had been part and parcel of their previous involvement in selling drugs with males. Moreover, this was a gang characterized by close, familial-like relationships among its female members. Joe-Laidler and Hunt (1997) extended Lauderback et al.'s (1992) analysis of PHP, comparing the social contexts of violence for young women in PHP with the social contexts facilitating violence among female gang members in other gangs in San Francisco. Although members of PHP were African American, the vast majority of other young women were Latina (with a small number of Samoans), and were in female groups affiliated with male gangs.

Joe-Laidler and Hunt (1997) found important differences in young women's exposure to violence across gang types, and report that girls in auxiliary gangs were exposed to a greater variety of violence-prone situations, many of which were tied to their associations with young men. The young women in PHP described violence occurring in three types of situations: violence associated with the drug trade, fights with girls in other gangs (over both men and turf), and intimate partner violence at the hands of their male partners. In contrast, young women in auxiliary gangs were subject to more violence-prone situations: violence in the context of gang initiations, conflicts with rival gang members—both male and female[10]—and conflicts *among* homegirls in the same gang (over reputation, respect, jealousies over males, and fights instigated by males), as well as intimate partner violence at the hands of boyfriends.

Joe-Laidler and Hunt's (1997) findings offer further evidence that dynamics resulting from the gendered social organization of gangs shapes young women's exposure to and participation in violence. Though additional research is needed on the role of ethnicity in shaping girls' gang experiences, there appears to be a relationship between the ethnic composition of gangs and their gender organization, as well as young women's experiences in gangs (see also Moore & Hagedorn, 1996). Contemporary research on African American gang girls has not found evidence of a strongly sexualized component of their gang activities (J. Miller, 2001a). However, in his research on Chicana gang members in Phoenix, Portillos (1999) reports that gang girls' sexuality was often used as a means of setting up rival gang males. In contrast to my portrait of African American girls in majority-male gangs as "one of the guys," Portillos describes Chicana gang girls constructing an oppositional femininity that is clearly differentiated from (and subordinate to) male gang members' gang masculinity.

As this research suggests, gender plays a complicated role in girls' gang participation, including their involvement in delinquency and violence. It intersects with ethnicity and culture, and is a structural determinant of girls' experiences rather than simply a result of individual differences between young women and young men. For some girls, and in some contexts, delinquency is part of the allure of gang life. But evidence suggests that some girls (as well as boys) are fairly ambivalent about their criminal involvement, even though they report finding it fun or exciting at times. On one hand, it brings them status and recognition within the group, as well as economic remuneration; on the other, it can get them into trouble with the law or put them at greater risk for being victimized by rival gang members or others on the streets.

But for girls in particular, many aspects of gang involvement, including delinquency, go against dominant notions of appropriate femininity. This shapes girls' experience within and outside of their gangs, often locking, them into what Swart (1991) describes as a series of double binds. This point brings me to the last topic I want to touch on—the consequences of gang involvement for girls. Here I will focus on two issues. First, what are the consequences of gang involvement for girls while they are active in gangs? Second, what evidence do we have about the long-term consequences of gang involvement for young women? Though young people often turn to gangs as a means of meeting a variety of needs within their lives, it is often the case that their gang affiliation does more harm than good by increasing their likelihood of victimization and decreasing their opportunities and life chances.

CONSEQUENCES OF GANG INVOLVEMENT FOR GIRLS

Girls' gang participation can be viewed as transgressing social norms concerning appropriate feminine behavior; thus a number of scholars have discussed gang girls as constructing an "oppositional" or "bad girl" femininity (see Hagedorn & Devitt, 1999; Messerschmidt, 1995; Portillos, 1999). Research, however, has consistently shown that youth gangs—with the exception of autonomous female gangs—are by and large male dominated in structure, status hierarchies, and activities, even as young women are able to carve meaningful niches for themselves (see Campbell, 1984; Fleisher, 1998; Hagedorn, 1998b; Joe-Laidler & Hunt, 1997; J. Miller, 2001a; Moore, 1991). Even young women in all-female gangs must operate within male-dominated street networks (see Lauderback et al., 1992; Taylor, 1993). Thus, while some scholars would suggest that because they are challenging traditional gender roles, girls' gang participation can be viewed as liberating, most researchers highlight what Curry (1998) refers to as the "social injury" associated with gang involvement. During the course of their gang involvement, girls face a number of risks and disadvantages associated with gender inequality. Moreover, there is some evidence of long-term detrimental consequences for gang-involved young women (Moore, 1991; Moore & Hagedorn, 1996).

Research has shown that girls in gangs face social sanctions, both within and outside the gang, for not behaving in gender appropriate ways. For instance, Swart (1991) suggests that girls' experiences in gangs are complicated by the contradictions they face as they balance deviant and gender norm expectations. On the one hand, he argues, "the female gang member's behavior must be 'deviant' to those outside of the gang in order to ensure her place within the gang itself" (p. 45). On the other hand, if it is too deviant, it risks the danger of offending other gang members who maintain certain attitudes about appropriate female conduct when it comes to issues of sexual activity, drug use, violence, and motherhood. The likelihood of such social sanctions, however, is shaped by the gender composition of girls' gangs. As I described, young women accepted as "one of the guys" are better able to escape disapproval, particularly with regard to their participation in gang delinquency (see Miller & Branson, 2000).

Thus, Swart's findings are complicated, as Curry (1998) notes, by evidence that also suggests that young women's gang involvement provides a means of resisting limitations placed on them by narrow social definitions of femininity, which they recognize as limiting their options in an environment in which they are already quite restricted. Campbell (1987), for instance, found that "gang girls see themselves as different from their [female] peers. Their association with the gang is a public proclamation of their rejection of the lifestyle which the community expects from them" (pp. 463–464; see also J. Miller, 2001a). Likewise, Taylor's (1993) study of female gang members in Detroit found young women highly critical of the entrenched misogyny on the streets and the difficulties females often face in interacting in these environments.

Regardless of girls' awareness of gender inequality, it remains an inescapable element of their experiences within gangs and brings with it particular sorts of consequences. For instance, there is a clear sexual double standard in operation within gangs, as in American society as a whole (Campbell, 1990; Fleisher, 1998; J. Miller, 2001a; Moore, 1991; Portillos, 1999; Swart, 1991). Moore (1991) suggests that some young men viewed young women as sexual objects, "a piece of ass," or "possessions" (pp. 52–53), while young women, though recognizing gender inequalities in their gangs, on the whole wanted to see themselves as respected by male members. Girls' dating options were narrowed as well. Being a gang member and having the look of a gang member was stigmatizing for girls, making them less attractive to boys outside the gang. On the other hand, male gang members frequently had girlfriends outside the gang who were "square," and these "respectable" girls were looked to by the boys as their future (Moore, 1991, pp. 74–76; see also Fishman, 1995).

Moreover, research suggests that rather than challenging this sexual double standard, young women often reinforce it in their interactions with one another. Several studies reveal that gang girls create hierarchies among themselves, sanctioning other girls both for being too "square" and for being too promiscuous. Typically, the sexual double standard is reinforced by girls as sanctions against those they perceive as too sexually active. Girls have not been found to gain status among their peers for sexual promiscuity (Campbell, 1990; J. Miller, 2001a; Swart, 1991); rather, they are expected to engage in serial monogamy. On the whole, the sexual double standard tends to disadvantage girls in their relationships with boys but also interferes with the strength of their own friendship groups (Campbell, 1987).

My research suggests additional problems exacerbated by gender inequality within gangs. Attention to the association between gang membership and delinquency has overlooked an equally important relationship: that between gang membership and victimization. Though few studies have been attentive to this question, there are reasons to consider it an important one. There is strong evidence that participation in delinquency increases youths' risk of victimization (Lauritsen, Sampson, & Laub, 1991). Given ample evidence linking youths' participation in gangs with increases in delinquency, it seems self-evident that gang membership likely increases youths' victimization risks. In my research, gang girls were significantly more likely than nongang girls to have been sexually assaulted,[11] threatened with a weapon, and stabbed, and to have witnessed stabbings, shootings, drive-bys, and homicides (J. Miller, 2001a).

Moreover, gender inequality in gangs and young men's greater participation in serious gang crime suggests that victimization risks within gangs will be shaped by gender. Because girls are less likely than their male counterparts to engage in serious forms of gang crime, they face less risk of victimization at the hands of rival gang males, because they are less likely to engage in those activities that would increase their exposure to violence. This lesser risk is bolstered to the extent that norms or rules exist against male gang members targeting rival females (Joe-Laidler & Hunt, 1997; J. Miller, 2001a). Thus girls' lesser risk is especially the case with regard to lethal and potentially lethal violence, particularly because young women themselves rarely engage in gun violence (Hagedorn & Devitt, 1999; J. Miller, 2001a).

For example, in an analysis of St. Louis homicide data (Miller & Decker, 2001), we found that women were more than twice as often (17% vs. 8%) nongang homicide victims as they were gang homicide victims. Moreover, the vast majority of female gang homicide victims were not the intended targets of these killings: the modal, and by far predominant, pattern for female gang homicides was for the victim to be killed when suspects opened fire into a group. In contrast, the majority of male gang homicide victims were the intended targets. Likewise, Hagedorn (1998b, p. 197) reports that female gang members in his sample reported having been shot at an average of 0.33 times, compared to 9.1 times for male gang members, a ratio of 27:1.

However, because leadership and status hierarchies in mixed-gender gangs are typically male dominated, and because girls are less likely to engage in those activities that confer status within the gang, they are often viewed as lesser members within their gangs. This devaluation of young women can lead to girls' mistreatment and victimization, especially by members of their own gang, because they aren't seen as deserving of the same respect (see Joe-Laidler & Hunt, 1997; J. Miller, 2001a). These problems are further exacerbated by the sexual double standard described above, as well as high rates of intimate partner violence among gang youth as documented by Joe-Laidler and

Hunt (1997; see also Fleisher, 1998). One particularly troubling issue for some gang girls is the use of sexual initiations for entree into the gang. Both my research and that of Portillos (1999) uncovered the use of this practice—having sexual relations with multiple male gang members—among gangs, though in neither instance did we find it to be the primary initiation pattern for girls.[12] When this occurs, girls are highly stigmatized and disrespected by other gang members, both male and female. They are viewed as promiscuous and sexually available, thus increasing their subsequent mistreatment. In addition, they are viewed as taking the "easy" way in and are not seen as valuable members of the gang (J. Miller, 2001a; Portillos, 1999).

Moreover, I found that the stigma could extend to female gang members in general, creating a sexual devaluation that all girls had to contend with. Nonetheless, there appears to be tremendous variation in girls' experiences within gangs. Among the girls in my study, some were able to carve a niche for themselves that put them, if not exactly in the same standing as young men, at least on a par in terms of much of their treatment. Other young women were severely mistreated, and there was a range of experiences in between. Ironically, those young women most respected within the gang were more likely to face gang-related victimization at the hands of rivals. Those young women defined as "weak" by their lack of participation in gang-related fighting and delinquency were more likely to face abuses at the hands of their gang peers (J. Miller, 2001a).

Thus far, I have specifically discussed the impact of gang involvement for girls while they are in their gangs. What about after they leave? Few studies offer evidence of the long-term consequences of gang involvement for girls (see Moore, 1991; Moore & Hagedorn, 1996). However, the available evidence suggests that young women in gangs are at greater risk than others for a number of problems into and within their adult lives. Whereas many opportunities for legitimate success are gravely limited for young women living in impoverished communities, the negative consequences associated with gang membership can prove crippling. Gang membership exacerbates already troubled lives (Fleisher, 1998). Moore and Hagedorn (1996) note that although many young women turn to gangs as a means of dealing with multiple life problems, "for most women, being in a gang does have a real impact on later life" (p. 215).

Moore's (1991) research on Chicano/a gang members in Los Angeles found that ex-gang members could be divided into three categories: *tecatos, cholos,* and *squares.* She reports that approximately a quarter of the males in her study, and "a much smaller proportion of the female sample" (p. 125) were *tecatos*—heroin addicts involved in street life; about a third of the men but more of the women were *cholos*—persisting in gang and criminal involvement into adulthood. Women and men in this category typically had not held down regular jobs and had unstable marriage patterns, often characterized by early marriage and childbearing, followed by early divorce (Moore, 1991, pp. 125–127). Finally, she reports that whereas around 40% of the males in her sample went on to lead conventional lives ("squares"), this was the case for fewer of the women[13] (p. 127).

While Moore's Los Angeles research concerned individuals who had been in gangs in the 1950s and 1970s, her more recent work with Hagedorn (Moore & Hagedorn, 1996) compared these with contemporary African American and Latina gang members in Milwaukee, Wisconsin. They report that substantially fewer of these women continued their gang involvement into adulthood, concluding that "for women—but not for men—the gang was almost completely an adolescent experience" (p. 209). Latinas were more likely to be involved in drug sales and use into adult-hood, compared with African American women. Moore and Hagedorn (1996) conclude:

> For Latinas in both cities, gang membership tended to have a significant influence on their later lives, but for African American women in Milwaukee, the gang tended to be an episode. There is much less sense in Milwaukee that gang girls of any ethnicity were as heavily labeled in their communities as were Chicana gang girls in Los Angeles. (p. 210)

It seems reasonable to suggest that the earlier a girl exits the gang, the greater her chances for a better life. Some evidence suggests that childbearing and the child care responsibilities that result often facilitate young women's maturation out of gangs (J. Miller, 2001a; Moore & Hagedorn, 1996). However, though having children may expedite girls' leaving their gangs, doing so does not necessarily increase their chances for successful lives. Partly this is because stable marriages and jobs are less available in the current socioeconomic climate in urban communities in the United States than in the past. Communities where many gangs are located have dwindling numbers of males in the marriage pool; moreover, skyrocketing rates of incarceration and lethal violence have greatly contributed to this shortage (Moore & Hagedorn, 1996; Wilson, 1996). Considering the high unemployment rates in most gang neighborhoods, many young men have few conventional opportunities and are increasingly likely to continue their gang and criminal involvement into adulthood (Klein, 1995). The bleak futures that await the men in their communities often makes marriage no longer a desirable component of gang-involved women's lives (Moore & Hagedorn, 1996). The attacks on many social programs have also negatively affected women's lives after gang membership. Moore and Hagedorn (1996) observe,

> Ironically, the most important influence on gang women's future may be the dismantling of the nation's welfare system in the 1990s. This system has supported women with children who want to stay out of the drug marketing system and in addition has provided a significant amount of cash to their

communities. Its disappearance will deepen poverty and make the fate of gang women ever more problematic. (p. 217)

These issues are of vital importance for gang-involved young women and represent an area strongly in need of further research.

CONCLUSION

This chapter has addressed a number of issues concerning young women's involvement in gangs—the extent of their gang involvement, why they become involved, and what their experiences in gangs are like, including their participation in delinquency and exposure to violence. As I have shown, young women join gangs in response to a myriad of problems in their lives. Gang involvement, though, tends to exacerbate rather than improve their situation. It increases the likelihood that young women will engage in delinquency and exposes them to risks of victimization, at the hands of both rival gangs and gang peers. Though young women are not as involved in the most serious forms of gang violence as young men, and gangs are less likely to be life threatening for their female than their male members, nonetheless, gang involvement often narrows young women's life options even further (see Moore, 1991).

A number of suggestions for policy and practice emerge from this overview. With regard to prevention, the research highlights several notable issues. Girls begin hanging out with gang members quite early and often join gangs in the first years of their teens. Thus prevention efforts must begin quite early. In addition, a series of risk factors appears to converge for girls, increasing the likelihood that gangs become an alluring option. These include living in neighborhoods where gangs are in close proximity; having multiple problems in the family, including violence and drug abuse; and having siblings or multiple family members in gangs. Most significant, it appears to be the convergence of such risk factors that particularly heighten girls' risks for gang involvement. Prevention efforts should be targeted especially to girls exposed to these problems. However, as Maxson and Whitlock (Chapter 2, this volume) suggest, etiological research on female gang involvement has not identified clear risk factors for girls, above and beyond those identified for girls' risks for delinquency. Their suggestions regarding gender-specific prevention approaches appear prudent, given the state of our knowledge about these issues.

Findings presented in this chapter also have implications for gang intervention with young women. Most notable is the need to recognize *variations* in young women's experiences and activities within and across gangs. My research suggests that although in some instances gender-specific interventions may be useful (particularly in dealing with sexual assault and abuse), it is also the case that some features of gang programming for young men are likely to be important for girls as well. For example, though girls are rarely as involved in serious violence as boys, it is nonetheless the case that group processes, conflicts, and rivalries provoke girls' participation in confrontations with rival gang members in ways similar to those of young men. Thus, interventions for girls need to take such issues into account (see Klein, 1995).

Intervention strategies should also be tailored to meet the diverse needs of female gang members, with sensitivity to ethnic and cultural differences. In addition, given variations across gangs, specific knowledge about girls' gangs can provide suggestions for effective approaches. Specifically, attention to the gender composition and organization of girls' groups is likely to provide important information about girls' victimization risks and their exposure to violence-prone situations (Joe-Laidler & Hunt, 1997). In particular, the level and nature of young women's participation in gang crime may be an indicator of the particular types of victimization risks these young women face: Girls who are heavily involved in street crime are at heightened risk for physical violence such as assaults and stabbings; other young women are at greater risk for ongoing physical and sexual mistreatment by male gang members (J. Miller, 2001a; Miller & Brunson, 2000). Most important is the need to recognize that young women in gangs are not a monolithic group and should be approached accordingly.

Unfortunately, responses to gangs and gang members are often primarily punitive in nature, disregarding the social, economic, and personal contexts that cause gang participation. This punitive orientation toward gang members means that gang-involved youths are not seen as in need of assistance and protection, and this—coupled with the problems they face in their daily lives—has further detrimental effects on these young people (see Fleisher, 1998; Moore & Hagedorn, 1996). Moreover, programming and policies targeted specifically to the needs of female gang members have been scant (see Curry, 1999). Given the findings I have detailed above, the best course of action with regard to young women's gang involvement should involve policies that consider the social, economic, and personal contexts that influence gang participation, gang crime, and young women's victimization within these groups. Initiatives that actually consider the best interest of youths are needed in order to rationally respond to gangs and young women's involvement in these groups.

NOTES

1. This title is borrowed appreciatively from Anne Campbell's (1984) monograph of the same name—recognized by many as the force behind contemporary research on young women in gangs.
2. Part of this discrepancy is likely attributable to differences in youths' perceptions of what constitutes membership in their gangs. See Hagedorn and Devitt (1999) and

Miller and Brunson (2000) with regard to the gendered social construction of gangs and gang membership.

3. However, family poverty was not a significant predictor of gang membership for young women in the RYDS study (Thornberry, 1998).

4. Although the RYDS study did not find family violence to be a significant risk factor for female gang involvement (Thornberry, 1998), there is a growing body of literature supporting the link between childhood maltreatment and youths' subsequent involvement in delinquency (see Smith & Thornberry, 1995; Widom, 1989). Maxson and Whitlock (Chapter 2, this volume) note that studies of risk factors for gang membership are better at distinguishing gang and nongang youth among males than females. They suggest that "male gang members may be more distinctive than their nongang counterparts than is true for females," and that prevention programming for girls, given our current state of knowledge, may be most successful in targeting girls' risks for delinquency more generally rather than risks for gang involvement.

5. Recent evidence suggests that girls' supportive relationships in gangs may be stronger in all-female gangs and those with a substantial number of female members than in gangs that are numerically or ideologically male dominated. See my discussion later in this chapter of Joe-Laidler and Hunt (1997), J. Miller (2001a), Miller and Brunson (2000), and Peterson et al. (2001) regarding the impact of gendered gang structure on member activities and delinquency.

6. Taken individually, a majority of girls fit within each category: 96% described living in neighborhoods with gangs (vs. 59% of nongang girls). Of these, 69% explicitly described their neighborhood and peer networks as factors in their decisions to join. Likewise, 71% recognized family problems as contributing factors (26% of nongang girls reported similar problems); and 71% had siblings or multiple family members in gangs, or described the influence of gang-involved family members on their decisions to join (compared to a third of the nongang girls who had gang members in their immediate family or multiple gang members in their extended family). In all, 90% of the gang members in the study report two or more dimensions of these risk factors; and fully 44% fit within the overlap of all three categories. In contrast, only a third of the nongang girls experienced a multiple of these risk factors for gangs, and only four nongang girls (9% vs. 44% of gang girls) reported all three dimensions.

7. In my study, differences between gang and nongang girls did not emerge in school measures, nor did gang members describe school contexts as contributing to their decisions to join. This may be a result of differences across sites, or the result of sampling or methodological differences (see Esbensen & Winfree, 1998, for a discussion of sampling and methodology).

8. This is particularly the case since boys in all-male gangs also reported lower rates of gang delinquency than youths in gangs with both male and female membership.

9. And note that girls in majority-male gangs reported more individual delinquency than boys in all-male gangs.

10. In fact, Joe-Laidler and Hunt note that fights between rival girls were often instigated by males, who reportedly enjoyed watching females fight. Though they describe rules excluding girls from fighting males from rival gangs, young women sometimes got caught in these conflicts.

11. Sexual assault requires some clarification. In all, 25 gang girls (52%) in my study had been sexually assaulted a total of 35 times. Most of the sexual victimization young women reported occurred in the context of their families or by men they were exposed to through family members. On the whole, the gang context did not seem to increase girls' risk of sexual assault as it did for their risk of other violent crime. However, as I discuss, this is not to suggest that sexual assaults in gangs did not occur or that other forms of sexual exploitation were not present. In fact, as I will discuss, the less girls were involved in gang crime, the more vulnerable they appeared to be to sexual exploitation and other mistreatment within the gang.

12. In Portillos's (1999) research, girls from the neighborhood could be viewed as "born into" the gang by virtue of their close connections to the neighborhood, and girls could also be beaten in as a means of gaming status. It was also the case in his research that when girls were "trained into" gangs, this was not always consensual. In my research most girls were beaten or jumped into their gangs, though there was more fluidity in St. Louis because of gangs' strong neighborhood dimensions. It is notable that Joe and Chesney-Lind (1995) did not report initiation rituals among gang youth in their study in Hawaii, and Joe-Laidler and Hunt (1997) do not describe initiations for PHP members, but they do for members of other gangs.

13. Moore (1991) notes that this finding is partly an artifact of the underrepresentation of "square" women in her sample. She notes, "Some such women refused the interview because their husbands would not allow them to discuss their 'deviant' adolescence; others refused because they were afraid that they would be questioned about what they now define as 'deviance'—particularly about sexual activity" (p. 130). Moore concludes, "These views offer a poignant confirmation of the stigma attached to women's gang membership" (p. 130).

WHAT IS THE STATUS OF GIRLS IN STREET GANGS?

By Michel Dorais,
Patrice Corriveau,
and Peter Feldstein

U nlike the United States, where an increasing number of girls are joining or forming gangs, Canada is thought to have few female gang members, and most of these generally remain in the peripheral circle.[8] Machismo among gang members is one obvious explanation; another is stricter parental control over girls, whose socialization takes place more in the private sphere than in public (on the street). Girls simply have less opportunity to join a gang than do boys.

Some scholars believe that the small numbers of girls identified as gang members merely reflect the hesitancy of law enforcement personnel to identify and treat them as such. But that perception is starting to change. U.S. research over the last two decades has found that active female participation in criminal gang activities is on the rise (Taylor 1993: 10; Esbensen et al. 1999). Schalet et al. (2003: 128) noted the emergence of female-only gangs which, following the example of male gangs, are involved in prostituting other girls. Other American studies have estimated that girls represent anywhere from 20 to 45 per cent of gang members in that country.[9] The much smaller estimates for Canada reflect a distinctly different reality here.[10]

Since girls are less likely than boys to be suspected of criminal activities, their involvement can be useful in deceiving the police or the civic authorities. Therefore, gangs often use girls as accomplices in money laundering, counterfeiting, credit card theft, fencing of stolen property, and other offences. Their role tends to be that of dissimulation rather than intimidation, force, or violence (although girls are perfectly capable of these). Rarely do they command or initiate violent crimes, although they may act violently under the orders or influence of a male leader.

While the role of girls in gangs is changing, no observer of the phenomenon has any illusions that large numbers of girls will become full-fledged members. The few who achieve this status will be perceived and treated as boys, in many respects. They too will have to undergo the punching initiation and do battle with girls from rival gangs. But their femininity will never disappear altogether, far from it, and this is evident in the motives for such fights, which are frequently triggered by a perceived attack on a girl's "sexual reputation." This is of enormous importance to an aspiring female gang member. She cannot allow herself to be perceived by the boys as a mere sex object, much less a whore. To do so is to instantly lower her status to a dangerous level because of the unwritten rule whereby boys must attract and seduce girls yet show outward contempt for them. One of the most terrifying displays of this contempt is the "gang bang."

A gang bang is a ritual gang rape in which a girl is forced to have sex with several gang members at once or in rapid succession. If the same girl is subjected to more than one of these incidents, the initial one is sometimes referred to as the "sex-in." Another practice is the "roll-in," where the girl rolls a die to determine how many sexual partners she has to satisfy on the spot. Many other variations are possible.[11] One girl remembered: "My ex told me, 'We're going to see some people.' We got there and there were some guys sitting around drinking. They asked him to go get something, beer I think. As soon as he left, the guys started touching me, asking me to get undressed, telling me they wanted to 'try me.' They said, 'It's no problem, everybody's okay with it' … I didn't know what to do. I let it happen. My ex and I never discussed it again." In another case, a new recruit was told by her female recruiter, "There's a party and you're going to be initiated. We all went through it. Just do what the guys tell you. You don't want to look like an idiot."

The main point cannot be overstressed: the gang bang is not a fun orgy but rather a purposeful assault committed by gangs that operate prostitution rings. Its main role appears to be that of sexually desensitizing both the victim and the assaulters in preparation for their respective roles in prostitution. Most obviously, it conditions the girl to have forced sex without thinking of it as rape. It is not just the traumatic bodily experience she is living through, but the simultaneous and incongruous reassurance that no trauma is being inflicted. Message: when men are having fun, you are having fun too. It does not matter what your body is telling you. The predictable post-traumatic stress symptoms the girl may experience, such as loss of sexual sensation or even a feeling of being cut off from her own body, reinforce the "normality" of submission to men's desires, however extreme, and thus create the docility that is the underage prostitute's main asset (from the pimp's standpoint, of course). She's "been there"; it's no big deal. The fear of the gang bang may itself be enough to intimidate a girl into what she sees as the lesser evil: having unwanted sex with one or more gang members, followed by paid non-consensual sex. Girls who participated in gang bangs may be reminded of their initiation with the message; you were willing to "do" anybody that night, so why turn down a paying client now? One girl recollected: "It was only later that I realized what had happened. One night I was in a bar, and all of a sudden I woke up somewhere, and all these guys were standing there expecting me to suck their dicks. I think they put something in my drink. Since that night I haven't been the same. I feel absolutely mortified."

Somewhat less obviously, the gang bang plays the role of desensitizing the boys. They cannot be allowed to nurture any feelings of love or exclusivity toward the girls whom they induct, or to resent the girls' treatment at the hands of the gang, since such feelings would limit their ability to pimp the girls without compunction. In this business, love interferes with profit margins, and so love must be vanquished by inculcating contempt. When the boys imitate their leaders (mimetism, after all, plays a pivotal role in street gangs) by "sharing" their girlfriends in a gang bang, they learn to redefine "manliness" as intense sexual desire coupled with domination of the women who allow them to fulfil it and emotional insensitivity to their needs. They enter into a pact to stand strong, as boys, against their own human emotions. An intriguing element of this pact, which we were unable to explore further in this research project, is that the act of sharing the same girl while others look on may allow the boys to have sexual feelings in male company, an experience otherwise strictly off limits in the macho world of gangs. There appears to be a homoerotic element at work here in which voyeurism and sexual promiscuity play a role.

In this way the gang bang "breaks" the boy for the role of sex slaver, just as it breaks the girl for the role of sex slave. Subsequently, as our respondents related, the gang reinforces this message by subjecting any pimp who lets a girl keep some of her earnings to ridicule and contempt. A real man must be in control, they tell him; he cannot let himself be controlled by a girl. It should be noted that by no means all boys are eager participants in the gang bang: knowing full well what lies in store for their girlfriends, they may go to great lengths to postpone the "official introduction" to the other gang members.

In short, the gang bang, like the punching initiation, puts a brand on the participants' bodies in a manner analogous to the gang's marking of geographical territory. The outward signs of allegiance (jewels, clothing, accessories, tattoos) are really only the culmination of an allegiance already more deeply inscribed in the body. The gang bang physically trains its participants, willing or unwilling, in the social and gender hierarchy by which they will be ruled and from which so the gang leaders tell them there is no escape.

Scholars and practitioners disagree on how common or systematic gang bangs are. Most of our respondents hold the belief that they are quite common, but each gang evidently has its traditions. Researching gang bangs is especially difficult in that many young women decline to report them. As we have seen, the acute cognitive dissonance laid over the event may lead girls to consider as group sex what was undoubtedly an instance of rape. Miller (2001) found that while all of her female respondents confirmed the existence of the practice, none admitted having participated in it. Given their depiction of it as a game, an unavoidable initiation, or a hurdle to be overcome, one wonders if they adopted the point of view of the boys who abused them. Cote (2004) found that when teenage girls were questioned by the Montreal police, even those who had participated in a gang bang did not consider it to be an instance of sexual assault. They claimed that they had consented.

Indeed, there appears to be a culture of silence among girl gang members around the phenomenon of the gang bang. No girl wants to be known as a slut, "the one who did all the boys." As well, many girls are reticent to use the term prostitution to describe their activities. Instead of using words that force them to look these experiences squarely in the face, they may think of them and describe them as survival sex: sex made necessary by the circumstances of the moment. Their core self image is at stake, but there is more: their image in the eyes of the rest of the gang is critical to their well-being. A girl who admits the facts is simply compounding the stigma that will inevitably surround her. Instead she learns to keep her status as a sex object a secret, thus striving to maintain outward respectability and distinguish herself from the pack (Chesney-Lind and Shelden 2004).

But there are few non-sexualized positions available for girls in gangs, and these are hotly contested. Furthermore, these positions often require the girl to act as a recruiter of other girls for prostitution. Thus the dilemma: to keep her reputation intact, she must arrange for the other girls' reputations to be ruined. A dichotomy rapidly emerges between the girls who manage to preserve their sexual reputation and those who do not. The losers are doubly stigmatized: by the boys and men who exploit them and by the girls who despise them (Chesney-Lind and Shelden 2004; Schalet et al. 2003; Burris-Kitchen 1997). As a result, girl-on-girl abuse in gangs has increased (Lucchini 1996: 34), as each girl seeks to protect her sexual status by denigrating the others. Schalet, Hunt, and Joe-Laidler (2003: 117) note that the importance accorded by girls to their sexual respectability varies depending on male and female sex roles in their culture of origin. For example, sexual freedom is more widely accepted among African-Americans than Latinos.

Within the overall variation in North American gang typology, there are three general types of gangs that allow for girls' involvement.[12] Undoubtedly the most frequent type in the United States and Canada exploits girls for sexual purposes, notably prostitution (Totten 2,000). The second type admits young women or girls in non-sexual roles. They have a lesser status than the boys and are generally in the minority; their main role is as accomplices in various crimes. In this context it is especially important for a girl to keep up her sexual status, since there may be opportunities for her to move from an auxiliary to a more active role (Huff 1990; Miller 1998). The third type are girl-only gangs, which tend to reproduce the culture of male gangs and may also involve victimization of other girls. No one in gang culture, whether male or female, questions the culture of machismo that reigns.

What is the Status of Girls in Street Gangs?

PowerPoint by:
Erika Brown
Lawren Fuggins
Rocio Ramirez

Introduction

► Over the last two decades, more females are joining and participate in criminal gang activity than previous but are not reported
like men because girls have less opportunities to join gangs and
stricter parental control.

► Studies have estimated that females represent anywhere from
20-45% of gang members in the US.

► Law enforcement have a hard time identifying females as gang
members and are reflected by the uncertainty to treat them as
legitimate gang members.

Initiation

- ► Females undergo the courting initiation and battle other females from rival gangs.
- ► "Motives for such fights, are frequently triggered by a perceived attack on a girl sexual reputation." (pg 28) The reputation of an aspiring female gang member is highly important.
- ► Some outward signs of allegiance are jewels, clothing, accessories, and tattoos.
- ► Men must also attract and seduce females to show their power over the female. i.e. "Gang Bang"

Initiation Cont.

- ► "**Gang bang** is a ritual gang rape in which a girl is forced to have sex with several gang members at once or in rapid succession" (pg 29).
- ► Another practice is "**roll-in**" which is when a female rolls a die to determine how many sex partners she has to encounter on the spot.
- ► Gang bang is not an excitable sex act but is rather an assault to prep females and sexually desensitize them to partake in prostitution operations.

Gender & Working Roles

- Since females are less likely to be suspected, their involvement in crimes make it easier to deceived the local authority.
- Females are usually persuaded to do money laundering, counterfeiting, credit card theft, fencing of stolen property, and other several offences.
- Recruitment is done by other female gang members to occupy the prostitution ring and to keep their reputation intact.

Mental Trauma of Female Gang Members

- When a man is feeling pleasure, the female should too; It does not matter what your body is telling you.
- The predictable post-traumatic stress symptoms the girl may experience: lost of sexual sensation or even a feeling of being cut off from her own body.
- Reinforces the common notion of **submission** to men's desires and creates the notion of complacency which is the main value of the young female prostitute (from the pimp's point of view).
- The **FEAR** of the gang bang itself may be enough for a female to rather have unwanted sex with one or more gang members.

The Gang Bang Effect

- ► Male gang members cannot be attached mentally and emotionally with a female gang member because having feelings will limit the ability to be able to pimp them; love interferes with profit margins and so love must be removed by instilling inferiority.
- ► By sharing their girlfriends in a gang redefine their "manliness" as an extreme sexual desire with superiority over the women who allow them to dominate and provide emotional insensitivity to their needs.

Gang Bang Effect Cont.

- ► "An intriguing element of this pact, which we were unable to restore further in this research project is that the act of sharing the same girl while others look on may allow the boys to have sexual feelings in a male company, an experience otherwise strictly off limits in the macho world of gangs, there appears to be a homoerotic element at work here in which voyeurism and sexual promiscuity play a role." (Pg 31)

Conclusion

- A gang bang physically trains its willing and unwilling participants in the social and gender hierarchy; there's no escape.
- Female respondents confirmed that gang bangs do exist but none admitted in participating in them (Miller 2001).
- "No girl wants to be known as a slut, 'the one that did all the boys'"(pg 33).
- The female's self-image in the eyes of the gang is crucial to her well-being.

Conclusion cont.

- There are three general type of gangs that allow for females involvement: sexual exploitation (prostitution), accomplices in various crimes, and female-only gangs that reproduce the culture of male gangs (including victimizing other female).

DRUGS AND GANGS

INITIATION OF DRUG USE, DRUG SALES, AND VIOLENT OFFENDING AMONG A SAMPLE OF GANG AND NONGANG YOUTH

By Finn-Aage Esbensen,
Dana Peterson,
Adrienne Freng,
and Terrance J. Taylor

rug use, drug sales, and violent offending are often considered the domain of gangs and their members, and the co-occurrence of these behaviors has been widely documented. Less attention, however, has been given to the temporal sequencing of these criminal events. That is, do youths join gangs and then begin their involvement in drug use, drug sales, and violent offending? Do youths already engage in these activities prior to joining the gang? Or, are these events that occur simultaneously? And importantly, why is this issue of interest? We believe that there are three main reasons for pursuing this line of inquiry: to provide a description of adolescent offending, to advance ideas for theory development and testing, and to inform gang prevention and intervention policy. Of some concern is simply the accuracy of the stereotype that after youths join gangs they become involved in drug use,

Finn-Aage Esbensen, Dana Peterson, Adrienne Freng, Terrance J. Taylor, "Initiation of Drug Use, Drug Sales, and Violent Offending Among a Sample of Gang and Nongang Youth," *Gangs in America III* ed. by C. Ronald Huff, pp. 37-50. Copyright © 2001 by SAGE Publications. Reprinted with permission.

drug sales, and violent offending. Is this media image borne out in research? From a theoretical perspective, do gangs attract youths who are already quite delinquent or do gangs facilitate initiation of delinquency, especially drug trafficking and violence? These competing questions pit social control theory against social learning theory. Or, is it that a combination of these two perspectives best explains the relationship between gang affiliation and involvement in illegal activities? From a policy perspective, knowledge of the initiation patterns may also be of some value. Depending on the transition pattern, prevention or intervention strategies may be the more suitable approach for addressing the gang problem.

In this chapter we utilize two samples of students to describe typologies of offenders and to disentangle the initiation patterns of these activities. A cross-sectional study of students provides the basis for describing typologies of offenders. For the latter objective, we use 4 years of data from the National Evaluation of the Gang Resistance Education and Training (G.R.E.A.T.) program to examine whether gang membership precedes involvement in drug use, drug sales, and violent offending or whether these activities are already part of the future gang members' behavioral repertoire prior to joining the gang.

LITERATURE REVIEW

There is a considerable body of research that has noted the co-occurrence of drug use and/or drug sales with other forms of delinquency, including gang membership (e.g., Elliott, Huizinga, & Menard, 1989; Fagan, Weis, & Cheng, 1990; Huizinga, Loeber, Thornberry, & Cothern, 2000; van Karnmen, Maguin, & Loeber, 1994). Case studies of gangs have documented the prevalence of drug use, drug trafficking, and/or violent offending among gang members (e.g., Decker & Van Winkle, 1996; Hagedorn, 1988; Moore, 1990). General survey samples have also produced data sets that confirm the co-occurrence of these behaviors among a larger population of adolescents. Investigation of the relationship among gang membership, drug use, drug sales, and violence has become increasingly important given the "proliferation of U.S. cities with street gang activity" (Maxson & Klein, 2001, p. 173).

Representative of the general survey approach, in 1986, the Office of Juvenile Justice and Delinquency Prevention (OJJDP) funded three projects collectively known as the Program of Research on the Causes and Correlates of Delinquency. Researchers from three universities collaborated on this project, conducting general surveys of "high-risk" youth in Denver, Colorado; Pittsburgh, Pennsylvania; and Rochester, New York. The Denver Youth Survey (DYS) and the Rochester Youth Development Study (RYDS) both contained survey information about gang involvement, and both of these studies are ongoing as of 2001. The DYS is a household probability sample consisting of

1,530 youth aged 7 to 15 during the first year of data collection. These youth completed annual face-to-face interviews that lasted between 50 and 90 minutes. The RYDS is a school-based sample composed of approximately 1,000 students who completed one-hour interviews every 6 months. Although the sampling procedures and frequency of interviews varied, the two projects used comparable questions to measure a variety of factors, including gang affiliation, self-reported delinquency, and drug use. These two studies have produced several important investigations of the role of gangs in violence, examining changes across time (Bjerregaard & Smith, 1993; Esbensen & Huizinga, 1993; Thornberry, Krohn, Lizotte, & Chard-Wierschem, 1993). Another schoolbased study, the Seattle Social Development Project, recently has contributed to this emerging body of gang literature derived from a general youth sample (e.g., Battin, Hill, Abbott, Cataiano, & Hawkins, 1998; Hill, Howell, Hawkins, & Battin-Pearson, 1999). Of particular relevance to the current inquiry is the finding from these studies that self-reported delinquency increases substantially after a youth has joined a gang. These studies, however, relied upon more global measures of delinquency and rates of offending rather than individual initiation. As such, they did not address the issue of whether the' individual youths were involved specifically in violence and drug sales prior to joining the gang.

On the basis of decades of gang research, whether utilizing law enforcement data, case studies or ethnographic studies, qualitative interviews, or general surveys, there is very little question concerning the heightened levels of delinquency and drug use among gang members. Representative of the extent to which gang members are involved in delinquency, estimates from the RYDS and the DYS are that gang members account for well over one half of the self-reported delinquency among youths in those studies. Thornberry and Burch (1997), for instance, reported that gang members accounted for 86% of serious delinquent acts, 69% of the violent offenses, and 70% of drug sales over a 4-year period, although gang youths (youths who were gang members at some time during the study period) represented only 30% of the sample. Similar results were reported for the Denver Youth Survey (Esbensen & Huizinga, 1993), the Seattle Social Development Project (Battin-Pearson, Thornberry, Hawkins, & Krohn, 1998), the G.R.E.A.T. Evaluation (Esbensen & Winfree, 1998), and in Huff's (1998) four-city study.

Drug trafficking has been widely attributed to gangs, and there is considerable agreement that gang youths are significantly more active in this arena than are nongang youths. There remains a question, however, concerning the extent to which gangs control drug sales. Some researchers maintain that the organizational structure of the typical youth gang is not conducive to organized drug trafficking. That is, youth gangs tend to be loosely organized with ephemeral leadership and to lack financial resources and cohesiveness; all traits deemed necessary for organized drug distribution (e.g., Klein, 1995; Moore, 1990; Spergel, 1995). In contrast, others have identified a subset of gangs that are primarily drug-selling gangs (Fagan, 1989; Taylor, 1989). In other research conducted in St. Louis and Kansas City, Decker and Van Winkle (1996) and Fleisher (1998), respectively, reported that profits from drug sales were generally kept by individuals and were not produced as a collective activity by the gang and subsequently not seen as gang property. Thus, these authors suggest that although gang members may be involved in drug selling, it is not common for the gangs themselves to be organized for that purpose. Whether drug sales are an organized gang activity or not, the consensus is that, "Drug use, drug trafficking, and violence overlap considerably in gangs" (Howell, 1998, p. 11).

In their review of the literature examining the co-occurrence of youth gangs, drug use, drug sales, and violence, Howell and Decker (1999) focused their attention more on general societal trends. In that report they examined such relationships as the introduction of crack cocaine and the rise in youth violence and homicides, and the increase in gang violence and drug trafficking across time. In this chapter, our focus is on the extent to which individuals are involved in these activities and whether there is a specific pattern of initiation into these activities; that is, we examine the within-individual change across time.

Prior gang research has, for the most part, not addressed the issue of whether drug use, drug sales, and violent offending precede gang involvement, whether they co-occur, or whether they are a product of joining the gang. There is a small body of research that has examined transition from one type of drug use to another or the transition from drug use to delinquency (e.g., Clayton, 1992; Elliott et al., 1989; van Kammen & Loeber, 1994; van Kammen et al., 1994; Yamaguchi & Kandel, 1984). These questions of initiation patterns are of both theoretical and practical importance. If we can identify a pattern or sequencing of behavior, we are better able to target interventions that may inhibit progression from one behavior to another.

Some longitudinal researchers have addressed the question of whether gangs recruit already delinquent youth (a "selection" model) or whether the gangs socialize new members into delinquent activity (a "social facilitation" model). Thornberry and colleagues (1993) and Esbensen and Huizinga (1993) found support for a facilitation and an "enhancement model" that incorporates both processes: Gang members appear to be active in delinquent activity prior to joining the gang, but their level of delinquency increases greatly during their period of membership and declines after leaving the gang, although it does remain at levels more elevated than for those who were never in a gang.

With respect to policy, considerable attention has been paid to prevention, intervention, and suppression approaches of responding to gang proliferation. If the selection model were the dominant pattern, it would seem logical to employ a general delinquency prevention program coupled with a targeted gang intervention. If the social facilitation model were dominant, targeted interventions with gang members would be recommended.

In this chapter, we explore two questions: (a) What are the prevalence rates for drug use, drug sales, and violent offending for gang and nongang youth? Is there offense specialization or as Klein (1995) argues, "cafeteria-style" delinquency? And importantly, (b) What is the temporal sequencing of these behaviors? Is there a selection, a social facilitation, or an enhancement effect?

CURRENT STUDY

The analyses reported in this chapter are based upon two separate studies, one cross-sectional and one longitudinal, that were part of the National Evaluation of the Gang Resistance Education and Training (G.R.E.A.T.) program. The cross-sectional study was conducted during the spring semester of 1995. Approximately 6,000 eighth-grade students enrolled in 42 different public schools in 11 cities across the continental United States completed anonymous group-administered questionnaires. From fall 1995 through fall 1999, a longitudinal study of slightly more than 2,000 students who were surveyed each year was conducted in six different cities (the analyses in this chapter utilize the 1995–1998 data). At the outset of this investigation, these students were enrolled in seventh grade (sixth in one site), representing 22 schools. The same questions were included in both studies so that we could replicate the analyses with the two samples.

In both studies, cities were purposively selected to allow for evaluation of the G.R.E.A.T. program. Clearly, only those cities with the program were included. A second consideration for site selection was geographical location. Even with a relatively small number of cities, we sought sites that would provide geographical diversity and varying levels of urbanization. A third criterion was the cooperation of the school districts and the police departments in each site. The cross-sectional cities were: Kansas City, Missouri; Las Cruces, New Mexico; Milwaukee, Wisconsin; Omaha, Nebraska; Orlando, Florida; Philadelphia, Pennsylvania; Phoenix, Arizona; Pocatello, Idaho; Providence, Rhode Island; Torrance, California; and Will County, Illinois. The longitudinal cities included the following: an east coast city (Philadelphia, Pennsylvania); a west coast location (Portland, Oregon); the site of the G.R.E.A.T. program's inception (Phoenix, Arizona); a midwest city (Omaha, Nebraska); a small city and home of the research project (Lincoln, Nebraska); and a small "border town" with a chronic gang problem (Las Cruces, New Mexico).

When conducting research with minors, a more restrictive code of ethics is applied than that guiding research involving adults. In addition to providing the standard information to potential respondents (i.e., information on the potential benefits and risks, the voluntariness of their participation, the purposes of the research, the procedures to be followed, the degree of confidentiality), researchers must also secure consent from the parents of the minors. Two different types of parental consent may be used by researchers: active parental consent and passive parental consent. Passive parental consent requires the researcher to inform parents or legal guardians about the research and to provide them with the opportunity to refuse to allow their child's participation in the research. Under this provision, absent a refusal, parental consent is implied and the child is included in the research. Active parental consent is more rigorous and more difficult to attain. Under this standard, the researcher must obtain a signed consent form from the parent or legal guardian providing permission for the child to participate in the study. Absent a signed consent form, it is assumed that the parent has withheld permission and the child is excluded from study participation.

Passive consent procedures were used in 10 of the 11 cross-sectional sites (one school district required active parental consent procedures), but active parental consent was used in the longitudinal study. In no school did more than 2% of parents return refusal forms under the passive consent procedures; in fact, no refusals was the norm at most schools. Under the active consent procedures, many students were excluded from participation, in spite of concerted efforts to obtain the parental permission.

In all the longitudinal sites, the same active consent procedures were followed. Prior to the planned surveys, three direct mailings were made to parents of potential survey participants. Included in the mailings were a cover letter, two copies of the parent consent form for student participation, and a business reply envelope. With substantial Spanish-speaking populations in Phoenix and Las Cruces, mailings to parents in these cities included Spanish versions of the cover letter and the consent form. In addition to the mailings, all parents not responding after the second mailing were contacted by telephone. School personnel also cooperated by distributing consent forms and cover letters at school. Teachers in all classrooms involved in the evaluation assisted with this process, rewarding students with a new pencil upon return of the forms. Some teachers agreed to allow us to offer incentives such as pizza parties for classrooms in which a minimum of 70% of students returned a completed consent form. Other teachers offered incentives of their own, including earlier lunch passes and extra credit points.

These procedures resulted in an overall response rate of 67% (57% providing affirmative consent and 10% withholding consent), with 33% of parents failing to return the consent forms. For a more detailed discussion of the active consent process and examination of the effects of active consent procedures on the representativeness of the sample, consult Esbensen, Miller, Taylor, He, and Freng (1999).

QUESTIONNAIRE COMPLETION RATES

The completion rates for the longitudinal student surveys were excellent. Of the 2,045 students for whom active parental consent was obtained, 1,761 (86%) students completed surveys during the second year of data collection. For the third-and fourth-year surveys, retention rates were 76% and 69%, respectively. Given the multisite, multischool sample, combined with the fact that respondents at five of the six sites made the transition from middle school to high school between the year-2 and year-3 surveys, this completion rate is commendable.

For the third-and fourth-year surveys, considerable difficulty was introduced into the retention of the student sample. As the cohort moved from middle school to high school, combined with normal mobility patterns, students were enrolled in more than 10 different high schools in each of four sites (Omaha, Phoenix, Portland, and Philadelphia), and by the last data collection effort, participating students were enrolled in more than 100 different schools. It was necessary to contact officials at these schools, whether fewer than 10 respondents or more than 100 were enrolled at the school. In some instances, these new schools were in different districts, which required approval from the necessary authorities to survey their students.

MEASUREMENT

Considerable debate surrounds the definition of gang membership (see, e.g., the writings of Curry & Decker, 1998; Decker & Kempf-Leonard, 1991; Klein, 1995; Winfree, Fuller, Backstrom, & Mays, 1992). Some self-report surveys have relied on a single item to determine gang status of respondents (e.g., Bjerregaard & Smith, 1993), whereas others have used multiple items to assess gang status (e.g., Esbensen & Huizinga, 1993; Esbensen & Winfree, 1998; Hill et al., 1999). In previous work with the cross-sectional data from this study, we examined the definitional issue in considerable detail. We investigated the effect of different definitions on the demographic composition of the resultant gangs and the attitudes and illegal involvement of gang members (Esbensen, Winfree, He, & Taylor, 2001). All respondents in that study answered the following two questions: "Have you ever been a gang member?" and "Are you now in a gang?" Those respondents indicating current gang membership were then asked to answer a number of questions about their gang, including organizational characteristics of the gang and the types of illegal activities in which gang members were involved. We then examined the demographic, attitudinal, and behavioral characteristics of "gang members" based on five increasingly more restrictive definitions (the most restrictive definition included only those youth who indicated that they were current and "core" gang members, that their gang was engaged in illegal activities, and that the gang had several types of organizational qualities). Clearly, the more restrictive definitions resulted in the identification of fewer gang members. Further, with each additional criterion, the remaining gang youth were more antisocial in their reported attitudes and behaviors. The largest change, however, remained the difference between those youth who had never been in a gang and those who acknowledged gang affiliation at some time. Based on this previous research, we chose in this chapter to use the single item reflecting current gang membership as our measure of gang status. Due to our interest in establishing the year of gang joining, use of the "ever" measure ("Have you ever been a member of a gang?") would have been inappropriate. This decision was also driven by practical considerations—maintaining as large a sample of gang members as possible in order to have an adequate sample size for any meaningful analyses.

Our dependent measures are drawn from respondents' self-reports of delinquency involvement. "Drug use" consisted of the reported use of three substances: marijuana, inhalants, and other illegal drugs. Although we initially had included alcohol and tobacco, we decided that these behaviors are too prevalent in the adolescent population to be of sufficient utility in this particular area of study. "Drug sales" consisted of two items: selling marijuana and selling other illegal drugs. The violence measure consisted of three items: attacking someone with a weapon, shooting at someone, and robbing someone. Initially we had included a fourth item, "hit someone with the idea of hurting them," but we found the prevalence rate of this behavior was such that it confounded the analyses. General delinquency is so prevalent in the sample that to better assess the relationship between gang affiliation and serious delinquency (those behaviors of most interest to public policy debates), we restricted our summary measures to what can be considered serious forms of drug use, drug sales, and violence. This high prevalence is demonstrated by the fact that by the fourth year of data collection, only 12% of the complete sample had *not* initiated general delinquent behavior (measured by a 17-item general delinquency scale). This is in sharp contrast to the finding that 57% of the nongang youth never initiated the three serious behaviors noted above.

ANALYSIS STRATEGY

Our first objective was to provide a description of the two samples in terms of the extent to which they were nonoffenders, committed only one type of offense, or were involved in multiple types of offending. We classified respondents in the two samples into one of eight types of offenders. Excluding gang member status, respondents could be classified as: (a) nonoffenders, meaning that they reported no instances of drug use, drug sales, or violence; (b) single offenders, having initiated only one of the three activities (3 possibilities); (c) double offenders, engaging in two of the three behaviors (3 possible combinations); or (d) triple offenders, engaging in all three behaviors. Our primary interest in this chapter, however, is to determine which of these behaviors was initiated first. The cross-sectional data are not suitable for answering this question because we cannot establish the temporal ordering with only one data point. This question calls for within-individual change over time, so multiple data points for the same individuals are needed. Thus, to answer this question, longitudinal panel data are required.

Complicating the classification of respondents is what is referred to as a "left-hand censoring" problem—that is, some respondents already will have initiated two or more of the behaviors by the first data collection point and thus we cannot determine which occurred first. Depending on the research design, there may also be a "right-hand censoring" problem—that is, a respondent may initiate behaviors after the completion of the research, thus not allowing for assessment of the sequencing of events.

RESULTS

The cross-sectional study consisted of 5,935 eighth-grade students. Sample demographics are as follows: 48% were male; 30% lived in single-parent households; 42% were white, 26% were African American, and 19% were Hispanic; their average age was 14; and the majority had parents who had some college education. After excluding incomplete surveys (i.e., those with missing data on one or more of the key variables), we were left with 5,485 (92.5%) usable questionnaires for the analyses reported in this chapter.

The longitudinal sample consisted of 2,045 students for whom active consent was obtained. The analyses reported in this chapter rely on questionnaires completed during 4 years of the longitudinal study—1995 through 1998. These years encompass Grades 7 through 10 in five of the sites and Grades 6 through 9 at the sixth site. Based on demographic data provided during the first year of data collection, this sample is quite similar to the cross-sectional sample: 47% male; 52% white, 16% African American, 18% Hispanic; an average age of 12 at the study's outset; and 27% residing in single-parent households.

Table 3.1 Typologies of Delinquent Behavior for Eighth Graders in the Cross-Sectional Data Set

	Total, Percentage (n = 5,485)	Nongang, Percentage (n = 4,935)	Gang, Percentage (n = 393)
Nonoffender	65	68	15
Drug use only	17	17	14
Violence only	4	4	4
Drug sales only	1	1	2
Use & violence	3	3	10
Use & sales	5	4	14
Sales & violence	0.4	0.3	2
Use, sales, & violence	6	3	40

NOTE: Percentages do not add to 100 due to rounding.

With respect to the offender types, the most common typology in the cross-sectional study was the nonoffender; fully 65% of the sample had not initiated any of the three behaviors (see Table 3.1). Another 22% reported participating in only one activity, with drug use being the most common. Only 14% of this large sample had initiated two or more behaviors at the time of data collection during spring semester of eighth grade. This figure is important to highlight; although general delinquency is quite rampant, serious offending (behaviors of specific interest in this study) is relatively infrequent. Examination of gang and nongang youth reveals the extent to which the gang youths are more highly involved in delinquency than are the nongang youths. Whereas slightly more than 10% of the nongang youth report initiation of two or more of these behaviors, this figure is in excess of 65% among the gang youths.

A similar classification of the longitudinal sample reflects stability across samples. In order to approximate the cross-sectional sample, we used data collected during the year in which this longitudinal sample was in eighth grade (the second-year data). As shown in Table 3.2, more than three fourths of the longitudinal sample had not yet initiated the three types of delinquency measured in these analyses and only 9% had initiated two or more activities. Among the gang and nongang youths, the pattern resembled that reported for the cross-sectional respondents.

Table 3.2 Typologies of Delinquent Behavior for Eighth Graders in the Longitudinal Data Set

	Total, Percentage (n = 1,684)	Nongang, Percentage (n = 1,591)	Gang, Percentage (n = 66)
Nonoffender	77	79	15
Drug use only	11	11	14
Violence only	3	3	8
Drug sales only	0.4	0.3	2
Use & violence	2	1	12
Use & sales	3	3	18
Sales & violence	1	1	0
Use, sales, & violence	3	2	32

NOTE: Percentages do not add to 100 due to rounding.

INITIATION PATTERNS

Examination of initiation patterns is limited to the longitudinal sample. Given our research interest, we had to restrict our analyses to those cases for which we had complete data across all four time points (1,091 or 53%). The left-hand censoring problem (i.e., youths who had already initiated two or more behaviors) further reduced our sample for the transition analyses to 883 youths (43% of the active consent sample). Of these youths, the issue then became one of identifying the year in which they initiated one or more of the four behaviors in question. With four variables (drug use, drug sales, violent offending, and gang membership) measured at four points in time, there are a total of 64 possible patterns of initiation (e.g., drug use and gang membership in the same year followed by drug sales the next year and no violence initiation represents one possible pattern of initiation).

To facilitate discussion of the initiation patterns, we first report the overall prevalence of the behaviors for the restricted sample. During the 4-year data collection period, 42% of the youths had initiated drug use, 16% had initiated drug sales, 16% had initiated serious violence, and 7% reported joining a gang. These prevalence rates suggest that it is a small subset of the sample that will have initiated multiple types of offenses.

The next step in the analysis was to identify the initiation patterns. Table 3.3 reveals that for the vast majority of survey participants, no initiation pattern could be determined. For fully 89% of the restricted sample, the youths had either not initiated any of the behaviors, had initiated only one of the behaviors, or had initiated two or more behaviors in the same year with no subsequent initiations. Among the gang youths, 14% reported only joining a gang; 6% initiated only one of the other delinquency types; and 35% co-initiated two or more delinquency types in the first year. We are thus left with a small sample of youths to test our main point of inquiry—the role of gangs in drug use, drug sales, and violence.

Table 3.3 Initiation of Behaviors for the Longitudinal Sample

	Total, Percentage (n = 883)	Nongang, Percentage (n = 832)	Gang, Percentage (n = 57)
No pattern discernible	89	92	55
Nonoffender	54	57	14
One behavior only	27	28	6
Two or more behaviors co-initiated in same year	9	7	35
Pattern discernible	11	8	45

Table 3.4 Bivariate Initiation Sequences Among Gang Members, n 51

	Drug Use, Percentage	Drug Sales, Percentage	Violence, Percentage
Never initiate behavior			
Behavior before gang	18 22	37 10 18	35 16 14
Gang before behavior	14		

We now turn our attention to the transition patterns for the sample of gang youths (see Table 3.4). It is important to note that even with our large sample of youths, we are restricted to examining the actual initiation patterns of only 51 gang youths. For parsimony, we examine three bivariate transitional possibilities—whether gang membership preceded, followed, or occurred simultaneously with drug use, drug sales, and violent offending. When the gang youth initiated the behavior in question, the most common pattern was for the behavior in question to be initiated during the same year the youth reported joining the gang. For example, 47% reported joining a gang the same year they started using drugs. Similarly, 35% initiated violence and drug sales the same year of gang joining. Interestingly, more than one third of the gang youth did not initiate violent offending or drug sales during the 4-year study period. No clear pattern emerged for the remaining youths with regard to the initiation of the behavior, either before or after joining the gang. Clearly, there is no conclusive evidence that joining a gang causes drug use, drug sales, or violence among gang members or that youths who are already involved in these activities join gangs.

CONCLUSION

Our purpose in pursuing this particular line of inquiry was to explore the two questions posed at the outset of this chapter: (a) What are the prevalence rates for drug use, drug sales, and violent offending for gang and nongang youth? Is there offense specialization or, as Klein (1995) argues, cafeteria-style delinquency; and, importantly, (b) What is the temporal sequencing of these behaviors? Is there a selection, a social facilitation, or an enhancement effect?

With respect to the first question, these analyses confirm what others have reported: Gang members are disproportionately involved in drug use, drug sales, and violent offending. Furthermore, it appears that the gang members participate in a more diverse range of illegal activities than do the nongang youth. Whereas more than 90% of non-gang youth in both samples indicated that they were either nonoffenders or involved in only one of the three types of illegal behaviors, more than 60% of gang members in each sample indicated that they engaged in two or more of the activities. We realize that our focus on serious forms of delinquency may well underestimate prevalence rates and subsequently the observed co-occurrence of delinquent activities. Therefore, the fact that the majority of gang youth reported involvement in two or more of these forms of delinquency is quite noteworthy, especially given the relatively young age of the cross-sectional sample and the longitudinal sample used in the typology analyses.

With respect to the second question, these analyses suggest that an enhancement model best fits the data. The most common pattern of initiation into drug use, drug sales, violent offending, and gang membership was for the delinquent activity to be initiated during the same year as joining the gang. These analyses do not allow us to conclude that joining a gang is a precursor to involvement in drug use, drug sales, or violent offending, or that delinquency is a precursor to gang joining. Although participation in these activities is considerably more common among gang members, a sizable minority of the gang members does not report engaging in drug selling or violence, although we acknowledge that we may have a right-hand censoring problem. That is, some of these gang members may simply not have initiated the behaviors prior to the conclusion of the current study period.

Several limitations to the study reported here should be discussed. First, to assess initiation patterns from one behavior to another, it may be desirable to have more frequent data collection points, or to ask respondents specific questions to determine at what point during the year an event occurred. The annual data upon which our analyses relied provide only a crude estimate of initiation; that is, it is difficult to disentangle the actual initiation pattern accurately. With weekly or monthly recording of illegal activity, it would be possible (perhaps) to determine the initiation patterns for those gang members who co-initiate in the same year.

Second, we chose to restrict our measures of offending to what can be considered serious criminal activity. This meant excluding more common types of delinquency (minor assault) and drug use (alcohol and tobacco). Our concern here was not the transition in offending from minor to serious, but rather the extent to which joining a gang is associated with involvement in serious forms of delinquency. One consequence of this decision to restrict the analyses to serious offending is that it made our task more difficult. That is, the prevalence of the selected behaviors is relatively low. Therefore, there are few individuals who have actually engaged in two or more of the offenses, making it difficult to assess initiation patterns.

The fact that there is a low prevalence rate of involvement in these behaviors, although posing a problem for these analyses, is encouraging news. Involvement in delinquent activities may be quite common in a general sample of adolescents, but serious offending is relatively rare. For research purposes, it is worth noting how difficult it is to examine low prevalence behaviors in a general sample. From the active consent sample of 2,045 youths, we were ultimately limited to a sample of 51 gang members to conduct the necessary analyses. It is difficult to examine the effects of gang membership with so few cases.

Where does this leave us? Although these analyses are exploratory in nature, they do provide a descriptive picture of within-individual change in offending across 4 years. Several policy-related suggestions seem relevant. First, even with this young sample, a sizable proportion of youths is already engaged in drug use by eighth grade. Thus, it is clear that drug prevention efforts need to target youth prior to eighth grade. To date, many school-based drug prevention programs have targeted elementary school-aged youth, without much apparent success. Recently, one of the more popular programs (DARE) announced plans to implement the program in middle schools, thereby focusing their efforts on the age at which drug use initiation generally occurs. It will be interesting to see if this strategy will be more successful. There is also evidence in these analyses for general delinquency prevention efforts. Whereas the prevalence rates are low for violent offending and joining a gang, the fact remains that youth aged 13, 14, and 15 are getting involved in serious forms of offending. With respect to the effect of gangs on behavior, the analyses reported in this chapter, although limited by the data, are supportive of the enhancement model. It appears that delinquent youth are attracted to gangs and that gangs facilitate involvement in delinquency. For gang policy, this suggests that it is feasible to promote both prevention strategies and targeted intervention. Programs such as the Comprehensive Community-Wide Approach promoted by the Office of Juvenile Justice and Delinquency Prevention (OJJDP), though difficult to implement and evaluate, find support in the analyses reported here (see Howell, 2000, for an overview of programs and strategies).

Initiation of Drug Use, Drug Sales, and Violent Offending Among a Sample of Gang and Nongang Youth

Nikita Nickols
Amber Elis

Sociology 362:40
Gangs and Adolescents Subcultures
December 4, 2010

Article

► **Purpose**
► The purpose of this article is to figure out the sequence of events that leads to youth gang members joining a gang, and eventually being involved in drug dealing. The author looked to answer the following questions in the article.

1. Do youths join gangs and then began their involvement in drug use, drug sales, and violent offending?
2. Do youths already engage in these activities prior to joining the gang?
3. Is there any relationship between gang affiliation and involvement in illegal activity?
4. Is it possible for youth to just be involved in one delinquent or illegal activity?

Article

▶ The author also wrote three main reasons why the answers to these questions are important:

1. To provide a description of adolescent offending
2. To advance ideas for theory development and testing
3. To inform gang prevention and intervention policy makers

Article

▶ <u>**Summary**</u>

▶ The author questioned if the relationship of gang affiliation vs. the actually involvement of violent offending.

▶ This article is a 4 year cross sectional, and longitudinal study from a program called Gang Resistance Education and Training (GREAT.) The study was the same. They wanted to see if gang involvement had a outcome of eventually violent offending, and drug use, and dealing.

▶ The article used eight other research articles that had similar formats. They all found that in some way the majority of the youth that joined gangs were already delinquent in some way and the involvement of drug use and sales increased after they became gang members.

▶ One issue that was not brought up was in which order does drug use, drug sales, and violent offending occur.

▶ The data was collected through self reporting surveys.

Statistics

► <u>Gender</u>
► 5,935 eighth grade students.
► 48% were male 52% were female.
► The average age was 14 years old.
► <u>Race</u>
► 42% white
► 26% African American
► 19% Hispanics
► 27% resided in single parent households
► **<u>Location (State or town)</u>**
► **Some of the cross sectional cities were Kansas City, Missouri; Orlando, Florida; Las Cruces, New Mexico; Phoenix, Arizona; Torrance, California; and Will County, Illinois**

Results

	Total Percentage (n=4,935)	Nongang, Percentage (n=4,935)	Gang, Percentage (n=393)
Nonoffender	65	68	15
Drug use only	17	17	14
Violence only	4	4	4
Drug sales only	1	1	2
Use & violence	3	3	10
Use & sales	5	4	14
Sales & violence	0.4	0.3	2
Use, sales, & violence	6	3	40

Results

- ► Cross Sectional Data
- ► 65% of the sample had not initiated in any pf the three behaviors.
- ► 22% participated in only one activity with drug use being the most common.
- ► 14% Initiated two or more behaviors.
- ► Most gang members are already showing some kinds of delinquency prior to joining a gang, for those that end up leaving the their delinquent behaviors declines afterwards. It will still be higher then those that never joined a gang at all.
- ► It was hard to figure out the sequence of events that lead to violent offending.

Additional Sources

- ► <u>Article: Youth Gangs in Schools</u>
- ► This article examined 3 main topics
  1. Charactertics of gangs in school.
  2. Reasons for greater gang prevalence in some schools.
  3. Impact of gangs on victiminization at school.
- ► Students reported that marijuana, cocaine, crack, uppers, and downers were readily available at their school.
- ► Twenty-eight percent of students reported that gang members attended their school.

Discussion Continued:

- Is it possible for youth to just sell drugs?
- Jay-Cent, and Jay Z, 50 Notorious B.I.G were all involved in drugs sales.
- However they had no involvement in drug use, gang membership, or violent offending behavior.
- These group of young men represent nongang youth who are involved in drug trafficking.
- Youth gangs tend to be loosely organized with ephemeral leadership and lack financial resources and cohesiveness; all traits deemed necessary for organized drug distrubution (e.g.,Klein, 1995; Moore, 1990; Spergel, 1995).

References

- Benson, Finn-Aage., Freng, Adrienne., Peterson, Dana., and Taylor, Terrance. J. 2000. "Initiation of Drug Use, Drug Sales, and Violent Offending Among a Sample of Gang and Nongang Youth." *Department of Justice.* 94:1. 37–52
- Howell, James, C., and Lynch, James, P. 2000. "Youth Gangs in Schools." *U.S. Department of Justice.* 445:153. 1–9
- "The Youth Gangs, Drugs, and Violence Connection." Juvenile Justice Bulletin. 1999. Retrieved December1, 2010. (*http://www.ncjrs.gov/pdffiles/93920.pdf*)

GANG JOINING AND RISK FACTORS

PRECURSORS AND CONSEQUENCES OF MEMBERSHIP IN YOUTH GANGS

By Richard L. Dukes,
Rubén O. Martinez,
and Judith A. Stein

Explanations of gang membership were studied in a population of 11,000 secondary school students. Lower self-esteem, perceived academic ability, psychosocial health, and bonds with institutions appeared to precede gang membership (selection model). Greater drug use, greater delinquency, greater fear of harm, and being armed were precursors and consequences of gang membership (facilitation and selection models). "Wannabes" were partway between nonmembers and members. Findings were consistent with gang membership as a result of lack of social integration.

In the wake of drive-by shootings by heavily armed teenagers, reports of young people from the inner city moving to the heartland to sell drugs and guns, and media saturation in music, movies, and news, gang violence has received renewed attention in academia (Cummings & Monti, 1993; Hagedorn, 1991; Huff, 1989, 1993; Monti, 1993; Sanders, 1994). In fact, after little consideration for almost 20 years, gangs have been resuscitated as an explanation for crime by young people (Campbell, 1991). In addition to reasons mentioned above, the resurgence of interest

Richard L. Dukes, Ruben O. Martinez, Judith A. Stein, "Precursors and Consequences of Membership in Youth Gangs," *Youth and Society*, vol. 29, no. 2, pp. 139-165. Copyright © 1997 by SAGE Publications. Reprinted with permission.

also may be due to a societal emphasis on law and order, the War on Drugs, and an aging population (Curry & Spergel, 1988; King, 1993; Moore, 1993; Spergel, 1992). A recent Gallup poll showed that adults viewed fighting, violence, and gangs as the biggest problem confronting public schools (Associated Press, 1994). Laws at every level have been passed in an effort to stem criminal behavior associated with youth gangs (Jackson & Rudman, 1993). Suppression, intervention, and prevention have become watchwords, and many communities have organized themselves to address the "gang problem" (Spergel et al., 1994).

Social scientific knowledge about youth gangs and how their members differ from nongang youths is limited and controversial. More specifically, little is known about how gang members differ from young members of the general population. This research examines the relationship between gang membership and delinquency using self-report data from a survey of youths.

Current lack of knowledge about youth gangs is due in part to a shift in research emphasis during the 1970s from etiology to control (Klein & Maxson, 1989; Short, 1990). Recently, a renewed interest in understanding basic gang processes has resulted in an emerging body of qualitative and quantitative research. Case studies have been particularly fruitful (See Campbell, 1991; Hagedorn, 1988; MacLeod, 1987; Moore, 1991; Sanchez Jankowski, 1991; Sanders, 1994; Vigil, 1988). Survey approaches to the study of gangs—especially longitudinal studies—also have been useful (Bowker & Klein, 1983; Esbensen & Huizinga, 1993; Fagan, 1989; Thornberry, Krohn, Lizotte, & Chard-Wierschem, 1993).

The link between gang membership and delinquency is virtually indisputable (Curry & Spergel, 1992; Esbensen & Huizinga, 1993; Fagan, 1989). Strong links also have been made between gang membership and lower socioeconomic status (Hirschi, 1969; Lasley, 1992; Miller, 1974), adolescence (Lasley, 1992; Thornberry et al., 1993), being male (Esbensen & Huizinga, 1993; Harris, 1988), ethnic minority status and identity (Gray-Ray & Ray, 1990; Hagedorn, 1988; Vigil, 1988), and lack of influence by parents (Fagan, 1989; Fagan, Piper, & Moore, 1986). General agreement on these issues led Moore (1993) to warn researchers of a tendency to stereotype every young minority male as a violent, drug-using gang member. Despite the increased focus on gangs, gaps in knowledge still exist about the etiology of gangs and the temporal relationship between gang membership and criminal behavior.

DELINQUENCY AND SOCIAL CONTROL

There are several theories of delinquency and gang activity (e.g., cultural deviance, social strain, differential association, and learning theory). One of the most influential and empirically supported theories on crime and delinquency is the psychosocial control theory by Hirschi (1969). Like other control theorists, Hirschi emphasized internal control as the mechanism for explaining conformity and delinquency. His work is derived from Durkheim's concept of *integration.* Through socialization, individuals develop a strong conscience and a strong personal sense of morality that prevents delinquent behavior. An individual who is detached from societal institutions is more likely to become delinquent than one who is integrated. After becoming delinquent, the individual may turn to other delinquents for support and confirmation. Association with these others (and subsequent societal sanctions against deviant behavior) lead to further decrease in integration.

Hirschi (1969) identified poor family relations and failure in school as indicators of a lack of bonding and increased potential for delinquency. According to Hirschi, the *social bond* is made up of four elements: attachment, commitment, involvement, and belief. Children who are attached to their parents, committed to long-term goals (e.g., careers), involved in conventional activities (e.g., chores, homework, sports), and believe in the morality of the law are not likely to become delinquent.

More recently, Gottfredson and Hirschi (1990) presented a new version of psychosocial control theory. They identified six features of adolescents who have high self-control: (a) ability to defer gratification; (b) persistence in a course of action; (c) tendency to be cautious, cognitive, and verbal; (d) a tendency to engage in long-term pursuits; (e) valuation of cognitive and academic skills; and (f) altruism and sensitivity to the feelings of others. Accordingly, self-control is inversely related to delinquency.

Recently, Esbensen, Huizinga, and Weiher (1993) questioned the utility of Hirschi's (1969) ideas. Using data collected from youths living in high-risk neighborhoods, these researchers found that involvement in conventional activities did not insulate adolescents from delinquency, nor did these nondelinquent activities distinguish gang members from the other delinquent youths. Also, in contrast to Hirschi's view, Esbensen et al. found that youths who expressed toleration of criminal activity by their peers were more likely to become gang members and to engage in criminal activity themselves than were youths who were less tolerant of transgressions by their peers (p. 109). In other words, youths who are bonded to peers (albeit delinquent ones) are likely to engage in delinquent behavior. Is social control theory wrong, as suggested by Esbensen et al., or does social bonding make a difference in the delinquency or nondelinquency of adolescents?

GANGS AND DELINQUENCY

Although virtually all studies of gangs show a relation between membership and delinquency, Thornberry et al. (1993) noted a dearth of empirically based explanations for it.

They reviewed the following three types of models that can account for the relationship: (a) a selection model, whereby already delinquent youths are recruited by gangs; (b) a social facilitation model, whereby gangs involve "normal" persons in delinquency; and (c) an enhancement model, which combines the previous two models. The selection model implies that gangs only concentrate delinquent youths. They do not necessarily influence the members. The social facilitation model identifies threats to group status, cohesion, and solidarity as sources of aggressive, violent responses by gang members. The enhancement model posits the selective recruitment of high-risk adolescents (those disposed toward delinquency if not already delinquent) as well as facilitation of delinquency by the gang.

Using data from a multiwave panel study, Thornberry et al. (1993) provided empirical support for the enhancement model, which combines selection and facilitation. The adolescents they studied were no more delinquent than nongang youths before joining a gang; however, gang members engaged in more delinquent behavior, and adolescents who left the gang became less delinquent after doing so. Curry and Spergel (1992) found that gang involvement predicted delinquency but that delinquency did not effectively predict gang involvement. Similarly, Esbensen et al. (1993) found that gang members reported higher rates of criminal activity than did nongang street offenders and nongang youths. These findings support the facilitation model over that of selection, although it is likely that gangs recruit from pools of youths who want to be gang members ("wannabes").

In addition to the types of members studied by Thornberry et al. (1993) and other researchers, in this article, we examined wannabe gang members on measures of self-esteem and psychosocial health, bonding, delinquency, and drug use. By including wannabes, we can test the competing models outlined above. According to the facilitation model, we would expect wannabes to be less delinquent than gang members and indistinguishable from nonmembers. If the selection explanation is more tenable, wannabes should be more delinquent than nonmembers and indistinguishable from gang members. This test was embedded in a broader model-building process to create a theoretical context for the explanation involving other key constructs from theories of social integration.

METHODS

Data were gathered from the population of secondary school students in six districts in the Pikes Peak region of Colorado. An anonymous questionnaire was distributed to students during regular class time in November 1992 as part of a continuing community-wide effort to examine problems confronting youths. The triennial survey has been conducted since 1983 as a joint venture between local school districts and the Center for Social Science Research at Colorado University, Colorado Springs.

The instrument appeared in two forms that were randomly assigned to respondents. Both forms contained a core of 66 items that measured background variables; gang membership; use of alcohol, tobacco, and other drugs; and delinquency. Form A contained 21 additional items on self-concept of academic ability, education, religion, and work. Form B contained 36 additional items on family, psychosocial health, fear of being harmed, attitudes toward police, and resistance to peer pressure.

Variables

The instrument contained a set of items that measured characteristics of the social background of the respondent. These characteristics were likely to have preceded membership in a gang. The instrument also contained an item that measured the degree of affiliation with a youth gang. It asked, "Would you consider yourself to be a member of a gang?" Responses were received from 11,023 students. Five ordinal response categories stated, "No, never, and I would not like to be a member of a gang" (9,477 responses; 86.0%), labeled *confirmed nonmembers;* "No, but I would like to become a member" (434 responses; 3.9%), labeled *wannabes;* "No, not currently, but I was a member of a gang in the past" (513 responses; 4.7%), labeled *former gang members;* "Yes, I'm a member of a local or neighborhood gang" (251 responses; 2.3%), labeled *local gang members;* "Yes, I'm a member of a local set of a national gang" (348 responses; 3.1%), labeled *national gang members.* Spergel et al. (1994) refer to wannabes as recruits. They also note that there are large alliances of gangs known as "nations" and that such gang conglomerates have thousands of members, In this study, current members of gangs made up 5.4% of the population of students. Among gang members, 58.1% reported being in a local set of a national gang.

Other variables were predicted to be related to the degree of gang affiliation. Some of them were likely to be precursors of gang membership, but others were likely to be consequences of it. Overall, they included measures of self-esteem, self-derogation, self-concept of academic ability, and purpose in life. Other variables measured resistance to peer pressure, bonding to family, education, police, and ethnic pride. A final set of variables included measures of drug use, delinquency, fear of being hurt, and carrying a weapon for self-defense.

Self-Esteem and Psychological Health

Items on the Self-Esteem Scale (Rosenberg, 1965, 1979) were factor analyzed using maximum likelihood solution and oblique rotation. Two factors were extracted similar to those reported by Kaplan and Pokorny (1969). Items 1, 3, 4, 7, and 10 loaded onto a factor labeled Self-Esteem. Items 2, 6, and 9 loaded onto a factor labeled Self-Derogation. Items 5 and 8 did not load onto either factor at least .5, so they were dropped. Most items here and below had loadings of at least .7, and all but one of the factor analyses below were confirmatory, because the composition of each scale was predicted beforehand.

Factor analysis showed that the six items on the questionnaire that measured self-concept of academic ability (Items 1 to 6 from Brookover, Beady, Flood, Schweitzer, & Wisenbaker, 1979; see the appendix) loaded onto a single factor. A typical item stated, "Think of other students in your class. Do you think you can do school work better than, the same as, or poorer than the other students in your class?" Responses were recorded on a 5-point scale.

The five items on the questionnaire from the Purpose in Life Scale (Items 9,13,16,18, and 19 from Crumbaugh, 1968, based on Frankl's [1969] concepts; see the appendix), a measure of psychosocial health, also loaded together. A typical item stated, "My life is. ..." The 6-point response scale was anchored by *empty, filled only with despair* and *running over with exciting, good things*.

Five Likert-type items on the questionnaire were from the Ethnic Identity Scale (Phinney, 1992, 1993). Four items loaded on a factor named Ethnic Pride (Items 6, 11, 14, and 20; see the appendix). A typical item stated, "I have a lot of pride in my ethnic group and its accomplishments."

Bonding

Three Likert-type items on the questionnaire measured resistance to peer pressure. The items loaded together on a single factor. A typical item stated, "I usually give in to my friends when they pressure me."

Family bonds were measured by three Likert-type items that also loaded highly together. A typical item stated, "My parents never really understand me." Because this item measured a lack of bonding, responses were reflected (i.e., reverse-coded).

Police bonds were measured by three Likert-type items that also loaded on a single factor. One item stated, "Police officers would rather try to catch you doing something wrong than try to help you." When agreement with an item represented a lack of bonding, responses were reflected.

Educational bonds were measured by items that measured the importance of good grades, the importance of a successful career as an adult, and the amount of education the respondent would like to complete. The three items loaded onto a single factor. Religious bonds were measured by a single item that asked about the importance to the respondent of religion and religious beliefs. A scale of work asked how many hours per week the respondent worked in a paid job and how much money she or he earned. The two items were highly correlated ($r = .75$; $p < .001$).

Use of Alcohol, Tobacco, and Other Drugs

A scale of use of drugs legal for adults measured the frequency of use of substances that were illegal for adolescents to use but that were legal for adults. The scale contained measures of use of beer, wine, liquor, and cigarettes. Responses were recorded on 7-point scales that ranged from *never tried* to *over 15 times* in the last month. Factor analysis showed that items measuring the use of these substances loaded onto a single factor.

Based on factor analysis, a scale of use of illegal drugs was constructed. Included in this scale were measures of frequency of use of amphetamines, LSD, cocaine powder, crack cocaine, steroids, inhalants, and other illegal drugs. Marijuana use loaded approximately .5 on both drug use scales, so it was kept as a separate, single indicator.

Delinquency, Fear, and Carrying a Weapon

A scale of delinquency contained 12 items that factored together. The scale contained items that measured frequency during the previous 12 months of fighting, group fighting, injuring others, being injured, stealing, trespassing, selling illegal drugs, getting into trouble with school authorities, getting into trouble with police, receiving traffic tickets, drinking before getting into trouble, and getting into trouble as a result of gang activity.

A scale of fear of being hurt was made up of four items having a common stem that asked, "How often do you feel that someone might try to harm or injure you?" Specific items said, "at school," "going to and from school," "while out with friends," and "at other times." Responses were recorded on 5-point response categories that ranged from *never, rarely, some days, most days,* and *every day.* The items loaded onto a single factor.

A single item asked, "During the last month, how often have you carried a gun or a knife for self-defense?" Answers were recorded into response categories as above.

Analyses

Two methodological approaches were used to analyze the data and test the competing models: (a) log-linear models, ANCOVAs, and ANOVAs; and (b) latent variable structural equation models. In the log-linear models and the ANOVAs, the scale items were weighted by their factor loadings and then were added together to form composites. In the structural equation models, for which we used EQS (Bentler, 1995), the untransformed items were hypothesized as indicators of their underlying latent variables. Comparing the two types of statistical analysis, the composites contained more measurement error than the latent variables, which are relatively error free, but as reported below, results of the two approaches were similar.

RESULTS

Affiliation with Gangs

Background variables were examined in a hierarchical log-linear model for their ability to predict gang membership. Best predictions were found for the following dichotomous variables: (a) ethnic background (Native American, Black, Latino vs. Asian, White, mixed), (b) gender (male and female), (c) living arrangements (not living with either parent vs. living with at least one parent), and (d) an indicator of socioeconomic status represented by father's educational deficit (father less than high school graduate vs. father at least a high school graduate). The dichotomies were created as a result of bivariate tables (not shown) that revealed large gaps in percentages of gang members across the categories of the independent variables.

Results of the multiway frequency analysis were consistent with previous research. The aggregate interactions were not statistically significant, so they were not examined further; however, the aggregate main effects were statistically significant, so the analysis proceeded with examination of the separate effects of independent variables. Findings showed that each of them was significant beyond the .0001 level (see Table 1), and the percentage differences were marked.

Gang membership was associated with being Native American, Black, or Latino. Among these ethnic groups, 13% (230 out of 1,704) of the respondents reported being in a gang. Among Asians, Whites, and students from the mixed racial group, only 4% (369 out of 9,319) reported being gang members.

Gang membership was associated with being male. Among males, 8% (405 out of 5,242) reported being gang members. Among females, 3% (194 out of 5,781) reported being gang members.

Gang membership was associated with living away from both parents. Among respondents living away, 16% (104 out of 632) reported being gang members. Among respondents living with parents 5% (495 out of 10,391) reported being gang members.

Gang membership was associated with low levels of socioeconomic status as measured by father's education. Among respondents whose fathers had not graduated from high school, 14% (113 out of 821) reported being gang members. Among respondents whose fathers had graduated from high school, 5% (486 out of 10,202) reported being gang members.

Although statistically significant interactions were not observed, the effects of membership in multiple categories of risk were striking. For instance, among the 27 respondents who were Native American, Black, or Latino, male, living away from both parents, and whose fathers did not graduate from high school, 12 (44%) reported being gang members. Among the 4,448 respondents who were Asian, White, or of mixed racial background, female, living with at least one parent, and whose fathers had graduated from high school, only 43 (1%) reported being gang members.

CROSS-GROUP COMPARISONS AND EXPLANATION OF GANG MEMBERSHIP

Mean scores for scales of esteem, bonds, and deviance were computed across categories of degree of gang membership (see Table 2). Each scale was standardized, so the grand mean was zero, and standard deviation was one. The deviations from the grand mean were adjusted for covariates of racial group, gender, living arrangement, and father's education. Using F ratios, the differences among means for all scales were statistically significant. Betas are presented in the last column of Table 2 to give an approximate idea of the degree of statistical association. These betas showed the effects of degree of affiliation with a gang on the other measures after the effects of the other variables (covariates in the ANCOVA) were removed. One can see that the associations for measures of esteem and bonding were lower than the associations for measures of deviance.

Table 1 Log-Linear Model of Gang Membership

Effect	df	Partial X2	Probability
Native American, Black, or Latino	4	208.30 130.18 85.18	.0001 .0001 .0001
(0,1) Male (0,1)	4	77.62	.0001
Live away from both parents (0,1)	4		
Educational deficit of father (0,1)	4		

Unfortunately, the F ratios could not show which of the group means were different from each other, and the pattern of differences was substantively important. Using the Scheffé test, differences of .20 were statistically significant at the .001 level for the core items on the questionnaire that were administered to the population, and deviations of .40 were statistically significant at the .001 level for the optional items from Form A or Form B that were administered to half the population.

In Table 2, scale means were computed for each category of gang membership. The Scheffé test was necessary because a significant difference between adjacent categories represented support for one of the explanations of gang membership presented by Thornberry et al. (1993). For example, if the selection model was a credible explanation, the differences among the groups should have been a result of persistent individual characteristics and not membership in a gang per se. Therefore, the difference between nonmembers and wannabes would have been large and statistically significant (see

Gap 1 in Table 2), and the differences among wannabes, former members, and the two groups of gang members would have been small and not statistically significant.

TABLE 2 Standardized Mean Differences on Precursors and Consequences of Degree of Affiliation with Gang, Controlling for Racial Group, Gender, Living Arrangement, and Father's Education

	Confirmed Nonmember	Gap 1: Selection	Wannabe	Former Member	Gap 2: Facilitation	Local Member	National Member	βa
Esteem								
Self-esteem	.04	>	-.34	-.18		-.28	-.24	.11
Self-derogation	-.03	<	.20	.22		.15	.03	.07
Self-concept of academic ability	.06	>	-.42	-.25		—54	-.26	.15b
Purpose in life	.07	>	-.54	-.32		-.59	-.50	.18b
Ethnic pride	.02	>	-.26	.03		-.07	-.22	.07
Resistance to peer pressure	.05		-.33	-.26	>	-.50	-.48	.15 b
Bonds								
Family	.07	>	-.53	-.41		-.65	-.50	.19b
Police	.07		-.22	-.50	>	-.74	-.82	.22b
Education	.09	>	-.63	-.32		-.55	-.82	.25b
Religion	.04		-.21	-.14		-.31	-.28	.09b
Work c	-.05		-.07	.31	>	.40	.55	.14 b
Deviance								
Use legal drugs	-.12	<	.37	.74	<	.82	1.24	.33
Use marijuana	-.10	<	.20	.42	<	.69	1.37	.31
Use illegal drugs	-.11	<	.22	.31	<	.68	1.67	.34
Delinquency	-.20	<	.50	1.02	<	1.43	2.16	.53
Fear being hurt	-.08	<	.30	.39	<	.67	1.25	.26b
Carry a weapon	-.13	<	.28	.80	<	1.13	1.66	.39b

a.   All F ratios were significant beyond the .001 level.

b.   Measure appeared on Form A or Form B of the instrument. Statistics computed on half the cases. Mean differences of .40 were required for statistical significance at .001 level. Other measures required a mean difference of .20.

c.   Age also was controlled.

Conversely, if the social facilitation model was a credible explanation, the differences among the groups should have been most pronounced across membership categories. That is, the differences among nonmembers, wannabes, and former members should have been small and not statistically significant because none of these respondents belonged to a gang at the time of the survey. Likewise, differences among local and national members should have been small and nonsignificant because both sets of respondents were members of gangs at the time of the survey; however, the difference between nonmembers and members should have been large and statistically significant. In particular, the difference between wannabes and local gang members should have been large and statistically significant (see Gap 2 in Table 2). If differences fit both patterns, then the enhancement (or mixed) model was a more credible explanation than either of the other two.

SELF-ESTEEM AND RELATED MEASURES

The analysis of self-esteem supported the selection model. The highest mean on self-esteem was for confirmed nonmembers (.04). Using the Scheffé test, the differences between confirmed nonmembers and wannabes (-.34) was greater than .20, so the difference was statistically significant. In Table 2, this difference is shown by the greater-than symbol in the column labeled *Gap 1*. Also, the means for the other groups were not different from each other at the .001 level. These two findings supported the selection model.

The analysis of derogation partially fit the selection model. Mean derogation was lowest for confirmed nonmembers (-.03), and means for wannabes and former members were higher to a statistically significant degree (shown by the less-than symbol in Gap 1 of Table 2). This finding supported the selection model. Also, it was supported by the finding that the means for wannabes, former gang members, local gang members, and national gang members were not different from each other to a statistically significant degree. One finding did not support the selection model. The mean for confirmed nonmembers was not lower to a statistically significant degree than the means for local gang members and national gang members.

Findings for self-concept of academic ability partially supported the selection model. Scores for confirmed nonmembers were the highest (.06). Scores for wannabes (-.42) and local gang members (-.54) were lower than the mean score for confirmed nonmembers to a statistically significant degree (shown by the greater-than symbol in Gap 1 of Table 2). Because the Scheffé test was computed on half the sample, a difference of .40 was needed for statistical significance at the .001 level. Further support of selection came from the finding that the means for wannabes, former gang members, local gang members, and national gang members were not different from each other to a statistically significant degree. One finding did not support selection. The means for former gang members and national gang members were not lower to a statistically significant degree than the mean for confirmed nonmembers.

Findings for purpose in life, a measure of psychosocial health, strongly supported selection. Means for wannabe gang members (-.54), local members (-.59), and national gang members (-.50) were lower than the mean for confirmed nonmembers (.07) on the Purpose in Life Scale (shown by the greater-than symbol in Gap 1 of Table 2). The mean difference between confirmed nonmembers (.07) and former gang members (-.32) just missed statistical significance using the criterion of a .40 difference at the .001 level.

The analysis of ethnic pride showed that confirmed nonmembers and former gang members had the highest levels of ethnic pride. Wannabes and national gang members had the lowest ethnic pride. The differences in means between confirmed nonmembers and wannabes supported the selection model (shown by the greater-than symbol in Gap 1 of Table 2).

The analysis of resistance to peer pressure supported both selection and facilitation, so the enhancement or mixed model was the most credible explanation. The mean for confirmed nonmembers was the highest of any group (.05), and it was higher than the means for local gang members (-.50) and national gang members (-.48) to a statistically significant degree. Differences among the three groups of nonmembers and among the two groups of members were not statistically significant. Findings supported the facilitation model, as shown by the greater-than symbol in Gap 2 of Table 2.

BONDING

Cross-group differences in bonding also appear in Table 2. Because data on bonding were available for only half of the cases, differences of at least .40 were necessary for statistical significance at the .001 level.

The analysis of family bonds showed strong support for selection. The mean for confirmed nonmembers (.07) was the highest of any group. The differences between this mean and those for all of the other groups were statistically significant. Furthermore, no other group mean was significantly different from any of the remaining means.

The pattern of means for police bonds followed the one for resistance to peer pressure (above). Analysis of means for educational bonds supported the selection model. Analysis of the item on religious bonds showed no statistically significant differences between any pair of means, so none of the explanations were supported.

An interesting pattern emerged for work. As the degree of involvement with gangs became greater, the involvement with work also became greater. The means presented in Table 2 included an additional adjustment for grade in school, because a greater number of older students worked. Means for confirmed nonmembers (-.05) and wannabes (-.07) showed they worked the least, and these means were not different from each other to a statistically significant degree. Local gang members (.40) and national gang members (.55) worked the most, and these means were not different from each other to a statistically significant degree. Differences between confirmed nonmembers and wannabes on one hand and local gang members and national gang members on the other hand were statistically significant. The mean for former gang members was in the middle, and it was not different from any other mean to a statistically different degree. Findings supported a facilitation model in which increased affiliation with a gang appeared to create a greater involvement in work.

Typically, the most recent job reported by respondents was lawn work, restaurant work, retail sales, office work, or child care (not shown in the table). Although 62% of confirmed nonmembers reported working in one of these standard job categories, only 45% of the national gang members did so. Could gang members have been engaged in illegal activities that they reported as work? If so, the percentages of students who reported working in "other" job categories should have been the reverse of the percentages above. In fact, 14% (660 out of 4,549) of confirmed nonmembers reported working in an other job category, and 36% of national gang members reported working in an other job category.

DEVIANCE

On all six measures related to deviance, the means increased with the degree of gang affiliation. On the measures of use of legal drugs, use of marijuana, use of illegal drugs, delinquency, and frequency of carrying a weapon, statistically significant differences appeared between confirmed nonmembers and wannabes. These differences supported a selection explanation. On use of marijuana, use of illegal drugs, and delinquency, a statistically significant difference was observed between former gang members and local members. These differences supported a facilitation explanation. Together, these two sets of findings supported the enhancement or mixed model.

The scale for fear of being hurt was based on half the cases, so a difference between means of .40 was required for statistical significance. The mean for confirmed nonmembers (-.08) was lower than the means for local gang members (.67) and national gang members (1.25) to a statistically significant degree. Furthermore, differences between pairs of means for confirmed nonmembers, wannabes (.30), and former members (.39) were not statistically significant. Finally, the difference between the means for local gang members and national members was statistically significant. Findings supported a facilitation explanation. On the measure of frequency of carrying a weapon, statistically significant differences were observed for each group versus each other group.

In addition to consideration of each scale separately, it is instructive to examine the columns of the table, too. Overall, confirmed nonmembers clearly had the best scores of any group, and wannabe gang members had the worst scores of any group. This contrast supported the selection model. The findings for measures of esteem from

Table 2 generally supported the selection model. The findings for bonds and deviance supported both selection and facilitation, so the enhancement or mixed model was the most credible explanation.

STRUCTURAL EQUATION MODEL

As an extension of path analysis, factor-analytical structural equation models allow testing of relations among time-ordered components of a causal model. Additionally, structural equation models offer advantages over traditional path analysis by eliminating some measurement error and by offering a single summary measure of the fit of the model to the data.

A presumed causal ordering of components of a model of gang membership emerged from the previous analyses. The order of the components was as follows: (a) background variables; (b) attitudinal measures such as self-esteem, bonding, and related variables; (c) degree of gang membership; and (d) behavioral measures such as delinquency and drug use. Logic showed background variables came first in time. The analyses in Table 2 showed the selection model to be strongest for self-esteem, bonding, and related variables. Finally, the facilitation model was clearly the best explanation of delinquency and drug use in research by Thornberry et al. (1993), and evidence for facilitation also was found in the analysis above. This convergence supported treating delinquency and drug use as results of the degree of gang membership.

A second-order factor analysis was conducted on the factors within each group of components described above in an attempt to simplify the relations among them. Unfortunately, measures of self-concept of academic ability, and bonding with education, religion, and work appeared only on Form A of the questionnaire, whereas purpose in life and bonding with family and police appeared on Form B. Thus, separate second-order factor analyses and structural equations modeling were conducted on measures from Form A or from Form B. Results for Form A were slightly more interesting, so they are presented below.

The three primary factors and the single variable associated with deviant behavior loaded together. Use of drugs legal for adults, use of illegal drugs, use of marijuana (the single item), and delinquency were used as indicators of a latent variable, labeled *deviant behavior*.

As suggested by theoretical reasoning and by the empirical results reported above on various deviance measures, the degree of involvement in a youth gang was treated as an interval variable (Bollen & Barb, 1981). Furthermore, theory and preliminary results reported in Table 2 showed that bonding was inversely related to the degree of involvement in a youth gang, which, in turn, was related inversely to deviance. Second-order factor analysis of Self-Esteem, Self-Concept of Academic Ability, and Ethnic Pride showed that these factors could not be combined into a single latent variable. Likewise, a second-order latent variable for bonding was not found, so the best-fitting selection of these components (and all four background variables) were incorporated into the structural equations model presented in Figure 1.

Three latent variables (including the second-order variable of deviant behavior) and the variable of degree of gang membership were the main components of the model. Beginning in the nucleus of the model, the degree of involvement in a youth gang, as predicted, increased deviant behavior (regression coefficient = .49, $p < .001$). Second, emphasis on education was inversely related to degree of involvement in a gang (-.21, $p < .001$). Third, emphasis on education was inversely related to deviant behavior (-.26, $p < .001$). Fourth, self-concept of academic ability predicted emphasis on education (.73, $p < .001$).

Background variables used in the earlier analysis to predict the degree of involvement in a gang were used to predict the major variables in the model. Being female led to less involvement in a gang (-.08, $p < .001$), less delinquent behavior (one of the primary factors predicted by deviant behavior) (-. 14, $p < .001$), an increased emphasis on education (.12, $p < .001$), and a belief that one can complete a graduate education (a measured variable that was an indicator of self-concept of academic ability) (.10, $p < .001$).

Living with at least one parent led to less involvement in a youth gang (-.10, $p < .001$). Racial minority group membership increased the degree of involvement in a

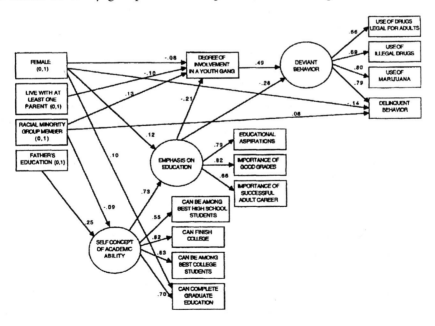

Figure 1: Structural Equation Model of Gang Membership and Deviance

youth gang (. 13, $p < .001$) and increased delinquent behavior (.08, $p < .001$). Also, racial minority status predicted a lower self-concept of academic ability (see Dukes & Martinez, 1994; Martinez & Dukes, 1987, 1991; Turner & Turner, 1982). Finally, father's education increased the self-concept of academic ability (.25, $p < .001$). Overall, demographic variables had small, statistically significant effects in predicted directions on the main variables of the model.

The comparative fit index (CFI; Bentler, 1995) of .98 showed a near maximum degree of fit between the hypothesized model and the data. Ideally, the saturated matrix of all variables and all possible relations would not be significantly different from the restricted matrix that is represented by the paths in the model. Although the model of gang membership and deviance fit the data exceptionally well, the very large number of cases in the data set resulted in statistical significance at the .001 level for the χ^2 of 577.62 with 61 degrees of freedom.

DISCUSSION

Results indicated that nearly 1 of every 20 youths in public secondary schools in the Pikes Peak region was an active gang member at the time of the survey. Together with wannabes and former members, almost 3 of every 20 youths in the region were impacted by membership in a gang. Self-reported data showed that youths from many different backgrounds were affiliated with gangs. Ethnic minority young men from poor backgrounds who were living away from their parents clearly were more at risk than other youths.

Young women were less involved in gangs than young men, but the effect was smaller than might be expected from previous research. Campbell (1991) argued that the mechanism of gang membership is similar for males and females (also see Esbensen & Huizinga, 1993; Esbensen et al., 1993). Being female did not influence the latent variable of deviant behavior to a statistically significant degree. Rather, female gender had a specific negative effect only on delinquency, a well-established finding (Esbensen & Huizinga, 1993); the deviant behavior latent variable had various forms of substance use as major components, and presumably, the gender groups did not differ in their drug usage.

Additional analyses (not presented) revealed that a major difficulty in predicting which respondents were gang members was the fact that many students had characteristics of gang members but they were not members. From the nucleus of the model emerged a picture of the process by which some at-risk students become mainstreamers and more pro-social. They feel good about their abilities as students, and they translate this self-confidence into educational bonds and an orientation toward education as a ladder to a successful career as an adult. These students generally are not interested in becoming gang members, and their behaviors are less deviant. Thus, findings support the results of Reyes and Jason (1993) who found that low-risk minority youths were more satisfied with school and had a social group free of gang members.

Overall, the findings complemented and extended those of Thornberry et al. (1993). Because the earlier study did not examine self-esteem or bonding, current findings of support for the selection model extend the earlier ones and support Hirschi's (1969) notion that low self-esteem and lack of bonding may lead to gang membership. This result is contrary to the findings of Esbensen et al. (1993).

On measures of delinquency and drug use, Thornberry et al. (1993) found evidence for the facilitation model. Our analyses also supported facilitation. Additionally, our analysis dealt with respondents who were not gang members and did not want to be as well as respondents who were not members but wanted to be. Thornberry et al. examined only the former type of nonmember. Our findings showed pronounced differences between these two major categories of nonmembers, and these differences, almost by themselves, resulted in our finding that a selection process played an important part in gang membership. In general, active members of gangs and respondents who wanted to become gang members reported lowest scores on measures of self-esteem, psychosocial health, and ethnic identity. Gang members tended to be persons with identity problems who did not feel good about themselves, had less confidence in their academic abilities, had lower feelings of purpose in life, and had weak attachments to their ethnic group. These individuals appeared to be less integrated into societal institutions, as shown by our measures of social bonds. These results support those of Baron and Tindall (1993), who found that adolescents with weak social bonds were the most delinquent.

In fact, youths who wanted to become gang members had the lowest level of self-esteem of any group. Being in a gang seemed to improve the self-esteem of the members, and consistent with Thornberry et al. (1993), so did leaving the gang. The self-esteem factor seems to be central to the process of joining gangs, participating as a member, and leaving them. If the wannabes are the ones who actually join gangs, then gangs seem to enhance their self-esteem. Initially, the gang may provide support and affirmation, but later, it may become a negative point of reference, and members who leave it feel better about themselves.

Wannabes and active gang members reported less ability to resist peer pressures, greater detachment from their families, greater social distance from police, and lesser academic orientation and aspirations. In control theory, these youths would be considered to have low levels of self-control (Hirschi, 1969; Gottfredson & Hirschi, 1990). Certainly, they reported being more detached socially from institutions, and they were more susceptible to peer influences that may have encouraged delinquent acts.

Our data supported the enhancement model for deviance. Wannabes reported higher levels of delinquency than nonmembers. Current gang members reported the highest rates of delinquency, and former members reported intermediate levels of delinquency (also see Esbensen & Huizinga, 1993). The enhancement model emphasizes both the selective recruitment of high-risk adolescents and the facilitation of delinquency by the gang. Somewhere in this process, minority gang-related youths develop a sense of ethnic pride, which may sustain them as they struggle to leave the gang and try to succeed in mainstream society.

A lack of integration into societal institutions may predispose individuals toward delinquency, because internal controls that are developed through socialization are weak and relatively ineffective (Hirschi, 1969; Gottfredson & Hirschi, 1990). Weak social bonds leave individuals susceptible to the influences of delinquent peers who may provide the insecure person with a "family," albeit one that is riddled with tension and conflict. This scenario applies most completely to adolescents who are living apart from their parents.

Like Hirschi's (1969) theory, the structural equation model suggests that an emphasis on getting students interested in education and the promise of later successful careers as adults facilitates decreased involvement with gangs. The model relies on achievement (and indirectly on social class) as an explanation for gang affiliation, and it suggests that programs that fall short of transforming the relation between education and social class are likely to address the symptoms rather than the causes of gangs and deviant behavior. Add race to these factors, and the system of social stratification in the United States is brought more sharply into focus. Gangs are the outcome of social stratification processes that create poor, disenfranchised communities that are subjected to stigma and repression in a systematic fashion (Esbensen & Huizinga, 1990; Moore, 1991; Padilla, 1992; Vigil, 1988). Members of gangs are individuals struggling to understand themselves and their devaluation in the public institutions of society. Gangs provide a vehicle by which devalued adolescents can insulate themselves, at least temporarily, from the negative judgments others have made of them (Padilla, 1992).

STUDY LIMITATIONS

All data were based on self-reports. Strengths and weaknesses of this approach are well known. Second, the oldest respondents in the sample were 19, and all of them were enrolled in school at the time of the survey. School dropouts and older gang members were not included in the data. Third, the population that was studied came from one city, so additional research is needed to determine generalizability of the findings. Fourth, respondents were allowed to define what they meant by the term *gang*. Imprecision in the term could have resulted in measurement error. Finally, a cross-sectional population survey such as the one used in this research is not a substitute for a longitudinal study; however, the use of wannabes and embedding the test within a broader model may have allowed a better test of the selection-facilitation explanation than a survey from a single point in time that did not incorporate these additional features. Of course, the causal sequence of events would have been demonstrated more convincingly by use of multiple waves.

APPENDIX

Items That Loaded Onto a Single Factor

Self-Esteem (from Rosenberg, 1979)

1. On the whole I am satisfied with myself.
2. At times I think I am no good at all.
3. I feel that I have a number of good qualities.
4. I am able to do things as well as most people.
5. I feel I do not have much to be proud of.
6. I certainly feel useless at times.
7. I feel that I am a worthwhile person.
8. I wish I could have more respect for myself.
9. I am inclined to feel that I am a failure.
10. I take a positive attitude toward myself.

Self-Concept of Academic Ability (from Brookover, Beady, Flood, Schweitzer, & Wisenbaker, 1979)

1. Think of your friends. Do you think you can do school work better than, the same as, or poorer than your friends?
2. Think of other students in your class. Do you think you can do school work better than, the same as, or poorer than the other students in your class?
3. When you finish high school, do you think you will be one of the best students, about the same as most, or below most of the students?
4. Do you think you could finish college?
5. If you went to college, do you think you would be one of the best students, about the same as most, or below most of the students?
6. If you want to be a doctor or a teacher, you need more than four years of college. Do you think you could do that?

Purpose in Life (from Crumbaugh, 1968)

7. My life is empty, filled only with despair/running over with exciting good things.
8. I am a very irresponsible person/very responsible person. 16. With regard to suicide, I have thought of it seriously as a way out/never given it a second thought.
9. Facing my daily life tasks is a source of pleasure and satisfaction/a painful and boring experience.
10. My life is in my hands and I am in control of it/out of my hands; controlled by external factors.

Ethnic Pride (from Multigroup Ethnic Identity Measure; Phinney, 1992)

1. I am happy that I am a member of the group I belong to.
2. I have a strong sense of belonging to my own ethnic group.
3. I have a lot of pride in my ethnic group and its accomplishments.
4. I feel good about my cultural or ethnic background.

REFERENCES

Associated Press. (1994, August 26). Violence seen as biggest problem in schools. *The Gazette*, p. A4.

Baron, S. W., & Tindall, D. B. (1993). Network structure and delinquent attitudes within a juvenile gang. *Social Networks, 15,* 255–273.

Bender, P. M. (1995). EQS: *Structural equations program manual.* Encino, CA: Multivariate Software.

Bollen, K. A., & Barb, K. H. (1981). Pearson's r and coarsely categorized measures. *American Sociological Review, 46,* 232–239.

Bowker, L. H., & Klein, M. W. (1983). The etiology of female delinquency and gang membership: A test of psychological and social structural explanation. *Adolescence, 18,* 740–751.

Brookover, W., Beady, C., Flood, P., Schweitzer, J., & Wisenbaker, J. (1979). *School social systems and student achievement.* New York: Praeger.

Campbell, A. (1991). *The girls in the gang* (2d ed.). Cambridge, MA: Basil Blackwell.

Crumbaugh, J. (1968). Cross-validation of purpose-in-life test based on Frankl's concepts. *Journal of Individual Psychology, 24,* 74–81.

Cummings, S., & Monti, D. J. (1993). Public policy and gangs: Social science and the urban underclass. In S. Cummings & D. J. Monti (Eds.), *Gangs* (pp. 305–320). Albany: State University of New York Press.

Curry, G. D., & Spergel, I. A. (1988). Gang homicide, delinquency, and community. *Criminology, 26,* 381–405.

Curry, G. D., & Spergel, I. A. (1992). Gang involvement and delinquency among Hispanic and African-American adolescent males. *Journal of Research in Crime and Delinquency, 29,* 273–291.

Dukes, R. L., & Martinez, R. (1994). The impact of ethgender on self-esteem among adolescents. *Adolescence, 29,* 105–115.

Esbensen, F., & Huizinga, D. (1990). Community structure and drug use: From a social disorganization perspective. *Justice Quarterly, 7,* 691–709.

Esbensen, F., & Huizinga, D. (1993). Gangs, drugs, and delinquency in a survey of urban youth. *Criminology, 31,* 565–589.

Esbensen, F., Huizinga, D., & Weiher, A. W. (1993). Gang and non-gang youth: Differences in explanatory factors. *Journal of Contemporary Criminal Justice, 9(2),* 94–116.

Fagan, J. A. (1989). The social organization of drug use and drug dealing among urban gangs. *Criminology, 27,* 633–669.

Fagan, J. A., Piper, E. S., & Moore, M. (1986). Violent delinquents and urban youth. *Criminology, 23,* 439–466.

Frankl, V. E. (1969). *The will to meaning.* New York: New American Library.

Gottfredson, M., & Hirschi, T. (1990). *A general theory of crime.* Stanford, CA: Stanford University.

Gray-Ray, P., & Ray, M. C. (1990). Juvenile delinquency in the Black community. *Youth & Society, 22,* 67–84.

Hagedorn, J. M. (1988). *People and folks: Gangs, crime and the underclass in a rust belt city.* Chicago: Lake View.

Hagedorn, J. M. (1991). Gangs, neighborhoods, and public policy. *Social Problems, 38,* 529–541.
Harris, M. G. (1988). *Cholas: Latino girls and gangs.* New York: AMS.

Hirschi, T. (1969). *Causes of delinquency.* Berkeley, CA: University of California Press.

Huff, C. R. (1989). Youth gangs and public policy. *Crime & Delinquency, 35,* 524–537.

Huff, C. R. (1993). Gangs and public policy: Macrolevel interventions. In A. P. Goldstein & C. R. Huff (Eds.), *The gang intervention handbook* (pp. 463–475). Champaign, IL: Research Press.

Jackson, P., & Rudman, C. (1993). Moral panic and the response to gangs in California. In S. Cummings & D. J. Monti (Eds.), *Gangs* (pp. 257–276). Albany: State University of New York Press.

Kaplan, H. B., & Pokorny, A. D. (1969). Self-derogation and psychosocial adjustment. *Journal of Nervous and Mental Disease, 149,* 421–434.

King, A.E.O. (1993). African-American males in prison: Are they doing time or is the time doing them? *Journal of Sociology and Social Welfare, 20,* 9–27.

Klein, M. W., & Maxson, C. L. (1989). Street gang violence. In N. A. Weiner & M. E. Wolfgang (Eds.), *Violent crime and violent criminals* (pp. 198–234). Newbury Park, CA: Sage.

Lasley, J. R. (1992). Age, social context, and street gang membership: Are "youth" gangs becoming "adult" gangs? *Youth & Society, 23,* 434–451.

MacLeod, J. (1987). *Ain't no makin' it.* Boulder, CO: Westview.

Martinez, R., & Dukes, R. L. (1987). Race, gender, and self-esteem among youth. *Hispanic Journal of Behavioral Science, 9,* 427–443.

Martinez, R., & Dukes, R. L. (1991). Ethnic and gender differences in self-esteem. *Youth and Society, 22,* 318–338.

Miller, W. B. (1974). American youth gangs: Past and present. In A. S. Blumberg (Ed.), *Current perspectives on criminal behavior* (pp. 210–239). New York: Alfred A. Knopf.

Monti, D. J. (1993). Origins and problems of gang research in the United States. In S. Cummings & D. J. Monti (Eds.), *Gangs* (pp. 3–26). Albany: State University of New York Press.

Moore, J. (1991). *Going down to the barrio: Homeboys and homegirls in change.* Philadelphia, PA: Temple University.

Moore, J. (1993). Gangs, drugs, and violence. In S. Cummings & D. J. Monti (Eds.), *Gangs* (pp. 27–46). Albany: State University of New York Press.

Padilla, F. M. (1992). *The gang as an American enterprise.* New Brunswick, NJ: Rutgers University.

Phinney, J. S. (1992). The multigroup ethnic identity measure: A new scale for use with adolescents and young adults from diverse groups. *Journal of Adolescent Research, 7,* 156–176.

Phinney, J. S. (1993). A three-stage model of ethnic identity development in adolescence. In M. E. Bernal & G. P. Knight (Eds.), *Ethnic identity: Formation and transmission among Hispanics and other minorities* (pp. 61–79). Albany: State University of New York Press.

Reyes, O., & Jason, L. A. (1993). Pilot study examining factors associated with academic success for Hispanic high school students. *Journal of Youth and Adolescence, 22,* 57–71.

Rosenberg, M. (1965). *Society and the adolescent self-image.* Princeton, NJ: Princeton University Press.

Rosenberg, M. (1979). *Conceiving the self.* New York: Basic Books.

Sánchez Jankowski, M. S. (1991). *Islands in the street: Gangs and American urban society.* Los Angeles: University of California Press.

Sanders, W. B. (1994). *Gangbangs and drive-bys: Grounded culture and juvenile gang violence.* New York: Aldine De Gruyter.

Short, J. F. (1990). Gangs, neighborhoods, and youth crime. *Criminal Justice Research Bulletin, 5,* 1–11.

Spergel, I. (1992). Youth gangs: An essay review. *Social Service Review, 66(1),* 121–140.

Spergel, I., Curry, D., Chance, R., Kane, C, Ross, R., Alexander, A., Simmons, E., & Oh, S. (1994). *Gang suppression and intervention: Problem and response* (Research Summary). Washington, DC: Office of Juvenile Justice and Delinquency Prevention.

Thornberry, T. P., Krohn, M. D., Lizotte, A. J., & Chard-Wierschem, D. (1993). The role of juvenile gangs in facilitating delinquent behavior. *Journal of Research in Crime and Delinquency, 30,* 55–87.

Turner, C. B., & Turner, B. F. (1982). Gender, race, social class, and self evaluation among college students. *Sociological Quarterly, 23*,491–507.

Vigil, D. (1988). *Barrio gangs: Street life and identity in southern California.* Austin: University of Texas Press.

ABOUT THE AUTHORS

Richard L. Dukes is a professor of sociology and the director of the Social Science Research Center at the University of Colorado at Colorado Springs. He obtained his Ph.D. from the University of Southern California. Recent publications include "Prejudice Toward Persons Living With a Fatal Illness" (Psychological Reports, 1995, with H. C. Denny) and "An Appraisal of Simulation and Gaming on the 25th Anniversary of S&G" (Simulation and Gaming, 1994). Interests include gaming and simulations, youth lifestyles, self-esteem among youths, and social stratification.

Rubén O. Martinez is assistant provost at the University of Southern Colorado. He obtained his Ph.D. from the University of California, Riverside. Recent publications include "The Impact of Ethgender on Self-Esteem Among Adolescents" (Adolescence, 1994, with R. L. Dukes) and "Ethnic and Gender Differences in Self-Esteem" (Youth & Society, 1991, with R. L. Dukes). Interests include the education of ethnic minority youths, higher education issues, and environmental concerns. He was an American Council on Education (ACE) Fellow in 1994–1995 at the University of Southern Colorado.

Judith A. Stein, Ph.D., is a research psychologist specializing in measurement and psychometrics in the Department of Psychology, University of California, Los Angeles. She has been coordinating, designing, and performing collaborative studies that encourage innovative applications of structural equation modeling. Recent publications include "Three-Year Follow-Up of Drug Abuse Resistance Education: D.A.R.E." (Evaluation Review, 1996, with R. L. Dukes and J. B. Ullman) and "An Evaluation of D.A.R.E. (Drug Abuse Resistance Education) Using a Solomon Four Group Design With Latent Variables" (Evaluation Review, 1995, with R. L. Dukes and J. B. Ullman).

Precursors and Consequences of Membership in Youth Gangs

Richard L. Dukes
Ruben O. Martinez
Judith A. Stein

PowerPoint by:
Lakisha Blackman
Alfredo Perez
Daryoush Zolfaghari

Precursors and Consequences of Gang Membership in Youth Gangs according to the article are *"Explanations of gang membership studied in a population of 11,000 secondary school students. Lower self-esteem, perceived academic ability, psychosocial health, and bonds with instructional apparel to precede gang membership info structuring delinquency and social control."*

Delinquency is a key component of the three models. It accounts for the variable of relationship between delinquency and gang memberships. (Thornberry et al 1993)

Selection model: whereby already delinquent youths are recruited by gangs. Selection model implies that "gangs only concentrate delinquent youths. They do not influence their members.

Social facilitation model: whereby gangs involve "normal persons" in delinquency. Social facilitation model "identifies threats to group status, cohesion, and solidarity" as a source of aggression with a violent response by gang members.

Enhancement model; identifies with both models, selection recruitment of high risk delinquent youth adolescence towards delinquency if not already delinquent as well as facilitation of delinquency by the gang.

Self Esteem and Psychosocial Health

► Self-esteem in association with social strain and learning relates to poor self-control, poor family bonding relationships and failure in school creates an increased potential for delinquency and gang membership creating a social bond of attachment, commitment, involvement, and belief within the gang.

► Psychosocial health the most influential and empirically supported explains how individuals develop a strong conscience through socialization after being delinquent, individual may turn to other delinquents for support and confirmation of gang cultural deviance and social strain. Youth who can tolerate criminal activity and extreme violence.

Bonding

► Bonding pertains to integration. After becoming delinquent youth adolescence leads to integration of peers who engage in delinquent behavior whether it be by socialization amongst peers or societal institutionsapparel to proceed gang membership such as juvenile, jail or prison institutions.

Methods

- ► Gathered data from population of secondary school students
- ► Anonymous questionnaire in two forms that were randomly assigned
- ► Similarities and differences

Variables

- ► Measured characteristics of social background
- ► Measured the degree of affiliation with a youth gang
- ► 11,023 total responses

Methods cont.

Self-Esteem and Psychosocial Health

- ► Items on the Self-Esteem Scale (Rosenberg, 1965, 1979) were factor analyzed
- ► Items measured youth's concept of academic ability
- ► Psychosocial Health

Bonding

- ► Items measured resistance to peer pressure
- ► Family bonds
- ► Police bonds
- ► Educational bonds
- ► Religious bonds

Methods cont.

Use of Alcohol, Tobacco, and other Drugs

► Measures use of drugs/substances legal for adults but illegal for adolescents
► i.e. status offenses (Bartollas, Schmalleger, 2010)
► Also measured use of illegal drugs

Delinquency, Fear, and Carrying a Weapon

► Measured frequency of delinquency in the past 12 months
► Scale of fear of being hurt
► Whether or not youth has carried a weapon in the past month

Predicting Gang Membership

Variables that helped predict gang membership:

1. Ethnic background
2. Gender
3. Living arrangements
4. Socioeconomic status represented by father's educational deficit

Predictions continue

Ethnic background – reporting being in a gang:
  Native American, Blacks, Latino – 13% (230 out of 1,704)
  Whites, Asian – 4%

Gender associated with gang membership:
  Males- 8% (405 out of 5,242)
  Females – 3%

Predictions continue cont.

Living Arrangements :
  Living away from both parents -16%
  Living at home with parents -5%

Father's Education:
  Not High school graduate – 14% gang membership
  High school graduate – 5% no gang membership

Results from Study

- 1 out of 20 was involved with gangs.
- 3 our of 20 were impacted by gangs.
- Ethnic minority, poor background, , living away from home – more at risk to join gang.
- Women were less involved than men.
- Study supports the Selection Model (Thornberry)
  - Low self esteem & lack of bonding = higher risk of joining gang.
  - Gangs recruit these type of youths.

Work Cited

- Bartollas, Clemens and Schmalleger, Frank. 2010. *Juvenile Delinquency*.8th ed. Upper Saddle River, NJ: Prentice Hall.
- Walker—Barnes, Chanequa. 2001. "Perception of Risk Factors for Female Gang Involvement among African American and Hispanic Women." Youth and Society. November 17, 2010. (http://www.streetgangs.com/academic/perceptions_risk.pdf)

MOVING RISK FACTORS INTO DEVELOPMENTAL THEORIES OF GANG MEMBERSHIP

By James C. Howell,
and Arlen Egley Jr.

Several quantitative longitudinal studies of youth gang members—particularly those embedded in well-designed studies of large, representative samples of children and adolescents—have expanded interest in risk factors for gang membership. Drawing on recent research findings, this article aims to review and synthesize risk factors for gang involvement and to integrate these in a theoretical explanation of youth gang membership. Research-supported risk factors from other studies are combined with variables in Thornberry et al.'s interactional theory of gang membership to form a broader developmental theory of gang involvement. Program and policy implications are also drawn.

Keywords: youth gang; risk factors; theory; developmental

K nowledge of risk factors for youth gang membership has grown exponentially during the past decade. The expanded breadth of this research literature is owed mainly to recent gang research on two fronts. Gang member studies were imbedded within four large-scale longitudinal studies of adolescents in Denver,

James C. Howell, Arlen Egley, Jr., "Moving Risk Factors into Developmental Theories of Gang Membership," *Youth Violence and Juvenile Justice*, vol. 3, no. 4, pp. 334-354. Copyright © 2005 by SAGE Publications. Reprinted with permission.

Colorado (Denver Youth Survey), Rochester, New York (Rochester Youth Development Study), Pittsburgh, Pennsylvania (Pittsburgh Youth Study), and Seattle, Washington (Seattle Social Development Project).[1] Second, youth gang studies using other types of research designs, including ethnographic studies (e.g., Decker & Van Winkle, 1996; Horowitz, 1983; W. B. Miller, Geertz, & Cutter, 1962; Moore, 1978,1991; Moore & Hagedorn, 2001; Short, 1974,1996; Vigil, 2002) and cross-sectional adolescent surveys (Curry, 2000; Curry & Spergel, 1992; Decker & Curry, 2000; Esbensen, 2000; Esbensen & Deschenes, 1998; Gottfredson & Gottfredson, 2001; Le Blanc & Lanctot, 1998; Lynskey, Winfree, Esbensen, & Clason, 2000; Maxson, Whitlock, & Klein, 1998; Winfree, Bernat, & Esbensen, 2001), have also made important contributions to cumulative knowledge of gang risk factors.

We focus in particular in this review on prospective longitudinal quantitative studies because the level of proof is higher in these kinds of studies.[2] This is because longitudinal research designs permit measurement of the risk factors at an earlier point in time than the outcome variable—gang membership in this case. Thus, longitudinal research designs are stronger than cross-sectional studies for determining causal relationships. Because cross-sectional studies measure both risk factors and outcomes at the same point in time, the causal ordering cannot be determined with certainty; what appears to be a predictor could well be an outcome of gang membership. Similarly, sorting out causal factors in ethnographic studies is a particularly difficult task because the focus of these observational studies is on gang life, not on distinguishing adolescents who join from those who do not (Eitle, Gunkel, & Gundy, 2004).

We examine recent research on risk factors for gang membership within the context of Thornberry and colleagues' (Thornberry, Krohn, Lizotte, Smith, & Tobin, 2003; Thornberry, Lizotte, Krohn, Smith, & Porter, 2003) theoretical model of gang membership, itself an extension of Thornberry's interactional theory of delinquency (Thornberry, 1987; Thornberry & Krohn, 2001). Their new gang membership interaction theory adopts a life-course perspective that we attempt to expand with a broader developmental theory of gang involvement that takes into account risk factors for delinquency that precede gang membership, often by several years. We view gang involvement as a stepping stone in individual delinquent careers.

We also make some observations on the program and policy relevance of gang membership risk factors. What is the value of knowing the risk factors for gang membership? How can they be addressed in programming? What are the implications for gang control policy?

We do not consider here the influence of protective factors because research on their effects on gang membership, and delinquency as well, is yet in its infancy.[3] In general, research on protective factors has been slower to develop than research on risk factors in part because of conceptual issues. Factors traditionally have been designated as either risk factors or protective factors; however, recent research shows that some factors may have risk effects but no protective effects, and other factors may have both effects (Stouthamer-Loeber, Wei, Loeber, & Masten, 2004). There also is evidence that, like risk factors, protective factors may have main effects on delinquency. There are other protective factor research issues (Stouthamer-Loeber et al., 2004) including ambiguity about variables that are associated with better and worse outcomes within high-risk groups, use of the term in inconsistent ways, and researchers who have sometimes focused more on concurrent rather than predictive protective factors. Numerous possible protective factors have been suggested in the gang literature (Bjerregaard & Smith, 1993; Esbensen, Huizinga, & Weiher, 1993; Hill, Howell, Hawkins, & Battin-Pearson, 1999; Howell, 2004; Maxson et al., 1998; Thornberry, Krohn, et al., 2003; Walker-Barnes & Mason, 2001; Whitlock, 2002; Wyrick, 2000). Unfortunately, the gang field is far from reaching consensus with respect to evidence-based protective factors, hence we cannot justify including them here because our aim is to synthesize research-supported variables. Nevertheless, research on protective factors for gang involvement is important because it has been demonstrated in the broader field of juvenile delinquency that problem behaviors are significantly more likely to occur when individuals experience a preponderance of risk factors over protective factors in the major developmental domains (Browning & Huizinga, 1999; Smith, Lizotte, Thornberry, & Krohn, 1995; Stouthamer-Loeber et al., 2004).

SUMMARY FINDINGS FROM LONGITUDINAL RISK FACTOR STUDIES OF GANG MEMBERSHIP

Researchers organize the risk factors for serious and violent delinquency according to five developmental domains (sometimes called risk factor levels): individual, family, school, peer group, and community. This framework has its origins in developmental psychologist Bronfenbrenner's (1979) conceptualization of the different spheres of influence that affect a child's behavior, namely relations in the family, the peer group, and the schools. Subsequent research on risk factors for adolescent problem behaviors added two other important risk factor domains: individual characteristics and community conditions (Hawkins, Catalano, & Miller, 1992). Indeed, research shows that risk and protective factors in these five domains function as predictors of juvenile delinquency, violence, and gang membership at different stages in social development as affected by the timing of the respective spheres of influence (Loeber & Farrington, 1998; Thornberry, Krohn, et al., 2003).[4] Although multiple pathways to gang membership are conceivable, a developmental model that includes the gang pathway is useful for marking stages or transitions in offender career development.

Recent youth gang research has produced three seminal findings with respect to the effect of risk factors on the likelihood of gang membership. First, risk factors for gang membership span all five of the risk factor domains (family, peer group, school, individual characteristics, and community conditions). In Seattle, risk factors measured at ages 10 to 12 in each of the five domains predicted gang joining at ages 13 to 18 (Hill et al., 1999). Second, risk factors have a cumulative effect; that is, the greater the numbers of risk factors experienced by the youth, the greater the likelihood of gang involvement. For example, youth in Seattle possessing seven or more risk factors were 13 times more likely to join a gang than were children with no risk factor indicators or only one risk factor indicator (Hill et al., 1999). Third, the presence of risk factors in multiple developmental domains appears to further enhance the likelihood of gang membership. For youth in the Rochester study (Thornberry, Krohn, et al., 2003; Thornberry, Lizotte, et al., 2003), a majority (61%) of the boys and 40% of the girls who exhibited elevated risk in all domains self-reported gang membership. In contrast, only one third of the boys and one fourth of the girls who experienced risk in a simple majority of the domains joined a gang. Thus, gang theories not only need to address multiple risk factors, they also need to address risk factors in multiple developmental domains.

THORNBERRY AND COLLEAGUES' PATH MODEL OF THE ORIGINS OF GANG MEMBERSHIP

Thornberry and colleagues' (Thornberry, Krohn, et al., 2003; Thornberry, Lizotte, et al., 2003) path model of the origins of gang membership for males, derived from their own interaction theory (Thornberry, 1987; Thornberry & Krohn, 2001), contains three fundamental premises (Thornberry & Krohn, 2001, p. 292). First, their theory adopts a developmental or life-course perspective that posits that the causes of behavior are not set or determined in childhood. Rather, "behavior patterns continue to unfold and change across the person's life, in part because of the consequences of earlier patterns of behavior" (Thornberry, Krohn, et al., 2003, p. 83). Second, their theory emphasizes behavioral interactions and bidirectional causality: "Behavior patterns emerge from interactions between the person and his or her environment and not simply from the environment acting upon the individual" (Thornberry & Krohn, 2001, p. 293). Third, their theory incorporates the effect of both social structural influences and social-psychological processes, whereby the former "influences and to some extent determines the initial values of process variables at early stages in the life course" (p. 293).

Stated briefly, the causal model of gang involvement in Thornberry and colleagues' (Thornberry, Krohn, et al., 2003, pp. 83–86) interactional theory of gang membership begins with the more distal structural variables and progresses to the more proximal processual variables. Thus, neighborhood-level variables (e.g., disorganization, concentrated disadvantage, poverty) and family-structural variables (e.g., parental education, family structure) generally exert influence on the risk of gang membership indirectly through the inhibition and/or attenuation of prosocial bonds. The weakening of conventional bonds (e.g., parental and school attachment) elevates risk for antisocial influences (e.g., delinquent peer association), the internalization of antisocial values (e.g., delinquent beliefs), and such precocious behaviors as early dating. The cumulative effect of disadvantage moving from more distal to more proximal variables in turn increases levels of acting out, individual stress, and involvement in delinquency. Consequently, antisocial influences, delinquent behaviors, and life stressors (negative life events) increase the chances that the excitement, protection, and other perceived social benefits of gang membership "will be viewed as a viable means of adjustment to the adolescent's somewhat bleak world" (p. 86).[5]

Thornberry and colleagues (Thornberry, Krohn, et al., 2003) tested their path model in a series of logistic regression equations for males in the Rochester study. The overall results provided considerable empirical support for this adapted version of Thornberry's (1987) interactional theory. As hypothesized by the authors, the initial effect of the more distal structural variables decreased as the more proximal process variables were added sequentially to the model.[6] The authors summarize the results by noting: "A large part of the initial effects of the structural variables is indirect ... flowing through later process variables" (Thornberry, Krohn, et al., 2003, p. 93). Two variables, school performance and antisocial influences, largely mediated structural disadvantage effects on gang membership (p. 93).

Thornberry and colleagues' (Thornberry, Krohn, et al., 2003) gang membership theory needs to be tested in other cities. As they aptly note, the gang phenomenon in Rochester may be different in some important respects compared to longer standing gang problem cities such as Chicago or Los Angeles, where gang involvement is often intergenerational (see the discussion on this point in Thornberry, Krohn, et al., 2003, pp. 189–192). Causal processes may also be different in late gang problem onset localities. The overwhelming majority of gang problem localities first experienced the emergence of gangs within the last 15 years of the 20th century (Howell, Egley, & Gleason, 2002), and the youth gangs in the newer gang problem localities are distinctly different in their demographic characteristics and patterns of criminal involvement from the gangs in the jurisdictions where gang problems began much earlier. Klein and Maxson (1996) also provide evidence that younger gangs noticeably differ from older gangs across a number of structural attributes (e.g., size, age range, subgrouping, and territoriality).

Thornberry and colleagues' (Thornberry, Krohn, et al., 2003) gang membership theory also needs to be tested for girls; it was examined only for boys in the study sample because of an insufficient number of female cases. However, the researchers did include girls in their bivariate analyses of risk factors, and although tentative, the pattern of findings across risk factor domains was notably similar to that of males in the study. Male gender remains a stronger predictor of gang involvement, but attention to female involvement has increased in recent years. In some localities, girls represent between one fourth and one third of current gang members (Esbensen & Deschenes, 1998; Esbensen, Deschenes, & Winfree, 1999; Esbensen & Winfree, 1998; Thornberry, Krohn, et al., 2003).

AN EXTENSION OF THORNBERRY AND COLLEAGUES' GANG MEMBERSHIP THEORY

Before proceeding in this endeavor, two caveats are in order. First, our theoretical focus pertains solely to gang joining. We do not attempt to explain why gangs form in communities (for broad community-level explanations, see Fleisher, 1998; Moore, 1998; Thrasher, 1927/2000). Nor do we attempt to explain the escalation and de-escalation of gang delinquency and violence (see Decker, 1996, for a discussion of this group-level phenomenon).

The principal modification we propose is an extension of Thornberry and colleagues' (Thornberry, Krohn, et al., 2003) theory downward to younger age groups, specifically from preschool age through childhood, because their theory was tested on teenage boys, ages 13 and older. Other gang risk factor studies have included preteens. The youngest participants in two gang member risk factor studies, in Seattle (Hill et al., 1999) and Montreal (Craig, Vitaro, & Tremblay, 2002), were 10-year-olds. Several elements of Thornberry and colleagues' (Thornberry, Krohn, et al., 2003) gang theory have been tested in other sites, as seen Table 1. The theoretical significance of many of these risk factors is discussed below. We also draw on ethnographic and cross-sectional studies that help explain how particular risk factors may operate. Several of the study sites included females, thus the expanded theoretical model may have applicability for girls and boys. This, of course, is an empirical issue.

To extend the age span of Thornberry and colleagues' (Thornberry, Krohn, et al., 2003) gang membership theory downward, our developmental model (see Figure 1) encompasses antecedents of gang membership from birth through adolescence.[7] Studies suggest that antecedents of gang involvement begin to come into play long before youths reach a typical age for joining a gang. For the highest-risk youth, a stepping-stone pattern appears to begin as early as ages 3 to 4 with the emergence of conduct problems, followed by elementary school failure at ages 6 to 12, delinquency onset by age 12, gang joining around ages 13 to 15, and serious, violent, and chronic delinquency onward from midadolescence.[8] This complete sequence, incorporating gang involvement, has not been fully demonstrated empirically. However, there is strong research support for the remaining transitions, from one stage of problem behaviors and delinquency to the next (Loeber & Farrington, 1998, 2001a). For example, Loeber's (Loeber et al., 1993) Pathways Model, which has gained substantial empirical support (Howell, 2003, p. 53), illustrates key stepping stones in escalating delinquent behavior, beginning with stubborn behavior, defiance, and disobedience in early childhood. Children who display these behaviors are at risk for later avoidance of authority figures, including truancy and running away from home, which in turn places them at increased risk for progressing along overt (violent) and covert (property crime) pathways that include more serious behavior. Gang involvement (physical fighting) is an intermediate step in Loeber's overt pathway.

We include factors contained in Thornberry and colleagues' (Thornberry, Krohn, et al., 2003, pp. 83–86) interaction theory of gang membership and suggest other factors that might strengthen their theory. We incorporate risk factors shown to predict gang membership in other longitudinal studies of gang membership, particularly the Denver Youth Survey, the Rochester Youth Development Study, the Pittsburgh Youth Study, and the Seattle Social Development Project. Table 1 contains risk factors for gang membership from prospective longitudinal studies of representative child and adolescent samples.[9]

Table 1. Risk Factors for Gang Membership in Prospective Longitudinal Studies

Community or neighborhood risk factors
Availability of or perceived access to drugs (Hill, Howell, Hawkins, & Battin-Pearson, 1999)
Neighborhood youth in trouble (Hill et al., 1999)
Community arrest rate (Thornberry, Krohn, Lizotte, Smith, & Tobin, 2003)
Feeling unsafe in the neighborhood (Kosterman et al., 1996)
Low neighborhood attachment (Hill et al., 1999)
Neighborhood residents in poverty or family poverty (Hill et al., 1999; Thornberry, Krohn, et al., 2003)

Availability of firearms (Bjerregaard & Lizotte, 1995; Lizotte, Krohn, Howell, Tobin, & Howard, 2000; Lizotte, Tesoriero, Thornberry, & Krohn, 1994; Thornberry, Krohn, et al., 2003)
Neighborhood disorganization (Thornberry, 1998; Thornberry, Krohn, et al., 2003)
Neighborhood drug use (Thornberry, Krohn, et al., 2003) Family risk factors
Family structure (Hill et al., 1999[a]; Thornberry, Krohn, et al., 2003)
Family poverty (Hill et al., 1999; Thornberry, Krohn, et al., 2003)
Family transitions (Thornberry, Krohn, et al., 2003)[b]
Family financial stress (Eitle, Gunkel, & Gundy, 2004)
Sibling antisocial behavior (Hill et al., 1999)
Low attachment to parents or family (Eitle et al., 2004; Thornberry, Krohn, et al., 2003)
Child maltreatment (Thornberry, Krohn, et al., 2003)
Low parent education level (Thornberry, Krohn, et al., 2003)
Parent proviolent attitudes (Hill et al., 1999)
Family management: low parent supervision, control, or monitoring (Hill et al., 1999; Lahey, Gordon, Loeber, Stouthamer-Loeber, & Farrington, 1999[c]; Thornberry, Krohn, et al., 2003)
Teenage fatherhood (Loeber et al., 2003) School risk factors
Low achievement in elementary school (Craig, Vitaro, & Tremblay, 2002; Hill et al., 1999)
Negative labeling by teachers (as either bad or disturbed) (Esbensen, Huizinga, & Weiher, 1993)
Low academic aspirations (Bjerregaard & Smith, 1993; Hill et al., 1999; Thornberry, Krohn, et al., 2003)
Low school attachment (Hill et al., 1999)
Low attachment to teachers (Thornberry, Krohn, et al., 2003)
Low parent college expectations for participant (Bjerregaard & Smith, 1993; Thornberry, Krohn, et al., 2003)
Low degree of commitment to school (Thornberry, Krohn, et al., 2003)
Low math achievement test score (Thornberry, Krohn, et al., 2003)
Identified as learning disabled (Hill et al., 1999)

Peer group risk factors
Association with peers who engage in delinquency or other problem behaviors (Bjerregaard & Lizotte, 1995; Bjerregaard & Smith, 1993; Eitle et al., 2004; Hill et al., 1999; Lahey et al., 1999c)
Association with aggressive peers (Craig et al., 2002; Lahey et al., 1999[c]) Individual risk factors
Violence involvement (Hill et al., 1999; Thornberry, Krohn, et al., 2003)
General delinquency involvement (Curry, 2000; Hill et al., 1999; Esbensen & Huizinga, 1993; Thornberry, Krohn, et al., 2003)
Aggression or fighting (Craig et al., 2002; Lahey et al., 1999c)
Conduct disorders[d] (Lahey et al., 1999)
Externalizing behaviors (disruptive, antisocial, or other conduct disorders; Craig et al. ,2002; Hill et al., 1999)
Early dating (Thornberry, Krohn, et al., 2003)
Precocious sexual activity (Bjerregaard & Smith, 1993; Thornberry, Krohn, et al., 2003)
Antisocial or delinquent beliefs (Hill et al., 1999; Thornberry, Krohn, et al., 2003)
Hyperactive (Craig et al., 2002; Hill et al., 1999)
Alcohol or drug use (Bjerregaard & Smith, 1993; Hill et al., 1999; Thornberry, Krohn, et al., 2003; Thornberry, Krohn, Lizotte, & Chard-Wierschem, 1993)
Early marijuana use and early drinking (Hill et al., 1999)
Depression (Thornberry, Krohn, et al., 2003)
Life stressors[e] (Eitle et al., 2004; Thornberry, Krohn, et al., 2003)
Poor refusal skills (Hill et al., 1999)

NOTE: Race or ethnicity and gender are excluded.

a.   The Social Development Research Group study compared three family structures: no parents in home, one parent only, and one parent plus other adults. The last structure was the strongest predictor.

b.   This risk factor predicted stability of gang membership.

c.   Significant effects were observed only in early adolescence.

d.   As measured in this study, conduct disorder symptoms include bullying, fighting, lying, cruelty toward animals, attacking people, running away from home, fire setting, theft, truancy, and vandalism. Most of these behaviors are illegal and when detected may result in arrest and court adjudication as a delinquent.

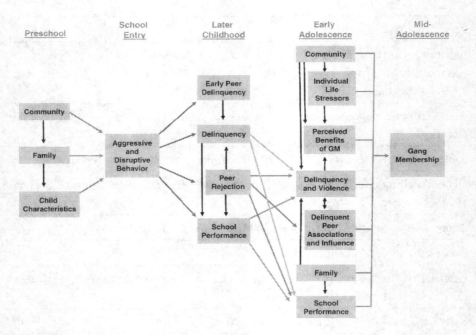

Figure 1. *A Developmental Model of Gang Involvement*

___

e.　　In the Rochester study, these consisted of failing a course at school, being suspended or expelled from school, breaking up with a boyfriend or girlfriend, having a big fight or problem with a friend, or the death of someone close. Eitle and colleagues (2004) measured different types of violent events, traumas, and other major adverse events that occurred in preadolescents' lives (before age 12).

Our theoretical model incorporates four developmental stages: preschool, school entry, childhood, and adolescence.[10] Preschool factors predict early child conduct problems such as aggressive and disruptive behavior during school entry (Coie & Miller-Johnson, 2001), and these problem behaviors predict childhood delinquency, which, coupled with other risk factors in all developmental domains, increases the probability of delinquent activity and gang involvement during adolescence. The influence of risk factors for delinquency varies with age (Lipsey & Derzon, 1998; Loeber & Farrington, 1998, 2001a), and by the time youths enter high school, most of the risk factors affecting gang involvement have long been established. We discuss each of the developmental stages in turn.

In this first developmental stage, child characteristics and community and family deficits produce aggressive and disruptive behavior disorders by the time of school entry (Burke, Loeber, & Birmaher, 2002; Coie & Miller-Johnson, 2001; Kalb & Loeber, 2003; Loeber & Farrington, 2001a) and in turn delinquency and school performance problems in later childhood (Loeber & Farrington, 2001a).[11] The theoretical linkage between structural community (macrolevel) factors and delinquency at the individual level is mediated primarily by family variables (Thornberry & Krohn, 2001). We hypothesize that lack of "social capital" (Coleman, 1988,1990) is an important by-product of "concentrated disadvantage" (McNulty & Bellair, 2003, p. 11) in impoverished, distressed, and crime-ridden communities.[12] We suggest that, when combined with family and child deficits, concentrated disadvantage increases the odds of disruptive behavior disorders in children by the time of school entry and of delinquency later during childhood. Families with a harsh child punishment profile are overrepresented in such disadvantaged neighborhoods, and serious delinquency tends to occur more quickly in youngsters residing in these communities (Loeber et al., 2003).

When linked with certain family and child characteristics, concentrated disadvantage impedes socialization of children (Loeber et al., 2003; Tremblay, 2003). Important family variables in the preschool stage include low parental education (human capital) and a host of family problems (Loeber & Farrington, 2001a) including a broken home, parental criminality, poor family or child management, abuse and neglect, serious marital discord, and young motherhood (Pogarsky, Lizotte, & Thornberry, 2003). Pivotal child characteristics during the preschool period include a difficult temperament and impulsivity, typically described as aggressive, inattentive, and sensation-seeking behaviors (Keenan, 2001; Loeber & Farrington, 2001a).

Taken together, concentrated disadvantage at the community level, family problems, and certain child characteristics lead to early childhood problems (aggression and disruptive behavior), and each of these four variables in turn increases the likelihood of delinquency in childhood and gang membership in adolescence.

THE SCHOOL ENTRY STAGE

Early childhood aggression and disruptive behaviors (Coie & Miller-Johnson, 2001) including stubbornness, defiance, disobedience, and truancy following school entry are products of dysfunctional families (Kalb & Loeber, 2003), particularly in disadvantaged communities. Aggressive and disruptive behaviors are likely to be followed by rejection by prosocial peers, thus opening the door to antisocial or deviant peer influences, which predict delinquent activity in later childhood and early adolescence

(Coie & Miller-Johnson, 2001). The link between physical aggression in childhood and violence in adolescence is particularly strong (Brame, Nagin, & Tremblay, 2001; Broidy et al., 2003).

It is important to note that most disruptive children do not become child delinquents, nor do most child delinquents engage in delinquency in adolescence (Loeber & Farrington, 2001a). From one fourth to one third of disruptive children are at risk of becoming child delinquents, and about a third of all child delinquents later become serious, violent, and chronic offenders.[13] However, as Thornberry and Krohn (2001) note, "the earlier the onset, the greater the continuity" (p. 297).

THE LATER CHILDHOOD STAGE

In the third developmental stage, later childhood, other risk factors (causal variables) that explain gang membership begin to come into play. Children who are involved in delinquency, violence, and drug use at an early age are at higher risk for gang membership than are other youngsters (Craig et al., 2002; Hill et al., 1999; Lahey, Gordon, Loeber, Stouthamer-Loeber, & Farrington, 1999). More than one third of the child delinquents in the Montreal and Rochester samples became involved in crimes of a more serious and violent nature during adolescence, including gang fights (Krohn, Thornberry, Rivera, & Le Blanc, 2001). As Thornberry and Krohn (2001) state, "In brief, very early onset offending is brought about by the combination and interaction of structural, individual, and parental influences" (p. 295).

Peer rejection in the early school years may lead to greater susceptibility to the influence of deviant peers including more aggressive youths (Coie & Miller-Johnson, 2001, p. 192). Aggressive and antisocial youths begin to affiliate with one another in childhood (Cairns & Cairns, 1991; Coie & Miller-Johnson, 2001), and this pattern of aggressive friendships may continue through adolescence (Cairns & Cairns, 1994). A Montreal study suggests that displays of aggression in delinquent acts, at age 10 or perhaps younger, may be key factors leading to gang involvement (Craig et al., 2002). Peers rated gang members as significantly more aggressive than non-gang members at ages 10 to 14.

The negative consequence of delinquent peer associates is one of the most enduring findings in empirical delinquency research (Warr, 2002). Associations with delinquent peers increase delinquency. In turn, involvement in delinquency leads to more frequent associations with delinquent peers (Elliott & Menard, 1996; Thornberry, Lizotte, Krohn, Farnworth, & Jang, 1994). Early peer delinquency thus increases delinquency involvement in later childhood, which in turn increases the likelihood of gang membership in early adolescence (Craig et al., 2002; Eitle et al., 2004; Hill et al., 1999). Weakened social bonds as a result of delinquency may be an important interaction effect of this process (Thornberry & Krohn, 2001).

Poor school performance (poor grades and test scores) in later childhood is likely to result from prosocial peer rejection, child delinquency, and family problems (Thornberry & Krohn, 2001). Other school-related variables that lead to gang involvement include low achievement in elementary school (Craig et al., 2002; Hill et al., 1999) and low school attachment and having been identified as learning disabled (Hill et al., 1999).

Factors that weaken the student-school bond (commitment to school) in the later childhood stage contribute to delinquency and gang membership. The poor school performance of children is one side of the coin; poor-quality schools (poorly organized and functioning) are the other side (Durlak, 1998). A contemporary indicator of poor-quality schools is zero-tolerance policies that produce high suspension, expulsion, and dropout rates. In addition to alienating students from schools and teachers, thus weakening the student-school bond, these policies release many youths from adult supervision during the day and after school, potentially exposing them to deviant influences on the streets (Vigil, 2002).

THE EARLY ADOLESCENCE STAGE

The remainder of our expanded theoretical model incorporates only risk factors that predict gang involvement. Children who are on a trajectory of worsening antisocial behavior are more likely to join gangs during adolescence (Esbensen & Huizinga, 1993; Hill et al., 1999; Lahey et al., 1999), and they tend to have more problems than do non-gang members (Craig et al., 2002). Gang entry might be thought of as the next developmental step in escalating delinquent behavior (Esbensen & Huizinga, 1993; see also Lahey et al., 1999). Future gang members not only evidence a large number of risk factors (Hill et al., 1999), they are likely to show risk factors in multiple developmental domains (Thornberry, Krohn, et al., 2003) including community or neighborhood, family problems, school problems, delinquent peer influence, and individual characteristics. Each of these risk domains is considered next.

Community or neighborhood risk factors. As Tremblay (2003) states, "As children grow older, they are more and more negatively influenced by their environment" (p. 192). Community or neighborhood risk factors that have been shown to predict gang membership in early adolescence include availability or perceived access to drugs, neighborhood youth in trouble, feeling unsafe in the neighborhood, and low neighborhood attachment (Hill et al., 1999; Kosterman et al., 1996). Other important neighborhood risk factors consist of high community arrest rates, high drug use, and neighborhood disorganization (see Table 1). Availability of firearms may also be an important community variable (Bjerregaard & Lizotte, 1995; Lizotte, Krohn, Howell, Tobin, & Howard, 2000).

Communities that suffer from concentrated disadvantage may lack the necessary collective efficacy (informal control and social cohesion) among residents to ameliorate the negative effects of concentrated disadvantage (Morenoff, Sampson, & Raudenbush, 2001; Sampson, 1997). This condition is likely exacerbated by the prevalence of crime in the community, the availability of drugs, and soon, all that weaken neighborhood attachment.

Family risk factors. Family-level factors can be divided into two groups—structural variables and social process variables. Nonintact family (not living with both biological parents) is a key structural variable, and family management problems typically characterize family process variables. However, structural variables are often mediated by family process variables and thus are typically only indirectly associated with gang membership. For example, for Thornberry and colleagues (Thornberry & Krohn, 2001; Thornberry, Krohn, et al., 2003; Thornberry, Lizotte, et al., 2003), structural adversity affects such factors as parenting deficits and the development of strong family bonds.

Family influences begin to fade in adolescence (Lahey et al., 1999; Lipsey& Derzon, 1998; Thornberry, Lizotte, et al., 2003), and studies do not clearly distinguish the family influences on gang membership that remain in adolescence from those that are potent at an earlier point. In the Rochester study, a nonintact family and low parent education predicted gang membership in early to mid adolescence. Poor parental attachment to child, low parental supervision, and child maltreatment emerged as significant family process variables in the bivariate analysis of risk factors, but only for males (Thornberry, Krohn, et al., 2003, p. 66). Another family structural variable, family transitions (change in parent figures), predicted stable gang membership in a separate bivariate analysis (Thornberry, Krohn, et al., 2003, p. 71). Only one additional family structure variable (family poverty) has been examined in other longitudinal studies (Hill et al., 1999). Family process variables associated with gang membership in other quantitative longitudinal studies (see Table 1) include sibling antisocial behavior, family financial stress, and parents' proviolent attitudes. Several ethnographic studies suggest that family conflict and child victimization in the home may have greater importance as risk factors for gang membership for girls than for boys (Fleisher, 1998; J. A. Miller, 2001; Moore, 1978; Moore & Hagedorn, 2001).

Important family risk factors for gang involvement are not limited to at-risk youths' families of origin; these also extend to the families that youths create. Among males, teenage fatherhood may predict gang membership (Loeber et al., 2003). Parental criminality may also prove to be an important variable; this factor has not been researched in longitudinal gang member risk factor studies.

School risk factors. Poor school performance on math tests predicts gang membership for males (Thornberry, Krohn, et al., 2003). Other school risk factors identified in the Rochester bivariate analysis include low academic aspirations, low attachment to teachers, low college expectations of the parent for the child, and low degree of commitment to school. Negative labeling by teachers (as either bad or disturbed) is another important predictor (Esbensen et al., 1993). Feeling unsafe at school may also predict gang involvement (Gottfredson & Gottfredson, 2001). Students who feel vulnerable at school may seek protection in a gang.

Peer risk factors. Along with peer delinquency, Thornberry and colleagues (Thornberry, Krohn, et al., 2003; Thornberry, Lizotte, et al., 2003) included delinquent beliefs as a component of antisocial influences in their gang membership theory, and the latter factor proved to be significantly related to gang membership, whereas surprisingly delinquent peers did not. Other studies show that association with delinquent or antisocial peers and aggressive peers during childhood and early adolescence is a predictor of gang membership (see Table 1).

Associates of gang members are also part and parcel of a community's gang problem because of their active involvement in delinquency (Curry, Decker, & Egley, 2002). Theories of gang membership need to account for close associates of gang members because several variables distinguish associates of gang members from nongang youths (Eitle et al., 2004): preteen exposure to stress, early deviance, early peer deviance, and family attachment. Interestingly, increased preteen stress exposure was associated with increased gang involvement in this study even when the remaining three variables were controlled.

Individual risk factors. Studies have identified more risk factors for gang membership in the individual domain than in any other domain (see Table 1). Early involvement in delinquency and violent behavior in the Seattle study and delinquency involvement in early adolescence in the Rochester study predicted gang membership. Both of these studies also show that the risk of gang involvement is elevated for youngsters who use alcohol or drugs, who are involved in other forms of delinquency, and who hold antisocial or delinquent beliefs (Hill et al., 1999; Thornberry, Krohn, et al., 2003). Experiencing life stressors is another important individual risk factor at the early adolescence stage (Eitle et al., 2004; Thornberry, Krohn, et al., 2003).

Violent victimization is another potentially important individual variable (Peterson, Taylor, & Esbensen, 2004), also seen in ethnographic studies (Decker & Van Winkle, 1996; Fleisher, 1998; J. A. Miller, 2001; Moore, 1991). This is a relatively powerful predictor of individual violence (Shaffer & Ruback, 2002), and personal victimization is related to individual involvement in violence and aggression, which are predictors of gang membership (Craig et al., 2002; Hill et al., 1999; Lahey et al., 1999).

Early dating predicted male gang membership in the Rochester gang theory (Thornberry, Krohn, et al., 2003), and this was also significant for females in the bivariate analysis. Precocious sexual activity was a significant risk factor for gang membership among males but not among females in the bivariate analysis in the Rochester study (Thornberry, Krohn, et al., 2003, p. 66). Depression showed a similar pattern. Interestingly, low self-esteem did not prove to be a statistically significant predictor in the Rochester study (p. 66). Also, Denver Youth Survey data show that youth who were involved in drug use, gang involvement, and delinquency tended to have higher self-esteem (Tiet & Huizinga, 2003).

PERCEIVED BENEFITS OF JOINING A GANG

Although this is not a risk factor as such, personal reasons for joining a gang are an important source of motivation. Among the various reasons youth give for joining a gang, the following are most common. First, related to social reasons, youth join to be around friends and family members (especially siblings or cousins) who already are part of the gang. Second, regarding protection, youth join for the presumed safety they believe the gang can afford (Decker & Curry, 2000; Decker & Van Winkle, 1996; Peterson et al., 2004; Thornberry, Krohn, et al., 2003). Also reported by youth, albeit far less frequently, are more instrumental reasons for joining a gang such as selling drugs or making money (Decker & Van Winkle, 1996).

PROGRAM IMPLICATIONS

What are the program implications of the risk factors for gang membership? In other words, can this information be diffused into practice? How can this be done?

Use of the science-based risk and protection framework of the public health model helps structure the delinquency prevention enterprise in communities (U.S. Department of Health and Human Services, 2001). The public health model is a user-friendly conceptual model for practitioners because of widespread public familiarity with applications in the health arena, such as the prevention of cardiovascular diseases. It has been demonstrated that research-based prevention programs and activities can be successfully promoted by providing community stakeholders with training and technical assistance in risk-protection assessment and strategic prevention planning (Hawkins, Catalano, & Arthur, 2002). Several hundred communities have been successfully engaged in risk and protection-focused delinquency prevention programming, some with impressive results (Hawkins et al., 2002), but nothing has been reported regarding risk-focused gang prevention programming. The compilation of risk factors for gang membership in this article serves as the basis for such an undertaking.

The comprehensive gang prevention, intervention, and suppression model (Spergel, 1995) is a flexible framework that guides communities in developing and organizing a continuum of programs and strategies. Although the results of a six-site evaluation were mixed, when it was well-implemented in three of the communities, the comprehensive gang model effectively guided interagency initiatives in Chicago, Illinois, Mesa, Arizona, and Riverside, California, in developing services and strategies that contributed to reductions in gang violence and drug-related offenses (Spergel et al., 2003; Spergel, Wa, & Sosa, 2004).[14] However, general deterrence effects (at the project-area level) were not as strong as the program effects at the individual-youth level. None of the sites attempted to implement risk focused primary prevention programs; the deliberate emphases in the sites were on intervention and suppression. The successful sites implemented social intervention (outreach and crisis intervention), opportunities provision (education, job, cultural), suppression, and organizational change strategies.

The National Youth Gang Center has developed a strategic planning tool, an operating system, that communities can use to implement the comprehensive gang model and risk-focused prevention (see http://www.iir.com/nygc/). The tool includes research-based risk factors and indicators and information on promising and effective juvenile delinquency and gang programs and strategies that address specific risk factors among various age groups. It incorporates a problem-solving approach to gang-related crime, for example in the engaging of participating sites in an analysis of crime trends involving gang members, in the identification of hot spots, and in the targeting of high-rate gang offenders and violent gangs. To complement the use of the strategic planning tool, an assessment protocol, which any community can use to assess its gang problem and to promote the development of a data-driven continuum of gang prevention, intervention, and suppression programs and strategies, is available (National Youth Gang Center, 2002a). Resource materials that assist communities in developing an action plan to implement the comprehensive gang model are also available (National Youth Gang Center, 2002b). This operating system does not reference the comprehensive gang model as if it were a prescriptive program model; rather, it contains user-friendly tools that empower communities to assess their gang problem, to inventory existing program resources, to identify gaps, and to select preferred solutions from a menu of research-based program and strategy options.

As a general observation, overreliance on one strategy or another is unlikely to produce fundamental changes in the scope and severity of a community's gang problem (Curry & Decker, 2003). Prevention programs are needed to prevent youth from developing problem behaviors, becoming delinquent, and perhaps joining gangs. These can potentially reduce the predominant risk factors for gang involvement and increase protective factors (that are yet to be identified) in each community. Intervention programs are needed to rehabilitate delinquents and separate gang-involved youths from gangs. Suppression activities by law enforcement officers, prosecutors, courts, and correction officers should target the most violent gangs and high-rate gang-involved offenders. There was considerable evidence in the Chicago (Little Village Project) demonstration of the comprehensive gang model that a balanced approach at the individual gang member level contributed to a reduction of violence arrests at the gang and community levels and also improved the perception of residents about the scope and severity of the gang problem (Spergel et al., 2003).

CONCLUSION

Gang involvement can prove to be a critical turning point in an adolescent's life. It may greatly amplify involvement in serious and violent delinquency, which in turn will likely lead to precocious, off-time, and unsuccessful transitions that could bring disorder to the life course in a cascading series of difficulties including school dropout, early pregnancy or early impregnation, teen motherhood, and unstable employment (Thornberry, Krohn, et al., 2003, pp. 179–180). Although many risk factors for gang involvement have been demonstrated and reviewed here, they are part of a longer developmental sequence. That is, the accumulation of risk factors in early childhood and adolescence contribute to known risk factors for gang involvement.

As suggested by Thornberry and colleagues (Thornberry, Krohn, et al., 2003), this process is distinctively interactional. To illustrate, structural deficits lead to parental deficits, weakened social bonds, poor school performance, and rejection by prosocial peers, which leads to delinquent peer associations and delinquent beliefs, which leads to delinquency, which further reduces social bonds and enhances delinquent peer associations, which leads to gang involvement and serious, violent, and chronic offending. As Thornberry and colleagues explain, this sequence is not specifically unidirectional but is rather bidirectional where current behaviors are influenced by antecedent risk variables, which in turn diminish the chances of alleviating risk and extricating gang-involved youths from the process leading to seriously antisocial outcomes. Through this evolving bidirectional sequence in which prosocial choices become less and less available, gang involvement becomes an increasingly viable perceived alternative for meeting an adolescent's immediate needs and alleviating stress.

We have offered a developmental model of gang involvement that extends Thornberry and colleagues' (Thornberry, Krohn, et al., 2003) gang theory downward to younger predelinquent and delinquent levels. In building on their pioneering theoretical contribution, our developmental model suggests a broader perspective of gang involvement, beginning with antecedent problem behaviors that emerge in early childhood. Our developmental model adds a theoretical explanation (Coie & Miller-Johnson, 2001) of early childhood problems (aggressive and disruptive behaviors) and links these to problems in later childhood (early peer delinquency, delinquency, peer rejection, and poor school performance) and subsequently to a host of risk factors for gang membership during adolescence. Although our theory rests on the shoulders of Thornberry and Krohn's (2001) developmental theory of delinquency and their theory of gang involvement (Thornberry, Krohn, et al., 2003; Thornberry, Lizotte, et al., 2003), we attempted to extend their theory down to younger age groups by the addition of predictors of delinquency and gang membership from other studies and by suggesting developmental stepping stones to gang involvement.

Risk factor studies will be enriched by continued use of theory to guide empirical inquiries, as exemplified in the empirical test of Thornberry and colleagues' (Thornberry, Krohn, et al., 2003) path theory. Through the attentive practice of specifying theoretical concepts and their relationships (i.e., theoretical propositions) in advance, one can avoid contributing to what Thornberry and colleagues (Thornberry, Krohn, et al., 2003) refer to as "a somewhat atomized view of gang members that is focused on individual variables" (p. 77).

In the same vein, it is important to avoid gang programming that is similarly atomized in the expectation that a single program or strategy (such as an after-school program) will solve the problem. There is no magic bullet for combating gangs. A comprehensive continuum of programs and strategies is needed. Tools that empower communities to systematically assess their gang problem, to inventory existing resources, and to develop and implement a continuum of gang prevention, intervention, and suppression strategies and programs are available.

Authors' Note: Work on this article was supported by Cooperative Agreement 95-JD-MU-K001 with the Institute for Intergovernmental Research, National Youth Gang Center, from the Office of Juvenile Justice and Delinquency Prevention (OJJDP), U.S. Department of Justice. Points of view or opinions expressed herein are those of the authors and do not necessarily represent the official position or policies of the OJJDP or the U.S. Department of Justice. We want to thank John P. Moore, director of the National Youth Gang Center, for his support of this work and the anonymous reviewers of this journal for their helpful comments.

NOTES

1. See Howell (2003, p. 82) for a listing of the research reports on gang members published to date in the four studies. Pittsburgh Youth Study researchers subsequently published an additional report (Gordon et al., 2004).

2. Longitudinal gang studies are not the only valuable methods, of course, and these are costly and difficult to design and implement. Other gang study methods, including ethnographies, case studies, and cross-sectional surveys, can make valuable contributions toward understanding gang involvement and can also play important roles in the context of community initiatives that combat gangs. For example, cross-sectional student surveys can determine the prevalence of risk factors that need to be addressed in prevention programming and the geographical location of programs. Ethnographic and case studies can be used to describe existing gangs and their activities, thus informing interventions.

3. These are conditions that, presumably, either counter the initial influence of risk factors or increase resilience to them and thus inhibit the development of problems even in the face of risk exposure.

4. It should be noted that risk factors in these domains also predict a variety of other problem behaviors in childhood and adolescence (Loeber & Farrington, 1998, 2001a).

5. The life stressors consist of failing a course at school, being suspended or expelled from school, breaking up with a boyfriend or girlfriend, having a big fight or problem with a friend, and/or the death of someone close.

6. One neighborhood structural variable, area disorganization, did not significantly increase the odds of gang membership. This finding serves as a reminder of the important distinction between the influence community-level factors have on the emergence and character of gang activity and gang membership risk itself (Bursik & Grasmick, 1993). Put differently, most youths in disadvantaged, gang-problem neighborhoods do not join gangs (Klein, 1995).

7. The very early factors (ages 0–3) are not discussed herein. Readers should consult Loeber and Farrington (2001b). Future expansion of our proposed model should take these into account. Readers should note that we do not depict the bidirectional effects in Figure 1. This is an empirical matter.

8. Studies do not clearly specify the typical child delinquency age of onset. In the Rochester sample, the very youngest onset group (onset at 4–10 years of age) had the highest prevalence rate for both serious and violent offenses during the early adult years, roughly ages 19 to 22 (Krohn, Thornberry, Rivera, & Le Blanc, 2001, p. 83). These researchers suggest that "our focus should be on those children who exhibit delinquent behavior during very early school years" (p. 90).

9. Readers are cautioned that citations to more than one study for a given risk factor do not necessarily mean that exact replications have occurred. The given variable could well have been operationalized differently and/or measured using different indicators.

10. The age range for childhood is approximately ages 4 to 12 (which overlaps with the preschool and school-entry periods), and the range for adolescence is ages 13 to 25.

11. Disruptive behavior disorders include conduct disorders such as aggression and oppositional defiant disorder (Burke, Loeber, & Birmaher, 2002).

12. Social capital refers to the quality of social relations in an individual's environment, especially the relations between children and adults that inhibitor facilitate access to resources (Coleman, 1990). Broadly defined, social capital includes the availability of services to children and families (National Research Council, 1993) that facilitate positive youth development (National Research Council & Institute of Medicine, 2002, pp. 6–10). In other words, the absence of social capital has the effect of knifing off developmental opportunities.

13. The Study Group on Very Young Offenders compiled the following list of warning signs for later problems among disruptive chi ldren during the preschool years (Loeber & Farrington, 2001 b, p. xxiv): (a) disruptive behavior that is either more frequent or more severe than that of other children of the same age; (b) disruptive behavior such as temper tantrums and aggression that persists beyond the first 2 to 3 years of life; and (c) a history of aggressive, inattentive, or sensation-seeking behavior in the preschool years.

14. Drug-related arrests of program clients were not reduced significantly in Riverside.

REFERENCES

Bjerregaard, B., & Lizotte, A. J. (1995). "Gun ownership and gang membership." *Journal of Criminal Law and Criminology*, 86, 37–58.

Bjerregaard, B., & Smith, C. (1993). "Gender differences in gang participation, delinquency, and substance use."*Journal of Quantitative Criminology*, 9, 329–355.

Brame, B., Nagin, D. S., & Tremblay, R. E. (2001). "Developmental trajectories of physical aggression from school entry to late adolescence." *Journal of Child Psychology and Psychiatry and Allied Disciplines*, 42, 503–512.

Broidy, L. M., Tremblay, R. E., Brame, B., Fergusson, D., Horwood, J. L., Laird, R., et al. (2003). "Developmental trajectories of childhood disruptive behaviors and adolescent delinquency: A six-site, cross-national study. " *Developmental Psychology*, 39(2), 222–245.

Bronfenbrenner, U. (1979). *The ecology of human development, experiments by nature and design.* Cambridge, MA: Harvard University Press.

Browning, K., & Huizinga, D. (1999). *Highlights of findings from the Denver Youth Survey* (Fact Sheet106). Washington, DC: U.S. Department of Justice, Office of Juvenile Justice and Delinquency Prevention.

Burke, J. D., Loeber, R., & Birmaher, B. (2002). "Oppositional defiant disorder and conduct disorder: A review of the past 10 years, Part II." *Journal of the American Academy of Child and Adolescent Psychiatry*, 41, 1275–1293.

Bursik, R. J., Jr., & Grasmick, H. G. (1993). *Neighborhoods and crime: The dimensions of effective community control.* New York: Lexington.

Cairns, R. B., & Cairns, B. D. (1991). "Social cognition and social networks: A developmental perspective." In D. J. Pepler & K. H. Rubin (Eds.), *The development and treatment of childhood aggression* (pp. 249–278). Hillsdale, NJ: Lawrence Erlbaum.

Cairns, R. B., & Cairns, B. D. (1994). *Lifelines and risks: Pathways of youth in our time.* New York: Cambridge University Press.

Coie, J. D., & Miller-Johnson, S. (2001). "Peer factors and interventions." In R. Loeber & D. P. Farrington (Eds.), *Child delinquents, development, intervention, and service needs* (pp. 191–209). Thousand Oaks, CA: Sage.

Coleman, J. S. (1988). "Social capital in the creation of human capital." *American Journal of Sociology,* 94, 95–120.

Coleman, J. S. (1990). *Foundations of social theory.* Cambridge, MA: Harvard University Press.

Craig, W. M., Vitaro, C. G., & Tremblay, R. E. (2002). "The road to gang membership: Characteristics of male gang and non-gang members from ages 10 to 14." *Social Development,* 11(1), 53–68.

Curry, G. D. (2000). "Self-reported gang involvement and officially recorded delinquency." *Criminology,* 38, 1253–1274.

Curry, G. D., & Decker, S. H. (2003). *Confronting gangs: Crime and community* (2nd ed.). Los Angeles: Roxbury.

Curry, G. D., Decker, S. H., & Egley, A., Jr. (2002). "Gang involvement and delinquency in a middle school population." *Justice Quarterly,* 19, 275–292.

Curry, G. D., & Spergel, I. A. (1992). "Gang involvement and delinquency among Hispanic and African-American adolescent males." *Journal of Research in Crime and Delinquency,* 29, 273–291.

Decker, S. H. (1996). "Collective and normative features of gang violence." *Justice Quarterly,* 13, 243–264.

Decker, S. H., & Curry, G. D. (2000). "Addressing key features of gang membership: Measuring the involvement of young members." *Journal of Criminal Justice,* 28, 473–482.

Decker, S. H., & Van Winkle, B. (1996). *Life in the gang: Family, friends, and violence.* New York: Cambridge University Press.

Durlak, J. A. (1998). "Common risk and protective factors in successful prevention programs." *American Journal of Orthopsychiatry,* 68, 512–520.

Eitle, D., Gunkel, S., & Gundy, K. V. (2004). "Cumulative exposure to stressful life events and male gang membership." *Journal of Criminal Justice,* 32, 95–111.

Elliott, D. S., & Menard, S. (1996). "Delinquent friends and delinquent behavior: Temporal and developmental patterns." In J. D. Hawkins (Ed.), *Delinquency and crime: Current theories* (pp. 2867). New York: Cambridge University Press.

Esbensen, F. (2000). "Preventing adolescent gang involvement: Risk factors and prevention strategies." *Juvenile Justice Bulletin*, Youth Gang Series. Washington, DC: U.S. Department of Justice, Office of Justice Programs, Office of Juvenile Justice and Delinquency Prevention.

Esbensen, F., & Deschenes, E. P. (1998). "A multi-site examination of gang membership: Does gender matter?" *Criminology*, 36, 799–828.

Esbensen, F., Deschenes, E. P., & Winfree, L. T. (1999)." Differences between gang girls and gang boys: Results from a multi-site survey." *Youth and Society*, 31, 27–53.

Esbensen, F., & Huizinga, D. (1993). "Gangs, drugs, and delinquency in a survey of urban youth." *Criminology*, 31, 565–589.

Esbensen, F., Huizinga, D., & Weiher, A. W. (1993). "Gang and non-gang youth: Differences in explanatory variables." *Journal of Contemporary Criminal Justice*, 9, 94–116.

Esbensen, F., & Winfree, L. T. (1998). "Race and gender differences between gang and non-gang youths: Results from a multi-site survey." *Justice Quarterly*, 15, 505–526.

Fleisher, M. S. (1998). *Dead end kids: Gang girls and the boys they know*. Madison: University of Wisconsin Press.

Gordon, R. A., Lahey, B. B., Kawai, E., Loeber, R., Stouthamer-Loeber, M., & Farrington, D. P. (2004). "Antisocial behavior and youth gang membership: Selection and socialization." *Criminology*, 42(1), 55–88.

Gottfredson, G. D., & Gottfredson, D. C. (2001). *Gang problems and gang programs in a national sample of schools*. Ellicott City, MD: Gottfredson Associates.

Hawkins, J. D., Catalano, R. F., & Arthur, M. W. (2002). "Promoting science-based prevention in communities. " *Addictive Behaviors*, 27, 951–976.

Hawkins, J. D., Catalano, R. F., & Miller, J. Y. (1992). "Risk and protective factors for alcohol and other drug problems in adolescence and early adulthood: Implications for substance abuse prevention." *Psychological Bulletin*, 112, 64–105.

Hill, K. G., Howell, J. C., Hawkins, J. D., & Battin-Pearson, S. R. (1999). "Childhood risk factors for adolescent gang membership: Results from the Seattle Social Development Project." *Journal of Research in Crime and Delinquency*, 36, 300–322.

Horowitz, R. (1983). *Honor and the American dream: Culture and identity in a Chicano community*. New Brunswick, NJ: Rutgers University Press.

Howell, J. C. (2003). *Preventing and reducing juvenile delinquency: A comprehensive framework*. Thousand Oaks, CA: Sage.

Howell, J. C. (2004). "Youth gangs: Prevention and intervention." In P. Allen-Meares & M. W. Fraser (Eds.), *Intervention with children and adolescents: An interdisciplinary perspective* (pp. 493514). Boston: Allyn & Bacon.

Howell, J. C., Egley, A., Jr., & Gleason, D. K. (2002). *Modern day youth gangs*. Juvenile Justice Bulletin, Youth Gang Series. Washington, DC: U.S. Department of Justice, Office of Juvenile Justice and Delinquency Prevention.

Kalb, L. M., & Loeber, R. (2003). "Child disobedience and noncompliance: A review." *Pediatrics*, 111, 641–652.

Keenan, K. (2001). "Uncovering preschool precursor problem behaviors." In R. Loeber & D. P. Farrington (Eds.), *Child delinquents: Development, intervention, and service needs* (pp. 117–134). Thousand Oaks, CA: Sage.

Klein, M. W. (1995). *The American street gang.* New York: Oxford University Press.

Klein, M. W., & Maxson, C. L. (1996). *Gang structures, crime patterns and police responses.* Los Angeles: Social Science Research Institute, University of Southern California.

Kosterman, R., Hawkins, J. D., Hill, K. G., Abbott, R. D., Catalano, R. F., & Guo, J. (1996, November). *The developmental dynamics of gang initiation: When and why young people join gangs.* Paper presented at the annual meeting of the American Society of Criminology, Chicago.

Krohn, M. D., Thornberry, T. P., Rivera, C., & Le Blanc, M. (2001). "Later careers of very young offenders." In R. Loeber & D. P. Farrington (Eds.), *Child delinquents: Development, intervention, and service needs* (pp. 67–94). Thousand Oaks, CA: Sage.

Lahey, B. B., Gordon, R. A., Loeber, R., Stouthamer-Loeber, M., & Farrington, D. P. (1999). "Boys who join gangs: A prospective study of predictors of first gang entry." *Journal of Abnormal Child Psychology, 27,* 261–276.

Le Blanc, M., & Lanctot, N. (1998). "Social and psychological characteristics of gang members according to the gang structure and its subcultural and ethnic makeup." *Journal of Gang Research,* 5,15–28.

Lipsey, M. W., & Derzon, J. H. (1998). "Predictors of violent or serious delinquency in adolescence and early adulthood: A synthesis of longitudinal research." In R. Loeber & D. P. Farrington (Eds.), *Serious and violent juvenile offenders: Risk factors and successful interventions* (pp. 86–105). Thousand Oaks, CA: Sage.

Lizotte, A. J., Krohn, M. D., Howell, J. C., Tobin, K., & Howard, G. J. (2000). "Factors influencing gun carrying among young urban males over the adolescent-young adult life course." *Criminology,* 38,811–834.

Lizotte, A. J., Tesoriero, J. M., Thornberry, T. P., & Krohn, M. D. (1994). "Patterns of adolescent firearms ownership and use." *Justice Quarterly,* 11, 51–73.

Loeber, R., & Farrington, D. P. (Eds.). (1998). *Serious and violent juvenile offenders: Risk factors and successful interventions.* Thousand Oaks, CA: Sage.

Loeber, R., & Farrington, D. P. (Eds.). (2001a). Child delinquents: Development, intervention, and service needs. Thousand Oaks, CA: Sage.

Loeber, R., & Farrington, D. P. (Eds.). (2001b). Executive summary. In R. Loeber & D. P. Farrington (Eds.), Child delinquents: Development, intervention, and service needs (pp. xix-xxxi). Thousand Oaks, CA: Sage.

Loeber, R., Farrington, D. P., Stouthamer-Loeber, M., Moffitt, T. E., Caspi, A., White, H. R., et al. (2003). The development of male offending: Key findings from fourteen years of the Pittsburgh Youth Study. In T. P. Thornberry & M. D. Krohn (Eds.), Taking stock of delinquency: An verview of findings from contemporary longitudinal studies (pp. 93–136). New York: Kluwer Academic/Plenum.

Loeber, R., Wung, P., Keenan, K., Giroux, B., Stouthamer-Loeber, M., Van Kammen, W. B., & Maughan, B. (1993). Developmental pathways in disruptive child behavior. Development and Psychopathology, 5, 103–133.

Lynskey, D. P., Winfree, L. T., Esbensen, F., & Clason, D. L. (2000). Linking gender, minority group status, and family matters to self-control theory: A multivariate analysis of key self-control concepts in a youth gang context. Juvenile and Family Court Journal, 51(3), 1–19.

Maxson, C. L., Whitlock, M., & Klein, M. W. (1998). Vulnerability to street gang membership: Implications for prevention. Social Service Review, 72(1), 70–91.

McNulty, T. L., & Bel lair, P. E. (2003). Explaining racial and ethnic differences in serious adolescent violent behavior. *Criminology*, 41, 709–748.

Miller, J. A. (2001). One of the guys: Girls, gangs and gender. New York: Oxford University Press.

Miller, W. B., Geertz, H., & Cutter, H. S. G. (1962). Aggression in a boys' street-corner group. Psychiatry, 24, 283–298.

Moore, J. W. (1978). Homeboys: Gangs, drugs and prison in the barrios of Los Angeles. Philadelphia: Temple University Press.

Moore, J. W. (1991). Going down to the barrio: Homeboys and homegirls in change. Philadelphia: Temple University Press.

Moore, J. W. (1998). Understanding youth street gangs: Economic restructuring and the urban underclass. In M. W. Watts (Ed.), Cross-cultural perspectives on youth and violence (pp. 6578). Stamford, CT: JAI.

Moore, J. W., & Hagedorn, J. M. (2001). Female gangs. Juvenile Justice Bulletin, Youth Gang Series. Washington, DC: U.S. Department of Justice, Office of Juvenile Justice and Delinquency Prevention.

Morenoff, J. D., Sampson, R. J., & Raudenbush, S. W. (2001). Neighborhood inequality, collective efficacy, and the spatial dynamics of urban violence. *Criminology*, 39, 517–559.

National Youth Gang Center. (2002a). OJJDP comprehensive gang model: Assessing your community's youth gang problem. Washington, DC: Office of Juvenile Justice and Delinquency Prevention.

National Youth Gang Center. (2002b). OJJDP comprehensive gang model: Planning for implementation. Washington, DC: Office of Juvenile Justice and Delinquency Prevention.

National Research Council. (1993). Losing generations: Adolescents in high risk settings. Washington, DC: National Academy Press.

National Research Council & Institute of Medicine. (2002). Community programs to promote youth development. Washington, DC: National Academy Press.

Peterson, D., Taylor, T. J., & Esbensen, F. (2004). Gang membership and violent victimization. Justice Quarterly, 21, 793–815.

Pogarsky, G., Lizotte, A. J., & Thornberry, T. P. (2003). The delinquency of children born to young mothers: Results from the Rochester Youth Development Study. *Criminology*, 41, 1249–1286.

Sampson, R. J. (1997). Collective regulation of adolescent misbehavior: Validation results from eighty Chicago neighborhoods. Journal of Adolescent Research, 12, 227–244.

Shaffer, J. N., & Ruback, R. B. (2002). Violent victimization as a risk factor for violent offending among juveniles. Juvenile Justice Bulletin. Washington, DC: U.S. Department of Justice, Office of Justice Programs, Office of Juvenile Justice and Delinquency Prevention.

Short, J. F., Jr. (1974). Youth, gangs and society: Micro-and macro sociological processes. The Sociological Quarterly, 15, 3–19.

Short, J. F., Jr. (1996). Personal, gang, and community careers. In C. R. Huff (Ed.), Gangs in America (2nd ed., pp. 221–240). Thousand Oaks, CA: Sage.

Smith, C. A., Lizotte, A. J., Thornberry, T. P., & Krohn, M. D. (1995). Resilient youth: Identifying factors that prevent high-risk youth from engaging in delinquency and drug use. In J. Hagan (Ed.), Delinquency in the life course (pp. 217–247). Greenwich, CT: JAI.

Spergel, I. A. (1995). The youth gang problem. New York: Oxford University Press.

Spergel, I. A., Wa, K. M., Choi, S., Grossman, S. F., Jacob, A., Spergel, A., & Barrios, E. M. (2003). Evaluation of the Gang Violence Reduction Project in Little Village: Final report summary. Chicago: School of Social Service Administration, University of Chicago.

Spergel, I. A., Wa, K. M., & Sosa, R. V. (2004). The comprehensive, community-wide gang program model: Success and failure. Chicago: School of Social Service Administration, University of Chicago.

Stouthamer-Loeber, M., Wei, E., Loeber, R., & Masten, A. S. (2004). Desistance from persistent serious delinquency in the transition to adulthood. Development and Psychopathology, 16, 897–918.

Thornberry, T. P. (1987). Toward an interactional theory of delinquency. Criminology, 25, 863–891.

Thornberry, T. P. (1998). Membership in youth gangs and involvement in serious and violent offending. In R. Loeber & D. P. Farrington (Eds.), Serious and violent juvenile offenders: Risk factors and successful interventions (pp. 147–166). Thousand Oaks, CA: Sage.

Thornberry, T. P., & Krohn, M. D. (2001). The development of delinquency: An interactional perspective. In S. O. White (Ed.), Handbook of youth and justice (pp. 289–305). New York: Plenum.

Thornberry, T. P., Krohn, M. D., Lizotte, A. J., & Chard-Wierschem, D. (1993). The role of juvenile gangs in facilitating delinquent behavior. Journal of Research in Crime and Delinquency, 30, 55–87.

Thornberry, T. P., Krohn, M. D., Lizotte, A. J., Smith, C. A., & Tobin, K. (2003). Gangs and delinquency in developmental perspective. New York: Cambridge University Press.

Thornberry, T. P., Lizotte, A. J., Krohn, M. D., Farnworth, M., & Jang, S. J. (1994). Delinquent peers, beliefs, and delinquent behavior: A longitudinal test of interactional theory. Criminology, 32, 601–637.

Thornberry, T. P., Lizotte, A. J., Krohn, M. D., Smith, C. A., & Porter, P. K. (2003). Causes and consequences of delinquency: Findings from the Rochester Youth Development Study. In T.

P. Thornberry & M. D. Krohn (Eds.), Taking stock of delinquency: An overview of findings from contemporary longitudinal studies (pp. 11–46). New York: Kluwer Academic/Plenum.

Thrasher, F. M. (2000). The gang—A study of 1,313 gangs in Chicago. Chicago: New Chicago School Press. (Original work published 1927)

Tiet, Q. Q., & Huizinga, D. (2003). Dimensions of the construct of resilience and adaptation among inner-city youth. Journal of Adolescent Research, 17, 260–276.

Tremblay, R. E. (2003). Why socialization fails: The case of chronic physical aggression. In B. B. Lahey, T. E. Moffitt, & & A. Caspi (Eds.), Causes of conduct disorder and juvenile delinquency (pp. 182–224). New York: Guilford.

U.S. Department of Health and Human Services. (2001). Youth violence: A report of the Surgeon General. Rockville, MD: U.S. Department of Health and Human Services, National Center for Injury Prevention and Control; Center for Mental Health Services, National Institutes of Health, National Institute of Mental Health.

Vigil, J. D. (2002). A rainbow of gangs: Street cultures in the mega-city. Austin: University of Texas Press.

Walker-Barnes, C. J., & Mason, C. A. (2001). Ethnic differences in the effect of parenting on gang involvement and gang delinquency: A longitudinal, hierarchical linear modeling perspective. Child Development, 72, 1814–1831.

Warr, M. (2002). Companions in crime: The social aspects of criminal conduct. New York: Cambridge University Press.

Whitlock, M. L. (2002). Family-based risk and protective mechanisms for youth at-risk of gang joining. Unpublished doctoral dissertation, University of California, Los Angeles.

Winfree, L. T., Jr., Bernat, F. P., & Esbensen, F. A. (2001). Hispanic and Anglo gang membership in two southwestern cities. The Social Science Journal, 38, 105–117.

Wyrick, P. A. (2000). Vietnamese youth gang involvement (Fact Sheet 2000–01). Washington, DC: Office of Juvenile Justice and Delinquency Prevention.

James C. (Buddy) Howell, Ph.D., is a senior research associate with the National Youth Gang Center. His research interests include youth gangs, juvenile justice, public crime policies, and diffusion of research-based practice.

Arlen Egley Jr. is a senior research associate with the National Youth Gang Center. He received his Ph.D. in criminology and criminal justice from the University of Missouri St. Louis in 2003. His research interests include juvenile delinquency and violence, youth gangs, and public policy responses to these issues.

Moving Risk Factors Into Developmental Theories of Gang Membership

- ► Basic tenet of risk factor approach: Often multiple rather than single pathways to adverse outcomes.
- ► Risk Factors-individual or environmental hazards that increase an individual's vulnerability to negative developmental outcomes (Small and Luster 1994)
    - Multiple Risk Factors-Multiple and often overlapping risk factors in individual's background that lead to adverse outcomes.

Developmental Domains or Risk Factor Levels

1. Individual
2. Family
3. School
4. Peer Group
5. Community

Framework from developmental psychologist Bronfenbrenner (1979) conceptualization of different spheres of influence that affect a child's behavior.

Moving Risk Factors Into Developmental Theories of Gang Membership

Broader developmental theory of gang involvement sought.

► Longitudinal Studies
   1. Denver Youth Survey
   2. Rochester Youth Development Study
   3. Pittsburgh Youth Study
   4. Seattle Social Development Project
► Ethnographic Studies
► Cross-Sectional Studies

Aim is to synthesize research-supported variables.

Life Course Perspective

► Thornberry et al. Interactional Theory of Gang Membership.
► Life course perspective
   — Expanded with broader developmental theory that takes into account risk factors for gang membership that precede gang membership.
   — Gang involvement stepping stone in individual delinquent careers.

What is the Value of Knowing Risk Factors?

► What is the value of knowing risk factors for gang membership?
► How can they be addressed in programming?
► What are the implications for gang control policies?

Protective Factors

► Problem behaviors significantly more likely to occur when individuals experience a preponderance of risk factors over protective factors in major developmental domains.

Resilience Explains Why Numerous Youth Manage to Resistance Joining Gangs

▶   Resilience Has Been Defined As:
    —   Manifestations of competence in children despite exposure to stressful events (Garmezy, Masten, and Tellegen 1984).
    —   "Resilience is the ability to thrive, mature, and increase competence in the face of adverse circumstances. These circumstances may include biological abnormalities or environmental obstacles. Further, the adverse circumstances may be chronic and consistent or severe and infrequent. To thrive, mature, and increase competence, a person must draw upon all of his or her resources: biological, psychological, and environmental." (Gordon 1995)

Some Earlier Findings

1. Risks factors span all five domains.
2. Risk factors have cumulative effect.
    —   Risk factors measured at 10–12 predict gang joining at 13–18 (Seattle).
    —   7 or more, 13 times more likely to join (Seattle).
3. Multiple risk in multiple developmental domains increases risk exponentially.

Expanded Path Model (Thornberry, Krohn, et al., 2003)

► Derived from Interactional Theory

1. Developmental/Life Course Perspective-causes of behavior not set or determined in childhood, rather behavior patterns change and unfold across the person's life.

2. Behavioral interactions and bidirectional causality.

3. Social structural influences and socialpsychological processes.

Added younger age groups to include antecedents of gang memberships, birth-adolescence.

Preschool Stage

► Preschool-predict early childhood conduct problems e.g. aggressive, disruptive behavior during school entry.

— Childhood Characteristics-difficult temperament/impulsivity, aggressive, inattentive, and sensation-seeking (Keenan, 2001)

— Community Deficits-lack of social capital is by-product of "concentrated disadvantage" e.g. impoverished, distressed, crimeridden communities.

— Family Deficits-harsh child punishment, low parental education (human capital), broken home, parental criminality, poor family/child management, abuse/neglect, serious martial discord, young motherhood (Pogarsky, Lizotte, & Thornberry, 2003).

School Entry Stage

► Early childhood aggression and disruptive behaviors (stubbornness, defiance, disobedience, and truancy) following school entry are products of dysfunctional families (Kalb & Loeber, 2003).
  — Rejection by prosocial peers
  — Vulnerable to antisocial or deviant peers influences

► Physical aggression in childhood linked to violence in adolescence (Broidy et al., 2003)

Childhood Stage

Early onset offending is brought about by the combination and interaction of structural, individual and parental influences.

► Causal variables
  — Delinquency, violence, drug use
  — Aggressive and antisocial youths affiliate and form friendships through adolescence.
    ▷ Association with delinquent peers increase delinquency, and involvement in delinquency leads to more frequent associations with delinquent peers.
► Poor school performance-low achievement in elementary, low school attachment, and learning disabilities.
► Poor quality schools-zero tolerance policies (high suspension, expulsion, dropout rates (Vigil, 2002)

Early Adolescence Stage

1. Community or neighborhood risk factors-drugs (access/use), youth in trouble, feeling unsafe, low neighborhood attachment, high arrest rates, neighborhood disorganization, firearms.

2. Family Risk Factors-

   — Structural Variables-Nonintact family, low parental education, family transitions, poverty

   — Social Process Variables-Family management problems, poor attachment to child, low parental supervision, child maltreatment, sibling antisocial behavior, financial stress, parents' proviolent attitudes.
      ▷ Family conflict, child victimization (girls)
      ▷ Teen fatherhood, parental criminality (boys)

3. School Risk Factors-Math (boys), low academic aspirations, low attachment to teachers, low college expectations for child by parent, low commitment to school, negative labeling, feeling unsafe.

4. Peer Risk Factors-delinquent beliefs, delinquent or anti-social peers, preteen stress, early peer deviance, family attachment.

5. Individual Risk Factors-early delinquency/violent behavior, alcohol, drugs, life stressors, violent victimization.

   — Early dating, precocious sexual activity and depression (males),

U.S. Department of Health and Human Services

- ▶ Public Heath Model
- ▶ Need Comprehensive Gang Prevention, Intervention, and Suppression Model (Spergel, 1995).
    - — Social intervention (outreach, crises intervention)
    - — Opportunity Provision (education, job, cultural)
    - — Suppression
    - — Organizational Change Strategies
- ▶ Need Risk-Focused Gang Prevention Programming
    - — California Endowment
- ▶ See National Youth Gang Center Planning Tool.

MOVING RISK FACTORS INTO DEVELOPMENTAL THEORIES OF GANG MEMBERSHIP: HOMEWORK ASSIGNMENT

Please define the following terms/concepts using the article. Additionally, provide one example for each term from your reading. Please bring your homework to the next class!

1. **Youth Gang**

2. **Risk Factors**

3. **Longitudinal Study Research Design(s)**

4. **Ethnographic Study Research Design(s)**

5. Cross-Sectional Study Research Design (s)

NEIGHBORHOOD DISADVANTAGE, SOCIAL CAPITAL, STREET CONTEXT, AND YOUTH VIOLENCE

By Stacy De Coster,
Karen Heimer,
and Stacy M. Wittrock

This article integrates arguments from three perspectives on the relationship between communities and crime—constrained residential choices, social capital, and street context perspectives—to specify a conceptual model of community disadvantage and the violence of individual adolescents. Specifically, we propose that status characteristics (e.g., race, poverty, female headship) restrict the residential choices of families. Residence in extremely disadvantaged communities, in turn, increases the chances of violent behavior by youths by influencing the development and maintenance of community and family social capital, and by influencing the chances that youths are exposed to a criminogenic street context. We assess our conceptual model using community contextual and individual-level data from the National Longitudinal Study of Adolescent Health. Our findings suggest that individual or family status characteristics influence violence largely because of the communities in which disadvantaged persons and families reside. Although we find that

Stacy De Coster, Karen Heimer, Stacy M. Wittrock, "Neighborhood Disadvantage, Social Capital, Street Context, and Youth Violence," *The Sociological Quarterly*, vol. 47, no. 4, pp. 723-753. Copyright © 2006 by John Wiley & Sons, Inc. Reprinted with permission.

community social capital does not predict individual violence, both family social capital and measures of an alternative street milieu are strong predictors of individual violence. Moreover, our street context variables appear to be more important than the social capital variables in explaining how community disadvantage affects violence.

A central focus in contemporary criminology has been identifying structural characteristics of communities that are associated with crime and violence (e.g., Bursik 1984; Taylor and Covington 1988; Bellair 1997; Sampson, Raudenbush, and Earls 1997; Baller et al. 2001; Rosenfeld, Messner, and Baumer 2001; Morenoff, Sampson, and Raudenbush 2001). Most of this research has focused on neighborhood rates of crime.[1] However, recent studies have begun to explore how community-level features impact individuallevel differences in crime and violence (e.g., Simcha-Fagan and Schwartz 1986; Peeples and Loeber 1994; Aneshensel and Sucoff 1996; Elliott et al. 1996; Simons et al. 1996; McNulty and Bellair 2003a,b). An advantage of studies that use community-level as well as individual-level data (i.e., contextual studies) is that they are able to assess the extent to which community characteristics mediate the effects of individual status characteristics, such as race and poverty status, on individual violence.

The issue of whether communities mediate the effects of status characteristics on violence is one that has been at the core of community and crime theorizing for several decades (see Shaw and McKay 1942) and is one that links criminological studies more broadly to research and theorizing on residential segregation (e.g., Wilson 1987; Massey and Denton 1988,1993; Massey 1990). Although it seems to be accepted as a truism that communities play a core role in explaining the effects of race and poverty of individuals on their participation in violence, little research bears directly on this issue because studies that focus on individual violence and crime seldom include measures of community structure. A couple of recent studies have addressed this gap by examining the impact of racialized residence patterns on violence (McNulty and Bellair 2003 a,b). However, research has not yet teased apart how family poverty, as well as race, restricts residence and steers some families into communities that foster violence and crime among youths. This is an important next step, given debates in urban sociology over the relative impact of race versus poverty on residential patterns (e.g., Wilson 1987; Massey and Denton 1988; Massey 1990; Morenoff and Sampson 1997), and macrolevel criminological research that attempts to tease apart the overlapping effects of race and poverty at the neighborhood and city levels of analysis (e.g., Krivo and Peterson 2000; Vélez, Krivo, and Peterson 2003). It also seems important to try to tease apart the contributions of family structure, especially female headship, to restrictions in residential patterns because family structure varies by race and poverty and is influential in the prediction of crime and violence (see Shihadeh and Steffensmeier1994; Parker and Johns 2002).

A second advantage of contextual studies is that they are able to assess the joint effects of proximal (e.g., family and peer contexts) and more distal (e.g., communities) social contexts on the violent behaviors of individuals. The few existing studies of communities and crime that include proximal measures of both social bonds to families and deviant peer associations show that deviant peers are more important than family bonds for understanding the relationship between community characteristics and individual crime (e.g., Elliott et al. 1996; Cattarello 2000; McNulty and Bellair 2003a). This suggests that models of communities and crime that do not include nonconventional relationships and other aspects of an alternative criminal or street context—a context characterized by violent behaviors, opportunities for violence, and embeddedness in violent relationships—may be incomplete. Moreover, theoretical discussions in the community and crime literature suggest the relevance of street context for understanding links between race, community disadvantage, and violence (see Sampson and Wilson 1995; Shihadeh and Flynn 1996; Peterson and Krivo 1999). Yet, recent reviews of the literature continue to lament the lack of empirical attention to criminogenic street contexts and other nonconventional aspects of communities and social relationships (see Sampson et al. 2002; Kubrin and Weitzer 2003a). As such, we specify a model linking community characteristics to individual violence that considers conventional aspects of communities—social capital and social bonds—as well as nonconventional aspects of communities—a criminogenic street context.

Our approach to understanding the relationship between community characteristics and violence uses community-level contextual data and individual-level data to assess the importance of variables derived from three perspectives on the relationship between communities and crime—constrained residential choices, social capital, and street context perspectives. The constrained residential choices perspective suggests that minority and poor individuals will be more likely to engage in violence largely because of residential constraints that concentrate them in disadvantaged communities. The social capital and street context perspectives provide insights into the mechanisms through which these disadvantaged communities lead to individual violence. We add to recent research in this tradition in the following ways. First, we consider the distinct contributions of race, poverty, and female headship to residential patterns, which in turn affect the likelihood of adolescent violence. Second, we incorporate several indicators of a criminogenic street context. Studies assessing the mechanisms linking communities to crime have tended to focus on weak or attenuated conventional culture (e.g., Warner 2003; Browning, Feinberg, and Dietz2004) or to focus rather narrowly on deviant peer associations (see Sampson, Morenoff, and Gonnon-Rowley's 2002 review). We include a set of variables to capture exposure to criminogenic street context and assess whether these variables as a set help to explain the effects of community disadvantage on violence.[2]

We begin by discussing research on the ways in which residential patterns are constrained by individual and family characteristics, such as race, income, and female headship. Next, we discuss theoretical arguments that link residential location—particularly socioeconomic disadvantage of communities—to violent crime and delinquency. In doing this, we highlight arguments from both social capital and street context perspectives. Finally, we derive hypotheses about residential constraints, social capital, and criminogenic street context and test them using panel data from the National Longitudinal Study of Adolescent Health, or Add Health (Udry 2003), which includes data on individuals and on the communities in which they reside.

RACE, POVERTY, AND CONSTRAINED RESIDENTIAL CHOICES

Research in urban sociology shows that residence patterns in the United States are systematically restricted by characteristics of individuals and families (e.g., Wilson 1987; Massey and Gross 1991; Alba and Logan 1993; Massey and Denton 1993; South and Deane 1993). This research often focuses on the racial segregation of disadvantaged urban neighborhoods that arises because of economic constraints and discriminatory practices. For instance, Wilson (1987) proposes that middle-class blacks moved out of urban ghettos when legal barriers to racial segregation were reduced by civil rights legislation, leaving behind the "truly disadvantaged," or the most impoverished black families who did not have the resources to take advantage of opportunities to relocate. Essentially, as legal barriers to discrimination were toppled, black middle-class families who had the resources to relocate migrated out of the most disadvantaged areas in significant numbers; this resulted in the concentration of impoverished black residents in inner cities, who became socially as well as economically isolated (Wilson 1987, 1996).

Bursik and Grasmik (1993) also emphasize the constraints that prevent lower-income families from residing in higher-status communities. Specifically, they discuss instances where residents of high-status areas have successfully attempted to protect the reputation of their communities by making it difficult for lower-income families to maintain homes in their communities. Thus, family economic status plays a role in predicting residential patterns for both economic (lack of financial resources) and social (attempts of local residents to defend territories against lower-class residents) reasons (see Wilson 1987; Bursik and Grasmik 1993). The focus on economics in these discussions, particularly Wilson's (1987), coalesces with what Massey (1985) refers to as the spatial assimilation model of minority residential location (see also Alba, Logan, and Bellair 1994; Logan, Alba, and Leung 1996). This model posits that racial segregation in residential patterns results primarily from racial differences in economic resources.

An alternative model of minority residential location, the place stratification model, posits that black residential location is influenced primarily by discriminatory practices on the part of real estate agents ("the dual housing market"), white residents of areas, banks, and local governments (see Massey and Denton 1988,1993; Logan et al. 1996; Krivo et al. 1998). Consistent with the place stratification model, criminologists have discussed instances in which adult residents of white communities have endorsed the use of delinquency to discourage black families from moving into their communities (see Heitgerd and Bursik 1987; Skogan 1990). These arguments suggest that discriminatory practices and attempts to defend white territories against black families may have hindered the ability of middle-class black families to translate income into residence in more advantaged community locations (see also Massey and Fong 1990; Massey and Gross 1991; South and Deane 1993).

The emphasis on racial discrimination and the inability of middle-class black families to move into advantaged community locales in the place stratification model has been viewed often as a challenge to Wilson's (1987) proposal that middle-class black families have migrated out of disadvantaged, ghetto areas. However, Morenoff and Sampson (1997) provide a resolution to this discrepancy by differentiating between core ghetto areas and areas that lie on the periphery of these ghetto areas. Whereas impoverished black families are likely to reside in the core ghetto, black families with financial resources may migrate out to the periphery of the ghetto, which remains highly segregated. Such a pattern suggests that Wilson's (1987, 1996) argument that impoverished blacks are socially isolated is not necessarily at odds with the argument that racial discrimination produces and reinforces residential segregation.

In sum, previous research and theorizing has forged links between the status characteristics of individuals or families and the characteristics of communities. Specifically, research indicates that impoverished and black families are likely to reside in disadvantaged areas—characterized by extreme poverty, welfare dependency, isolation from conventional role models, and disproportionately high rates of female-headed households (e.g., Wilson 1987; Massey and Denton 1993; Krivo et al. 1998). These areas are characterized also by high rates of crime and violence (e.g., Liska and Bellair 1995; Morenoff and Sampson 1997; South and Messner 2000). A core premise of research and theorizing on communities and crime is that the relationship between the structural characteristics of a neighborhood and crime rates in the neighborhood are not simply a reflection of the characteristics of the people residing in these areas (e.g., Shaw and McKay 1942; Bursik and Grasmick 1993). Instead, the structural characteristics of the neighborhoods in which impoverished and black individuals and families are able to make their residence are central for understanding why these individuals become involved in crime and violence (e.g., Shihadeh and Flynn 1996; Peterson and Krivo 1999; Vélezetal. 2003).[3]

The most direct way to assess this premise is to evaluate the extent to which the effects of individual status characteristics on individual violence are explained by measures of neighborhood disadvantage. Until recently, surprisingly few studies examined both individual and neighborhood contextual effects, perhaps because of the paucity of data containing information on both individuals and communities. Recent works by McNulty and Bellair (2003a,b), however, have begun to examine how individual and community characteristics work together, particularly with regard to the interplay between individual's racial statuses and neighborhood disadvantage. More specifically, McNulty and Bellair (2003a,b) show that the association between race (black versus white) and violent delinquency is accounted for by neighborhood disadvantage. This research is an important first step. However, better understanding the link between individual and community-level processes requires consideration of the impact of poverty as well as race and family structure in shaping residential patterns and violence. This is especially important given ensuing debates concerning whether poverty and/ or family structure explain the impact of race on residence (e.g., Wilson 1987; Massey 1990) and/or violence (e.g., Shihadeh and Steffensmeier 1994; Krivo and Peterson 2000; Parker and Johns 2002; Vélezetal 2003).

Whereas macrolevel studies often cannot disentangle the separate effects of race, poverty, and female headship on crime (Land et al. 1990), it is possible to disentangle these effects at the individual level, given the large samples included in recent self report surveys. In this study, we use data from the Add Health survey to examine the non-overlapping effects of racial status, family poverty, and female headship on residence in extremely disadvantaged communities, which may increase the likelihood that youths are exposed to and engage in violence, all else constant. The question then becomes, how precisely is disadvantaged community context translated into the violence of individuals?

THE TRANSLATION OF COMMUNITY DISADVANTAGE INTO INDIVIDUAL VIOLENCE

Social Capital and Informal Social Controls

The question of how community disadvantage translates into individual violence has been the focus of much theory and research on communities and crime. In discussing the mechanisms through which community characteristics influence violence and crime, theoretical arguments often emphasize the importance of formal and informal community controls (e.g., Shaw and McKay 1942; Sampson and Groves 1989; Gottfredson et al. 1991; Bursik and Grasmick 1993; Sampson et al. 1997). Specifically, these arguments propose that formal and informal mechanisms of social control break down in urban communities and in communities characterized by concentrated disadvantage and social isolation.

This general argument is central to social disorganization theory (Shaw and McKay 1942; Sampson and Groves 1989), the systemic model (Kasarda and Janowitz 1974; Bursik and Grasmick 1993), and perspectives that focus on community social capital (Sampson and Wilson 1995) and collective efficacy (Sampson 1997; Sampson et al. 1997). For present purposes, we draw on the concept of social capital because it dovetails with our emphasis on the importance of both community and family contexts for understanding individual violence. In fact, Coleman (1990:300) defines social capital as the relationships between actors that "in here in family relations and in community organizations and that are useful for the cognitive or social development of a child or young person." Thus, this concept encompasses both community and family relations.

Generally, community social capital consists of interrelations or ties between families or individuals within a community. Some key dimensions of community-based social capital include the closure of social networks, community supervision, and the connectedness of individuals in the community (see Coleman 1988; Sampson 1997; Short 1997; Kubrin and Weitzer 2003a). An example of closure would be a case in which a youth's parents are friends with the parents of the youth's friends (Coleman 1988). In this case, the parents can share the task of supervision and parenting. Community supervision similarly entails the sharing of supervisory tasks among residents in a community. This concept, however, focuses more broadly on the ability and willingness of community residents to supervise the behavior of residents through informal surveillance and direct intervention (see Bursik and Grasmick 1993). Finally, the social connectedness of individuals in communities can be found in organizational participation and in community friendships (Sampson 1997). These community-based forms of social capital are the fundamental components of social organization emphasized in Shaw and McKay's (1942) social disorganization theory.

In the family context, social capital consists of interrelations or ties between individuals within a family. For instance, Coleman (1990) discusses intergenerational closure, or relationships between parents and children within a family, as an important component of familial social capital. Such social relationships parallel the emotional attachments between parents and children emphasized in Hirschi's (1969) social control theory (see Hagan, MacMillan, and Wheaton 1996). Thus, the mechanisms linking community structure to individual violence in a social capital model combine arguments from social disorganization theory at the community level and social control theory at the individual level. These mechanisms parallel also the concepts of private and parochial control emphasized in Bursik and Grasmick's (1993) systemic model of social disorganization. Family social capital is a rather clear example of private control because this control is grounded on intimate, primary groups and is achieved through the threatened withdrawal or allocation of social support and sentiment (see Hunter 1985; Bursik and Grasmick 1993). Community-based capital is more consistent with parochial control because this control—including supervision of local teens and participation in organizations—relies on the relatively weak ties of secondary groups.

Overall, our discussion of social capital encompasses arguments from social disorganization, social control, and systemic theories of crime. In doing so, this model posits that structural aspects of communities either facilitate or inhibit the creation of community based and family-based social capital, which in turn affect individual participation in violence.

Criminal or Street Context

In line with the social capital approach, Anderson's (1997, 1999) ethnographic research on inner-city ghetto communities highlights the role of family processes in mediating the relationship between communities and violence. Specifically, his research shows that in the most disadvantaged areas of the inner-city ghettos, "decent" parents compensate for problems in the community by giving their children a clear message of their care and concern. Anderson (1999) notes, however, that youth from decent homes eventually must learn to deal with the reality of the streets, which can undermine significantly the ability of parents and families to control youth. This does not imply that the family is not an efficacious force in the inner city. It does suggest, however, that the effects of family-based social capital may be diminished by exposure to the street.

Anderson (1999) emphasizes that this street context is produced by the structural problems of the inner city. Specifically, concentrated disadvantage and social isolation from conventional institutions produce a context in which violence becomes a central component of life. Some of the important elements of this street milieu include the experience of and exposure to violence. When discussing exposure to violence, Anderson notes that younger children often witness the disputes of older people, which are resolved regularly through aggression and violence. These disputes teach youth that "might makes right," thereby promoting their own use of violence in future situations.

In addition to witnessing violence, youth in disadvantaged areas often experience violence at the hands of others in the community. It is not surprising, therefore, that an additional element of the street culture is a sense of hopelessness based on the belief among community youth that they could die violently at a young age. Indeed, Anderson (1999) notes that youth in the most disadvantaged communities readily accept this fate, which allows them to live on the edge and engage in behaviors, such as violence, without considering the effects that such behaviors may have on their futures.

Sampson's (1997) statements about the importance of culture in linking communities to crime are consistent with the aspects of criminogenic street context discussed thus far. Specifically, he proposes that youth in disadvantaged communities are likely to see violence as a way of life because they are likely to have role models who do not control their own violence and are likely also to witness violent acts in their community. To this, Sampson (1997) adds that the availability of and easy access to firearms and other weapons in disadvantaged communities increases the chances that youth will experiment with violence (see also Anderson 1999).

Each of these arguments can be viewed as consistent with traditional learning theories of crime (Sutherland 1947; Akers 1998). Easy access to firearms provides the opportunity for youth to engage in violence, and witnessing role models engage in violence likely provides them with techniques and definitions of violence. An additional element of street context is the embeddedness of youth in relationships that promote violence, which can be conceptualized as associations with deviant or criminal peers (see also Hagan and McCarthy 1997).

Overall, this discussion proposes that a criminogenic street context may emerge in extremely disadvantaged communities as a byproduct of poverty and other problems in the community. The street milieu—which increases the chances of embeddedness in deviant peer relationships, easy access to firearms, witnessing street violence, personal experiences with violent victimization, expectations that future victimization could result in death—subsequently impedes the ability of "decent" families to control the violent behaviors of youths. This underscores the combined importance of community, family, and peer contexts for understanding violent delinquency.

HYPOTHESES

In the remainder of this article, we draw from the literature discussed previously to propose and test hypotheses about variation in serious violent delinquency. We begin with the expectation—based on much individual-level research on delinquency—that youths' violence will be associated with individual and family characteristics, such as race, ethnicity, female headship, and family socioeconomic disadvantage, as well as age and sex. A major question of our study is whether the associations between these factors and violence are in part because of their impact on residence patterns, specifically on residence in disadvantaged communities. In other words, we are interested in assessing the assertion that the effects of individual and family status characteristics on violence are explained partially by residence in disadvantaged communities. While this is a common assertion, research has not yet thoroughly addressed whether or not community disadvantage can account for the separate effects of race, poverty status, and family structure on adolescent violence. Thus, we assess the following hypothesis:

Hypothesis One: The effects of individual and family status characteristics—especially family disadvantage, female headship, race, and ethnicity—on violent delinquency will be reduced when a measure of community disadvantage is added to the model.

Following the recent burgeoning of research on social capital and crime, we expect that when parents participate in community organizations, neighbors help to supervise youths, and parents know their children's friends and friends' parents (i.e., high network closure), youths will be less likely to engage in serious violence. Connections between individuals within families, or family social bonding from a control theory perspective, can be considered a form of social capital and should reduce the chances of violence by youths. These effects should emerge beyond the effects of individual characteristics, family disadvantage, and community disadvantage. Furthermore, following other research (e.g., Sampson and Groves 1989; McNulty and Bellair 2003b; Sampson 2004), we expect these social capital variables to help account for the effect of residing in socially and economically disadvantaged locales. This is because concentrated social and economic disadvantage may undermine the formation of social capital because families in these communities may lack the resources and institutional support needed to invest in social ties at the family and/or community level (Coleman 1988; see also Sampson et al. 1997; Sampson and Raudenbush 1999; Morenoff et al. 2001). This lack of social capital and informal social control subsequently frees youth in structurally disadvantaged communities to engage in violence and crime. This discussion generates the following hypothesis:

> Hypothesis Two: Family-based and community-based social capital—network closure, community participation, collective supervision, and family cohesiveness—will reduce the chances that youths engage in violence and will reduce the effect of disadvantaged communities on violence.

We also expect that youths who encounter criminogenic street contexts will be more prone to violence than other youths. Based on the literature reviewed previously, we consider criminogenic street contexts to include the presence of deviant peers, easy accessibility of guns, and a violent street environment that, following Anderson (1999), can be expected to result in youths' witnessing episodes of serious street violence, being subject to past violent victimization, and generally, expecting that life might be cut short by violent victimization in the future. Youths who encounter elements of this criminogenic context can be expected to be more likely than other youths to aggress and to solve problems with violence. Moreover, the work of Anderson and others suggests that this criminogenic street context is more likely to arise in extremely disadvantaged communities (Wilson 1987; Fagan and Wilkinson 1998). Specifically, Anderson (1999) proposes that people in disadvantaged and socially isolated communities are acutely aware that society has forgotten them and denies them access to legitimate means of resolving conflicts and problems, and this can lead to the emergence of a street context that promotes the use of violence to respond to conflicts (see also Kubrin and Weitzer 2003b). Youth and families in disadvantaged areas are exposed to this street environment on a daily basis. Although "decent" families may try to protect their children from the lessons of the street through the development of strong relationships, they constantly are in competition with the pervasive street environment. Despite the recent popularity of this argument, there is limited quantitative research on the links between community disadvantage, criminogenic street context, and serious violence by individual youths. From this literature, we derive and test the following hypothesis:

> Hypothesis Three: Exposure to elements of criminogenic street contexts—deviant peers, easy access to guns, witnessing serious street violence, experiencing violent victimization in the past, and expecting that future violent victimizations could be lethal—will increase the chances that youths engage in violent delinquency and will reduce the effect of disadvantaged communities on violence.

DATA, MEASUREMENT, AND MODEL SPECIFICATION

Data

We assess these predictions using the data from the National Longitudinal Study of Adolescent Health, or the Add Health Study (Udry 2003). Add Health is a nationally representative, probability-based survey of U.S. adolescents in grades 7 through 12 between 1994 and 1996 (Harris et al. 2003). These data are particularly well suited for our study because they include individual-level information on individual and family status characteristics, community characteristics, social capital, aspects of criminogenic street context, and self-reported violent delinquency. The data also include community-level information on census tracts in which individuals are located, which allow us to link individual characteristics with a measure of community disadvantage. Finally, we exploit the longitudinal nature of the data by assessing the effects of variables capturing individual and family characteristics, community disadvantage, social capital, and street context at wave 1 on subsequent violence measured at wave 2.

Add Health is based on a multistage cluster design in which the clusters were sampled with an unequal probability (Chantala and Tabor 1999). At the first stage, 80 high schools and 52 middle schools ("feeder schools") were sampled with replacement in 1994 and 1995. At the second stage of sampling, individual adolescents and parents were sampled from the school rosters and from those identified at the first stage, and were administered the wave 1 in-home questionnaire in 1995. The response rate for the wave 1 in-home questionnaire was 78.9 percent. The wave 2 in-home questionnaire was administered in 1996 to adolescents only. The attrition rate from wave 1 to wave 2 was 28.3 percent and 13,750 youths completed the wave 2 interview (Harris et al. 2003). The Add Health study design incorporates systematic sampling methods and implicit stratification to ensure that this sample of respondents are representative of U.S. schools in terms of region of the country, urbanicity, school type, ethnicity, and school size (Harris et al. 2003). In all of our analyses, we use the sample weights provided with the data, which are designed to account for the sampling design as well as the attrition from wave 1 to 2.[4]

We use variables from the first two waves (1995–1996) of the in-home questionnaire data, from the youth and parent interviews. In addition, we use the contextual data (from the Census and other agencies) on the tracts in which respondents reside. The inclusion of both of these sources of data—individual as well as independent measures of community-level characteristics—is an important strength of the Add Health for our study. We use the data from the 11,207 individuals who remain after listwise deletion of missing data.

Measurement of Variables

We present estimates for a series of five models. Each model adds a block of covariates, corresponding to our theoretical predictions. Appendix A contains descriptions of these variables and Appendix B reports descriptive statistics. Our first model includes variables that represent individual and family status characteristics, as well as other control variables. We include the following individual and family characteristics, all measured at wave 1: youth's race (black or other), Latino ethnicity, residence in a female-headed household, parents' high school education, the family's receipt of public assistance, gender, and age.[5] All of these variables, with the exception of age, are binary. Black racial status is coded 1 if the youth reports that she/he is African American or black and 0 otherwise. Latino ethnicity is coded 1 if the youth reports that she/he is Latino and 0 otherwise. Residence in a female-headed household is coded 1 if the respondent reported living with only a residential mother, aunt, grandmother, or any combination of the three, and if there was no male adult present in the household.[6] Parents' high school education or less is coded 1 if the parent respondent reports that the highest level of education achieved by her/himself or her/his spouse is a high school degree or less. Receipt of public assistance is coded 1 if parents reported at least one of the following conditions, and 0 otherwise: parent or spouse received public assistance, generally; any member of the household received Aid to Families with Dependent Children (AFDC) in the last month; any member of the household received food stamps in the last month;

and any member of the household received a housing subsidy or lived in public housing in the last month. Gender is coded 1 for male, 0 for female.[7] Age ranges from 12 to 21.

Our second block of variables, all measured at the level of the census tract and drawn from government data, is designed to capture neighborhood context.[8] Here we include a binary variable coded 1 if the respondent lives in an urban neighborhood, and 0 otherwise. We also include a variable created through principal components analysis that includes indicators associated with high levels of community disadvantage, following previous research (e.g., Wilson 1987; Land, McCall, and Cohen 1990; Krivo and Peterson 1996; Sampson et al. 1997; Morenoff, Sampson, and Raudenbush 2001). The variables that are entered into our principal components score include the proportion of the population that is black, proportion of households that are female headed, proportion of ever married men who are divorced or separated, total unemployment rate, male unemployment rate, median household income, and proportion of the population with income below the poverty line. This index has a Cronbach's alpha of 0.74. Our construction of this index follows other studies' measures of economic disadvantage (e.g., Sampson et al. 1997; Sampson and Morenoff 2004) and adds theoretically relevant variables capturing the presence of employed and married adult male role models.[9]

The next model that we estimate adds youth's prior serious violence to the covariates described previously. This is a composite variable that captures the range of youths' serious violent offending before the wave 1 interview (see Appendix A for further details). We include this variable because it affords some control for unmeasured, unchanging characteristics of individuals, and thus results in a conservative estimate of the associations between variables in our model than would be possible if we omitted a measure of prior violence.[10] This includes self-reports of the following types of violence (see Appendix A for full description): engaged in a serious fight during the previous 12 months; used or threatened to use a weapon to get something from someone during the previous 12 months; hurt someone badly enough to need bandages or care from a doctor or nurse during the previous 12 months; shot or stabbed someone during the previous 12 months; ever used a weapon in a fight. Add Health contains only categorical information on youths' self-reported violence, and most youths reported that they had engaged in the forms of serious violence listed previously either one or two times in the past year (one of the categorical choices in the Add Health interview), or not at all in the past year. We therefore created a 0 to 1 variable for each type of violence, with 0 corresponding to no serious violence in the past year, and 1 corresponding to 1 or more violent delinquent acts in the past year. We then summed across the five types of serious violence to produce a serious violence index comprising six categories, ranging from 0 to 5. This violence index thus captures the range of youths' involvement in forms of serious violence. As we discuss later, we also discuss results from supplementary analyses in which the outcome variables are the separate measures contained in the violence index.

We next estimate a model that adds a set of variables capturing conventional social capital at the wave 1 interview. These variables are designed to measure network closure, parents' participation in organizations, collective supervision, and family cohesiveness. We measure network closure using the parent's report of how many parents of her/his child's friends she/he has talked to in the four weeks preceding the interview. This is the same variable that Coleman (1988) identifies as a good measure of this concept. Parental participation in organizations is a four-item composite variable measured by the parent's report of being a member of different community organizations or participating in fund-raising at his/her child's school. Collective supervision is a two-item composite variable that includes the parent respondent's report of whether neighbors share in the supervision of children in the neighborhood, following previous research (e.g., Sampson and Groves 1989). Specifically, we use the parent's response to items asking whether she/he would tell a neighbor if she/he saw the neighbor's child getting into trouble, and whether she/he thought the neighbor would do the same. We create a family cohesiveness variable using a principal components analysis that combines the youth's wave 1 self-reports about attention received from the family, understanding by the family, and having fun with the family. The Cronbach alpha for this principle component is 0.78.

Finally, we estimate a model that adds variables that capture different aspects of criminogenic street context, all measured at wave 1.[11] We specify these variables at wave 1 to ensure that the temporal ordering matches the causal ordering of our theoretical arguments. We first include deviant peer associations, measured by youths' reports of their friends' use of drugs, alcohol, and cigarettes. While this measure does not capture associations with violent peers (and such a measure is not available in the Add Health), exposure to peers who engage in deviance in any form—even substance use—is an important dimension of a criminogenic context. Moreover, research on the generality of deviance shows that youths who use controlled substances are more likely than other youths to engage in other types of crime, including violence (e.g., Osgood et al. 1988).

We measure the accessibility of guns as a binary variable, through youths' self-reports that they have "easy" access to guns in their homes. This is not simply a measure of gun availability, but rather captures youths' perceptions that they have "easy" access to guns in their homes. We also include a binary variable capturing youths' self-reports of witnessing serious street violence (i.e., a stabbing) in the year prior to the wave 2 interviews.[12] Expectation of lethal violence is measured by youths' perceptions of the likelihood that they could die from a serious violent victimization by age 21. Finally, we include a composite variable capturing youths' experiences with serious violent victimization, including being stabbed or shot in the past year.

Our outcome variable, involvement in serious violent delinquency during the year between the wave 1 and wave 2 interviews, is measured identically to the measure of prior serious violence and comprises a six-point ordinal scale, as described above.

Again, this variable captures the range of involvement in serious violent offenses and captures important differences in involvement in violence across individuals.

Model Specification and Estimation

Three basic features of the data must be accounted for in our statistical models: First, the dependent variable is measured on a six-category ordinal scale; it is therefore more appropriate to use an ordinal-response rather than a continuous-response regression model. Second, the sampling design uses schools as the primary sampling units, which produces potential within-cluster correlation. Third, we must incorporate sampling weights to account for the unequal weights probability sampling. To account for all three features of these data, we weight the data and use generalized estimating equations to estimate correlated response ordinal logit models in our analyses of serious violence (Lipsitz, Kim, and Zhao 1994).

To be more specific, we define Yh(i) to be the six-category ordinal response for the hth respondent within school i (i.e., cluster i). The response distributions are modeled as functions of covariates {xh(i)} through the ordinal logit regression model:

$$\log \text{odds } (Yh(i) > k) = \beta k + \beta xh(i), k = 0,1,2,3,4; h = 1,\ldots, ni; I = 1, \ldots, 147.$$

Here, β is the vector of regression coefficients. We use generalized estimating equations that are identical to the multinomial likelihood equations that treat all *n1* + ... + n147 = 11,207 observations as independent and weight each contribution according to its sampling weight. These estimates of β from the estimating equation are consistent, even when there is significant within-cluster correlation (Lipsitz et al. 1994). We compute estimates of standard errors that are valid when there is within-cluster correlation using an empirically adjusted covariance matrix. We used SAS GENMOD to estimate our models.

To assess the robustness of our findings using the index of violence, we also report the results of logistic regression analyses on two of the violent acts included in the index—engaging in a serious fight and shooting or stabbing someone in the past 12 months. We use the same procedures discussed previously in estimating these models.

RESULTS

The results of our analyses provide general support for the arguments we develop above. To summarize, our results suggest that individuals and families may be constrained in their residential choices, and this has some consequences for violent delinquency. In addition, aspects of both conventional social capital and criminogenic street contexts influence the likelihood of violence. We present our findings in Table 1.

We begin by discussing model 1, which reveals how violence varies across race, ethnicity, family disadvantage, and sex. Specifically, the results for model 1 show that blacks, Latinos, and men are more likely than their comparison groups to have been involved in a broader range of serious violence, measured at wave 2. Youths from disadvantaged families—those that are female headed, receive public assistance, and that are headed by adults whose highest education is a high school degree or less—are also likely to have higher scores on our wave 2 violence measure than other youths.

Model 2 shows that although urban residence has no effect, community disadvantage has a significant effect on serious violent delinquency that is beyond the effects of the variables in model 1. Moreover, adding community disadvantage to the equation appears to result in some decreases in the effects of the individual and family characteristics on violence reported in model 1. The most notable decrease is the effect of race, but there also appear to be some decreases in the effects of Latino ethnicity, family's receipt of public assistance, and parents' education. The implication of this, consistent with our discussion of the literature, is that minorities and disadvantaged families experience constrained residential choices and are more likely to reside in disadvantaged communities, which in turn translates into a higher likelihood of youth violence.

Beyond this, we note that the effects of several youth and family disadvantage variables continue to be associated with violent delinquency, even after community disadvantage is controlled. Model 2 shows that Latino youths and those from female-headed families receiving public assistance are more likely to be violent than their counterparts, regardless of whether they live in an extremely disadvantaged community.

Model 3 adds youths' prior involvement in serious violence. Not surprisingly, the association between prior violence and subsequent violence is highly significant, consistent with the stability of delinquency demonstrated in previous research. Moreover, once prior violence is controlled, the associations between violence and Latino ethnicity, public assistance, and female headship become non significant. This makes sense, given the high level of stability in violence across the two waves and the association between ethnicity and family disadvantage reported in model 1. Nevertheless, we note that the association between community disadvantage and violence remains statistically significant (model 3). This is an important finding. Even after taking account of individuals' own propensity for violence as measured by past behavior (and thus accounting for unmeasured, unchanging characteristics of individuals), youths who live in more disadvantaged communities are more likely than youths in other neighborhoods to score higher on our measure of serious violent delinquency at wave 2. The coefficient associated with residence in a disadvantaged community in model 3 indicates that a standard deviation increase in the principal component score for disadvantaged communities is associated with a multiplicative change of about 1.09 (or 9 percent increase) in the odds that youths will engage in more serious violence, even when all of the other variables in this model are controlled.

Model 4 adds our variables designed to capture conventional social capital. Counter to our expectation, we find no significant effects of network closure, parental participation in community organizations, or collective supervision on the range of violent offending of youth. We note, however, that the weak associations between these variables and youths' violence are not entirely inconsistent with previous research. Indeed, Warner and Wilcox Rountree (1997) note that "while acceptance of the importance of local social ties seems strong within modern social disorganization theory, there really is quite limited support for this assumption" (p. 522). To the extent that there is support for social ties, it may be limited to property crimes. For instance, the structural-level study of Sampson and Groves (1989) found stronger effects of social capital variables on property crime than on violent crime. Similarly, Johnstone (1978) reported that family status better explained violent crime than did community status. Such findings have prompted some researchers to suggest that community-based social capital may be less important for predicting violent crimes than it is for predicting property crimes (see Bursik and Grasmick 1993; Peeples and Loeber 1994).

Table 1. Parameter Estimates for the Ordinal Logistic Regression Model of Violent Delinquency

Variables	Model 1	Model 2	Model 3	Model 4	Model 5
Individual/family characteristics					
Youth's sex (male)	0.974*** (0.058)	0.976*** (0.058)	0.592*** (0.073)	0.651*** (0.075)	0.690*** (0.077)
Youth's black racial status	0.163* (0.082)	0.027 (0.095)	-0.171 (0.108)	-0.126(0.107)	-0.028(0.106)
Youth's Latino ethnicity	0.300*** (0.087)	0.239** (0.085)	0.156(0.086)	0.165(0.089)	0.169(0.088)
Youth's age	-0.034 (0.020)	-0.032 (0.020)	-0.039* (0.020)	-0.060** (0.020)	-0.126*** (0.024)
Female-headed household	0.243** (0.080)	0.218** (0.081)	0.083 (0.081)	0.055 (0.079)	0.000 (0.078)
Parent education high school or less	0.185* (0.081)	0.151 (0.082)	0.072 (0.084)	0.067 (0.084)	0.071 (0.083)
Parent receiving public assistance	0.334*** (0.100)	0.265** (0.098)	0.140(0.069)	0.114(0.114)	0.117(0.114)
Neighborhood context					
Urban neighborhood		0.092 (0.072)	0.048 (0.487)	0.041 (0.067)	0.050 (0.069)
Community disadvantage		1.989** (0.674)	1.498* (0.728)	1.503* (0.716)	1.055 (0.696)
Involvement in prior violence					
Youth's involvement in prior violence			0.970*** (0.033)	0.938*** (0.033)	0.817*** (0.035)
Conventional social capital					
Network closure				0.004(0.018)	0.004(0.019)

Parents' participation in organizations	-0.066 (0.040)	-0.051 (0.040)
Collective supervision	0.002 (0.044)	0.006 (0.046)
Family cohesiveness	-5.363*** (0.927)	-3.779*** (0.934)
Criminogenic street context		
Deviant peer associations		0.356*** (0.036)
Accessibility of guns		0.038 (0.092)
Witness serious violence		0.427*** (0.093)
Expectation of lethal victimization		0.002 (0.047)
Past violent victimization		0.184 (0.119)

*p< 0.05, **p< 0.01, ***p < 0.001.

Note: Standard errors are in parentheses.

N= 11,207.

Yet, we find that family cohesiveness has a substantial deterrent effect on youth violence, which offers partial support for Hypothesis 2 (model 4). Our findings regarding the set of social capital variables are generally consistent with Hirschi's (1969) social control theory and with Bursik and Grasmick's (1993) conclusion that private controls, or controls within primary groups, may be more important for predicting crime and violence than are parochial controls, or controls within secondary community groups. We discuss this issue further in the conclusions.

Overall, our measures of social capital do not appear to add much to our understanding of the link between community disadvantage and adolescent violence; indeed the coefficient associated with community disadvantage in model 3 is very similar to the coefficient in model 4, which adds the social capital variables.

Our fully specified model—model 5—is reported in the last column of Table 1. This model adds the variables we use to capture criminogenic street context. As we discussed previously, these variables rarely are included in research on communities and crime, and when they are included, they are not viewed as a set capturing street context but are treated more as control variables. The results from model 5 show that consistent with Hypothesis 3, two important aspects of street context have strong significant effects on the range of involvement in violent delinquency. First, we find that youth who are more embedded in deviant peer groups at wave 1 are more likely to engage in a range of violent acts at wave 2. This is the case even though our measure of peer deviance captures illicit substance use by youths' friends and not violent behavior. Indeed, a standard deviation unit increase in associations with deviant friends is associated with an increase of about 1.36 times (or 36 percent) in the odds that youths will subsequently commit serious violence. Second, we find that having witnessed serious violence (in the form of a stabbing) strongly increases the chances that youth report involvement in a range of violent acts.[13] Youths who reported witnessing serious violence at wave 1 are about 1.53 times (or 53 percent) more likely to report violent delinquency at wave 2 than youths who did not previously witness serious violence, even after previous violence and the other variables in the model are controlled.

We do not, however, find a significant relationship between violence and easy access to guns in the home. It may be that youths often obtain guns and other weapons from places other than home, which is not captured in our measure. We also do not find associations, net of the other variables in the model, between violent behavior and youths' expectations of lethal victimization or their previous experiences with serious violent victimization (i.e., being shot or stabbed).

The results from model 5 also show that the association between family bonds and youths' violence remains significant after the street-context variables are taken into account. Although the effect of family bonds clearly is diminished compared with its effects in model 4, it remains strong and a standard deviation unit increase in the principal components score for cohesive families translates into an decrease of about 15 percent in the odds that youths engage in future violent delinquency. In short, our findings suggest that families are somewhat efficacious in control ling violence, even when competing with the influences of the street. However, while a standard deviation unit increase in family cohesiveness reduces the odds of violence by about 15 percent, recall that witnessing violence and a standard deviation unit increase in deviant peer associations increase the chances of violence by 53 and 36 percent, respectively. We view these as important findings, considering that studies of communities and crime focus predominantly on the mediating effects of concepts related to social control— i.e., social capital and collective efficacy—without much consideration afforded to sub cultural or street context variables (see Sampson et al.'s 2002 review).

We note that the effects of community disadvantage are finally reduced to non significance once the street-context variables are controlled (model 5). This suggests that fully understanding the effects of structural disadvantage on violence requires considering youths' exposure to elements of criminogenic street context. The only individual characteristics that remain significantly associated with violence after our social process variables are considered are age and gender. This is consistent with the many studies that note that men and younger adolescents are consistently involved in more delinquency, even after social factors are taken into account.

Supplementary Analyses

To assess the robustness of our findings using the violence index, we repeated our analyses using the separate variables comprising the index as outcomes. Each of these was specified as a binary variable, as discussed previously. We report two of these models in Table 2, engaging in a serious fight and shooting or stabbing someone, which are the least serious and most serious items in the index, respectively. Our analyses of all of items comprising the index produce results very similar to those reported in Table 2. These supplementary analyses show clearly the same pattern of results reported in the final model of Table 1. These findings thus indicate that the story that unfolds in the analysis of our violence index holds for all of the individual forms of violence comprising our index.

CONCLUSIONS

The findings from our study suggest that violent delinquency is largely a product of individual status characteristics, family disadvantage, community disadvantage, weakened family bonds, and exposure to some elements of a criminogenic street milieu. More specifically, we find evidence consistent with the argument that minorities and disadvantaged families experience constrained residential choices, resulting in a greater likelihood of residing in disadvantaged communities. Living in these communities subsequently translates into a higher likelihood of youth violence.

Table 2. Parameter Estimates for the Logistic Regression of Select Individual Violence Items

Variables	Serious fight	Shot/stabbed
Individual/family characteristics		
Youth's sex (Male)	0.585*** (0.078)	1.403*** (0.246)
Youth's black racial status	-0.183(0.115)	0.493(0.271)
Youth's Latino ethnicity	0.202* (0.099)	0.338 (0.288)
Youth's age	-0.109*** (0.025)	-0.140(0.079)
Female-headed household	0.020 (0.086)	-0.149(0.234)
Parent education high school or less	0.013(0.082)	0.308 (0.230)
Parent receiving public assistance	0.103(0.119)	0.007 (0.247)
Neighborhood context		
Urban neighborhood	-0.008(0.072)	0.320 (0.263)
Community disadvantage	0.765 (0.646)	1.984(2.217)
Involvement in prior violence		
Youth's involvement in prior violence	0.716*** (0.051)	0.463*** (0.080)
Conventional social capital		
Network closure	0.013(0.020)	-0.042 (0.065)
Parents' participation in organizations	-0.057(0.044)	0.049(0.118)
Collective supervision	0.010(0.048)	0.099(0.157)

Family cohesiveness	-3.749*** (1.086)	-6.625* (2.881)
Criminogenic street context		
Deviant peer associations	0.310*** (0.042)	0.544*** (0.109)
Accessibility of guns	0.001 (0.096)	-0.093(0.252)
Witness serious violence	0.452*** (0.114)	0.853*** (0.233)
Expectation of lethal victimization	-0.025(0.049)	-0.005(0.104)
Past violent victimization	-0.052(0.141)	0.109(0.258)

*p< 0.05, **p< 0.01, ***p< 0.001.

Note: Numbers in parentheses are standard errors.

Our exploration of the link between community disadvantage and violence shows that our measures of community social capital are relatively unimportant for understanding the relationship between community disadvantage and youth violence. None of our variables tapping direct experiences with elements of community social capital are associated with youth violence. Family cohesiveness does curb youth violence, however.

It is possible that our findings about the effects of community social capital may have been different if we had access to community-level measures of social capital—such as the densities of ties within neighborhoods and pervasiveness of collective supervision (Sampson et al. 2002). Unfortunately, there were very few individuals in many of the census tracts in Add Health, which precludes aggregating the data from individuals to develop reliable measures of community-level social capital. Yet, this is an important issue to consider in future data collection efforts. There may be instances in which families are not embedded within the social relationships within their community, even though there are strong community relationships surrounding them. And the likelihood of violence among adolescents whose families are embedded in community relationships in tight-knit communities may differ from the likelihood of violence among those whose families are not embedded in community relationships within the same tight-knit communities. Fully assessing this possibility, which bears out in ethnographic research (see Furstenberg et al. 1999), would require studying the interaction between individual-level reports of family's ties and a measure of aggregate strength of family ties at the community level.

Future research linking community disadvantage to violence by individual youth may also want to consider including additional measures of social ties. In particular, such research could incorporate measures of the extent to which families and communities are mobilized to enact social ties for the good of the community (e.g., Sampson et al. 1997), as well as measures of public social ties—ties between communities and external resources (e.g., Vélez 2001). Inclusion of these measures may show that social ties are more important for understanding links between community disadvantage and violence by youth than what our study reports.

Although we did not find that youths who directly experienced higher levels of community social capital were less violent than other youths, our analysis did support our hypothesis about exposure to criminogenic street context. Specifically, youths who have more deviant friends and have witnessed violence are more likely to engage in serious violence. Moreover, our set of variables capturing criminogenic street context together reduce the association between community disadvantage and youth violence to non significance. Therefore, understanding the links between community disadvantage and violence seems to require careful consideration of exposure to criminogenic street context. Future research should go beyond existing work to develop a more thorough assessment of the important elements of criminogenic street context and to move beyond individual exposure to try to assess whether individual-and community-level norms and beliefs about appropriate uses of violence play a part in linking community disadvantage to violence.

The findings from the present study contribute to the literature in several ways. First, we go beyond existing macro level research to show that the relationship between violence and individual level, race, ethnicity, poverty, parents' education, and female headship can be explained in part by the types of communities in which families and individuals reside. Although there is widespread acceptance among criminologists that community structural disadvantage creates race, ethnicity, and poverty differences in violence, empirical research has not thoroughly examined whether community-level measures of disadvantage (measured apart from individuals' perceptions of disadvantage) do indeed account for variations across race, ethnicity, and family disadvantage in violence measured at the individual level.

More specifically, we show that race (black compared to nonblack) differences in violence result largely because of residence in disadvantaged communities. This individual-level finding is at least consistent with the arguments of macro level criminologists about the strong association between racial composition and poverty rates of communities (e.g., Krivo and Peterson 2000). By contrast, we find that residence in disadvantaged communities does not fully explain the effect of family disadvantage—measured by female headship, low levels of parent education, and family receipt of welfare—on participation in violent delinquency. Disentangling of the effects of race and family disadvantage or poverty as we have done here represents another contribution of this research.

A second contribution of our findings is that they highlight the importance of exposure to criminogenic street context in studies of communities and crime. As we noted previously, the effects of community disadvantage on violence are finally reduced to nonsignificance in our final model, which adds our street-context variables. Strong family cohesiveness reduces violence but does not appear to explain the negative consequences of extreme community disadvantage. This suggests that family bonds do not operate in isolation but combine with elements of a criminogenic street context to explain variation in violence across individuals. This is consistent with Anderson's (1999) argument that "decent" families can serve as a buffer to the problems of the inner city, although the ability of families to do so can be undermined by the street culture. It is also consistent with the original formulations of social disorganization theory (Shaw and McKay 1942), as well as learning theories. This finding suggests generally that future research should continue to explore the dual roles of oppositional street context and family cohesiveness in explaining serious violence and in mediating the relationship between structural aspects of communities and the violence of individuals within communities.

Finally, our article demonstrates that studies of individual violence can benefit from considering research in urban sociology and theories in criminology that focus on rates of crime and violence across communities. This emphasizes the importance of including both community-level and individual-level measures in future research on violent delinquency.

ACKNOWLEDGMENTS

Our research was supported by a grant from the College of Humanities and Social Science at North Carolina State University and by funding from the National Consortium on Violence Research. The authors are grateful to Joseph B. Lang for his statistical advice. The data for this study are from the Add Health project, a program project designed by J. Richard Udry (PI) and Peter Bearman, and funded by grant P01-HD31921 from the National Institute of Child Health and Human Development to the Carolina Population Center, University of North Carolina at Chapel Hill, with cooperative funding from 17 other agencies. Persons interested in obtaining data files from the National Longitudinal Study of Adolescent Health should contact Add Health, Carolina Population Center, 123 West Franklin Street, Chapel Hill, NC 27516–2524 (http://www.cpc.unc.edu/addhealth). Neither the funding agencies nor the collectors of the data bear any responsibility for the analyses and interpretation drawn here.

NOTES

1. Although studies in the communities and crime tradition also focus on victimization or suitable targets and fear of crime (see Wilcox Rountree and Land 1996; Markowitz et al. 2001; Wilcox, Land, and Hunt 2003), we focus here on research that more pointedly targets the causes of crime.

2. When studies have included variables that tap what we call criminogenic street context, they have tended to treat these as control variables entered before variables like community disadvantage (e.g., McNulty and Bellair 2003a).

3. Research on communities and crime juxtaposes composition or selection arguments with arguments focusing on emergent properties of communities (see Sampson 1985). Our theoretical discussion and empirical assessment of residential constraints take into consideration composition/ selection; discussion and assessment of community effects, social capital, and street context are consistent with perspectives focusing on emergent properties.

4. There were a few variables with nontrivial missing data that were not addressed in the sampling weights, namely, information on network closure, parent's participation in organizations, and collective supervision. We reestimated our models using mean substitution for missing data, and found no meaningful differences in the findings reported here.

5. We include only ascribed characteristics and characteristics of families over which adolescents have no control (i.e., poverty status) as factors determining selection into disadvantaged communities. This is consistent with Sampson et al. (2002) argument that the strategy of entering individual, family process, and peer variables as controls alongside neighborhood characteristics confounds the "importance of both long-term community influences and mediating developmental pathways regarding children's personal traits and dispositions, learning patterns from peers, family socialization, and more" (p. 469).

6. Seventeen cases were deleted from the analysis because the respondents reported multiple residential mothers and/or multiple residential fathers. Although some researchers advocate the use of additional measures of family structure (see Parker and Johns 2002), we focus on female headship because it is linked most often to family disadvantage and thus is part of the nexus of factors that constrains residential choices and leads to selection into disadvantage communities.

7. Twenty-three cases were deleted from the analysis because the respondents' reported sex was different in wave 1 and wave 2 of the interviews.

8. Studies demonstrate that residents in particular areas tend to disagree about the exact boundaries of their neighborhood (see Furstenberg et al. 1999), which renders the measurement of appropriate neighborhood units problematic. Given these constraints on systematic measurement of neighborhoods and given restrictions on available data generally, researchers often have used census tracts in their analyses of urban crime (Krivo and Peterson 1996; Crutchfield, Glusker, and Bridges 1999; Peterson, Krivo, and Harris 2000; McNulty and Bellair 2003a). Census tract boundaries are drawn by census tract committees to account for natural boundaries and population characteristics in a way that creates units that are meant to represent natural social aggregates. Research on appropriate units of analysis reports that use

of census tract aggregates does not produce substantially different results from aggregates such as block groups (see Gephart's 1997 review).

9. We also estimated models that included measures of residential stability and neighborhood crime but found that these variables were highly associated with our community disadvantage index, and we could not disentangle their separate effects. Our principle components analyses indicated that the reliability of the community disadvantage scale was decreased when these variables were added to the factor.

10. Moreover, youths' violence may influence their family relationships, relationships between their families and community members, and their exposure to violence and delinquent peers. It is much less likely that youths' prior violence leads to residence in a disadvantaged community. Thus, the ordering of variables in our models corresponds to our theoretical expectations about temporal order.

11. Although these indicators do not capture all that is likely important about a criminogenic street context, they do capture many of the elements of street context discussed in literature addressing oppositional or criminal street milieus (e.g., Sampson and Wilson 1995; Anderson 1999). Future quantitative research would benefit from inclusion of more direct assessments of neighborhood culture, not only context, such as some measure of aggregated neighborhood attitudes about violence and definitions favoring using violence as a means of gaining respect. Unfortunately, such measures are currently unavailable in datasets containing macro-and micro level information on communities and violence.

12. While this misses some situations of violence to which youths may be exposed, especially most instances of family violence, it does capture exposure to serious violence—namely stabbing—occurring in the street context. This is the only variable representing this construct available in the data and it clearly captures exposure to extreme violence.

13. In a supplementary analysis, we verified that the effect of witnessing serious violence remains significant in a model in which self-reported neighborhood crime is controlled.

REFERENCES

Akers, Ronald. 1998. *Social Learning and Social Structure*. Boston, MA: Northeastern University Press.

Alba, Richard D. and John R. Logan. 1993. "Minority Proximity to Whites in Suburbs—An Individual Level Analysis of Segregation." *American Journal of Sociology* 98:1388–427.

Alba, Richard D., John R. Logan, and Paul E. Bellair. 1994. "Living with Crime: The Implications of Racial/Ethnic Differences in Suburban Location." *Social Forces* 73:395–434.

Anderson, Elijah. 1997. "Violence and the Inner-City Street Code." Pp. 1–29 in Violence and Childhood in the Inner City, edited by Joan Mccord. New York: Cambridge University Press.
———1999. Code of the Street: Decency, Violence, and the Moral Life of the Inner City. New York: W.W. Norton.

Aneshensel, Carol S. and Clea A. Sucoff. 1996. "The Neighborhood Context of Adolescent Mental Health." Journal of Health and Social Behavior 37:293–310.

Baller, Robert D., Luc Anselin, Steven F. Messner, Glenn Deane, and Darnell F. Hawkins. 2001. "Structural Covariates of U.S. County Homicide Rates: Incorporating Spatial Effects." Criminology 39:561–90.

Bellair, Paul. 1997. "Social Interaction and Community Crime: Examining the Importance of Neighborhood Networks." Criminology 35:677–703.

Browning, Christopher R., Seth F. Feinberg, and Robert D. Dietz. 2004. "The Paradox of Social Organization: Networks, Collective Efficacy, and Violent Crime in Urban Neighborhoods." Social Forces 83:503–34.

Bursik, Robert J., Jr. 1984. "Urban Dynamics and Ecological Studies of Delinquency." Social Forces 63:393–413.

Bursik, Robert J., Jr. and Harold G. Grasmick. 1993. Neighborhoods and Crime. New York: Lexington.

Cattarello, Anne M. 2000. "Community-Level Influences on Individuals' Social Bonds, Peer Associations, and Delinquency: A Multilevel Analysis." Justice Quarterly 17:33–61.

Chantala, Kim and Joyce Tabor. 1999. "Strategies to Perform Design-Based Analysis Using the Add Health Data." Carolina Population Center University of North Carolina at Chapel Hill. Retrieved September 6, 2006 (http://www.cpc.unc.edu/projects/addhealth/files/weight1 .pdf).

Coleman, James S. 1988. "Social Capital in the Creation of Human Capital." American Journal of Sociology 94 (Supplement):S95–S120.
———1990. Foundations of Social Theory. Cambridge, MA: Belknap Press of Harvard University Press.

Crutchfield, Robert D., Ann Glusker, and George S. Bridges. 1999. "A Tale of Three Cities: Labor Markets and Homicide. "Sociological Focus 32:65–83.

Elliott, Delbert S., William Julius Wilson, David Huizinga, Robert J. Sampson, Amanda Elliott, and Bruce Rankin. 1996. "The Effects of Neighborhood Disadvantage on Adolescent Development." Journal of Research in Crime and Delinquency 33:389–426.

Fagan, Jeffrey and Deanna Wilkinson. 1998. "Guns, Youth Violence, and Social Identity in Inner Cities." Pp. 105–88 in Crime and Justice, Vol. 24, edited by Michael Tonry and Mark Moore. Chicago, IL: University of Chicago Press.

Furstenberg, Frank F., Thomas Cook, Jacquelyn Eccles, Glenn Elder, and Arnold Sameroff. 1999. Managing to Make It: Urban Families and Adolescent Success. Chicago, IL: University of Chicago Press.

Gephart, Martha A. 1997. "Neighborhoods and Communities as Contexts for Development." Pp 1-43 in Neighborhood Poverty: Context and Consequences for Children, Vol. 1, edited by Jeanne Brooks-Gunn, Greg J. Duncan, and Lawrence Aber. New York: Russell Sage Foundation.

Gottfredson, Denise C., Richard J. McNeil, III, and Gary D. Gottfredson. 1991. "Social Area Influences on Delinquency: A Multilevel Analysis." Journal of Research in Crime and Delinquency 28:197–226.

Hagan, John, Ross MacMillan, and Blair Wheaton. 1996. "New Kid in Town: Social Capital and the Life Course Effects of Family Migration on Children." American Sociological Review 61:368–85.

Hagan, John and Bill McCarthy. 1997. Mean Streets: Youth Crime and Homelessness. New York: Cambridge University Press.

Harris, Kathleen Mullan, Francesca Florey, Joyce Tabor, Peter S. Bearman, Jo Jones, and J. Richard Udry. 2003. The National Longitudinal Study of Adolescent Health: Research Design. Retrieved September 6, 2006 (http://www.cpc.unc.edu/projects/addhealth/design).

Heitgerd, Janet L. and Robert J. Bursik, Jr. 1987. "Extracommunity Dynamics and the Ecology of Delinquency." American Journal of Sociology 92:775–87.

Hirschi, Travis. 1969. Causes of Delinquency. Berkeley, CA: University of California Press.

Hunter, Albert. 1985. "Private, Parochial, and Public Orders: The Problem of Crime and Incivility in Urban Communities." Pp. 230–42 in The Challenge of Social Control, Citizenship, and Institution Building in Modern Society, edited by Gerald D. Suttles and Mayer N. Zald. Norwood, NJ: Ablex.

Johnstone, John W. C. 1978. "Juvenile Delinquency and Family: Contextual Interpretation." Youth and Society 9:299–313.

Kasarda, John D. and Morris Janowitz. 1974. "Community Attachment in Mass Society." American Sociological Review 39:328–39.

Krivo, Lauren J. and Ruth D. Peterson. 1996. "Extremely Disadvantaged Neighborhoods and Urban Crime." Social Forces 75:619–50.

———2000. "The Structural Context of Homicide." American Sociological Review 65:547–59.

Krivo, Lauren J., Ruth D. Peterson, Helen Rizzo, and John Reynolds. 1998. "Race Segregation and the Concentration of Disadvantage: 1980–1990." Social Problems 45:61–80.

Kubrin, Charis E. and Ronald Weitzer. 2003a. "New Directions in Social Disorganization Theory." Journal of Research in Crime and Delinquency 40:374–402.

———2003b. "Retaliatory Homicide: Concentrated Disadvantage and Neighborhood Culture." Social Problems 50:157–80.

Land, Kenneth C., Patricia L. McCall, and Lawrence E. Cohen. 1990. "Structural Covariates of Homicide Rates: Are There Any Invariances across Time and Social Space?" American Journal of Sociology 95:922–63.

Lipsitz, S. H., K. Kim, and L. Zhao. 1994. "Analysis of Repeated Categorical Data Using Generalized Estimating Equations." Statistics in Medicine 13:1149–63.

Liska, Allen E. and Paul E. Bellair. 1995. "Violent Crime Rates and Racial Composition: Convergence over Time." American Journal of Sociology 101:578–610.

Logan, John R., Richard D. Alba, and Shu-Yin Leung. 1996. "Minority Access to White Suburbs: A Multiregional Comparison." Social Forces 74:851–81.

Markowitz, Fred E., Paul E. Bellair, Allen E. Liska, and Jianhong Liu. 2001. "Extending Social Disorganization Theory: Modeling the Relationships between Cohesion, Disorder, and Fear." Criminology 39:293–319.

Massey, Douglas S. 1985. "Ethnic Residential Segregation: A Theoretical Synthesis and Empirical Review." Sociology and Social Research 69:315–50.

———1990. "American Apartheid: Segregation and the Making of the Underclass." American Journal of Sociology 96:329–57.

Massey, Douglas S. and Nancy A. Denton. 1988. "The Dimensions of Residential Segregation." Social Forces 67:281–315.

———1993. American Apartheid: Segregation and the Making of the Underclass. Cambridge, MA: Harvard University Press.

Massey, Douglas S. and Eric Fong. 1990. "Segregation and Neighborhood Quality: Blacks, Hispanics, and Asians in the San Francisco Metropolitan Area." Social Forces 69:15–32.

Massey, Douglas S. and Andrew B. Gross. 1991. "Explaining Trends in Racial Segregation, 1970–1980." Urban Affairs Review 27:13–35.

McNulty, Thomas L. and Paul E. Bellair. 2003a. "Explaining Racial and Ethnic Differences in Serious Adolescent Violent Behavior." Criminology 41:709–46.

———2003b. "Explaining Racial and Ethnic Differences in Adolescent Violence: Structural Disadvantage, Family Well-Being, and Social Capital." Justice Quarterly 20:1–31.

Morenoff, Jeffrey D. and Robert J. Sampson. 1997. "Violent Crime and the Spatial Dynamics of Neighborhood Transition in Chicago." Social Forces 76:31–64.

Morenoff, Jeffrey D., Robert J. Sampson, and Stephen W. Raudenbush. 2001. "Neighborhood Inequality, Collective Efficacy, and the Spatial Dynamics of Urban Violence." Criminology 39:517–59.

Osgood, D. Wayne, Lloyd D. Johnston, Patrick M. O'Malley, and Jerald G. Bachman. 1988. "The Generality of Deviance in Late Adolescence and Early Adulthood." American Sociological Review 53:81–93.

Parker, Karen F. and Tracy Johns. 2002. "Urban Disadvantage and Types of Race-Specific Homicide: Assessing the Diversity in Family Structures in the Urban Context." Journal of Research in Crime and Delinquency 39:277–303.

Peeples, Faith and Rolf Loeber. 1994. "Do Individual Factors and Neighborhood Context Explain Ethnic Differences in Juvenile Delinquency?" Journal of Quantitative Criminology 10:141–57.

Peterson, Ruth D. and Lauren J. Krivo. 1999. "Racial Segregation, the Concentration of Disadvantage, and Black and White Homicide Victimization." Sociological Forum 14:465–93.

Peterson, Ruth D., Lauren J. Krivo, and Mark A. Harris. 2000. "Disadvantage and Neighborhood Violent Crime: Do Local Institutions Matter?" Journal of Research in Crime and Delinquency 31:31–63.

Rosenfeld, Richard, Steven F. Messner, and Eric P. Baumer. 2001. "Social Capital and Homicide." Social Forces 80:283–309.

Rountree Wilcox, Pamela and Kenneth C. Land. 1996. "Burglary Victimization, Perceptions of Crime Risk, and Routine Activities: A Multilevel Analysis across Seattle Neighborhoods and Census Tracts." Journal of Research in Crime and Delinquency 33:147–80.

Sampson, Robert J. 1985. "Race and Criminal Violence: A Demographically Disaggregated Analysis of Urban Homicide." Crime and Delinquency 31:47–82.

———1997. "Collective Regulation of Adolescent Misbehavior: Validation Results from 80 Chicago Neighborhoods." Journal of Adolescent Research 12:277–44.

———2004." Networks and Neighbourhoods: The Implications of Connectivity for Thinking about Crime in the Modern City." Pp. 157–66 in Network Logic: Who Governs in an Interconnected World? edited by Helen McCarthy, Paul Miller, and Paul Skidmore. London: Demos.

Sampson, Robert J. and W. Byron Groves. 1989. "Community Structure and Crime: Testing Social Disorganization Theory." American Journal of Sociology 94:774–802.

Sampson, Robert J. and Jeffrey D. Morenoff. 2004. "Spatial (Dis)Advantage and Homicide in Chicago Neighborhoods." Pp. 145–70 in Spatially Integrated Social Science, edited by Michael Goodchild and Donald Janelle. New York: Oxford University Press.

Sampson, Robert J., Jeffrey D. Morenoff, and Thomas Gannon-Rowley. 2002. "Assessing Neighborhood Effects: Social Processes and New Directions in Research." Annual Review of Sociology 28:443–78.

Sampson, Robert J. and Stephen W. Raudenbush. 1999. "Systematic Social Observation of Public Spaces: A New Look at Disorder in Neighborhoods." American Journal of Sociology 105:603–51.

Sampson, Robert J., Stephen W. Raudenbush, and Felton Earls. 1997. "Neighborhoods and Violent Crime: A Multilevel Study of Collective Efficacy." Science 277:918–24.

Sampson, Robert J. and William Julius Wilson. 1995. "Race, Crime, and Urban Inequality." Pp. 3754 in Crime and Inequality, edited by John Hagan and Ruth D. Peterson. Stanford, CA: Stanford University Press.

Shaw, Clifford R. and Henry D. McKay. 1942. Juvenile Delinquency and Urban Areas. Chicago, IL: University of Chicago Press.

Shihadeh, Edward S. and Nicole Flynn. 1996. "Segregation and Crime: The Effect of Black Social Isolation on the Rates of Black Urban Violence." Social Forces 74:1325–52.

Shihadeh, Edward S. and Darrell J. Steffensmeier. 1994. "Economic Inequality, Family Disruption, and Urban Black Violence—Cities as Units of Stratification and Social Control." Social Forces 73:729–51.

Short, James. 1997. Poverty, Ethnicity, and Violent Crime. Boulder, CO: Westview Press.

Simcha-Fagan, Ora and Joseph E. Schwartz. 1986. "Neighborhood and Delinquency: An Assessment of Contextual Effects." Criminology 24:667–99.

Simons, Ronald L., Christine Johnson, Jay Beaman, Rand D. Conger, and Les B. Whitbeck. 1996. "Parents and Peer Group as Mediators of the Effect of Community Structure on Adolescent Problem Behavior." American Journal of Community Psychology 24:145–65.

Skogan, Wesley. 1990. Disorder and Decline: Crime and the Spiral of Decay in American Cities. New York: Free Press.

South, Scott J. and Glenn Deane. 1993. "Race and Residential Mobility: Individual Determinants and Structural Constraints." Social Forces 72:147–67.

South, Scott J. and Steven S. Messner. 2000. "Crime and Demography: Multiple Linkages, Reciprocal Relations." Annual Review of Sociology 26:83–106.

Sutherland, Edwin H. 1947. Principles of Criminology, 4th ed. Philadelphia, PA: Lippincott.

Taylor, Ralph B. and Jeanette Covington. 1988. "Neighborhoods Changes in Ecology and Violence." Criminology 26:553–89.

Udry, J. Richard. 2003. The National Longitudinal Study of Adolescent Health (Add Health), Waves I & II, 1994–1996; Wave III, 2001–2002 [MRDF]. Chapel Hill, NC: Carolina Population Center, University of North Carolina at Chapel Hill.

Vélez, Maria B. 2001. "The Role of Public Social Control in Urban Neighborhoods: A Multi-Level Analysis of Victimization Risk." Criminology 39:837–64.

Vélez, Maria B., Lauren J. Krivo, and Ruth D. Peterson. 2003. "Structural Inequality and Homicide: An Assessment of the Black-White Gap in Killings." Criminology 41:645–72.

Warner, Barbara. 2003. "The Role of Attenuated Culture in Social Disorganization Theory." Criminology 41:73–97.

Warner, Barbara D. and Pamela Wilcox Rountree 1997. "Local Social Ties in a Community and Crime Model: Questioning the Systemic Nature of Informal Social Control." Social Problems 44:520–36.

Wilcox, Pamela, Kenneth C. Land, and Scott A. Hunt. 2003. Criminal Circumstance: A Dynamic Multicontextual Criminal Opportunity Theory. New York: Aldine de Gruyter.

Wilson, William Julius. 1987. The Truly Disadvantaged: The Inner City, the Underclass, and Public Policy. Chicago, IL: University of Chicago Press.

1996. When Work Disappears: The World of the New Urban Poor. New York: Knopf/Random House.

Wave 1 Individual/Family Status Characteristics

Youth's Sex	Binary variable, coded 1 if the youth is male, 0 if female. (youth data)
Youth's Black Racial Status	Binary variable, coded 1 if youth is black, 0 if non-black. (youth data)
Youth's Latino	Binary variable, coded 1 if the youth is Latino, and 0 otherwise.
Ethnicity	(youth data)
Youth's Age	Youth's age in years, ranging from 12 to 21. (youth data)
Female-Headed	Binary variable, coded 1 if female-headed household, 0 if not
Household	female-headed household. We constructed this variable using
	the household roster items from the youth interview, which allowed us to identify all persons living in the youth's home and their relationship to the youth. If a respondent reported living with only a residential mother, aunt, grandmother, or any combination of the three, and if there was no male adult present in the household, they were considered to be living in a female headed household. Residential mother includes biological mother, stepmother, adoptive mother, foster mother, or other mother. (youth data)
Parent Education	Binary variable, coded 1 if highest level of education of the most
High School Grad Less	highly educated parent was high school degree or less, and 0 or
	otherwise. If the household was a single-parent household, we
	measured parent's education as the highest level of education achieved by the single parent. If the household was a two-parent household, we measured parent's education as the highest level achieved by either parent. If parent data were missing, we substituted the youth's report of parents' education. (parent and youth data)

Parent Receives	Binary variable, coded as 1 if the parent receives public
Public Assistance	assistance, such as food stamps, AFDC or a housing subsidy, 0 if
	no type of pubic assistance is received. Receipt of public assistance is measured by the parent respondent's self-report of at least one of the following conditions: parent or spouse received public assistance, generally; any member of the household received AFDC in the last month; any member of the household received food stamps in the last month; and any member of the household received a housing subsidy or lived in public housing in the last month. Parent's reports of welfare receipt were supplemented by the youth's report that his/her residential mother and/or residential father received some form of public assistance to allow for recovery of some cases where parents' reports were missing. (parent and youth data)
Prior Violence	Range of violent delinquency in which the youth reported
	involvement during the 12 months prior to the wave 1 interview. Youth were asked whether (in the past 12 months) they had engaged in the following: a serious fight, used or threatened to use a weapon to get something from someone, hurt someone badly enough to need bandages or care from a doctor or nurse, shot or stabbed someone. We also included youths' reports of whether they had ever used a weapon in a fight, to allow for greater comparability with the wave 2 measure of violence, which includes youth reports of using a weapon in a fight in the past 12 months. We coded any involvement in each of these behaviors 1, and summed across the items to produce a six category variable ranging from 0–5. (youth data)

Wave 1 Community Context

| Urban Neighborhood | Binary variable, coded 1 if neighborhood is completely urbanized, and 0 otherwise. (contextual data) |
| Community | Principle component score. The component includes |

Disadvantage	proportion of the population that is black, propor tion of
	households that are female-headed households with own children and no husband present, the proportion of males ever married that are separated or divorced, total unemployment rate, male unemployment rate, median household income, and the proportion of individuals with income in 1989 below the poverty line. All items were measured at the census-tract level, (contextual data) (Cronbach's $\alpha = 0.74$)

Wave 1 Conventional Social Capital

Network Closure	Parent response to the question, "How many parents of your
	child's friends have you talked to in the last four weeks?" (Coded 0 = none; 1 = one; 2 = two; 3 = three; 4 = four; 5 = five; 6 = six or more) (parent data)
Parents' Participation	Sum of parent responses to four items about involve ment in in Organizations
	The items are coded 1 if parents reported
	participating in the following, and 0 otherwise: Parent/teacher organization; Hobby or sports group, such as a bowling team or ham radio club; Civic or social organization, such as Junior League, Rotary, or Knights of Columbus; school fund-raising or volunteer work for youth's school, such as supervising lunch, chaperoning a field trip, etc. (parent data)
Collective (coded as	Mean of parent responses to the following questions
Supervision might,	1 = definitely would not, 2 = probably would not, 3 =
	4 = probably would, 5 = definitely would):
	•"If you saw a neighbor's child getting into trouble, would you tell your neighbor about it?"
	•"If a neighbor saw your child getting into trouble, would your neighbor tell you about it?"
	(parent data)
Family Cohesiveness	Principle component score created from the youth data using principle components analysis. (Cronbach's $\alpha = 0.78$) The component includes the following items (coded as 1 • not at all, 2 = very little, 3 = somewhat, 4

= quite a bit, 5 = very much) "How much do you feel
that your family pays attention to you?" "How much
do you feel that people in your family understand
you?"
"How much do you feel that you and your family have
fun
together?"
(youth data)

Wave 1 Criminogenic Street Context

Deviant Peer
drugs and
Associations
lows (coded 0

Mean of youth reports of their friends' involvement in

smoking. The items included in the scale are as fol-

to 3):
"Of your three best friends, how many smoke at least
one cigarette a day?"
"Of your three best friends, how many drink alcohol
at least once a month?"
"Of your three best friends, how many use marijuana
at least once a month?"
(Cronbach's α = 0.77) (youth data)

Accessibility of Guns
guns in

Binary variable of youth report of the accessibility of

her/his home, coded 1 if easily accessible and 0 if not
easily
accessible. (youth data)

Exposure to Violence
a stabbing

Binary variable of youth report that she/he witnessed

in the previous year, coded 1 if yes and 0 if no. (youth
data)

Expectation of Lethal
be killed by Victimization
chance; 2 = some chance, but

Youth report of her/his perception that she/he could
age 21 (coded as 1 = almost no

probably not; 3 = a 50–50 chance; 4 = a good chance;
5 = almost
certain). (youth data)

Past Violent
personal

Sum of two items from the youth interview capturing

Victimization being shot · · · violent victimizations in the previous year, including and being stabbed. The items are each coded as 1 if the event was experienced once or more, and 0 if the event was never experienced. (youth data)

WAVE 2 YOUTH VIOLENCE

Violent Delinquency · · · This is the range of types of violent delinquency in which the youth reported involvement during the 12 months prior to the wave 2 interview. Youths were asked whether (in the past 12 months) they had engaged in the following: a serious fight, used a weapon in a fight, used or threatened to use a weapon to get something from someone, hurt someone badly enough to need bandages or care from a doctor or nurse, you have shot or stabbed someone. We coded any involvement in each of these behaviors 1, and summed across the items to produce a six category variable ranging from 0–5. (youth data)

APPENDIX B. Descriptive Statistics*

	Mean	SD	Minimum	Maximum
Wave1 Individual/Family Characteristics				
Youth's Sex (male)	0.487	0.500	0	1
Youth's Black Racial Status	0.206	0.404	0	1
Youth's Latino Ethnicity	0.161	0.368	0	1
Youth's Age	15.754	1.585	12	21
Female-Headed Household	0.224	0.417	0	1
Parent Education High School or Less	0.368	0.482	0	1
Parent Receiving Public Assistance	0.155	0.362	0	1
Youth's Involvement in Prior Violence	0.633	0.977	0	5
Wave 1 Neighborhood Context				
Urban Neighborhood	0.536	0.499	0	1
Community Disadvantage (principal component)	-0.002	0.056	-0.130	0.354
Wave 1 Conventional Social Capital				

	Mean	SD	Min	Max
Network Closure				
Parents' Participation in Organizations	2.116	0.799		
Collective Supervision	1.899	0.948	0	6
Family Cohesiveness (principal component)	4.111	0.000	0	4
	0.789	0.038	1	5
Wave1 Criminogenic Street Context			-0.110	0.053
Deviant Peer Associations				
Accessibility of Guns	0.800	0.223		
Witness Serious Violence	0.874	0.416	0	3
Expectation of Lethal Victimization	0.115	1.645	0	1
Past Violent Victimization	0.319	0.802	0	1
	0.059	0.255	1	5
Wave 2 Youth Violence			0	2
Violent Delinquency	0.369	0.831	0	5
Items included in the violence scale:				
Serious Fight	0.196	0.041		
Used Weapon in Fight	0.398	0.198	0	1
Used/Threatened Weapon to Get Something	0.034	0.081	0	1
Hurt Someone	0.181	0.273	0	1
	0.017	0.131	0	1
Shot/Stabbed Someone			0	1

*Note: The descriptive statistics presented here are unweighted.

PUBLIC POLICY, CIVIL GANG INJUNCTIONS, AND GANGS

GANGS AND PUBLIC POLICY

PREVENTION, INTERVENTION, AND SUPPRESSION

By C. Ronald Huff

his volume includes contributions from some of the nation's leading scholars and practitioners on the subject of gangs. The foregoing chapters not only contribute to the growing body of knowledge concerning gangs but also have many implications for public policy formulation, implementation, and evaluation. All too often we forget to ask the question, "So what?" What are the implications for the ways in which society chooses to address the gang problem?

This closing chapter will attempt to pull together some of the implications of the collective research presented in this book for public policy—specifically for prevention, intervention, and suppression.[1] Those three elements are essential ingredients in any community's approach to the gang problem, and if the community can combine these components in a balanced manner, it is more likely that it can develop a comprehensive, rather than fragmented, strategy that will address not only the immediate short term challenge of *controlling* gang-related crime but also the longer-term challenge of *preventing* it. As Kent Shafer and I noted in Chapter 9, the most typical response of a community, when initially confronted with an emerging gang problem, is to rely solely or heavily on law enforcement and its expertise in suppression. We tried to summarize some of the dangers inherent in over reliance on that approach. In this chapter, drawing on the collective contributions in the preceding chapters, I outline an alternative to that approach that will serve communities much better in the longer term.

PREVENTION

All of us grew up hearing that "an ounce of prevention is worth a pound of cure." Never has that axiom been more accurate than with respect to the problem of gang-related crime and, in fact, crime in general. Our society has recently been pursuing an extraordinarily expensive policy agenda that tends to rely heavily on suppression and the extensive use of incarceration. In human history, it is rare for a society to incarcerate such a large proportion of its citizens, often removing them from the productive labor force (and, in the U.S., often from the rolls of taxpayers as well) and imprisoning them at great cost to the public, while also disrupting their families and causing many of their families to receive public assistance, thus driving up the costs even farther. In fact, the recent rates of incarceration in the United States put us in such illustrious company as the gulags of the former Soviet Union.

Let us compare this policy preference with our perspective on health care in the United States. By analogy, if we pursued similar policy preferences in health care, we would concentrate our public expenditures solely on those at the end of the medical care continuum—those who are dying. We would not focus on preventive health measures, even though they are much less expensive in the long run. Instead, we'd concentrate on end-of-life care, such as hospices and units for terminal cancer patients. Like-wise, the massive investment we've been making in prisons represents a public policy choice—a choice to concentrate our resource expenditures and our hopes on a policy of punishment and incapacitation for criminal behavior after it has occurred. But by then, the offender has already been transformed into a criminal, thus damaging his or her life chances. And by then, there are victims whose victimization might have been prevented.

Among the strategies available to us for attempting to prevent gang-related crime, *primary prevention* is the foundation on which we should build. In this approach, it is not necessary for us to identify specific individuals who are *likely* to become gang members or to engage in gang-related criminal behavior. The rationale for this approach is as follows: By providing effective programs to *entire groups* we will be able to involve a number of individuals who, without such programming, would become involved in gang-related crime. Programs of this genre include both community-wide approaches (e.g., the Communities That Care model and the Spergel/OJJDP comprehensive community strategy) and those that target specific groups (e.g., DARE and G.R.E.A.T., which concentrate on entire classes of school children). Careful evaluation of such programs is essential, and we know that our programmatic efforts must continue to be refined as we understand their effects and are able to improve their content.

But what do we know about the optimal target groups for such prevention efforts? Those that focus on entire communities and seek to engage the citizens and their local agencies and organizations in the effort to build human capital are addressing many of the points raised in the preceding chapters. But what about those that target specific groups for the purpose of primary prevention? Some of the research reported in this volume and elsewhere suggests that an optimal age to focus on the prevention of such high risk behaviors as using drugs and joining gangs might be between 10 and 12; in other words, children in the fifth to seventh grades in school. For example, interviews with 140 gang members in Ohio, Florida, and Colorado indicate that their first association with a gang occurred at ages ranging from about 12% to 13, and they then joined a gang about 6 months to 1 year after their first association. Those data also demonstrated that their first arrest occurred after they began their involvement with the gang. At the aggregate level, this relationship was invariant across all samples in all three states (Huff, 1998b).[2]

Further, evidence for this recommended target age range is provided in this volume by Esbensen, Peterson, Freng, and Taylor (Chapter 3) and by Miller (Chapter 12). Esbensen et al.'s data, based on part of a national evaluation of the G.R.E.A.T. program, showed that delinquent activity most commonly began in the year in which the youth joined a gang, and they found that a sizeable proportion of their sample was using drugs by the eighth grade. Miller, focusing on female involvement in gangs, recommended that prevention efforts begin prior to age 12, although she also recommended targeting such prevention efforts to girls with specific risk factors (an example of *secondary* prevention, rather than primary prevention).

Also, it is important to ask whether some current efforts at prevention may be targeting students *too early.* Should such programs be targeting classes of third graders, for example? Do the lives of third graders generally provide the kind of context in which such prevention programming is likely to be perceived as relevant and therefore more likely to be efficacious? It seems more likely that the kinds of behavioral rehearsal and other social learning techniques employed in such programming will be perceived as relevant only in the context of the day-to-day, lived experience of the children being targeted. Arguably, third graders would rarely be at a point where anticipatory socialization techniques would be salient to their lived experience. So, the challenge is to introduce such prevention programming at an optimal time—a time that fits into a range between the loss of "childhood innocence" and the beginning of significant adolescent peer pressures toward conformity—including conformity to deviant and delinquent behavioral expectations of some individuals and groups.

What kinds of programming might be useful at this age range? Interestingly, both Maxson and Whitlock (Chapter 2) and Miller (Chapter 12) commented on the importance of conflict resolution skills. Although their chapters focused on female involvement in gangs, the literature on male gang behavior suggests that conflict resolution skills would be no less important for boys, as well. Both boys and girls need to develop their social competence and their problem-solving and conflict resolution skills, not only to resist such high-risk behaviors as joining a gang or using or selling drugs, but also to prepare them for the everyday challenges they will face as citizens living and working in increasingly diverse communities and organizations in which conflict is an expected and normal part of daily life. Many of these skills can be taught in the schools, whose leaders can also improve their working partnerships with the community and their development of comprehensive safety and security plans, as recommended by Trump (Chapter 8), to prevent gang-related violence, as well as the kinds of tragedies that have been reported in recent years, though still quite rare statistically.

Prevention can, and should, also occur at the macrolevel, of course. Cureton (Chapter 6), Hagedorn (Chapter 7), Vigil and Yun (Chapter 11), and Fleisher (Chapter 13) all make this point—each in his own way. Taken collectively, those chapters provide powerful evidence for and advocacy of a stronger commitment to enhance economic opportunity for all our citizens, rather than to allow the illegal opportunity structure to compete for "job creation" in our cities (drug dealers are often more "equal opportunity employers" than are legitimate businesses); to celebrate, rather than to marginalize, diversity; and to focus our longer-term efforts on the development of human capital for our citizens and "social glue" for our communities, rather than to pursue policies that result in disinvestment, despair, multigenerational unemployment, and gangs in many of our communities. Zhang (Chapter 14) focuses on sociocultural and macrolevel factors and how they affect those who have immigrated to the United States from China. His documentation of, and insights into, the breakdown of social control in the families of Chinese immigrants whose children have broken the law provides additional evidence of the need for more effective efforts to support families and children in a society with a demanding and highly segmented economy that often contributes to disruptions in social control.

Finally, with respect to prevention, we lack a comprehensive youth policy perspective at the federal, state, and local levels of our society. By that, I mean a coordinated effort to assign a very high priority to the welfare of children and to ask ourselves when formulating public policies how they are likely to affect the welfare of our children. Although our children are our nation's most important resource for the future, we often pay more attention, in the public policy arena, to our physical infrastructure than to our human infrastructure. For example, it is unclear why, in a nation with such enormous economic resources, children should have to live in poverty and other conditions that greatly constrain their life chances and often contribute to their involvement in the alternative illegal economic opportunities made available to them. A coordinated effort at the national, state, and local levels to strengthen neighborhoods and families could help address the issues raised in Bursik's insightful discussion (Chapter 5) and could enhance the chances that the kind of "social capital" described by Bursik can be transferred to children by their parents and other adults in the community, thus increasing the chances that they will become law-abiding citizens, rather than-being forced to adapt to the "code of the street" (Anderson, 1999), which may often mean gang-related crime and violence in response to the daily, lived experience of marginalization.

INTERVENTION

Discussing prevention, I referred to an early "window of opportunity" for prevention that I believe occurs around ages 10 to 12. My own research has also indicated a second window of opportunity—this one for *intervention* with those who have already committed a criminal or delinquent act. This second opportunity occurs between the time gang members are arrested for property crimes (which typify first arrests for most gang members) and their subsequent involvement in more serious offenses. This period, according to my data (see Huff, 1998b), lasts about 1½ or 2 years. Intervention during that period affords us a chance to divert young offenders from the gang subculture before they further endanger their own lives and victimize other citizens. Successful intervention at this stage, through such programs as prosecutorial diversion targeting first-time, gang-involved property offenders, can save lives (of both the offenders and the victims) and can save society the enormous costs associated with arresting, convicting, and incarcerating serious offenders.

Although the best thing we can do is to prevent someone from ever becoming an offender, the second best thing we can do is to remove an offender from the pool of offenders. In the case of gang members, Decker and Lauritsen's research (Chapter 4) provides evidence that we have another window of opportunity for intervention when a gang member is confronted with the reality of a violent event and may be more motivated at that point to leave the gang. They advocate more detailed studies of the factors and processes associated with leaving the gang, as well as crime desistance in general. Why, for example, do some gang members decide to leave the gang in response to a violent event, but others stay? As Decker and Lauritsen note, there may be important developmental and maturational variables at work that we simply do not understand well. Gang members' decisions may be driven by the cumulative nature of their experiences, by differential support networks, and by other key factors that we have not identified at this point.

The research reported by Braga, Kennedy, and Tita (Chapter 17) also has important implications for intervention strategy. The "pulling-levers" approach (a form of suppression), when combined with intervention at optimal times (as discussed by Decker & Lauritsen) and appropriate social services, can yield effective results, as has been shown in Boston, for example, in addressing problems associated with gangs and guns. Their work has stimulated other communities to examine the factors associated with the local supply of guns and how youth obtain those weapons. Some of the renewed efforts I have witnessed include a more aggressive stance toward obtaining information when juveniles with guns are taken into custody. For example, a youth might be asked to provide information concerning how he or she obtained the gun, with a clear statement that the cooperativeness of the youth will be taken into account in determining the prosecution's recommendation concerning a proper disposition of the case. On the other hand, failure to provide information about how the weapon was obtained will also be taken into account by the prosecutor's office. If the youth states that the gun was obtained from an adult, then law enforcement is immediately instructed to investigate and, if appropriate, arrest the adult involved, who is then prosecuted aggressively. Finally, if the adult is convicted, the prosecutor's office works cooperatively with the news media to ensure heavy news coverage, with the rationale of promoting general deterrence by "getting the word out" that adults who furnish weapons to youth will be aggressively targeted for prosecution and conviction. This blend of intervention and suppression strategies provides a useful transition to the final focus of this closing chapter: suppression.

SUPPRESSION

Finally, several chapters in this volume have focused on issues that are important in any discussion of suppression. Clearly, suppression is a necessary but not sufficient strategy for dealing with gang-related crime. I always ask my students, when discussing gangs, "Who invented the DARE Program?" They seldom know that it originated in the Los Angeles Police Department (LAPD) in recognition of the fact that law enforcement simply cannot successfully deal with the gang problem via arrests only. The LAPD recognized that it was essential that prevention efforts begin with young children, before they became involved with gangs.

The LAPD is, of course, a police organization that has evolved from a nationally respected model to one that has witnessed a series of challenges that have called into question the department's relationship with minority citizens and the overzealous and lawless behavior of some of its elite gang unit officers in the Rampart Division. In Chapter 9, Kent Shafer and I focus on the advantages to be gained by changing the culture of law enforcement organizations from a paramilitary, suppression-focused approach to one that views law enforcement as partners with the community, rather than engaging in a war against the community. The fact is that most citizens are on the side of law enforcement, and even in the highest crime areas, most citizens do not want crime and violence, and want to find ways of dealing with them. The community-oriented, problem-solving approach to policing has much to recommend it, and it also seems to offer greater potential for addressing the gang problem, because community policing officers are likely to obtain more information that is relevant than are officers assigned to a centralized unit.

One useful tool for law enforcement, in improving its understanding of gang incidents and how they are distributed spatially, is the Orange County Gang Incident Tracking System described by Meeker and Vila (Chapter 10). The changing nature of gang turf and gang-related crimes is such that they cut across jurisdictions. This requires cooperation among law enforcement agencies, including a shared database whenever possible. Meeker and Vila also found that communication among these entities is essential to the success of such collaborative efforts. Their discussion of the issues associated with such shared databases is important for those who are now confronting emerging and/or growing gang problems. Properly utilized, such shared databases have great potential.

Finally, Geis's discussion of civil injunctions (Chapter 16) has enormous implications for scholars, policymakers, and practitioners as we consider where, or if, civil injunctions should be employed as weapons in dealing with the gang problem. As Geis points out, such injunctions are often drafted in impermissibly broad language and have great potential for misuse and abuse, given the broad discretion afforded law enforcement officers in the United States. Such injunctions clearly have the potential to be utilized for the "profiling" of certain groups (generally minorities), who may then be harassed and/or arrested, even though no criminal behavior was evident on their part. Geis eloquently argues that in this case, "the cure is worse than the disease," so to speak, because the freedoms that we all cherish so much are endangered whenever any of us is deprived of them without due process of law and without proof beyond a reasonable doubt that we have committed a crime. We must, then, ask ourselves whether, were we to apply a balancing test (our interest in preserving our freedom to associate with each other as we please vs. our desire to control gang-related crime), it is worth the tradeoff involved in allowing law enforcement the discretion to enforce such civil injunctions.

It is fitting that we conclude a volume on the subject of gangs with such a cautionary note, because gangs are not *the* problem; they are instead a *dependent* variable—a *symptom* of more fundamental, causally prior independent variables that have numerous dysfunctional consequences for our society, one of which is gang-related crime. The underlying factors that contribute to the formation of gangs and to gang-related crime have been well documented in this book and its two preceding editions. It is my hope that we will continue to make progress in our understanding of gangs and that we will improve our ability to translate that research into sound public policy and programmatic initiatives because in the end, our research demonstrates that gangs generally have two kinds of victims—those who join the gang and those who are victimized by the gang. As a society, we have a responsibility to try to prevent both kinds of victimization.

NOTES

1. For an overview and assessment of appropriate prevention and intervention strategies, see Goldstein and Huff (1993), Klein (1995), and Tonry and Farrington (1995).

2. Longitudinal cohort studies have provided extensive data that demonstrate the relationship between gang membership and criminal behavior. See Esbensen and Huizinga (1993, pp. 565–589); Thornberry, Krohn, Lizotte, and Chard-Wierschem (1993, pp. 55–87); and Battin, Hill, Abbott, Catalano, and Hawkins (1998, pp. 93–115).

Gangs and Public Policy
Prevention, Intervention, and Suppression

C . Ronald Huff

PowerPoint by: Cecil Silva
Martha Mendoza
► Ebony La'Starr Jones

Prevention

► This Chapter will attempt to pull together some of the implications of the collective research presented in this book for public policy specifically for prevention, intervention, and suppression. Golden and Huff (1993)Klein (1995) and Tony and Farrington (1995).

► Those three elements are essential ingredients in any community's approach to gang problem, and if the community can combine these components in a balanced manner, it is more likely that it can develop a comprehensive, rather than fragmented, strategy that will address not only the immediate short challenge of *controlling* gang-related crime but also the longer-term challenge of *preventing* it.

- In human history, it is rare for a society to incarcerate such a large proportion of its citizens, often removing them from the productive labor force (and, in the U.S., often from the rolls of taxpayers as well) and imprisoning them at great cost to the public, while also disrupting their families and causing many of their families to receive public assistance, thus driving up the cost even farther.
- The massive investment we've been making in prisons represents a public policy-choice to concentrate our resource expenditures and our hopes on a policy of punishment and incapacitation for criminal behavior after it has occurred. But by then, the offender has already been transformed into a criminal.
- For attempting to prevent gang-related crime, primary prevention is the foundation in which we should build. It is not necessary for us to identify specific individuals who are likely to become gang members to engage in related criminal behavior.
- An approach is as follows: By providing effective programs to *entire groups*. For example: D.A.R.E. and Great (e.g., the Communities That Care model and the Spergel/ OJJDP COMPHEHENSIVE COMMUNITY STATEGY)

- Children joining gangs from 10–12 yrs old. (5th graders-7th)
- For example: 140 gang kids were interviewed from Ohio, Florida and Colorado indicated that their first association with a gang occurred at 12½ to 13 years of age. Within, 6 month to a 1 year they would join a gang. (Huff,1998).
- Esbensen et al.'s data based on a national evaluation of the G.R.E.A.T program, showed that the delinquent activity began the first year which the youth joined the gang, and they a sizeable proportion of their sample was using drugs by the eighth grade.
- Although our children are our nation's most important resource for the future, we often pay more attention, to public policy arena, to our physical infrastructure than to our human infrastructure.
- Prevention can and should occur.
- Finally, with respect to prevention, we lack a comprehensive youth policy perspective at the federal, state and local levels of our society.

Intervention

- Intervention is the second window of opportunity in attempting to gain control of the gang problem.
- Occurs between the time gang members are arrested for the first time and their subsequent involvement in more serious offenses. (Huff, 1998)
- This period usually lasts about 1½ or 2 years.
- Intervention during this period presents a chance to divert adolescents from the gang subculture before they further endanger their lives and the lives of others. (Huff, 1998)

Intervention (continued)

- Another window of opportunity in the intervention phase is when a gang member is confronted with the reality of a violent event. This may motivate the adolescent gang member to want to leave the gang. (Huff, 1998)
- The "pulling-levers" approach (a form of suppression) when combined with intervention and appropriate social services, can yield effective results. (Decker & Lauritsen)

- Evidence suggests that the human service or social intervention strategy, which was predominant in the 1950s and 1960s in addressing the problem of youth gangs, was replaced in the 1970s and 1980s by a law enforcement or suppression strategy (Spergel & Curry, 1991).
  - Spergel's analysis of the effectiveness of gang intervention strategies indicates that, as a primary strategy, Community Organization was perceived to be more effective in "emerging" gang problem settings than in "chronic" settings. Further, as a primary strategy, Opportunities Provision was seen to be more effective in settings where the gang problem was "chronic"; for example, gangs such as the "Crips" and "Bloods," which were established in the 1980s and are still active.

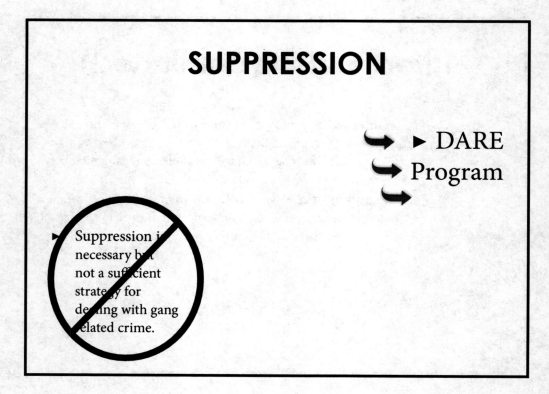

SUPPRESSION

▶ DARE
Program

- Suppression is necessary but not a sufficient strategy for dealing with gang related crime.

- LOS ANGELES (AP) — Anti-gang legislation and police crackdowns are failing so badly that they are strengthening the criminal organizations and making U.S. cities more dangerous.

- Mass arrests, stiff prison sentences often served with other gang members and other strategies that focus on law enforcement rather than intervention actually strengthen gang ties and further marginalize angry young men, according to the Justice Policy Institute, a Washington, D.C

LAPD

➢ Departments Relationship with minority citizens
➢ Rely solely or heavily on law enforcement and its expertise in suppression

Change is GOOD!

➢ Changing the culture of law enforcement organization

➢ Suppression—focused approach to one that views law enforcement as partners with the community.

► Policing – greater potential for addressing the gang problem
► Useful tool for law enforcement—understanding gang incidents and how they are distributed spatially
► Ex/ Orange County Gang Incident Tracking System
► Shared Database for emerging and/ or growing gang problems
► Civil injunctions—weapons in dealing with the gang problem … Good or Bad?

Conclusion

Prevention, Intervention, and Suppression are essential ingredients in any community's approach to a gang problem.

Refrences

► http://www.usatoday.com/news/nation/2007-07-18-gang-report_N.htm
► http://www.athabascau.ca/courses/crjs/360/gangs_intervention.html
► http://www.athabascau.ca/courses/crjs/360/gangs_what_works.html

NEW APPROACHES TO THE STRATEGIC PREVENTION OF GANG AND GROUP-INVOLVED VIOLENCE

By Anthony A. Braga,
David M. Kennedy,
and George E. Tita

number of jurisdictions have been experimenting with new problem-solving frameworks to prevent gang and group-involved violence. These new strategic approaches have shown promising results in the reduction of violence. Pioneered in Boston, these new initiatives have followed a core set of activities to reduce violence. These activities have included the "pulling levers" focused deterrence strategy, designed to prevent violence by and among chronic offenders and groups of chronic offenders; the convening of an interagency working group representing a wide range of criminal justice and social service capabilities; and jurisdiction-specific assessments of violence dynamics, perpetrator and victim characteristics, and related issues such as drug market characteristics and patterns of weapons use and acquisition. All of these initiatives have been facilitated by a close, more or less real-time, partnership between researchers and practitioners. In many jurisdictions, an initial interest in "juvenile violence" or "gun violence" has shifted, as the problem assessments have proceeded, to a focus on understanding and controlling violence, regardless of age or weapon type, associated with chronic offenders and groups of chronic offenders. This chapter traces the development of these new problem-solving frameworks, discusses the commonalities and divergences across jurisdictions that have experimented with these approaches, and synthesizes the key elements of the new strategic prevention frameworks.

THE DEVELOPMENT OF THE NEW STRATEGIC
PREVENTION FRAMEWORKS: THE BOSTON GUN PROJECT

The Boston Gun Project was a problem-solving enterprise expressly aimed at taking on a serious, large-scale crime problem—homicide victimization among young people in Boston. Like many large cities in the United States, Boston experienced a large, sudden increase in youth homicide between the late 1980s and early 1990s. Boston youth homicide (ages 24 and under) increased 230%—from 22 victims in 1987 to 73 victims in 1990 (Braga, Kennedy, Waring, & Piehl, 2001). Youth homicide remained high well after the 1990 peak; Boston averaged 44 youth homicides per year between 1991 and 1995 (Braga et al., 2001). The Boston Gun Project proceeded by (a) assembling an interagency working group of largely line-level criminal justice and other practitioners; (b) applying quantitative and qualitative research techniques to create an assessment of the nature of, and dynamics driving, youth violence in Boston; (c) developing an intervention designed to have a substantial, near-term impact on youth homicide; (d) implementing and adapting the intervention; and (e) evaluating the intervention's impact (Kennedy, Piehl, & Braga, 1996). The Project began in early 1995 and implemented what is now known as the Operation Ceasefire intervention, which began in the late spring of 1996.

The trajectory of the Project and of Ceasefire is by now well known and extensively documented (Kennedy et al., 1996; Kennedy, Braga, & Piehl, 1997; Kennedy, 1997; Kennedy, 1998; Kennedy, 2001; Braga et al., 2001). Briefly, the working group of law enforcement personnel, youth workers, and researchers diagnosed the youth violence problem in Boston as one of patterned, largely vendetta-like ("beef") hostility among a small population of chronically criminal offenders, and particularly among those involved in some 60 loose, informal, mostly neighborhood-based groups (these groups were called "gangs" in Boston, but were not Chicago or LA-style gangs). As this diagnosis developed, the focus of the project shifted from its initial framework of "juvenile violence" and "gun violence" to "gang violence." The Operation Ceasefire "pulling-levers" strategy was designed to deter violence by reaching out directly to gangs, saying explicitly that violence would no longer be tolerated, and backing up that message by "pulling every lever" legally available when violence occurred (Kennedy, 1997,1998). Simultaneously, youth workers, probation and parole officers, and later churches and other community groups offered gang members services and other kinds of help. The Ceasefire Working Group delivered this message in formal meetings with gang members; through individual police and probation contacts with gang members; through meetings with inmates of secure juvenile facilities in the city; and through gang outreach workers. The deterrence message was not a deal with gang members to stop violence. Rather, it was a promise to gang members that violent behavior would evoke an immediate and intense response. If gangs committed other crimes but refrained from violence, the normal workings of police, prosecutors, and the rest of the criminal justice system would deal with these matters. But if gang members hurt people, the Working Group focused its enforcement actions on them.

A central hypothesis within the Working Group was the idea that a meaningful period of substantially reduced youth violence might serve as a "firebreak" and result in a relatively long-lasting reduction in future youth violence (Kennedy et al., 1996). The idea was that youth violence in Boston had become a self-sustaining cycle among a relatively small number of youth, with objectively high levels of risk leading to nominally self-protective behavior such as gun acquisition and use, gang formation, tough "street" behavior, and the like: behavior that then became an additional input into the cycle of violence (Kennedy et al., 1996). If this cycle could be interrupted, a new equilibrium at a lower level of risk and violence might be established, perhaps without the need for continued high levels of either deterrent or facilitative intervention. The larger hope was that a successful intervention to reduce gang violence in the short term would have a disproportionate, sustainable impact in the long term.

A large reduction in the yearly number of Boston youth homicides followed immediately after Operation Ceasefire was implemented in mid-1996. As discussed earlier, Boston averaged 44 youth homicides per year between 1991 and 1995. In 1996, with Ceasefire in place for roughly half the year, the number of Boston youth homicides decreased to 26 and then further decreased to 15 youth homicides in 1997, a level below that characteristic of Boston in the pre-epidemic period. The low level of youth homicides has continued through 1998 (18) and 1999 (15; Braga & Kennedy, 2001). A formal evaluation of Operation Ceasefire revealed that the intervention was associated with a 63% decrease in the monthly number of Boston youth homicides, a 32% decrease in the monthly number of shots-fired calls, a 25% decrease in the monthly number of gun assaults, and, in one high-risk police district given special attention in the evaluation, a 44% decrease in the monthly number of youth gun assault incidents (Braga et al., 2001). The evaluation also suggested that Boston's significant youth homicide reduction associated with Operation Ceasefire was distinct when compared with youth homicide trends in most major U.S. and New England cities (Braga et al., 2001).

At first blush, the effectiveness of the Operation Ceasefire intervention in preventing violence may seem unique to Boston. Operation Ceasefire was constructed largely from the assets and capacities available in Boston at the time and deliberately tailored to the city's particular violence problem. Operational capacities of criminal justice agencies in other cities will be different, and youth violence problems in other cities will have important distinguishing characteristics. However, the basic working group problem-solving process and the pulling-levers approach to deterring chronic offenders are transferable to violence problems in other jurisdictions. A number of cities have begun to experiment with these analytic frameworks and have experienced some encouraging preliminary results. Consistent with the problem-solving approach, these cities have tailored the approach to fit their violence problems and operating environments.

Minneapolis, Minnesota

Homicide in Minneapolis, traditionally a city with a very low homicide rate, increased dramatically from 59 victims in 1994 to 97 victims in 1995. In 1996, the number of homicides remained unusually high at 83 victims. In response to these unprecedented increases, a group of community members, law enforcement officers, government officials, and corporate representatives retained Police Executive Research Forum (PERF) and Harvard University researchers to help analyze their homicide problem and develop appropriate preventive strategies (Kennedy & Braga, 1998). The Minneapolis problem-solving enterprise was organized as an integrated academic-practitioner partnership and involved a working group composed of Minneapolis Police Department officers, Hennepin County probation officers, local and federal prosecutors, ATF field agents, and other local, state, and federal criminal justice agency representatives.

Using a blend of quantitative and qualitative exercises, the research team closely examined all homicide incidents between January 1994 and May 1997. The problem analysis revealed that homicide victims and offenders tended to have criminal histories, often substantial ones, and committed a wide variety of crimes including drug offenses, property crimes, disorder offenses, weapons offenses, and violent crimes (Kennedy & Braga, 1998). Many homicide victims and offenders were under probation supervision, sometimes at the time of the homicide incident. Gang-related violence played an important role in Minneapolis homicides. Reviews with Minneapolis practitioners suggested that Minneapolis did indeed have both "native" and Chicago-style gangs, plus groups linked to other cities and to Native Americans. Nearly 45% of the homicide incidents were considered to be gang related (Kennedy & Braga, 1998). Of all homicide incidents during the period examined, 26% of the victims and slightly more than 45% of the offenders were gang members (Kennedy & Braga, 1998). Some 32 active gangs with about 2,650 members were identified as being central to gang violence in Minneapolis; these individuals represented less than 3.5% of Minneapolis residents between the ages of 14 and 24 (Kennedy & Braga, 1998). These gangs tended not to be territorial, but operated fluidly geographically across Minneapolis and other local jurisdictions.

The working group decided that the results of the problem analysis supported the use of a pulling-levers ceasefire-style intervention. The working group responded to outbreaks of gang violence with a wide variety of criminal justice activities focused on the gang or gangs in question, communicated this new policy directly to gangs and gang members as the implementation unfolded, and matched the criminal justice intervention with social service and community-based interventions wherever possible (Kennedy & Braga, 1998). A key element in the enforcement portfolio was the creation, in the Hennepin County Probation Department, of a small number of field probation officers dedicated to the project and detailed to conducting home visits, street enforcement, and the like, in the company of Minneapolis Police Department officers.

The enforcement phase of the operation was kicked off by selecting a particularly violent gang, the Bogus Boyz, that was ultimately largely dismantled through the use of federal weapons prosecutions. The Minneapolis working group pursued a wide variety of means to deliver the deterrence message to the target audience. The Mayor and the enforcement team held a press conference to announce the Bogus Boyz arrests and their antiviolence rationale; teams of police and probation officers made home visits to troublesome gang members and paid special visits to gang-involved victims of gang violence (often in the company of their friends) in the hospital where they would warn against retaliation; and posters detailing the city's new gang violence policy were displayed prominently in the Hennepin County jail for viewing by the arrestees.

Although a formal evaluation of this effort has not been conducted, preliminary findings suggest that the intervention had an impact on homicide. After the intervention was implemented in June 1997, monthly homicide counts during the summer of 1997 showed a sharp reduction compared to monthly counts of homicide over the previous two summers (1995, 28 victims; 1996, 41 victims; 1997, 8 victims; Kennedy & Braga, 1998). After the initial success of the operation, adherence to the core strategy by the agencies involved slackened, and homicide in the city increased, though not to the levels observed immediately prior to the initial intervention.

Baltimore, Maryland

Baltimore has long suffered from high yearly counts of homicides. During the 1990s, however, Baltimore experienced more than 300 homicides per year between 1990 and 1997, with a 30-year peak of 353 homicides in 1993 (Kennedy, Braga, & Thomson, 2000). In 1996 and 1997, Baltimore had the fourth highest homicide rate in the United States among cities with more than 250,000 residents (Pastore & Maguire, 1999).

Beginning in 1998, with the support of the Baltimore Safe and Sound Campaign, a working group composed of Baltimore Police Department officers, Baltimore State's Attorney's Office and U.S. Attorney's Office prosecutors, probation and parole officers, juvenile corrections officers, federal law enforcement agencies (ATF, FBI, and DEA), and Harvard University researchers engaged in a problem-solving enterprise to unravel the dynamics underlying the homicide problem, develop a comprehensive violence reduction strategy, and implement the strategy (Kennedy et al., 2000).

The research team began the homicide problem analysis by obtaining official data on 303 homicide victims and 211 homicide suspects from 1997. A close examination of the criminal history data revealed that 74% of the victims and 87% of the suspects had adult and/or juvenile charges filed against them in court (Kennedy et al., 2000). Some 53% of the victims and 68% of the offenders had been under either adult or juvenile court-ordered supervision. Among those with criminal records, victims averaged about 8 prior charges and offenders nearly 10 prior charges; these prior offenses include a wide range of violent, drug, and property offenses (Kennedy et al, 2000). Using semi-structured qualitative data collection techniques, the research team closely examined the circumstances of the homicide victimizations. About 20% of the homicide incidents involved an ongoing dispute that was not about drug business between individuals or groups. Disputes involving drug business were involved in 18% of the homicides, and street drug robberies characterized 10% of the homicides. The remaining incidents were characterized as the result of robberies (nonstreet drug, 10%), spontaneous arguments (9%), domestic violence (6%), other circumstances (4%), or unknown circumstances (22%). Some 59% of the incidents occurred in or near a street-level drug market, and about 46% of the suspects and 37% of the victims were members of a drug organization or some recognized neighborhood criminal network (Kennedy et al., 2000). The project research identified some 325 drug groups in Baltimore that ranged in nature from rather sophisticated drug organizations, to structured neighborhood groups or "gangs" that sold drugs, to loose neighborhood groups that sold drugs (Kennedy et al., 2000).

The overall picture that emerged from this research suggested that violent groups of chronic offenders immersed in Baltimore's drug markets were responsible for the bulk of the city's homicides. As such, the working group felt that a pulling-levers-focused deterrence strategy was a promising way to reduce the city's homicide problem. Unlike Boston and Minneapolis, the sheer number of groups, the high homicide rate—averaging nearly one a day—and the clear role of street drug activity as a driver of the violence made the idea of an operation focused solely on groups implausible. Instead, the Baltimore strategy took *violent street drug market areas* as the basic unit of work. The basic operational idea was to take these areas in turn, reaching out to the groups in a particular area, "calming" the violence, establishing a maintenance strategy for the area, and then expanding the operation to new areas.

The first application of Operation Safe Neighborhoods, as the operation was called, focused on a very violent drug market area in the Park Heights neighborhood (Kennedy et al., 2000). The strategy proceeded by delivering a benchmark intervention that focused a varied menu of criminal justice operations on the violent groups in the target area. Selected members of the violent groups, usually those members on probation or under some form of criminal justice supervision, were then required to attend a forum where the new strategy was explained to the offenders. The forum was supplemented by a variety of other communication strategies, including the posting of fliers in the area and direct one-on-one communications with offenders on the street. Beyond the communication of cause and effect between violent behavior and law enforcement actions, the offenders were also offered access to social intervention and opportunity provision programs organized by the Safe and Sound Campaign. The violence prevention strategy was designed to ensure compliance in the targeted area, and new violent areas were addressed until the strategy was implemented citywide. Although a formal evaluation of the strategy has not been completed, preliminary analyses suggest that the intervention was associated with a 74% reduction in shootings and a 22% reduction in homicides in Park Heights during the 5 months following the intervention relative to shootings and homicides in the target area during the same time period one year earlier (Kennedy et al., 2000).

Boyle Heights, City of Los Angeles, California

In March 1998, the National Institute of Justice (NIJ) funded RAND to develop and test strategies for reducing gun violence among youth in Los Angeles. In part, the goal was to determine which parts of the Boston Gun Project might be replicable in Los Angeles. In designing the replication, RAND drew a clear distinction between the process governing the design and implementation of the strategy (data-driven policy development, problem solving, working groups) and the elements and design (pulling levers, collective accountability, retailing the message) of the Boston model. Processes, in theory, can be sustained and adaptive, and as such can be utilized to address dynamic problems. By singling out process as an important component, the RAND team hoped to make clear that process can affect program effectiveness independently of the program elements or the merits of the actual design (see Tita, Riley, & Greenwood, 2001, for a detailed analysis of the project).

The Los Angeles replication is unique in several important ways. First, the implementation was not citywide, but only within a single neighborhood (Boyle Heights) within a single Los Angeles Police Department Division (Hollertbeck). The project site, Boyle Heights, also differs from other sites in that the population is relatively homogenous. Well over 80% of the residents are Latinos of Mexican origin. The same is true for the gangs, many of which were formed prior to the Second World War. These gangs are clearly "traditional" gangs, with memberships exceeding a hundred members. The gangs are strongly territorial, contain age-graded substructures, and are intergenerational in nature (Maxson & Klein, 1996).

Unlike the other cities where gang and group-involved violence is a rather recent phenomenon, Los Angles represents an attempt to reduce gun violence in a "chronic gang city" with a long history of gang violence and an equally long history of gang reduction strategies. The research team first had to convince members of the local criminal justice and at-large community that the approach we were espousing differed in important ways from these previous efforts to combat gangs. In fact, it does—the RAND project was not about "doing something about gangs," but rather "doing something about gun violence" in a community where gang members committed an overwhelming proportion of the gun violence. The independent analysis of homicide files confirmed the perception held by police and community alike that gangs were highly overrepresented in homicidal acts. From 1995 to 1993, 57% of all homicides had a clear gang motivation. Another 25% of the homicides could be coded as "gang related" because they involved a gang member as a victim or offender but were motivated for reasons other than gang rivalries.

The analysis found very little evidence that drug dealing motivated much of the violence. Among the 90 gang-motivated homicides, less than 10% (8) also included a drug component. Law enforcement officials from the working group were skeptical and insisted, "These kids are ... being killed because of [dope]." The group revisited the homicide files with the gang detective personally responsible for assembling the cases. In the end, 4 homicides out of the 90 were recoded: Three homicides that were originally coded "gang-motivated only" were changed to "gang-/drugmotivated" and 1 case was recoded from "gang-/drug-motivated" to "gang-motivated only" (Tita et al, 2001).

Given the social organization of violence in Boyle Heights, the multidisciplinary working group fully embraced the pulling-levers-focused deterrence strategy developed in Boston. The processes of communicating the message have also been formally adopted, though to date this has been accomplished through personal contact rather than in a group setting. Police, probation, community advocates, street gang workers, a local hospital, and local clergy are all passing along the message of collective accountability for gangs continuing to commit gang violence.

It is too early to comment on any successes that the actual implementation of the strategy has had on reducing gun violence. However, participants are encouraged that in 2000, a year in which the citywide homicide rate in Los Angeles increased by 30% (and is being attributed to a rise in gang violence), homicide within the Hollenbeck area decreased by 15%. This at least suggests that the working group process and the collection and sharing of information among agencies may be responsible for some level of proactive responses to potential incidents of violence, as opposed to purely reactive responses.

STRATEGIC APPROACHES TO COMMUNITY SAFETY INITIATIVE IN FIVE CITIES

The Strategic Approaches to Community Safety Initiative (SACSI) is a U.S. Department of Justice pilot project that follows the Boston Gun Project's strong emphasis on partnerships, knowledge-driven decision making, and ongoing strategic assessment (Coleman, Holton, Olson, Robinson, & Stewart, 1999). The project is spearheaded by U.S. Attorneys and has been implemented in five cities—Indianapolis, Indiana; Memphis, Tennessee; New Haven, Connecticut; Portland, Oregon; and Winston-Salem, North Carolina. The crime problems addressed vary across the cities and range from gun violence (Indianapolis, Portland, and Winston-Salem), to community fear (New Haven), to sexual assault (Memphis). Several of the sites have adopted pulling-levers strategies that are well enough along to discuss here. In addition, although not formally part of SACSI, U.S. Attorneys have spearheaded pulling-levers operations in High Point, North Carolina, and in Omaha, Nebraska. We will discuss these operations as a group.

The Indianapolis project's working group is composed of Indiana University researchers and federal, state, and local law enforcement agencies (McGarrell & Chermak, 2001). During the problem analysis phase, the researchers examined 258 homicides from 1997 and the first 8 months of 1998 and found that a majority of homicide victims (63%) and offenders (75%) had criminal and/or juvenile records. Those with a prior record often had a substantial number of arrests. The working group members followed the structured qualitative data gathering exercises used in Boston to gain insight into the nature of homicide incidents. The qualitative exercise revealed that 59% of the incidents involved "groups of known chronic offenders" and 53% involved drug-related motives such as settling business and turf disputes (McGarrell & Chermak, 2001). It is worth noting that the terminology "groups of known chronic offenders" was used because there was not a consensual definition of *gang*, and the reality of much gang activity in Indianapolis is of a relatively loose structure (McGarrell & Chermak, 2001).

The working group developed two sets of overlapping strategies. First, the most violent chronic offenders in Indianapolis were identified and targeted for heightened arrest, prosecution, and incarceration (McGarrell & Chermak, 2001). Second, the working group engaged the pulling-levers approach to reduce violent behavior by groups of known chronic offenders (McGarrell & Chermak, 2001). The strategy implemented by the Indianapolis working group closely resembled the Boston version of pulling levers. The communications strategy, however, differed in an important way. The deterrence and social services message was delivered in meetings with high-risk probationers and parolees organized by neighborhoods. Similarly, home visits to probationers and parolees were generally organized by neighborhood. As the project progressed, when a homicide or series of homicides involved certain groups or gangs, the working group attempted to target meetings, enforcement activities, and home visits on the involved groups or gangs (McGarrell & Chermak, 2001). The research team has not yet completed a formal evaluation of the intervention. However, homicides citywide in Indianapolis fell from roughly 150 a year in the 2 years preceding the intervention to 100 in the year following implementation (Edmund F. McGarrell, personal communication, March 25, 2001). In addition, a preliminary analysis following an application of the pulling-levers approach in the Brightwood neighborhood suggests that the approach significantly reduced gun assaults and robbery incidents in the targeted area (McGarrell & Chermak, 2001).

High Point, North Carolina, is a city that began experiencing a quite severe street homicide problem in the mid-1990s. Working with Kennedy, U.S. Attorney Walter Holton, members of his staff, and members of the High Point police department determined that the problem fit the groups-of-chronic-offenders mold and instituted a pulling-levers strategy in late 1998. The High Point working group was quite robust and, in addition to the usual state and local actors, included very active participation by ATF, FBI, and DEA. As in Indianapolis, High Point followed a mixed strategy that focused both on repeat drug, gun, and violent offenders and on violent groups. The working group identified several hundred violent offenders and held a series of meetings with them; these meetings were formatted such that community representatives and service providers met privately with the offenders first, then enforcement representatives met with them subsequently. The operation was launched in the wake of the federal prosecution of a repeat gun offender, a prosecution that was then heavily "marketed" to offenders through the meeting process. In addition, as violence occurred in the community, the groups involved were identified and targeted for enforcement.

Homicides in High Point had numbered 14 (5 firearm) in 1994; 11 (9 firearm) in 1995; 11 (8 firearm) 1996; 16 (11 firearm) in 1997; and 14 (14 firearm) in 1998. After the operation began in late 1998, homicides fell to 5 (2 firearm) in 1999 and 9 (8 firearm) in 2000. According to High Point officials and the U.S. Attorney's office, none of the 1999 or 2000 homicides was the drug/gang type targeted by the strategy (Caren Johnson, personal communication, March 26, 2001).

The Winston-Salem operation is similar to High Point's, with an interesting elaboration. The Winston-Salem SACSI team was quite deeply focused on preventing juvenile offending. As the problem assessment proceeded, it became clear to the Winston-Salem team that juvenile offending, especially violent offending, was often the result of juveniles being incorporated into the criminal activity of older offenders, for instance as drug couriers and enforcers. Therefore, while maintaining its focus on juveniles and holding meetings with juvenile offenders, the Winston-Salem working group also sought to break this cycle by holding meetings with older offenders in which they were warned quite explicitly that incorporating juveniles into their illegal activity would result in focused state and federal enforcement attention (Coleman et al., 1999). In Winston-Salem, SACSI has focused on the four areas of the city that account for the vast majority of juvenile violent offenses. In these four areas, since the implementation of the SACSI strategy in September 1999, the city has seen a 36% reduction in juvenile violent offenses and a 60% reduction in the use of firearms by juveniles (Caren Johnson, personal communication, March 26, 2001).

Stockton, California

Beginning in mid-1997, criminal justice agencies in Stockton began experimenting with the pulling-levers approach to address a sudden increase in youth homicide. The Stockton Police Department and other local, state, and federal law enforcement agencies believed that most of the youth violence problem was driven by gang conflicts and that the pulling-levers approach used in Boston might be effective in reducing. Stockton's gang violence problem. The strategy was implemented by the Stockton Police Department's Gang Street Enforcement Team and grew into what is now known as Operation Peacekeeper as more agencies joined the partnership. The Peacekeeper intervention is managed by a working group of line-level criminal justice practitioners; social service providers also participate in the working group process as appropriate. As street gang violence erupts or when it comes to the attention of a working group member that gang violence is imminent, the working group follows the Boston model by sending a direct message that gang violence will not be tolerated and pulling all available enforcement levers to prevent violence while continuing communications and providing social services and opportunities to gang members who want them.

To better document the nature of youth homicide in Stockton, the working group retained Harvard University researchers to conduct an analysis of youth (age 24 and under) homicide incidents between 1997 and 1999 (see Braga, Thomson, & Wakeling, 2000). The research revealed that many offenders and victims involved in youth homicide incidents had noteworthy criminal histories and criminal justice system involvement. Following the same qualitative research methods used in Boston and elsewhere, gang-related conflicts were identified as the motive in 48% of the youth homicides. The research analysis also revealed that there were 44 active gangs with a total known membership of 2,100 individuals. Most conflicts among Stockton gangs fall into three broad categories: Asian gang beefs, Hispanic gang beefs, and African American gang beefs. Within each broad set of ethnic antagonisms, particular gangs form alliances with other gangs. Conflicts among Asian gangs were among clusters of different gangs composed mostly of Laotian and Cambodian youth. Conflicts among Hispanic gangs mainly involved a very violent rivalry between Norteño gangs from Northern California and Sureño gangs from Southern California. African American gangs tended to form fewer alliances and divided along well-known Blood and Crip lines. The research also suggested that Operation Peacekeeper was a promising approach to preventing gang violence as youth homicides in Stockton dropped by 54% between 1997 (24) and 1998 (11) and remained low in 1999 (14).

KEY ELEMENTS OF THE NEW APPROACHES

The available research evidence suggests that these new approaches to the strategic prevention of gang and group-involved violence have generated promising results. It is important to recognize that, with the exception of the Boston experience, rigorous evaluations of the interventions implemented in the various cities have not been completed. As such, these promising results should be interpreted with caution. Nevertheless, there are some core elements of this approach that seem to be the key ingredients in their apparent success. These key elements are worth delineating here.

Recognizing that violence problems are concentrated among groups of chronic offenders who are often, but not always, gang involved. Research has demonstrated that the character of criminal and disorderly youth gangs and groups varies widely both within cities and across cities (see, e.g., Curry, Ball, & Fox, 1994; Maxson & Klein, 1995). The diverse findings on the nature of criminally active groups and gangs in the jurisdictions described in this chapter certainly support this assertion. The research also suggests that the terminology used to describe the types of groups involved in urban violence matters less than their behavior. Gangs, their nature, and their behavior remain central questions for communities, police, and scholars. At the same time, where violence prevention and public safety are concerned, the gang question is not the central one (Kennedy, 2001). The more important observation is that urban violence problems are in large measure concentrated among groups of chronic offenders and the dynamics between and within these groups (Kennedy, 2001). This is an old observation in criminology, and is essentially well known among line law enforcement personnel, prosecutors, probation and parole officers, and the like. These new strategies offer a way of responding to this reality without setting the usually unattainable goals of eliminating chronic offending and/or eliminating criminal gangs and groups.

At the core of much group and gang violence is a dynamic or self-reinforcing positive feedback mechanisms. The research findings indicate that groups of chronic offenders are locked in a self-sustaining dynamic of violence often driven by fear, "respect" issues, and vendettas. The promising reductions observed in the cities engaging these strategic crime prevention frameworks suggest that the "firebreak hypothesis" may be right. If this cycle of violence among these groups can be interrupted, perhaps a new equilibrium at a lower level of risk and violence can be established. This may be one explanation for the rather dramatic impacts apparently associated with what are in fact relatively modest interventions.

The utility of the pulling-levers approach. The pulling-levers deterrence strategy at the heart of these new approaches was designed to influence the behavior, and the environment, of the groups of chronic-offenders that were identified as the core of the cities' violence problems. The pulling-levers approach attempted to prevent gang and group-involved violence by making these groups believe that consequences would follow violence and gun use and that they would, therefore, choose to change their behavior. A key element of the strategy was the delivery of a direct and explicit "retail deterrence" message to a relatively small target audience regarding what kind of behavior would provoke a special response and what that response would be.

Several of these sites have modified Boston's basic approach in interesting ways. Indianapolis and the North Carolina sites have incorporated a focus on individual dangerous offenders as well as on groups, and Indianapolis has a focus on neighborhoods as well. Indianapolis has also extended the strategy to felons returning from prison, warning them as part of the release process about the new enforcement regime to which they will be exposed. Winston-Salem has incorporated an intriguing attempt to prevent juveniles from being drawn into criminal activity. Those sites using Boston-style offender call-ins have developed their own variations on that theme, whereas Minneapolis and the Boyle Heights project in Los Angeles have relied on one-on-one outreach to their target populations. In addition, none of the sites have working groups or sets of partners that look exactly like Boston's or like each other's. This all fits with the original idea behind the Boston project and the pulling-levers idea, which was that the intervention and the logic behind the intervention were both flexible, open to adaptation according to local conditions, local preferences, and the strengths and weaknesses of variable sets of partners (Kennedy, 1997, 2001).

Drawing on practitioner knowledge to understand violence problems. The experiences, observations, local knowledge, and historical perspectives of police officers, street workers, and others with routine contact with offenders, communities, and criminal networks represent an underutilized resource for describing, understanding, and crafting interventions aimed at crime problems (Kennedy et al., 1997). The semi-structured qualitative research performed by the academics in these initiatives essentially refined and specified existing practitioner knowledge. Combining official data sources with street-level qualitative information helped to paint a dynamic, real-life picture of the violence problem.

Convening an interagency working group with a locus of responsibility. Criminal justice agencies work largely independent of each other, often at cross-purposes, often without coordination, and often in an atmosphere of distrust and dislike (Kennedy,

2001). This is also often true of different elements operating within agencies. The ability of the cities to deliver a meaningful violence prevention intervention was created by convening an interagency working group of line-level personnel with decision-making power that could assemble a wide range of incentives and disincentives. It was also important to place on the group a locus of responsibility for reducing violence. Prior to the creation of the working groups, no one in these cities was responsible for developing and implementing an overall strategy for reducing violence.

Researcher involvement in an action-oriented enterprise. The activities of the research partners in these initiatives depart from the traditional research and evaluation roles usually played by academics (see, e.g., Sherman, 1991). The integrated researcher/ practitioner partnerships in the working group setting more closely resembled policy analysis exercises that blend research, policy design, action, and evaluation (Kennedy & Moore, 1995). Researchers have been important assets in all of the projects described above, providing what is essentially "real-time" social science aimed at refining the working group's understanding of the problem; creating information products for both strategic and tactical use; testing—often in a very elementary, but important, fashion—prospective intervention ideas; and maintaining a focus on clear outcomes and the evaluation of performance. They have begun to produce accounts both of basic findings and of intervention designs and implementation processes that will be helpful to other jurisdictions. In addition, in several sites, researchers played important roles in organizing the projects.

CONCLUSION

We have provided here an account of a number of related violence prevention efforts. We underscore, again, that none of these have been fully evaluated, nor have they used desirable controlled experimental designs. However, we interpret the cumulative experience described above as supportive, at this preliminary stage, of the proposition that the basic Boston approach has now been replicated, with promising results, in a number of disparate sites.

If this is true, it suggests that there was nothing particularly unique about either the implementation or the impact of Operation Ceasefire in Boston. It suggests further that the fundamental pulling-levers framework behind Ceasefire can be successfully applied in other jurisdictions; with other sets of partners; with different particular activities; and in the context of different basic types of gangs and groups. Further operational experience and more refined evaluation techniques will tell us more about these questions, as experience and analysis continue to accumulate. At the moment, however, there appears to be reason for continued optimism that serious violence by gangs and other groups is open to direct and powerful prevention strategies.

New Approaches to the Strategic Prevention of Gang and Group-Involved Violence

PowerPoint by: Guadalupe A.
Rodriguez
Merycela Ochoa

Introduction

► A number of jurisdictions have been experimenting with many strategies to end gang and group-involved violence.
   these strategies have shown some positive results in reducing violence.
► Such approaches include the "pulling-lever" deterrence strategies which is designed to prevent violence committed by chronic offenders.
   1. by the coming together of interagency working groups.
   2. jurisdiction review on violence dynamics, victim characteristics, and also issues focusing on the drug market and weapons.

The Development of the New Strategic Prevention Frameworks: The Boston Gun Project

► The Boston Gun Project was a project targeted towards the serious problem of homicide among the youth in Boston.
  ▷ "Boston youth homicide (ages 24 and under) increased 230%—from 22 victims in 1987 to 73 victims in 1990." (Braga, Kennedy, Waring, & Piehl, 2001)
► The Boston Gun Project progressed by
  a) putting together a interagency group of workers in criminal justice and in other fields.
  b) applying quantitative and qualitative research towards what drives the youth violence in Boston.
  c) developing an intervention to create a significant impact on youth homicide.
  d) applying and becoming accustomed to the intervention.
  e) evaluate the impact of intervention (Kennedy, Piehl, & Braga, 1996).
► Then, in 1996 The Boston Gun Project started the Operation Ceasefire Intervention.

Operation Ceasefire Intervention

► Operation Ceasefire Intervention focused more on "gang violence " than on "gun violence" or "juvenile violence" because of the hostility among small groups offenders or neighborhood groups in Boston.
  ▷ "The Operation Ceasefire "pulling-levers" strategy was designed to deter violence by reaching out directly to gangs, saying explicitly that violence would no longer be tolerated, and backing up that message by "pulling every lever" legally available when violence occurred" (Kennedy, 1997, 1998).
► Groups of people then started offering different services and other kinds of help for these gang members. Their message for them was to not involve themselves with gangs and to stop the violence.
► Following immediately after the Operation Ceasefire, the Boston average from youth homicide reduced from 44 youth homicides to 15 youth homicides in 1997. (Braga & Kennedy, 2001).
► Other cities have started implementing their own strategies on gang violence and have found them to have a positive impact
  ▷ Cities such as Minneapolis, Baltimore and Los Angeles.

Minneapolis, Minnesota

- It has always been a city with low homicide rate, however, in 1997 the numbers increased from 59 victims to 97 victims in a year.
  - ▷ Because of these astonishing numbers, community members, government officials, etc., retained PERF and Harvard University researchers to help analyze the homicide problem and to develop appropriate preventive strategies. (Kennedy & Braga, 1998).
- The research team found that most of the victims and the offenders had some sort of criminal histories.
- Gang-related violence played an important part in Minneapolis homicide.
  - ▷ Nearly 45% of the homicide incidents were considered to be gang related. (Kennedy & Braga, 1998).
- The enforcement phase of this operation started off by selecting one of the most violent gangs, the Bogus Boyz. The city held a press conference and announced their arrests and also their policy for nonviolence. The probation and police officers made home visits to the troubled gang members and made visits to those members in the hospitals ,due to gang violence, to warn them about retaliation and not to do it.
- This intervention did have a great impact on reducing homicide.

Baltimore, Maryland

- Baltimore has always had a high homicide rate.
  - ▷ "during the 1990s, Baltimore experienced more than 300 homicides per year between 1990 and 1997" (Kennedy, Braga, & Thomson, 2000).
  - ▷ A group of officers and law enforcement got together to figure out a strategy on reducing the violence.
- They examined past homicide cases and found that 74% of victims and 87% of suspects had adult or juvenile charges filed against them in court. (Kennedy et al., 2000).
- The research identified around 325 different drug groups in Baltimore.
  - ▷ So this suggest that the Baltimore's drug markets were the ones responsible for the majority of the cities homicide.
- Operation Safe Neighborhood—reach out to violent street drug market areas, establish a maintenance strategy for this area, and then expand it to a new area.
- They would take selected members of the gang and explain to them their prevention strategy. They were given access to interventions and programs organized by Safe and Sound Campaign.
- Analysis shows that the intervention was associated with 74% reducing in shooting and 22% reductions in homicides during the 5 months following the intervention(Kennedy et al., 2000).

Boyle Heights, Los Angeles, California

▶ In March of 1998 National Institute of Justice(NIJ) funded a test strategy RAND(Research and Analysis) to reduce gun violence among youth in L.A

▶ Goal: Determine which parts of Boston Gun Project might be replicable in LA. (In designing the replication RAND drew a clear distinction between the process of governing the design and implementation of the strategy and the elements and design of the Boston model(data-driven policy development, problem solving, working groups)

 ▷ (see Tita, Riley, & Greenwood, 2001, for a detailed analysis of the project

Implementation Strategies

▶ LA replication is unique
▶ Not city wide (single neighborhood)
▶ Homogenous
▶ 80% of residents were Latinos of Mexican origin
▶ Formed after WWII
▶ Traditional gangs with membership exceeding hundred members
▶ Territorial (Maxton & Klein,1996).

RAND Project Analysis

- ► Gun Violence
- ► Homicide Acts
- ► 1995 to 1998, 57% of all homicides had clear gang motivation another 25% could be coded as gang relationship

Safety Initiatives in Five Cities

- ► The Strategic Approaches to Community Safety Initiative (SACSI)
- ► Indianapolis, Indiana
- ► Memphis, Tennessee
- ► New Haven Connecticut
- ► Portland, Oregon
- ► Winston-Salem, North Carolina
- ► The crime problems addressed vary across the cities and range from
- ► Gun violence Indianapolis, Portland, Winston-Salem)
- ► Community fear (New Haven)
- ► Sexual assault (Memphis)

Indianapolis Project

- ► The Working group developed two sets of overlapping strategies
  - ► Most violent chronic offenders were identified and targeted heightened arrest, prosecution, and incarceration
  - ► Group engaged pulling-levers approach to reduce violent behavior by groups of known chronic offenders
  - ► At the High Point, North Carolina followed a mixed strategy that focused both on repeat drug, gun and violent groups
    - ▷ Homicide numbered from 14(5 firearm) in 1994; 11(9 firearm) in 1995; 11 (8 firearm) 1996; 16 (11 firearm) in 1997; and 14 (14 firearm) in 1998
    - ▷ (Caren Johnson, personal communication, March 26, 2001).

Experiments

- ► In mid-1997 criminal justice agencies in Stockton began experimenting pulling-levers approach to address a sudden increase in youth homicide
- ► Operation Peacekeeper
  - ▷ criminal justice practitioners
  - ▷ social services providers
- ► 1997–1999 Analysis of offenders and victims involved in youth homicide incidents had net worthy criminal histories, and criminal justice system involvement (age 24 and under)
- ► 48% of Gang Related conflict were identified as a motive of the youth homicide
- ► 44 active gangs with a total known membership of 2100 individuals.
- ► Asian gang beefs (Braga, Thomson, & Wakeling, 2000)
- ► Hispanic gang beefs
- ► African American gang beefs

Key Elements of New Approaches

- ► Recognizing that violence problems are concentrated among group of chronic offenders who are often, but not always, gang involved. (Curry, Ball & Fox, 1994; Maxton & Klein, 1995)
- ► At the core of much group and gang violence is a dynamic or self-reinforcing positive feedback mechanisms
- ► The utility of the pulling-levers approach
- ► Drawing n practitioner knowledge to understand violence problems
- ► Convening and interagency working group with a locus of responsibility
- ► Researcher involvement in an action-oriented enterprise

Work Cited

- ► Braga, A. A, Kennedy, D. M, & Tita, G. E. New approaches to the strategic prevention of gang and group-involved violence. 271–284.
- ► Jordan, J, The boston strategy to prevent youth violence. 2010. 14 Nov. 2010<http://www.sasnet.com/bostonstrategy/programs/02_bostjob-sproj.html>.
- ► Objectives analysis. effective solutions.. 21 Apr. 2010. 14 Nov. 2010<http://rand.org/about/>.

CIVIL BANISHMENT OF GANG MEMBERS
CIRCUMVENTING CRIMINAL DUE PROCESS REQUIREMENTS?

By Stephanie Smith

ang-related violence is a serious problem facing communities across the United States. Gangs have taken over neighborhoods and have left innocent citizens terrified to enter public spaces. Part of what makes the gang problem in America so staggering is that conventional crime-fighting techniques have proven particularly ineffective at reducing gang activity. Faced with growing gang problems and an inability to stop gangs through conventional techniques, communities have begun to turn to the civil justice system as an alternative.

For example, Cicero, Illinois, recently passed a gang free zones ordinance allowing the town to exile gang members through civil banishment.[3] The ordinance is believed to be the first of its kind in the nation[4] and creates a unique civil remedy against gang violence that could serve as a model for other communities.[5] Under the ordinance, following a civil administrative hearing, gang members found by a preponderance of the

Stephanie Smith, "Civil Banishment of Gang Members: Circumventing Criminal Due Process Requirements?" *The University of Chicago Law Review,* vol. 67, no. 4, pp. 1461-1487. Copyright © 2000 by University of Chicago Law School. Reprinted with permission.

evidence to have engaged in gang-related criminal activity are ordered to leave Cicero and face severe fines if they return.[6]

While gang violence is a serious problem, there are limits to the measures communities can take to combat gangs. Gang members' constitutional rights constrain the range of alternatives available, as evidenced by a recent Supreme Court decision striking down a Chicago gang loitering ordinance even though the city claimed its enforcement reduced gang-related crime.[7] Therefore, it is important to examine the constitutionality of civil responses like the Cicero ordinance before it is enforced or other cities decide to enact similar measures. This Comment provides an analytic framework for evaluating civil responses to the gang problem in America. Civil responses are attractive because they are less expensive and the government faces a lower burden of proof;[8] however, when the civil justice system is used to administer serious penalties, the constitutional concerns outlined in this Comment should be considered.

This Comment argues that civil banishment is unconstitutional because it actually administers a criminal penalty through a civil hearing and therefore provides inadequate procedural safeguards to gang members. Furthermore, even if civil banishment ordinances, such as the one Cicero has enacted to combat gangs, were reclassified as criminal and the relevant procedural safeguards that are currently lacking were added, courts would still be unlikely to enforce banishment of gang members because state laws often proscribe or severely limit the use of banishment as a criminal penalty. Therefore, this Comment argues that the Cicero ordinance should not be enforced, and other cities should not adopt civil banishment procedures in the ongoing war against gangs.

Part I of this Comment explores the growing problem of gang violence in America, the ineffectiveness of conventional techniques for combating this violence, and the creative techniques that cities have begun to use to combat it. Part I also focuses on civil banishment remedies, such as the ordinance passed by the town of Cicero. Part II discusses the nature of the distinction between civil and criminal penalties and argues that civil banishment imposes a criminal penalty though a civil hearing in violation of constitutional due process protections. Finally, Part III argues that courts would not enforce a civil or criminal banishment of gang members in light of existing state banishment law.

I. THE GROWTH OF GANG VIOLENCE IN AMERICA AND LAW ENFORCEMENT RESPONSES

Gang violence is a staggering problem facing cities across America.[9] Traditional criminal law enforcement methods have proven inadequate, and communities have had to respond with innovative law enforcement techniques.[10] This Part briefly describes the overwhelming problem of gang violence in America and the creative responses of communities to mounting urban chaos. This Part then focuses on civil banishment remedies, such as the innovative gang free zones ordinance passed by the town of Cicero, Illinois.

A. Gang Violence in America

Gang violence is a pervasive problem ravaging cities around the country and leaving innocent citizens afraid to enter public spaces.[11] Recently Justice Thomas stated that in many cities, "gangs have virtually overtaken certain neighborhoods ... causing fear and lifestyle changes among law-abiding residents."[12] Gangs reportedly exist in 94 percent of major cities and are present in at least 1,130 cities of all sizes in America.[13] One estimate reports that there are over sixteen thousand gangs in the nation, over five hundred thousand gang members, and nearly six hundred thousand annual gang-related crimes.[14] In Chicago alone, for example, it has been estimated that there were 132 criminal street gangs in 1996 and that between 1987 and 1994 these gangs were "involved in 63,141 criminal incidents."[15]

Part of what makes the gang problem so staggering is that conventional crime-fighting techniques have been ineffective at stopping gang activity.[16] Gang members establish control over areas of cities and avoid arrest by only committing criminal offenses when they know officers are not in the vicinity.[17] While most people who intend to commit crimes will not do so if an officer is present, the prevalence of gang crime coupled with gang members' ability to avoid being caught makes fighting gangs with the traditional criminal justice system difficult. Furthermore, gang members often intimidate potential witnesses into refusing to testify or to report crimes in the first place.[18] While under-reporting is problematic in other areas of criminal law as well, it seems particularly prevalent in the gang context given people's fear of gangs.[19] Traditional methods of enforcement are still important, but communities and prosecutors have found that they need "more tools" in the fight against gangs because conventional criminal sanctions have not reduced gang activity sufficiently.[20]

B. Community Responses

Faced with the inability to stop gang crime through conventional techniques, communities have begun to turn to the civil justice system as an alternative because of its more lenient standards of proof and lower litigation costs.[21] The most common innovative measure, first championed in California, is an anti-gang civil injunction issued pursuant to courts' nuisance abatement powers.[22] Under this approach, cities identify gang turfs, gang members, and unlawful or antisocial gang activity.[23] The cities then file civil suits requesting that the court declare the gang to be a public nuisance and enjoin the named defendants, "numbering from a dozen to over three hundred," from engaging in a variety of activities.[24] While the injunctions are tailored to individual cases, many share common provisions such as prohibiting gang members from committing illegal acts, from associating in public with other gang members, and from harassing innocent third parties.[25]

These measures have been criticized as effectively banishing street gang members from public spaces[26] without sufficient proof of specific crimes and harming minority communities.[27] Additionally, the injunctions have been denounced as unconstitutionally vague[28] and violative of gang members' right to due process of law.[29] However, a divided California Supreme Court upheld the constitutionality of using injunctions to abate the public nuisance of gangs.[30] Some commentators have praised the measures,[31] and communities that have used the injunctions have "declared them to be unqualified successes."[32] The use of anti-gang injunctions has spread throughout the country, showing the desire of communities to use the civil justice system to bolster their efforts to reduce gang activity.

C. Civil Banishment and the Cicero Gang Free Zones Ordinance

In their search for innovative ways to combat gang crime, some towns have not stopped at the filing of public nuisance suits. For example, the town of Cicero, Illinois has adopted another, more aggressive technique in its battle against street gangs: civil banishment of gang members.[33] Cicero has been faced with growing gang problems in recent years.[34] Last April, the town passed a controversial ordinance making the town a gang free zone.[35] Under the ordinance, the Superintendent of Police can request that the Town Attorney bring a civil action against a street gang member to banish the accused from Cicero.[36] The complaint must allege evidence that the street gang member "engaged in gang-related criminal activity in the community which presents a clear and present danger to the public order and safety."[37] The hearing on the complaint is conducted in front of an administrative hearing officer designated by the Town Board, not a criminal court judge.[38] The ordinance does not indicate how the hearing officer is selected or what position the hearing officer holds in the town. "If the hearing officer finds that the accused is a gang member and has engaged in gang-related criminal activity," the accused is effectively banished from the town by an order to "vacate his residence."[39] The order to vacate is to be enforced by the Superintendent of Police, and if the gang member stays within Cicero or subsequently reenters Cicero, he is fined $500 for each day he is present in the town.[40] Although a one-year probationary period may be granted if the accused renounces all gang activity,[41] the banishment from Cicero lasts indefinitely under the ordinance, and there is no provision allowing the accused to seek permission to visit the town for any reason.

In the hearing under the ordinance, the rules of evidence do not apply. For example, "hearsay shall be admissible" to determine if the accused has been involved in gang-related activity.[42] More importantly, during this civil proceeding, the town only has to prove involvement in gang-related activity by a preponderance of the evidence,[43] lower than the "beyond a reasonable doubt" standard required in criminal cases.[44] However, the accused does have a "right to discovery and to be represented by an attorney" at the hearing.[45]

Even though Cicero has not enforced the ordinance to date, the ordinance has nonetheless had effects on the community. In the wake of its passage and the surrounding publicity, it has been reported that people have left Cicero to avoid potential enforcement actions.[46] Furthermore, other cities have considered adopting similar measures and Cicero hopes to be a model to other communities throughout the nation.[47]

When Cicero passed the ordinance, many thought it was an extreme, and likely unconstitutional, measure.[48] Some commentators thought that the ordinance was unconstitutionally vague,[49] while others thought it impermissible because it punishes someone for his status.[50] Other commentators criticized the treatment of minors under the ordinance[51] and expressed reservations about pushing gang members into surrounding communities.[52] Still others expressed concern that the ordinance would work along racial lines.[53] However, none of these reports focused on the fact that the ordinance is imposing a criminal penalty through a civil hearing. Other cities that model the Cicero ordinance could likely draft their ordinances so as to avoid many of the constitutional challenges, such as vagueness. However, the criminal-civil distinction problem implicates the two most important features of Cicero's ordinance that other communities could not simply draft around: the civil nature of the proceeding and the punishment of banishment. This Comment argues that civil banishment exceeds the limit on the extent to which the civil system can be used to supplant the criminal system in combating gangs, because banishment is an extremely severe punishment. Furthermore, this Comment argues in Part III that banishment of gang members from an entire city would likely be struck down under existing state law even if criminal procedural protections were provided. Therefore, other cities modeling Cicero's ordinance could not draft around the two central features of Cicero's ordinance to save their measures from invalidity.

II. CIVIL BANISHMENT IMPOSES A CRIMINAL PENALTY THROUGH A CIVIL HEARING

For years the law has distinguished between criminal and civil proceedings.[54] This Part details the tests that courts and commentators have used to determine if an action is criminal or civil and explores recent Supreme Court applications of these tests. Although the distinction between civil and criminal actions has been rapidly collapsing in recent years,[55] this Part argues that it is still important to draw the distinction in many cases, especially where a serious loss of liberty such as banishment is at stake. This Part then argues that civil banishment is a criminal penalty couched as a civil one, and that a court should not allow this deprivation of constitutional procedural protections guaranteed in criminal proceedings.

A. The Criminal-Civil Distinction

The division between criminal and civil law is deeply ingrained in English and American law,[56] and the Supreme Court continues to take the distinction seriously.[57] The distinction is important because many constitutional procedural safeguards are only available in criminal proceedings. For example, the Self-Incrimination Clause in the Fifth Amendment is expressly limited to "any criminal case,"[58] and the Sixth Amendment protections of the rights to a speedy trial, trial by jury, confrontation of witnesses, compulsory process, and assistance of counsel are only available to the accused in "criminal prosecutions."[59] Furthermore, other constitutional protections, such as the Double Jeopardy Clause protection against repeat punishment for the same offense and the requirement of proof beyond a reasonable doubt, have been limited to the criminal context by the Supreme Court.[60] Therefore, properly classifying a proceeding as criminal or civil is extremely important to determine the constitutional rights of defendants.[61]

The paradigmatic distinction between the two types of proceedings is that the criminal law is punitive while the civil law is compensatory.[62] However, this paradigm of the criminal-civil distinction has been rapidly collapsing[63] in large part due to the recognition that the civil system can be used, not only to compensate, but also to deter undesirable behavior in the same way that the criminal system deters.[64] Many legislative bodies are now turning to civil law techniques to stop antisocial behavior because they are less expensive and unencumbered by the rigorous constitutional protections associated with criminal trials.[65] However, given the lack of many procedural safeguards in a civil proceeding, it is still important to ensure that criminal sanctions are not being administered through a civil proceeding in violation of a defendant's constitutional rights. It is helpful when making the criminal-civil distinction to recognize that core criminal remedies are incarceration and the stigma associated with criminal conviction, while the core civil remedies are injunctions or monetary damages to compensate for injuries.[66] There are heightened procedural protections in the criminal justice system because criminal penalties typically deprive defendants of more than just property, which implicates larger liberty interests. Some commentators have suggested that constitutional criminal procedural protections should be applied to a proceeding, even if it is labeled as civil, if the punishments are as severe as those authorized by criminal laws.[67]

B. Tests for Determining the Nature of a Proceeding

There is no simple test to use when determining if an action classified as civil is "really" criminal. In *United States v Ward*,[67] the Supreme Court outlined a two-part test to determine whether the action should be considered civil or criminal: (1) did the legislative body indicate "either expressly or impliedly a preference for one label or the other"; and (2) despite the civil label, is the "statutory scheme ... so punitive either in purpose or effect as to negate [legislative] intention."[69] Demonstrating a willingness to defer to the legislature, the Court stated that "only the clearest proof" will suffice to override legislative intent under the second part of the test and transform a proceeding denominated as civil into a criminal one.[70]

Under *Ward's* first prong, a court must ascertain the legislature's preference. Some commentators have dubbed this test the "legislative label approach" because the Court will usually ratify the legislature's decision to classify an action as civil or criminal.[71] However, even proponents of the legislative label approach admit that there are types of cases that are appropriately classified as criminal regardless of legislative intent.[72] For example, one commentator has argued that if the punishment in the proceeding is only consistent "with the view that the underlying conduct punished was criminal," then the proceeding should provide criminal constitutional protections.[73] Therefore, it is important to examine a proceeding to determine if, despite its civil legislative label, it is in fact a criminal proceeding for the purpose of constitutional protections.

In *Hudson v United States*,[74] the Court reaffirmed the *Ward* rule[75] and stated that the seven-factor test from *Kennedy v Mendoza-Martinez*[76] serves as a "useful guidepost[ ]" when determining whether, despite the legislative label, a civil remedy is in fact a criminal penalty.[77] In *Mendoza-Martinez*, the Supreme Court developed a seven-factor comparative test for courts to use to determine whether a civil proceeding is in reality a criminal one requiring attendant constitutional procedural safeguards.[78] The seven factors are: (1) "[w]hether the sanction involves an affirmative disability or restraint"; (2) "whether it has historically been regarded as a punishment"; (3) "whether it comes into play only on a finding of scienter"; (4) "whether its operation will promote the traditional aims of punishment—retribution and deterrence"; (5) "whether the behavior to which it applies is already a crime"; (6) "whether an alternative purpose to which it may rationally be connected is assignable for it"; and (7) "whether it appears excessive in relation to the alternative purpose assigned."[79]

Despite considerable deference to the legislature, the Supreme Court has allowed serious sanctions to be imposed through civil proceedings only when the sanction was limited to the deprivation of property or when the sanction has historically been administered through civil proceedings.

In a series of cases, the Court has demonstrated a willingness to allow punitive forfeitures of property through the civil system. In *Bennis v Michigan*,[80] the Court allowed the civil confiscation of an innocent party's property that had been used without her knowledge by someone else in the commission of a crime.[81] In *United States v Ursery*,[82] the Court held that a federal conviction for manufacturing marijuana, following a civil forfeiture action seizing property used to facilitate the same offense, did not violate the Double Jeopardy Clause because civil forfeitures "do not constitute 'punishment' for purposes of the Double Jeopardy Clause."[83] Finally, in *Hudson*, the Court held that the Double Jeopardy Clause did not bar a criminal prosecution for violating banking statutes subsequent to the civil imposition of monetary penalties and debarment for the same conduct.[84]

The Court has also ratified the civil label of a proceeding when it reflects a long-standing legislative and judicial practice of administering a particular sanction through the civil justice system. In *Kansas v Hendricks*,[85] the Court held that potentially indefinite involuntary civil commitment of sexually violent predators did "not establish criminal proceedings" and therefore did not violate the Double Jeopardy or Ex Post Facto Clauses.[86]

While the Court has narrowed the gap between the civil and criminal justice systems through these cases imposing serious sanctions, it continues to assess each proceeding under the *Ward* test. Thus, the banishment of gang members in a legislatively labeled civil proceeding must still be carefully evaluated to determine whether it is in reality a criminal sanction depriving defendants of procedural safeguards. This Comment argues that, despite the Supreme Court's deference to legislative intent and its reluctance to provide criminal procedural protections to proceedings denominated as civil, the civil banishment of gang members is so extreme that it should be recognized as a criminal punishment.

C. Application of the Court's Tests to the Cicero Ordinance and Civil Banishment

Despite its civil label, this Part argues that civil banishment pursuant to measures such as Cicero's gang free zones ordinance is so punitive in purpose and in effect that courts applying the *Ward* test would ignore the civil legislative label and provide the constitutional protections of criminal proceedings to defendants.

In determining the constitutionality of civil banishment, the *Ward* test applies.[87] The result of part one of the test will be clear; in passing the ordinance, the legislature will demonstrate its intent to create a civil proceeding. For example, the Cicero ordinance unambiguously states the legislature's preference under part one of the *Ward* test. The preamble to the ordinance states that the town's intent was "to create a *civil* remedy against street[ ] gangs and their members" because their activities "present[ ] a clear and present danger to public order and safety."[88] Having attempted to create a civil penalty under the first part of the *Ward* test, the analysis proceeds to the second part.[89]

[84] 522 US at 103–05 (holding that Double Jeopardy Clause was not violated by subsequent criminal prosecution, even though the prior civil proceedings deprived the defendants of their livelihood, because Congress intended the monetary penalties and debarment sanctions to be civil in nature and there was not the "clearest proof" required to show that the penalties and debarments were in fact criminal).

Under this part of the *Ward* test, the legislature's intent will only be negated where there is the "clearest proof" that the "statutory scheme [is] so punitive either in purpose or effect as to negate [legislative] intention."[90] Under a straightforward application of this part, civil banishment is punitive enough to negate the legislative label. Banishing someone from a town is far more serious than typical civil penalties.[91] Furthermore, as will be discussed in Part III, banishing gang members under the ordinance would likely be found to be excessive under current banishment law and is unlikely actually to achieve the goal of reducing overall gang-related activity. Banishing gang members also seems excessively punitive in light of available alternatives, such as criminally prosecuting the underlying behavior or seeking civil public nuisance injunctions against the gang members' behavior itself without banishing individuals from their homes. Therefore, given the excessive nature of banishment, a court would likely find that the clear proof needed to negate the civil label is present and criminal procedural protections should be provided despite the legislative intent to create a civil proceeding.

As an alternative to this facial application of the second part of the *Ward* test, the *Mendoza-Martinez* factors[92] provide a list of considerations to use in making this determination.[93] First, banishment involves "an affirmative disability or restraint"[94] even though it does not involve the paradigmatic criminal punishments of imprisonment or detention.[95] For example, under the Cicero ordinance, accused gang members whom the hearing officer finds to have engaged in gang-related criminal activity are "ordered to vacate [their] residence[s]" in Cicero,[96] and are fined $500 a day if they are found within the town thereafter.[97] One could argue that this is not a physical restraint on gang members because they are free to live in any other community they choose. However, while the banishment may not be a typical physical restraint, it does impose a disability on gang members by restraining them from living in Cicero. Furthermore, this may not be an affirmative disability or restraint because a gang member, in theory, could pay the fine and stay within Cicero. However, the high daily fine for remaining in the town effectively expels gang members because they are unlikely to be willing to incur the high cost associated with remaining there. Therefore, civil banishment is effectively removing individuals from the entire community just as imprisonment would. This is a greater affirmative disability or restraint than a large onetime fine or civil forfeiture.

Second, banishment has "historically been regarded as punishment."[98] Justice Brewer stated that "banishment of a citizen is punishment, and punishment of the severest kind."[99] Black's Law Dictionary defines banishment as a *"punishment* inflicted upon criminals, by compelling them to leave a country for a specified period of time, or for life."[100] Typically, banishment is imposed as a condition of probation or parole,[101] further indicating that it is historically associated with punishment.

The third factor to consider is whether sanctions pursuant to the ordinance "come[ ] into play only on a finding of *scienter.*"[102] The Cicero ordinance does not directly contain any mens rea or subjective mental element requirement before an accused gang member may be banished from the town. However, the ordinance does require that the hearing officer find that the accused "has engaged in gang-related criminal activity" before ordering him to leave Cicero.[103] Although the analysis under this factor may initially seem unclear, it ultimately points to negating legislative intent to create a civil penalty because the gang-related criminal activity necessary for banishment would require scienter. The scienter requirement would exist in any civil banishment ordinance that was premised on prior criminal behavior as the condition to initiate banishment proceedings.

The next factor to consider is whether the sanction will "promote the traditional aims of punishment—retribution and deterrence."[104] The Cicero ordinance seeks to promote the traditional aims of criminal law rather than the traditionally compensatory aims of civil law.[105] The ordinance seeks to deter gang-related activity that is viewed as a danger to the public safety.[106] The ordinance is aimed at reducing risks caused by gang members' activity and seeks retribution for past gang-related criminal activity. It is not focused on compensation for actual injuries because the moving party, the town,[107] does not seek any damages under the ordinance.

The fifth *Mendoza-Martinez* factor focuses on whether the ordinance applies to behavior that is "already a crime."[108] This factor is somewhat difficult to apply literally because civil banishment does not usually penalize specific behavior. For example, the Cicero ordinance allows the town to banish gang members if they are found to have engaged in any gang-related criminal activity that "presents a clear and present danger to the public order and safety."[109] However, this also argues for placing the ordinance on the criminal, rather than civil, side of the criminal-civil distinction because the ordinance can only apply if the accused has been involved in a dangerous activity that could be punished criminally.

The sixth factor to consider is whether an alternative purpose for civil banishment may be assigned.[110] Banishment may serve a broad deterrent purpose in addition to stopping an individual's conduct. For example, in addition to its primary purpose of ridding Cicero of existing gang members, the Cicero ordinance seeks to deter others from becoming gang members or committing gang-related criminal offenses. This deterrent purpose is a traditional goal of criminal law. However, an alternative deterrent purpose of the ordinance is insufficient to negate the legislative intent and turn the civil sanction into a criminal one.[111] Therefore, the results under this factor standing alone do not argue in favor of declaring the Cicero ordinance to be criminal in nature.

The final *Mendoza-Martinez* factor asks whether the ordinance "appears excessive in relation to the alternative purpose assigned."[112] Gang-related crime and violence is a major problem that has resisted traditional law enforcement techniques,[113] and the goals of deterring others from becoming gang members or committing gang-related crimes and protecting the community are clearly admirable and desirable. However, banishing people from a town seems to be an extreme measure to accomplish these purposes. As will be discussed in Part III, banishing gang members from a town would likely be found to be excessive under current state banishment law and is unlikely to actually achieve the goal of reducing overall gang-related activity. So banishing someone from an entire town, even a gang member, also argues in favor of denominating the punishment as criminal because it is excessive in relation to the alternative deterrent purposes of the ordinance. Therefore, the results of the analysis under all but one of the seven *Mendoza-Martinez* factors argue in favor of the position that Cicero is imposing a criminal punishment through a civil hearing.

Advocates of civil banishment might point to recent Supreme Court decisions allowing the imposition of serious sanctions through the civil system, but reliance on these precedents would be misguided. As noted in Part II.B, the Court has allowed the legislature to establish civil forfeiture proceedings that complement criminal penalties, but the Court has been reluctant to expand these civil sanctions beyond taking property. Civil banishment goes beyond the simple levying of a fine or the taking of property; it deprives the defendant of freedom in the same way revoking a person's citizenship or imprisoning her deprives her of freedom.

An advocate of civil banishment might point to *Hendricks* as the strongest case for upholding civil banishment. In *Hendricks,* the Court held that potentially indefinite involuntary civil commitment of sexually violent predators was constitutionally permissible.[114] *Hendricks* is inapposite. First, the Kansas statute at issue in *Hendricks* provides for civil commitment only of a person who "suffers from a mental abnormality or personality disorder which makes the person likely to engage in the predatory acts of sexual violence."[115] The civil system has traditionally been used to commit the mentally ill since colonial times.[116] The legislature in *Hendricks* did not attempt to implement a civil statute that inflicted a punishment that is disfavored in the civil justice system. By contrast, as discussed in Part III below, banishment has long been disfavored, even in the criminal context, and it has never been used extensively like the commitment of the mentally ill.

In *Hendricks*, the Court stressed that Kansas had "disavowed any punitive intent"[117] in the law allowing for the civil commitment of sexually violent predators and that the law did "not implicate either of the two primary objectives of criminal punishment: retribution or deterrence."[118] The Court found that Kansas was "not seeking retribution for a past misdeed" because it used past criminal conduct solely as evidence of "mental abnormality" or evidence that the person would likely be dangerous in the future."

On the other hand, civil banishment does implicate the traditional goals of criminal punishment. For example, the Cicero ordinance requires that the hearing officer find that the accused has "engaged in gang-related criminal activity"[120] and does not specify that the past conduct is to be used only as evidence of potential future dangerousness. It seems instead that Cicero is seeking retribution for past criminal gang activity.

The Court in *Hendricks* also found that Kansas did not intend the civil commitment to serve the traditional deterrent purpose of criminal punishment because the people Kansas sought to confine were "by definition" incapable of "exercising adequate control over their behavior."[121] The threat of confinement is therefore unable to deter such persons.[122] In contrast, the Cicero ordinance serves the traditional criminal law objective of deterring gang-related activity by providing probation if the accused agrees to cease participation in illegal gang activity and threatening banishment if he does not.[123] There is no indication that the gang members are not capable of being deterred.

The *Hendricks* Court also indicated that the state did not intend for commitment to last any longer than necessary and did not intend for the commitment to be punitive.[124] The Court stressed that civil confinement under the Kansas law was only potentially, and not definitely, of unlimited duration, with a provision for immediate release upon a showing that the confined person is "safe to be at large."[125] In contrast, civil banishment would be for unlimited duration unless a city established a system to readmit gang members who demonstrate that they are no longer engaged in gang activity. For example, the Cicero ordinance indefinitely banishes gang members who do not opt for the one-year probation period and has no provision for readmitting them to the city if they later renounce gang activity.[126]

Finally, Kansas provided "numerous procedural and evidentiary protections" to confine the civil commitments to "only a narrow class of particularly dangerous individuals."[127] While one could argue that the provision of heightened procedural protections makes the Kansas statute more criminal in nature than the Cicero ordinance, the Court saw these protections as demonstrating the care that Kansas was taking to narrow the scope of civil commitment under the act.[128] In contrast, the Cicero ordinance specifically provides low evidentiary standards[129] and indicates the town's intent to cast a broad net and remove as many gang members as possible. Other civil banishment ordinances would have to share this feature of the Cicero ordinance to have a sufficient impact given the large number of gang members in many communities. Furthermore, one could argue that with Kansas already providing "strict procedural safeguards,"[130] the Court did not have to be as concerned that Kansas was depriving people of constitutional criminal procedural protections.

Taken together, these differences indicate that there is more "clear proof" that the Cicero ordinance establishes criminal proceedings, despite its civil label, than the Court had before it in *Hendricks*. Therefore, the Court would be unlikely to let the civil denomination of banishment stand even though it let civil confinement survive in *Hendricks*.

Despite the Supreme Court's usual deference to legislative preference, civil banishment is "so punitive [ ] in purpose [and] effect"[131] that courts should negate the civil label and classify the proceeding as criminal. Furthermore, the Cicero Gang Free Zones Ordinance is distinguishable from recent Supreme Court cases, even *Hendricks*, that have allowed serious punishments through civil hearings. [132]

III. BANISHING GANG MEMBERS UNDER EXISTING BANISHMENT LAW

Even if the enactors of an ordinance banishing gang members properly classify the proceedings as criminal and provide the constitutionally required procedural protections, banishment imposed on gang members is unlikely to be upheld by courts. This Part discusses the current state of banishment law with a focus on intrastate, rather than interstate, banishment because the Cicero method (banishment from a single community), is effecting an intrastate banishment. This Part examines the general reluctance of courts to uphold banishment conditions. This Part then argues that banishing gang members should not be allowed by courts under the existing law because it is not narrowly tailored, it is unnecessarily severe and restrictive, and it merely pushes gang members into other areas, creating dissension between neighboring communities.

A. Current Banishment Law

1. Interstate banishment.

Historically, banishment was a severe form of criminal punishment used to rid communities of undesirable individuals.[133] Banishment reflects a community's view that it does not want to take the time to rehabilitate an offender, or that it sees an offender as incapable of rehabilitation and that the community feels that its safety is best served by expelling the offender from the community.[134] At the federal level, "[t]here is no banishment prohibition in the United States Constitution,"[135] and banishment was not cruel and unusual punishment at common law.[136] However, the majority of federal and state courts that have addressed interstate banishment have held it to be illegal,[137] and at least fifteen state constitutions explicitly prohibit banishing people from the state:[138] The majority of courts that have rejected interstate banishment have found that it is not related to the rehabilitative and deterrent goals of the criminal justice system and that it raises serious interstate comity problems when one state "make[s] other states a dumping ground for [its] criminals."[139]

2. Intrastate banishment.

Despite the fairly uniform rejection of interstate banishment, states do not agree on whether intrastate banishment may be imposed as a criminal sentence or a condition of probation or parole.[140] Banishment cases are "uncommon,"[141] and the majority of states have not addressed the intrastate banishment issue.[142] However, some states have indicated a willingness to uphold intrastate banishment conditions in limited circumstances[143] while others prohibit intrastate as well as interstate banishment." When determining the validity of a banishment order, courts typically look to at least three general factors. First, the banishment must be "related logically to the rehabilitative purposes of the sentence."[145] Second, the prohibited area in the banishment condition must be tailored in some way to fit the underlying crime.[146] Finally, the banishment condition cannot be "unnecessarily severe and restrictive."[147]

Under these guidelines, the determination of the legitimacy of a banishment condition is highly fact specific.[148] In cases of egregious misconduct, such as sexual abuse of a child, courts tend to permit more sweeping banishment conditions to protect past victims.[149] Generally, courts seem to prefer banishment conditions barring individuals from crime-ridden areas or locations frequented by past victims to those prohibiting individuals from entering entire communities.[150]

B. Banishment of Gang Members

Civil banishment effectively imposes an intrastate banishment of gang members by ordering them to leave a town. This Part argues that a court is unlikely to uphold such a condition under existing banishment law.

First, banishment of gang members does not serve any rehabilitative purpose. One could argue that removing gang members from a town is likely to sever their ties to their gang and reduce the likelihood that they will engage in further gang-related conduct.[151] Civil banishment, however, simply orders gang members to leave town and does not rehabilitate them in any way or try to reduce their future criminal behavior in other communities. On the other hand, this factor is not dispositive because the cases requiring a rehabilitative purpose have been in the probation context,[152] where rehabilitation is clearly the goal. Supporters could argue that the goal of civil banishment measures, such as the Cicero ordinance, is not gang member rehabilitation but rather community protection and that banishing gang members is therefore serving the underlying goals of the measures.[153]

Second, banishment of gang members such as that effected by the Cicero ordinance is not narrowly tailored geographically to match gang members' offenses as required in most intrastate banishment cases.[154] A gang free zones ordinance simply banishes gang members from the entire town, not only from specific areas where they engaged in criminal behavior. A court is unlikely to uphold such a broad geographic restriction that is unrelated to specific offenses. For example, there is no indication that the underlying criminal activity, required for banishment under the Cicero ordinance,[155] must be similar to the egregious crimes such as child sexual abuse and murder that have led courts to uphold such broad geographic banishment conditions.[156] For this reason, a court is unlikely to uphold a broad banishment condition even to stop the serious threat of gang activity.[157]

Finally, a court is likely to find that banishment of gang members is unnecessarily severe and restrictive. For example, overlapping with the previous factor, the fact that banishment under the Cicero ordinance is from the entire town makes the condition overly restrictive. Furthermore, most banishment conditions allowed by courts are limited in duration,[158] while banishment under the Cicero ordinance is permanent. The ordinance contains no provision specifying a period of time for the banishment and no provision for an excluded gang member to seek readmission to the town. A final indication that the banishment condition is overly restrictive is that it does not allow the banished gang member to enter the town for any reason.[159]

In addition to these factors generally considered in determining the legality of intrastate banishment conditions, the banishment of gang members is unlikely to be upheld because it merely pushes gang members into other regions, creating dissension between neighboring communities. Typically, comity concerns are discussed in interstate banishment cases.[160] However, the same principles apply to intrastate banishment. When a town tries to "dump" gang members into surrounding cities, serious problems between communities may arise if gang members join new gangs and continue to commit gang-related crimes in their new community.[161]

Finally, banishment is unlikely to be upheld because of the likelihood of enforcement along racial lines. In a comprehensive commentary on banishment, one commentator argues that banishment should be per se unconstitutional and recognizes as specific problems that banishment may be used as a "vehicle of racial discrimination in certain cases" and as a "means of effecting the political makeup of a [community]" by banishing minority citizens disproportionately and redistributing votes.[162] For example, critics of the Cicero ordinance have argued that it will work along racial lines.[163] While all criminal law enforcement is open to attack as discriminatory, banishing citizens deprives them of the right to vote in future elections to change current community policies and makes discretion particularly dangerous. Furthermore, if a court in fact allowed banishment through the civil, rather than criminal, justice system contrary to the argument in Part II, the lack of procedural safeguards would likely lead to a higher rate of wrongful convictions that would exacerbate the racial bias problem.

In light of these considerations and the factors generally used to determine the legality of intrastate banishment conditions, a court is unlikely to uphold the banishment of gang members.

CONCLUSION

Gang-related crime in America is staggering and communities are understandably searching for new ways to control gang violence. Communities are turning away from ineffective traditional criminal law techniques and are looking to innovative civil methods to fight gangs. The town of Cicero, Illinois has tried the novel measure of banishing gang members from the town pursuant to a civil administrative hearing.

However, civil banishment imposes a criminal penalty through a civil hearing and deprives gang members of important constitutional procedural protections. Despite the Supreme Court's strong preference for deferring to the civil or criminal label affixed to statutes by legislatures and the high burden of proof a challenger must meet to overcome the legislative denomination, the civil banishment of gang members is likely to transcend its civil legislative label.

Furthermore, even if Cicero provided the necessary procedural protections and recognized the criminal nature of the ordinance, courts would be unlikely to enforce the banishment of gang members under existing banishment law. Banishment imposed on gang members is not tailored in any way to a gang member's criminal behavior but is instead an unnecessarily broad geographical restriction from the entire town. Furthermore, banishment pushes gang problems into surrounding communities and is prone to discriminatory enforcement along racial lines.

While cities should pursue innovative ways to combat the serious problems of gang-related crime, communities should not be allowed to deprive gang members of criminal due process protections or to simply shift their problems into surrounding areas by banishing gang members. Cities should pursue stepped-up enforcement of petty crimes committed by gang members or nuisance abatement injunctions that are more narrowly tailored than broad banishment from an entire town to combat gang-related crime. The Cicero ordinance should not be enforced and other communities should not enact similar measures.

NOTES

1. †B.S. 1996, Rice University; J.D. Candidate 2001, The University of Chicago.
2. See notes 11–12 and accompanying text.
3. See note 10.
4. 3 An Ordinance Providing for the Enforcement of Gang Free Zones in the Town of Cicero ("Gang Free Zones Ordinance"), Ordinance No 111–99 (Apr 1999), amending Cicero Code of Ordinances ch 25.
5. 4 See Illinois Town Sues Gangs for Damages, AP (May 12,1999) (describing Cicero's gang free zones law as "an extraordinary ordinance ... believed to be the first of its kind in the nation").
6. See note 47 and accompanying text.
7. Gang Free Zones Ordinance § 25–300(a)(F)-(G), 25–300(c)(A)-(B).
8. City of Chicago v Morales, 527 US 41, 48–51 (1999) (holding that Chicago gang loitering ordinance was unconstitutionally vague).
9. See notes 60–61 and accompanying text (proof beyond a reasonable dodbt standard limited to criminal context); note 65 and accompanying text (civil law techniques less expensive than criminal procedures).
10. See Gregory S. Walston, *Taking the Constitution at Its Word: A Defense of the Use of Anti-Gang Injunctions*, 54 U Miami L Rev 47, 47 (1999) (stating that gang violence is no longer confined to inner cities but has "erupted to threaten virtually all neighborhoods in America"); Terence R. Boga, Note, *Turf Wars: Street Gangs, Local Governments, and the Battle for Public Space*, 29 Hary CR-CL L Rev 477,477 (1994) (stating that "gang violence has escalated to the point of ubiquity, resulting in the mutilation and death of countless participants and innocent bystanders").[10] See Walston, 54 U Miami L Rev at 48 (cited in note 9) ("The rising problem of gang violence has overwhelmed conventional law enforcement techniques."); Matthew Mickle Werdegar, Note, *Enjoining the Constitution: The Use of Public Nuisance Abatement Injunctions Against Urban Street Gangs*, 51 Stan L Rev 409, 410 & n 6 (1999) (noting that gang-related crime has "proven highly resistant to traditional crime fighting methods" and citing numerous reports of the failure of traditional law enforcement methods to effectively stop gangs); Boga, Note, 29 Harv CR-CL L Rev at 477 (cited in note 9) (noting that "there is growing sentiment that new law enforcement techniques are necessary to stymie [ ] mounting urban disorder").
11. See Gary Stewart, Note, *Black Codes and Broken Windows: The Legacy of Racial Hegemony in Anti-Gang Civil Injunctions*, 107 Yale L J 2249,2249 (1998) (stating that gang members are holding innocent people "hostage[ ] in the 'hood' leaving [them] afraid for their lives in public spaces").

12. *City of Chicago v Morales,* 527 US 41, 99–100 (1999) (Thomas dissenting) (also stating that citizens are often relegated to the status of prisoners in their own homes) (internal quotation marks omitted).

13. See Marilyn Tower Oliver, *Gangs: Trouble in the Streets* 7 (Enslow 1995).

14. See G. David Curry, Richard A. Ball, and Scott H. Decker, *Estimating the National Scope of Gang Crime from Law Enforcement Data,* in C. Ronald Huff, ed, *Gangs in America* 21, 31 (Sage 2d ed 1996) (providing table with estimated numbers of gangs, members, and gang crimes in cities of different sizes, for selected counties, and for the nation as a whole).

15. *Morales,* 527 US at 99 (Thomas dissenting) (discussing Chicago gang violence statistics).

16. See note 10.

17. *Morales,* 527 US at 45–47 (describing Chicago city council findings that led to the enactment of the invalidated Gang Congregation Ordinance prohibiting criminal street gang members from loitering).

18. Walston, 54 U Miami L Rev at 48 (cited in note 9) (describing reasons that gang violence has "overwhelmed conventional law enforcement techniques").

19. See notes 11–12 and accompanying text.

20. Art Barnum, *County Files Anti-Gang Suit: Unused State Law Cited in Civil Case Against Twenty Two West Chicago Defendants,* Chi Trib 1 (Oct 5,1999) (quoting State Attorney's justification for seeking a civil injunction against gang leaders in Cicero, Illinois barring their gang activities).

21. See notes 61 and 65 and accompanying text.

22. See, for example, Walston, 54 U Miami L Rev at 48 (cited in note 9) (stating that in the search for improved gang prevention, the most effective new technique is "enjoining the gang as a public nuisance"); Werdegar, Note, 51 Stan L Rev at 411 (cited in note 10) (noting that California has "pioneered the use of public nuisance law to obtain sweeping civil injunctions" against gang members); Stewart, Note, 107 Yale L J at 2249 (cited in note 11) (stating that many state and local governments "have adopted new criminal and civil approaches designed to abate the 'nuisance' of gang existence").

23. Werdegar, Note, 51 Stan L Rev at 416–17 (cited in note 10) (discussing processes cities use to obtain nuisance abatement injunctions against gangs).

24. Id.

25. Id at 417 (discussing typical provisions under nuisance abatement injunctions).

26. See Boga, Note, 29 Harv CR-CL L Rev at 492 (cited in note 9) (stating that municipalities are "on the verge of decreeing that [street gang members] are not suitable for any public space at any time").

27. See Stewart, Note, 107 Yale L J at 2250–51 (cited in note 11) (criticizing anti-gang civil injunctions as harming minority communities and perpetuating "racial stigma and oppression").

28. See Werdegar, Note, 51 Stan L Rev at 427–28 (cited in note 10) (discussing problems of arbitrary and discriminatory enforcement allowed under anti-gang injunctions). See also *Gallo v Acuna*, 929 P2d 596,629–30 (Cal 1997) (Mosk dissenting) (concluding anti-gang injunction violated vagueness and overbreadth doctrines).

29. See Werdegar, Note, 51 Stan L Rev at 433–34 (cited in note 10) (discussing the constitutional due process issues raised by the lack of procedural safeguards in civil anti-gang injunction cases); Stewart, Note, 107 Yale L J at 2266–67 (cited in note 11) (noting that civil hearings entitle defendants to "much less stringent and comprehensive" due process guarantees). .

30. *Acuna*, 929 P2d at 608–14 (holding that the nuisance abatement injunction issued against gang members did not violate their First Amendment rights of free speech or association and was not impermissibly overbroad or vague).

31. Walston, 54 U Miami L Rev at 53 (cited in note 9) (stating that "[b]ecause it is unreasonable to expect the common citizen to constantly be subjected to the inherent intimidation and violence of criminal street gangs, anti-gang injunctions present the proper solution for resolving the conflict between the interests of public safety and the civil liberties of gang members").

32. Werdegar, Note, 51 Stan L Rev at 411 (cited in note 10) (discussing the evident approval of anti-gang injunctions by law enforcement, politicians, and the courts).

33. See Eric Slater, *Suburb Gives Gang Members 60 Days to Leave*, Austin AmericanStatesman A12 (May 2, 1999) (stating that measures taken by Cicero are "stricter than any now on the books").

34. See Robert Becker and Rob D. Kaiser, *Cicero Taking Its Gang Fight to Court: Suits Seek Millions and Judicial Orders to Restrict Activities*, Chi Trib 1 (May 12,1999) (reporting that police have identified eighteen gangs in Cicero); Pam Belluck, *Capone's Old Haven in Illinois Wants to Evict Gang Members*, Deseret News A6 (May 9, 1999) (stating that Cicero officials reported sixty-four shootings and fifteen homicides in 1998 and twenty-four shootings and two homicides in the first four months of 1999, almost all gang related). In comparison, approximately one-quarter, or 175, of Chicago's 700 homicides in 1998 were gang related. See Steve Mills, *One Step to Reform, Two Steps Back: Corruption, Brutality Charges Still Tarnish Police*, Chi Trib 1 (Feb 11, 1999).

35. See Tammy Webber, *Illinois Suburb OKs Anti-Gang Ordinance*, AP (Apr 28,1999) (reporting that the Cicero ordinance making the town a gang free zone was passed by 95 percent of the voters and unanimously enacted by the Town Board).

36. Gang Free Zones Ordinance § 25–300(a)(C).

37. Id.

38. Id § 25–300(a)(E). However, a gang member can file an appeal from an order to leave Cicero with the Circuit Court of Cook County. See id § 25–300(a)(J).

39. Id § 25–300(a)(G).

40. Id § 25–300(a)(G), 25–300(c)(A)-(B).

41. Id § 25–300(a)(H). See also § 25–300(a)(I) (for individuals sixteen and younger the ordinance allows for a probationary period if the parents of the accused agree that the accused will cease gang activity).

42. Id § 25–300(a)(E).

43. Id § 25–300(a)(F).

44. See note 61 and accompanying text.

45. Gang Free Zones Ordinance § 25–300(a)(E).

46. See Rob D. Kaiser, *Suits Targeting Gangs Have Town Split in Two*, Chi Trib 1 (metro section) (May 13,1999) (relaying anecdotal evidence that six or seven people have left Cicero already out of fear of banishment); Slater, *Suburb Gives Gang Members 60 Days to Leave*, Austin American-Statesman at A12 (cited in note 33) (reporting that Cicero town president Betty Loren-Maltese thinks a lot of families will "see the handwriting on the wall and will leave").

47. See John Flink, *Alderman Urges Cicero-style Law to Battle Gangs*, Chi Trib 3 (metro section) (May 19,1999) (reporting Waukegan alderman suggesting that town look into prohibiting gangs); Betty Loren-Maltese, *Ridding Cicero of Gangs*, Chi Trib 14 (May 4, 1999) (quoting Cicero town president stating that Cicero's ordinance will serve as a model for other communities and that the town had already received over thirty requests from other municipalities for copies of the ordinance).

48. John Kass, *Cicero Keeping Streets, Alleys Safe from Little Hoopsters*, Chi Trib 3 (May 18, 1999) (stating that, because of the ordinance, constitutional scholars think Cicero's town president is "wacky").

49. See, for example, Stephen E. Sachs, *When Only "Good People" Have Rights*, St. Louis Post-Dispatch B15 (Aug 10,1999) (stating that the Cicero ordinance is likely to be unconstitutional because its expansive definition of street gang "opens up the door for arbitrary and discriminatory enforcement" and quoting Northwestern University law professor Dan Polsby as saying that "[s]ome ordinances are unconstitutional, but this one is unconstitutional as hell").

50. *Town's Anti-Gang Laws Raise Eyebrows: Legal Experts Believe Attempts to Kick Out All Gangsters are Unconstitutional*, Salt Lake Trib Dl (Apr 29,1999) (quoting the executive director of the ACLU as stating that the ordinance is unconstitutional "because [it] charge[s] somebody for their status[,] … not a crime").

51. See, for example, Editorial, *Gang Busting*, Daily Athenaeum (Apr 29, 1999) (noting that when gang members under age eighteen are forced to leave under the ordinance, their parents have to "move out with them or send them to live with out-of-town relatives").

52. See, for example, Brian Knowlton, *Cicero, Illinois to Gangs: Get Out of Town*, Intl Herald Trib 3 (Apr 30, 1999) (expressing concern that the ordinance allows Cicero to "foist" its problems on other towns).

53. See, for example, *Illinois Town Sues Gangs for Damages*, AP (cited in note 4) (quoting University of Chicago Professor Stephen Schulhofer as saying that "[w]hat you worry about is when something like this gives (the town) the power to sweep every Latin kid off the street"); Slater, *Suburb Gives Gang Members 60 Days to Leave*, Austin American-Statesman at A12 (cited in note 33) (reporting that opponents of the ordinance are concerned that it will "work along racial lines" against the influx of Latinos into predominantly white Cicero). But see Editorial, *Try Again on Gangs*, Chi Sun-Times 31 (June 14,1999) (stating that among those targeted by the ordinance are members of a Caucasian gang, the Nobel Knights).

54. See, for example, Susan R. Klein, *Redrawing the Criminal-Civil Boundary*, 2 Buff Crim L Rev 679, 679 (1999) (stating that "[o]ne of the most profound boundaries our justice system has drawn is that between the terrain of civil and criminal law").

55. See notes 63–64 and accompanying text.

56. See Kenneth Mann, *Punitive Civil Sanctions: The Middleground Between Criminal and Civil Law*, 101 Yale L J 1795, 1803 (1992) (discussing historic division between criminal and civil law dating back to the fourteenth and fifteenth centuries).

57. See, for example, Stephen J. Schulhofer, *Two Systems of Social Protection: Comments on the Civil-Criminal Distinction, with Particular Reference to Sexually Violent Predator Laws*, 7 J Contemp Legal Issues 69, 78 (1996) (stating that the Court takes the distinction seriously and that there are "good grounds for its durability").

58. US Const Amend V.

59. US Const Amend VI.

60. See *United States v Ward*, 448 US 242, 248 (1980) (stating that these protections "while not explicitly limited to one context or the other, have been so limited" by the Court to the criminal context).

61. See, for example, John C. Coffee, *Paradigms Lost: The Blurring of the Criminal and Civil Law Models-And What Can Be Done about It*, 101 Yale L J 1875, 1888 (1992) (stating that civil penalties "could provide the means for evading constitutional safeguards" guaranteed in the criminal context).

62. See, for example, Mann, 101 Yale L J at 1799, 1807–09 (cited in note 56) (discussing the respective paradigmatic purposes of criminal and civil law); Coffee, 101 Yale L J at 1884 (cited in note 61) (stating that "the criminal law prohibits, while the civil law prices"); Mary M. Cheh, *Constitutional Limits on Using Civil Remedies to Achieve Criminal Law Objectives: Understanding and Transcending the Criminal-Civil Law Distinction*, 42 Hastings L J 1325, 1354–55 (1991) (noting that commentators state that "recompense of the injured ... is the hallmark of a civil proceeding" while criminal punishment is traditionally for seeking retribution).

63. See, for example, Carol S. Steiker, *Punishment and Procedure: Punishment Theory and the Criminal-Civil Procedural Divide*, 85 Georgetown L J 775, 783–84 (1997) (discussing the increasing "blurring or destabilization" of the criminal-civil distinction); Coffee, 101 Yale L J at 1875 (cited in note 61) (stating that the "line between civil and criminal penalties is rapidly collapsing"); Cheh, 42 Hastings L J at 1327 (cited in note 62) (stating that the "current phenomenon of civil remedies blending with criminal sanctions never has been more actively or consciously pursued").

64. See *United States v Ursery*, 518 US 267, 292 (1996) (noting that deterrence "may serve civil as well as criminal goals"). See also Mann, 101 Yale L J at 1845–47 (cited in note 56) (discussing the rise of deterrence theory in law); Steiker, 85 Georgetown L J at 784–87 (cited in note 63) (discussing how the growth of "law and economics" has challenged the distinction between civil and criminal sanctions by recasting them as "related parts of a unitary scheme of state control of private behavior"); Richard A. Posner, *Economic Analysis of Law* 187,190 (Little, Brown 3d ed 1986) (arguing that tort remedies and criminal sanctions can both be effective deterrents). See also Steiker, 85 Georgetown L J at 787–97 (cited in note 63) (arguing that changes in cognitive and behavioral sciences and the similarity between modern modes of criminal punishment and civil regulation have also led to the collapse of the criminal-civil distinction in many cases).

65. See, for example, Steiker, 85 Georgetown L J at 780 (cited in note 63) (stating that the high cost of criminal procedure has led legislators to pursue "civil avenues to address what might more plausibly be classified as criminal conduct"); Cheh, 42 Hastings L J at 1345 (cited in note 62) (noting that the use of civil remedies is growing in part because they are "easier to use, more efficient, and less costly than criminal prosecutions").

66. See Mann, 101 Yale L J at 1809 (cited in note 56) (discussing the paradigmatic differences between criminal and civil remedies). See also *Kennedy v Mendoza-Martinez*, 372 US 144, 168 (1962) (holding that whether the sanction is an affirmative disability or restraint is a factor in determining whether it is criminal); Coffee, 101 Yale L J at 1878 (cited in note 61) (noting criminal law's goal of maximizing stigma and censure); Cheh, 42 Hastings L J at 1352 (cited in note 62) (noting that commentators have argued that the stigma and social condemnation associated with criminal proceedings distinguish them from civil ones).

67. See Cheh, 42 Hastings L J at 1350–51 (cited in note 62) (noting the appeal of the "sanction equivalency approach" but also the flaw in the approach because huge punitive damage awards have long been accepted as civil); George Fletcher, Comment, *The Concept of Punitive Legislation and the Sixth Amendment: A New Look at* Kennedy v. Mendoza-Martinez, 32 U Chi L Rev 290,292 (1965) (arguing for criminal procedural protections when there are "grave" penalties).

68. 448 US 242 (1980).

69. Id at 248–49 (stating that whether a penalty is civil or criminal "is a matter of statutory construction").

70. Id at 249.

71. See Klein, 2 Buff Crim L Rev at 683 (cited in note 54) (stating that the Supreme Court in the last few terms has routinely "bless[ed] whatever label a legislature places on a sanction"); Cheh, 42 Hastings L J at 1330,1359–60 (cited in note 62) (advocating legislative label approach because it provides a clear test for making the criminal-civil distinction and because it recognizes that criminal proceedings are public statements of societal boundaries and moral rules and therefore only something the public, through the legislature, has designated as criminal should be treated as such by a court).

72. See Ward, 448 US at 248–49 (noting that there will be cases in which the legislative intention of creating a civil penalty will be negated); Cheh, 42 Hastings L J at 1361–64 (cited in note 62) (noting that there are two types of cases that should be considered criminal regardless of the legislative label).

73. See Cheh, 42 Hastings L J at 1363 (cited in note 62) (stating that if the punishment "so dramatically expresses societal disapproval that its imposition can only be legitimated through the ceremony of a criminal conviction," the legislative label should not be followed in making the criminal-civil distinction). See also Fletcher, Comment, 32 U Chi L Rev at 292 (cited in note 67).

74. 522 US 93 (1997).

75. Id at 96 (reaffirming the rule established in Ward).

76. 372 US 144 (1963).

77. 522 US at 99–100 (noting usefulness of Mendoza-Martinez factors but also stressing that "only the clearest proof will suffice to override legislative intent and transform what has been denominated a civil remedy into a criminal penalty") (citations omitted).

78. 372 US at 167–69 (holding that the loss of citizenship for draft dodging was a criminal punishment that required a "criminal trial and all its incidents" and articulating a seven-factor test to determine if a statute is penal or regulatory in character).

79. 372 US at 168–69.

80. 516 US 442 (1996).

81. Id at 452–53 (holding that civil forfeiture was appropriate because it "serve[d] a deterrent purpose distinct from any punitive purpose" regardless of the party's innocence in the crime committed in her car).

82. 518 US 267 (1996).

83. Id at 270–71, 287–92 (holding that "in rem civil forfeitures are neither 'punishment' nor criminal for purposes of the Double Jeopardy Clause" because Congress intended the proceedings to be civil and because, given the proceedings' important non-punitive, deterrence goals, there is little proof that the proceedings are "so

punitive in form and effect as to render them criminal despite Congress' intent to the contrary").

84. 521 US 346 (1997).

85. Id

86. Id at 361–69 (holding that Kansas statute providing for the civil confinement of sexually violent predators did not establish criminal proceedings under the *Ward* test because the state's intent to create a civil proceeding was clear from the placement of the law in the probate code, rather than in the criminal code, and the defendant had failed to "satisfy [the] heavy burden" of showing that the statute was so punitive as to negate the state's intention).

87. See text accompanying notes 68–70, 74–77.

88. Gang Free Zones Ordinance, Preamble (emphasis added).

89. *Ward,* 448 US at 248–49 (stating that the first part of test to determine if a proceeding is criminal or civil involves determining the legislative intent and that if the intent is to create a civil penalty, then the second part of the test must be considered).

90. Id.

91. See Mann, 101 Yale L J at 1809 (cited in note 56) (discussing the paradigmatic criminal and civil remedies).

92. See text accompanying notes 78–79.

93. See text accompanying notes 74–77.[94] *Mendoza-Martinez,* 372 US at 168.

94. See Mann, 101 Yale L J at 1809–10 (cited in note 56) (discussing the paradigmatic criminal and civil remedies).

95. Gang Free Zones Ordinance § 25–300(a)(G).

96. Id § 25–300(c)(A)-(B).

97. *Mendoza-Martinez,* 372 US at 168.

98. *United States v Ju Toy,* 198 US 253,269 (1905) (Brewer dissenting) (condemning Court's denial of writ of habeas corpus to individual forbidden from reentering United States). See also Jonathan Elliot, ed, 3 *The Debates in the Several State Conventions on the Adoption of the Federal Constitution* 555 (Taylor & Maury 2d ed 1854) ("[I]f a banishment [from a country] be not a punishment, ... it will be difficult to imagine a doom to which the name can be applied.").

99.

100. *Black's Law Dictionary* 97 (West 6th ed 1991) (emphasis added).

101. See Wm. Garth Snider, *Banishment: The History of Its Use and a Proposal for Its Abolition under the First Amendment,* 24 New Eng J on Crim and Civ Confinement 455, 456 (1998) (noting that banishment is "often a condition of probation or parole" and discussing implications for how banishment is applied).

102. *Mendoza-Martinez,* 372 US at 168.

103. Gang Free Zones Ordinance § 25–300(a)(G).

104.*Mendoza-Martinez*, 372 US at 168. This continues to be a factor; however, the presence of a deterrent aim alone will be "insufficient to render a sanction criminal, as deterrence may serve civil as well as criminal goals." *Hudson*, 522 US at 105 (internal quotations omitted).

105.See notes 62 and 66 and accompanying text.

106.Gang Free Zones Ordinance, Preamble.

107.Id § 25–300(a)(A), (C) (stating that the Superintendent of Police shall file a hearing request under the ordinance and the Town Attorney shall draft the complaint). Having a government entity as the moving party is a traditional characteristic of the criminal rather than civil law. See Mann, 101 Yale L J at 1812 (cited in note 56) (discussing the difference in the moving party in criminal and civil proceedings and noting that the government is typically the moving party in a criminal proceeding while private parties typically control a civil one).

108.*Mendoza-Martinez*, 372 US at 168.

109.Gang Free Zones Ordinance § 25–300(a)(G).

110.*Mendoza-Martinez*, 372 US at 168–69.

111.See *Hudson*, 522 US at 105 (stating that the "mere presence" of a deterrent purpose "is insufficient to render a sanction criminal, as deterrence may serve civil as well as criminal goals") (internal quotations omitted).

112.*Mendoza-Martinez*, 372 US at 169.

113.See Part I.A.

114.*Hendricks*, 521 US at 361–69.

115.Id at 357 (discussing the Kansas civil commitment statute).

116.Id at 357 (noting that the Court has "consistently upheld" civil commitment of "people who are unable to control their behavior and who thereby pose a danger to the public health and safety" and listing sources that trace the history of civil commitment in the eighteenth and nineteenth centuries and colonial America).

117.Id at 368.

118.Id at 361–62.

119.Id at 362.

120.Gang Free Zones Ordinance § 25–300(a)(G).

121.*Hendricks*, 521 US at 362.

122.Id at 363.

123.Gang Free Zones Ordinance § 25–300(a)(H).

124.*Hendricks*, 521 US at 364 (noting that if the state seeks to detain someone under the statute for more than one year, a court must find beyond a reasonable doubt that the "same standards as required for the initial confinement" are met).

125.Id at 364.

126. The ordinance does provide for a one-year probationary period if the accused renounces gang activity, Gang Free Zones Ordinance § 25–300(a)(H), but there is no provision for ending the banishment once a gang member is ordered to leave the city.

127. *Hendricks,* 521 US at 364–65 (noting that Kansas's choice to afford "procedural protections does not transform a civil commitment proceeding into a criminal prosecution").

128. Id at 364 (stating that the "numerous procedural and evidentiary protections afforded [by Kansas] demonstrate that the Kansas legislature has taken great care to confine only a narrow class of particularly dangerous individuals, and then only after meeting the strictest procedural standards").

129. Gang Free Zones Ordinance § 25–300(a)(E)-(F).

130. *Hendricks,* 521 US at 368.

131. *Ward,* 448 US at 248–49.

132. *Hendricks,* 521 US at 369 (allowing potentially indefinite civil confinement for sexually violent predators).

133. See text accompanying notes 98–101. See also Snider, 24 New Eng J on Crim and Civ Confinement at 459–65 (cited in note 101) (discussing historical uses of banishment dating back to the Codes of Hammurabi and the Old Testament).

134. See Snider, 24 New Eng J on Crim and Civ Confinement at 456 (cited in note 101) (discussing the penological bases for banishment).

135. *Ray v McCoy,* 174 W Va 1,321 SE2d 90, 95 (1984) (Miller concurring).

136. *People v Baum,* 251 Mich 187,231 NW 95, 96 (1930) (discussing the fact that banishment to criminal colonies was common in England).

137. Snider, 24 New Eng J on Crim and Civ Confinement at 466 (cited in note 101) (noting that most state and federal courts addressing legality of interstate banishment have declared it illegal and discussing their reasons for doing so).

138. Id at 465 (discussing state prohibitions on banishing or exiling individuals from the state).

139. *Commonwealth v Pike,* 428 Mass 393,701 NE2d 951, 960–61 (1998) (invalidating a condition of probation prohibiting a party from entering Massachusetts during the period of his probation). See also *Baum,* 231 NW at 96 (stating that "permit[ting] one state to dump its convict criminals into another ... would tend to incite dissension, provoke retaliation, and disturb that fundamental equality of political rights among the several states which is the basis of the Union itself").

140. See Snider, 24 New Eng J on Crim and Civ Confinement at 470 (cited in note 101) (stating that most courts hold that any banishment sentence is illegal but that some courts have upheld intrastate banishment conditions).

141. *People v Harris,* 238 Ill App 3d 575, 606 NE2d 392, 396 (1992) (noting that "banishment cases are for the most part, uncommon").

142. A survey of state case law revealed that the following states have not addressed intra-state banishment conditions: Arkansas, Arizona, Colorado, Connecticut, Delaware, Florida, Hawaii, Idaho, Indiana, Kansas, Kentucky, Louisiana, Maine, Massachusetts, Maryland, Michigan, Missouri, Montana, Nebraska, Nevada, New Hampshire, New Mexico, New York, North Dakota, Ohio, Oklahoma, Pennsylvania, Rhode Island, South Carolina, South Dakota, Tennessee, Utah, Vermont, Washington, West Virginia, Wisconsin, and Wyoming. The District of Columbia has also not addressed intrastate banishment conditions.

143. A survey of state case law reveals that Alabama, Alaska, California, Georgia, Illinois, Minnesota, Mississippi, Oregon, and Texas have considered intrastate banishment conditions and upheld them in limited circumstances, or indicated a willingness to do so. See *Beavers v State,* 666 S2d 868,871 (Ala Crim App 1995) (holding that banishment from a county pursuant to a parole condition was allowed because it was voluntarily accepted); *Peratrovich v State,* 903 P2d 1071, 1079 (Alaska Ct App 1995) (holding that before imposing condition banishing defendant from his home, the judge must have good reasons for rejecting lesser restrictions); *Jones* v *State,* 727 P2d 6, 7–8 (Alaska Ct App 1986) (holding that an area restriction must be connected to underlying offense, must not be overly severe, and must be related to rehabilitation of the offender); *People v Watkins,* 193 Cal App 3d 1686, 1689 (1987) (upholding very narrow banishment condition because it was related to the defendant's crimes and preventing future criminality); *People v Beach,* 147 Cal App 3d 612, 620–23 (1983) (striking banishment condition that was not necessarily rehabilitative and "was unreasonably broad in light of the desired goal"); *In re White,* 97 Cal App 3d 141, 147–52 (1979) (modifying and limiting banishment condition because there was "little factual nexus" between condition and future criminality except in small area defendant was banished from and the condition was unduly harsh); *State v Collett,* 232 Ga 668, 208 SE2d 472, 474 (1974) (upholding condition banishing the defendant from seven counties in Georgia for one year, as there was no showing that the one-year period was unreasonable and no showing that banishment was unrelated to the defendant's crime); *United States v Cothran,* 855 F2d 749, 752 53 (llth Cir 1988) (upholding banishment condition requiring defendant to stay out of Georgia county because defendant could enter the county with permission); *Adams v State,* 2000 Ga App LEXIS 35, *2 (holding that banishing defendant from several Georgia counties for thirty years was not unreasonable); *Sanchez v State,* 234 Ga App 809, 508 SE2d 185, 186 (1998) (invalidating sentence banishing defendant from state and noting that banishment from areas within Georgia must be logically related to rehabilitation of the defendant); *Wyche v State,* 197 Ga App 148, 397 SE2d 738, 739 (1990) (banishment from five county area of Georgia, for four-year period, not unreasonable); *Kerr v State,* 193 Ga App 165, 387 SE2d 355, 359 (1989) (banishment permissible if it is for a reasonable duration and bears logical relationship to

the rehabilitative purpose of the punishment); *Parrish v State,* 182 Ga App 247, 355 SE2d 682, 683–84 (1987) (defendant must show that banishment is unreasonable or unrelated to rehabilitative purpose of sentence in order to have banishment set aside); *Edwards v State,* 173 Ga App 589, 327 SE2d 559, 561 (1985) (banishment of convicted criminal from a county is a permissible condition of probation); *Wilson v State,* 151 Ga App 501, 260 SE2d 527, 530–31 (1979) (banishment not per se violative of public policy and is within broad discretion of trial judge); *In re J.G.,* 295 Ill App 3d 840, 692 NE2d 1226, 1229 (1998) (holding that geographical restrictions as condition of juvenile probation must be reasonably related to the underlying crime and rehabilitation, and that in the instant case banishment had nothing to do with the "delinquent acts or rehabilitation"); *People v Pickens,* 186 Ill App 3d 456, 542 NE2d 1253, 1257 (1989) (holding that probation condition imposing geographic restriction from fifty block area was allowable because the probationer could obtain permission to reenter the area for legitimate reasons and this "remove[d] the taint of banishment from the restriction"); *State v Holiday,* 585 NW2d 68, 70–71 (Minn Ct App 1998) (finding ordinance could not allow for banishment of trespasser from all public housing because of overbreadth concerns); *Cobb v State,* 437 S2d 1218, 1221 (Miss 1983) (upholding probation condition requiring probationer to remain 125 miles outside of the county in which he committed his crime); *Martin v Board of Parole and Post-prison Supervision,* 327 Or 147, 957 P2d 1210, 1212, 1216–17 (1998) (upholding condition barring defendant convicted of sexually abusing a child from entering most of the victim's county); *Owens v Board of Parole,* 113 Or App 507, 834 P2d 547, 549 (1992) (holding that condition barring sex offender from entire county of victim was overbroad but indicating that more narrow restrictions would be allowed); *State v Ferre,* 84 Or App 459, 734 P2d 888, 889–90 (1987) (same); *State v Jacobs,* 71 Or App 560, 692 P2d 1387, 1389 (1984) (invalidating condition banishing probationer from entire town and holding that condition must be more "narrowly drawn" to fit specific crime); *Johnson v State,* 672 SW2d 621, 623 (Tex Ct App 1984) (holding that banishing defendant from county was not reasonably related to rehabilitation and was unduly restrictive of defendant's liberty).

144. A survey of state case law reveals that Iowa and North Carolina have considered intrastate banishment conditions and have essentially prohibited them. See *Burstein v Jennings,* 231 Iowa 1280, 4 NW2d 428, 429 (1942) (holding that trial court had no right to order defendant to stay out of county); *State v Churchill,* 62 NC App 81, 302 SE2d 290, 292–93 (1983) (noting that a North Carolina court has no power to issue a banishment sentence and that North Carolina defines banishment broadly to include banishment from "a city, place, or country, for a specific period of time, or for life"); *State v Setzer,* 35 NC App 734, 242 SE2d 509, 511 (1978) (noting that there is a well settled prohibition on banishment in North Carolina, but finding that restriction from area in and around courthouse was not illegal banishment); *State v Culp,* 30

NC App 398, 226 SE2d 841, 842 (1976) (holding that condition requiring defendant to move his trailer home constituted impermissible banishment from situs of trailer).

145. *Sanchez,* 508 SE2d at 186 (stating that banishment must be related to rehabilitative purposes of a probation sentence). See also *Commonwealth v Pike,* 428 Mass 393, 701 NE2d 951, 959–60 (listing cases in which conditions banishing probationers from small geographic areas were upheld because they "served the goals of probation" and noting that "banishment from a large geographical area ... struggles to serve any rehabilitative purpose") (internal citations omitted).

146. See *Jones,* 727 P2d at 8 (reversing condition of probation prohibiting the defendant from being within a forty-five block area in part because there was no "clear nexus between the area and [defendant's] misconduct"); *Martin,* 957 P2d at 1217 (upholding condition barring defendant convicted of sexually abusing a child from entering most of the victim's county); *Jacobs,* 692 P2d at 1389 (invalidating condition banishing probationer from an entire town because the condition should have been "more narrowly drawn" to the offense).

147. *Jones,* 727 P2d at 8 (reversing condition of probation prohibiting the defendant from being within a forty-five block area in part because it was unreasonably restrictive). See also *Holiday,* 585 NW2d at 70 (construing a Minneapolis ordinance as banishing a trespasser from only a few properties and not all public housing to avoid overbreadth concerns); *Owens,* 834 P2d at 549 (invalidating parole condition barring a sex offender from an entire county because the restriction was unnecessarily broad to accomplish the goal of protecting the victim); *Ferre,* 734 P2d at 889–90 (reversing an order barring probationer from an entire county because it was broader than necessary to protect the victims).

148. See Snider, 24 New Eng J on Crim and Civ Confinement at 472–73 (cited in note 101) (noting that the "illegality of banishment turns upon the circumstances under which the condition is imposed").

149. See *Cobb,* 437 S2d at 1221 (upholding five-year probation condition requiring probationer to remain 125 miles outside of the county in which he shot his nephew); *Martin,* 957 P2d at 1216–17 (upholding condition barring defendant convicted of sexually abusing a child from entering most of the victim's county).

150. See, for example, *Holiday,* 585 NW2d at 71 (invalidating an order banishing an individual from all public housing projects when he had only trespassed in one); *Jacobs,* 692 P2d at 1389 (banishment condition barring probationer from entire town should have been "more narrowly drawn" to the offense and to protecting past victims).

151. See Michael George Smith, Note, *The Propriety and Usefulness of Geographical Restrictions Imposed as Conditions of Probation,* 47 Baylor L Rev 571, 586–87 (1995) (noting that banishing individuals from an area to get them out of the way serves no rehabilitative purpose but that it "could break a chain of social contacts that has proven to cause criminal behavior in the past"). Smith's argument that removing

people from their established community may break social contacts that have facilitated criminal behavior may be particularly persuasive in the gang context due to the potential problems gang members might face if there are only rival gangs in the town in which they relocate. Consider Jeffrey Fagan, *Gangs, Drugs, and Neighborhood Change*, in Huff, ed, *Gangs in America* 39,41 (cited in note 14) (discussing that gangs have certain "turfs" and that fights are common among gangs). However, given the large number of gangs, it is likely that many gang members will in fact be able to find a new gang to associate with in the community that they move to and will continue to commit gang-related crime. Consider James F. Short, Jr., *Foreword: Diversity and Change in U.S. Gangs,* in Huff, ed, *Gangs in America* vii, xi (stating that "most gangs are neither very stable in membership [n]or very cohesive").

152. See note 145 and accompanying text.

153. See Slater, *Suburb Gives Gang Members 60 Days to Leave,* Austin American-Statesman at A12 (cited in note 33) (quoting Cicero town president as stating that her "concern is protecting the residents of the town of Cicero").

154. See text accompanying note 146.

155. Gang Free Zones Ordinance § 25–300(a)(G).

156. See text accompanying note 149.

157. The broad nature of the civil banishment of gang members from an entire town is one feature that distinguishes it from the more narrowly tailored nuisance abatement injunctions that have withstood a constitutional challenge in California. See notes 22, 30, and accompanying text. For example, unlike the broad provisions in the Cicero ordinance, nuisance abatement injunctions are focused on more specific behavior and on more targeted problem areas of the community. See notes 22–25 and accompanying text; Werdegar, Note, 51 Stan L Rev at 416 (cited in note 10) (noting that a city will identify and focus on a neighborhood "with an unusually high crime rate that is known to be the turf of a particular urban street gang"). The more narrow focus of nuisance abatement injunctions threatens the liberty interest of gang members less than a broad banishment from an entire town, so a court is more likely to uphold an injunction against a gang than a broad banishment condition exiling them from the entire town. Furthermore, courts have traditionally issued nuisance abatement injunctions, see Werdegar, Note, 51 Stan L Rev at 414 (stating that public nuisance doctrine is "centuries-old"), while they have traditionally been reluctant to allow banishment, see notes 137–40 and accompanying text. This also makes the nuisance injunctions easier to defend because a court seems more likely to use the established public nuisance doctrine in innovative ways to combat gangs than it is to increase the use of the generally disfavored banishment remedy.

158. Compare *Bagley v Harvey,* 718 F2d 921, 925 (9th Cir 1983) (holding that parole condition banishing defendant from the state of Washington was not cruel and unusual punishment because the banishment was not permanent—defendant could return at

the end of his parole term), with *Dear Wing Jung v United States,* 312 F2d 73, 76 (9th Cir 1962) (holding that condition requiring alien to leave the United States was the equivalent of permanent banishment from the United States and as such was "either a 'cruel and unusual' punishment or a denial of due process of law").

159. This factor would likely be particularly persuasive in an Illinois court because Illinois has held that allowing a probationer to enter a prohibited area for a legitimate reason "removes the taint of banishment" from a condition. *People v Pickens,* 186 Ill App 3d 456, 542 NE2d 1253, 1257 (1989) (holding that a court may impose a condition barring a defendant from certain areas if the banishment is reasonably related to the offense "*provided* that, if the defendant has a legitimate and compelling reason to go to that area or place, he may apply to a specified authority for specific permission" to do so).

160. See note 139 and accompanying text.

161. See Snider, 24 New Eng J on Crim and Civ Confinement at 456–57 (cited in note 101) (stating that "if one is banished from one community, he is necessarily relegated to another [and] [a]rguably, the community in which the offender now must reside will find him equally as repugnant as the one from which he was banished").

162. Id at 503–06 (discussing banishment as a means of political and racial oppression).

163. See note 53 and accompanying text.

Civil Banishment of Gangs: Circumventing Criminal Due Process Requirements?

PowerPoint by:
Joe Gordon
Mario Hernandez
Jeremy Napial

Gang Violence in America

▶ "Gangs have virtually overtaken certain neighborhoods ... Causing fear and lifestyle changes among law-abiding residents"

—Justice Thurman Thomas

City of Chicago v. Morales, 527 US 41, 99–100 (Thomas Dissenting)

Gang Violence in America

- Los Angeles Gang Related Crime Statistics-2008
- Homicides-167
- Aggravated Assaults-2830
- Rapes-40
- Robberies-2568
- Carjackings-111
- Kidnappings-53
- Arsons-3
- Criminal Threats-852
- Extortion-43

Los Angeles Police Department
City Wide Gang Crime Summary:
December 2008

Problem With Gang Violence

- With gang violence, can be extremely difficult to identify those explicitly responsible for crime.
- Crime often occurs when gang members know law enforcement is out of the area
- Gangs use intimidation to keep witnesses from testifying

Need For Another Method

► Communities yearn for alternative methods that allow law enforcement to police gangs.

Alternative Law Enforcement Responses to Gang Violence

► Civil injunctions, namely: The STEP Act
► California Penal Code Section: 186.22a.
► Part 1 of Crimes and Punishments
► Title 7 of Crimes against Public Justice
► Ch. 11 Street Terrorism and Enforcement Prevention Act

California Penal Code

Civil Banishment in Cicero, Illinois

Ordinance No. 111–99 passed in April 1999

Allows cities to exile gang members from Cicero, Il without a criminal trial

---

Civil Banishment in Cicero, Illinois continued.

▶ Police superintendent can bring a request to the Town Attorney to banish the accused from Cicero

▶ The complaint has to show that the accused has participated in gang activity and represents a "Clear and Present Danger" to the people of Cicero

▶ The hearing is conducted in front of an administrative hearing officer designated by the Town Board*

▶ The accused has the right to an attorney

▶ If the accused is found guilty by the hearing officer, the accused to vacate his home and is then banished from the city

Civil Banishment in Cicero, Illinois continued.

► If the suspect refuses to leave the city, or re-enters without permission, a $500 dollar a day fine is levied
► If the gang member renounces gang ties, they may be permitted to return to Cicero, however they will hold a probationary status for 1 year

Civil Banishment Ordinance

► The traditional rules of evidence do not apply
► Hearsay can be admitted into the testimony
► The burden of proof is far lower than a criminal trial
► A criminal penalty is imparted on the accused by a civil hearing

Civil Banishment: Impose A Criminal Penalty Process Requirement

► What is a civil and criminal action?
► Supreme Court Rulings
► Is Banishment violation of constitution rights.

Civil and Criminal Distinction

► Supreme Court takes Distinction between Civil Seriously
  ▷ Constitutional rights have to be invoke for criminal trials
    — Constitutional rights have to be invoke for criminal trials
    — 5thAmendment: Self—Incrimination Clause. Expressly limited to "any criminal case."
    — 6th Amendment: tights to a speedy trial trial by jury conformation of witness, compulsory process, etc.
    — Double Jeopardy: cannot be charged for the same crime twice.

► Paradigmatic difference between civil is compensatory and criminal is punitive.
  ▷ How ever civil cases have been compensate, but also deter undesirable behavior as used in the criminal system does.
  ▷ Civil system has been used to avoid criminal sanctions provided by for criminal procedures for constitutional rights.

Test to Determine the Nature of a Proceeding

► Several ways to test if a case is civil or criminal
  ▷ Supreme Court cases
    — United States V. Ward: two part test used
      ▷ did the legislative body indicate "either expressly or impliedly a preference for one label or the other…"
      ▷ despite the civil label, is the "statuary scheme… so punitive either in purpose or effect as to negate {legislative} intention"

Test to Determine the Nature of a Proceeding

► Hudson v. United States:
  ► reaffirmed Wards rule and used 7 factors test from Kennedy V. Mendoza-Martinez; in order to see if a case is in fact criminal and not civil as legislative body proclaimed

Continued...

► *Kennedy V Mendoza-Martinez*-Court came up with 7 factors to determine if civil cases are really criminal to require constitutional safe guards.
  ▷ whether the sanction involves an affirmative disability or restraint
  ▷ whether it has historically been regarded as a punishment
  ▷ whether comes into play only on a finding of scienter
  ▷ whether it's operation will promote the traditional aims of punishment-retribution and deterrence
  ▷ whether the behavior to which it applies is already a crime
  ▷ whether an alternative purpose to which it may rationally be connected is assignable for it
  ▷ whether it applies excessive in relation to the alternative purpose assigned.

Continued...

► More case examples
  ▷ *Bennis V. Michigan*: allowed the civil confiscation of an innocent part's property without her knowledge.
  ▷ *United States V. Ursery*: Courts held a federal conviction of a manufacture marijuana facilities and civil forfeiture action seizing property for the same offense, did not violate the Double Jeopardy Clause.
  ▷ *Hudson* did not bar a criminal prosecution for banking statues subsequently to the civil imposition of money penalties and debarment which were the same.

Application of the Courts to Test the Cicero Civil Banishment Ordinance

▶ Under the Wards test the ordinance does create a civil penalty under the 1st part, but in the 2nd part that the banishment of the ordinance is so punitive either in purpose or effect negates it's intention.

▶ Justice Brewer sated "banishment of a citizen is punishment , and punishment of the severest kind."

▶ The scienter has come into play where an officer has to accused a gang member in a "gang-related criminal activity." in order for the banishment to take effect. Which is criminal.

▶ The ordinance does seek to deter gang-related activity which is viewed as a danger to public safety. Does not focus does injured for these crimes from the moving party.

▶ *Mendoza-Martinez* factor focus on that the ordinance has to come from a criminal crime.

Application of the Courts to Test the Cicero Civil Banishment Ordinance

▶ Civil banishment deprives citizens from their freedom in the same way as if revoking the persons citizenship.

▶ *Kansas v. Hendricks* set the procedures for the civil commitment of prisoners convicted as sex offense.

  ▷ Court found that Kansas did not intend the civil commitment to deterrent purpose for criminal punishment.

  ▷ Kansas procedures made more criminal in nature than the ordinance in Cicero.

▶ The Court would less likely to allow civil denomination of banishment despite the civil

Banishing Gang Members Under Existing Banishment Law

- ► Current Banishment Law
- ► Interstate banishment
  - ▷ Security through expulsion
  - ▷ Majority illegal
- ► Intrastate banishment
  - ▷ Criminal sentence or condition of probation/parole
  - ▷ 3 general factors
    - — Related logically to the rehabilitative purposes of the sentence
    - — Prohibited area in the banishment condition must be tailored in someway to fit the underlying crime
    - — Cannot be unnecessarily severe and restrictive

Banishment of Gang Members

- ► Does not serve any rehabilitative purpose
- ► Does not narrowly tailored geographically to match gang members' offenses as required in most intrastate banishment cases.
- ► A court is likely to find that banishment of gang members is unnecessarily severe and restrictive.
- ► Unlikely to be upheld because of the likelihood of enforcement along racial lines

Conclusion

► Imposes a criminal penalty through civil hearing and deprives gang members of constitutional procedural protections
► Banishment pushes gang problems into surrounding areas and exacerbates discriminatory enforcement along racial lines

Works Cited

► Los Angeles Police Department: Gangs and Operations Support Division. "The Los Angeles Police Department Citywide Gang Crime Summary." *LAPD Online*. December 31, 2008. http://www.lapdonline.org/crime_maps_and_compstat/content_basic_view/24435 (accessed November 30, 2010).
► Smith, Stephanie. "Civil Banishment of Gang Members: Circumventing Criminal Due Process Requirements?" *The University of Chicago Law Review*, 2007: 1461–1487.

"IT'S GETTING CRAZY OUT THERE"

CAN A CIVIL GANG INJUNCTION CHANGE A COMMUNITY?

By Cheryl L. Maxson,
Karen M. Hennigan,
and David C. Sloane

RESEARCH SUMMARY:

Civil gang injunctions are an increasingly popular gang suppression tactic. This article reports on the first scientific evaluation of the community impact of this strategy. San Bernardino residents in five neighborhoods were surveyed about their perceptions and experience of crime, gang activity, and neighborhood quality 18 months before and 6 months after the issuance of an injunction. Analyses indicated positive evidence of short-term effects in the disordered, primary injunction area, including less gang presence, fewer reports of gang intimidation, and less fear of confrontation with gang members, but no significant changes in intermediate or long-term outcomes except lower fear of crime. Comparison of this injunction area with a previous one suggested that improvements in neighborhood dynamics might accrue over the long term. Negative effects were observed in the secondary, less disordered injunction area.

POLICY IMPLICATIONS:

This study suggests that the strategic suppression of gang member activities may translate into modest immediate improvements in community safety and well-being. Furthermore, the findings suggest that law enforcement use caution regarding the size of an injunction area and the type of gang targeted by the tactic. Coupling an injunction with

efforts to improve neighborhood social organization and provide positive alternatives for gang members might substantially improve its effectiveness.

KEYWORDS: Street Gangs, Civil Gang Abatement, Community Organization, Neighborhood Safety

One weekend in November 2002, a drive-by shooting on the west side of San Bernardino, California left two teenagers and one adult wounded. A 15-year-old resident of the area told a reporter, "It's getting crazy out there" (Fisher et al, 2002). Living on a block where an 11-year-old recently had been stabbed during a burglary, she seemed to be stating the obvious. Police responded by instituting a civil gang injunction (CGI)—a process whereby selected gang members are prohibited from engaging in such activities as loitering at schools, carrying pagers and riding bicycles, or face arrest—against a local gang. They hoped that by curtailing the gang's activities, they could diminish residents' sense of insecurity and promote a safer, healthier community. As a local newspaper editorialized, the injunction would help a neighborhood where residents "suffer emotional distress, their children cannot play outdoors, and their pets must be locked up inside" (Staff Reports, 2002).

The 2002 National Youth Gang Survey (NYGS) found active youth gangs in more than 2,300 cities and 550 other jurisdictions served by county law enforcement (Egley and Major, 2004). Youth that join gangs account for most serious and violent crimes committed by adolescents, and offending rates are elevated during active periods of membership (Thornberry et al., 2003). Gang members are notoriously resistant to intervention, and gang interventions are equally resistant to evaluation. In concluding a volume reporting nine separate police gang interventions, Decker (2003:290) warns "that we lack even basic knowledge about the impact of interventions on gangs and youth violence" and this ignorance "should be a clarion call to police, legislators, researchers, and policymakers" to critically evaluate interventions.

The CGI is an increasingly popular anti-gang strategy. Although civil court injunctions to prohibit gang activity at specific locations date back to 1980, the first injunction against a gang and its members is credited to the Los Angeles city attorney in 1987 (see Los Angeles City Attorney Gang Prosecution Section, 1995).[10] Injunction activity increased at a moderate pace until the mid-1990s when it dramatically accelerated. Our interviews with gang officers and prosecutors and reviews of practitioner reports and media accounts yielded 37 separate CGIs in Southern California between 1980 and 2000. In the four-year period from 1996 to 1999, a Southern California gang was enjoined, on average, every two months. As of July 2004, at least 22 injunctions had been issued in the city of Los Angeles alone. This growth in injunction activity has been fostered by how-to workshops sponsored by the California Association of District Attorneys, detailed training manuals (see Los Angeles County District Attorney, 1996, for an early example), and local descriptions in practitioner publications (Cameron and Skipper, 1997; Genelin, 1998; Mazza, 1999). Gang injunctions have also received widespread attention in local and national media.

Although most injunctions have occurred in California, law enforcement agencies nationwide are searching for new tools to combat the growth and impact of gangs in their neighborhoods. A nationwide interview survey of police officers in jurisdictions that the 1999 NYGS indicated had developed a CGI found a high rate of confusion about the tactic and confirmed 11 jurisdictions in 7 states outside California have obtained a CGI (Maxson, 2004). Anecdotally, police and public officials claim the tactic is very effective in eliminating gang activity. Yet, relatively little systematic research on the effectiveness of injunctions has been completed.

This article presents the findings of an evaluation of the impact of a CGI implemented in the Verdugo Flats neighborhood of San Bernardino, California, in Fall 2002. The research focuses on changes in the quality of life in this neighborhood, rather than on the injunction's effects on the targeted gang members or on levels of crime. The study's findings have clear implications for gang and crime researchers, law enforcement agencies that anticipate using this strategy, civil court judges who are asked to limit the activities of gang members to achieve more community order, and community members wondering if this strategy can improve their neighborhoods.

CIVIL GANG INJUNCTIONS

After conducting interviews with law enforcement gang specialists and reviewing the practitioner literature, we concluded that the CGI is a relatively flexible tool to combat gangs (Maxson, et al., 2003). Allan examined the variation in provisions in 42 injunctions requested by prosecutors and found that injunctions addressed "local gang

---

10   The historical information on CGIs was gathered from documents prepared by prosecutors (see particularly Castorena, 1998 and Whitmer and Ancker, 1996), newspaper articles, and interviews with police gang experts and injunction practitioners.

problems with customized provisions based on specific local circumstances" (2004:241). The procedures used vary among jurisdictions within and outside California, the state where most of them have been issued (Maxson, 2004). Here, we describe the process of obtaining and implementing CGIs as it is generally understood in California.

Implementing a CGI is an elaborate process. Police officers, often in collaboration with prosecutors, gather evidence that members of a street gang represent a public nuisance in their neighborhood, in violation of California Civil Code sections 3479 and 3480.[11] Evidence used to support an injunction includes the criminal history of gang members, written declarations by officers familiar with the neighborhood, and sometimes, declarations from community members that describe the effects of specific nuisance activities on neighborhood residents. The prosecutor uses the declarations and other materials to craft the injunction, working with officers to select the gang members to be named, the geographic area to be covered, and the specific behaviors that will be prohibited.[12]

The number of gang members, the size of the area, and the type of prohibited activities varies considerably.[13] The number of gang members can range from a handful to the hundreds, and the initial string of names often is followed by "and any other members."[14] The targeted area can be a housing complex, several square blocks, or an entire city, but most often CGIs are spatially based, neighborhood-level interventions intended to disrupt the gang's routine activities. Prohibited behaviors include illegal activities such as trespass, vandalism, drug selling, and public urination, as well as otherwise legal activities, such as wearing gang colors, displaying hand signs, and carrying a pager

---

11 Nuisance is defined by section 3479 as "Anything which is injurious to health, or is indecent or offensive to the senses, or an obstruction to the free use of property, so as to interfere with the comfortable enjoyment of life or property, or unlawfully obstructs the free passage or use, in the customary manner, of any navigable lake or river, bay, stream, canal, or basin, or any public park, square, street, or highway." According to section 3480, "A public nuisance is one which affects at the same time an entire community or neighborhood, or any other considerable number of persons, although the extent of the annoyance or damage inflicted upon individuals may be unequal."

12 Recent research on the formation of police gang units argues that law enforcement responses to gangs originate from a host of organizational factors, rather than from a rational assessment of the seriousness of local gang problems (Katz, 2001; Katz et al., 2002; see also, Decker, 2003). Any decision to pursue a CGI reflects these organizational, as well as other environmental, features.

13 Maxson et al. (2003) and Allan (2004) discuss the legal and procedural issues evident in the legal literature. For a detailed description of injunction forms in California and elsewhere, see also Maxson, 2004.

14 A recent CGI was issued against an estimated 1000 members of Oxnard's Colonia Chiques gang, precluding any identified gang member from congregating in a 6.6-square-mile area that covers more than a quarter of the city.

or signaling passing cars, behaviors associated with drug selling. Nighttime curfews are often imposed. Most disturbing to legal scholars and advocates is the commonly applied prohibition against any two or more named gang members associating with one another (Bjerregaard, 2003; Geis, 2002; Stewart, 1998).

The prosecutor files the application for a temporary restraining order (TRO) in civil court, and a hearing is scheduled. All named gang members are served notice of the hearing and the injunction. At this hearing, the judge considers the submitted evidence, hears testimony, and entertains questions from targeted individuals. Occasionally, legal counsel represents individuals, but as a rule, defendants are not provided with public counsel in civil proceedings.[15] Judges have at times challenged the inclusion of certain individuals, the size of the targeted area, and the scope of prohibitions. If the preliminary injunction is issued at this hearing, targeted individuals must be served again with amended papers before the injunction can be enforced. Offenders can be prosecuted in either civil or criminal court for violation of a valid court order and fined up to $1000 and/or incarcerated for up to six months. Some prosecutors seek enhanced bail amounts for arrested offenders, which can translate into significant jail time. The preliminary injunction can be in effect for a limited time, such as a year, or indefinitely. Prosecutors may seek a permanent injunction and can add individuals or provisions to an existing injunction with relative ease. A few gang injunctions have been denied, but judges usually approve them, particularly because the California Supreme court upheld a San Jose injunction in the Acuna case (People ex rel. Gallo v. Acuna, 929 P.2d 596, 1997).

The tactics used for implementation vary from one injunction to the next. Sometimes a special unit is tasked with enforcement. In other instances, the whole patrol force is alerted to the conditions of the injunction. No registry records the number of arrests resulting from injunctions. Interviews with law enforcement officials suggest the number varies widely, from very few to as many as several hundred.

THEORY: HOW CGIS MIGHT REDUCE GANG ACTIVITY

The criminological and social psychological literatures suggest several processes that might be relevant to understanding injunction effects on neighborhoods and gang members. First, social disorganization theory provides a foundation for predicting changes in social relationships. Resident participation in developing and implementing a gang injunction may spark a process of community engagement in efforts to build informal social control, social capital in the form of social networks, and supportive

---

15   In addition to pro bono services sometimes offered by private attorneys, occasionally a judge will grant public counsel.

organizational structures (Bursik and Grasmick, 1993; Greene, 2004). Even if neighborhood residents are not engaged in the injunction activities directly, reducing the level of the immediate threat of the gang may lay a foundation for improving the quality of neighborhood life by strengthening collective efficacy (Sampson et al., 1997). As levels of intimidation and fear ease, a community may be able to organize and become involved in the process of reversing the deterioration of the physical and social order in their community, with its attendant effects on fear of crime and civic engagement.

Practitioners often note these anticipated effects (see excellent examples in Los Angeles City Attorney Gang Prosecution Section, 1995 and Los Angeles County District Attorney, 1996). The goals of injunctions typically are couched in community policing terms, such as solving specific community crime, disorder, and fear problems (Allan, 2004; Greene, 2003; Stewart, 1998). As Ventura County prosecutor Karen Wold envisioned when seeking an injunction against the Colonia Chiques gang in Oxnard, California, "Parents can take their kids to the park again" (Wolcott, 2004). Higher levels of community involvement and greater impact on community environments might be expected from injunctions developed and implemented with this philosophical orientation, as compared with other forms of gang enforcement (Decker, 2003).

Second, two theories address how injunctions might influence individual gang members. Deterrence theory predicts that sure, swift, and severe sanctions will deter criminal behavior. Although the penalties for injunction violations are not severe, the notifications of hearings and injunction papers might make targeted gang members believe that they are being closely watched and more likely to be apprehended and prosecuted for violations (Grogger, 2002; Klein, 1993). Practitioners contend that issuance of the injunction has a profound effect on gang members. Longtime community gang intervention activist Father Greg Boyle was cited in a recent press report, "I mean eight minutes after one was filed here on the Eastside, I had kids in my office saying, 'Get me a job'" (Fremon, 2003). Low arrest rates would presumably erode this perception.

In addition, social psychological theory suggests that group identity causes individuals to feel less responsible for their behavior, and influences them to conform to situation-specific group norms (cf., Postmes and Spears, 1998; Spears et al., 2001). In gangs, situation-specific norms promote violent and antisocial behavior (Decker and Van Winkle, 1996; Vigil, 1988, 2002). A gang injunction holds individuals personally accountable for their actions which could weaken gang identity and decrease levels of participation in gang-related behavior, especially among noncore members (cf., Ellemers et al., 2002). In this process of holding individuals responsible for their gang activities, identification with the gang might decline, as could the overall gang cohesiveness. Alternatively, if the injunction sends the message that law enforcement is targeting the group rather than individuals, fringe members might react with increased loyalty to fend off the perceived group level threat and gang cohesiveness might increase (Klein, 1995).

Each theoretical perspective points to different evaluation designs to assess potential outcomes of CGIs. Deterrence and individuation might be tested by interviews with targeted gang members and the examination of changes in crime patterns. Community social disorganization theory suggests the assessment of changes in community perceptions of intimidation, fear, disorder, and neighborhood efficacy. This latter approach is adopted in this study.

Proclamations of the success of gang injunctions surface regularly in practitioner publications and media accounts. Many jurisdictions have multiple injunctions, and presumably, repetition of the strategy follows a positive experience. We have illustrated these success claims and the anecdotal evidence marshaled to support them elsewhere (Maxson et al., 2003). In these accounts, changes in crime rates are sometimes noted, but without adequate comparison with equivalent areas or offenders.

Three independent evaluations of injunctions have used official crime data to measure outcomes. Maxson and Allen (1997) conducted a process evaluation of a CGI in Inglewood, California. Their brief assessment of reported crime in the target area suggested little support for a positive effect. A legal advocacy organization conducted a statistical analysis of various crime indicators in 19 reporting districts including and surrounding the Blythe Street injunction implemented by the Los Angeles Police Department in the San Fernando Valley (ACLU, 1997). The authors concluded that this injunction increased violent crime.

In the most rigorous study of crime patterns to date, Grogger (2002) assessed changes in reported serious violent and property crimes for 14 injunctions obtained in Los Angeles County between 1993 and 1998. Grogger compared crime trends in the injunction areas with those in matched comparison areas. Pooling the injunction areas, he found that violent crime decreased during the year after injunctions by roughly 5% to 10%. This effect was concentrated in reductions in assault, rather than in robbery. He found no effect in property crimes and no evidence that injunctions caused crime to increase in adjoining areas. Because all injunctions were aggregated in this analysis, it was unclear whether some injunctions were more effective than others. Moreover, he could not identify offenses committed by gang members or the specific individuals targeted by the injunctions. Still, this study is the first scholarly report of positive effects of injunctions on crime in neighborhoods targeted by CGIs.

The community disorganization perspective suggests that injunctions should improve patterns in community processes, such as neighborhood relationships, disorder, and informal social control. The evaluation in this study addresses community-level outcomes rather than the individual gang member outcomes suggested by deterrence and individuation. Because the few evaluations of injunctions conducted to date consider the impact on criminal behavior, this study is the first to focus on neighborhood processes.

Conceptually, we expect that community-level effects of an injunction would unfold over time. If injunctions cause gang members to modify their behavior in the community, then the more immediate effects for neighborhood residents should be reduced gang visibility, graffiti, instances of gang intimidation, and fear of gang victimization. Only later should these benefits result in reduced fear of crime more generally, less crime victimization, and improved community order. Long term, residents in neighborhoods may experience increased neighborhood social cohesion and informal social control, more collective and neighborhood social efficacy, more willingness to call police in threatening situations, and improved perceptions of police authority.

SAN BERNARDINO AND THE VERDUGO FLATS INJUNCTION

An interview survey of more than two dozen Southern California police agencies with significant gang populations using multi-agency collaborations to combat them found that San Bernardino presented several advantages for the research. First, the San Bernardino Police Department (SBPD) had already conducted three injunctions (two against territorial street gangs and one against prostitutes along a main boulevard) before our first contact with them in Spring 2000. Second, the gangs that they were considering for further injunctions seemed excellent targets for studying the impact on communities. Third, the department welcomed our inquiry and proved very helpful in all regards.

San Bernardino is roughly 60 miles east of Los Angeles in the rapidly growing Inland Empire. In 2000, over 185,000 people lived in the city. Although the city is part of one of the fastest expanding economic areas in Southern California, it is also home to many poor minorities. Almost half of the population is Latino, roughly 18% are African Americans and about 30% are white. More than one in five of the residents in this city was born outside the United States, with another 20% born outside of California. Over one third of the population speaks only Spanish at home. The city has experienced gang activity for decades, and gangs have been expanding in the city throughout the last one third of a century. Although other Southern California cities were experiencing marked declines in violent and property crimes during the period of this study, reported crime in San Bernardino increased substantially between 2002 and 2003. San Bernardino police officials were quoted in local media reports as attributing the rise in crime rates to "continued economic problems, high rates of gang membership and a large number of parolees" (Warren, 2003: B5).

In Summer 2002, five shootings and one assault suggested that the Verdugo Flats gang was actively defending its territory against a failed intrusion by an African-American gang. Verdugo Flats is a large Latino gang that has claimed a sizeable swath of southwestern San Bernardino since the 1970s. SBPD reported that the gang had roughly 150 members as of August 2001, a 20% increase from two years before. They noted repeatedly that Verdugo Flats is "turf-oriented," claiming territory through extensive graffiti and intimidation of residents. SBPD officers stated that the combination of heightened violence and the inter-racial nature of the gang fight led San Bernardino authorities to move to file the long considered injunction on August 5, 2002.

Nineteen members of the gang were included in the requested injunction. The court instituted a TRO on September 24, 2002, prohibiting them from 22 activities. Prohibited activities included behaviors associated with selling drugs, trespass, a nighttime curfew, public order offenses (fighting, drinking, urinating, littering, vandalism, and graffiti), and public association with any other defendant.

SBPD officials implemented the injunction using procedures developed in their previous experiences. The enjoined individuals were named at patrol meetings, photographs of the individuals were placed on the wall of the room where patrol officers get their briefings, and Metropolitan Enforcement Team (MET) officers provided the primary enforcement for the injunction. As in earlier injunctions, the SBPD initiated a "sweep" of the injunction area right after they obtained the injunction. They searched homes of parolees and probationers and checked on outstanding warrants. They catalogued paraphernalia, photographs, and clothing.

After the initial implementation activities, SBPD continued to monitor the individuals named in the injunction, kept patrol officers informed, and attempted to ensure that the injunction restrictions were enforced. MET officers trained patrol officers to use the appropriate forms to arrest enjoined gang members and made sure that the in-house computer would notify patrol officers if an injunction member was stopped and identified. One police informant noted that he came in several times on his day off to work with patrol officers who had apprehended an enjoined individual. From the inception of the Verdugo Flats CGI in September 2002 until January 2004, five individuals were arrested related to the injunction. Arrested individuals were liable for enhanced bail of up to $25,000.

RESEARCH DESIGN AND METHODOLOGY

A community assessment survey was conducted twice—once before the injunction and once shortly after the injunction was imposed—to test the impact of the immediate change on neighborhood residents' attitudes and perceptions. We predicted that specific experiences of gang intimidation, fear of gang members, and visibility of the gang members and graffiti would all decrease within the first six months after the injunction. We also tested the impact on more intermediate outcomes: fear of crime, crime victimization, and perceived level of social disorder. We included long-term survey measures of neighborhood social cohesion, informal social control, collective efficacy, neighborhood efficacy, and willingness to call the police and trust in the police, although we expected that these changes would evolve over a longer period of time. Table 1 summarizes the measures used for each outcome variable.[16]

In addition to the residents of the injunction area called Upper Flats, four other neighborhoods were surveyed to control for local history such as crime trends in the city between the first and second waves of the survey. Two comparison areas were chosen because they had similarly high levels of social disorder, but they varied in the level of territorial gang activities. These areas were suggested by two police informants who had focused on gang crime in San Bernardino for several years and were very familiar with gang activities in this part of the city. North Area, located about a mile northeast of Upper Flats, is high in crime and physical and social disorder, the latter confirmed both by the authors' visual tour of the area and by residents' responses on the Wave 1 survey.[17] SBPD sources repeatedly confirmed that North Area had no territorial gang presence over the course of the study. The second area, Seventh Street, is a territorial gang area, about a half-mile north of Upper Flats where a gang injunction had been filed in 1997. The two remaining areas, immediately south of Upper Flats, were defined as one area during the pre-injunction survey. When the Flats injunction was filed, part of this area was included in the injunction. We renamed that portion of the southern area Lower Flats, and the remaining comparison area was named South Area. The South Area served as a good comparison for the Lower Flats injunction area, because both had comparably lower social disorder before the injunction was filed (see Footnote 8).

------

16   We consulted several surveys before beginning this one, including our sources for an earlier community policing survey for the Los Angeles Police Department (Maxson et al., 1999), among which were the New Jersey City Public Housing Resident Survey, University of Texas at Arlington Social Work Citizen Survey, University of Wisconsin Survey Research Laboratory Citizen Attitudes and Victimization Survey, the Chicago Community Policing Resident Survey, the Spokane Police Department and Washington State University Crime and Criminal Justice Survey, and the Joliet Police Department School Neighborhood Questionnaire. Other surveys from which we adapted additional material include the Denver Youth Study, the National Crime Victimization Survey, the University of California at Irvine Fear of Crime and Gangs Survey, the Chicago Neighborhood Study (Sampson et al., 1997), and others. In the second wave, we added a series of questions regarding community organization; these were adapted from the Harvard Social Capital Benchmark. Table 1 reports the measures used in analyses reported here. In constructing these measures, we considered the distribution of individual items and assessed all scales for reliability.

17   Residents' perception of social disorder in the five study areas in the Wave 1 surveys confirmed the observations and opinions of the police informants. Two homogeneous subsets were identified post hoc by the Dunnett test. Upper Flats, North Area, and Seventh Street were equivalent in perceived level of social disorder before the injunction (M = 2.35, 2.52, and 2.27 respectively) and were higher than Lower Flats and South Area (M = 1.75 and 1.63).

Beyond serving as comparisons for residents' perceptions about gangs, safety, and their community, these four comparison neighborhoods were also chosen as possible sites for displaced Verdugo Flats Gang activity because of the injunction.

Table 1. Summary OF Measures for Immediate, Intermediate, and
Long-Term Outcomes

	Item	Response Options
Immediate Outcomes		
See gang members hang out	How often have you seen gang members?[1]	Never/rarely/sometimes/monthly/more
See new graffiti	How often have you seen new graffiti or gang tags?	Never/rarely/sometimes/monthly/more
Been hassled by gang members	How often has someone you know been hassled by gang members?[1]	Never/rarely/sometimes/monthly/more
Young persons bullied by gang members	How often have young persons been bullied by gang members?[1]	Never/rarely/sometimes/monthly/more
Frightened by gang member	How often have you or a family member felt frightened by a gang member?[1]	Never/rarely/sometimes/monthly/more
Gang activities made you anxious	How often have gang activities made you feel anxious at home in the evening or night?[1]	Never/rarely/sometimes/monthly/more
Any intimidation by gang members	Count if any of the four items above happened[1]	Never/ever for any of four items above
Fear confrontation with gang member	How much do you fear that you or a member of your family will be confronted by a gang member in the neighborhood?	Not at all fearful/a little fearful/fearful/very Fearful
Intermediate Outcomes		
Fear of crime	How much do you fear that your home will be entered or damaged while you are away; that your car will be damaged or stolen; that you or a member of your family will be	Not at all fearful/a little fearful/fearful/very Fearful

	hurt by someone in the neighbor-hood; that you or a family member will be hurt even if you stay indoors?	alpha=.88 (W1); .90 (W2)
Perceived level of social disorder	How often has [13 possible prob-lems] occurred?[1]	Never/rarely/sometimes/monthly/more
Any violent victimiza-tion (or attempted)	How many times has someone robbed or tried to steal something from you by force; physically attacked you or attempted to do so; threatened or attacked you with a weapon?[1]	Not at all/yes to any of 3 items
Any property victim-ization (or attempted)	How many times has someone damaged or vandalized your home, eg. ... stolen or tried to steal something belonging to you like your vehicle; something from inside your home or garage (not vehicle); something outside in your yard or in your vehicle?[1]	Not at all/yes to any of 4 items

[1] These questions included "in the last six months, in your neighborhood. ..."

Long-Term Outcomes		
Social cohesion	People around here are willing to help their neighbors; This is a close-knit community; People in this neighborhood can be trusted; People in this neighborhood generally do not get along with each other; People in this neighborhood do not share the same values (r).	How strongly do you agree or disagree with these statements: strongly disagree/disagree/ neither agree nor disagree/agree/strongly agree alpha=.71 (W1); .78 (W2)
Informal social control	How likely is it that a neighbor would do something: If someone was letting trash pile	Very unlikely/unlikely/neither likely nor

	up in their yard or on their steps; if some young children were causing minor damage to	unlikely/likely/very likely
	a building in your neighborhood; if a suspicious stranger was hanging around the	alpha=.83 (W1); .82 (W2)
	neighborhood; if youth in the neighborhood were getting into trouble?	
Collective efficacy	Sum of standardized social cohesion and informal social control scales	
Believe neighborhood can solve problems	If there is a problem in this neighborhood, how likely is it that people who live here can	Very unlikely/unlikely/neither likely nor
	get it solved?	unlikely/likely/very likely
Willing to call police if a gang member	How likely or unlikely is it that you would call the police if a gang member threatened	Very unlikely/unlikely/neither likely nor
threatens	someone in your family?	unlikely/likely/very likely
Trust police	The police in my neighborhood can be trusted; the police in my neighborhood treat	How strongly do you agree or disagree with
	people fairly; the police in my neighborhood are respectful of people?	these statements: strongly disagree/disagree/ neither agree nor disagree/ agree/strongly alpha=.86 (W1); .86 (W2)

Surveys were completed with 797 San Bernardino residents in five neighborhoods 18 months before and 1229 residents six months after the issuance of the injunction. Roughly two thirds were Latino, with the remainder equally distributed among other ethnic categories. All participants were adults (35–40% were 18–34 years, 40–45% were 35–54 years, and about 20% were over 54 years in the two surveys); two thirds were women. Census data were used to assess whether the achieved sample characteristics in Wave 1 roughly approximate the population it was designed to represent.[18]

18   Our ability to conduct a direct comparison to census data is limited to the five demographic variables for which there is a good match between our measurement categories and the census survey: age, gender, and education level of the respondent; home ownership; and the respondent's length of residency. Gender comparisons are rough approximations because the census data available are reported for the entire population, whereas our respondents were limited to adults. Our residential stability measure asked about length of time lived in the neighborhood, whereas the census asks if the respondent has moved within the last five years. We selected the Wave 1 sample as the best

A hybrid survey procedure[19] was used to promote response rates in these difficult-to-survey neighborhoods. After five contacts to sampled addresses in support of the self-administered survey, trained field staff approached remaining addresses for a door-step interview using the same protocol. Adjusted response rates were 64% for Wave 1 and 73% for Wave 2.[20]

---

comparison because it was conducted just after the 2000 Census. Finally, the neighborhoods selected for our study are only roughly approximated by census block boundaries. Statistical comparisons of the two data sources reveal significant differences in all five areas on gender and educational attainment, and in a few areas on the other three variables. In all areas, survey respondents are disproportionately women and more educated when compared with the census population. It has implications for more limited generalizability of our findings to men and less educated persons. Beyond that, only scattered differences between the Census and the Wave 1 achieved sample were found. In Seventh Street, older individuals are more likely to respond to the survey. Homeowners disproportionately participated in the study in Upper Flats and North Area. In North Area and Lower Flats, survey respondents were less likely to have lived in the neighborhood for less than five years, but the Census incorporates any move, whereas our survey counted only moves from outside the neighborhood. In most areas, the match on age, homeownership, and residential stability between the Wave 1 and the census population was acceptable.

19   In our earlier work surveying highly disordered neighborhoods, we tested the efficacy of using a self-administered versus a telephonic personal interview survey approach. Anonymous self-administered surveys were more effective in these areas because residents seemed to be more forthcoming about their fears and perceptions than they were in personal interviews. (Explanations for survey mode differences are the subject of much debate, see Dillman, 2000 and Hennigan, Maxson et al., 2002). However, the self-administered approach in these communities resulted in lower than optimal response rates even after accruing responses over a three-month period according to Dillman's methods (Dillman, 1978, 1991). Consequently, for this work, we developed a hybrid approach for surveying in these areas that maximized the responses received from self-administered surveys (SA) and followed-up with face-to-face doorstep interviews (FTF) to achieve a higher response rate. Critical to the interpretation of comparisons across areas over time is the comparability of the ratio of SA to FTF achieved. In all except the South Area, the ratios were equivalent. More SA surveys were returned from the South Area in Wave 2 than in other areas, which created a bias toward less favorable neighborhood descriptions and more fear there. The direction of this bias, counter to the hypotheses and findings reported, suggests that differences between South and Lower Flats might be even stronger than indicated here. Furthermore, there were no interactions on any of the outcomes reported here between survey mode and wave. There were two significant mode by wave by area interactions on significant outcome effects. Testing the effects within survey mode revealed the reported differences were observed within both modes, but they were stronger within the FTF mode.

20   See Maxson et al., 2004, for a detailed statement of study areas, survey procedures, response rates, sample characteristics, the demographic comparability of the Wave 1 and Wave 2 achieved

Three sets of analyses were conducted. The first set compared the primary injunction area, Upper Flats, with North Area, the highly disordered neighborhood with no discernible territorial gang. The principal hypotheses for this first analysis predicted that residents in the primary injunction area would experience a positive change after the injunction on the immediate outcome variables relative to any change that occurred in its comparison area. We compared differences in the change over time in these two areas by examining their interaction in an analysis of variance using wave and area as factors. Significant interactions in the predicted direction were interpreted as support for the principal hypotheses. These analyses were repeated comparing change in the secondary injunction area, Lower Flats, with change in its control, South Area. A second set of analyses compared the same pairs of areas, testing whether similar change had occurred for each intermediate and long-term outcome.

A third set of analyses assumed that the Seventh Street area was characterized by similar neighborhood experiences before to implementation of its injunction as those in the Upper Flats primary injunction area. Both areas, as described by police informants, had been high-crime, active gang territories before their injunctions. Outcomes from the Wave 2 survey were compared between the earlier injunction area and the new one. We predicted that long-term effects, unlikely to have developed in the recent injunction area, would evidence higher levels in the older injunction area. These effects were tested using t-tests and chi-square analyses.

RESULTS

Immediate Outcomes

Our analyses supported the predictions that the gang injunction would have an impact on gang visibility almost immediately, and consequently they have an impact on the level of intimidation by gang members and the level of fear of gang members experienced by residents relatively soon after the injunction was filed and enforced. The top third of Table 2 shows the results of comparisons between Upper Flats and North Area, the two high disorder neighborhoods. Respondents living in Upper Flats reported seeing gang members hanging out in their neighborhoods less often than respondents in North Area, after the injunction than before. Although graffiti decreased in both

---

samples, and correspondance with U.S. Census data. We found no concern for methodological artifacts introduced by demographic shifts in any of the areas surveyed except for Lower Flats, where the Wave 2 demographics suggested an increase in renters and newcomers to the neighborhood.

areas, no significant difference appeared between the two areas on change in the level of graffiti from Wave 1 to Wave 2.

Fewer respondents in Upper Flats reported being hassled, frightened, or made anxious by gang members after the injunction than respondents in North Area. From Wave 1 to Wave 2, the percent of residents who reported experiencing any kind of intimidation fell eight percentage points in Upper Flats and rose by six percentage points in North Area. Similarly, fear of confrontation with a gang member decreased in Upper Flats over this time while it increased in North Area.

A different pattern of results emerged among immediate outcomes in the low disordered areas. Comparing the secondary injunction area, Lower Flats, with South Area, the top third of Table 3 shows respondents in Lower Flats reported more rather than less gang visibility than the low-disorder comparison South Area, and made to feel anxious by gang activity more rather than less often. The two low-disorder areas did not vary from wave-to-wave on any other immediate outcome measures.

Table 2. *Means And Tests of Area by Wave Interactions in Two High Disorder Areas on the Immediate, Intermediate, and Long-Term Outcomes*

	Upper Flats		North Area		Main Effect for Area	Main effect for Wave	Statistical test of predicted interaction
	W1 n= 287	W2 n = 384	W1 n = 227	W2 n =322			
Immediate Outcomes							
See gang members hanging out	2.86	2.53	2.88	2.90	*		F (1,1189) = 4.38, p = 0.037
See new graffiti	2.54	2.44	2.95	2.67	*	*	*ns
Been hassled	1.55	1.47	1.62	1.80	*		F(1,1183) = 4.31, p = 0.038
Young persons bullied	1.51	1.46	1.56	1.71	*		ns
Frightened by gang member	1.51	1.57	1.53	1.92	*	*	F (1,1186) = 5.69, p = 0.017
Gang activities made	1.95	1.76	1.88	2.02			F (1,1183) = 4.18,

you anxious						p = 0.041
Any intimidation by gang members	55%	47%	55%	61%		Wave1 X², ns; Wave2 X² = 13.18; df = 1,695; p<0.001
Fear confrontation with gang member	2.11	1.99	2.04	2.33	*	F(1,1192) = 10.32, p = 0.001

Intermediate Outcomes						
Fear of crime	2.14	2.03	2.17	2.28	*	F(1,1213) = 5.16, p = 0.023
Perceived level of social disorder	2.35	2.17	2.52	2.46		*	ns
Violent victimization (or attempted)	19%	23%	18%	29%		*	ns
Property victimization (or attempted)	48%	52%	54%	59%			ns

Long-Term Outcomes						
Social cohesion	2.95	3.04	2.84	2.80	*	ns
Informal social control	3.01	3.06	2.98	2.95		ns
Collective efficacy	2.98	3.05	2.91	2.87	*	ns
Belief neighborhood can solve problems	2.78	2.91	2.77	2.75		ns
Willing to call police if a gang member threatens	3.76	3.91	3.67	4.05		*	ns
Trust police	3.42	3.41	3.41	3.28		ns

INTERMEDIATE OUTCOMES

The gang injunction was also predicted to affect several intermediate outcomes if the influence of the injunction on gang intimidation and fear was strong and pervasive. Intermediate outcomes are less immediate because changes in gang behavior are just one of many factors in neighborhoods that may influence fear of crime, perceived level of disorder, and victimization. The analyses summarized in the middle of Table 2 showed little carryover of the injunction's impact to these more general outcomes. Residents of the primary injunction area, Upper Flats, reported less fear of crime than residents in North Area, but no significant differences on perceived social disorder or victimization.

Table 3. *Means and Tests of Area by Wave Interactions in Two Low-Disorder Areas on the Immediate, Intermediate, and Long-Term Outcomes*

	Lower W1 n = 72	Flats W2 n = 107	South W1 n = 42	Area W2 n = 104	Main effect for Area	Main effect for Wave	Statistical test of predicted interaction
Immediate Outcomes							
See gang members hanging out	1.72	2.06	1.73	1.51			* $F(1,315) = 5.97$, p = 0.015
See new graffiti	2.11	2.23	1.82	1.62			* ns
Been hassled	1.20	1.38	1.20	1.12			ns
Young persons bullied	1.23	1.43	1.23	1.14			ns
Frightened by gang member	1.22	1.41	1.27	1.20			ns
Gang activities made you anxious	1.37	1.56	1.56	1.28			* $F(1,312) = 6.58$, p = 0.011
Any intimidation by gang members	38%	42%	41%	26%			ns
Fear confrontation with gang member	1.49	1.71	1.28	1.38			* ns
Intermediate Outcomes							
Fear of crime	1.62	1.88	1.58	1.58			* ns

Perceived level of social disorder	1.75	2.06	1.63	1.61	F (1,321) = 4.44, p = 0.036
Violent victimization (or attempted)	6%	23%	2%	8%	Wave 1 X2, ns; Wave 2 X2 = 9.27; *df* = 1, n = 209, p = 0.002
Property victimization (or attempted)	28%	43%	36%	25%	Wave 1 X2, ns; Wave 2 X2 8.19; *df* = 1, n = 209, p = 0.004
Long-Term Outcomes					
Social cohesion	3.36	3.24	3.50	3.40	ns
Informal social control	4.04	4.22	4.31	4.35	ns
Collective efficacy	3.43	3.32	3.46	3.47	ns
Belief neighborhood can solve problems	3.29	3.11	3.25	3.59	F (1,315) = 4.28, p = 0.039
Willing to call police if gang member threatens	3.50	3.39	3.41	3.54	ns
Trust police	3.61	3.59	3.45	3.64	ns

Table 3 shows the results on these more general outcomes when comparing the secondary injunction area, Lower Flats, with its comparison, South Area. Both of these areas were low in disorder and victimization at Wave 1, but Lower Flats increased in perceived social disorder and victimization in the post-injunction survey relative to South Area.

LONG-TERM OUTCOMES

The long-term outcomes measured include neighborhood social cohesion, informal social control, collective efficacy, perceived neighborhood efficacy, and willingness to call and trust the police, which are indicators of the police's and community's ability to work together to combat crime. As a group, these outcomes might be influenced by changes set in motion by successful gang injunctions if the community became empowered as a result of changes in disorder, fear, and safety. However, statistical tests failed to reveal significant changes in the predicted direction on the long-term outcomes in the injunction areas relative to their comparison areas, as shown in Tables 2 and 3.

Contrary to predictions, perceived neighborhood efficacy decreased in the secondary injunction area, Lower Flats, relative to South Area. Residents here were less inclined to believe that the community could solve its problems after the injunction than before. Taken with the results of analyses in these areas above, lower neighborhood efficacy is consistent with the unexpected perceptions of higher gang visibility and disorder in the secondary injunction area.

As noted, Seventh Street is the territory of an active gang that had undergone an injunction five years before the second survey. Comparing the primary current injunction area, Upper Flats, with this area provides an opportunity to consider the impact on long-term outcomes as well as on immediate and intermediate ones. The results, as provided in Table 4, show that these two areas are not significantly different as regards immediate and intermediate outcomes when comparing the Wave 2 surveys. However, four of the six long-term outcomes showed significant differences between the two areas, with more favorable conditions in Seventh Street than in Upper Flats. One possible interpretation of these findings is that neighborhood social cohesion, collective efficacy, neighborhood efficacy, and willingness to call the police were higher in the Seventh Street Area than in Upper Flats because their gang injunction had been in place over a longer period of time. Although consistent with our hypotheses, the research design does not permit us to definitively rule out plausible alternative interpretations.

OUTCOMES BY AGE, ETHNICITY, AND GENDER

Each of the analyses reported were repeated adding age (18 to 34 vs. 35 and older), ethnicity (Hispanic vs. Nonhispanic), and gender as factors. No significant interactions with these demographics qualified the findings reported in comparison within the high-disorder areas. One triple interaction was significant in comparisons of Upper Flats and South Area. Older respondents showed an increase in trust, whereas younger respondents showed a decrease in trust in South Area, with little change from wave to wave in Upper Flats ($F = 6.88$; $df = 1,294$; $p = 0.009$). The findings reported in Tables 2–4 are robust across age, gender, and ethnicity.

Table 4. *Means and Tests by Area Comparing Two High-Disorder Injunction Areas on Wave 2 Immediate, Intermediate, and Long-Term Outcomes*

	Upper Flats	Seventh Street	Statistical Tests	
	W2	W2	t test or chi-square	
	n = 384	n = 312		
Immediate Outcomes				
See gang members hanging out	2.53	2.49	ns	
See new graffiti	2.44	2.4	ns	
Been hassled	1.47	1.54	ns	
Young persons bullied	1.46	1.55	ns	
Frightened by gang member	1.57	1.56	ns	
Gang activities made you anxious	1.76	1.8	ns	
Any intimidation by gang members	47%	52%	ns	
Fear confrontation with gang member	1.99	2.1	ns	
Intermediate Outcomes				
Fear of crime	2.03	2.04	ns	
Perceived level of social disorder	2.17	2.24	ns	
Violent victimization (or attempted)	23%	20%	ns	
Property victimization (or attempted)	52%	42%	$X^2(1) =$	: 7.687, p = 0.006
Long-Term Outcomes				
Social cohesion	3.04	3.16	$t(606)^1 =$	= 2.132, p = 0.033
Informal social control	3.06	3.2	ns	
Collective efficacy	3.05	3.18	$t(622)^1 =$	= 2.329, p = 0.020
Belief neighborhood can solve problems	2.91	3.12	$t(620)^1$	= 2.611, p 0.009
Willing to call police if a gang member threatens	3.91	4.16	$t(688) =$	= 2.813, p = 0.005

Trust police	3.41	3.46	ns

[1] adjusted for test with unequal variances.

DISCUSSION OF FINDINGS

Our analyses provide evidence of short-term effects of a CGI on the primary neighborhood targeted. Our surveys of community residents reveal less gang presence in the neighborhood, as compared with changes in the primary control area. Furthermore, fewer residents report acts of gang intimidation and residents express less fear of confrontation with gang members.

Police reported no territorial gang presence in the primary comparison area, but residents reported substantial gang activity on the pre-injunction survey. As crime increased in the city over the two-year period between the surveys (Warren, 2003), gang fear and intimidation increased in the disordered control area (North Area) but not in the neighborhood with the new injunction (Upper Flats). Thus, this strategy seemed to yield salutary effects in the primary injunction area: Immediate benefits accrued to residents' experience of gang visibility, intimidation, and fear.

These immediate benefits did not extend to the intermediate or long-term outcome indicators. Only in fear of crime did the primary injunction area show a relative decrease. No significant relative changes were observed on the other intermediate outcomes, perceived social disorder or crime victimization. Little evidence was found that immediate effects on residents translated into larger improvements in neighborhood quality, such as neighborhood social cohesion, informal social control, collective efficacy, and police/community relationships, although reductions in fear of crime and gang visibility, fear, and intimidation may be precursors to such change in the long run.

We found tantalizing hints of such changes in the comparison of the new injunction area (Upper Flats) with a contiguous area in which an injunction had been implemented five years before the second survey (Seventh Street). The two areas had similar levels of gang visibility, fear, and intimidation, but the longstanding injunction area showed favorable levels of social cohesion, neighborhood and collective efficacy, and willingness to call the police if a gang member threatened residents. If we assume the two areas had similar neighborhood characteristics at baseline before their injunction, these results are consistent with the view that community improvements will accrue once fear and intimidation are mitigated by implementation of a CBI. However, as the similarity of immediate outcomes might indicate, these gains are continually threatened by the persistence of gang activities.

Theories of social disorganization provide a context for interpreting changes brought about by the injunction. There was no direct community involvement in the development or implementation of the Flats injunction—a typical pattern identified in other studies as well (Allan, 2004; Maxson, 2004)—so the absence of relative change in collective efficacy or relationships with police is not surprising. The immediate changes in gang intimidation and fear in the primary injunction area may yet spark a dynamic of community improvement, as would be predicted from social disorganization theory. In this near-term assessment, reducing intimidating gang activity did not net this community the broader benefits of neighborhood social capital. The community-level processes apparently heightened in the older injunction area may have been initiated by an earlier lowering of gang intimidation and fear there. The comparison between the two injunction communities is consistent with an interpretation of community change: willingness to engage with police in crime control efforts, a perspective that neighbors can and will intervene to resolve incipient crime problems, and greater social bonds among neighbors.

The decreases in gang visibility, gang intimidation, and fear of gang crime in Upper Flats also could be the result of individual level processes such as deterrence or social identity-mediated deindividuation spawned by the injunction. The apparent decrease in intimidating gang behavior suggests that this injunction did not spur an increase in gang cohesion over the short term, although it could be triggered at a later date.

The unexpected expansion of the territory covered by the Flats injunction into the less disordered injunction area (Lower Flats) provided the opportunity to investigate the impact on a neighborhood with considerably less gang activity. Our comparison of this secondary injunction area with a similarly low-disorder, contiguous community produced results that caution those who would promulgate the efficacy of gang injunctions in diverse settings. Lower Flats evidenced negative impacts, relative to its comparison area (South Area): more gang visibility, anxiety, social disorder, and property victimization, and less faith that a neighborhood can solve its problems. Why didn't this injunction work as well in this area? We can speculate about several possible explanations.

The secondary injunction area might have been the locale for the displacement of gang activity from the primary injunction area. This area was surveyed as a comparison area before the injunction because of its potential vulnerability to displacement. Analysis showed that the location of police contacts with named gang members before the issuance of the injunction took place almost exclusively in the primary injunction area. The increased gang activity in Lower Flats also might have reflected the unanticipated consequences of increased suppression activities. This view would argue that police over-reached by including this neighborhood with less gang activity and less social disorder in the injunction. Suppression activities may have backfired by building cohesiveness (Klein, 1995) or oppositional defiance (Sanchez-Jankowski, 1991) among the targeted gang members who lived or were active in this area.

Finally, these negative results may be a reflection of weaknesses in the study design or methodology that affected the secondary area comparisons in particular. The area experienced substantial demographic change, with generally more renters and less residential longevity in the neighborhood. Our controls for these demographic changes did not change our conclusions[21] but such transitions may foster neighborhood dynamics that increase gang activity, independent of intervention efforts. We are cautious about drawing broad generalizations about the negative outcomes detected in the secondary injunction area.

IMPLICATIONS FOR FURTHER RESEARCH

Very little empirical research has been conducted investigating the impact of civil gang injunctions, despite their increasing popularity with law enforcement agencies. This study is the first that examines potential effects on community residents. Future studies that replicate the essential method of this research are needed in a variety of contexts: different injunction forms and implementation procedures, gang structures, law enforcement and court venues, and community environments. Given the expanding interest in this type of intervention, surprisingly little sound information is available regarding the effects on gang members or communities. A primary limitation of this study derives from its uniqueness: Any generalization of findings from one study of one injunction on one gang is clearly premature. The effects detected in this study reflect modest improvements in only the primary injunction area, and these may not be replicated in future studies.

Knowledge about injunctions could be improved substantially by the inclusion of other data collection components. An ethnographic component might address the activities and group processes in the gang targeted for an injunction before, during, and after implementation. Structured interviews with gang members, coupled with ethnographic field observation methods, are the optimal approach to investigating how injunctions do or do not work. A spatial analysis of gang and nongang crime in the targeted and comparison communities could inform the discourse on injunction impact and displacement.

An expanded longitudinal survey design is necessary to trace the long-term impacts of injunctions on community residents. Subsequent survey waves, conducted on an annual basis, could chart changes in community characteristics, such as social cohesion and informal social control, and neighborhood efficacy and policy/community

---

21   The only difference was observed in the homeownership category on the intermediate outcome of perceived level of social disorder. The increase in social disorder in Lower Flats relative to South Area was observed only among renters.

relationships that might be precipitated by the injunction intervention. The tenets of community social disorganization theory suggest that interventions like injunctions can produce positive community change and that these must be measured over an extended period of time. The tentative interpretation of differences in the new injunction area as compared with the previous injunction neighborhood would be ameliorated if these communities were surveyed over a longer period.

Just one area was available for each comparison with an injunction area. Our positive conclusions rest on differences detected between the primary injunction area and one similarly disordered comparison area. Visual inspection of the trends plotted on graphs suggests that the observed differences were more the result of negative changes in the comparison area than positive changes in the injunction area. The neighborhood that was selected as a comparison area possibly suffered from situational or idiosyncratic assaults on community health. Future research should include several comparison areas that mimic the intervention area at the baseline survey point.

POLICY IMPLICATIONS

The CGI against the Verdugo Flats gang in San Bernardino seems to have decreased the visibility of the gang, episodes of gang intimidation, fear of gang confrontations, and fear of crime in the targeted community. These effects are encouraging for law enforcement agencies wishing to experiment with this strategy. Coupled with the findings from another study that found small reductions in violent crime levels in injunction areas (Grogger, 2002), this study suggests that strategic suppression of gang member activities may translate into modest improvements in community safety and well-being. We recommend further experimentation with this strategy, if such efforts are coupled with a program evaluation that continues to build on the assessment of the intervention's effects.

The recent history of gang intervention policy and practice is not a positive record. Rigorous evaluations of gang programs are rare, and positive evidence of intervention is even more rare (see Decker, 2003; Klein and Maxson, 2005). One of the more visible recent efforts is Boston's Operation Ceasefire, which combined a focused deterrence strategy ("pulling levers") with activism from community groups and youth service providers (Kennedy, 1998; McDevitt et al., 2003). Researchers determined that implementation of Operation Ceasefire was associated with declines in youth homicides and gun assaults, but potential changes in community characteristics, such as those included in this study, were not monitored (Braga et al., 2001). Thus, we cannot weigh the relative merits of a CGI with other approaches to targeted deterrence, particularly those that may mobilize community participation in support of the intervention.

The study findings offer some guidelines for further refinement of the CGI strategy and recommendations for restraint or caution in some aspects. The negative results that emerged in the secondary injunction area argue for caution to be exercised when determining the geographic area to be covered by an injunction. Law enforcement and judicial practitioners should review spatial depictions of gang activity and crime to ensure that the area within which individual conduct is to be constrained is limited to spaces most often frequented by gang members. No evidence exists that expanding the geographic reach of the injunction reduces the displacement of gang activity. During the most recent campaign for mayor of Los Angeles, the incumbant proposed a citywide gang injunction, albeit with few details regarding the logistics or legality of such an operation (Faussett, 2005). Our findings would argue against such a broad geographic expansion of CGIs.

The Verdugo Flats gang—and most gangs included in the injunctions studied by Grogger—is a traditional, territorial gang. This type of gang is assumed by law enforcement to be most appropriate for injunctions, because of the geographic limitations imposed (Maxson et al., 2003). An alternative argument can be made for the viability of injunctions against specialty drug gangs, because they are more organized and have clear leadership (Klein, 1995). Until more is known about the mechanisms whereby injunctions reduce gang activity, limiting the strategy to the gang forms that have produced positive results thus far is advisable.

This study found tentative support for salutary injunction effects on community residents and neighborhoods. Theory and research on communities suggest that these effects could be substantially increased if injunction development and implementation engaged community residents in a process of neighborhood empowerment and improvement. Social networks and both formal and informal community organizations provide social capital through which neighborhoods can continue on a positive trajectory.

The positive effects of injunctions might be expanded if this strategy was coupled with the provision of skill-development and treatment resources for targeted gang members. The serving of injunction papers may open a window of opportunity for change. Offering a carrot of positive opportunity for vocational, educational, or personal growth with the stick of promised incarceration for violation of the injunction prohibitions may provide more immediate and long lasting change in negative gang behavior than that obtained from an injunction implemented alone.

McGloin's article in this volume suggests that better targeting of gang intervention efforts might derive from network analyses that identify gang "cut-points." She argues that key cut individuals provide a crucial structural or communication link between subunits or cliques within a gang. Conversely, CGIs target individuals whom police, and sometimes residents, have identified as central, or the most active, members of gangs. Each method supposes that targeting such individuals will help law enforcement better intervene in gang activities, by removing individuals crucial to gang functioning. Certainly, network analysis provides an empirical approach to identifying interactional linkages among group members. Identifying the role that cut-point individuals play regarding communication, leadership, and the fostering of criminal activity is an important step in better understanding gang linkages. Whether cutting off these cutpoints would have a lasting effect of weakening the gang, diminishing gang cohesiveness, or reducing criminal activity is a necessary next step in evaluating the efficacy of a network analysis.

Studying the sociometrics of a gang before planning an intervention is a sound recommendation, especially when information about linkages is derived from expert knowledge about gang interactional patterns. For example, Fleisher (2002) conducted interviews with gang members and neighborhood residents. As noted by McGloin, the results of such an analysis might lead to program support and services for less centrally involved gang members, while limiting suppression efforts to a few, critical targets. Furthermore, the structured collection of systematic information about individual activities may avoid reliance on more general perspectives that, as McGloin notes, "may tap into myths and perceptions rather than specific information and expertise." Such general perceptions may have led officers to include the Lower Flats area in the injunction, to the detriment of the success of this particular gang intervention.

Finally, even successful law enforcement suppression programs have limited utility as a solution to violent gang activity. As Bjerregaard states in reference to the anti-gang legislation that is sweeping the nation (2003: 186–187):

> Perhaps the biggest problem with these approaches is that they provide only temporary solutions and ignore the real problems that have contributed to the increase in both gangs and gang-related activity in our society. By focusing on gang suppression, we take the emphasis off of identifying and eradicating the ultimate causes of gang development and gang membership.

If CGIs crack the window of opportunity for change in communities, then public officials must seize this moment to put in place social policies that might check the economic disadvantage and social inequities that spawn gangs in communities. If they succeed, it might get a little less crazy out there.

REFERENCES

Allan, Edward L., Civil Gang Abatement: The Effectiveness and Implications of Policing by Injunction. New York: LFB Scholarly Publishing LLC.

American Civil Liberties Union (ACLU) of Southern California 1997 False Premises, False Promises: The Blythe Street Gang Injunction and Its Aftermath. Los Angeles: ACLU Foundation of Southern California.

Bjerregaard, Beth, Antigang legislation and its potential impact: The promises and pitfalls. Criminal Justice Policy Review 14:171–192.

Braga, Anthony A., David M. Kennedy, Elin J. Waring, and Anne M. Piehl, Problem-oriented policing, deterrence, and youth violence: An evaluation of Boston's Operation Ceasefire. Journal of Research in Crime and Delinquency 38:195–225.

Bursik, Robert J. and Harold G. Grasmick, Neighborhoods and Crime: Dimensions of Effective Community Control. Lexington, Mass.: Lexington Books.

Cameron, Jeffrey R. and John Skipper, The civil injunction: A preemptive strike against gangs. The FBI Law Enforcement Bulletin (November):11–15.

Castorena, Deanne, The History of the Gang Injunction in California. Los Angeles: Los Angeles Police Department Hardcore Gang Division.

Decker, Scott H., Policing Gangs and Youth Violence. Belmont, Calif.: Wadsworth.

Decker, Scott H. and Barrick Van Winkle, Life in the Gang: Family, Friends, and Violence. New York: Cambridge University Press.

Dillman, Don A., Mail and Telephone Survey: The Total Design Method. New York: Wiley. 1991 The design and administration of mail surveys. Annual Review of Sociology 17:225–249.

Mail and Internet: The Tailored Design Method. 2nd ed. New York: Wiley.

Ellemers, Naomi, Russell Spears, and Bertjan Doosje, Self and social identity. Annual Review of Psychology 53:161–186.

Egley, Arlen Jr. and Aline K. Major, Highlights of the 2002 National Gang Survey. OJJDP Fact Sheet. FS200401. Washington, D.C.: Office of Justice Programs, U.S. Department of Justice.

Faussett, Richard, Mayor vows to pursue a citywide gang injunction. Los Angeles Times (March 29).

Fisher, Michael, Ben Goad, and Lisa O'Neil Hill, Two areas face renewed violence. The (Riverside) Press-Enterprise (November 18).

Fleisher, Mark S., Doing field research on diverse gangs: Interpreting youth gangs as social networks. In C. Ronald Huff (ed.), Gangs in America. 3d ed. Thousand Oaks, Calif.: Sage.

Fremon, Celeste, Flying the flag: The debate over the latest gang crackdown. LA Weekly (July 18–24).

Geis, Gilbert, Ganging up against gangs: Anti-loitering and public nuisance laws. In C. Ronald Huff (ed.), Gangs In America. 3d ed. Thousand Oaks, Calif.: Sage.

Genelin, Michael 1998 Community prosecution: A difference. Prosecutor's Brief 3: 13–17.

Greene, Jack C., Gangs, community policing and problem solving. In Scott H. Decker (ed.), Policing Gangs and Youth Violence. Belmont, Calif.: Wadsworth.

Police youth violence interventions: Lessons to improve effectiveness. In Finn Esbensen, Larry Gaines and Steve Tibbetts (eds.), American Youth Gangs at the Millennium. Long Grove, Ill.: Waveland.

Grogger, Jeffrey, The effects of civil gang injunctions on reported violent crime: Evidence from Los Angeles County. Journal of Law and Economics 45:69–90.

Hennigan, Karen M., Cheryl L. Maxson, David Sloane, and Molly Ranney,Community views on crime and policing: Survey mode effects on bias in community surveys. Justice Quarterly 19:564–587.

Katz, Charles M., The establishment of a police gang unit: An examination of organizational and environmental factors. Criminology 39:301–338.

Katz, Charles M., Edward R. Maguire, and Dennis W. Roncek, The creation of specialized police gang units: A macro-level analysis of contingency, social threat and resource dependency explanations. Policing 25:472–506.

Kennedy, David M., Pulling levers: Getting deterrence right. National Institute of Justice Journal (July).

Klein, Malcolm W., Attempting gang control by suppression: A misuse of deterrence principles. Studies in Crime and Crime Prevention. Annual Review 88–111.

The American Street Gang: Its Nature, Prevalence and Control. New York: Oxford University Press.

Klein, Malcolm W. and Cheryl L. Maxson forth Street Gang Patterns and Policies. New York: Oxford University Press, coming

Los Angeles City Attorney Gang Prosecution Section, Civil gang abatement: A community based policing tool of the office of the Los Angeles city attorney. In Malcolm W. Klein, Cheryl L. Maxson, and Jody Miller (eds.), The Modern Gang Reader. 1st ed. Los Angeles: Roxbury Publishing. Los Angeles County District Attorney (LACDA) SAGE: A Handbook for Community Prosecution.

Maxson, Cheryl L., Civil gang injunctions: The ambiguous case of the national migration of a gang enforcement strategy. In Finn Esbensen, Larry Gaines, and Steve Tibbetts (eds.), American Youth Gangs at the Millennium. Long Grove, Ill.: Waveland.

Maxson, Cheryl L. and Theresa L. Allen, An Evaluation of the City of Inglewood's Youth Firearms Violence Initiative. Los Angeles: Social Science Research Institute, University of Southern California.

Maxson, Cheryl L., Karen Hennigan, and David C. Sloane, For the sake of the neighborhood? Civil gang injunctions as a gang intervention tool. In Scott H. Decker (ed.), Policing Gangs and Youth Violence. Belmont, Calif.: Wadsworth.

Maxson, Cheryl L., Karen Hennigan, David C. Sloane, and Kathy A. Kolnick, Can Civil Gang Injunctions Change Communities? A Community Assessment of the Impact of Civil Gang Injunctions. Draft Final Report to the National Institute of Justice. Los Angeles: Social Science Research Institute, University of Southern California (April).

Maxson, Cheryl L., Karen Hennigan, David C. Sloane, and Molly Ranney, The Community Component of Community Policing in Los Angeles: Final Report to the National Institute of Justice. Los Angeles: Social Science Research Institute, University of Southern California (August).

Mazza, Susan, Gang abatement. The San Diego experience. Law Enforcement Quarterly 288:11.

McDevitt, Jack, Anthony A. Braga, Dana Nurge, and Michael Buerger , Boston's youth violence prevention program: A comprehensive community-wide approach. In Scott H. Decker (ed.), Policing Gangs and Youth Violence. Belmont, Calif.: Wadsworth.

McGloin, Jean M., Policy and intervention: Consideration of a network analysis of street gangs. Criminology & Public Policy (this issue).

Postmes, Tom and Russell Spears, Deindividuation and antinormative behavior: A meta-analysis. Psychological Bulletin 123:238–259.

Sampson, Robert J., Stephen W. Raudenbush, and Felton Earls, Neighborhoods and violent crime: A multilevel study of collective efficacy. Science 277:918–924.

Sanchez-Jankowski, Martin, Islands in the Street: Gangs and American Urban Society. Berkeley, Calif.: University of California Press.

Spears, Russell, Tom Postmes, Martin Lea, and Susan E. Watt , A SIDE view of social influence. In Joseph P. Forgas and Kipling D. Williams (eds.), Social Influence: Direct and Indirect Processes. Philadelphia, Pa.: Psychology Press.

Staff Reports, Bernardino injunction issued against local gang. San Bernardino County Sun Newspaper (September 24).

Stewart, Gary, Black Codes and broken windows: The legacy of racial hegemony in antigang civil injunctions. Yale Law Journal 107:2249–2279.

Thornberry, Terence P., Marvin D. Krohn, Alan J. Lizotte, Carolyn A. Smith, and Kimberly Tobin, Gangs and Delinquency in Developmental Perspective. Cambridge, U.K.: Cambridge University Press.

Vigil, James Diego 1988 Barrio Gangs: Street Life and Identity in Southern California. Austin: University of Texas Press., A Rainbow of Gangs. Austin, Texas: University of Texas Press.

Warren, Jennifer, Decline in violent crime seen statewide. Los Angeles Times (October 16):B5.

Whitmer, John and Deanne Ancker 1996 The history of the injunction in California. In LACDA (ed.), SAGE: A Handbook for Community Prosecution.

Wolcott, Holly 2004   Officials seek injunction against Oxnard's Colonia Chiques gang. Los Angeles Times (March 25).

CASE CITED

People ex rel. Gallo v. Acuna, 1997.

Cheryl Maxson is an Associate Professor in the Department of Criminology, Law and Society at the University of California's Irvine campus. Dr. Maxson's general interests are juvenile delinquency and violence, street gangs, and juvenile justice policy and programs.

Karen Hennigan is a Research Assistant Professor at the Center for Research on Crime and Social Control, Department of Psychology at the University of Southern California. Dr. Hennigan's interests include the role of community, group and social identity in interventions, survey and evaluation research design and methods, and law enforcement and criminal justice programs and policies.

David Sloane is a Professor in the School of Policy, Planning, and Development at the University of Southern California. Dr. Sloane's research includes studies on community planning and policy, urban cultural landscapes, and the historical development of urban places.

"It's Getting Crazy Out There": Can a Civil Gang Injunction Change a Community?

PowerPoint by:
Marlyn Alas
Meghan Bacca
Francisco Figuroa

How is a CGI Implemented?

A process whereby selected gang members are prohibited from engaging in such activities as loitering at schools, parks, carrying pagers, and riding bicycles, or face arrest- against a local gang.

1. Police along with Prosecutors gather evidence that members of a street gang represent a public nuisance.
   - Criminal history
   - Written declarations by officers familiar with the neighborhood
2. Select members to be named based on declarations
3. Pick geographic area to be covered in injunction
4. Specific behaviors that will be prohibited
5. Prosecutor files for temporary restraining order
6. Members named in injunction are served notice of injunction hearing.
   - Defendants are not provided public counsel
7. If implemented members must be served again before the injunction can be enforced.

(Maxson, p. 581)

Verdugo

- Verdugo Flats precluded from congregating from Grant to Third streets and from Medical Center Drive to I-215.
- Verdugo Flats is by far the largest gang in the city with about 3,000 members, police said. Affiliate gangs include Seventh Street and Mount Vernon. (knowgangs.com)
- "Turf Oriented"
  - ▷ Graffiti
  - ▷ Intimidation
- 19 members
- 22 Activities

San Bernardino Police Department

- Already had conducted three gang injunctions.
  - ▷ One against prostitutes.
  - ▷ Two against territorial street gangs.
- Department welcomed study and was helpful
- Gangs they were considering for further injunctions seemed excellent targets for studying the impact on communities.
- San Bernardino has eight police officers and a sergeant assigned to its gang unit.
- The city has an estimated 3,038 gang members. (www.co.san-bernardino.ca.us/sheriff)

Different Types of Surveys Used and Why They Worked:

- ► Self- Administered Survey (SA)-two were used, once before the injunction and once shortly after the injunction was imposed.
- ► Face to Face doorstep interviews (FTF)- interviews in which the surveyor goes to the home/apartment of the interviewee instead of telephonic or selfadministered survey.
- ► Community Assessment surveys were given before and shortly after the injunctions were imposed in order to accurately measure the change in perception in the neighborhood.
- ► Surveys completed with 797 SB residents in five neighborhoods 18 months before and 1229 residents six months after the injunction.
- ► To promote responds rates due to below optimum rates with a SA surveys, a hybrid survey procedure of SA survey and FTF was used to boost response rates successfully.

Social Disorganization Theory

- ► provides a foundation for predicting changes in social relationship. Resident participation in developing and implementing a gang injunction may spark a process of community engagement in effort to build informal social control, social capital in the form of social networks, and supportive organizational structures. (Bursik and Grasmick, 1993; Greene, 2004)
- ► Even if neighborhood residents are not engaged in the injunction activities directly, reducing the level of the immediate threat of the gang may lay a foundation for improving the quality of neighborhood life by strengthening collective efficacy (Sampson et al., 1997) As levels of intimidation and fear ease, a community might be able to organize and become involved in the process of reversing the deterioration of the physical and social order in their community, with its attendant effects on fear of crime and civic engagement.

Deterrence Theory

▶ Predicts that sure, swift, and severe sanctions will deter criminal behavior. Although the penalties for injunction violations area not severe, the notifications of hearings and injunction papers might make targeted gang members believe that they are being closely watched and more likely to be apprehended and prosecuted for violations (Grogger, 2002: Klein, 1993).

▶ Practitioners contend that issuance of the injunction has a profound effect on gang members.

Immediate Outcomes:
Comparing the Upper Flats, North Area, Lower Flats and the South Area

▶ Respondents living in the Upper flats reported seeing less gang members hanging out in their neighborhood less often that reported in North Area, after the injunction than before.

▶ Although graffiti decreased in both areas, no significant difference appeared between the two areas on change in the level of graffiti from Wave 1 to Wave 2.

▶ Fewer respondents in Upper Flats reported being hassled, frightened, or made anxious by gang members after the injunction that respondents in North Area.

▶ Lower Flats reported more rather than less gang visibility than the low disorder comparison South Area, and made to feel anxious by gang activity more rather than less often.

▶ The two low-disorder areas did not vary from wave-to-wave on any other immediate outcome measures.

Social Psychological Theory

► Group identity causes individuals to feel less responsible for their behavior, and influences them to conform to situationspecific group norms (cf., Postmes and Spears, 1998; Spears et al., 2001)

► A gang injunction hold individuals personally accountable for their actions, which would weaken gang identity and decrease levels of participations in gang related behavior, especially among noncore members (cf., Ellemers et al., 2002). In this process of holding individuals responsible for their gang activities, identification with the gang might decline, as could the overall gang cohesiveness.

Intermediate Outcomes:

► The gang injunction was also predicted to affect several intermediate outcomes if the influence of the injunction on gang intimidation and fear was strong and persuasive.

► Residents of the primary injunction area, Upper Flats, reported less fear of crime than the residents of North Area but no significant differences on perceived social disorder or victimization.

► Both of these areas were low in disorder and victimization at Wave 1, but Lower Flats increased in perceive social disorder and victimization in the post-injunction survey relative to South Area.

Long Term Outcomes:

▶ The long-term outcomes measured include neighborhood social cohesion, informal social control, collective efficacy, perceived neighborhood efficacy, and willingness to call and trust the police.

▶ Residents were less inclined to believe that the community could solve its problems after the injunction than before. Upper Flats, within this area provides an opportunity to consider the impact on long-term outcomes as well as on immediate and intermediate ones.

▶ Four of the six long-term outcomes showed significant differences between the two areas, with more favorable conditions in Seventh Street than in Upper Flats.

▶ Older respondents showed an increase in trust.

▶ younger respondents showed a decrease in trust in South Area, with little change from wave to wave in Upper Flats.

References:

Bursik, Robert J. and Harold G. Grasmick 1993 Neighborhoods and Crime: Dimensions of Effectiveness Community Control. Lexington, Mass: Lexington Books. Ellemers, Naomi, Russell Spears, and Bertjan Doosje2002 Self and Social Identity. Annual Review of Psychology 53:161–186.

Civil Banishment of Gang Members: Circumventing the Criminal Due Process Requirements? (n.d.). (Reprinted from Civil Banishment of Gang Members: Circumventing the Criminal Due Process Requirements?, Vol. 64, pp. 1461–1487, by S. Smith, 2000)

Grogger, J. (2002). *The Effects of Civil Gang Injunctions on Reported Violent Crime: Evidence from Los Angeles County (Journal of Law and Economics, Trans., Vol. 45, pp. 69–90).*

Klein, Malcolm W. 1993 Attempting gang control by suppression: A misuse of deterrence principles. Studies in Crime and Crime Prevention. Annual Review 88–111.

Postmes, Tom and Russell Spears 1998 Deindividuation and antinormative behavior. A meta-analysis. Psychological Bulletin 123:238–259.

Sampson, Robert J., Stephen W. Raudenbush, and Felton Earls 1997 Neighborhoods and Violent crime: A multilevel study of collective efficacy. Science 277: 918–924

Spears, Russell, Tom Postmes, Martin Lea, and Susan E. Watt 2001 A SIDE view of social influence. In Joseph P. Forgas and Kipling D. Williams (eds.), Social Influences: Direct and Indirect Processes. Philadelphia, Pa: Psychology Press.

PRISON GANGS AND DESISTANCE

LEGAL INNOVATION AND THE CONTROL OF GANG BEHAVIOR

By Eva Rosen
and Sudhir Venkatesh

ABSTRACT

This review considers one of the most prominent methods of combating gang activity in the second half of the last century, namely the deployment of legal strategies to prevent gang formation and intervene in existing gang structures. These include highly formalized strategies, such as the enactment of legislative decrees such as injunctions that limit the association of gang members in public space, as well as informal procedures in which communities create an indigenous and localized set of norms and juridical procedures to fight gang activity. Research on legal tactics and gang control in the past few decades has shown that the formative understanding of the city as a social ecology of distinct and separate communities, in which social institutions and residents are largely attuned to activity occurring within their boundaries, remains at the heart of social policy formulation with respect to youth delinquency. The

Eva Rosen, Sudhir Venkatesh, "Legal Innovation and Control of Gang Behavior," *Annual Review of Law and Social Science*, vol. 3, pp. 255-270. Copyright © 2007 by Annual Reviews. Reprinted with permission.

review addresses these major legal innovations and the debates surrounding them.

INTRODUCTION

Crime rates have been falling nationally. Yet American social science, the popular media, and law enforcement organizations continue to expend considerable time and energy on understanding the causes and consequences of criminal behavior. In particular, there has been sustained interest in the behavior of street gangs (see Coughlin & Venkatesh 2003).

The role of street gangs as organized entities perpetuating criminal activity is not a new phenomenon. However, each particular historical period bears witness to different types of gang delinquency and correlatively unique strategies for gang abatement strategies. This article considers one of the most prominent methods of combating gang activity that arose in the past three decades, namely the deployment of legal strategies to prevent gang formation and intervene in existing gang structures. These include highly formalized strategies, such as the enactment of legislative decrees that limit the association of gang members in public space, as well as informal procedures in which communities create an indigenous and localized set of norms and juridical procedures to fight gang activity.

Note that this article focuses its attention on urban gang activity. Many of the legal strategies occur in suburban and exurban areas as well; however, in most cases, they have been developed in the context of metropolitan areas and then exported outward. Thus, the focus on urban gangs has relevance for wider explorations. The article also focuses on the U.S. case.

HISTORY: GANGS AND THE URBAN ECOLOGY

Efforts to combat street gangs are at least a century old. Some of the earliest works on American urban gangs arose as a part of the Chicago School of sociology. This perspective on the city was developed by social scientists at the University of Chicago in the early twentieth century and had considerable influence on how Americans (in and out of the academy) looked at, and responded to, patterns of human behavior in the emerging metropolis. Thrasher's [1963 (1927)] seminal work, *The Gang*, examined 1313 street gangs in Chicago neighborhoods. Thrasher's comprehensive view of the city's gangs was not intended to combat gang activity. Nevertheless, it was motivated in the spirit of sociology at that time, whereby theorization was inextricably linked to the pragmatic need to spur action and reform. Thrasher developed a systematic portrait of gang formation and reproduction in the city, and, in this research initiative, he paid particular attention to the institutions that played a role in curbing juvenile delinquency. Like his peers at the University of Chicago, where much of the leading research on delinquency was taking place, Thrasher tried to combine scientific reasoning with pragmatism.

The early twentieth century Chicago School writings culminated in the influential "social disorganization" theory (Shaw & McKay 1942). Clifford Shaw and Henry McKay portrayed juvenile delinquency as an "ecological" problem: Communities with high rates of gang activity were those in which local residents, groups, organizations, etc., either failed to transmit values to young people or failed to exercise adequate social control. These authors stayed true to the reigning human ecology model of the city by focusing their efforts on local communities—these were the areas where delinquency had its etiology, and hence where the solutions must be targeted. The human ecology framework for understanding urban structure and process posited that the city is a composite of discrete and distinct natural areas (Venkatesh 2001). People experienced much of their daily lives within their neighborhoods, so early scholars thought, and the view of urban gangs reflected this sentiment: Politicians employed the gang to bring out the vote; gangs protected turf, which meant they stayed within the boundaries of a specified natural area; gang members could be an indigenous security force for neighborhood residents; and so on (Venkatesh 1999, Suttles 1968).

The social disorganization perspective was deeply influential for much of the twentieth century. Gang activity was thought to be an ecological (local) problem, and, as the welfare state grew in the twentieth century, antigang initiatives were in fact joint efforts in which government (at various levels) funded social workers, who then combed streets, parks, and alleys to find wayward youth. In line with the ecological perspective, the objective was to reintegrate young people into youth centers, schools, employment agencies, worksites, and other so-called mainstream social institutions that would control their behavior and transmit proper values to the youth—what Spergel (1995) has called the social work approach to fighting gangs. Because street gangs were largely comprised of adolescents, this approach tended to be effective: Social workers focused their energies on individuals who were naturally aging out of the gang and in need of work and income for their families. This crime fighting tactic also worked because of a thriving urban industrial economy that offered employment for youth.

This so-called social work approach to gang intervention changed radically after the 1960s. The reasons driving the shifts are complex, but they include the retrenchment of the welfare state; the concomitant lack of support of the American public for government-based programs that helped poor and needy communities (Rieder 1985); the changing profile of street gangs from adolescent peer groups to assemblies of teenagers as well as young adults; and the move away from penal welfarism toward a punitive model of policing that placed "less emphasis on the social contexts of crime and measures of state protection and more on prescriptions of individual/family/ community responsibility and accountability" (Muncie 2007, p. 20). In major urban areas, one saw that enforcement agencies—e.g., police, FBI, specialized tactical units dedicated to narcotics trafficking—took the lead in targeting gangs where once social workers, public health officials, and the clergy worked the streets. Along with these historical shifts, after the 1960s one saw a profound increase in street gang membership and gang-related violence (this history is presented in greater detail in Coughlin & Venkatesh 2003).

It would be easy to argue that the change in gang activity necessitated novel approaches. Klein (1995) argues that street gangs' primary activity was inactivity, but more recently, in Chicago (which was not dissimilar to other major urban areas in the Northeast, Midwest, and select western municipalities such as Los Angeles), gang-related homicides increased five times from 1987 to 1994 (see Block et al. 1996 for more background). The rate of street gang crime in the two most dangerous parts of the city was 76 times that of the two safest areas. Part of the increase in crime occurred because, as recent studies have argued, street gangs became more entrepreneurial. Furthermore, many of the most developed street gangs were in minority inner-city communities. In these areas, the gangs attempted to control underground economies that included drug trafficking, prostitution, and extortion of legitimate businesses (Collins 1979, Hagedorn 1991, Jankowski 1991, Padilla 1992, Spergel 1995, Sullivan 1989, Taylor 1990, Venkatesh 2000).

As many scholars have pointed out, perhaps the most important catalyst for this change in gang organizations was the trade of crack cocaine, which altered fundamentally the urban street gang and its modus operandi (see Venkatesh & Levitt 2000, Levitt & Venkatesh 2000). With their shift in orientation toward business (and away from petty delinquency and the protection of neighborhood turf), the gang's primary goal was to control geographic areas to solidify their drug sales. This led to an increase in violence both within and between gangs. And, as a consequence, law enforcement shifted its approach. For example, beginning in Chicago (Padilla 1992), municipal police departments began to merge their gang and narcotics divisions to respond more effectively to the conflation of gangs and organized criminal entrepreneurship.

GANGS AND THE LAW

In considering the past three decades of legal tactics to combat gangs, we can detect patterns of change and continuity. We should begin by noting that there have been several reconceptualizations of the city that have sought to move mainstream social science and public policy away from the human ecology paradigm (Zukin 1980). However, the most influential paradigm for understanding how cities work—and correlatively, how social behavior like gang activity operates within urban areas—remains the eco-logical paradigm. It is no surprise, therefore, that the strategies reviewed here share with their predecessors the need to work within the rich matrix of institutional and personal relationships at the community level. We refer to this, in the context of the law, as "localism" (Schragger 2001).

To elaborate, the new legal tactics that are being used to combat gangs are over-whelmingly directed at empowering local entities that might already have some estab-lished capacity to exercise social control over young people. In this sense, they resemble the earlier social work approach, but the key difference is that the funds and leadership arise through legislation and the agencies (e.g., prosecutors, judges, police) that carry out the law. The key in this approach is to decentralize criminal justice interventions to deploy a greater share of resources (and accountability) to persons, groups, and institu-tions operating at the community level—i.e., to those stakeholders (including police, block clubs, storeowners, clergy, etc.) whose boundaries are in a particular geographi-cally bounded community. One can contrast this to the highly centralized modality of antidelinquency in Europe—e.g., The Netherlands, Germany, and France.[10]

These legally driven initiatives have been motivated by a belief that gangs and drug trafficking (and drug-related violence) are synonymous: The popular catchphrase that arose in the early 1980s is the "gang and drug problem." This perspective is not without some justification, as noted above (Skolnick 1994). The proliferation of drug sales among urban (and in some cases, suburban, exurban, and rural) gangs was cited by inner-city residents as often as were poverty and poor educational systems as a cause of the swell in gang violence.

Perhaps the most common use of the law as a gang-fighting tool lies in the creation of legislative decrees, called injunctions, to limit the free association of street gangs in

---

10 Perhaps the most recognizable of the U.S. variants is the so-called community policing strategy in which law enforcement officials, residents, and neighborhood associations work collectively to identify problems and devise anticrime initiatives. The birth of community policing in major U.S. urban areas may be viewed in part as a willingness of municipal government to support residents' desire to take back control of streets from street gangs (see Skogan 1986). For a review of community policing, see Muncie 2007, who explains that young people were increasingly governed "through the motifs of 'crime and disorder' (Simon & Burns 1997) in which an obsession with regulation—whether the regulation occurs through families, schools, or training programmes—encourages a generalised mistrust and fear of young people." The essay also reviews use of informal social control activities, wherein residents acted outside the police, as well as use of community courts, which were additional measures developed by locally based constituencies to combat gangs (Fagan 1993, Venkatesh 2006, Venkatesh & Murphy 2007).

the public theaters of the neighborhood.[11] These include park areas, streets and street-corners, playgrounds (in and outside of schools), alleyways, beachfronts, boardwalks, and so on. The State of California has been at the vanguard in this area, and many other states have attempted to replicate its policing strategies. In the 1980s, various California municipalities began to experiment with public nuisance laws as a means of combating the street gang. The objective was to combat gang crime by banishing gang members from publicspace. In 1987, for example, the City of Los Angeles passed the first gang injunction against the Playboy Gangster Crips. The injunction was seen as a creative method of providing the community with the tools to effectively combat gang crime locally. The media and police agencies represented the tactic as a success—e.g., they cited drops in major felonies and gang-related crime (Yoo 1994, p. 218). San Jose, Norwalk, Long Beach, San Francisco, and San Diego also put in place or attempted measures to ban gangs from public space.

In 1988, the California legislature enacted the Street Terrorism Enforcement and Prevention Act (STEP) to prevent gang crime. Those individuals understood by law enforcement to be known and active gang members were prohibited from associating with other active gang members when the gathering was for purposes of carrying out a crime. STEP sought to disrupt patterns of gang association and activity at the root of gang crime, stating that "[a]ny person who actively participates in any criminal street gang with the knowledge that its members engage in or have engaged in a pattern of criminal gang activity, and who willfully promotes, furthers, or assists, in any felonious conduct by members of that gang, shall be punished by imprisonment in a county jail for a period not to exceed one year." It is worth noting that to bring about an indictment the act requires more than mere association: Law enforcement must also prove knowledge of criminal activity and active participation.

Subsequent attempts to limit free association of street gangs followed. From 1992 to 1994 there were seven injunctions obtained in California: People ex rel. Gallo v. Carlos

---

11   These injunctions are based on the declaration of the gang as a public nuisance. A public nuisance, according to California Civil Code Section 4379, is anything that is "injurious to health ... or is indecent or offensive to the senses, or an obstruction to the free use of property, or unlawfully obstructs the free passage or use, in the customary manner, or any ... public park, square, street, or highway." A prosecutor may apply for an injunction after first showing that a gang is a public nuisance. There are three steps that are usually followed in obtaining an injunction: (a) a temporary restraining order, in which the prosecutor makes a request directly to a judge and must prove that the gang is a public nuisance (typically the prosecuting officer produces statements made by the police and community members); (b) a preliminary injunction, in which the framework for the permanent injunction is established and put into play until the end of the trial; (c) the permanent injunction, which is the result of a trial in which the prosecution is successful.

Acuna, People ex rel. City Attorney v. Avalos, People ex rel. Fletcher v. Acosta, People v. Blythe Street Gang, People ex rel. Jones v. Amaya, City of Norwalk v. Orange Street Locos, and People v. "B" Street Boys. Several behaviors were specifically prohibited, including association with other gang members, forced entry (in many cases gang members demanded or forced entry into residents' homes to elude arrest), wearing and using gang signs and clothing, use of cell phones and beepers (to promote gang business), local movement (to prevent members from eluding arrest), and harassment of residents, and some cities also instituted adult curfews. Astvasadoorian (1998) claims a significant impact for neighborhoods with antigang injunctions: "[C]rime has consistently decreased where these injunctions have been issued" (see Astvasadoorian 1998 for statistics and cities). But others claim that this effect is temporary and comes at the expense of civil liberties (Stewart 1998, Werdegar 1999).

Chicago and the State of Illinois were also at the forefront of the development of legal strategies aimed at combating gangs (as noted, Chicago had already merged its narcotics and gang divisions, an act that laid the groundwork for cooperation between police and federal officials interested in breaking up the street gang as an organized criminal unit). Toward the end of the 1980s, Chicago's inner-city communities—many of which were disproportionately poor and African American—became deleteriously affected by gang violence, including drive-by shootings, open-air drug dealing, extortion, and fighting (see Venkatesh & Levitt 2000). Neighborhood groups pressed the city council to come up with effective legislation that could curb gang activity.

Negotiations between block clubs, churches, youth centers, schools, etc., and the mayor and city council officials eventually led to the 1992 Chicago's Gangs Congregation Ordinance. The purpose of the ordinance was to prevent gang members from congregating in public areas before they moved on to more serious crimes (as a result of their association in public). As Schragger (2001) points out, Chicago police did not exercise surveillance over the entire city looking for gang members, but instead they targeted particular areas (blocks, parks, etc.) that they felt were saturated with dangerous street gang activity—i.e., they created "no-gang loitering areas." Police would first warn the suspected individual gang members; if the group did not leave the area in question, law enforcement would proceed to make an arrest. The Supreme Court struck down the ordinance in City of Chicago v. Morales (1999) (hereafter referred to as Morales).

There is much disagreement about the effectiveness of Chicago's antigang strategy, and a study of the key debates (along with efforts in California at the same time) points to the central issues that arise when the law is used to combat gangs (cf. Smith 2000). Critics of Chicago's use of this antiloitering or quality-of-life measure suggested that police officers would target African Americans disproportionately because the information regarding known gang members was highly incomplete; in their efforts to target known areas of gang activity, law enforcement was disproportionately moving into minority areas when the statistics did not necessarily provide justification for them to do so (Stewart 1998, Boga 1993). Supporters, in contrast, believed that law enforcement finally had a tool to combat gang activity; they also pointed out that the ordinance was different from previous antiloitering ordinances owing to the limits placed on police discretion (Astvasadoorian 1998, Kennedy 1997; see also Livingston 1999).

Other important legal tools arose in the 1980s and 1990s, such as increased criminal penalties for gang activity (including heightened penalties for gang activity occurring near schools), sweeps,[12] juvenile curfews (see Harvard Law Review 1994), relaxed standards for admission of evidence of gang membership, tougher defense tactics in search and seizure situations such as the "no-knock narcotics search warrant" (see Allegro 1989), and public nuisance laws. However, measures such as these had minimal impact on gang activity unless they worked in conjunction with the enjoining of gangs through public nuisance laws, which was by far the most widespread measure. Attacking gangs via protecting public space was innovative in part because nuisance and quality-of-life statutes called on provisions in civil procedure instead of criminal law (this had several important consequences for defendants; for example, there was no need to prove guilt beyond a reasonable doubt and no requirement for either a trial jury or for defense counsel).

Municipal law enforcement tended to be at the forefront of efforts to prevent gangs from occupying public space. When federal agencies intervened, they too turned to the law for antigang prevention efforts, but they sought to apply federal racketeering statutes that approached the street gang as an organized criminal enterprise. In its original intent, the RICO (Racketeer Influenced and Corrupt Organizations) statute was meant to address legitimate businesses that had been infiltrated by criminality (Atkinson 1978). However, in the past few decades it has been used to address organized crime and gang activity (for detailed discussion, see Lynch 1987, Ploscowe 1963, Bonney 1993). Decker et al. (1998) have investigated to what extent the street gang is becoming part of organized crime, with results that vary according to the gang and geographic location. To invoke the RICO statutes, prosecutors must demonstrate that the gang is a

---

12   In 1994, the Chicago Housing Authority (CHA) created the Operation Clean Sweep program. This antigang and crime control strategy rested on the use of surprise searches of public housing apartments. The use of so-called sweeps received attention because law enforcement officials did not obtain warrants before searching individual homes for contraband. To avoid potential legal issues surrounding violation of Miranda protections, the CHA used its own private police force—instead of public law enforcement officers—to carry out the constitutionally questionable strategy. The procedure brought about immediate criticism from civil rights advocates who argued that the constitutional rights of the poor were being trampled upon. Five thousand residents signed a petition that they supported the use of the sweeps to enforce law and order. In April 1994, a federal district court in northern Illinois issued a ruling that the sweeps were unconstitutional and so banned the use of sweeps.

collective enterprise intent on promoting economic gain and that there is criminal activity furthered by this enterprise. The problems with this method include determining who is a gang member and defining precisely the nature and mission of gang activity (see Needle & Stapleton 1983). Also, the preventative benefits seem to arise after the gang has attained a fairly substantial degree of organization—i.e., the legislation does not provide tremendous support for small-scale gangs even if they are oriented toward commercial pursuits (Goldstein 1990, Sheldon et al. 1997, Skolnick 1994, Walker 1994).

It is the so-called "broken windows" perspective that provides the theoretical background for antigang injunctions (Wilson & Kelling 1982, Kelling & Coles 1996). In 1982, James Wilson and George Kelling published an article in Atlantic Monthly that offered a new set of explanations for the causes of neighborhood crime. Wilson & Kelling divide urban residents into "law-abiding citizens" and "disreputables," a position similar to contemporary arguments by Kennedy (1997) and Anderson (1999), who distinguish between "street" and "decent" families. Wilson & Kelling tied social disorder together with physical disorder; the simple version is that a window left broken and unrepaired sends a signal of diminished collective care for the neighborhood, which makes the area a petri dish for criminals who believe that few locals will stop them in their efforts. The patterns are cyclical in that "untended behavior leads to the breakdown of social controls" (Wilson & Kelling 1982), which then leads to increased atomization of community members. In the end, the community becomes "vulnerable to criminal invasion" (Wilson & Kelling 1982). An example of this thesis may be found in Glazer's (1997) discussion of graffiti. Glazer writes that "the proliferation of graffiti, even when not obscene, confronts the subway rider with the inescapable knowledge that the environment he must endure for an hour or more a day is uncontrolled and uncontrollable, and that anyone can invade it to do whatever dam age and mischief the mind suggests."[13]

The initial empirical results supported the broken windows theory. In one systematic study based on 40 urban neighborhoods, Skogan (1990, pp. 18–20) found a causal link between disorder and crime. He writes, "Disorder not only sparks concern and fear of crime among neighborhood residents; it may actually increase the level of serious crime. Disorder erodes what control neighborhood residents can maintain over local events and conditions. It drives out those for whom stable community life is important, and discourages people with similar values from moving in. It threatens house prices

---

13   As a solution to increased neighborhood crime and disorder, Wilson & Kelling (1982) advocate such tactics as police foot patrol to increase contact and trust at the neighborhood level, which would thereby promote a sense of safety. The authors find that placement of police on foot patrol increased the perception of safety among residents. The crime rate (violent crime) did not decrease, but people felt safer. The authors argue that they were in fact safer, even though the crime rate did not decline.

and discourages investment. In short, disorder is an instrument of destabilization and decline" (Skogan 1990, p. 3).[14,15]

The broken windows perspective was cited by critics as providing theoretical support for the use of gang abatement strategies that involve enjoining the street gang (Astvasadoorian 1998, Kennedy 1997, Wilson & Kelling 1982). According to this perspective, small signs of social disorder that are not directly of harm may nevertheless have a contributing impact on crime (see Schragger 2001 for a review). Thus, even seemingly insignificant incidents of disorderliness must be criminalized because this will create the perception of order and safety, which will then lead to decreases in the likelihood of criminal activity. To create this order, society must criminalize "disreputable" behavior (Wilson & Kelling 1982). As noted here, the most common tool of criminalization has been the enjoining of gangs by policing public space.

The broken windows theory runs a fine line between encouraging more community social control and infringing upon civil liberties of gang members. Some critics have charged that the injunction gives police too much discretion in determining what behavior or people are disreputable (Stewart 1998). Wilson & Kelling (1982) have countered this criticism by suggesting that it is possible to train police in proper procedure, but this argument is not developed in any meaningful way. They write that the criminalization of such behavior "exist[s] not because society wants judges to punish vagrants or drunks, but because it wants an officer to have the legal tools to remove undesirable persons from a neighborhood when informal efforts to preserve order in the streets have failed" (Wilson & Kelling 1982).

We can point to other theoretical justifications for the use of civil injunctions as a means to curb gang activity (Kahan 1998). Economic analyses of criminal behavior must take into account the values of individuals and communities that produce the behavior. In other words, one must understand the social meaning that individuals attach to gang membership, whether they are affiliated with the gang or simply tolerate their presence in the neighborhood. By looking at differential levels of interest in gang

---

14   More recent work by Sampson and colleagues (1997) has questioned the links of social and physical disorder, emphasizing instead the shared levels of trust and willingness to help one another that exist in a neighborhood—i.e., collective efficacy. In a 1995 survey in Chicago, Sampson demonstrated that this collective efficacy, defined as "social cohesion among neighbors combined with their willingness to intervene on behalf of the common good," is linked to reduced violence (Sampson et al. 1997). The authors recognize the link between public disorder and small crime with the larger issue of violent crime; however, rather than emphasizing this causal link, Sampson posits at the center of the equation the community's capacity to respond to low-order public disorder.

15   Astudy conducted by Harcourt (1998) reviews the work of Skogan and Sampson and finds that Harcourt's own data in New York City do not support Skogan's claim that reducing disorder deters more serious crime.

membership and willingness to accept high gang activity, this perspective attempts to understand why some communities have much more gang crime than others (Horowitz 1987; Kahan 1998, p. 613). This theory moves us away from strategies like so-called crackdowns in which heightened policing is used to break up the gang organization—the use of tactical units, for example, is not favored because it reinforces the attraction of gang membership for young people and adds strength to the meaning of gang behavior for youth (Kahan 1998, p. 614). Instead, the key to combating gang activity lies in the eradication of the avenues through which gangs disseminate information about themselves and attract other youth. One method is to curb gang interaction through gang loitering laws and youth curfews that limit the public behavior of street gangs. These interventions act on the principle that gangs impart much of their power through how they are perceived by community members.

A related perspective on social meaning puts into relief the difference between the community's norms and shared understandings of crime and social order and those of the wider society (Meares & Kahan 1998b). In this view, a representative body of residents and organizations may legitimately suspend certain protected privileges, allow greater police discretion than is publicly accepted, and otherwise act in contradistinction to prevailing social norms. Here, the primary debate has been around the issue of rights: Do communities have the capacity to define social rights based on their own norms, when these rights may contradict those protected by the general laws of the land (Alschuler & Schulhofer 1998, Meares & Kahan 1998a)? There is extensive research documenting the existence of differential norms regarding law and order, particularly among disadvantaged and/or minority communities (Anderson 1999, Meares Muncie 2007, Jankowski 1991, Pattillo Suttles 1968, Venkatesh & Murphy 2007, Venkatesh 2000). However, these studies have not informed the debate on the need to bend the law in order to adhere to local norms for conduct.

DEBATING INJUNCTIONS

There has been some legal support for the use of antigang injunctions, such as those that prohibit association of gang members in public space. This view is primarily illustrated by the 1997 California Supreme Court decision in People ex rel. Gallo v. Carlos Acuna upholding the constitutionality of the public nuisance laws enjoining gangs. The court (hereafter "Acuna court") ruled that "acts or conduct which qualify as public nuisances are enjoinable as civil wrongs or prosecutable as criminal misdemeanors" (Astvasadoorian 1998). In the original complaint, the City of San Jose declared that the gang was a public nuisance and injurious to residents' health and senses (Acuna 1997, 14 Cal. 4th at 1103). The California Court of Appeal struck down 15 of the 24 provisions owing to their unconstitutionally overbroad or vague nature that could allow for infringement on defendants' First Amendment rights; however, the city appealed parts of this decision. In response, the Acuna court ruled that the injunction neither violated the First Amendment rights of the gang members nor was unconstitutionally over-broad or unduly vague. The Acuna court reviewed the history of antigang injunctions in California and ruled that such injunctions did not violate First Amendment freedom of association and were not vague or overbroad.

According to the Acuna court, the injunction did not violate First Amendment rights because the relationships in question were not of an intimate or intrinsic nature and therefore are not protected by the First Amendment. Furthermore, the court ruled that the injunction was not overbroad as it applied only to the 38 gang members in question. Nor was it found to be overbroad in curbing the defendants' right to association; the injunction only applied to a small area in Rocksprings, not to anywhere outside this location. Finally, as the First Amendment does not protect violence—a primary activity attributed to the gang members in Rocksprings—the court did not find the injunction to be overbroad in prohibiting activities of the gang members. Defendants argued that they could not be prohibited from associating with each other, particularly if there is no clear intent to perpetrate illegal acts. However, owing to the consistent—even daily—nature of the illegal and violent acts, the Acuna court deemed it unnecessary to demonstrate specific intent to commit a crime.

The broken windows perspective played an important role in the arguments of those defending the Acuna decision. The notion that public association was sui generis a threat could be traced to the idea that reducing the attractiveness of the physical landscape—gangs made areas unsafe for public traffic—leads to greater crime (Astvasadoorian 1998). Once again, the ecological view of communities was brought into the legal terrain to defend a particular program of action to combat gangs.

Critics responded to the Acuna decision with various arguments, most of which centered on the notion that such injunctions curbed free association as protected by the Constitution (Werdegar 1999, p. 411; Stewart 1998). For Werdegar and others (Poulos 1995, Boga 1993) there are both legal and practical reasons for ensuring that injunctions are not used to enjoin gang members, including the high margin of error in these injunctions. Specifically, it is simply too difficult to identify with any sufficient degree of certainty the gang membership status of individual occupants of a public space (Werdegar 1999, p. 416). Community members and police officers—especially those police who are not assigned to a regular beat and are therefore unfamiliar with the neighborhood and the locals—may not know which of the gang members is responsible for making the noise, causing the disturbance, or committing a certain crime. They may not always recognize the youth in question with a high level of assuredness. In other words, the injunction is potentially vague.

This constitutional vagueness challenge is based on the right to due process in the Fifth and Fourteenth Amendments—the Fifth Amendment requires sufficient and clear warning of any prohibited behavior, and the Fourteenth Amendment requires that the law be enforced justly and equitably, avoiding arbitrariness and discrimination. In 1972, Papachristou v. City of Jacksonville struck down a vagrancy ordinance with the vagueness doctrine, setting a precedent that removed vagrancy ordinances from the books all across the country.

A primary supporter of the Acuna decision, Deputy City Attorney of Los Angeles Raffy Astvasadoorian, challenged the critics who charge that such injunctions infringe upon First Amendment rights: "No rational person would assert that a group of people who conjointly and consistently violate the law have a constitutionally protected right to do so. In the context of crime prevention, and gang crime and violence in particular, this type of reasoning is utter nonsense" (Astvasadoorian 1998). Like Wilson & Kelling (1982), Astvasadoorian asserts that the nature of gang crime—in that it involves a group of people—renders it in a class of its own meriting special legal treatment.

Another critique of public nuisance laws as a gang abatement strategy suggests that there is no need to develop entirely new legal tactics to combat gang crime. The search for innovation hides the fact that the solution lies in improved implementation of existing provisions. Boga (1993), for example, argues that existing law offers ample ammunition to combat gang crime, with no further need to invoke injunctions. "Nuisance abatement orders preventing gang members from congregating publicly operate on this [...] faulty principle. Rather than apply existing laws to punish illicit activities, they seek to criminalize all meetings by gang members regardless of their motivation" (Boga 1993, p. 11).

Judge Lee Sarokin (1996, p. 381), a retired judge on the U.S. Circuit Court of Appeal, extended this position to develop the so-called brussels sprouts analogy:

> What did you do as a kid if you had brussels sprouts on the plate? You moved them around, spread them around to make it look as if there were less, but they were still there and someone in authority usually required you to deal with them. If you will forgive me for abusing this metaphor, we have three choices as I see it: (1) we can dump the brussels sprouts in the garbage, which is really what we have been doing all of these years; (2) we can spread them around, hide them under the mashed potatoes, and make it look like we are really dealing with the problem; or (3) we can deal with them, absorb them into ourselves and society, and make us all healthier.

Sarokin does not advocate the unbridled use of antiloitering initiatives, but he does believe that the basic proposition of broken windows theory is correct—i.e., that low-level crime and disorder foster more violent crime. He advocates rehabilitation of individuals, which harkens back to the social work strategy that was in vogue in the mid-twentieth century.

Boga (1993) considers three acceptable methods of legally combating gang crime without resorting to the injunction based on the public nuisance law. The first is the use of California's STEP Act, which creates the substantive offense of participation in a criminal street gang (see Boga 1993, p. 6). Secondly, for states that do not have such legislation, Boga cites the acceptable use of drug loitering ordinances. These laws only target such "gatherings that directly injure public health and safety" rather than the general prohibition of public congregation in abatement injunctions (Boga 1993, p. 6). Finally, Boga suggests using probation and parole systems to achieve the same goal as the public nuisance laws, which can be more unfair and unreliable. For Boga, the use of public nuisance laws is more of an effort to banish street gangs from public space than to combat crime. He writes that "by means of this civil remedy, cities are effectively banishing street gangs from the realm of public space" (Boga 1993, p. 7).

Some have suggested that not only do antigang injunctions violate First Amendment rights, but they are also racist in their effects. Stewart (1998, p. 2251) draws explicit links between vagrancy laws and their use in controlling undesirable peoples, and the more recent use of public nuisance laws. In the Papachristou v. City of Jacksonville (1972) decision, vagrancy laws were said to perpetuate arbitrary enforcement of the law, which led to discrimination against certain unpopular groups. This decision was a landmark case for striking down vagrancy laws all over the country that unfairly targeted racialized/ethnic minority groups (Stewart 1998, p. 2258; also see Stuntz 1992). Stewart claims that antigang injunctions target minority groups in a similarly unfair fashion.

Finally, the use of injunctions has been criticized because it allows police to exercise great discretion. In 1999, the Illinois Supreme Court (in the Morales decision) deemed Chicago's gang loitering ordinance unconstitutional. In Justice Stevens's opinion, the law was impermissibly vague in authorizing police to disperse gang members found loitering in public spaces (Morales 119 S.Ct. at 1861–62). A coalition of scholars, community groups, and law enforcement felt betrayed by this decision to invalidate the ordinance (see Roberts 1999). They did not believe that the police discretion was too great, and they felt that the ruling took away a powerful tool of communities to combat crime—the so-called realist interpretation is one in which practical considerations regarding crime control supersede abstract considerations regarding civil rights (cf. Meares & Kahan 1998b). Some portrayed the use of antiloitering ordinances as tame compared with more punitive measures that result in mass incarceration of minorities (Rosenthal 2000). In contrast, others argued that the ordinance would lead to arbitrary and discriminatory police action and represented a breach of constitutional rights (cf. Werdegar 1999, Stewart 1998). Both supporters and critics in Illinois had hoped that the Morales decision would help them make sense of the host of laws and ordinances—at the city and state level—that had been passed regarding the scope of police discretion and the protection of civil liberties. In this respect, Morales offered little help.

Researchers suggest that legal tactics and sanctions will be only minimally useful because they fail to take into account the role of the street gang in the lives of youth. Boga calls for the need to provide alternative communal associations, so that youth do not believe the gang to be the only game in town. Researchers have suggested that gangs provide emotional and social supports and services, which could be provided more effectively by community based organizations (Brotherton & Barrios 2003; Jankowsi 1991; Pattillo 1998; Spergel 1990,1995). Some of these researchers argue for increased funding of local organizations that outreach to troubled youth [Jankowski (1991) revives the need for social worker indoctrination, in which trained case workers intervene in the lives of gang members and reconnect them with mainstream institutions]. Mayer (1993) argues that current antigang initiatives are driven by fear and are not appropriate responses to gang violence and crimes. He cites a faulty definition of youth gangs as the root of the misdirected efforts. For example, many define a criminal street gang as an organization, association, or group engaging in criminal acts such as assault, robbery, homicide, and/or drug trafficking. Other characteristics include a common name or identifying symbol and a sense of group identity. However, counter to this well-accepted definition, youth gangs are not necessarily characterized by a convergence of strong social ties, criminal purpose, and outward manifestations of gang consciousness. Mayer (1993) argues that incorporation of these fallacies into current antigang initiatives undermines their effectiveness and leads to abuse of their power.

Others have suggested that the contemporary street gang is really a commercial enterprise (cf. Bourgois 1996; Jankowski 1991; Padilla 1992; Venkatesh 1997, 2000). These researchers seek to add greater historical specificity to the popular conception of the gang as a group of petty delinquent teenagers. In this framework, prevention and intervention efforts would have to include provisions for individual members to earn income outside the street gang—and, of course, preferably in the legitimate mainstream economic market. This could take several forms: e.g., a jobs program could target older adults who remain in gangs to supplement income by offering them other meaningful employment; a community-based vocational training program could increase the human capital of individuals.

Meares (1998) moves in a different direction by suggesting that social scientists return to social disorganization theory when constructing interventions. An individual's propensity to commit a crime is mediated by the community structures in which they live, she suggests, and less by individual factors such as unemployment and poverty. A focus on individual incentive to break the law should be replaced with a focus on the characteristics of communities that help support criminal activity. Meares emphasizes the evolution from Shaw & McKay's (1942) disorganizational theory to modern-day theorists' "differential organizational theory" (Meares 1998, p. 195). For Meares, the "(loitering) ordinances that empower police officers to assist residents directly in community guardianship are an example of law enforcement strategies that could improve community social organization" (p. 223). Like Livingston, Meares argues that ordinances are a feasible alternative to other, stigmatizing legal options: "[U]nlike the reverse sting procedure, curfews and loitering laws do not have redistributive properties that directly contribute to the perception of poor minorities that the criminal justice scales are being 'righted.' They focus instead on all in poor communities, regardless of race. They remove signs of disorder, making room for the community leaders to establish order" (Meares 1998, p. 223).

CONCLUSION

This article has reviewed a recent development in social organization of street gang activity, namely a shift in the societal strategies to combat neighborhood gangs. Unlike earlier historical periods, in the past three decades law enforcement officials, in conjunction with community stakeholders, have turned to legal tactics as a mechanism for gang prevention and intervention. Two assumptions lie at the core of these strategies: First, effective antigang strategies should be local (cf. Hanson 1970, Frug 1993). That is, individuals, groups, and community associations can play an important role in legal tactics to fight gangs, whereas in the past these local entities were largely relegated to the sphere of counseling, social work, and nonpunitive initiatives. Second, gangs need to operate in public to survive; take away their freedom of association and one dramatically reduces the likelihood that gangs will be able to function.

These two premises have resulted in varying forms of social intervention. The most widespread tactic has been to utilize legal injunctions to deter a gang presence in public areas of a neighborhood—e.g., street corners, parks, school playgrounds. City and state governments in particular have sought to prohibit street gang members from meeting with each other, with the assumption that the ostensible purpose of such convenings is to plan and carry out the gang's criminal activities. These injunctions have had varying success, and to date there is no systematic social science research that has evaluated the impact of antiloitering and related injunctions on gang-related crime. Instead, the effects of the injunctions have been to raise wider issues concerning the rights of poor people to control how their neighborhoods are protected and how laws are enforced. As important, these injunctions have not always survived constitutional challenges—the Morales decision in Chicago presents the clearest case of a court rescinding injunctions on the basis of violations of rights to freedom of association (in addition to related issues such as vagueness, limited checks on police discretion, and differential impact on minority groups).

The so-called philosophy of "localism" (Schragger 2001) that undergirds these legal tactics has led to the development of other antigang initiatives, but research is similarly equivocal. Community policing, which began forcefully in Chicago, has been replicated throughout American cities, but there is no definitive assessment to date on the effectiveness of this enforcement strategy for the prevention of gang activity. Vigils and other take-back-the-night strategies, in which residents harass gang members and attempt to make them uncomfortable occupying public spaces, are similarly ineffective for crime prevention, although they may have secondary effects such as promoting feelings of solidarity among community residents. And informal social control strategies, whether vigilante justice movements (Venkatesh 2006) or statesanctioned community courts, have not been subjected to any systematic evaluation [see Fagan & Malkin (2003) for a study on a community justice center in Red Hook, Brooklyn; Merry (1993) has reviewed the literature on community mediation in the United States]. One thing is certain: The formative understanding of the city as a social ecology of distinct and separate communities, in which social institutions and residents are largely attuned to activity occurring within their boundaries, remains at the heart of social policy formulation with respect to youth delinquency. Broken windows theory is one of the more recent manifestations of the notion that highly localized tactics (e.g., fighting graffiti and vandalism, reappropriating public space) are preferred in controlling antisocial youth behavior. Despite the effectiveness of federally driven initiatives that have dismantled the gang, such as the use of RICO-based strategies, the preference among law enforcement, policy makers, and the general public is to allow residents and collective actors at the community level, such as police and block club presidents, to take a greater role in gang intervention. More research will be needed to determine whether these new efforts have attained their objectives in keeping families and communities safer.

DISCLOSURE STATEMENT

The authors are not aware of any biases that might be perceived as affecting the objectivity of this review.

LITERATURE CITED

Allegro DB. 1989. Police tactics, drug trafficking, and gang violence: why the no-knock warrant is an idea whose time has come. Notre Dame Law Rev. 64:552–70

Alschuler AW, Schulhofer SJ. 1998. Antiquated procedures or bedrock rights? A response to Professors Meares and Kahan. Univ. Chicago Leg. Forum 1998:215–44

Anderson E. 1999. Code of the Street: Decency, Violence, and the Moral Life of the Inner City. New York: Norton. 352 pp.

Astvasadoorian R. 1998. California's two-prong attack against gang crime and violence: the Street Terrorism Enforcement and Prevention Act and anti-gang injunctions. J. Juvenile Law 19:272–300

Atkinson J. 1978. "Racketeer Influenced and Corrupt Organizations," 18 U.S.C. §§ 1961–68: broadest of the federal criminal statutes. J. Crim. Law Criminol. 69(1):1–18

Block CR, Christakos A, Jacob A, Przybylski R. 1996. Street Gangs and Crime: Patterns and Trends in Chicago. Research Bulletin. Chicago: Ill. Crim. Justice Inf. Auth.

Boga TR. 1993. Turf wars: street gangs, local governments, and the battle for public space. Harvard Civil Rights-Civil Lib. Law Rev. 29:477–504

Bonney LS. 1993. The prosecution of sophisticated urban street gangs: a proper application of RICO. Catholic Univ. Law Rev. 42:579–614

Bourgois P. 1996. In Search of Respect: Selling Crack in El Barrio. New York: Cambridge Univ. Press. 407 pp.

Brotherton D, Barrios L. 2003. Between Black and Gold: The Street Politics of the Almighty Latin King and Queen Nation. New York: Columbia Univ. Press City of Chicago v. Morales et al., 527 U.S. 41 (1999)

Collins HC. 1979. Street Gangs: Profiles for Police. New York: NY City Police Dep.

Coughlin BC, Venkatesh SA. 2003. The urban street gang after 1970. Annu. Rev. Sociol. 29:41–64

Decker SH, Bynum T, Weisel D. 1998. A tale of two cities: gangs as organized community groups. Justice Q. 15:395–426

Fagan J. 1993. The political economy of drug dealing among urban gangs. In Drugs and the Community: Involving Community Residents in Combatting the Sale of Illegal Drugs, ed. RC Davis, AJ Lurigio, SP Rosenbaum, pp. 19–54. Springfield, IL: Thomas

Fagan J, Malkin V. 2003. Theorizing community justice through community courts. Fordham Urban Law J. 30:857–953

Frug J. 1993. Decentering decentralization. Univ. Chicago Law Rev. 60:253

Glazer N. 1997. Unsolved mysteries. New Republic. June 23, p. 29

Goldstein H. 1990. Problem-Oriented Policing. New York: McGraw Hill. 206 pp. Hagedorn JM. 1991.

Gangs, neighborhoods, and public policy. Soc. Probl. 38(4):529–42 Hanson R. 1970. Toward a new urban democracy: metropolitan consolidation and decentralization. Georgia Law J. 58:863

Harcourt BE. 1998. Reflecting on the subject: a critique of the social influence conception of deterrence, the broken windows theory, and order-maintenance policing New York style. Mich. Law Rev. 97(2):291–389

Harvard Law Review. 1994. Juvenile curfews and gang violence: exiled on Main Street. Harvard Law Rev. 107(7) :1693–710

Horowitz R. 1987. Community tolerance of gang violence. Soc. Probl. 34(5):437–50 Jankowski MS. 1991. Islands in the Street: Gangs and American Urban Society. Berkeley: Univ. Calif. Press. 382 pp.

Kahan DM. 1998. Social meaning and the economic analysis of crime. J. Leg. Stud. 27(2):609–22

Kelling GL, Coles CM. 1996. Fixing Broken Windows: Restoring Order and Reducing Crime in our Communities. New York: Free Press. 319 pp.

Kennedy R. 1997. Race, Crime, and the Law. New York: Pantheon Books. 538 pp.

Klein MW. 1995. The American Street Gang, Its Nature, Prevalence, and Control. New York: Oxford Univ. Press. 270 pp.

Levitt SD, Venkatesh SA. 2000. An economic analysis of a drug selling gang's finances. Q. J. Econ. 115(3):755–89

Livingston D. 1999. Gang loitering, the court, and some realism about police patrol. Supreme Court Rev. 1999:141–202

Lynch GE. 1987. RICO: the crime of being a criminal, Parts I & II. Columbia Law Rev. 87:661–764

Mayer JJ. 1993. Individual moral responsibility. Wake Forest Law Rev. 28(4):943–86

Meares TL. 1998. Social organization and drug law enforcement. Am. Crim. Law Rev. 35(2):191–228

Meares TL, Kahan DM. 1998a. Black, white, and gray: a response to Alschuler and Schulhofer. Univ. Chicago Leg. Forum 1998:245–60

Meares TL, Kahan DM. 1998b. The wages of antiquated procedural thinking: a critique of Chicago v. Morales. Univ. Chicago Leg. Forum 1998:197

Merry S. 1993. Sorting out popular justice. In The Possibility of Popular Justice: A Case Study of Community Mediation in the United States, ed. SE Merry, N Milner, pp. 31–66. Ann Arbor: Univ. Mich. Press

Muncie J. 2007. Youth justice and the governance of young people: global, international, national, and local contexts. In Youth, Globalization, and the Law, ed. SA Venkatesh, R Kassimir, pp. 17–60. Stanford, CA: Stanford Univ. Press. 352 pp.

Needle J, Stapleton WV. 1983. Handling of Youth Gangs. Reports of the National Juvenile Justice Assessment Centers. Washington, DC: US Dep. Justice

Padilla F. 1992. The Gang as an American Enterprise. New Brunswick, NJ: Rutgers Univ. Press Papachristou v. City of Jacksonville, 405 U.S. 156 (1972)

Pattillo ME. 1998. Sweet mothers and gangbangers: managing crime in a black middle-class neighborhood. Soc. Forces 76(3):747–74

Pattillo ME. 1999. Black Picket Fences: Privilege and Peril among the Black Middle Class. Chicago: Chicago Univ. Press. 283 pp.

People ex rel. Gallov. Carlos Acunaetal., 14 Cal.4th1090 (1997)

Ploscowe M. 1963. New approaches to the control of organized crime. Ann. Am. Acad. Polit. Soc. Sci. 347:74–81

Poulos P. 1995. Chicago's ban on gang loitering: making sense of vagueness and overbreadth in loitering laws. Calif. Law Rev. 83(1):379–418

Rieder J. 1985. Canarsie. Cambridge, MA: Harvard Univ. Press. 290 pp.

Roberts DE. 1999. Race, vagueness, and the social meaning of order-maintenance policing. J. Crim. Law Criminol. 89(3):775–836

Rosenthal L. 2000. Gang loitering and race. J. Crim. Law Criminol. 91(1):99–160

Sampson R, Raudenbush SW, Earls F. 1997. Neighborhoods and violent crime: a multilevel study of collective efficacy. Science 277:918–24

Sarokin HL. 1996. Civil rights or nuisance: How should the judge-citizen view a vagrant's behavior? Mich. Law Policy Rev. 1:379–82

Schragger RC. 2001. The limits of localism: gang anti-loitering law and local government. Mich. Law Rev. 100(2):371–472

Shaw C, McKay H. 1942. Juvenile Delinquency and Urban Areas. Chicago: Univ. Chicago Press Sheldon RG, Tracy SK, Brown WB. 1997. Youth Gangs in American Society. Belmont, CA: Wadsworth. 360 pp.

Skogan W. 1986. Fear of crime and neighborhood change. Crime Justice 8:203–39

Skogan W. 1990. Disorder and Decline: Crime and the Spiral Decay in American Neighborhoods. New York: Free Press. 218 pp.

Skolnick JH. 1994. Justice Without Trial: Law Enforcement in Democratic Society. New York: Macmillan. 312 pp.

Simon D, Burns E. 1997. The Corner: A Year in the Life of an Inner City Neighborhood. New York: Broadway Books. 560 pp.

Smith S. 2000. Civil banishment of gang members. Univ. Chicago Law Rev. 67:1461

Spergel I A. 1990. Youth gangs: continuity and change. Crime Justice 12:171–276

Spergel IA. 1995. The Youth Gang Problem: A Community Approach. New York: Oxford Univ. Press. 346 pp.

Stewart G. 1998. Black codes and broken windows. Yale Law J. 107(7):2249–80

Stuntz WJ. 1992. Implicit bargains, government power, and the Fourth Amendment. Stanford Law Rev. 44(3):553–91

Sullivan M. 1989. "Getting Paid": Youth, Crime, and Work in the Inner City. Ithaca, NY: Cornell Univ. Press. 275 pp.

Suttles GD. 1968. Social Order of the Slum: Ethnicity and Territory in the Inner City. Chicago: Univ. Chicago Press. 243 pp.

Taylor CS. 1990. Dangerous Society. East Lansing: Mich. State Univ. Press

Thrasher FM. 1963 (1927). The Gang: A Study of 1313 Gangs in Chicago. Chicago: Univ. Chicago Press. 388 pp.

Venkatesh SA. 1997. The social organization of street gang activity. Am. J. Sociol. 103(1):82–111 Venkatesh SA. 1999. Community-based interventions into street gang activity. J. Community Psychol. 27(5):551–67

Venkatesh SA. 2000. American Project: The Rise and Fall of a Modern Ghetto. Cambridge, MA: Harvard Univ. Press. 360 pp.

Venkatesh SA. 2001. Chicago's pragmatic planners: American sociology and the myth of community. Soc. Sci. Hist. 25(2):275–317

Venkatesh SA. 2006. Off the Books. Cambridge, MA: Harvard Univ. Press. 426 pp.

Venkatesh SA, Levitt SD. 2000. Are we a family or a business? Theory Soc. 29(4):427–62 Venkatesh SA, Murphy AK. 2007. Policing ourselves: law and order in the American ghetto. In Youth, Globalization, and the Law, ed. SA Venkatesh, R Kassimir, pp. 124–62. Stanford, CA: Stanford University Press. 352 pp.

Walker S. 1994. Sense and Nonsense about Crime and Drugs. Belmont, CA: Wadsworth. 320 pp. Werdegar MM. 1999. Enjoining the constitution. Stanford Law Rev. 51(2):409–45

Wilson JQ, Kelling GL. 1982. Broken windows. Atlantic Mon. 249(3):29–38

Yoo CS. 1994. The constitutionality of enjoining street gangs as public nuisances. Northwest. Univ. Law Rev. 89:212–67

Zukin S. 1980. A decade of new urban sociology. Theory Soc. 9:575–601

Legal Innovation and the Control of Gang Behavior

Eva Rosen and Sudhir Venkatesh

PowerPoint by: Randi Windom, Lavene Mays, Vinlecia Harris

History: Gangs and the Urban Ecology

► One of the earliest works on American urban gangs came from the Chicago School of Sociology.
► This perspective had considerable influence on how Americans (in and out of the academy) looked at, and responded to, patterns of human behavior in cities.
► "juvenile delinquency is an ecological (community) problem
► communities with high rates of gang activity were those in which local residents, groups, organizations, ect., either failed to transmit values to young people or failed to exercise adequate social control." (Shaw & McKay)
► Early scholars from the university believed that since people experienced much of their daily lives within their neighborhoods or their ecology, this is where fighting gangs had to occur.
► Politicians employed the gang to bring out the vote; gangs protected turf, which meant they stayed within the boundaries of a specified natural area; gang members could be an indigenous security force for neighborhood residents..." (Venkatesh 1999, Suttles 1968)

History: Gangs and the Urban Ecology (cont.)

- The social disorganization perspective, thought of by Shaw & McKay in 1942 was so influential that it brought about a solution which tried to rid young people from gangs.
- Since gang activity was thought to be an ecological problem, a new approach, in which the government funded social workers, to crack down on gang activity was put into action. The objective was to reintegrate young people into youth centers, schools, employment agencies, work sites, mainstream social institutions that would control their behavior and transmit proper values to the youth.
- This new approach was successful the majority of gang members were adolescents, social workers focused on individuals who were ageing out of the gang and needed work and income to help these adolescents get out of gangs.

Gangs And The Law

- Ecological Paradigm: the most influential paradigm for understanding how cities work-and additionally, how social behavior like gang activity operates within urban areas.
- Localism: the need to work within the rich matrix of institutional and personal relationship at the community level.
- There were new legal tactics utilized to combat gangs, and the differences between such tactics and the social work approach was that the funds and leadership came from the legislation and the agencies that carry out the law. (e.g. prosecutors, judges, police).
- This approach was made to decentralize criminal justice interventions to deploy a greater share of resources to persons, groups, and institutions operating at community level.

Gangs And The Law (cont.)

- In 1988, the Street Terrorism Enforcement and Prevention Act (STEP), was enacted by the California legislature , to prevent gang crime.
  - ▷ To stop disrupt patterns of gang association
  - ▷ To end the root of gang crime
- This act targeted individuals understood by law enforcement to be known and active gang members. They were prohibited from gathering and association with other active gang members for purposes of carrying out a crime. Utilizing this legislation law enforcement must prove knowledge of criminal activity and active participation.
- Subject to imprisonment in the county jail up to 1 year.
  - ▷ Crime has consistently decreased where these injunctions have been issued

---

Gangs And The Law (cont.)

- <u>Racketeer Influenced and Corrupt Organization (RICO)</u>
  - ▷ Municipal law enforcement tended to be at the forefront of efforts to prevent gangs from occupying public space. When federal agencies intervened, they too turned to the law for anti-gang prevention efforts.
  - ▷ To invoke the RICO statutes, prosecutors must demonstrate that the gang is a collective enterprise, intent on promoting economic gain and that there is criminal activity furthered by this enterprise.
  - ▷ Problems with this method is determining who is a gang member and defining precisely the nature and mission of gang activity.
  - ▷ The preventative benefits seem to arise after the gang has attained a fairly substantial degree of organization.
  - ▷ This type of legislation does not adequately (or fairly) address small-scale gangs that do not have large entrepreneurial pursuits.

Gangs And The Law (cont.)

- ► Untended Behaviors
  - ▷ Leads to the breakdown of social controls
  - ▷ Increased atomization of community members
  - ▷ Community becomes "vulnerable to criminal invasion
- ► Glazer's (1997) discussion of graffiti
  - ▷ An example from the reading "Proliferation of graffiti, even when not obscene, confronts the subway rider with the inescapable knowledge that the environment he must endure for an hour or more a day is uncontrolled and uncontrollable, and that anyone can invade it to do whatever damage and mischief the mind suggests."(pg445)
  - ▷ Initial empirical results supported the broken windows theory. In one systematic study based on 40 urban neighborhoods, Skogan (1990-pp. 18–20) found a casual link between disorder and crime.
  - ▷ Disorder not only sparks concern and fear among neighborhood residents
  - ▷ Drives out those who stable community life is important
  - ▷ Discourages people with similar value from moving in
  - ▷ Increases the level of serious crimes
  - ▷ Threatens house prices and discourages investment
  - ▷ Broken windows theory runs a fine line between encouraging more community social control and infringing upon civil liberties of gang members. Some critics have charged that the injunction gives police too much discretion in determining what behavior or people are disreputable (Stewart 1998).

Gangs And The Law (cont.)

- ► Injunctions: the most common use of the law as a gang-fighting tool to limit the free association of street gangs in the public theaters of the neighborhood.
- ► Some of the public places included:
  - — Park Areas
  - — Streets and Street corners
  - — Playgrounds (in and outside of schools)
  - — Alleyways
  - — Beachfronts
  - — Boardwalks ect.

The objective was to combat gang crime by banishing gang members from public space.

Broken Windows

- ▶ Perspective that provides the theoretical background for anti-gang injunctions (Wilson & Kelling 1982, Kelling & Coles 1996). Published and article entitled Atlantic Monthly that offered a new set of explanations for the causes of neighborhood crime.

- ▶ Who distinguish between "street" and "decent families"
- ▶ Social order together with physical order
- ▶ Broken Window—If a window is left broken and unrepaired sends a signal of diminished collective care for the neighborhood, which makes the area a Petri dish for criminals who believe that few locals will stop them in their efforts.

Home Boy Industries

- ▶ Father Greg Boyle priest who started the largest gang intervention program
- ▶ Home Boy Industries—company motto proclaims, "Nothing stops a bullet like a job", has grown from a small bakery in East Los Angeles into the largest gang-intervention program in the country. Helping gang members correct their lives and find felony friendly employers.
  - ▷ Provides services for mental health
  - ▷ Counseling
  - ▷ Tattoo removal
  - ▷ Job placement
  - ▷ Educational programs
- ▶ Offers Five Businesses in addition to rival gang members whom work side by side daily
  - ▷ Bakery
  - ▷ Silkscreen studio
  - ▷ Café
  - ▷ Landscaping service
  - ▷ Retail store

Debating Injunctions

— There have been several arguments opposing the legality (and effectiveness) of Injunctions

— Injunctions have been called overly vague and an infringement of civil liberties

— There is also major concern in how these laws are applied by law enforcement as outsiders may not know the difference between a group of gang members and a group of non-gang affiliated youth

— These issues were raised and injunctions upheld in the case People ex rel. Gallo v. Carlos Acuna California Supreme Court 1997

— Supporters of Injunctions often rely heavily on the broken window theory to support this type of legislation

Brussels Sprout Analogy

▶ Judge Lee Sarokin utilized the brussels sprout analogy in regards to discussing the gang issue

▶ This analogy draws on the experience many experienced as children when there were vegetables we didn't want to eat; there were three ways to deal with brussels sprouts throw them away, move them around, deal with and absorb them

▶ Judge Sarkon does believe in the basic premises of the broken window theory however he does not believe the anti-loitering laws are effective

▶ He believes in rehabilitating individuals which is similar to the social work approach

Alternatives to Legal Tactics

- ► Researcher do not believe that legal actions will eliminate ganging behavior
- ► Instead many believe there must be alternative outlets for youth group association
- ► Currently there are some groups that are classified as being gangs (by outsiders) when they are social groups
- ► The roles of gangs that are ignored are the emotional and social ties it gives to members, if community organizations can assist in filling this gap then the negative aspects associated with ganging behavior can be curbed
- ► Further as gangs are seen as being a means for economic advantages another way to curb ganging behaviors would be to make jobs and job training accessible to ganging and at risk youth
- ► Utilizing Social disorganization theory society one can look at lessening negative ganging phenomenon by moving to eradicate neighborhood shortcomings (poverty, unemployment, low education rates) as these shortcomings lead to an increased propensity of illegal behavior in individuals

Achieving Peace in the Streets:
How Legislative Efforts Fail in Combating Gang Violence in Comparison to Successful Local Community-Based Initiatives One Matthew Cannata 1999

- ► Ganging is ingrained in American society it is not something that will just go away
- ► Many ganging youth view courts and jails as inevitable and therefore are not particularly deterred by the use of those punishments, thus making them ineffective
- ► Community based programs that address the needs of the community do more to curb violence associated with ganging behavior
- ► For example Boston Ten Point Coalition

  - — violence is a crime problem not a social problem
  - — only a small number of youth cause problems and they can be identified
  - — community leaders should have informal say when it comes to arrests
  - — if police act inappropriate they should be held accountable

- ► This had some success in Boston and has many programs including a Cease fire program
- ► This program was called the "Boston Miracle" due to how it affected large drops in criminality especially fatalities associated with gangs in Boston

Conclusion

▶ There are many legislative tactics that are currently being utilized to address the gang issue in America. The effectiveness of said actions have not had the success they intended however changing legislation can only occur with continued research filtered to legislatures and the public at large. A paradigm shift must occur in America to address the ganging problem effectively.

Works Cited

— Rosen, Eva and Sudhir Venkatesh. 2007. "Legal Innovation and Control of Gang Behavior" Pp 439–451 in Gangs and Adolescent Subcultures Reader edited by La Tanya Skiffer. San Diego, CA: Cognella Academic Press/University Readers.

— Kim, Jen. 2010. "On The Job: Give Gangs Their Daily Bread." *Psychology Today*. Retrieved [November 6, 2010] (www.psychologytoday.com)

— Cannata, Mattew. 2009." Achieving Peace in the Streets: How Legislative Efforts Fail in Combating Gang Violence in Comparison to Successful Local Community-Based Initiatives." *New England Journal on Criminal & Civil Confinement* Vol.35 (Issue 1); p243–276. Retrieved [November 8, 2010] (http://0-web.ebscohost.com.torofind.csudh.edu/ehost/search?vid=1&hid=13&sid=07a4ab16-d064-4bc1-95c7-097cf6afee56%40sessionmgr4).

GOING HOME, STAYING HOME
INTEGRATING PRISON GANG MEMBERS INTO THE COMMUNITY

By Mark S. Fleisher
and Scott H. Decker

Recidivism rates in the United States and Canada have hovered at approximately 60 percent for decades. To explain why six out of 10 former inmates return to prison, it is reasonable to assume that imprisonment, even under the best conditions, cannot prepare inmates adequately for productive life in a mainstream community. Prison gang members encounter challenges to post-imprisonment community life that non-gang members may not encounter or encounter with similar intensity. This article argues that the burden of inmate readjustment should fall on communities rather than on individual former inmates, and that successful community integration requires communitywide planning and an understanding of the realities of a gang lifestyle.

Keywords: community integration, community mobilization, prison gangs, rehabilitation

INTRODUCTION

I t is arguable that most prison gangs are either street gangs imported into prisons (Jacobs, 1974) or prison equivalents of street gangs rather than the highly structured, traditionally defined prison gangs such as the Mexican Mafia, Texas Syndicate, and others described in the prison gang overview. Prison gangs are chronic, serious, criminal organizations. Prison gang groups are qualitatively and quantitatively different from the street and/or youth gangs that have occupied the attention of gang researchers (Decker & Van Winkle, 1996; Fleisher, 1998).

We would argue that the study of gangs needs a strong bifurcation between the hard-core criminals in the Mexican Mafia and Aryan Brotherhood, among others, and the youthful adolescents and young adults whose gang membership is transitory (Esbensen & Huizinga, 1993, Thornberry, 1998), whose crime is opportunistic (Klein, 1995), and whose behavior is focused more on drinking and drug use (Fagan, 1989) than on organized drug distribution, prostitution, gambling, and contract murder. Prison gang members are those men whose criminal lifestyles have become entrenched and difficult to break. These chronic gang offenders are the focus of this article.

This article focuses on two major topics. First, there is a discussion of issues affecting community integration (as opposed to reintegration) of former inmates who are also gang members as they moved into their home communities after release. Second, there are realistic, proactive proposals offered to community leaders that will enable them to meet the challenge of integrating former prison gang members. Street gangs in prison and traditional prison gangs—known also as disruptive groups and security threat groups (STGs) (Fleisher & Rison, 1999, discusses the characteristics of disruptive and STGs)—will be lumped and referred to as prison gangs for the purpose of this article.

Mark S. Fleisher, PhD, is a Professor in the Department of Criminal Justice Sciences, Illinois State University, Normal, Illinois.

Scott H. Decker, PhD, is a Professor in the Department of Criminology and Criminal Justice, University of Missouri, St. Louis.

In dealing with the first topic, we chose the word integration rather than reintegration for a specific reason. Research among youthful and adult gang members suggests these men probably were not integrated well into lawful economic networks in the community before they entered prison; rather, these men spent their lives in impoverished communities where they as well as their parents and other relatives had low-paying jobs and other social and economic difficulties and personal problems such as addictions, which threatened and/or worsened these men's link to legitimate employment markets. Street research shows that post-imprisonment, these men easily can reestablish neighborhood-based ties to gang social networks. A newly released gang-affiliated former inmate, within hours or minutes of returning home, can be selling drugs on a street corner. The challenge for community interventionists is one of finding realistic mechanisms to integrate into the lawful community former prisoners who are gang members. This is a formidable challenge and one not being met with standard forms of parole.

The rich literature on community intervention strategies and gang crime suppression lacks a specific approach prescribing the best practices of integrating prison gang members into the legitimate community. Community gang crime is a difficult problem for law enforcement and social service agencies to handle but when we add to an already difficult intervention problem the issue of prison gang members returning home, the challenges escalate and urgency is added to the need to create effective means of facilitating adult gang members' integration into the legitimate community. Suggestions offered here are a step in outlining the arguments that lead toward creating realistic approaches to the community integration of prison gang members.

The arguments advanced and the insights offered in this article are based on our numerous years of community gang research among youthful and adult gang members in cities such as St. Louis, Kansas City, Seattle, and Champaign (Illinois). In addition to conducting years of street gang research (Fleisher, 1995, 1998), Fleisher was employed by the Federal Bureau of Prisons as a correctional worker in a high-security penitentiary (Fleisher, 1989) and then as a regional administrator. Decker and Curry have years of community gang research and have collaborated closely with communities and police departments on community gang-related issues (see Curry, Ball, & Decker, 1996; Curry & Spergel, 1992; Decker, Bynum, & Weisel, 1998; Decker, Pennell, & Caldwell, 1996; Decker & Van Winkle, 1995). The observations and recommendations offered in this article are extracted from our professional experiences and are issues that communities must face if they are to develop effective strategies in response to prison and street gang members returning home.

STATE AND FEDERAL PRISON DEMOGRAPHICS: THE CONTEXT FOR PRISON GANGS

The number of prison gangs and prison gang members currently in American prisons is unknown. Correctional agencies consider data and information on prison gangs and their members to be law enforcement intelligence because prison gangs often pose egregious threats to institution security. With the need for controlling information and keeping it out of the hands of prison gang members themselves and their allies on the street, correctional agencies carefully guard such data. Despite that, however, we can get a general overview of the nature of the risk that prison gangs may pose to institutions by looking at publicly available correctional data. Table 1 documents the escalating rate of confinement in state and federal corrections since 1990. If we assume that at least one third of inmates have some tie to a prison gang, either as a member or an associate, that suggests there are nearly 400,000 gang members or affiliates inside American prisons.

The principal factors that have influenced such growth in federal and state prison populations also lead to the suggestion that the influence of prison gangs will not diminish inside prisons (Beck & Mumola, 1998). Such factors include: a 39 percent rise in the number of parole violators returned to state and federal prisons; a 4 percent increase in new court commitments; a decrease in release rates from 37 percent (1990) to 31 percent (1997); and an increased in average time serviced from 22 months (1990) to 27 months (1997). Four percent of America's prisoners will not be released. As inmates serve longer terms and as prisons receive more recidivists, the dilemma of controlling prison gangs escalates along with the prisoner population.

Table 1 State and Federal Prison Popultions and Incarceration Rates in the 1990s

On December 31		Number of inmates	Sentenced prisoners per 100,000 resident population	
	Federal	State	Federal	State
1990	65,526	708,393	20	272
1995	100,250	1,025,624	32	379
1996	105,544	1,077,824	33	394
1997	112,973	1,129,180	35	410
1998	123,041	1,178,978	38	423

Source: Data from Beck, A.J., & Mumola, C.J. Prisoners in 1998, Bulletin NCJ-175687. Washington, DC: U.S. Department of Justice.

The size of correctional agencies has expanded differently with some experiencing massive growth with others experiencing relatively little. Table 2 shows the highest and lowest inmate populations and incarceration rates. The three agencies with the highest inmate populations also have experienced serious challenges with prison gang management. When inmate populations expand, the risk of prison gangs also expands. Likewise, when incarceration rates are high, it is realistic to assume that the wide net of arrest and conviction will be cast over violent and non-violent drug offenders, many of whom will enter prison with street gang affiliations.

Table 3 shows offense types of convicted inmates in state and federal prisons. These data show that nearly half of state prison inmates serve convictions on violent offenses while slightly more than 60 percent of federal inmates serve sentences for drug offenses. Violent offenders serving sentences with violent and non-violent drug offenders set the stage for expansion of prison gangs.

Table 2 Three Highest and Lowest Jurisdictions for Prison Populations and Incarceration Rates

Prison populations Three highest jurisdictions	Number of inmates	Incarceration rates per 100,000 state residents	
California Texas Federal Bureau of Prisons Three lowest jurisdictions	161,904 144,510 123,041	Louisiana Texas Oklahoma	736 724 622
North Dakota Vermont Wyoming	915 1,426 1,571	Minnesota Maine North Dakota	117 125 128

Source: Data from Beck, A.J., & Mumola, C.J. Prisoners in 1998, Bulletin NCJ-175687. Washington, DC: U.S. Department of Justice.

Table 3 State and Federal Prisoners by Type of Offense, 1997

Type of Offense	Estimated Number of Prisoners			
	State 1,046,705	As a percentage of	Federal 88,018	As a percentage of
	Number	State prisoners	Number	Federal prisoners
Violent Offenses (murder, negligent manslaughter, sexual assault, robbery, assault, other violent)	494,349	47.2	13,021	14.7
Property Offenses (burglary, larceny/theft, motor vehicle theft, fraud, other property)	230,177	21.9	5,964	6.7
Drug Offenses (possession, trafficking, other drug)	216,254	20.6	55,069	62.5
Public-order Offenses (weapons, other public-order)	103,344	9.8	13,026	14.7

Source: Data from U.S. Department of Justice (1999). Substance abuse and treatment, state and federal prisoners, 1997, special report NCJ-172871. Washington, DC: U.S. Department of Justice.

Gang and correctional researchers as well as correctional administrators will agree that one of the most difficult current challenges for correctional administrators is managing the effect of prison gang activity. The other articles in the issue are devoted to that challenge.

We argue that the problem of prison gangs originates in the community and that community problems linked to gangs do not end when gang offenders are convicted and sentenced to prison. The link between prison gangs and the community is unexplored. Among other issues, we know little about how street gangs facilitate the criminal activity of prison gangs, how prison gangs select new members from among street gangs, and how prison gang members' family members, friends, and associates strengthen criminal conduct within correctional institutions by participating indirectly and directly in prison gang-related crime. It is also critical to note that no published reports suggest that prison-based gang suppression and intervention have the effect of reducing gang involvement and gang crime in communities after the release of prison gang-affiliated inmates. This last observation is critical: Data noted above show that 96 percent of prisoners will be released into the community. This suggests an out-of-sight, out-of-mind approach to street and prison gangs and opens the door for more community gang-related crime, which in turn stretches the resources of community-based social and law enforcement agencies. With prison inmate populations expanding and parole violations nearing 40 percent and with state prisons housing mostly recidivists, community integration is a vital social and economic challenge to communities. The data cited above on prison inmate populations and incarceration rates clearly suggest that California, Texas, Louisiana, and Oklahoma—among dozens of other communities in states across the country—either have or likely will have serious community-based gang-related problems.

CORE FEATURES OF GANGS: IMPEDIMENTS TO COMMUNITY INTEGRATION

Why do prison gangs pose such a difficult intervention problem? What can communities do about those problems? Gang research literature is clear on a number of issues affecting the emergence and perpetuation of community gangs; as long as these issues exist in the community, gangs will exist as well. Many issues have become axioms about street gangs and these often apply as well to prison gangs. These issues are critical in planning former prison gang members' community integration. We outlined a number of these key issues below.

First, gangs facilitate crime. This happens in at least two ways. A gang has a structure; some structures are formal such as those referred to in this issue in the editor's overview of prison gangs. Other gangs have informal structures. Nevertheless, a gang group is a network of members who align themselves with other members. In forming such alignments, members who share propensities for various types of crime, ranging in severity from shoplifting to homicide, may find each other and in that relationship, commit more serious crimes than they would have had they not been in a gang. Because a gang is a social group whose members commit a wide range of offenses, members likely may have opportunities to commit types of crime that they may have bypassed previously.

Because gang groups accelerate the frequency and severity of crime, such groups have a measurable effect on their members' criminal behavior. In short, individuals in gang groups commit more crime than they would outside such a group. Although there are no published analyses of such crime acceleration for prison gangs (street gangs in prison or traditional prison gangs), such acceleration is reported widely in the street gang literature (Esbensen & Huizinga, 1993; Thornberry, 1998) and arguably would be a reasonable assumption about the influence of a prison gang group on the behavior of individual members.

Second, gangs are social groups with longevity. Gangs often persist longer than individual members, especially the most criminal and problematic gang groups. A Vice Lord neighborhood of 30 years ago likely may still be a Vice Lord territory now. Even if gang members are convicted and imprisoned for long terms, new gang members replace them year after year. This suggests that structural and economic forces in the neighborhoods establish conditions necessary for gang emergence. When a gang-affiliated inmate returns home, even after a 10-year prison term, likely waiting there will be members of his or another gang who will offer criminal opportunities but not opportunities of lasting social and economic value within the mainstream community. Repeatedly arresting these gang members has little effect on reducing the propensity for the emergence and perpetuation of street gangs (Klein, 1995) if these are a community's only efforts to curb community gang crime.

Third, self-identification to a gang may persist for years and/or decades, especially among adult offenders with extensive criminal histories; the blood in/blood out rule shared among the major prison gangs, noted in the editor's overview, argues for the gang group's effort to retain long-term membership. By contrast, youth gang membership may be short term and transitory (Decker & Van Winkle, 1996; Esbensen & Huizinga, 1993; Thornberry, 1998).

Recent research in Champaign shows that men and women now in their 40s and 50s have retained since their youth a self-identification to a gang and with that affiliation have retained social ties with people whom they have know since their teens (Fleisher, 2000). A gang member may not choose to exploit his or her gang affiliation to further criminal activity; a gang affiliation may not be the only prerequisite necessary to engage in lucrative drug crime activities; and a gang affiliation may not isolate self-identified members of different gangs from one another in daily interactions.

This research shows that these gang-identified men's daily interactions are fluid and influenced more by friendship ties than gang affiliation. Members of different gangs freely interact on the street unless personal biases otherwise alter the friendship relationship. This finding has significant implications for post-imprisonment community integration of prison gang members and suggests that former inmates of different prison gang affiliations may be able to cooperate in the community even though penitentiary life precluded such cooperation. Such cooperation may align these men in employment sites, training programs, and treatment venues.

Fourth, adult gang members may be unwilling to relinquish a gang identity even if they are not active gang members. A gang identity and the social ties it brings are significant in a person's neighborhood identity and help to create a sense of belonging to a persistent social group. In this sense, a gang identity is a proxy for a person's social history, for better or worse, as we see it because in a gang neighborhood, a sense of belonging to a local-area gang network may be achieved only with gang affiliation, prison experience, and a cultivated knowledge of the street.

Fifth, gang members are poor and as such are outsiders in the mainstream community. Research literature is clear on the social and economic marginality of gang members, especially the hard-core gangsters who are most likely to be involved in criminal conduct serious enough to affect a prison term. In our many years of gang research, we have not known hard-core gangsters who were honor students, had offers to attend college, had supportive and loving parents, and had strong social bonds to community institutions such as schools, athletic teams, and civic organizations. The profile of the street gang member who eventually enters prison for violent and/ or drug-related offenses is the opposite of the characterization just noted. To such a sad picture, we realistically add the emotional and psychological deficits affected by violent victimization and post-traumatic stress (see Davis & Flannery in this issue) and multiple addictions.

Sixth, gang identity is linked to self identity. Street gang research shows that being a gang member may be a vital element in the self-definition of a gang member. Given that a formerly imprisoned gang member likely has failed at school and has few if any support ties to a mainstream community, a gang affiliation offers companionship, identity, and sense of belonging to a marginal community. Former prison gang members may not wish to shed the gang mantle. A gang identity may offer these men an identity in their neighborhoods that has social and economic value.

Try as we might, we most likely won't be able to strip the gang self-identification of a prison and/or street gang member. Adult criminals who claim a prison gang affiliation are likely to be serious offenders, especially those in high-security institutions. Preaching at them about the dangers of gang affiliation and/or threatening them with longer prison terms may move some prison gang members away from their gang groups but realistically will have little effect on the thousands of men who see themselves to be hard-core gangsters. Gangs are social groups and a sense of belonging and identity come with gang membership.

COMMUNITY RE-ENTRY AND INTEGRATION

Adult gang members who also are former inmates face especially difficult problems when they return to the community. These men entered prison with poor work skills, little education, and alienated from high paying employment; imprisonment does little to improve that situation and has worsened it in a number of ways. Former inmates are stigmatized by their "excon" status, which reinforces the middle-class notion of them as outsiders, and by virtue of serving 5-, 10-, or 15-year sentences or longer, have left community job markets behind. Imagine the economic plight of men imprisoned in the middle 1980s who return home in 1995. When these men were imprisoned, computers were not being used in most offices and the Internet was an abstraction. In 1995, the best, most highly paid employment was open to men and women with college diplomas and high-tech skills. A 30-year-old former inmate is faced with an employment market unfamiliar to him and competition for the best jobs from college graduates. Where does that leave, and lead, the former inmate who has gang ties to the local Vice Lords, Gangster Disciples, or Mexican Mafia? To be sure, even if former prison gang members want to straighten out their lives, they likely cannot get jobs paying enough money to keep them away from lucrative drug markets; and to complicate this picture even more, it will be highly unlikely that a former inmate and prison gang member will have the community social support necessary to assume a lawful lifestyle.

Prison anti-gang (or "deganging") programs have not been evaluated or at least such evaluations have not been distributed publicly. Even if such institution-based programs serve to improve prison social order, former inmates' home neighborhoods are not highly controlled environments and as such pose social and economic difficulties that a street gang affiliation can overcome easily. Neighborhood illegal drug markets are easy to exploit, especially for men who have spent their lives selling drugs. Prison-based education and vocational programs coupled with longer prison terms do not resolve problems related to either prison gang management or prison-to-community transition for former gang-affiliated inmates. Bossler's, Fleisher's, and Krienert's (2000) research among federal inmates shows that full-time, legal employment, even at middle to upper income levels, is often an insufficient buffer to engaging in lucrative illegal drug markets and other forms of high-profit economic crime.

Former prison inmates, especially those with low levels of education, face low wages, low levels of social support in communities, and few realistic opportunities to earn wages high enough to divert them from high-income street crime. A realistic assessment of the economic future of prison gang members who may have long histories of juvenile and adult

> Prison deganging programs have struggled to find a solution to the disorder of prison gangs as communities have struggled to find solutions to the disorder of street gangs.

arrests and convictions is poor. Add to this dim financial outlook the social instability typical among persistent criminals, which includes a shifting residential pattern and/or a reliance on local shelters for temporary residences, and a dim outlook worsens. For men facing this bleak future, resuming an active affiliation with a local gang is a productive and perhaps the only way to live a relatively stable social and economic lifestyle.

COMMUNITY INTERVENTION

Given the reality of the street gang life and its social and economic advantages for former prison gang members, community leaders have a daunting challenge. What can communities do to assist prison gang members looking for legitimate opportunities? Before we offer specific suggestions, it is necessary to remind readers of the realities of dealing with former inmates who are also gang members.

First, it is unlikely that such men will relinquish gang ties; they may tell parole officers they no longer hang out with gangsters and former gang crime partners but what they say and what they do in the neighborhood are different. Unless a gang affiliation requires a man to become actively involved in gang crime, it should not matter if a man claims to be a Gangster Disciple, Black Gangster, or some other gang. Gang affiliation is much more than a link to a social group whose members commit crimes. For men who have been gangsters for decades, it is a form of personal identity most will be unwilling to relinquish. Were a former inmate residing in a gang neighborhood to disassociate from all of his gang companions, he may have to sever ties with parents, aunts and uncles, cousins, siblings, grandparents, and his own children as well as life-long friends. Such a loss of social capital would isolate a former inmate and leave him without social support. Shedding such social ties is unrealistic and if it were required as a condition of parole, the stage would be set for a quick parole violation and return to prison. We must be sure to recognize that hanging out with gang members does not mean involvement in crime and/or gang crime necessarily. We also must keep in mind that gang neighborhoods offer low-income housing and also may offer low-skill jobs to former inmates and may be the most economically accessible and socially suitable place for former prison gang members.

Second, we must expect that some percentage of former inmates who may or may not be gang members will violate parole and/or commit new offenses. Parole violations and the commission of new crimes by repeat offenders may have less to do with the quality of community problems than with the social, economic, and emotional instability of former inmates. Sitting in the Champaign County Correctional Center on his way to yet another state prison term, the leader of the Mickey Cobras in Champaign said it this way: "When your life's a mess and you have nowhere to stay, jail's a good place to go" (Fleisher, 2000).

Keeping in mind the realities of street life for former prison gang members, community planning must be realistic, which means overcoming those realities. Asking too much of former inmates sets them and us up for failure. Each time a parolee violates his parole and is re-arrested, the cost to the community may be higher than the cost to the parolee. Former inmates/gang members often comment that when a fellow gang member returns to prison, he is "going home" (Fleisher, 2000). We have outlined below a number of steps communities may take to facilitate community integration. These steps occur at both an individual and a community level.

INDIVIDUAL-LEVEL INTERVENTION

Bossler, Fleisher, and Krienert (2000) and particularly Bossler (1999) show that the resilience given by jobs and stable interpersonal relations may be eroded quickly by the persistent abuse of alcohol and other drugs. This fact suggests that former inmates need long-term drug and alcohol treatment. This we already know; however, where that treatment occurs is critical to its success.

Long-term treatment in prison therapeutic communities does little to help inmates when they return home. Follow-up treatment conducted in community-based treatment centers located miles away from former inmates' neighborhoods sets the stage for failure. Such men who need treatment likely are unwilling to spend several dollars on bus fare if a bus can take them to the treatment center. At home, a former inmate may have a wife or girlfriend who drinks alcohol and smokes marijuana, or uses other drugs, and in the neighborhood, his companions do the same. The likelihood of him resisting drug use is reduced if he has to travel at his own expense to find support. Easily accessible community-based treatment centers, preferably in gang neighborhoods themselves, may be a first step in improving a recovering drug addict's chances of staying clean.

Returning home from prison sounds like a joyous event. It is not. In the reality of street life in a gang neighborhood, there are no yellow ribbons tied around trees and no placards welcoming home a former inmate. An inmate released after years of imprisonment may find "home" to be rather inhospitable: he may find that the house he left behind is occupied by strangers, boarded up, or torn down; if he finds his house, his bed now may be occupied by someone else; his friends, siblings, and cousins may be residing in other neighborhoods or may be in prison or dead; his former girlfriend may have a new suitor and more children; and his pre-imprisonment behavior, if it included violence and/or ripping off local residents, now may exclude him from local social networks or, worse yet, set him up for retaliatory violence even after years away from the neighborhood. These are the realities of returning home for many former inmates. A realistic approach to overcoming the "worst case" as noted here also would bolster the integration of former inmates whose return home is less risky; even in the best case, a former inmate must have a stable residence, find and keep a job, and surround himself with companions supportive of a straight lifestyle. These seemingly simple things are difficult to do in an impoverished gang neighborhood.

Given the realistic limitations already noted, communities may wish to develop, in cooperation with local social service, alcohol and drug treatment, employment training agencies, community homes or dormitories for former inmates that offer a variety of treatment services, job training and placement, and continuous, post-release social support of a year or longer. Such homes located in gang neighborhoods could operate as residential therapeutic communities (Yablonsky, 1997). A residential center that serves as the focal point for a variety of services for former inmates could streamline parole officers' requirement to visit parolees, enable service providers to meet clients' needs in an environment comfortable to the clients, and strengthen former inmates' social ties to the community.

COMMUNITY-LEVEL INTERVENTION

Parole agents' case loads are high and parole offices often are located dozens of miles from parolees' homes. There is only so much that a parole agent can do for a parolee if the agent sees the parolee once or twice every 60 to 90 days. It would seem reasonable that if correctional agencies would establish community-based parole offices in local neighborhoods, parole officers would have immediate access to parolees. While it may be difficult to establish such offices in large urban centers, metropolitan communities with populations of approximately 100,000 may be well-chosen test sites. Champaign, for instance, is such a community and dozens of former prison gang members return to specific, well-defined neighborhoods annually; but these men and women have few contacts with parole officers and fewer contacts with community members who can offer them employment. It is helpful to keep in mind that poor gang neighborhoods are social and economic isolates located in the midst of urban and suburban prosperity. A primary objective of a state correctional agency should be to create and sustain meaningful links between impoverished gang neighborhoods and community prosperity. Placing parole offices within gang neighborhoods may be a small first step toward achieving that objective.

Vocational training and substance abuse treatment may have little payoff if former inmates cannot find jobs. But one job for one former inmate, however, will not resolve the problem of neighborhood and family poverty. In poor neighborhoods like those that former prison gang members call home, households are often multigenerational and the household composition may shift from week to week. With a shift in household composition comes a shift in household economy. A job may help one former inmate but that same former inmate may be obligated to then assist his extended family of 6, 8, or 10 family members, all or most of whom may be unemployed. Add to that the fact that former inmates may be poorly skilled and have access only to menial work. Fast-food employment, for instance, embarrasses these men because they and we see those as teenage jobs (Fleisher, 2000). Even if these men accepted such employment, take-home pay is too low to support themselves and their families; if they abandon their families, they feel alone and alienated. Such economic and social pressure may push a former inmate back into lucrative street trades such as drug selling. Thus, the "one-job-per-inmate" strategy may be flawed from its inception when that strategy is tested against real-life social and economic demands in gang neighborhoods.

Former inmates' struggle to stay crime free can be heard on the streets in a gang neighborhood. The consequences of being poor, never having enough money to support themselves and their families, trying to get better paying jobs at low-skill levels are common topics among adult, former prison gang members. These men are aware of their difficulty and know well that if they move toward crime, the local police likely will knock on their door first.

A more difficult approach to integrating prison gang and non-gang members as well requires a long-term strategy to improve local neighborhood economies and strengthen the tie between local neighborhoods and its encompassing dominant community. Decker and Van Winkle (1996), Moore (1991), and Klein (1995) have shown clearly the relationship between community social organization and local economies and the emergence and perpetuation of gangs. However, creating long-term social and economic change in economically disadvantaged communities, such as described by Wilson (1987), has advantages and disadvantages from a communitywide planning perspective.

A major advantage of thinking broadly about community development rather than looking past the social and economic context of gang formation is that such a broad approach tackles head on the context of gang formation and offers a long-term remedy. Community development refers to the nature of the relationship among local residents and between local residents and schools and businesses as well as to the stake local residents have in community government (Bursik & Grasmick, 1993). By reducing the number and severity of risk factors, such as lowering unemployment for adults and reducing school truancy, communities can expect a reduction in gang crime and related problems. Such an approach requires careful planning and the participation of community stakeholders including representatives of the disadvantaged neighborhoods.

A major disadvantage of this approach is that it will not bring a quick, politically efficacious solution to the so-called gang and/or crime problem. Indeed, creating closer ties between residents of gang neighborhoods and the dominant community may be inimical to the wishes of community power brokers, voters, and even elected officials who believe that punishment means long prison terms and that such an approach is the only adequate way to respond to gangs and gang members.

Were a community to consider implementing a community development approach, the opinions of local residents must be included (Spergel, 1995). Fleisher's (2000) research in Champaign's gang neighborhoods has sought in part to understand the nature of local residents' ties to the dominant community, including the federal government. In these predominantly African-American neighborhoods, the prevailing attitude about the link between the neighborhoods and the broader community was expressed by a middle-aged member of the Black Gangsters who has been to state prison seven times and federal prison once: "Nobody—let me tell you that again—nobody in this here neighborhood wants the white man coming in and telling us what we need or what we should be doing. People in here know what they want, they just don't know how to get it. Sure there are folks up in here who will sell drugs and act stupid [gangbang] no matter what you do, but most folks don't want to do that stuff. If you want to do something around here, ask these people what kinds of jobs they want, what kinds of services they want, and how they want to get them things. But don't let no white man come up in here waving his finger in the black man's face telling him what he should be doing. Slavery days are over" (Fleisher, 2000).

As seen from inside gang neighborhoods, the dominant community is perceived to be criticizing poor persons for not trying harder to improve their lot in life. But with low levels of education and little familiarity with life outside of public housing projects and gang neighborhoods, poor persons are doing as well as they can, especially when they are isolated socially and economically. To be sure, long prison terms increase social and economic isolation within the dominant community by removing employable men who may link local neighborhoods to the dominant community. Prison sentences never improve the economic opportunities for former inmates who carry the label of ex-con.

While a "one-job, one-person" approach is necessary, such an approach is insufficient to prevent and/or intervene on the social and economic context of gang formation. Such an approach even may be insufficient for reasons already noted to reduce the likelihood that former (male and female) gang members will stay out of prison. A more productive approach first should include an assessment of the skills of the former inmates within gang neighborhoods and then should proceed to a realistic communitywide discussion of the best ways to link job skills to jobs. Local neighborhood small-scale businesses, such as car maintenance (tuneups, oil changes), barbering, beauty parlors, house painting, carpentry, and even cottage industries such as sewing (common in women's prisons) may encourage legal employment while allowing former inmates to remain within neighborhoods where they feel comfortable and are not treated as outsiders.

LINKING CORRECTIONS AND THE COMMUNITY

Facilitating the successful community integration of prison gang members is a difficult process, but it is achievable if community members and law enforcement officials have a clear understanding of the real life difficulties that former inmates/gang members encounter in the community. On an individual-level, these former inmates have low levels of education, substance addictions, and criminal records. Krienert's and Fleisher's article in this issue shows that gang membership can be seen as a proxy for risk factors of a severity greater than those of non-gang members. This means, among other things, that a community response to gang members must be more intense, prolonged, and targeted to balance the disabilities that former inmates/gang members bring back to the community.

On the neighborhood level, there are likely to be few if any jobs available in the poor neighborhoods. In the larger mainstream community, local employers may not find a gang-affiliated former inmate an attractive potential employee, especially when other potential employees with similar or better job skills without a felon record are easily available. Such an obstacle to employment surely would be the case in the dominant community, especially in the competition for high-paying jobs that require more technical skills than most former inmates have.

While some companies hire ex-cons (Tatge, 2000),

> Former prison inmates, especially those with low levels of education, face low wages, low levels of social support in communities, and few realistic opportunities to earn wages high enough to divert them from high income street crime.

such an approach is "one-person, one-job" and is driven by a corporate need to fill jobs rather than a need to develop poor communities. Even though one or even 100 former prison gang members may be helped temporarily, such an approach does little to improve local social and economic conditions in communities where, generation after generation, chronic features of life include joblessness, poverty, and street gangs.

Without a communitywide approach to building economic and social capital in poor neighborhoods, the families there would continue to suffer the well-documented deprivations of chronic poverty with little meaningful assistance from mainstream communities (Katz, 1993).

Prison deganging programs have struggled to find a solution to the disorder of prison gangs as communities have struggled to find solutions to the disorder of street gangs. We have argued that a solution to gang-affiliated social disorder must act at multiple levels, offering individuals, neighborhoods, and communities economic support. At the same time, however, a communitywide solution must strengthen the social and economic link between gang neighborhoods and the dominant community. Doing that would require that the dominant community pour job training and employment opportunities into poor neighborhoods with the direct participation of residents of those poor areas.

Prison systems can and should take the lead in such activity because they have a major stake in ensuring that former inmates go home and stay home. When inmates walk away from prisons, their supervision is passed to parole officials. Parole officers are likely to be charged with the responsibility of law enforcement officers rather than providers of opportunities to former offenders and their communities. However, even if parole officers want to help, they may not have the time or resources to actively assist former inmates in finding employment and supporting their other needs. In the end, inmates are passed from one agency to another until they are home again—older but with little else having changed for the better.

Correctional officials can develop a bridge between gang neighborhoods and the mainstream community. A telephone call from a state commissioner of corrections to a state attorney general or a governor could initiate a planning commission to establish realistic planning to overcome the obstacles of community integration. We already have suggested that such an approach would be to the long-term advantage of a correctional system and a community. Lower recidivism rates may reflect well on institutional corrections, but at the same time, a lower recidivism rate means less community crime. While recidivism has been a customary measure of the effectiveness of imprisonment as an intervention and a punishment, recidivism also may be a measure of a community's degree of meaningful support of former inmates. A number of steps, which are outlined below, can be taken to improve community support.

First, senior correctional officials should initiate tactical and strategic planning between themselves and local community agencies such as law enforcement, social welfare, community college, mental health and treatment, and small businesses. Correctional officials have inmate release and criminal history data, and such data can be useful to plan the type and level of community services. Data show (see Krienert & Fleisher in this volume) that gang-affiliated inmates have lower levels of employment and more serious drug problems than non-gang inmates. Treatment may be delivered in prison, but when these men are back in the community, drug use likely will resume. Knowing, for example, that 150 men will be released to a particular neighborhood during the next 18 months is information necessary to deliver drug treatment services to this specific group of former inmates.

Second, multimodal community-based service delivery systems should be developed, keeping in mind the realistic obstacles faced by former inmates and the realistic behavior we can expect from them. A multimodal system would provide a variety of complementary services, such as drug treatment, education, and vocational training, in one place. We would argue that it would be insufficient for a community to have drug treatment available somewhere in a community, education somewhere else, and vocational training in yet another place. Rather, it is essential to centralize those services in the neighborhoods where former inmates and their families reside. Doing that would enable easy reach to these services and may help to overcome the persistent attitude among gang members that social service agencies are more of an obstacle than an aid (Hagedorn, 1988). It is equally important for those services to be available when former inmates need them most such as late evenings and weekends. Social services, vocational training, and treatment services that operate at a city center Monday to Friday, from eight to five, are not likely to meet the needs of former inmates/gang members.

Accomplishing the task of centralizing drug treatment and other services in poor neighborhoods likely will strain the standard procedures that agencies use to offer such services. However, the realistic limitations on life in a gang neighborhood and the predications of the realistic behavior of gang members demand a change from a conventional approach if we wish to reduce recidivism, improve the future for former inmates, and lower levels of gang-based street crime.

Third, correctional institutions employ experts in the delivery of a wide variety of services to inmates. These staffers may be significant resources in the development of neighborhood-based service delivery in high-crime gang communities. Former inmates are not likely to intimidate prison workers and they may be used to train and support community agency staffers in learning the best practices of dealing with often-aggressive former inmates. Using prison workers as community mentors may strengthen local agencies' abilities to design programs that fit inmates' needs.

Fourth, we should reconfirm publicly our responsibility of ensuring that former inmates find a lawful place in the community. With nearly two million men and women in state and federal prisons in late 2000, overlooking the future needs of millions of currently imprisoned men and women is the equivalent of overlooking the needs of the residents of an area the size of metropolitan Denver. Nearly all of these prisoners will be released and as they serve their sentences, correctional agencies and communities should be planning what will happen to them after release and how they best can prepare for the day they go home. If the community approach is punitive, states will continue to build more prisons for recidivists. The consequences of avoiding a proactive approach to inmate integration are dire: Overlooking millions of today's prisoners has a high opportunity cost that our children will pay with higher taxes and/or less support for public education, higher education, and community-based initiatives.

Correctional institutions' programs in education and vocational training, and work opportunities in small-scale factories, culinary arts, welding, automotive repair, and the like may meet the needs of minimum-wage employment of today's former inmates. But communities change faster than prisons. Imagine returning home in the year 2000 having spent the last 20 years in prison. It may take inmates more than 30 to 60 days in a half-way house to learn how to negotiate in a community significantly different from the one they left in 1980 when there was no Space Shuttle, when computers did not sit on everyone's desks, and when no one held a Palm Pilot in one hand and cellular phone in the other.

A 25-year-old inmate imprisoned in 2000 on a federal drug conspiracy conviction may face 300 months in prison and would not be released until sometime around 2021. What economic opportunities will be available then to former inmates? Will welding and food service be desirable employment in 2021? To realistically prepare inmates for the future, we will have to do more than teach them to read and write, which were useful vocational skills in the early 20th century but are inadequate in the 21st century. Realistic planning for the release of millions of inmates should be done jointly between correctional and community agencies. We must move quickly to narrow the training gap that now prepares former inmates for 1940s-like jobs.

***

We have reviewed a range of issues that likely would influence the integration of prison gang members into their home communities. These are serious issues, we have argued, that will not be remedied with solutions of remedial education and basic vocational training. The risk factors producing delinquents who became members of street and prison gangs are enormously complex, and simple solutions will not reasonably meet the challenges of overcoming poverty, marginalization, class structure, and education deficits so extreme that research cited here has shown that the only way many gang members can earn a sufficient income is by selling illegal drugs.

Street and prison gang members are different in important ways from non-gang members. Gang members participate in social networks built on crime partnerships that accelerate the rate of crime as well as the severity of the crime committed. Despite the criminal conduct linked to gang groups, gangs do offer members a sense of identity and belonging as well as, paradoxically, a sense of security. Among middle-aged men, research shows that a gang identity is another element in one's distinctiveness in the community and asking men to relinquish such an identity might be the equivalent of asking them to relinquish their ties to family. We have argued that trying to strip men of a gang identity may be possible in prison because prison is a highly controlled, closed community operated by, in a real sense, a law enforcement agency. When on the street, however, a man's gang identity can be used to negotiate a place to reside, a source of income, and a ready-made set of friends.

A central theme is this article has been the critical need of community involvement in the post-release integration of prison gang members. These men were marginal community members before they were imprisoned and surely now that each one has an ex-con tag, their community lives won't get easier. Surely, communities will have many failures, that is, men whose criminal lives dominate their conduct and these men will end up in prison again. On the other hand, research has shown that most men want to live lawful lives but either do not know how or do not have the resources to accomplish it. These men need help. We are the only ones capable of helping them.

We have suggested that such help be a blend of services delivered to them in a way that meets their lifestyle. A pedantic approach requiring former inmates and gang members to meet "our conditions or else" is unreasonable and in the long run will be counterproductive as we repeatedly imprison men who were just released. Helping individual gang offenders is critical but we also must infuse with financial resources and social services the impoverished communities where most were reared. Research has shown that treating the individual and avoiding the more complex problem of community rehabilitation only allows the problem of street gangs to persist. With a concerted effort initiated by correctional officials, who indeed understand offender programming and treatment perhaps better than any other agencies in the criminal justice system, we can plan intervention strategies that work to lower recidivism and improve the lives of former inmates. Accomplishing that mission will improve community life as well.

REFERENCES

Beck, A.J., & Mumola, C.J. (1998). *Prisoners in 1998.* Bulletin NCJ175687. Washington, DC: U.S. Department of Justice.

Bossler, A. (1 999). *The role of employment in the lives of federal prisoners: An holistic approach.* Master's thesis, Department of Criminal Justice Sciences, Illinois State University, Normal, Illinois 61790.

Bossler, A., Fleisher, M., & Krienert, J. (2000, February). Employment and crime: Revisiting the resiliency effect of work on crime. *Corrections Compendium, 25,* 1 (2), 1–3, 16–18.

Bursik, R.J., & Grasmick, H.G. (1 993). *Neighborhoods and crime: The dimensions of effective community control.* New York: Lexington Books.

Curry, G.D., Ball, R.A., & Decker, S.H. (1996). *Estimating the national scope of gang crime from law enforcement data.* Washington, DC: National Institute of Justice.

Curry, G.D., & Spergel, I.A. (1992). Gang involvement and delinquency among Hispanic and African American adolescent males. *Journal of Research on Crime and Delinquency, 29,* 273–291.

Decker, S.H., Bynum, T.S., & Weisel, D.L. (1 998). Gang as organized crime groups: A tale of two cities. *Justice Quarterly, 15,* 395–423.

Decker, S.H., Pennell, S., & Caldwell, A. (1 996). *Arrestees and guns: Monitoring the illegal firearms market.* Washington, DC: National Institute of Justice.

Decker, S.H., & Van Winkle, B. (1995). Slingin' dope: The role of gangs and gang members in drug sales. *Justice Quarterly, 11,* 1001—1022.

Decker, S.H., & Van Winkle, B. (1996). *Life in the fang: Family, friends, and violence.* New York: Cambridge University Press.

Esbensen, F., & Huizinga, D. (1 993). Gangs, drugs and delinquency in a survey of urban youth. *Criminology, 31,* 565–590.

Fagan, J. (1 989). The social organization of drug use and drug dealing among urban gangs. *Criminology, 27,* 633–670.

Fleisher, M.S. (1989). *Warehousing violence.* Newbury Park, CA: Sage.

Fleisher, M.S. (1 995). *Beggars and thieves: Lives of urban street criminals.* Madison: University of Wisconsin Press.

Fleisher, M.S. (1 998). *Dead end kids: Gang girls and the boys they know.* Madison, WI: University of Wisconsin Press.

Fleisher, M.S. (2000–2001). *Adult male gang member residential mobility.* Unpublished field notes.

Fleisher, M.S., & Rison, R.H. (1999). Gang management in corrections. In P.M. Carlson & J.S. Garrett (Eds.), *Prison and jail administration.* Gaithersburg, MD: Aspen Publishers, Inc.

Hagedorn, J.M. (1988). *People and folks: Gangs, crime and the underclass in a rustbelt city.* Chicago: Lake View.

Jacobs, J.B. (1974). Street gangs behind bars. *Social Problems, 21,* 395–09.

Katz, M.B. (1993). Reframing the 'underclass' debate. In M.B. Katz (Ed.), *The "underclass" debate: Views from history.* Princeton, NJ: Princeton University Press.

Klein, M.W. (1995). *The American street gang.* New York: Oxford University Press.

Moore, J.W. (1991). *Going down to the barrio: Homeboys and homegirls in change.* Philadelphia: Temple University Press.

Spergel, I. (1995). *The youth gang problem.* New York: Oxford University Press.

Tatge, M. (2000). With unemployment low, a new group is in demand: Ex-cons. *The Wall Street Journal,* CV(81), 1, A8.

Thornberry, T. (1998). Membership in youth gangs and involvement in serious and violent offending. In R. Loeber & D.P. Farrington (Eds.), *Serious and violent juvenile offenders: Risk factors and successful interventions.* Thousand Oaks, CA: Sage Publications.

United States Department of Justice (1 999, January). *Substance abuse and treatment, state and federal prisoners, 1997.* Special Report NCJ-1 72871. Washington, DC: U.S. Department of Justice.

Wilson, W.J. (1 987). *The truly disadvantaged.* Chicago: University of Chicago Press.

Yablonsky, L. (1997). *Gangsters: Fifty years of madness, drugs, and death on the streets of America.* New York: New York University Press.

Going Home, Staying Home: Integrating Prison Gang Members into the Community (Fleisher & Decker, 2001)

1. Recidivism-60% US and Canada.
2. Community should be responsible for inmates readjustment to community life.
3. Communitywide Planning.

Prison Gangs

1. Chronic, serious, criminal organizations.
2. Here street gangs and prison gangs are discussed together....
3. Mexican Mafia, Texas Syndicate, Aryan Brotherhood.
   1. Drug distribution, prostitution, gambling, contract murder.
4. Need bifurcation between hard-core criminals versus transitory youthful adolescents and young adults in gangs.
   1. Drinking, drug use (Fagan, 1989).

Community Integration

1. Integration versus reintegration.
   — Impoverished communities, low paying jobs, social and economic difficulties, personal problems (addition).
2. Challenge is to find realistic mechanisms to integrate former prisoners who are gang members e.g., best practices.

Prison Demographics

1. Escalating rate of confinement since 1990s.
2. Nearly 400,000 gangs members in prisons.
   — 39% parole violators return.
   — 4% new court commitments.
   — Decrease in release rates 37 % (1990) to 31% (1997).
   — Increase in time served 22 months (1990) to 27 months (1997).
   — 4% will not be released.

Prison Demographics

1. California 161,904
2. Texas 144,510
3. Federal Bureau of Prison 123,041
4. North Dakota 915
5. Vermont 1,426
6. Wyoming 1,571
▶ Almost ½ state prison inmates (violent offense).
▶ 60% federal inmates (drug offenses).
▶ 96% prisons will return to communities.

Impediments to Community Integration

1. Gangs facilitate crime as a social group as they accelerate the frequency and severity of crime.
   — Individuals in gang groups commit more crime.
2. Gangs have longevity as social groups, they exist longer than individual members.
   — Structural and economic forces responsible.
3. Self-identification may persists for years/decades for adult offenders, but be transitory of youth members (Decker & Van Winkle, 1996).
   — Champaign men and women in 40s and 50s are still gang members (Fleisher, 2000).
   — Fluid interactions based on friendship ties not the gang.
   — Rival gang members may have friendship ties outside prison.

Impediments to Community Integration

4. Adult gang members may be unwilling to relinquish gang identity.
   — Sense of belonging, a person's social history.
5. Poverty and gangs-lack social bonds to community (schools, sports, civic orgs.)
   — Emotional and psychological deficits, violent victimization, PTSD, and multiple addictions.
6. Gang identity linked to self-identity-gang identity offers companionship, identity, sense of belonging.
   — In poor communities, this identity has social and economic value.

Community Re-entry and Integration

Adults gang members/former inmates enter with:
1. Poor work skills
2. Lack of education
3. Alienation from high-paying employment
▶ Stigmatized as ex-cons.
▶ Return after 5-, 10-, 15- years-new technology, internet…
▶ No community support e.g. Yellow Ribbon Campaign…
▶ Prison-Based anti-ganging or deganging programs lack evidence of success.
   — Prison based education and vocation programs…/longer terms.

Multimodal-Local Community Corrections Intervention

▶ Community integration-
— Should it matter is someone still claims gang ties?
— Lose of social capital difficult…
▷ Are we asking too much of former gang members?
1. Individual-level intervention-Residential Therapeutic Communities (Yablonsky, 1997).
— Long-term, local drug and alcohol treatment.
— Stable residence (dorms), job (employment training agencies), social capital support.
2. Community-level intervention-Community Development
— Community-based parole offices.
— Reject one-job-per-inmate model.
— Community Development-Improve local neighborhood economies and ties between neighborhoods…jobs/truancy.

GOING HOME, STAYING HOME: HOMEWORK ASSIGNMENT

Please define the following terms/concepts using this week's article. Additionally, provide one example for each term from your reading. Please bring your homework to the next class.

1. **Community Reintegration-**

2. **Community Integration –**

3. **Individual Level Intervention –**

4. **Community-Level Intervention –**

5. **Recidivism**

JOINING AND LEAVING GANGS

SELECTION AND FACILITATION EFFECTS ON SELF-REPORTED ANTISOCIAL BEHAVIOUR IN EARLY ADOLESCENCE

By Mons Bendixen,
Inger M. Endresen,
and Dan Olweus

ABSTRACT

Gang membership is repeatedly reported to be one of the strongest predictors of antisocial behaviour. However, whether this association primarily reflects a selection effect or whether it primarily is related to a facilitation of antisocial behaviour within the gang has scarcely been an object of empirical study. This paper examines how antisocial behaviour and gang membership are associated among adolescents across time, using longitudinal data from a representative sample of Norwegian adolescents (N = 1203). Initial cross-group comparisons revealed that gang members were markedly more involved in general antisocial behaviour than non-gang members not only during periods of active gang membership but also during other periods, thereby supporting the theory that there is a selection effect. This effect was smaller for violence than for other forms of antisocial behaviour. Results from longitudinal analyses that compared behavioural changes among gang members and non-gang members during periods when the gang members joined and left a gang demonstrated that active gang affiliation strongly

Mons Bendixen, Inger M. Endresen, Dan Olweus, "Joining and Leaving Gangs: Selection and Facilitation Effects on Self-Reported Antisocial Behaviour in Early Adolescence," *European Journal of Criminology*, vol. 3, no. 1, pp. 85-114.

621

facilitated general antisocial behaviour as well as violent behaviour. Taken together, the results give strong support to the theory that both selection and facilitation processes contribute to the association between gang membership and antisocial involvement.

INTRODUCTION

The association between an individual's involvement in antisocial behaviour and gang membership is one of the strongest and most consistent in the criminological literature (Elliott et al. 1985; Elliott and Menard 1996; Thornberry et al. 1994). Regardless of methodology and design, empirical studies repeatedly have shown that adolescents who are members of a gang are markedly more involved in antisocial behaviour than their non-member peers (for an overview, see Spergel 1990). The membership effect has been demonstrated across a great variety of behaviours such as theft, burglary, vandalism, truancy, drug sales and drug use, and is especially strong for more serious and violent offences (Thornberry et al. 1993).

Although the association between gang membership and antisocial behaviour appears indisputable, criminologists seem to disagree about the temporal sequence of the two factors, and whether the factors are causally linked or not. According to Thornberry and associates (1993), the *mechanisms* underlying this relationship are poorly understood owing to the lack of longitudinal data.

The general shortcoming of cross-sectional designs in disentangling temporal events makes these designs insufficient for drawing any conclusions regarding the nature of the link between antisocial behaviour and gang membership (Thornberry et al. 1993; Henry et al. 1994; Tonry et al. 1991: 27–9). To understand better how gang membership influences individuals' antisocial behaviour across time, members and non-gang members must be followed long enough to observe their behaviour before, during and after periods of active gang membership.

Thornberry and colleagues (1993) have outlined three models as a basis for exploring the temporal sequence and underlying processes for the strong gang-delinquency association. The first model focuses on the formation of the gang and the selective affiliation processes that take place prior to gang formation. In this model, it is assumed that gangs recruit members who already are delinquent, or at least have a high propensity for delinquency, before joining the gang (the *selection model*). The second model emphasizes the facilitation or social learning processes that take place within the gang and among gang members. In this model, gang membership is considered to be a major cause of the increased delinquency among gang members (the *social facilitation model*). The third model is based on a combination of the first two, and the underlying assumption is that social facilitation and selection processes may work together in forming the strong association between gang membership and antisocial behaviour. Thornberry et al. use the term *enhancement model* for this combined model. A short presentation of the three models, their theoretical basis and their implications for antisocial behaviour before, during and after active gang involvement follows.

EXPLANATORY MODELS

In the first model, it is assumed that peer selection is the main process accounting for the strong relationship between delinquent behaviour and gang membership. The *selection model* contends that gangs primarily attract adolescents already involved in antisocial and deviant behaviour and that virtually no new behaviour is generated at the individual level as an effect of joining a gang. Rather, the increased levels of antisocial and deviant behaviour associated with gangs are truly an effect of antisocial elements 'flocking together'. Several studies have found that adolescents tend to select friends with similar backgrounds, attitudes and personality traits as themselves (see review by Rowe et al. 1994). For example, Kandel (1978) found in her study of friendship pairs that the vast majority of friendship similarity in minor delinquency was the result of selection and the average influence effect was small. In their *General Theory of Crime*, Gottfredson and Hirschi claim that 'adventuresome and reckless children who have difficulty making and keeping friends tend to end up in the company of one another, creating groups made up of individuals who tend to lack self-control' (1990: 158). In short, they consider lack of *self-control* to be the primary determinant of crime and analogous acts through its interaction with *crime opportunity*. Gang members are assumed to perceive reduced risks of sanctions by diffusing and confusing the responsibility for their acts; gangs or groups 'act as a mask and a shield, as a cover for activities that would not otherwise be performed' (Gottfredson and Hirschi 1990: 209). Within this framework, the gang does not so much instigate the production of antisocial behaviour as reduce the probability of getting caught. However, even if gang membership may be perceived as an opportunity factor (Huang et al. 2001), opportunity is not considered to have an independent effect on antisocial behaviour beyond its interaction with self-control according to Gottfredson and Hirschi's theory. The predictions from the selection model are that *gang membership follows antisocial/delinquent behaviour,* and joining or leaving a gang is not likely to produce any major changes in antisocial behaviour at the individual level.

A largely different explanation for the strong gang-delinquency association is provided by the *social facilitation model*. This model, which emphasizes the socialization processes within the gang, does not consider gang members to be particularly different from non-members prior to or after their periods of active membership. The group norms and various social processes activated by the gang are thought to facilitate involvement in delinquency and violence, and gang membership is viewed to be a major cause of deviant behaviour. Changes in antisocial/delinquent involvement are assumed to follow changes in gang membership status.

This model is compatible with socialization theories, such as differential association theory or social learning theories (Sutherland and Cressey 1978; Akers 1997). The typical temporal sequence proposed by Akers is that associations with delinquent peers will precede delinquency: 'the sequence of events, in which deviant associations precede the onset of delinquent behavior, will occur more frequently than the sequence of events in which the onset of delinquency precedes the beginning of deviant associations' (1997: 69). The groups with which one is in differential association are essential in this theory, since they are assumed to provide the major social contexts in which all the mechanisms of social learning operate. According to the facilitation model, an *increase in antisocial/ delinquent behaviour after joining a gang is expected* and a *decrease after leaving the gang,* since the learned behaviour will no longer receive enough social support and reinforcement to be sustained.

The *enhancement model,* proposed by Thornberry et al. (1993), is a mixed model based on the assumption that both selection and social facilitation processes contribute to the association between gang membership and delinquent behaviour. In this model, gangs are assumed to recruit their members from adolescents who are already delinquent. Further, since gangs provide an atmosphere that encourages delinquency and sometimes makes it easier, delinquent behaviour will be facilitated.

Several authors have integrated aspects from control theory and social learning theory into combined explanatory models (for an overview, see Akers 1997; Thornberry and Krohn 1997). Thornberry (1987; Thornberry and Krohn 2001) has proposed an interactional theory of delinquency, which is considered to be a theoretical elaboration rather than a theoretical integration of prior theories. This perspective holds that both processes (deviant behaviour leading to deviant peer associations and deviant peers contributing to increased deviance) operate to produce deviant behaviour over the life course (Thornberry and Krohn 1997). In this theory, the fundamental cause of delinquency is assumed to be weakened social constraints (Thornberry 1987). However, what is required if the freedom resulting from weakened bonds is to be channelled into serious and prolonged delinquency is an interactive setting in which delinquency is learned, performed and reinforced (Thornberry 1987: 865). According to the *enhancement model* proposed by Thornberry et al. (1993, 2003), one would expect *higher rates of delinquency among gang members than among non-gang members before joining a gang* owing to social selection and *a significant increase after joining a gang* owing to the facilitation effect.

In the present study, the proposed mixed *enhancement model* will be examined along with the *facilitation model* and the *selection model.* We consider the models outlined by

Thornberry et al. (1993) to be a useful basis for an exploration of the contribution of selection and facilitation processes to the association between gang membership and antisocial behaviour or delinquency, and our design is clearly influenced by their study. Before turning to the description of the present study, we will discuss the available longitudinal research that has focused on these questions.

PRIOR RESEARCH

Prior published studies on how the level of involvement in antisocial behaviour is associated with joining and leaving antisocial gangs are scarce. Longitudinal studies examining this issue have been reported by Esbensen and Huizinga (1993), using data from the Denver Youth Study, by Thornberry et al. (1993, 2003), using data from the Rochester Youth Development Study, and by Lacourse et al. (2003), who used data from the Montreal Longitudinal Experimental Study. Recently, Gordon and colleagues (2004) reported on results from the Pittsburgh Youth Study. In addition, results from an unpublished study by Hill et al. (1996) using data from the Seattle Social Development Project have been briefly summarized by Thornberry (1998).

Esbensen and Huizinga (1993) concluded from their study of a 'highrisk' neighbourhood sample of principally African-American and Hispanic males and females that gang members were, compared with non-gang members, more involved in 'street offences' (theft, violence, selling drugs, etc.) and 'serious offences' (theft, violence, vandalism, fraud, etc.) prior to and after periods of active gang membership. To a lesser extent, this was also true for the category of 'illicit drug use'. During the year of active membership, however, Esbensen and Huizinga reported that the gang members' involvement was substantially higher than non-members' involvement irrespective of the offending category. In general, their analyses supported a mixed model, even if the social facilitation effect was stronger than the effect of social selection.

Thornberry et al.'s (1993) study involved a sample of boys from Rochester, New York. Separate analyses were performed on various groups of transient and stable gang members over a period of three years. The dependent variables were 'person offences' (violence), 'property offences' (including acts of vandalism, theft, joy-riding and fraud), 'drug sales', 'drug use' and a 'general delinquency' index covering the items from the first three categories. Regarding the transient gang members, who stayed in the gang for no more than one year, they concluded that their data were most consistent with the social facilitation model. A notable exception was the category 'property offences', which turned out to be relatively insensitive to changes in gang membership status. Transient gang members were not significantly more involved than non-members in any of the categories analysed in periods before and after active gang membership. This was also true of stable gang members (who were active gang members for at least two consecutive years), with the notable exception of the 'general delinquency' index, for which the analyses demonstrated selection as well as facilitation effects. Thornberry and associates maintained that the 'strongest support for the facilitation model is found in the analysis of the type of behavior most often associated with gangs crimes against the person' (1993: 80).

Recently, Thornberry and colleagues published additional analyses of the Rochester study including data from the fourth year (Thornberry et al. 2003). By applying more advanced multivariate models that also controlled for unmeasured characteristics of the individual, they were able to separate the effects of selection from those of facilitation. Similar to their earlier results, these new analyses showed that selection effects were generally small or modest across the various domains of antisocial behaviour, and facilitation effects were strong and consistent in these more recent analyses too.

Lacourse et al.'s (2003) study of violent behaviour among a sample of white, French-speaking adolescents of low socioeconomic status largely supported Thornberry et al.'s (1993) findings. The results from the Montreal study showed that transitions into delinquent groups significantly increased involvement in violent offending whereas transitions out of delinquent groups were associated with decreased levels of violent offending. Slightly elevated levels of violence were also present before joining delinquent groups, suggesting some selection effect. However, this effect was evident only among students with a history of childhood delinquent behaviour.

Thornberry's (1998) summary of the unpublished results from the Seattle sample suggests that the mean levels of violence were found to be especially elevated during the year of active gang membership and substantially reduced after active membership. Although the level of violence was somewhat higher before joining a gang, Thornberry (1998) concluded that the results were most consistent with the social facilitation model. The selection effect was less consistent and less powerful than the demonstrated facilitation effect.

Similarly to Thornberry et al.'s more recent results, Gordon and colleagues' (2004) also found evidence for selection effects across different delinquency outcomes in their study of a representative sample of boys in public schools in Pittsburgh. By using advanced multiple regression models they were able to adjust for unmeasured pre-existing individual differences as well as controlling for age, seasonality and calendar time trends. Still, the authors report that the most consistent finding was that the boys reported more drug sales, drug use, violent and property delinquency in periods when they were active members compared with periods before and after active gang involvement.

Although the most consistent findings regarding the gang-delinquency relationship have pointed to the strong socialization effects that take place within gangs, these recent studies indicate that selection processes are also at work. This is further underlined in a number of longitudinal studies that have uncovered *risk factors* for later gang membership through the use of different analytic methods. For example, bivariate analyses have shown that violence and externalizing problems (Hill et al. 1999) and conduct disorders and self-reported delinquency (Lahey et al. 1999) were among the strongest predictors for later becoming a gang member. In addition, Thornberry and colleagues (2003) found that violent delinquency predicted gang membership for males when the effects of other predictors across various domains were controlled for.

In sum, the Denver, Rochester, Montreal, Seattle and Pittsburgh studies clearly support a facilitative effect of gang membership across a variety of antisocial behaviours. Violent behaviour seems to be particularly strongly related to gang membership in demonstrating increased levels of offending mainly in periods of active membership. Still, the Denver Youth Study taken together with the more recent findings from the Rochester and Pittsburgh studies and the studies on risk factors for gang entry indicates that some selection effects are present.

Drawing strongly on the previous studies, this paper investigates how gang membership is associated with antisocial involvement across time in a representative sample of Norwegian, predominantly white, adolescents. More specifically, we want to examine the magnitude of the selection and facilitation effects for general antisocial behaviour and interpersonal violence. Questions raised are:

1. Do gangs primarily attract adolescents already involved in antisocial behaviour, or do gangs primarily facilitate antisocial behaviour?
2. Does the magnitude of these two effects differ between general antisocial behaviour and violence, as indicated in prior studies?

Since no results have yet been published from European studies on the longitudinal association between involvement in antisocial behaviour and gang membership, this study helps to show whether the conclusions drawn from North American studies can be more widely generalized.

METHODS

The present study is part of a large-scale, longitudinal research programme on 'The school as a context for social development' under the direction of Dan Olweus. The main focus of the project was on bullying in school and, particularly, on the effects of a school-based intervention programme in reducing such problems (see, e.g., Olweus 1991, 1993a, 1993b, 1994, 2005). The data used in the present study were collected in May/June 1983, here designated Time 1, in May/June 1984 (Time 2) and in May/June 1985 (Time 3). It should be noted that the Olweus Bullying Prevention Programme was implemented in the period between Time 1 and Time 2. It has been documented that the programme had positive effects on the level of bullying as well as on substance use and antisocial behaviour in general (e.g. Olweus 1991, 1994).

Sample

Data were collected from four relatively large cohorts of students from the city of Bergen in Norway. Bergen, with slightly more than 200,000 inhabitants, is the second-largest city in Norway. The subjects participating in the project were in grades 5–8 (according to the current grade designation system) at Time 1. However, only students in grades 7 and 8 were asked questions about membership of antisocial gangs.

Subjects in classes at the same grade, who were therefore of approximately the same age, were regarded as belonging to a cohort (Olweus and Alsaker 1991). The classes to be included in each cohort were selected at random from all those at the relevant grade in Bergen. Hence, each cohort is broadly representative of students in the relevant grade in schools in Bergen; also, students in Bergen are to a large extent representative of those throughout towns in Norway. Close comparisons between the cohorts are possible, because each is representative of students in the relevant grade, and the methods of selection used for students in each grade were the same.

A total of 56 classes (28 at each grade level) drawn from 28 elementary schools (grade 7) and 14 secondary/junior high schools (grade 8) participated. The modal age for students in grades 7 and 8 at the first measurement occasion (Time 1) was 13 and 14, respectively. The total number of students who answered the questionnaire on antisocial behaviour at Time 1 in these cohorts was 1292 (586 girls and 706 boys). This represents 93.8 percent of the total eligible sample of 1377 students. At Time 2, 79.8 percent of these students were still in the project, and 75.2 percent of the Time 1 students participated at Time 3. The number of students with valid longitudinal data at at least two of the three time points was 1203.

Previous analyses have shown that students who were particularly strongly involved in antisocial behaviour dropped out of the study in disproportionate numbers at Time 2 or Time 3 (Bendixen and Olweus 1999). This selective attrition may have reduced the initial selection effect for joining gangs because some of the most extreme subjects were not available for analysis.

Procedure

The subjects answered the questions about antisocial behaviour (as well as other relevant questions) in their regular classrooms. Two research assistants administered the questionnaires with the teacher absent. Each measurement occasion lasted for two or three school periods of 45 minutes each. The students were encouraged to give sincere answers to the questions, and they were told that their responses would be confidential (confidentiality was achieved by means of a code system). Detailed instructions about how to respond were written on the front page. The research assistants read this aloud in the class and an example was given. The assistants were available for help during the whole session.

Measurements

Two dependent variables were used in the present study: general antisocial behaviour (Total scale of antisocial behaviour, 17 items) and violent behaviour (Violence scale, 5 items on violence and causing trouble in public not covered by the total scale). The wording of the items covered by the scales is shown in the appendix. The scores on the total scale and the violence scale were based on item responses reflecting participation or nonparticipation in the depicted antisocial act in the specified period 'this spring term' (approximately five months). The response alternative 'at no time this spring' was coded as '0', whereas having committed the behaviour in question one or more times during the spring was coded as '1'. The scores on the items were added to form a composite score reflecting the variety of antisocial acts. A subject's variety score, which is a sum score, indicates the range or number of different offence types or antisocial acts of a certain category in the specified period admitted to by the subject. As an indicator of the internal consistency of the scales, Cronbach's alpha for the total antisocial behaviour scale (boys and girls in the two cohorts pooled) was .78 (Time 1), .81 (Time 2) and .76 (Time 3). The corresponding values for the violence scale were .61 (Time 1), .77 (Time 2) and .65 (Time 3). The raw stability coefficients (Pearson's r) between Time 1 and Time 2 (one-year interval) were .58 and .35 for the total scale and the violence scale, respectively. Between Time 1 and Time 3, the stability coefficients were .45 (total scale) and .30 (violence scale). More details about the development of the scales and their psychometric properties, reliability and construct validity are given in Bendixen and Olweus (1999).

The main independent variable in this study was gang membership. Although there is some controversy regarding the definition and identification of a gang (see Spergel 1990; Klein 1995; and Curry and Decker 1998 for reviews), the identification of a gang member is a rather straightforward process. According to Curry and Decker, 'the most powerful measure of gang membership is self-nomination' (1998: 6). Support for this assertion is found in a large number of studies using diverse methodologies such as self-reports, interviews and police records. On each of the three measurement occasions, cohort members were asked three questions: 'Have you (during the past five months): (1) Been a member of a group or gang that has vandalized property (destroyed things like benches, seats in a movie or a bus, telephone booths, etc.)? (2) Been a member of a group or gang that has bullied or pestered other people? (3) Been a member of a group or gang that has drunk alcohol and then been noisy and rowdy?' The survey questions differed somewhat from those posed by Thornberry et al. (1993) and Esbensen and Huizinga (1993). Thornberry and associates asked the respondents only whether they belonged to a street gang, without seeking any further information on the gang's illegal orientation or activity, colours, signs, organization or turf. Esbensen and Huizinga, on the other hand, asked follow-up questions in order to discriminate members of criminal gangs from respondents who were part of informal youth groups. Although the questions asked in this study differed somewhat from those used by Esbensen and Huizinga, the content of the questions was basically similar; both sets of questions clearly emphasized the antisocial or criminal dimension of gang activity.

On each of the three measurement occasions, between 9 percent and 11 percent of the students responded 'yes' to at least one of the three gang questions. The majority of the students were involved in 'drinking and disorder' gangs. Being a gang member in one domain (vandalism, bullying, or drinking and disorderly) was highly correlated with membership in another domain (Pearson's r for dichotomous items averaged .40), and Cronbach's alpha for the gang membership variable was above .60 on each of the three measurement occasions. However, there was a notable change of emphasis between the domains over the three measurement occasions. Among those who continued as gang members, an increasingly larger proportion got involved in the 'drinking and disorder' domain across time at the expense of involvement in the 'vandalism' and the 'bullying' domains. Acknowledging both the relatively strong inter-correlations between the three domains, and that the most common antisocial behaviour pattern during the adolescent years involves different types of behaviour (see, e.g., Klein 1984), we decided to treat gang membership as a single concept straddling the three domains. If cohort members answered 'yes' to one or more of the three gang questions on any measurement occasion, they were considered gang members.

Table 1 shows a sample matrix describing the gang affiliation of the various groups organized according to the stability of their membership. The transient gang members said they were active on one of the three measurement occasions only, whereas the stable gang members said they were active on two or three of the measurement occasions. Included in the matrix are students who completed the questionnaire on at least two of the three occasions (e.g. gang member at T1, absent at T2, not a gang member at T3 was classified as transient member, Time 1 only). Because the five-month reference period covers only approximately half of the total time-span of three years, we may have missed a few gang members who were active only between the reference periods. However, we do not think this problem is large. As described in Bendixen and Olweus (1999), the main advantage of using the five-month period ('this spring term') rather than the more conventional 12-month reference period was that it represented a more natural memory unit to the students.

As we can see from Table 1, 249 of the students (almost 21 percent of the sample of 1203) said they were gang members on at least one out of three measurement occasions.

Being a gang member was, however, a rather unstable characteristic. Three out of four gang members (190 out of 249) were active members at only one point in time, and are defined here as transient members. Gang members (both transient and stable) accounted for 24 percent of the male students and 17 percent of the female students; 38 percent of gang members were females. Despite this substantial involvement of females (see also Bjerregaard and Smith 1993 and Esbensen and Huizinga 1993), the stable gang members were predominantly boys. Gang members of both sexes were predominantly students from the older of the two age cohorts (two out of three).

Table 1 Sample matrix for describing antisocial gang affiliation at three times

	Time 1	Time 2	Time 3	n
Non-gang members	Non-active	Non-active	Non-active	954
Transient gang members				
Time 1 only	Active	Non-active	Non-active	77
Time 2 only	Non-active	Active	Non-active	50
Time 3 only	Non-active	Non-active	Active	63
Stable gang members				
Times 1 and 2 only	Active	Active	Non-active	19
Times 1 and 3 only	Active	Non-active	Active	13
Times 2 and 3 only	Non-active	Active	Active	17
Times 1, 2 and 3	Active	Active	Active	10

Analyses

In our early investigations we performed separate analyses on the different sub-groups of gang members, producing a rather complicated picture of the effects of gang membership on antisocial behaviour. Taking account of this complexity, two types of analyses were performed: (1) *cross-group analyses,* contrasting involvement in antisocial behaviour and violence for nongang members versus gang members in non-active periods; and (2) *longitudinal analyses* comparing (a) the same subjects in active versus nonactive periods of gang membership, and (b) change across time in antisocial and violent behaviour among gang members versus non-gang members (group by time effects). Initially, boys and girls were analysed together, but supplementary analyses were later performed on the male sub-sample.

Cross-group differences were analysed using independent samples *t*-tests for each of the three measurement occasions. When the assumption about equal variance in the groups compared was not met, the 'unequal variance' procedure in SPSS with corrected degrees of freedom was used. Profile analyses (the GLM repeated measures procedure in the SPSS package) were applied for comparisons of the cross-time changes.

In addition to tests of significance, effect sizes *(d)* were computed for independent and dependent samples using the formulas advocated by Cortina and Nouri (2000).[10] For the computations of effect sizes reflecting group differences over time, the mean differences in the scores between the two points of time were used in the formula. The main advantages of using effect sizes over tests of significance are that effect sizes permit more direct comparisons of results across studies, and that the magnitude of the selection and facilitation effects can be estimated. However, when the assumptions of homogeneity of variance and equal sample sizes are not met (as would be expected when comparing gang members with non-gang members), the calculated effect size estimates in these samples may be substantially different from those in the population and must be interpreted cautiously (Cohen 1977). To meet the risk of overestimation, we used separate variance t-values in Cortina and Nouri's formula (1.5).

Hypotheses

From the three explanatory models outlined in the introduction, several hypotheses can be generated:

- The *selection model* will be supported if:
  1. gang members are more involved in general antisocial behaviour and violence than are non-gang members whether or not they are currently active members (cross-group comparison), and
  2. changes in gang members' involvement in general antisocial behaviour and violence are virtually unrelated to whether they are entering or leaving gangs (cross-time comparison).
- the *social facilitation model* will be supported if:
  3. gang members are more involved in general antisocial behaviour and violence than are non-gang members only in periods when they are active members; in non-active periods their behaviour will not differ greatly from that of the non-gang members (cross-group comparison), and
  4. changes in gang members' involvement in general antisocial behaviour and violence are related to whether they are entering or leaving gangs (crosstime comparison).
- The *enhancement model* will be supported if hypotheses 1 and 4 are confirmed.

---

10   In estimating the effect size for independent samples with unequal group sizes, we used formula (1.5): $d = t\,[(1/n1) + (1/n2)]^{.5}$ in Cortina and Nouri (2000). Formula (1.5) was also used for estimating group differences for difference scores. In estimating the effect size for dependent (correlated) samples, formula (5.2): $d = tr\,[2(1\ r)/n]^{.5}$ in Cortina and Nouri (2000) was used.

General Antisocial and Violent Behaviour: Descriptive Analyses

Across the three time periods, approximately half of the sample of nongang members had committed at least one of the antisocial acts covered by the total scale of anti-social behaviour during the previous five months. In comparison, 80 percent of the transient gang members and more than 90 percent of the stable gang members had committed such an act. The gender difference in antisocial participation was negligible. Regarding violent behaviour, less than 10 percent of non-gang boys committed an act of violence during the previous five months. For girls who were not gang members the participation rate was markedly lower at 3.5 percent. By comparison, in the case of transient gang members, 25 percent of boys and 11 percent of girls participated in violence. Stable gang members demonstrated the highest rate of participation in violent behaviour: approximately 50 percent of the boys and more than 30 percent of the girls had committed an act of violence during the previous five months. In sum, these results suggest that, although general antisocial and violent behaviour was strongly linked to gang membership, not every gang member was involved in general antisocial behaviour and a fairly substantial proportion were not involved in violent behaviour.

The mean scores on the total scale of antisocial behaviour are shown in Table 2. The original variety scores, which reflect the number of acts (between 0 and 17) that an individual had committed, have been recalibrated so that the range is 0–100. The figures in Tables 2 and 3 were based on the total number of students responding at the time period in question: numbers are smaller for analyses requiring data from more than one time period for the same student. As can be seen from Table 2, gang members were markedly more likely to be involved in general antisocial behaviour than were non-gang members, and this remained true in periods before and after active gang membership, and particularly during periods of active gang membership.

Involvement in violent behaviour was lower than for general antisocial behaviour (see Table 3). However, the pattern of involvement observed for general antisocial behaviour was largely replicated for violent behaviour, suggesting that involvement in violent behaviour was particularly strong in periods of active gang membership.

Cross-group Differences

Between-groups t-tests were performed in order to examine hypotheses 1 and 3 regarding gang members' antisocial involvement in periods when not actively involved in gangs. These analyses contrasted non-gang members with gang members in non-active periods on each of the three measurement occasions. The results from the analyses are displayed in Table 4.

As can be seen from the upper panel of Table 4, non-active gang members scored significantly higher on the total scale of antisocial behaviour than did non-gang members at all the three points of time. At T1, *before* joining the gang, non-active gang members (covering the 'Time 2 only', 'Time 3 only' and 'Time 2 and 3 only' groups) scored 0.65 standard deviation units above non-gang members. Furthermore, the effect sizes *(d)* were moderate to large for non-active gang members at T2 (covering the 'Time 1 only', 'Time 3 only' and 'Time 1 and 3 only' groups) and moderate at T3 *after* active membership (covering the 'Time 1 only', 'Time 2 only' and 'Time 1 and 2 only' groups). Across the three time periods, the group differences averaged 0.59 standard deviation units, and were even more pronounced when boys were analysed separately *(d = 0.67)*. These results clearly support hypothesis 1 and the presence of a selection effect.

Table 2 Mean scale scores on the total scale of antisocial behaviour: age 13 and age 14 cohorts

	n	Time 1	Time 2	Time 3
Non-gang members	954	7.7	6.4	6.2
		(8.8)	(7.2)	(6.0)
Transient gang members				
Time 1 only	77	25.2	13.3	10.3
		(29.4)	(16.2)	(12.3)
Time 2 only	50	17.2	24.8	13.7
		(21.1)	(32.2)	(16.3)
Time 3 only	63	17.2	16.7	19.0
		(18.4)	(18.9)	(19.6)
Stable gang members				
Times 1 and 2 only	19	36.2	47.8	17.3
		(50.3)	(58.2)	(16.7)
Times 1 and 3 only	13	37.4	23.3	20.9
		(43.6)	(27.8)	(24.6)
Times 2 and 3 only	17	14.4	27.2	25.3
		(15.6)	(26.3)	(29.6)

	n	Time 1	Time 2	Time 3
Times 1, 2, and 3	10	43.1	44.5	43.1
		(47.2)	(43.8)	(45.1)

Note: Boys' scores in parenthesis.

The results for the violence scale, displayed in the lower panel of Table 4, showed that non-active gang members were significantly more involved in violent behaviour than were non-gang members on all three measurement occasions. However, the group differences were less marked than for general antisocial behaviour and averaged one fourth of a unit of standard deviation across the three time periods. For boys, the group differences were equally small and non-significant at Time 1 and Time 3 (before and after joining the gang). Although social selection seems to be a less crucial factor in explaining the association between gang membership and violent behaviour among adolescents, the presence of a small selection effect suggests that hypothesis 1 cannot be rejected.

Table 3 Mean scale scores on the violence scale of antisocial behaviour: age 13 and age 14 cohorts

	n	Time 1	Time 2	Time 3
Non-gang members	954	2.6	1.4	1.1
		(4.2)	(2.3)	(1.6)
Transient gang members				
Time 1 only	77	12.0	5.5	2.8
		(16.3)	(8.4)	(3.9)
Time 2 only	50	5.5	14.3	4.4
		(9.2)	(24.8)	(6.3)
Time 3 only	63	5.1	3.3	9.7
		(5.9)	(3.5)	(13.1)
Stable gang members				
Times 1 and 2 only	19	23.2	27.4	6.2
		(38.0)	(46.0)	(6.7)
Times 1 and 3 only	13	15.3	4.0	18.5
		(20.0)	(5.7)	(24.4)
Times 2 and 3 only	17	5.0	22.4	13.8

		(6.0)	(21.7)	(20.0)
Times 1, 2 and 3	10	29.0	28.9	20.0
		(33.8)	(25.7)	(20.0)

Note: Boys' scores in parenthesis.

Analyses with Repeated Measures

Two sets of profile analyses were carried out for further examination of the facilitative effect of active gang membership on antisocial and violent behaviour. First, we made a rough comparison of gang members' antisocial and violent behaviour in active versus non-active periods, using mean scores in active and passive periods for all gang members who were not active throughout and across all measurement occasions, with the subjects' sex as a between-groups factor. Second, we compared the profiles of gang members in periods of joining and leaving with those of non-gang members. If the profiles of the two groups were significantly different, this would appear as a significant interaction (Time x Group) effect in the analysis. In these analyses, subjects' sex was included as a covariate.

The within-group analyses clearly showed that gang members' involvement in general antisocial behaviour was markedly higher in periods of active membership than in non-active periods for the same individuals ($F(1,152) = 29.35$, $p < .001$). The overall effect size of this within-group difference was moderate ($d = 0.46$). The difference between active and non-active periods did not differ significantly for boys and girls (non-significant Time x Sex interaction).

Table 4 Between-group differences in antisocial and violent behaviour for non-gang members vs. gang members in periods of non-active membership: age 13 and age 14 cohorts

	Mean	score (s.d.)				
	Non-gang	Gang (non-active)	d.f.	t		d
Antisocial behaviour						
T1	7.7 (10.2)	17.0 (14.8)	129.3	6.56	***	0.65
	8.8 (10.6)	18.9 (15.8)	86.3	5.43	***	0.67
T2	6.4 (10.0)	15.6 (14.9)	127.0	6.47	***	0.64

	7.2 (11.3)	18.6 (15.8)	83.3	5.89	***	0.75
T3	6.2 (9.7)	12.2 (12.7)	132.6	4.85	***	0.49
	6.0 (9.8)	13.9 (13.4)	65.8	4.29	***	0.60
Violent behaviour						
T1	2.6 (8.9)	5.2 (12.7)	128.7	2.12	**	0.21
	4.2 (11.2)	6.9 (13.8)	90.7	1.66	n.s.	0.21
T2	1.4 (6.9)	4.4 (10.9)	125.5	2.83	**	0.28
	2.3 (9.0)	5.8 (12.8)	83.3	2.28	*	0.29
T3	1.1 (6.4)	3.7 (10.9)	125.3	2.47	*	0.25
	1.6 (7.9)	4.8 (13.1)	63.0	1.82	n.s.	0.26

Note: Boys' figures in italic.

t-and d-values are based on separate variance estimates.

*p < .05, **p < .01, ***p < .001, n.s. non-significant

As in the case of general antisocial behaviour, gang members were significantly more involved in violent behaviour in periods when they were active members than in periods when they were non-active (F(1,152) = 15.88, $p < .001$). The overall effect size of this difference was moderate (d = 0.42). However, a significant Time x Sex interaction (F(1,152) = 10.97, $p < .01$) was evident for violent behaviour; the difference between active and non-active periods was markedly larger for boys than for girls. In sum, these results show that active gang membership is associated with high levels of general antisocial behaviour as well as violent behaviour (supporting hypothesis 4). The following paragraphs describe the results of more detailed analyses of behavioural changes in gang members compared with non-gang members during periods when gang members leave or join gangs.

For gang members, four events were identified and analysed. Gang members could either be leaving or joining a gang between Time 1 and Time 2, or be leaving or joining a gang between Time 2 and Time 3. Students who joined or left a gang at a particular time were grouped together regardless of whether they were transient or stable gang members. Non-gang members, who constitute the vast majority of the cases analysed, by definition experienced no joining or leaving events across the three measurement occasions. Any change in behaviour for these subjects must be attributable to factors other than leaving or joining gangs, and these non-gang members serve as 'controls' in the analyses.

The results of the analyses of the total scale of antisocial behaviour are displayed in the upper panel of Table 5. Only interaction effects are reported. Significant Time x Group interaction effects were demonstrated for all events except for 'Joining between T2 and T3'. For the significant results, the effect sizes of the difference scores were generally large. On average, leaving or joining a gang produced a relative change in general antisocial behaviour of 0.68 of a standard deviation unit.

To give a clearer illustration of the interaction effects, we have in Figure 1 plotted the profiles for the joining, leaving and non-gang groups between Time 1 and Time 2. As can be seen from Figure 1, the profiles for the gang groups differed markedly from that of the non-gang members. Although the general antisocial behaviour for non-gang members decreased slightly between T1 and T2, the decrease for the leaving group was clearly more marked. Similarly, joining a gang between T1 and T2 markedly increased the level of antisocial behaviour.

For boys, the size of the effect of leaving on the total scale of antisocial behaviour was similar to the effect of joining (mean $d = 0.72$). These results strongly support hypothesis 4 about the facilitative effect of gang membership. A significant Time x Sex interaction effect was evident for changes in gang membership status between Time 1 and Time 2, suggesting that general antisocial behaviour changed more for boys than for girls when leaving or joining a gang.

For the violence scale (see the lower panel of Table 5), significant interaction effects were demonstrated across all events, including joining between T2 and T3. This is further illustrated in Figure 2, which clearly shows that violent behaviour for the joining group increased markedly between T2 and T3 whereas no behavioural change took place for non-gang members. Leaving the gang between T2 and T3 was strongly associated with reduced levels of violent behaviour.

Table 5 Interaction (time x group) effects for gang members vs. non-gang members with sex as a covariate: age 13 and age 14 cohorts

			d.f.	F				d
Antisocial behaviour								
Leaving between T1	and	T2	867	48.49	T	x	S	0.91
			(451)	(35.59)				(1.01)
Leaving between T2	and	T3	759	35.59				0.86
			(380)	(12.02)				(0.78)

Joining between T1	and	T2	858	42.87	T	x	S	0.90
			(447)	(35.42)				(1.06)
Joining between T2	and	T3	770	0.34 n.s.				0.05
			(400)	(0.32) n.s.				(0.03)
Violent behaviour								
Leaving between T1	and	T2	851	17.93	T	x	S	0.56
			(442)	(8.80)				(0.50)
Leaving between T2	and	T3	750	35.57	T	x	S	0.87
			(375)	(46.26)				(1.53)
Joining between T1	and	T2	842	50.82				0.98
			(438)	(42.36)				(1.16)
Joining between T2	and	T3	761	19.58				0.60
			(395)	(20.28)				(0.74)

Notes: Boys' figures in parenthesis. All F-values are significant at the $p < .01$ level except n.s. T x S: significant Time x Sex interaction. Effect sizes (d) are estimated from difference scores.

On average, leaving or joining a gang produced a relative change in violent behaviour of 0.75 standard deviation units. For boys, the facilitation effect was even stronger nearly one unit of standard deviation. A significant Time x Sex interaction effect was evident for *leaving* a gang at both time periods (boys' scores changed more than girls'). In sum, these results give strong support to hypothesis 4 and a facilitation effect.

DISCUSSION

Main Results

The main goal in the present study was to examine the contribution of selection and facilitation processes to the frequently demonstrated associations between gang

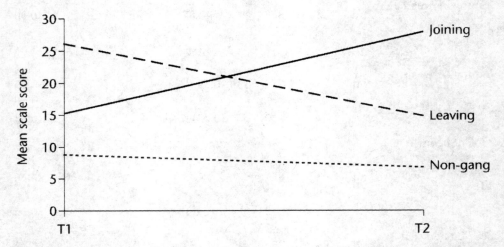

Figure 1 Mean variety scale scores for total antisocial behaviour: Non-gang members, and gang members joining and leaving between Times 1 and 2.

Figure 1 Mean variety scale scores for total antisocial behaviour: Non-gang members, and gang members joining and leaving between Times 1 and 2.

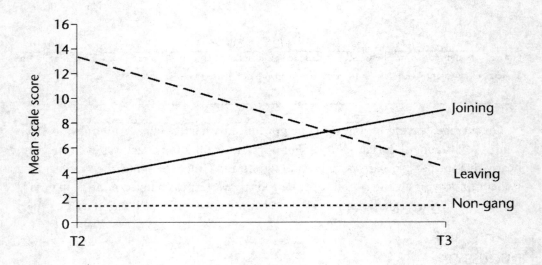

Figure 2 Mean variety scale scores for total violent behaviour: Non-gang members, and gang members joining and leaving between Times 2 and 3.

membership and delinquent and violent behaviour. Effects of both processes were demonstrated, in somewhat varying degree, for the two dependent variables.

The cross-group analyses demonstrated that gang members were significantly more involved in general antisocial behaviour than were their non-gang peers in periods when they were not active gang members (before, between and after periods of gang membership). These results support hypothesis 1 and the presence of a selection effect. The size of this selection effect was moderate in the sample as a whole, and somewhat stronger for boys when analysed separately. Moreover, the longitudinal analysis of gang members in active versus non-active periods demonstrated that they were significantly more involved in antisocial behaviour when they were active gang members compared with the passive periods. This result is clearly in accordance with hypothesis 4, and gives strong support to the view that active gang membership facilitates antisocial behaviour. In line with this, the longitudinal analyses comparing gang members after joining or leaving the gang with the non-gang group demonstrated that general anti-social behaviour in gang members increased after joining a gang and decreased after leaving as compared with the non-gang group. With the exception of students joining a gang between T2 and T3, these effects were strong. In demonstrating selection effects as well as strong social facilitation effects with respect to general antisocial behaviour, thus confirming both hypotheses 1 and 4, these results appear to be most consistent with the enhancement model.

With respect to involvement in *violent behaviour*, gang members again scored significantly higher than their non-gang peers in periods when they were not actively associating with the gang (before, between and after periods of gang membership). However, when boys were analysed separately, the effects at T1 and T3 were not significant, and the cross-group comparisons indicated only a small selection effect. The profile analyses, on the other hand, demonstrated that entering and leaving a gang were followed by marked changes in violent behaviour, suggesting a strong facilitation effect, especially for leaving between T2 and T3 and joining between T1 and T2. Further, the results from analyses of boys separately indicated an even stronger facilitation effect for boys than for girls.

Unlike the results for the total scale of antisocial behaviour, the facilitation effect for violent behaviour was marked also when joining between T2 and T3. Since the total scale of antisocial behaviour includes a larger proportion of less serious types of offending than the violence scale, the absence of a facilitation effect for the former when joining in this period may reflect an ageing-out effect. The results may suggest that, for nonviolent types of antisocial behaviour, subjects who joined a gang at Time 3 (when they were 15 and 16 years old) to some extent were less subject to conformity pressures than were those who joined at younger ages. Hence, age seems to influence what types of antisocial behaviour are facilitated in periods of active gang membership.

In conclusion, small but significant selection effects were demonstrated for the majority of the cross-group comparisons in violent behaviour, and the results from the profile analyses strongly supported the presence of facilitation processes. As in the case of general antisocial behaviour, these results are most consistent with the enhancement model (hypotheses 1 and 4), although facilitation rather than selection makes the strongest contribution to the enhanced level of violent behaviour.

Comparing the Current Results with Previous Studies

When comparing the results for the total scale of antisocial behaviour with the results from earlier studies, it is important to bear in mind that this scale covers mainly items on theft and vandalism. It differs somewhat from Thornberry and colleagues' 'general delinquency' and 'property offences' scales. The 'general delinquency' scale covers a broader range of acts compared with our total scale, and the 'property offences' scale is clearly more restricted. The total scale also differs markedly from Esbensen and Huizinga's 'street offences' and 'serious offences', which include more serious acts. The measure that is most comparable to our total scale is perhaps Esbensen and Huizinga's 'minor offences' and Gordon et al.'s 'property delinquency'.

The significant *selection effects* shown for the total scale of antisocial behaviour in the present study run counter to the findings reported from the Rochester study. In the latter, a selection effect was found only for the 'general delinquency' index, which in addition to property offences included both violence and drug selling. Besides, the selection effect was weak and restricted to stable gang members. In the Denver study, significant selection effects were reported only for 'street offences' and 'serious offences' (both including violence), but the 'minor offences' index used in the Denver study was not subject to separate analyses of selection effects. On the other hand, the Pittsburgh study reported selection effects for 'property delinquency' quite similar to those found in our study.

In addition, the strong *facilitation effects* demonstrated for the total scale of antisocial behaviour differ somewhat from the findings in the Rochester study. In Thornberry et al.'s (1993) study, a strong facilitation effect was found for all the included indices, with the exception of the 'property offences' index, which did not show systematic variation with gang membership. The facilitation effect for the total scale of antisocial behaviour found in our study seems to be more consistent with the results from the Denver study, where facilitation effects were found for all the offending categories. Unfortunately, separate analyses of facilitation effects were not performed on the 'minor offences' index in that study. Again, the facilitation effects in our study are largely comparable to those reported in the Pittsburgh study.

Turning to violent behaviour, both the small selection effects and the moderate to strong facilitation effects demonstrated in the present study seem to be more consistent with the results from prior studies. The results from the Denver study (Esbensen and Huizinga 1993), the Montreal study (Lacourse et al. 2003) and the Seattle study (in Thornberry 1998) demonstrated that gang members were only marginally more involved in violent behaviour in non-active periods compared with their non-gang peers. As noted above, a small selection effect was identified in the Rochester study (Thornberry et al. 1993) on the 'general delinquency' index for the stable gang members. Re-analyses of this panel study including data from year 4 (Thornberry et al. 2003) also showed a small selection effect for violent delinquency. Also, the results from the Pittsburgh study, as well as analyses of risk factors reported from the Rochester study and other studies (Hill et al. 1999; Lahey et al. 1999), suggest that some selection effect for violent behaviour may be present in gang members.

The relatively large selection effect demonstrated for general antisocial behaviour in this study and in the Pittsburgh study compared with the smaller effect reported from the Rochester study could reflect either (1) discrepancies in the content of the measures used, (2) differences in the applied analytical techniques, or (3) differences in sample characteristics. As noted above, our total scale of antisocial behaviour differs somewhat from Thornberry et al.'s (1993) 'general delinquency' and 'property offences'. It seems, however, that conceptual differences in the criterion variables are not large enough to account for the different findings.

The prevalence of gang membership in this study was not lower than in previous studies. Although the criterion for gang membership by and large was comparable across the studies, the addition of the term 'group' to the gang questions in our study may have widened the meaning of the questions slightly. Given the unique meaning of the word 'gang' for American youth (Esbensen et al. 2001), this addition may have led to a slight over-inclusion of gang members and a more heterogeneous sample of gang members. This could partly explain the low involvement in violence by gang members in our study, but it is also likely that violence is less common among Norwegian adolescents compared with North American youth in general.

Turning to differences in analytical techniques, the earlier studies merely reported on levels of significance for relatively small samples in their cross-group analyses. In the present study (as well as in the Pittsburgh Study), sub-groups of gang members with similar gang status were joined to form larger units for analysis, reducing the probability of Type I errors. Analyses of a large number of sub-groups with small n's, as in the Rochester Study, not only affect the true alpha level but also clearly reduce the power of the analyses. Estimates of effect sizes, on the other hand, provide information on the strength of the effects. Not only are effect sizes independent of group sizes, they also enable a more direct comparison of effects across studies.

With respect to sample characteristics, the age groups were largely comparable across the studies, all of which involved only adolescents in their early-and mid-teens. However, in contrast to earlier studies, the present study (and to some extent the

Pittsburgh study) was conducted on a largely representative sample of adolescents from a non-gang city. Becoming a gang member in a mid-sized city in Norway may be a more extreme choice than becoming a gang member in a high-risk area. Hence, the observed differences in selection effects could reflect a higher threshold for joining a gang in this study.

Conceptual Considerations and Theoretical Implications

Since self-reported gang membership and general antisocial and violent behaviour are highly correlated phenomena, it may be argued that they are merely different reflections of the same underlying dimension within a person, and that joining or leaving a gang would not cause changes in antisocial behaviour. This claim is a logical consequence of Gottfredson and Hirschi's assertion that self-reported peers' delinquency 'may merely be another measure of self-reported delinquency' (1990: 157). We do not share this concern for two reasons. First, gang membership as measured in our study is a state (an aspect of being), whereas antisocial behaviour is a set of actions (an aspect of doing). Although the two variables correlate, they are conceptually different. Second, and related to the first, the observed overlap between gang membership and antisocial behaviour is far from perfect, and self-reported gang membership does not assume involvement in general antisocial or violent behaviour. In fact, a number of students who were active gang members did not report any antisocial involvement. This was particularly true for violent behaviour, in which the majority of the gang members were not involved.

So far, the results are reviewed in the context of the three explanatory models the selection model, the social facilitation model and the enhancement model but the findings also have implications for traditional theories of criminal and analogous behaviour. Gottfredson and Hirschi's (1990) *General Theory of Crime* and social learning theory (Akers 1985, 1997) have offered different explanations of the strong gang-crime relationship, and they differ markedly in their beliefs in the gang's potential to change its members' level of antisocial behaviour. Gottfredson and Hirschi's theory does not anticipate an independent main effect for crime opportunity beyond its interaction with low self-control. Consequently, they claim that the criminal influence of the gang generally is small, owing to the fact that the gang primarily attracts persons lacking self-control. Our results for general antisocial and violent behaviour give little support to Gottfredson and Hirschi's notion. Not only does the theory have difficulties in explaining the relatively large behavioural changes following changes in gang membership status, but the small selection effects on violent behaviour also run counter to the theoretical predictions. Still, a more direct test of the theory's assumptions would involve an examination of how self-control interacts with gang membership across time.

In contrast to control theories, social learning theory recognizes the antisocial peer group and the gang as major independent factors affecting the onset, continuation and termination of the subject's antisocial behaviour. This theory does not exclude the possibility of social selection both selection and social facilitation processes may be operative but it emphasizes facilitation effects over selection effects in explaining the association between gang membership and antisocial behaviour. Our findings are encouraging for social learning theory in demonstrating moderate to strong facilitation effects, particularly in the case of violent behaviour. The results for antisocial behaviour clearly are compatible with combined or integrated models.

Compared with either control or social learning theories, interactional theory (Thornberry 1987) claims to have a less static view on the processes linking gang membership to antisocial behaviour. Although the interactive process cannot be studied directly in our longitudinal design, our results suggest that selection and facilitation processes work in a reciprocal manner. At least some of the gang members seem to be 'different kinds' of people, with a stronger orientation toward general antisocial behaviour than their non-gang peers before they join a gang. According to this theory, weakened social constraints against deviant behaviour increase the risk of seeking out others with a similar orientation to form gangs or groups. Once gangs are formed, the interaction with these peers further facilitates and stimulates these behaviour tendencies.

Limitations of This Study

Although this sample is largely representative of Norwegian adolescents, it still needs to be recognized that the ability to generalize from these findings is limited to the lower age continuum of the adolescent period (ages 13–16). Furthermore, and principally owing to the lower number of female gang members in the study, separate analyses of girls were not performed. Still, the analyses indicate that gang membership is less facilitative of violent behaviour among girls than among boys. This result may reflect a statistical bias associated with the higher prevalence of boys' violent behaviour and, until future studies have addressed this issue covering large enough cohorts of male and female gang members, this finding remains suggestive. Furthermore, the Olweus Bullying Prevention Programme introduced between Time 1 and Time 2 in this study may have affected the results somewhat. It has been demonstrated that the anti-bullying programme reduced the overall level of antisocial and violent behaviour on the second and third measurement occasions. This may have reduced the proportion of students joining antisocial gangs as well as the magnitude of the behavioural changes associated with changes in gang membership.

CONCLUSION

The current study has shown the facilitative effects of active gang membership on antisocial as well as violent behaviour, and most of these effects were quite strong. When young people joined a gang (except when this was between T2 and T3), their levels of violent and antisocial behaviour increased markedly; when they left a gang, this was followed by a marked decrease. The marked facilitation effect demonstrated in the present study fits well with previous studies in the case of violence, but less well in the case of general antisocial behaviour.

The present findings suggest that the association between gang membership and antisocial behaviour is considerably influenced by selection processes, and in this respect they differ markedly from the findings of earlier studies. Individuals with an antisocial orientation tend to seek the company of similar individuals in addition to being influenced by members of the gang. These results are more in line with recent findings from the Pittsburgh study and with the previous findings from studies of risk factors for joining antisocial gangs.

It was found that the students who joined gangs were more involved in violent behaviour, too, than were their non-gang peers in periods prior to and after active gang membership. However, these selection effects in the case of violent behaviour were markedly smaller than for antisocial behaviour, and two of the comparisons were non-significant when the male sample was analysed separately. These results indicate that the magnitude of selection effects is contingent upon the dependent variable in question.

APPENDIX

Total Scale of Antisocial Behaviour (17 items)
Avoided paying for such things as movies, bus or train ride, or food?
Scribbled on the school building, outside or inside, or on things belonging to your school?
Stolen money or other things from members of your family?
Cursed at a teacher?
Taken things worth less than NKr.200 from a store without paying?
Skipped one or two lessons?
Purposely destroyed or broken such things as windows, benches, telephone booths, or mailboxes?
Without permission taken a bicycle or a moped that did not belong to you?
Skipped school a whole day?

Had a violent quarrel with a teacher?
Signed someone else's name to get money or other things you wanted?
Purposely broken chairs, tables, desks, or other things in your school?
Purposely destroyed seats in a bus, a movie theatre, or other places?
Taken things worth more than NKr.200 from a store without paying?
Broken into a shop, house, or apartment and taken something?
Broken into a parking meter or the coin box of a pay phone?
Stolen a wallet or purse while the owner wasn't around?

Violence Scale (5 items)
Got into a fight at a private party?
Got into a fight in a public place (in the street, at a club or in a similar place)?
Beaten someone up so badly they probably needed a doctor?
Been noisy and rowdy in a public place (in the street, at a club or in a similar place)?
Taken part in a fight with the police?

ACKNOWLEDGMENTS

This research was supported by grants from the Norwegian Council for Research (NFR) to Mons Bendixen and Dan Olweus and grants to Dan Olweus from the Norwegian Public Health Association, the Norwegian Ministry of Children and Family Affairs (BFD) and, in earlier phases, the Norwegian Ministry of Education—these grants are gratefully acknowledged. We would also like to thank Terrence P. Thornberry for commenting on an earlier draft of this paper.

REFERENCES

Akers, R. L. (1985). *Deviant behavior: A social learning approach,* 3rd edn. Belmont, CA: Wadsworth.

Akers, R. L. (1997). *Criminological theories: Introduction and evaluation,* 2nd edn. Los Angeles, CA: Roxbury Publishing Company.

Bendixen, M. and Olweus, D. (1999). Measurement of antisocial behaviour in early adolescence and adolescence: Psychometric properties and substantive findings. *Criminal Behaviour and Mental Health 9,* 323–54.

Bjerregaard, B. and Smith, C. (1993). Gender differences in gang participation, delinquency, and substance use. *Journal of Quantitative Criminology 9,* 329–55.

Cohen, J. (1977). *Statistical power analysis for the behavioral sciences,* revised edn. New York: Academic Press.

Cortina, J. M. and Nouri, H. (2000). *Effect size for ANOVA designs.* Sage University Papers Series on Quantitative Applications in the Social Sciences, series no. 07–129. Thousand Oaks, CA: Sage.

Curry, G. D. and Decker, S. H. (1998). *Confronting gangs.* Los Angeles, CA: Roxbury Publishing Company.

Elliott, D. S. and Menard, S. (1996). Delinquent friends and delinquent behavior: Temporal and developmental patterns. In J. D. Hawkins (ed.) *Delinquency and crime: Current theories,* 28–67. Cambridge: Cambridge University Press.

Elliott, D. S., Huizinga, D. and Ageton, S. S. (1985). *Explaining delinquency and drug use.* Beverly Hills, CA: Sage.

Esbensen, F.A. and Huizinga, D. (1993). Gangs, drugs, and delinquency in a survey of urban youth. *Criminology 31,* 565–89.

Esbensen, F.-A., Winfree, L. T., Jr, He, N. and Taylor, T. J. (2001). Youth gangs and definitional issues: When is a gang a gang, and why does it matter? *Crime and Delinquency 47,* 105–30.

Gordon, R. A., Lahey, B. B., Kawai, E., Loeber, R., Stouthamer-Loeber, M. and Farrington, D. P. (2004). Antisocial behavior and youth gang membership: selection and socialization. *Criminology 42,* 55–87.

Gottfredson, M. R. and Hirschi, T. (1990). *A general theory of crime.* Stanford, CA: Stanford University Press.

Henry, B., Moffitt, T. E., Caspi, A., Langley, J. and Silva, P. A. (1994). On the 'Remembrance of things past': A longitudinal evaluation of the retrospective method. *Psychological Assessment 6,* 92–101.

Hill, K. G., Howell, J. C., Hawkins, J. D. and Batting-Pearson, S. R. (1999). Childhood risk factors for adolescent gang membership: Results from the Seattle Social Development Project. *Journal of Research in Crime and Delinquency 36,* 300–22.

Hill, K. G., Hawkins, J. D., Catalano, R. F., Kosterman, R., Abbott, R. and Edwards, T. (1996). The longitudinal dynamics of gang membership and problem behavior: A replication and extension of the Denver and Rochester gang studies in Seattle. Paper presented at the annual meeting of the American Society of Criminology, Chicago.

Huang, B., Kosterman, R., Catalano, R. F., Hawkins, J. D. and Abbott, R. D. (2001). Modelling mediation in the etiology of violent behavior in adolescence: A test of the social developmental model. *Criminology 39,* 75–107.

Kandel, D. B. (1978). Similarity in real-life adolescent friendship pairs. *Journal of Personality and Social Psychology 36,* 306–12.

Klein, M. W. (1984). Offence specialization and versatility among juveniles. *British Journal of Criminology 24,* 185–94.

Klein, M. W. (1995). *The American street gang: Its nature, prevalence, and control.* New York: Oxford University Press.

Lacourse, E., Nagin, D., Tremblay, R. E., Vitaro, F. and Claes, M. (2003). Developmental trajectories of boys' delinquent group membership and facilitation of violent behaviours during adolescence. *Development and Psychopathology 15*, 183–97.

Lahey, B. B., Gordon, R. A., Loeber, R., Stouthamer-Loeber, M. and Farrington, D. P. (1999). Boys who join gangs: A prospective study of predictors of first gang entry. *Journal of Abnormal Child Psychology 27*, 261–76.

Olweus, D. (1991). Bully/victim problems among schoolchildren: Basic facts and effects of a school based intervention program. In D. Pepler and K. H. Rubin (eds) *The development and treatment of childhood aggression*, 411–48. Hillsdale, NJ: Erlbaum.

Olweus, D. (1993a). *Bullying at school: What we know and what we can do*. Oxford: Blackwell Publishers.

Olweus, D. (1993b). Victimization by peers: Antecedents and long-term outcomes. In K. H. Rubin and J. B. Asendorpf (eds) *Social withdrawal, inhibition, and shyness in childhood*, 315–41. Hillsdale, NJ: Erlbaum.

Olweus, D. (1994). Annotation: Bullying at school: Basic facts and effects of a school based intervention program. *Journal of Child Psychology and Psychiatry and Allied Disciplines 35*, 1171–90.

Olweus, D. (2005). A useful evaluation design, and effects of the Olweus Bullying Prevention Program. *Psychology, Crime and Law 11*, 389–402.

Olweus, D. and Alsaker, F. D. (1991). Assessing change in a cohort longitudinal study with hierarchical data. In D. Magnusson, L. Bergman, G. Rudinger and B. Torestad (eds) *Problems and methods in longitudinal research*, 107–32. New York: Cambridge University Press.

Rowe, D. C., Woulbroun, E. J. and Gulley, B. L. (1994). Peers and friends as nonshared environmental influences. In E. M. Hetherington, D. Reiss and R. Plomin (eds) *Separate social worlds of siblings: The impact of nonshared environment on development*, 159–73. Hillsdale, NJ: Erlbaum.

Spergel, I. A. (1990). Youth gangs: Continuity and change. In M. Tonry and N. Morris (eds) *Crime and justice: A review of research*, vol. 12, 171–275. Chicago: University of Chicago Press.

Sutherland, E. H. and Cressey, D. R. (1978). *Criminology*, 10th edn. Philadelphia, PA: Lippincott.

Thornberry, T. P. (1987). Toward an interactional theory of delinquency. *Criminology 25*, 863-91.

Thornberry, T. P. (1998). Membership in youth gangs and involvement in serious and violent offending. In R. Loeber and D. P. Farrington (eds) *Serious & violent juvenile offenders: Risk factors and successful interventions*, 147–66. London: Sage.

Thornberry, T. P. and Krohn, M. D. (1997). Peers, drug use, and delinquency. In D. M. Stoff, J. Breiling and J. D. Maser (eds) *Handbook of antisocial behavior*, 218–33. New York: Wiley.

Thornberry, T. P. and Krohn, M. D. (2001). The development of delinquency: An interactional perspective. In S. O. White (ed.) *Handbook of youth and justice*, 289–305. New York: Plenum.

Thornberry, T. P., Krohn, M. D., Lizotte, A. J. and Chard-Wierschem, D. (1993). The role of juvenile gangs in facilitating delinquent behavior. *Journal of Research in Crime and Delinquency 30*, 55–87.

Thornberry, T. P., Krohn, M. D., Lizotte, A. J., Smith, C. A. and Tobin, K. (2003). *Gangs and delinquency in developmental perspective.* Cambridge: Cambridge University Press.

Thornberry, T. P., Lizotte, A. J., Krohn, M. D., Farnworth, M. and Jang, S. J. (1994). Delinquent peers, beliefs, and delinquent behavior: A longitudinal test of interactional theory. *Criminology 32*, 47–83.

Tonry, M., Ohlin, L. E. and Farrington, D. P. (1991). *Human development and criminal behavior: New ways of advancing knowledge.* New York: Springer-Verlag.

ABOUT THE AUTHORS

Mons Bendixen is a PhD student in the Faculty of Psychology, University of Bergen. His current position is associate professor in the Department of Psychology, Norwegian University of Science and Technology. His main research interests are the measurement and development of antisocial behaviour in adolescence and aggressive behaviour in intimate relationships. mons.bendixen@svt.ntnu.no

Inger M. Endresen has a doctoral degree in psychology from the University of Bergen. She is employed as a senior researcher at the Research Center for Health Promotion (HEMIL-senteret), University of Bergen. Her research interests are the development of empathic responsiveness and acting-out behaviour. Inger.Endresen@psyhp.uib.no\

Dan Olweus has a doctoral degree in psychology from the University of Umea, Sweden, and is a research professor of psychology affiliated with the Research Center for Health Promotion, University of Bergen. A major focus of his research has been on the development and reduction/prevention of bully/victim problems and antisocial behaviour in school. He also has a strong interest in social science research methodology. dan.olweus@psyhp.uib.no

CPSIA information can be obtained
at www.ICGtesting.com
Printed in the USA
FSOW02n1723061217
42081FS